OUT
FRONT.

Also by Don Shewey

SAM SHEPARD
CAUGHT IN THE ACT: NEW YORK ACTORS FACE TO FACE
(WITH SUSAN SHACTER)

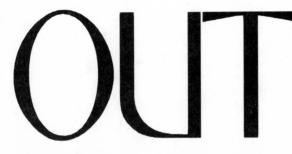

OUT

Contemporary Gay and Lesbian Plays

FRONT

Edited and with an introduction by
Don Shewey

GROVE PRESS
New York

Published by Grove Press
a division of Wheatland Corporation
920 Broadway
New York, N.Y. 10010

Library of Congress Cataloging-in-Publication Data

Out front: contemporary gay and lesbian plays / edited with an introduction by Don Shewey.
— 1st ed.
    p.   cm.
    Contents: Street theater / by Doric Wilson — Bent / by Martin Sherman — Execution of
justice / by Emily Mann — The well of horniness / by Holly Hughes — A weekend near
Madison / by Kathleen Tolan — Remedial English / by Evan Smith — Forget him / by
Harvey Fierstein — The Lisbon traviata / by Terrence McNally — The fairy garden / by
Harry Kondoleon — Jerker, or The helping hand / by Robert Chesley — As is / by William M.
Hoffman.
    Bibliography: p.
    ISBN 0-8021-1041-X   ISBN 0-8021-3025-9 (pbk.)
    1. Homosexuality—Drama. 2. Lesbianism—Drama. 3. Gays' writings, Ameri-
can. 4. Lesbians' writings, American. 5. American drama—20th century. I. Shewey,
Don.
PS627.H6709   1987
812'.52'080353—dc19
                   88-1257
                   CIP

Designed by Irving Perkins Associates
Manufactured in the United States of America
First Edition 1988

10 9 8 7 6 5 4 3 2 1

Dramatists Play Service, Inc., 440 Park Avenue South, New York, NY 10016. No stock or amateur performance of the play may be given without obtaining in advance the written permission of the Dramatists Play Service, Inc., and paying the requisite fee. All inquiries concerning rights other than stock and amateur rights should be addressed to Gilbert Parker, c/o William Morris Agency, Inc., 1350 Avenue of the Americas, New York, NY 10019.

The Fairy Garden, © copyright, 1982, by Harry Kondoleon. All rights reserved. CAUTION: Professionals and amateurs are hereby warned that *The Fairy Garden* is subject to a royalty. It is fully protected under the copyright laws of the United States of America, and of all countries covered by the International Copyright Union (including the Dominion of Canada and the rest of the British Commonwealth), and of all countries covered by the Pan-American Copyright Convention and the Universal Copyright Convention, and of all countries with which the United States has reciprocal copyright relations. All rights, including professional, amateur, motion picture, recitation, lecturing, public reading, radio broadcasting, television, video or sound taping, all other forms of mechanical or electronic reproduction, such as information storage and retrieval systems and photocopying, and the rights of translation into foreign languages, are strictly reserved. Particular emphasis is laid upon the question of readings, permission for which must be secured from the author's agent in writing. All inquiries concerning rights (other than stock and amateur rights) should be addressed to George P. Lane, c/o William Morris Agency, Inc., 1350 Avenue of the Americas, New York, New York 10019. The stock and amateur production rights in *The Fairy Garden* are controlled exclusively by the Dramatists Play Service, Inc., 440 Park Avenue South, New York, New York 10016. No stock or amateur performance may be given without obtaining in advance the written permission of the Dramatists Play Service, Inc., and paying the requisite fee. The music for the song in *The Fairy Garden*, and permission for its use in performance of the play, can be obtained directly from the composer: Gary S. Fagin, 600 West 11th Street, Apt. 5G, New York, N.Y. 10025.

Jerker, or the Helping Hand, copyright © 1985 by Robert Chesley. All rights reserved. Reprinted with permission.

As Is, copyright © 1985 by William M. Hoffman. Reprinted by permission of Random House, Inc. The author's preface first appeared in *Vogue*, © 1985 by Conde Nast Publications, Inc. CAUTION: Professionals and amateurs are hereby warned that *As Is*, being fully protected under the copyright laws of the United States, the British Empire including the Dominion of Canada and all other countries of the Copyright Union, is subject to royalty. All rights, including professional, amateur, motion picture, recitation, lecturing, public reading, radio and television broadcasting and the rights of translation into foreign languages, are strictly reserved. Particular emphasis is laid on the question of readings, permission for which must be obtained in writing from the author's agent. All inquiries should be addressed to the author's representative, Mitchell Douglas, International Creative Management, 40 West 57th Street, New York, N.Y. 10019.

TO BOB

CONTENTS

INTRODUCTION

PRIDE IN THE NAME OF LOVE:
NOTES ON CONTEMPORARY GAY THEATER

by Don Shewey

Gay theater has many valuable stories to share with the world: stories about self-discovery, about being fundamentally different from what everyone around one appears to be, about growing up to be radically different from one's parents, about forming relationships in which the rules have to be made up as one goes along. Like any minority-rooted theater with a political subtext, gay plays that pursue these themes constantly risk lapsing into limiting (if potentially liberating) ghetto talk, dimensionless propaganda, or sudsy melodrama. The best gay plays transcend these elements, as does all art that transforms the particular into the universal, but even those that don't still have an important social value that must not be underestimated. Throughout history, theater has provided an opportunity for a community to get together and talk about itself. And like all "ghetto theater," even the most simplistic gay plays serve the primitive function of affirming the existence of a mistreated minority, confirming its convictions, and acting as a corrective to neglect or abuse by the culture-at-large.

The image of gay life traditionally presented onstage—when it was there at all—was a distorted one: we had the choice of being frivolous fairies, psychotic bull-dykes, or suicidal queens. With the advent of the gay movement (which more or less coincided with the success of Mart Crowley's 1968 *The Boys in the Band*), gay people began demanding honest portrayals of ourselves onstage; we wanted positive images, role models, alternatives to heterosexual stereotypes. The result has been varied: gay theater by gay men and women, gay theater written and produced by heterosexuals, serious and sensationalistic, occasionally on Broadway, but much more often off. Some of the most acclaimed gay plays have, in fact, been performed only rarely or in the briefest of runs. For some, scripts don't even exist.

In *Gay Plays: The First Collection* (Avon, 1979), editor William Hoffman took the first step toward establishing a standard repertoire. The collection was divided equally between well-known hallmarks of gay theater and new scripts. An anthology ideologically confined to presenting "positive images" would have censored not only the somewhat dated anguish of Frank Marcus's Sister George and Lanford Wilson's Lady Bright, but also the biting critique of the gay world found in Robert Patrick's *T-Shirts*—and in doing so would have excluded a portion of our world that does exist. Hoffman's anthology reminds us that some of us *are* frivolous fairies, psychotic bull-dykes, and suicidal queens.

Before *The Boys in the Band*, the existence of gay characters was so rare that instances could be tallied in a matter of seconds. Since *Boys*, the self-identified gay theater has grown in strength and influenced the mainstream to the point where it is no longer remarkable for conventional plays to feature gay characters.

HAROLD: What I *am*, Michael, is a thirty-two-year-old, ugly, pockmarked Jew fairy—and if it takes me a while to pull myself together and if I smoke a little grass before I can get up the nerve to show this face to the world, it's nobody's goddamn business but my own.

—The Boys in the Band[1]

For all intents and purposes, gay theater began as a result of *The Boys in the Band*, much the same way the gay liberation movement began with the Stonewall rebellion in 1969, when a routine police raid on a Greenwich Village gay bar incited the patrons, led by drag queens, to fight back for the first time in history. In both cases, gays were a visible presence beforehand, but the event was the catalyst for a sudden eruption of activity. Yet while *The Boys in the Band* was undeniably a turning point in the evolution of gay theater, its influence must be documented through at least two entirely different histories: the history of the mass-media image of gays, and the history of contemporary theater made by gays themselves.

There are remarkable differences between mass images of gay men and lesbians, created for the most part by heterosexuals, and those created by gays on the journey to self-definition. Such differences are perhaps predictable, since most popularly known psychiatric research into homosexuality starts with a basically negative, or at least neutral and scholarly, attitude—"very much the way a scientist might look at bugs or monkeys as something that might perhaps have something to offer the higher form of species," to quote Allen Young.[2] On the other hand, "in the post-Stonewall gay-liberation literature, the writings of gay people [are concerned with] trying to communicate with each other and to reveal the reality of the gay experience to straight society"[3]—not to mention discovering the reality and setting it down for ourselves. And the job is a big one.

The history that leads up to *The Boys in the Band* and paves the way for *La Cage aux Folles* begins in the days when homosexuality was not allowed on the stage under any circumstances. *Sappho*, a play about the lesbian poet by Alphonse Daudet and Adolph Belot, was first performed in the United States in 1895, but when revived in 1900 it caused a great scandal and ultimately the play was banned. In 1926, Edward Bourdet's *The Captive*, "the tragedy of a young woman . . . who falls into a twisted relationship with another woman,"[4] and *Sex* by Jane Mast (better known as Mae West), which has a subplot concerning a male hustler, met similar fates, as did West's 1927 *The Drag*, whose main character was a man in conflict over his homosexuality, and her 1928 *Pleasure Man*, a backstage comedy featuring campy gay men as secondary characters. As late as 1944, theaters in New York refused to rent to the producers of Dorothy and Howard Baker's *Trio* because the play dealt with an older woman's "unnatural" feelings for a girl. On the other hand, Mordaunt Shairp's *The Green Bay Tree* (1932), which portrayed a wealthy bachelor's protective relationship with a working-class boy, was produced in London and New York without condemnation, presumably because the love between the two men never quite went so far as to speak its name.

When homosexuality did begin to whisper its name onstage, it was usually in melodramatic treatments of false accusation (Robert Anderson's *Tea and Sympathy,* Lillian Hellman's *The Children's Hour,* Arthur Miller's *A View from the Bridge,* Allen Drury's *Advise and Consent*), vice (William Inge's *The Boy in the Basement*), or violence (Inge's *Natural Affection* and *The Cell,* Frank Marcus's *The Killing of Sister George,* LeRoi Jones's *The Toilet*). By the 1950s and '60s, although somewhat more sympathetic portrayals of homosexuals had begun to filter into popular theater, the gay content was still largely between the lines, and often as not gays were still ultimately seen as unhappy and pathetic—not surprising, considering society's attitude toward homosexuals. New York state law officially prohibited the presentation of homosexuality onstage until 1967.

In the mass audience, commercial theater—the straight theater, if you will—the appearance of *The Boys in the Band* signaled another step in the increasing boldness (or tastelessness, as some would have considered it) of stage productions. Its four-letter words made it racy, and its homosexual milieu gave it an exotic attraction akin to that of a circus freak-show. The play's roaring success seemed to indicate that homosexuality was no longer a taboo subject—in fact, that it was commercially viable—and enabled other writers to deal with homosexuality on a more honest, open level without facing immediate commercial disaster. Simon Gray's *Butley,* Michael Cristofer's *The Shadow Box,* John Hopkins's *Find Your Way Home,* Miguel Pinero's *Short Eyes,* James Kirkwood and Nicholas Dante's *A Chorus Line,* and David Rabe's *Streamers* were among the first plays that presented openly gay characters in mainstream dramas. On the other hand, this new freedom opened the doors to a flood of sensational plays exploiting the topic of homosexuality for its novelty or shock value—as in the "kinky" use of gay characters to spice up a tepid farce about marital infidelity in *Norman, Is That You?.*

While theater was taking tiny steps ahead in its treatment of homosexuality, the subject was approached explicitly and with far greater sophistication in non-dramatic literature. Novels about gay life—such as John Rechy's *City of Night,* Gore Vidal's *The City and the Pillar,* and Jean Genet's *Our Lady of the Flowers*—were widely read and commercially successful decades before homosexuality was accepted onstage.[5] By comparison, film and television—more mass media than theater—were even slower about presenting honest portrayals of gay life.[6] Books are written and read in private and thus are far safer than other forms of artistic expression. A book does not judge, as parents, teachers, or friends may, or tell one's secret before one is prepared to face it or share it with others. Reading up on homosexuality, therefore, is often the first step toward identifying and then accepting one's gay identity, by virtue of its very solitary and private nature.

Theater, on the other hand, is public. To present homosexuality in the theater, someone (an author, speaking through an actor) has to stand up and say, "This is me. I am gay." Playwrights and performers tended to view homosexuals as "other," as "them"—which may explain the strange, strained nature of most gay characters before 1968. Characters who would have gone unnoticed had they appeared in a novel suddenly had stunning impact when seen live. *The Boys in the Band* represented another milestone—"the crossroads at which the homosexual American novel and the theater met."[7] As French critic Georges-Michel Sarotte points out, "The sight of men congregating, loving, laughing, crying like everyone else—whereas before they had existed only in novels or as members of a secret, infamous society—suddenly forced the audience to recognize that they were human beings like everyone else."[8]

The history of what could more accurately be called gay theater, separate from the appearance of gay characters in mainstream plays, is bound up with the burgeoning Off Off Broadway theater in New York and the politics of the gay movement. The accidental birth of Off Off Broadway is generally attributed to Joe Cino, whose Caffe Cino started out in 1958 as a bohemian hangout. In the beginning, the café's regular crowd of writers, painters, and artistically-minded refugees from small-town America began to read poetry and perform scenes from plays as an occasional entertainment. But before long the Cino had become a real theater, an anarchic, unpretentious, amazingly prolific collective of actors and writers. From the very beginning most—if not all—of the Cino core were gay.

Minor plays by established gay writers were a frequent feature of the Cino's programming—Oscar Wilde's fairy tale *The Happy Prince*, William Inge's *The Tiny Closet*, Noël Coward's *Fumed Oak* and *Still Life*, Jean Genet's *Deathwatch*, André Gide's *Philoctetes*, lots of Tennessee Williams's one-acts, and so on. But more important, the Cino attracted, inspired, and nurtured a number of young, untried playwrights—including Doric Wilson, H. M. Koutoukas, Lanford Wilson, and Robert Patrick—for whom gayness was an essential part of a new, freewheeling, sometimes whimsical, often campy theater. Among the significant gay plays that came out of the Cino are Patrick's *The Haunted Host*, in which an eccentric writer exorcises the ghost of an unhappy love affair, and Lanford Wilson's *The Madness of Lady Bright*, in which a lonely, aging drag queen goes to pieces and slowly puts himself back together.

After the Caffe Cino, other Off Off Broadway theaters sprang up. Among the first was the Judson Poets Theater, run by Al Carmines. The Judson attracted the vanguard of new playwrights, many of them gay. Among its most noted productions were Carmines's adaptations of the plays of Gertrude Stein and his musical *The Faggot*. With the founding of Ellen Stewart's La Mama Experimental Theater Club, the Off Off Broadway movement went into full swing, and the percentage of gay input was high.

In 1966, a group of flamboyant gay actors and writers put together a theater devoted to total outrageousness called the PlayHouse of the Ridiculous under the direction of Ronald Tavel and John Vaccaro. Gay camp and monstrous excesses were the specialties of productions such as *Screen Test*, in which a cruel director tortured a would-be star, and *Shower*, "a spoof on James Bond movies with 'Brechtian interludes,'"[9] and the theater acquired a large gay audience. A spinoff of the original group, led by writer-actor-director Charles Ludlam, became the Ridiculous Theatrical Company, which has flourished for twenty years as a classical comic theater in New York. The Ridiculous Theater as a genre was part product and part progenitor of a new tradition of gay camp/drag theater, whose participants range from groups like the Ballet Trockadero, the Cockettes, Hot Peaches, and Bloolips to performance artists such as Ethyl Eichelberger (best known for his vaudevillean portraits of legendary female characters such as Phedre, Medea, and Nefertiti), San Francisco-based puppeteer Winston Tong, John Kelly (who started out creating tiny German Expressionist operas in East Village punk clubs), British drag performer and political activist Neil Bartlett, and Split Britches, a lesbian troupe formed by Lois Weaver, Peggy Shaw, and Deborah Margolin.

The early Off Off Broadway movement, by rejecting the rules of traditional commercial theater both in style and in substance, instigated a renaissance in American playwriting. Just as Off Off Broadway incorporated the voices of emerging black playwrights, it also gave gay artists a forum for the unself-conscious exploration of their own lifestyles. And for gay audiences and gay theater people who found *The Boys in the Band* an only partly accurate representation of the gay world, who objected to its perpetuation of old stereotypes about gays being pathetic, neurotic, effeminate, incomplete people, Off Off Broadway provided a vital outlet. With the force of the post-Stonewall gay liberation movement behind it, the backlash against such limited portrayals of gays as Crowley's fueled a theatrical explosion.

One person who made the connection between the Off Off Broadway movement and gay politics was playwright-director Doric Wilson. Wilson, who was helping to start the Circle Repertory Theater at the time of the Stonewall uprising, noticed a viable, visible gay movement springing up and soon became involved with it. "I would run back and forth from the Circle to GLF [Gay Liberation Front] and then GAA [Gay Activists Alliance]," Wilson says, and he began to realize he didn't like the schizophrenia such splintering fostered. "We didn't like *Boys in the Band*, but on the other hand those of us who were creative did not like the idea of censorship," Wilson says. Pondering the dilemma *Boys in the Band* raised, the playwright wondered why more diverse creative gay voices weren't making themselves heard. Adamant that "there should be a place where authors and artists who want to deal with their gayness can have their work done, and done well, and done away from the marketplace where sensationalism is the rule of the day,"[10] Wilson established The Other Side of Silence (TOSOS) in February 1974.

Though it operated steadily for little more than three years, TOSOS broke ground for an ongoing theater run by and for gays. Its productions ranged from *Lovers*, an original musical by Peter del Valle and Steve Sterner, to classic plays by Noël Coward and Joe Orton, to Wilson's own Oscar Wildean fantasia *Now She Dances!* and *The West Street Gang*, a docudrama about anti-gay violence. Producer John Glines was associated with TOSOS for a short time before he left in 1976 to form his own theater, The Glines, which remained active for six years, producing mostly new scripts by writers such as George Whitmore (*The Rights*) and Jane Chambers (*Last Summer at Bluefish Cove*). Outside of New York, gay theaters were forming in Minneapolis (the Out and About Theater), San Francisco (Theatre Rhinoceros), London (Gay Sweatshop), and Los Angeles (Celebration Theatre). By 1983, the newly formed Gay Theatre Alliance counted forty theaters among its membership, including theaters in Amsterdam, Toronto, and Sydney. Today gay theaters from Atlanta to Anchorage form a network that has nurtured such playwrights as Robert Patrick, Victor Bumbalo, Robert Chesley, and Doug Holsclaw.

With the high percentage of gay talents working in every aspect of the business (writing, staging, composing, performing, and design), it was inevitable that professional theater would eventually intersect with the self-defined, noncommercial-oriented gay theater. No one could have predicted, however, that the catalyst would be a four-and-a-half-hour trilogy about a drag queen that contains explicit references to anal sex and a rousing conclusion in which a nice Jewish mother is told she can pack up her bunny slippers and go back to Miami if she can't accept her son's gay lifestyle. Even those who saw Harvey Fierstein's plays Off Off Broadway at La Mama when they premiered individually were not prepared for the cumulative effect of *The International Stud, Fugue in a Nursery,* and *Widows and Children First,* performed together as *Torch Song Trilogy.* Seen all at once, in a production mounted by The Glines and starring the author himself, the trilogy proved to be a powerful, profoundly moving statement and a masterpiece of drama.

Torch Song Trilogy is superbly theatrical in the way each play's interior structure tells part of the story itself. *The International Stud's* five fragmented, vaudeville-like scenes reflect the excitement and alienation of gay-bar life; *Fugue* delineates marriage and connection as it sings with the heightened lyricism of new love; and *Widows,* formally the most conventional of the three plays (though the most revolutionary in content), is full of slammed doors—conflict made concrete. Beyond the trilogy's structural ingenuity, explosive rhetoric, and disarming wit, however, Fierstein's triumph is in taking his audience deep into an "exotic" emotional situation (a bisexual triangle, a gay "family") and confronting the basic, even conventional dilemmas of modern life. The sexual revolution that permitted instant gratification didn't guarantee satisfaction, the trilogy shows. Liberation from the nuclear family, Fierstein suggests, brought its own problems: what to do with our longing for community, how to obliterate the pain of losing your lover to someone else, to cancer, to thugs on the street. *Torch Song Trilogy* doesn't provide answers to all the questions it raises, but it does give a model of how to come to terms with our common struggle for self-acceptance and—above all—love.

What's finally most remarkable about *Torch Song Trilogy* is that it portrays gay life not as an isolated phenomenon but in constant relation to the society at large. And the society it exposes is one whose sexual values have undergone an enormous upheaval, a contemporary revolution that has left gays and straights alike struggling to learn the new rules.

In the modern world, radical impulses are absorbed and defanged with sometimes frightening speed. The same year that the producer of *Torch Song Trilogy* aroused controversy by thanking his male lover on the television broadcast of the Tony Awards, producer Allen Carr commissioned Harvey Fierstein to write the book for a Broadway musical based on the hit French play and movie *La Cage aux Folles.* If the success of *Torch Song Trilogy* signaled a merging of visionary gay theater with mainstream culture, *La Cage aux Folles* seemed like a co-opting of gay tradition to revitalize the wheezing carcass of the Broadway musical. Still, within this artistically stultified and socially conservative genre, a long-running hit musical that celebrates the union of lovers who are neither young and beautiful nor heterosexual is in its own way unprecedented. A far cry from the self-hatred of *The Boys in the Band, La Cage aux Folles*'s anthem of pride in the name of love, Jerry Herman's now-classic "I Am What I Am," sounds a message of gay self-affirmation as passionate as that of Fierstein's:

ZAZA: I am what I am
      And what I am
      Needs no excuses
      I deal my own deck
      Sometimes the ace
      Sometimes the deuces
      There's one life
      And there's no return and no deposit
      One life
      So it's time to open up your closet
      Life's not worth a damn
      Till you can say—"Hey, world,
      I am what I am!"[11]

Before World War II, America cherished its image as a melting pot that dissolved all ethnic distinctions, assimilating immigrant experiences and minority characteristics in order to produce homogeneous middle-class citizens. The events of World War II, however, made it necessary for individuals with ethnic histories that differed from the white Anglo-Saxon norm to assert their differences from the American dream. The spectre of Hitler's death camps accentuated the necessity of a Jewish tribal consciousness for protection, even survival. Blacks and women who made vital contributions to American society during the war also found their identities thrown into question suddenly; the autonomy they had experienced made them unable and unwilling to recede to second-class status after the war was over. Along with the movements for these groups' basic rights came the Kinsey report in 1948, with its astonishing documentation that only fifty percent of the population is exclusively heterosexual throughout its adult life. A new group of human beings— not a freakish mutation or easily dismissed minority—entered American consciousness.

Then in the 1950s, American society was threatened with enforced conformity, personified by Senator Joseph McCarthy in his campaign against communism, homosexuality, and other "un-American activities." The ultimate rejection of McCarthyism was an expression of the real American impulse toward individual freedom. No longer could history be portrayed as the history of rich straight white men. The triumph over McCarthyism was the celebration of human diversity.

At the same time, however, no rich straight white man can be depended upon to rewrite history to include others who are not like him—and so collections like this one serve a crucial function. Jews, blacks, women, and gays can reclaim their own place in the continuity of history by making their voices heard, for "part of oppression," as Karla Jay says, "is having other people tell your story."[12] The struggle to assert disparate voices in the face of a rigidly narrow convention is an ongoing one— one the writers represented in this book share.

No play is more appropriate to open this anthology than Doric Wilson's comic dramatization of events on Christopher Street the night of June 27, 1969, when the Stonewall riots changed the course of history for gay men and lesbians. In the tradition of some of the earliest outfront gay theater, *Street Theater* is part social history, part documentary theater.

Other plays emphasized the documentary aspect more strongly. Jonathan Katz's *Coming Out*, for example, first produced in 1972 as a commemoration of Stonewall and later revived for a tour of New England, offered literary portraits of little-known figures from gay American history. Similarly, *Crimes Against Nature*, created by the Gay Men's Theater Collective from San Francisco, consisted of nine personal accounts by individuals in the process of overcoming obstacles on the path to establishing a gay identity. Unafraid of being seen as propagandistic, unconcerned with being accused of preaching to the already converted, these plays spoke directly to the social needs of their audiences, giving them a power that true theater seeks and rarely finds.

Not strictly documentary like those plays, *Street Theater* is a stylized comedy, a cartoonish parade of what the *Village Voice* called "a collection of gay culture icons."[13] It teams a leatherman bartender with the shady proprietor of a gay bar, undercover vice cops with street cruisers, two fork-tongued drag queens who mourn the death of Judy Garland with two gay intellectuals sizing up each other's political correctness, a lesbian mechanic with a sixties flower child, and a professorial closet queen with a naïve Midwestern boy new to Greenwich Village. Wilson deftly manipulates what seem like cardboard comic stereotypes from a 1930s musical, and even throws in Michael and Donald, straight out of *The Boys in the Band* with their sweaters tied around their necks. Yet in the process he lifts these familiar gay masks to show the human faces underneath as he skillfully traces the political alliances that led a motley group of disenfranchised women and men to decide they had nothing to lose by fighting back against the abuse of society and the law. The play closes with a classic exchange. Michael and Donald, self-hating homosexual victims, stand disdainfully on the sidelines and yell at the drag queens brawling with policemen, "You faggots are revolting!!" The professor, shedding his closet mentality to join the tribe, retorts, "You bet your sweet ass we are!"

Street Theater was first performed in 1982 by Theatre Rhinoceros, San Francisco's leading gay theater. The same year a production opened in New York at a tiny theater in Tribeca and then moved to the Mineshaft, the notorious and legendary leather bar and sex club. Crudely staged, with actors occupying a narrow walkway between two groups of spectators on benches and folding chairs, this gay history performed in a gay space was nonetheless electrifying. Its performance conjured memories of the Federal Theater's original New York production of Marc Blitzstein's 1937 radical opera *The Cradle Will Rock* about steel industry corruption and labor union gallantry, which defied the government's attempt to suppress its subversive anticapitalist message by going on in a disused theater without sets, lights, electricity, or any power but the bond between the show and its audience.

Martin Sherman's *Bent* begins on another famous night in gay history—Berlin, June 28, 1934, also known as "The Night of the Long Knives." Aided by Richard Plant's ground-breaking research on the persecution of homosexuals in Nazi Germany, Sherman's play focuses on a pair of lovers captured by storm troopers as they attempt to flee Germany after Hitler's purge (read: execution) of homosexuals in government. Rudy, the weaker, dies on a boxcar to Dachau. Having heard that prisoners wearing the pink triangle get the worst treatment, his lover Max bargains with train guards for the yellow star of a Jew. He earns it by committing a grotesque act: to convince the guards he isn't "bent," he rapes the corpse of a thirteen-year-old girl.

After a first act full of people and action and shifting scenes, *Bent*'s second half is restricted to the barren prison camp (a Beckett landscape) where Max carries rocks from one pile to another and back (a task not unlike that performed by South African prisoners in Athol Fugard's *The Island*). Sharing his labors is Horst, a man imprisoned for signing a petition for gay-rights pioneer Magnus Hirschfeld. Horst disapproves of Max's masquerading as a Jew; as the two grow closer, he chips away at Max's unwillingness to wear the pink triangle, to admit who and what he is. In the language of the play, Max's denial of his homosexuality is the act of a man afraid to surrender to love, a man who considers love antithetical to survival. Horst's message is that love is essential to survival. In a scene that is incongruous, exhilarating, and finally courageous, Max and Horst ultimately make love to each other with words alone, standing side by side at attention under the gaze of armed guards. For Max the discovery that he can express his true feelings even under the most brutal conditions and stay alive is a crucial breakthrough. In *Bent*, love is the ultimate act of defiance.

As both a graphic portrayal of gay oppression in a historical context and a tribute to the power of love, *Bent* is an emotional tour de force and a major contribution to the body of Holocaust literature. (Largely through the influence of this play, produced on Broadway in 1979 with Richard Gere in the starring role, the pink triangle was adopted as a symbol of contemporary gay pride.) Like all historical dramas, *Bent* is as much about the time in which it was written as the period it depicts. Not just a history lesson, it is also a polemic on contemporary gay male sexuality. In prison, Horst tries to convince Max that his inability to love stems from his penchant for sadomasochism and that S&M is a form of self-hatred. Sherman's suggestion that S&M, a fashionable practice in contemporary gay society, is as barbarous and psychotic as Nazi Germany's extermination of the Jews is a provocative one. The author sets up two opposing equations—love equals self-acceptance, and S&M equals self-hatred. Horst accepts his homosexuality, loves Max, and wants Max to reciprocate. Yet in its conclusion—a donning of the pink triangle and then a suicide, as if to confirm that it's better to die as the person you are than to live as someone you're not—Sherman brings up a troubling implication: that the only option for an open homosexual is suicide.

Based on the 1979 trial of Dan White for murdering San Francisco Mayor George Moscone and openly gay city supervisor Harvey Milk, Emily Mann's *Execution of*

Justice (first performed by the Actors Theatre of Louisville) is a documentary embellished with testimony from what the author terms "the uncalled witnesses." The play poses provocative and unanswered questions about antihomosexual prejudice and social justice in America. As Mel Gussow wrote in the *New York Times*, "Step by careful step, the author as investigative reporter—and skillful dramatist— creates a world in which a social structure becomes a fortress to subvert both law and morality."[14] The contrast between the weak prosecution of Dan White and the emotional defense exemplifies the co-opting of "morality" by right-wing forces in America, who have tried to confuse the public (or perhaps merely the media) into believing that "moral values" and "liberal values" are mutually exclusive—conveniently overlooking concern for the rights of the underprivileged and the jarring incongruity of bigotry and the tenets of Christian morality.

When *Execution of Justice* opened on Broadway in 1986, Richard Hummler wrote in *Variety*, "This nonprofit-spawned play, precisely the kind of material that the nonprofit theaters should be doing, may prove too unpleasant a dose of reality for today's increasingly escapist-oriented Broadway public."[15] He was right; the play lasted only a few days on Broadway. Yet Mann's play has had a long life outside of New York. By its very nature a true ensemble piece (*Justice* was originally commissioned by the Eureka Theater, an ensemble of actors and directors in San Francisco; its cast was large and deliberately eschewed leading roles), the play has been embraced as such by resident theaters in Baltimore, Seattle, San Francisco, Houston, Minneapolis, and Washington.

While *Execution of Justice* may seem to belong to the same genre of courtroom dramas as *Inherit the Wind*, in fact Mann invented a different form to tell this particular story—a collage structure relying on first-hand interviews, mixed-media imagery (including crucial excerpts from Robert Epstein and Richard Schmiechen's Oscar-winning documentary *The Times of Harvey Milk*), and even sound cues such as the haunting echo of Mary Ann White's high heels on the marble floor of a deserted church. This insistence on creating a structure appropriate to her material is a hallmark of contemporary feminist playwriting. Female playwrights from Caryl Churchill (*Cloud Nine, Top Girls*) to Ntozake Shange (*for colored girls who have considered suicide when the rainbow is enuf*), rather than employing old dramatic formulas generally created by men, have created a body of work unconventional in form as well as content. This revolution in dramatic form has had a liberating effect on women's theater and American theater in general. By calling attention to dramatic structure itself, by employing heightened language, these playwrights have rescued theater from the straitjacket of naturalistic drama, which has not escaped the influence of two generations of television soap operas and sitcoms.

Lesbian playwrights have gained much from such experimentation with dramatic form. Although the best-known lesbian playwright of our time was the late Jane Chambers, who wrote in a naturalistic vein (*A Late Snow, Last Summer at Bluefish Cove*), younger writers have been more adventurous. One of the few plays about black lesbians I have encountered is Alexis De Veaux's *No*. This cycle of poems, stories, and scenes (adapted for the stage by Glenda Dickerson at the New Federal Theater in 1981) fractures the political, social, sexual, and emotional experiences of young black gay women into more vivid fragments than any one character in a conventional play could be expected to hold together. If the structure of the play owes something to Ntozake Shange, the brassy directness of De Veaux's political invective and lush sensuality of her language are all her own.

Holly Hughes emerged from the East Village club scene that has nurtured art stars such as Keith Haring and Kenny Scharf, actress-comedienne Ann Magnuson and writer-director John Jesurun, as well as any number of young performance artists who mix dance, theater, music, and video with outspoken gay content, such as Tim Miller, John Bernd, Ishmael Houston-Jones, and John Kelly. Hughes shares the TV-bred instinct for savage parody and aggressive infantilism that characterizes many East Village performers, but unlike most of them she is primarily a writer who blends junk culture with poetry to make theater that has been labeled "dyke noir" by critic C. Carr. In her plays *The Well of Horniness*, *The Lady Dick*, and *Dress Suits to Hire*, "Hughes has gleefully invented herself a genre with little precedent," writes Carr. "From the hard-boiled fiction she loves, she's appropriated the tough guy talk, the lowlife mood, the shady shifty operators." As for the crime, "the *characters* are the crime—women who drive each other to emotional extremes, who put their sexuality upfront where everyone has to acknowledge it."[16]

The Well of Horniness is the kind of work that postmodern literary critics love to call a "text." Conceived as a lesbian porn flick, it premiered as a sketch at the WOW Cafe (a women-run theater and hangout in New York City), was adapted into a radio play, and then mutated into a strange hybrid of radio and theater. Anything but a straightforward picture of lesbian life on the Lower East Side, it reads like the dramatic equivalent of Kathy Acker's parodistic novels *Great Expectations* and *Don Quixote*, a pop mosaic encoded with partially digested scraps of cultural debris and half-rejected, half-embraced stereotypes of wicked sister-love.

Among the crop of mainstream gay plays that have emerged in the 1980s, it's interesting to note that many observe gay people finding new relationships with their families. Whereas the New York school of gay plays (Robert Patrick, Doric Wilson, Harvey Fierstein) tends to focus on modern-day metropolitan gay lifestyles, such works as Lanford Wilson's *Fifth of July*, William Finn's *March of the Falsettos*, Victor Bumbalo's *Niagara Falls*, and Timothy Mason's *Levitation* acknowledge that outside of New York and San Francisco there is no such thing as an exclusively gay lifestyle: you have to deal with the family. The lesbian mother in Caryl Churchill's *Cloud Nine* and the gay father in *March of the Falsettos* are particularly intriguing characters as they reflect a complicated struggle: how to adjust to the transition from a socially condoned relationship to one for which there is no accepted or acceptable model. Lin in *Cloud Nine* finds flexibility rewarding and ends up sharing her house with her five-year-old daughter, her married lover Vicky, and Vicky's gay ("I think I'm a lesbian") brother Edward. In William Finn's musical, on the other hand, two men accustomed to independence find negotiating a working relationship bewilderingly difficult. "Life's a sham, and every move is wrong," cry the exhausted lovers. "We've examined every move as we move along." What's refreshing about these plays is that they explore the content of gay lives rather than parading propaganda (see how happy we are) or melodrama (die, doomed queen).

In Kathleen Tolan's *A Weekend Near Madison*, Nessa, a famous feminist folk-singer, and her young female lover Sam have decided that they'd like to have a baby. To accomplish this goal, Nessa organizes a reunion of her college chums to select which of her male friends she would like to be the father of her child: her former boyfriend Jim, or his macho-pig brother Dave (whose own wife Doe is barren from complications after an abortion). The form of the play may sound overly familiar—both the domestic drama aspect and the college-chums reunion genre were practically patented by Michael Weller in *Moonchildren* and *Loose Ends*—but here the content is revolutionary in its subtle overhaul of established notions about gender. As critic Jan Stuart has noted, "When Doe confesses to her husband how much she needs him, it is not before realizing how powerfully her female identity has hitherto hinged on a capacity to make babies." Asked to father a child for the lesbian couple, Jim gets a taste of his sister-in-law's feminist rage at the thought that one's usefulness as a person could be reduced simply to one's sexual function. "Even Nessa," writes Stuart, "whose feminist polemics spew out in awkward funny gobs of contradictions, is given the final dignity (and humanity) of self-knowledge, as she locates the source of her contradictions in her own long-rooted experience of the nuclear family."[17]

Just as structural innovation distinguishes contemporary women's theater, fantasy and theatricality are hallmarks of gay male sensibility, and for much the same reason: to rescue imaginative space from the onslaught of heterosexual society. "Fantasy and ornament are the most genuinely subversive aspects of gay writing," Edmund White once remarked in a roundtable discussion on gay sensibilities. "Realism written with understatement and control subscribes to a conventional manner of seeing the world, of tracing causality, of defining character, of establishing hierarchies of importance. . . . Realism is a *legacy* of fantasy, the imitation of the fantasies of the past; and for that reason realism is almost always conservative. A fantasist, by contrast, sets herself or himself up as someone capable of re-imagining the world—and this challenge to order is perceived by cultural conservatives as 'wrong,' dangerous, anomalous, decadent. The anomaly is that an individual is exercising the right to *play* in a state of complete freedom, and this exercise becomes an invitation to readers to live lives of freedom."[18] This freedom, White noted, is shared by others left out of the consensus culture as gays are—minority writers such as Gabriel García Márquez, Maxine Hong Kingston, and Ishmael Reed.

Fantasy figures heavily in many of the plays in this anthology. The hero of Evan Smith's *Remedial English* is a character familiar from life but new to the theater—a lovestruck gay schoolboy obsessed with a classmate. When Sister Beatrice assigns the bright but underachieving Vincent to tutor one of her slower students, he is in heaven: his charge is Rob Andrews, Adonis of the boys' locker room. All day long Vincent daydreams, part Sal Mineo in *Rebel Without a Cause*, part heroine of *Gidget Gets a Sex-change*. His study date crashes and burns, though, when Rob turns out to be a heterosexual dumbbell who refers to Emily Dickinson as a "bitch" and whose response to Vincent's eloquent description of Gandhi's philosophy of civil disobedience is, "Nuke 'em!" First produced as part of the Dramatists Guild's Young Playwrights Festival at Playwrights Horizons in 1986, *Remedial English* introduced a fresh comic voice to the theater.

Like many of Harvey Fierstein's one-act plays, *Forget Him* is the contemporary equivalent of that feature of Greek dramatic festivals called the satyr play, which consisted of a comic treatment of a theme from a longer work. *Forget Him* continues the search for the ideal man begun by Arnold Beckoff in *The International Stud*, the first play of *Torch Song Trilogy*. Its hero, Michael, was a virgin when he enlisted Mr. Marlowe's dating service to find his ideal mate. When Marlowe succeeded in finding him a man who was rich, handsome, sexy, and more—deaf and blind— Michael thought he was happy. But now, after four years of living with a less-than- perfect man, Michael is tormented by the thought of "Him," the unblemished idol of his dreams whom he fears he's missing by sticking with Eugene. In a brief, surreal encounter, Michael is forced to admit the folly of his fantasy and to forget "Him."

In contrast to the essential innocence of *Remedial English* and *Forget Him*, the fantasies at work in Terrence McNally's *The Lisbon Traviata* are steamier—mari- nated in centuries of Italian music—as well as more lethal. The first act is the ultimate bitchy opera-queen conversation between Stephen, a famous playwright who hasn't written in a long while, and Mendy, his dear old friend and unrequited lover. The second act is the ultimate sordid lovers' quarrel between Stephen and his mate of eight years, Michael, who has spent the night with another man. McNally has made a career out of showing people at their worst; here, lovers in the throes of murderous jealousy are not a pretty sight. Yet there is something curiously moving in this portrait of a love so strong, so operatically intense, that it finally destroys.

In Harry Kondoleon's *The Fairy Garden*, chic Dagny consults with two male friends, Roman and Mimi, who are lovers, about whether to stay with her rich but despicable husband or run off with her sexy mechanic boyfriend. But in nine short scenes, everything rapidly shifts. The lovers break up, Dagny cuts off her husband's head and tosses it in the ice bucket, a real fairy appears (a *real* fairy?) to grant them one wish, and they decide to put the husband's head back on. Mimi falls in love with Dagny, the hated husband announces he's fallen in love with the fairy who is now disguised as a real woman (a *real* woman?), and the two couples go off. The mechanic shows up, only he's really a stripper and does his act for jilted Roman, who chases him off. Finally, Roman and the fairy have a confrontation and—in a dreamlike *coup de théâtre*—disappear in a vapor of memory and obliterated identity. Underneath the fabulistic designer facade of *The Fairy Garden* lies a modern romantic tragedy. The force from which all else flows is the passion for love, the unquenchable lust, the yearning for connection with the Other that defines the language and the form and the almost tropical feverishness of Kondoleon's writing.

Compared to television's live coverage every night of the latest election campaign or hostage crisis, theater may seem like a cumbersome form of communication, lagging years behind in dealing with the urgent issues of the day. Yet theater can also lead, asserting its ancient function as a public forum in which a community gathers to talk about itself. The best contemporary example is the theater's response to the AIDS crisis. William Hoffman's *As Is* and Larry Kramer's *The Normal Heart* took the lead in promoting education on AIDS and concern for the afflicted, a social obligation that the press, the government, even made-for-TV movies were slow to pick up on. The audiences for these and other plays about AIDS—Robert Chesley's

Jerker, for instance, or Doug Holsclaw's *The Life of the Party* (a spin-off of *The AIDS Show,* a revue first performed at San Francisco's Theatre Rhinoceros in 1984)—experienced something extraordinary. The line between what was happening onstage and what was happening in the lives of the audience was so fine that the script for these works seemed a mere pretext for the gathering of individuals collectively seeking information about this mysterious disease, seeking an outlet for anger, anxiety, and grief. These plays had a powerful impact on an audience that needed to bolster a still shaky sense of gay self-acceptance in order to face the medical horrors and political backlash sure to come.

While AIDS has become a global concern—"a social phenomenon, not just a public health issue," in the words of Dr. Steven Joseph, New York City Commissioner of Health—it struck first and deepest in the heart of the gay communities in New York and San Francisco, with their high populations of artists. Undoubtedly, it was this personal contact with AIDS that triggered such an immediate response from gay theater artists. *The Normal Heart,* Larry Kramer's report from the front lines about the formation in 1981 of Gay Men's Health Crisis (the primarily volunteer organization, co-founded by Kramer, that has become the model for AIDS service agencies around the world), is part autobiography and part jeremiad. Kramer's gripping and caustically comic portrait of personalities and politics inside New York's gay male community is wrapped around a love story between writer Ned Weeks and *New York Times* reporter Felix Turner.

As passionate as he is self-serving, Weeks (aka Kramer) directs his fury at two targets. First he excoriates the media (especially the *New York Times*) and the government (especially Mayor Koch) for turning a blind eye to an epidemic occurring in a population of homosexuals and drug addicts, while making major stories out of the comparatively far smaller Tylenol scare and an outbreak of Legionnaires' disease. But Weeks/Kramer is also angry at gay men for not being more militant in demanding attention be paid to the AIDS crisis. A polemicist at heart, Kramer frames all issues in black and white: you're either helping the cause (by following Kramer's outspoken example) or you're responsible for murdering fellow gays. When it comes to sex, gay men have only two choices: orgiastic promiscuity or celibacy. This message unpleasantly echoes some of the "conventional wisdom" of the psychiatric community and has made Kramer's work more appealing to straight audiences than gays. Still, infuriating and abrasive as it is, Kramer's play is nonetheless an impassioned call to political action. The longest running play ever to be performed at Joseph Papp's Public Theater, *The Normal Heart* has been produced around the world and is scheduled to be made into a film by Twentieth Century Fox.

In rich contrast to Kramer's revocation of sexual joy is Robert Chesley's *Jerker, or The Helping Hand: A Pornographic Elegy with Redeeming Social Value and A Hymn to the Queer Men of San Francisco in Twenty Telephone Calls, Many of Them Dirty.* The subtitle Chesley has supplied makes his play sound raunchier than it really is. While the dialogue between two strangers who conduct their entire relationship on the telephone is racy enough to have launched FCC sanctions against a California radio station for broadcasting part of it on the air, Chesley is less concerned that the audience share his characters' specific sexual fantasies than that they cherish the vitality of the sexual imagination in the face of death. As Stephen Holden wrote in the *New York Times*, *Jerker* points out "more bluntly than any other play dealing with AIDS how the epidemic has threatened one of the fundamental reasons for an entire community's very existence—its freedom of erotic expression—and challenged its hard-won self-esteem."[19]

Almost in passing, Chesley makes a quietly profound statement that deserves special mention. Departing from their usual masturbatory fantasies, toward the end of the play the character J.R. enchants his telephone companion Bert with a bedtime fairy tale about two young boys who battle their way through the Forbidden Forest to arrive at the castle of a handsome prince. "He questions us about each adventure, peril, and sorrow," J.R. recounts, "and from the answers he brings forth from us we understand that each one, even the most terrible, was a lesson on our journey to the palace; and we understand that we ourselves were lessons for others whose paths crossed ours in the Forest." In this storybook image, Chesley has found a way for gay men to find meaning in the AIDS crisis without guilt or resignation, placing our history in the continuum of human experience.

Where *The Normal Heart* focuses on political aspects of the AIDS crisis and *Jerker* concerns itself with sexuality, William Hoffman's *As Is* looks at AIDS from a personal and social point of view. This moving and humorous drama concerns two men who are former lovers and how they cope with the situation when one of them is diagnosed as having AIDS. In quick, deft strokes, Hoffman draws this complicated relationship in realistic detail. Yet the play itself is a kaleidoscope of dissolving scenes utilizing a corps of actors as a sort of Greek chorus who provide an objective context for the story as well as interacting with the main characters, playing friends, family, doctors, etc. With remarkable economy, Hoffman combines medical information, political background, social history of gay New York, and a catalogue of the shifting emotions that AIDS can produce both in the people who have it and those who care for them. Unlike Larry Kramer's unremitting despondence in *The Normal Heart*, Hoffman manages—without denying the toll that AIDS has taken or being Pollyanna-ish about the prospects of facing a life-threatening disease for which there is no known cure—to insist that where there is life, there is hope. Popular with audiences on Broadway, Off Broadway, and on cable television, around the country and around the world, *As Is* is the best play anyone has written yet about AIDS.

There will always be skeptics who question the validity, even the existence, of such a thing as "gay culture" or "gay sensibility," choosing to overlook or ignore the effects of a culture that raises us to be—does its best to make us be—heterosexual. But despite that culture, many of us are not heterosexual. Perhaps the essential strangeness of being gay is being something other than what one was brought up to be.

In the past, homosexual society was characterized by isolation and subterfuge; underground living produces a subculture. But as someone young enough to have been spared the isolation-and-subterfuge era, I've seen the direct benefit of open, if newborn, gay culture. The primary function of culture is to show us what to be, how to live, and time and time again I've been given the courage to be honest about my own feelings in a world that encourages me to hide them.

Having grown up in a strict household on Air Force bases around the country, I got the same negative messages from society, from homophobic psychotherapists, and from the Catholic Church that the previous generation of gay men did. Yet unlike them, I was also getting positive messages to counteract the gloomy ones. Even the offhand signs I received—Allen Ginsberg's casual remarks about his lover, Peter Orlovsky, in interviews, the description of a male character who "has a 'thing' about Mick Jagger" in the liner notes for the Broadway cast album of *Hair*, Jill Johnston's stream-of-consciousness column in the *Village Voice* covering lesbian communes and the New York bohemian art scene in the same breath—made a difference, letting me know that there was a way of living gay. While for previous generations the only "gay culture" was pornography, Mae West movies, Streisand records, and the opera, I was fortunate to have had the essays of Karla Jay and Allen Young, the writings of Edmund White and Dennis Altman, the cranky, defiant journalism of Arthur Bell and John Mitzel, the poems of Frank O'Hara and Judy Grahn, the plays of Robert Patrick and Harvey Fierstein.

By the time I was forming an adult identity, being gay meant coming out—a political act that was applauded, if only by other gays. It was relatively easy for me to follow the path that others had carved out of a wilderness: I had their fortitude as a model, whereas they had had mostly silence. I started writing for a gay newspaper and became part of the culture that had helped me; as my career progressed, I resisted attempts to suppress my gay identity. Even on the rare occasions when I was forced to hide my feelings, they were never a source of anguish or a threat to self-esteem but rather a gift to be cherished and safeguarded.

Coming out is not a one-time thing, however. When I moved to New York, I found myself living in the West Village—in the heart of the most visible gay culture on the East Coast. Still, as I went off to meet this editor or that one, friends would advise, "Don't let her know you're gay." In New York City! Disturbing but true: it takes as much courage to be openly gay in New York as it does almost anywhere else.

In the last decade, between the height of the disco era and the abyss of the AIDS crisis, gay culture has begun to infiltrate and to influence mainstream culture to the benefit of both, thanks to openly gay artists in every field of endeavor: visual art, pop music, the dance, the novel, film, journalism, performance art, and theater. Whether gay culture has validity for people who aren't gay depends on how much they really want to hear. But the courage to be who you are is something we all need. Questions of identity—who you know yourself to be versus who you allow yourself to be with others—as well as the importance of sex and love are more than obsessive themes in gay culture. They are significant issues for all of us in living our lives.

The plays in this anthology present a wide range of vastly divergent characters, dramatic forms, ethnic experience, sexual experience, political viewpoints, and visions of homosexuality. They don't adhere to any party line. I like to think that they represent the pluralistic reality of the gay and lesbian population of America, which in turn represents the democratic ideal of Western civilization. It would be naïve, however, not to acknowledge that there is an ongoing debate over which more accurately represents "the people's voice" in a democratic society: the individual will, or the majority rule. The tension is one that underlies all minority culture in

America. The despairing view is that by making one attribute the basis of our identity—whether it be sexual preference, race, or religion—we give others permission to persecute us on the same basis. The hopeful view is that we will come to see the richness in our differences and to cherish our differences as vital to our humanity. Between hope and despair, we live our lives.

June 1, 1987

FOOTNOTES

1. Mart Crowley, *The Boys in the Band*, in Harold Clurman, ed., *Famous American Plays of the 1960s*, New York: Dell Books, 1972, p. 352.
2. Quoted in Don Shewey, "The Gay Report," *Boston Phoenix*, May 29, 1979.
3. Ibid.
4. J. Brooks Atkinson, the *New York Times*, September 30, 1926, cited in Jonathan Katz, *Gay American History*, New York: Thomas Y. Crowell, 1976, p. 83.
5. For an extensive study of the homosexual novel in America throughout the twentieth century, see Roger Austen, *Playing the Game*, New York: Bobbs-Merrill, 1977.
6. For a thorough treatment of gay representation in cinema, see Vito Russo, *The Celluloid Closet*, New York: Harper & Row, revised 1987.
7. Georges-Michel Sarotte, *Like a Brother, Like a Lover*, New York: Anchor Press/Doubleday, 1978, p. 33.
8. Ibid.
9. Stefan Brecht, *Queer Theater*, Frankfurt: Suhrkamp, 1978, p. 108.
10. Interview with Don Shewey, August, 1976.
11. "I Am What I Am," lyrics and music by Jerry Herman, Jerryco Music Co./Edwin H. Morris & Co. (ASCAP), copyright 1983.
12. Quoted in Shewey, *Boston Phoenix*, cited above.
13. Robert Massa, *Village Voice*, December 7, 1982.
14. *New York Times*, March 29, 1984.
15. *Variety*, March 19, 1986.
16. C. Carr, "The Lady Is a Dick: The Dyke Noir Theater of Holly Hughes," *Village Voice*, May 19, 1987.
17. *New York Native*, October 10, 1983.
18. Quoted in John Hofsess, "Portraits of the Artist: Why Is Gay Art Gay?" *New York Native*, December 20, 1982.
19. *New York Times*, May 1, 1987.

ACKNOWLEDGMENTS

First of all, I'd like to thank all the playwrights in this anthology for the inspiring courage of their excellent work. In particular, Bill Hoffman was a big help to me in several stages of preparing this book. Terry Helbing, Betty Osborn, Glenda Dickerson, Nina Reznick, David Roggensack, and several people from the William Morris Agency—George Lane, Michael Traum, Peter Franklin, Gilbert Parker, and Peter Hagan—provided valuable assistance in tracking down authors, manuscripts, and permissions. I'd like to thank the many people who sent me scripts and suggestions for this anthology, especially Sky Gilbert and Neil Bartlett. My introduction is the evolutionary product of articles written over the years for the Jove Books anthology *Lavender Culture*, the *Soho News*, the *Boston Phoenix*, and the *Village Voice*, and I'd like to thank the editors who brought them about: Karla Jay and Allen Young, Tracy Young, Carolyn Clay, Ande Zellman, Sylviane Gold, and Ross Wetzsteon. The final form of the introduction owes much to the superior editorial suggestions of Helen Eisenbach. For the bibliography, Dennis Altman provided crucial research on Australian plays, Dee Michel passed along useful articles on gay theater in Los Angeles, and Alice Playten's subscription to *Time Out* allowed me to keep up with gay plays produced in London. For their general friendship, support, and encouragement, I'd like to thank Robert Boyle, Elinor Fuchs, Harry Kondoleon, and James Leverett.

For the many large and small ways they helped make this book possible, I owe a debt of gratitude to Jed Mattes, Sam Montgomery, and especially the late Luis Sanjurjo at ICM, and Walt Bode at Grove Press, who said yes to this project in the first place and provided unwavering, sensible, good-humored support from start to finish. Finally, special thanks, as ever, to Stephen Holden.

STREET THEATER

by
Doric Wilson

FOR
Tom Strogen,
Vernon Kroenig, and
Jörg Wenz—
and far too many others

Street Theater opened February 18, 1982, at Theatre Rhinoceros in San Francisco, California. The play was directed by Allan Estes with the following cast:

MURFINO	Ron Lanza
JACK	Harvey Hand
C.B.	Margaret Van Schenk
HEATHER	Maud Winchester
SEYMOUR	Joe Cappetta
CEIL	Duane Cropper
DONOVAN	Mark Merry
SIDNEY	David Vining
BOOM BOOM	Steev'n Lloyd
TIMOTHY	David Williston
MICHAEL	Alan Herman
DONALD	Brett Hirschi
JORDAN	Tom Ammiano
GORDON	Robert Ferguson

General manager for Theatre Rhinoceros: Lanny Baugniet; technical director: Raleigh Waugh; production manager and set design: Valentine Hooven; stage manager: Ted Skinner; costume design: Nick Papagallo; lighting design: Raleigh Waugh; sound design: Carl Carlson; assistant director: Christopher Guerin.

Street Theater opened in New York City, November 18, 1982, at the Basement. The production was produced by Ken Cook, TOSOS, and Bart in association with Terry Miller and Candida Scott Piel. Ken Cook replaced J. Kevin Hanlon as director. Meridian Theatre then moved the play to the Mineshaft on January 27. The cast, including the Mineshaft replacements, was as follows:

MURFINO	Harvey Perr
	Tony Nunziata
JACK	Nole Cohen
	Peter Boruchowitz
C.B.	Julia Dares
HEATHER	Maud Winchester
	Loreta Feldon
SEYMOUR	Joseph Smenyak
	Tony Torres
CEIL	Bill Blackwell
	Casey Wayne

DONOVAN	Michael Scully
	Tom Cahill
SIDNEY	Ivan Smith
	Daniel Holmberg
BOOM BOOM	Michael Bowers
	Philip Blackwell
TIMOTHY	David Williston
	J.J. La Britz
MICHAEL	Mel Minter
	Doug DeVos
DONALD	Archie Harrison
	Charles Poindexter
JORDAN	Vito Russo
	Terry Helbing
GORDON	Joel Jason
	Randy Carfagno

Stage manager: Warren Lalman. Stage manager for the Mineshaft: Gail Wilcox. Set design for the Basement: Valentine Hooven; lighting design: Nancy Haskell; hair: Ethyl Eichelberger.

The playwright gives special thanks to:

Richard Anderson, Bart, Bill Blackwell, Georges Caldwell and Castello, Jane Chambers and Beth Allen, Robert Chesley, Howard Cruse, Allan Estes, Dr. Ronald Grossman, Terry Helbing, John F. Karr, Rob Kilgallen, Jane Lowry, Mr. Marcus, Terry Miller, George Sardi, Teri Sheridan, Mark Thompson, Glenn Turner, Casey Wayne, Marjorie Wilson, Larry Clinton and the people of the Bar, Wally Wallace and the people of the Mineshaft, the Lesbian/Gay Freedom Day Committee of San Francisco, the staff, crew and family of Theatre Rhinoceros, TOSOS Theater Company and Meridian Gay Theatre, and most particularly to Jim Cronin. Without their love and support, *Street Theater* would not have been written.

CHARACTERS

MURFINO, a thug
JACK, heavy leather, keys left
C.B., a politically incorrect lesbian
HEATHER, a flower child
SEYMOUR, a vice cop
CEIL, a street queen
DONOVAN, apparently a pedestrian
SIDNEY, in the closet
BOOM BOOM, a street queen
TIMOTHY, new in town
MICHAEL, in analysis
DONALD, noncommittal
JORDAN, a student radical
GORDON, a new-left liberal

TIME

Late evening, the 27th of June, 1969.

SETTING

Christopher Street.

5

ACT I

No curtain. No scenery. The audience, arriving, sees an empty stage in half-light. The sound system plays a medley of upbeat golden oldies from the sixties, ending with the Lovin' Spoonful's "Summer in the City." MURFINO, a thug, enters stage right carrying a battered, empty garbage can. MURFINO is a standard cigar-stub-in-mouth slob. He wears a sweat-stained tank top and pressless pants. The stage lights come up as MURFINO places the can down stage left.

MURFINO (*to the audience, an unauthorized prologue*): This play is called *Street Theater* on account of it's all about this bunch of lowlifes. You know, juicebums, hopheads, oddballs, weirdos, queers—what you call your "artistic element." The usual gutter crud you got to expect to contend with down here in the Village.

(JACK, *heavy leather, keys left, enters stage left carrying an overly full plastic trash bag.* JACK *is the ominous image used to promote S&M establishments. His geniality and good humor come as a surprise to the uninitiated.*)

JACK (*giving the bag to* MURFINO): Here you go, Murfino.

MURFINO (*opening the bag*): What's this?

JACK: You forgot your lunch.

MURFINO: Garbage! (*Emptying a wide assortment of rubbish into the can, filling it to overflowing.*) We have to be this authentic?

JACK: It won't be Christopher Street without it.

MURFINO (*to the audience, referring to* JACK): The very "element" of which we were speaking.

JACK: Who, me? Artistic? I guess you could say that. (*Displaying a heavily tattooed arm.*) Sure, this body of mine is a walking museum.

MURFINO (*deprecating*): Since when do tattoos qualify as culture?

JACK: You haven't seen the latest addition to my collection. (*To the audience:*) This'll interest you . . . (*Slowly unbuttoning his fly.*) . . . it's a major masterpiece . . . a "multi-media" collage, painstakingly combining an extremely graphic design with a found object of which I'm inordinately fond—

MURFINO (*scandalized*): Put that away!

JACK (*teasing*): You don't want a private showing?

MURFINO: We don't want no "K-Y jokes" in this theater.

JACK (*buttoning his fly*): Your loss.

(*A smiling* JACK *exits stage right as C.B., a politically incorrect lesbian, enters stage right carrying a signpost with signs reading: CHRISTOPHER STREET, SHER-*

IDAN SQUARE and NO STANDING. C.B. styles herself "diesel dyke," dresses accordingly. Paternally maternal, C.B. is often described as a "good Joe." She wears her hair in a DA.)

MURFINO (*to the audience*): I'm here to see to it this show remains compatible to you the general public. Which means *no* pubic hair, *no* winking-and-giggling, *no* in-jokes elbow-nudging you in the rib cage. (*Confidentially.*) You want winking and giggling and pubic hair, later you should stop by this bar I happen to be associated with. Allegedly. (*Indicating stage left.*) Up the street, middle of the block. That's where your degenerate behavior belongs—in a bar, where it's profitable.

C.B. (*to* MURFINO): What are you telling them? (*To the audience:*) What's he been telling you?

MURFINO (*caught*): I'm . . . er . . . bidding them a cordial welcome to the 27th of June, 1969.

C.B. (*placing the signpost down stage right*): Yeah?

MURFINO: We are attempting to depict here an historical event . . . a date destined to live forever in the annals of anals. You want they should acquire an erroneous impression?

C.B. (*crossing upstage left*): They already have one.

MURFINO: So I'm setting them straight.

C.B. (*pulling a backdrop across upstage, left to right*): Swell, just what we need—to be set "straight."

(*The backdrop represents Christopher Street, circa 1969. It is a montage of Village impressions: tenements, highrises, the Jefferson Market Court House, the Women's House of Detention, the storefront of Village Cigars, the display window of a sedate antique shop, a slightly bent boutique offering men's swimwear, neon signs advertising Carr's, Danny's, Julius's and the Harbor bar, a fragment of the Mattachine Society's logo, etc. right of upstage center on the backdrop is the doorway of a brownstone.*)

MURFINO (*assisting* C.B. *with the backdrop*): Clearly you are unread and unawares of Therman Wilder (*sic*) whom I am emulating in this my introduction of them to our town here so to speak. (*To the audience:*) He was of your lavender leaning, Therman Wilder. Bet they never taught you that in school.

(HEATHER, *a flower child, enters stage left, carrying a fire hydrant painted a rainbow of Day-Glo colors.* HEATHER *is a beaded and fringed recent convert to the counterculture.*)

C.B. (*to* MURFINO): I was in that play. At Vocational High. The girl playing Emily got pregnant so I had to go on in the part. (*To the audience:*) You should have seen me, I wore my mother's wedding dress and everything. Mom was so proud of me, she cried for a week.

MURFINO: You blame her? Her one and only chance to see you in it?

C.B.: You'd like me to break both your legs? (*Transported into a gentle* EMILY.) "Goodbye to clocks ticking . . . and Mama's sunflowers . . . and food and coffee . . . and new ironed dresses . . . ."

HEATHER: That's beautiful.

C.B. (*embarrassed*): Oh, yeah, well . . .

HEATHER: Like, man, you're a poet.

C.B. (*blushing*): Naw. . . .

MURFINO (*to* HEATHER): What do you want?

HEATHER: Peace and love.

MURFINO: Spare us the pinko party line.

HEATHER (*referring to the hydrant*): They told me to bring this to you.

C.B. (*indicating downstage right*): Put it over there, kid, next to the street sign.

(C.B. *exits stage left.*)

MURFINO (*to* HEATHER): Yeah, over there . . . give the dogs some selection. (A *double take.*) Who messed up that fireplug?

HEATHER: Isn't it groovy?

MURFINO: It's all covered with paint.

HEATHER: You never saw psychedelic before?

MURFINO: Hydrants are supposed to be respectable. You know, *rusty.*

HEATHER (*pleased with herself*): I sent it on a trip.

MURFINO (*appalled*): You did this destruction?

HEATHER: Bringing beauty to the urban environment is my bag.

MURFINO: You have defaced public property.

HEATHER (*patiently*): Like, man, where have you been? This is the Dawning of the Age of Aquarius, all property belongs to the public.

(HEATHER *exits stage right.*)

MURFINO (*calling after* HEATHER): Not when this city owns it!

(SEYMOUR, *an undercover cop, enters stage right looking for* MURFINO. SEYMOUR *is somewhat disguised as an actual person. Constabulary to the core, his eyes are innocent of intelligence, he has cultivated the chin of a recruiting poster.*)

MURFINO (*to the audience, indicating the hydrant*): Look at that fireplug! What happens we should have a conflagration on this block? No self-respecting fireman's gonna touch a pansy plug like that.

SEYMOUR (*pulling* MURFINO *aside*): You and me, we need to talk!—Surreptitiously, if you see my drift.

MURFINO (*to the audience*): Don't let Seymour here worry you, he only looks like lowlife.

SEYMOUR (*to the audience*): I'm practicing a deception.

MURFINO (*to the audience*): He's undercover.

SEYMOUR (*to the audience, flashing his badge*): Vice squad, N.Y.P.D.

MURFINO (*to the audience*): Had you fooled, didn't he?

SEYMOUR (*to the audience*): Bet you thought I was an actual person.

MURFINO (*to the audience*): Seymour here specializes in "Convenience Surveillance."

SEYMOUR (*to the audience, clarifying*): Toilet Patrol.

MURFINO (*to the audience*): He's stationed behind the air vent in the "little boys' room" of the Sheridan Square I.R.T. subway station.

SEYMOUR (*to the audience*): Uptown side, second urinal to the left.

MURFINO (*to the audience*): You owe it to yourself to stop by and watch him work— he's an inspiration.

SEYMOUR (*to the audience, an open invitation*): Sure . . . feel free. . . .

(JACK *enters stage right carrying the sign for the Stonewall Inn.*)

JACK (*to* MURFINO): Where do you want your sign?

MURFINO: Where do you think? Over the door to my alleged bar.

JACK: How's it going to get there?

MURFINO: You're going to climb up and hang it.

JACK: Depends on what you're paying.

MURFINO: Consider it a contribution to Gay History.

JACK: I give at home.

MURFINO: As a favor to me?

JACK: Me, do you a favor? You won't even allow me past the door of that cesspool you operate.

MURFINO: Because we try to cater to what you might call a "clientele."

JACK: Which includes me.

SEYMOUR: It's Murfino's fault you don't look convincing?

JACK (*amused*): You're saying I don't fit in?

MURFINO: Get wise to yourself—

SEYMOUR: —that black leather jacket—

MURFINO: —those biker's boots—

SEYMOUR: —your general deportation (*sic*)—

MURFINO: —you're neither fish nor fruit.

JACK: So what am I?

SEYMOUR: You are feloniously misrepresenting yourself as a male.

JACK (*reaching for his fly*): Want to take a gander at my credentials?

MURFINO: How many times I got to tell you? We don't want to see that!

JACK: Just so there isn't any confusion.

SEYMOUR (*to* JACK): Your normal queer is supposed to be highly detectable.

MURFINO: It's part of Mother Nature's plan.

JACK (*baiting them*): It is?

MURFINO: Sure. . . .

SEYMOUR (*offering friendly advice*): People prefer other people to be immediately recognizable, otherwise people can become nervous.

JACK: I make you nervous?

SEYMOUR (*nervous*): Me? No. Not at all.

JACK: How can I best improve my image?

MURFINO: Invest in a pinkie ring.

JACK: It's that simple?

SEYMOUR: Naw, there's lots more to it than that.

JACK: You sound like an authority.

SEYMOUR (*modestly*): I've given it some study.

MURFINO (*a testimonial*): When it comes to moral turpitude, Seymour here's your man.

JACK (*setting* SEYMOUR *up*): Care to share your expertise?

SEYMOUR (*uncertain*): Give you some pointers?

MURFINO: This is hardly the time or place . . . what if a pedestrian should walk by?

JACK (*to* SEYMOUR): I'm eager to learn.

SEYMOUR: It isn't all that easy. Abnormality takes full time concentration.

JACK: So I've noticed.

SEYMOUR: It is not a path to be ventured upon lightly.

JACK: Funny, I might have thought otherwise.

SEYMOUR: It all starts with the wrist.

JACK: How so?

SEYMOUR (*an educator*): Your sexual malefactor has, between his arm and his hand, an absence of bone. (*He demonstrates.*)

JACK (*trying not to break up*): Do we know why?

MURFINO: Spineless fathers.

JACK (*displaying his fist*): So since I have a bone . . . ?

SEYMOUR: You're at a serious disadvantage.

JACK: How else can I qualify?

MURFINO: How much do you know about Broadway musicals?

JACK: Next to nothing.

SEYMOUR: You handy around the kitchen?

JACK: Nope.

MURFINO: How's your lisp?

JACK: Hardly competent.

(C.B. *and the stage crew enter stage left with a step unit which they place right of upstage center, corresponding with the doorway depicted on the backdrop. The stage crew exits,* C.B. *lingers.*)

SEYMOUR (*to* JACK): You're a difficult case.

JACK: I've been told that before. I've got an idea. Why don't we pick up a six-pack, hop on my Harley and head over to my pad where we can advance my education in private?

SEYMOUR: Are you having innuendos at my expense?

JACK (*mock innocence*): Honestly, officer, I'm only offering you a chance to become better acquainted with your handcuffs.

SEYMOUR: Try any of that suggestive stuff with me, I'll rack your ass.

JACK: How about we toss for it?

MURFINO (*trying to defuse the situation*): How about you hang my sign?

JACK: Where's the ladder?

SEYMOUR (*sneering*): You're a fairy—use your wings.

JACK (*not camp*): They're in the cleaners.

C.B. (*to* SEYMOUR, *as she joins them*): You casting aspersions at my buddy Jack?

SEYMOUR: What's it to you, doll face?

C.B.: Maybe you should apologize.

SEYMOUR: Maybe you should button your lip.

C.B.: Maybe you should—

MURFINO (*warning*): Seymour here is—

C.B. (*unimpressed*): I know "what" he is. Last week, "Seymour here" stumbled half-crocked into Cookies, pushed his fat ass between me and my sometimes fiancée Connie and suggested to her something on the order of "What you dykes really need is the cock of a good man."

SEYMOUR: A fact of life.

C.B.: To which I took issue.

SEYMOUR (*less cocky*): That was you?

C.B. (*sweetly*): That was me—the butch with the broken beer bottle.

SEYMOUR: Hey, babe, no offense. . . .

C.B.: I'm only sorry you had to depart in such a hurry.

SEYMOUR: What can I say? I'm a busy guy.

C.B.: What's your schedule like tonight?

SEYMOUR: I got prior commitments.

C.B.: You couldn't spare me a few minutes for a rematch?

MURFINO: We don't want no trouble on this street.

C.B. (*to* SEYMOUR): What's the matter, pork chop, run out of aphorisms?

JACK (*pulling C.B. away*): Forget it, C.B.

SEYMOUR (*the voice of authority*): Yeah, take a walk.

C.B. (*standing firm*): One round, Queensberry rules?

SEYMOUR: I refuse to deck a person reputed to be of the opposite sex.

C.B.: Unless you're married to her?

SEYMOUR: Let's keep my home life out of this.

JACK (*to* C.B.): Forget it, it's not worth the hassle.

SEYMOUR (*to* C.B.): It's rough stuff like this which gives you lesbos such a bad name.

C.B.: So hand your badge and your gun to Murfino, we'll reinforce my stereotype.

SEYMOUR: One more step in my direction, you're on your way to the Women's House of Detention.

C.B.: Yeah? It'll be old home week—the joint's full of females who fight back.

JACK (*maneuvering* C.B. *off right*): It's not worth it, C.B.

(JACK *and an unconsenting* C.B. *exit stage right.*)

MURFINO (*calling after* JACK): What about my sign?

SEYMOUR: Jeez, anywhere you go anymore, you run into overly sensitive perverts.

MURFINO: Ah, they got no gratitude.

SEYMOUR: I only stopped by to warn you. Word's gone down at the precinct, you're up for a raid tonight.

MURFINO (*staggered*): A raid?

SEYMOUR: Captain's been getting heat from the local community killjoys.

MURFINO: For which I pay off.

SEYMOUR: Relax, the raid'll be perfectly polite.

MURFINO (*skeptical*): Some consolation.

SEYMOUR: It's strictly routine . . . we'll be in and out, no problem.

MURFINO: Explain that to my partners in New Jersey.

SEYMOUR: You're the only one inconvenienced? The fellows on the squad aren't exactly thrilled at the prospect of entering an establishment of your persuasion.

MURFINO: You couldn't find it in your heart to raid some other bar? There's a great after-hours club right here in the vicinity. I recommend it highly. The Snake Pit.

SEYMOUR: We'll put it on the list.

MURFINO: For grief like this, I pay you five big ones a month?

SEYMOUR (*setting down the new terms*): Starting now, seven-fifty.

MURFINO: You already hit me for an increase!

SEYMOUR: That was Christmas, for Christ's sake.

MURFINO (*moaning*): Seven-fifty.

SEYMOUR: You add more water to the drinks.

MURFINO: This has to happen to me on a full-moon Friday night?

SEYMOUR: Alert your better customers.

MURFINO: And completely kill my cash register? You tell the captain to hold off with this raid until the last possible moment—give me a chance to drum up some early business.

SEYMOUR: Why not? No need for your whole night to be a bust.

MURFINO (*starting to exit left*): I should listen to my son. Always he's after me to get out of fag bars and into some wholesome profession . . . something respectable, like drug dealing.

(MURFINO *exits stage left with the Stonewall Inn sign as* CEIL, *a street queen, enters stage right.* CEIL *is a loud, brassy drag with a heart of maribou and breasts of birdseed.* CEIL *is dressed in lost-and-found gutter glamour. She crosses to the garbage can, rummages through the rubbish, shopping for a new ensemble.*)

SEYMOUR (*to* CEIL): Hey you . . .

CEIL (*come-hitheringly*): Talking to me, Thunder Thighs?

SEYMOUR: What do you think you're doing?

CEIL: Comparison shopping.

SEYMOUR: That garbage is the personal possession of this street. It is not to be removed. Never. By anyone.

CEIL (*leaning provocatively against the garbage can*): Really? So what's a girl supposed to wear?

(DONOVAN, *apparently a pedestrian, enters stage left. Masculine in his repression of personality,* DONOVAN *is dressed as a tourist.*)

CEIL (*to* DONOVAN, *peddling her many—if spurious—charms*): Well hello, handsome, in the market for some hanky-panky?

(DONOVAN *ignores* CEIL, *pretends to window shop.* SEYMOUR *watches* DONOVAN *with professional interest.*)

CEIL (*to* DONOVAN, *importuning*): Pssst, tall, dark, and timid, buy me a drink, we can talk terms.

(DONOVAN *ignores* CEIL, *continues to feign an interest in window shopping. Out of the corner of his eye, he watches* SEYMOUR. SEYMOUR, *smelling the pleasure and profit of entrapment, pretends the same. They begin the long, complex, and furtive saraband which was street cruising in the sixties.*)

CEIL (*to the audience, disgusted*): Wouldn't you know? Mutual attraction strikes again. They want you to think they're window shopping. They can keep it up for hours. And they will. Round and round and round the block, window after window after window, memorizing each and every item of merchandise on display. And you wonder why faggots are so hung up on material possessions?

(DONOVAN *moves to another window,* SEYMOUR *counters. They almost make eye contact.*)

CEIL (*to the audience*): Don't you love it? They almost made eye contact. Two or three more circuits around the block, they might even gather up the nerve to ask each other for a light. Or the time of day. The preliminaries can take forever, the sex they'll dispose of lickety-split.

(SEYMOUR *glares at* CEIL, *casually exits stage right, hoping to lure* DONOVAN.)

CEIL (*to* DONOVAN): He isn't your type . . . *I'm* your type.

(DONOVAN *ignores* CEIL, *takes* SEYMOUR's *bait, exits stage right in hot pursuit.*)

CEIL (*calling after* DONOVAN): I can show you a much better time! (*To herself as she digs through the garbage:*) Tonight isn't going to be my night. Friday night never is. (*Matter-of-factly:*) Any night never is. (*Deciding between a chenille bedspread and a shag rug.*) At least I'll be well dressed.

(SIDNEY, *in the closet, enters stage right.* SIDNEY *is an intellectual degenerated into a critic. Of middle age and advanced paranoia,* SIDNEY *is terrified he might be recognized. He wears a raincoat, hat, scarf, and sunglasses.*)

CEIL (*blocking* SIDNEY): The answer to a maiden's prayer! A man of discerning taste. (*blocking* SIDNEY.) Which of these nifty numbers is the real me? The chenille bedspread? Picture it as an evening dress . . . empire waist . . . possibly a bow . . . *or* . . . the shag rug . . . we're talking cocktail frock . . . micro-mini . . . cinch belt—

SIDNEY (*recoiling*): Away from me!

CEIL: I'm basically bashful myself—want a cheap date?

SIDNEY: Away from me, you . . . you . . . !

CEIL: Ten bucks, you can call me anything.

(SIDNEY *escapes from* CEIL, *exits stage left.*)

CEIL (*calling after* SIDNEY): Five, I pretend I don't even know you!

(BOOM BOOM, *another street queen, enters stage left. Très grande transvestite.* BOOM BOOM *is clearly depressed, her fine feathers trail, her two-inch eyelashes droop.* NOTE: *For the sake of authenticity, either* BOOM BOOM *or* CEIL *should be played black and proud.*)

CEIL (*to* BOOM BOOM): Hi ya, Boom Boom, how you doing?

BOOM BOOM (*gloomily*): Hi ya, Ceil.

CEIL (*concerned*): Hon, what's wrong?

BOOM BOOM: Mary, don't ask.

CEIL: You developed an aversion to sequins?

BOOM BOOM: Worse.

CEIL: They evicted you from the Port Authority Bus Terminal?

BOOM BOOM: Much worse.

CEIL: They caught you sneaking out of Smiler's with your bra full of Entenmann's?

BOOM BOOM: Worser even still.

CEIL (*eagerly*): Whatever can it be?

BOOM BOOM (*distrusting*): I'd rather not discuss it. (*Busying herself with the garment quandary.*) On you, the chenille.

CEIL: You think?

BOOM BOOM (*draping the chenille on* CEIL): You don't have the legs for Mary Quant.

CEIL: You do?

BOOM BOOM: Don't fidget. What do you want done with the bust?

CEIL: Perhaps a bow.

BOOM BOOM: Jackie exhausted the bow. Maybe a bunch of . . . (*Her eyes brim with tears.*) . . . a bunch of violets.

CEIL (*comforting*): Boom Boom, hon, tell Ceil what's wrong. You can confide in me, really you can.

BOOM BOOM: Promise you'll keep your mouth shut?

CEIL (*gleefully*): It's that good?! (*Catching herself.*) It's that bad?

BOOM BOOM: I *mean* it, Ceil, I don't want this spread around the streets.

CEIL: Cross my heart.

BOOM BOOM (*abashed*): I was hired.

CEIL (*shocked*): Please?! A job? Actual employment?

BOOM BOOM: Nine to five, no parole in sight.

CEIL: Doing what?

BOOM BOOM: Ruining my nails.

CEIL: What will Welfare say?

BOOM BOOM: They're highly disappointed in me.

CEIL: How could this calamity happen?

BOOM BOOM: Miss Witch at Unemployment dug up this Fourteenth Street Fagin who runs a fabric sweatshop who's too cheap to afford the luxury of sexual discrimination. He calls me "dearie." "You're late to work again, dearie, I'll have to dock your wages. You have two hands, dearie, keep 'em both occupied. Don't mutter, dearie, it isn't ladylike."

CEIL: You poor thing. (*Discarding the chenille.*) Who can concentrate on haute couture when one's own sister's in such dire distress?

BOOM BOOM: I'm a ruined woman.

CEIL: To me you'll always be a queen.

BOOM BOOM (*dabbing her eyes with a hankie*): In exile.

CEIL: You gotta try to see the bright side.

BOOM BOOM: There isn't one.

CEIL: Sure there is. (*Suddenly realizing.*) All the money you're making!

BOOM BOOM (*apprehensive*): Shush!

CEIL: Boom Boom, *we're* rich!

BOOM BOOM: Lower your voice!

CEIL: Just think of the vast implications of our sudden prosperity!

BOOM BOOM: "Our" prosperity?

CEIL: No more smooching up some stiff at the bar for the price of a beverage . . . no more cash-and-carry carhopping at the entrance of the Holland Tunnel . . . best of all, now I don't have to con Little John into robbing a bank to pay for my sex change.

BOOM BOOM: You blab one word about this, you won't need an operation.

CEIL: Why all the secrecy?

BOOM BOOM: When I was broke, I could bring home tricks—what were they going to steal? The sink? They already swiped that. Now that I'm a working woman, I have sex, I get rolled.

CEIL: You couldn't be more choosy about who you pick up?

BOOM BOOM: You be choosy, I'd rather make out. To be prepared, I went out today and blew half my salary on medical supplies. Bandaids, splints, cinctures . . . thank God I was a boy scout.

CEIL: You might want to call the emergency room at St. Vincent's . . . sort of put them on alert.

BOOM BOOM: Oh for the good old days when I was an unemployed street person and all my medicine cabinet contained was peroxide, Nair, and A-200.

(TIMOTHY, *a new boy in town, enters stage right. Freshfaced and polite,* TIMOTHY *is very young and equally disoriented.*)

TIMOTHY (*to* BOOM BOOM): Pardon me, ma'am, is this Green*wich* Village?

CEIL (*incredulous*): "Ma'am"?

BOOM BOOM (*to* TIMOTHY, *charmed*): New in town?

TIMOTHY: How can you tell?

CEIL: Gut instinct.

TIMOTHY: I arrived this morning. From Oregon.

BOOM BOOM (*enraptured*): You're a lumberjack!

CEIL (*ditto*): How exciting.

BOOM BOOM (*to* TIMOTHY, *fantasizing*): I can see you now—

CEIL (*ditto*): —high in those Sierras—

BOOM BOOM: —topping that tall timber.

TIMOTHY: We don't have trees where I come from.

CEIL (*disappointed*): You don't?

BOOM BOOM (*ditto*): No trees?

TIMOTHY: I guess they used to have some, but they cut them all down to make paper bags. Mostly now it's sand and wind and tumbleweeds.

CEIL: You're a cowboy!

BOOM BOOM: How romantic.

CEIL (*to* TIMOTHY, *fantasizing*): I can see you now—

BOOM BOOM (*ditto*): —riding that range—

CEIL: —breaking those broncos.

TIMOTHY: We don't have any of them anymore, either.

BOOM BOOM (*disillusioned*): No broncos.

CEIL (*ditto*): Figures.

TIMOTHY (*trying to be helpful*): My folks took me to a rodeo once. But I was too young to remember. My dad sells insurance.

BOOM BOOM (*less than impressed*): How . . .

CEIL (*ditto*): . . . er . . .

BOOM BOOM: . . . interesting.

CEIL: Yes.

TIMOTHY: I'm studying Motel Management at Central Christian. Or I was.

BOOM BOOM (*to* CEIL, *disapproving*): He's a dropout.

TIMOTHY (*flattered*): I am? Does that make me a hippy?

CEIL (*disdainful*): We hope not.

BOOM BOOM: We don't approve of hippies.

CEIL: Or long hair.

BOOM BOOM: All this free love—

CEIL: —cuts into profits.

TIMOTHY: I didn't mean to offend you.

BOOM BOOM (*relenting*): You didn't.

CEIL (*ditto*): You couldn't.

BOOM BOOM (*taking* TIMOTHY *by the arm*): We like you.

TIMOTHY: You do?

CEIL (*taking* TIMOTHY *by the other arm*): Absolutely.

TIMOTHY: You don't even know me.

BOOM BOOM (*pulling* TIMOTHY *in her direction*): That's easily remedied.

CEIL (*pulling* TIMOTHY *her direction*): I know a much nicer doorway.

BOOM BOOM (*holding firm*): Doorway. How typical.

CEIL (*holding firmer*): So where are you dragging him off to? The trucks?

BOOM BOOM (*to* CEIL): Let loose of him, you tramp!

CEIL: I saw him first, Miss Demeanor!

BOOM BOOM (*beginning a tug of war with* TIMOTHY): He's mine!

CEIL: Mine!!

BOOM BOOM: Mine!!!

TIMOTHY: Am I being mugged?!

CEIL: You wanna?

BOOM BOOM (*glaring at* CEIL): Such a kidder.

TIMOTHY: I don't have any money.

CEIL: We aren't after you for your money, honey.

BOOM BOOM (*an undulating introduction*): I'm Boom Boom.

CEIL: And I'm Ceil.

TIMOTHY (*still uncertain*): My mom warned me not to give my name to strangers.

BOOM BOOM: We seem strange?

TIMOTHY: No . . . I . . . er . . . (A *hunch*.) . . . are you?—

CEIL (*demurely*): Are we "what"?

BOOM BOOM (*ditto*): Don't be shy—

CEIL: —ask away.

TIMOTHY: Are . . . are you two ladies, whores?

BOOM BOOM: I'm a lady whore—Ceil's pure trash.

TIMOTHY: Wow! For-real females of the evening.

CEIL: Depending on the time of day.

TIMOTHY: Mom also warned me about you.

BOOM BOOM: How helpful of her.

CEIL (*to* TIMOTHY): And you couldn't wait to come looking for us.

TIMOTHY: Beg pardon, ma'am, but I came looking for Green*wich* Village.

BOOM BOOM: This is it.

TIMOTHY (*looking around*): This? I'm not sure what I expected. I know I'm not ready for . . . well . . . for all the buildings . . . and the buses . . . and the cabs . . . and . . . and . . .

CEIL: You were expecting maybe depravity?

TIMOTHY: Is that the same as "Vice Running Rampant"?

BOOM BOOM: Mom sure has a way with words.

CEIL (*to* TIMOTHY, *explaining*): That's what the buildings are for.

BOOM BOOM: They contain the "Vice."

TIMOTHY (*in awe*): They do?

CEIL: And the buses and the cabs—

BOOM BOOM: —carry all the people from where they live—

TIMOTHY (*catching on*): —down here to the buildings!

CEIL: Sure, because if they had to walk—

BOOM BOOM: —they'd be too tired to "Run Rampant."

TIMOTHY: So if I wander around, I'll find what I'm looking for?

CEIL (*motherly*): You wander around—

BOOM BOOM (*ditto*): —it'll find you.

TIMOTHY: It will?

CEIL: Count on it.

TIMOTHY: Guess maybe I should be moseying along.

BOOM BOOM: Have fun.

TIMOTHY: "Vice" is supposed to be fun?

CEIL: At first.

TIMOTHY (*overjoyed*): Hot damn! The way mom talked it down, I knew it had to be something special.

(TIMOTHY *exits stage left in search of forbidden fruits.*)

BOOM BOOM (*referring to* TIMOTHY): I used to be that young.

CEIL: I still am.

(MICHAEL *and* DONALD *from* The Boys in the Band *enter stage left, ostensibly out for a walk and a talk.* MICHAEL *and* DONALD *seem to exemplify all-American young manhood. Cleancut, sanitized, they are as slick and shiny as processed cheese. They wear chinos, penny loafers, and cashmere sweaters tied round their shoulders.*)

MICHAEL (*to* DONALD, *as they cross right*): . . . so I said to my psychiatrist, I hate myself.

DONALD: What did he say?

MICHAEL: He said I have every reason to hate myself.

DONALD (*skeptical*): That's a breakthrough?

MICHAEL: You have no idea how good I feel about how bad I feel.

DONALD: You're sure this shrink knows what he's doing?

MICHAEL: He's the staff consultant for the *New York Times.*

DONALD: Yes, but has he had any practical experience?

MICHAEL: This man has a seventy-eight percent cure rate.

DONALD (*doubtful*): Have you actually met any of his . . .

MICHAEL: His successes? He won't allow me to meet them. Not until I prove to him I have myself under psychosexual self-restraint.

DONALD: Uh-huh.

MICHAEL: He's afraid if they encounter me while I'm still in the infectious stage, they might relapse.

DONALD: You're sick.

MICHAEL: What do you think I've been trying to tell you?

(MICHAEL *and* DONALD *exit stage right.*)

CEIL (*referring to* MICHAEL *and* DONALD): There they go—

BOOM BOOM: —Michael and Donald.

CEIL: The boys in the band.

BOOM BOOM: Whatever happened to Emory?

CEIL: You didn't hear? He ran off with a married dentist from the Bronx. They opened a pet store in Miami.

(JORDAN, *a student radical, and* GORDON, *a new-left liberal, enter stage right in deep dispute.* JORDAN *and* GORDON *are humorlessly earnest, rigid in their convictions.* JORDAN *is a hard-eyed fanatic, he is pinned with a spectrum of buttons advocating every political cause except his own. He wears baggy corduroys and scuffy desert boots.* GORDON *is more orthodox in his unorthodoxy, more easygoing. He wears a rumpled tweed sports jacket and smokes a pipe.*)

JORDAN (*to* GORDON, *as they cross left*): . . . you're radically misinformed!

GORDON: You're politically naïve!

JORDAN: Gordon, read history . . . only first read Chairman Mao.

GORDON: Open your eyes, Jordan, wake up to the realities.

JORDAN: There is only one way society will ever be organized in a structure capable of enforcing personal freedom—through the discipline of anarchy.

GORDON: The one and only viable route to individual liberty is by working through the system.

JORDAN: Overthrowing the system.

GORDON: Integrating ourselves into the mainstream.

JORDAN (*contemptuously*): Reformer.

GORDON (*pityingly*): Pawn of the Kremlin.

JORDAN: Red baiter.

GORDON: Dupe.

JORDAN (*sees* BOOM BOOM *and* CEIL, *stiffens*): Gordon!

GORDON (*fearful*): What?

JORDAN: Don't look behind you.

GORDON (*frozen*): What is it? Republicans?

JORDAN (*with repugnance*): Men dressed as women.

(A *common enmity reconciles* JORDAN *and* GORDON.)

GORDON (*sneaking a peek*): Are you sure?

JORDAN: No doubt about it.

GORDON: How can you tell?

JORDAN: Their elbows.

(BOOM BOOM *and* CEIL *attempt to minimize their elbows.*)

GORDON: Disgusting.

JORDAN: Revolting. (*Loudly, for* BOOM BOOM *and* CEIL'S *benefit.*) Transvestites are the inevitable by-product of decadent capitalist imperialism.

BOOM BOOM (*a stage whisper to* CEIL): Ceil, the word's out! They know I'm working!

GORDON (*to* JORDAN): In a socially responsible democracy, crossdressers will be institutionalized.

JORDAN: Along with everyone over thirty.

(JORDAN *and* GORDON *exit righteously stage left.*)

CEIL (*outraged*): Over thirty?

BOOM BOOM (*calling after them*): Come back and say that to my face, Miss Thing!

CEIL (*to* BOOM BOOM): I'm telling you, Boom Boom, this night portends not at all well.

BOOM BOOM: I thought you were off Seconals.

CEIL: Seriously, I have a premonition.

BOOM BOOM: So have a blood test.

(SIDNEY *enters stage left, crosses right, stops, turns to confront the audience.*)

SIDNEY (*to the audience*): I know what you're thinking and you're wrong. I don't frequent this street. I don't frequent any street. I'm . . . er . . . I'm innocently walking my dog. Where is my dog? Yes, an interesting question. After thorough intellectual investigation—M.A., Yale—investigation both empirical and dialectical—critical analysis was my major—I have resolved this problem to my satisfaction. I have no dog. I do have an allergy to dogs. As my allergy has four feet and *as* a dog has four feet, I can be said to be walking the essence of Rover, if not the fact. I can hardly expect you to comprehend my logic, you've been denied my vast educational advantages. Suffice it to say, dog or no, I am definitely not "cruising." That would imply I'm a "homosexualist," which is, as a hypothesis, ludicrous. Yale men don't suck cock. Not with competence.

(SIDNEY *exits stage right.*)

BOOM BOOM (*to* CEIL, *referring to* SIDNEY): What did the closet queen say?

CEIL: Something about the Princeton rub.

BOOM BOOM: I have noticed recently a marked deterioration in the standard of faggot on this street.

CEIL: Tell me about it. Wherever one looks, one sees essential values disappearing faster than the flip.

BOOM BOOM: The times we live in.

CEIL: It gives one pause.

BOOM BOOM (*with marked solemnity*): Did you go uptown today?

CEIL (*ditto*): To the memorial service?

BOOM BOOM: Yeah.

CEIL (*a lump in her throat*): I wanted to, I couldn't face it.

BOOM BOOM (*ditto*): Me neither.

BOOM BOOM and CEIL (*woefully*): Judy.

CEIL: The homosexual's mater dolorosa.

BOOM BOOM: The drag queen's bread and butter.

CEIL: I'd rather remember her the way she was.

BOOM BOOM: Yeah, "fucked up"—not laid out.

CEIL (*gravely*): They bury her tomorrow.

BOOM BOOM: Ferncliff Cemetery—

CEIL: —Hartsdale, N.Y.

BOOM BOOM: I sent flowers.

CEIL: I sent a dozen Bennies.

BOOM BOOM: How thoughtful.

CEIL: She meant so much to me.

BOOM BOOM: To all of us.

CEIL: There *is* hope.

BOOM BOOM: Meaning?

CEIL (*significantly*): She had a son.

BOOM BOOM: So?

CEIL: So what better home life to make a faggot?

BOOM BOOM: Faggots aren't made, they're happenstance. That's why the quality's so inconsistent.

CEIL (*woefully*): He could've carried on the tradition, taught himself to lip sync.

BOOM BOOM: Maybe there's hope for Liza?

CEIL: Get real.

(JACK *and* C.B. *enter stage right.*)

JACK (*to* C.B.): . . . so last night I cleaned the valves, but this morning it started all over again . . . kind of a "crunchity-bang."

C.B. (*stopping short*): Sounds bad.

JACK (*worried*): How bad?

C.B.: I don't want to speculate, not until I've had a chance to look it over.

BOOM BOOM (*to* C.B.): Hi-ya, C.B.

CEIL (*to* JACK, *demurely*): Hi-ya, stud.

JACK (*friendly*): How ya doing?

C.B. (*ditto*): How's it going, girls?

CEIL: Me and Boom Boom have become persons of affluence.

BOOM BOOM: Didn't I tell you to shut up about that?

JACK (*cozying up to* BOOM BOOM): You come into an inheritance?

BOOM BOOM: Already they're after me for my money.

(SEYMOUR *enters stage left, crosses right.*)

CEIL (*referring to* SEYMOUR): Look who's back.

BOOM BOOM: He's cute. (*Vamping* SEYMOUR.) You're cute.

C.B. (*hissing*): He's a cop.

CEIL: He's a cop?

JACK: Planning to consort with the enemy?

CEIL: It's a thought.

BOOM BOOM: Have you no shame? Where's your sense of—

(DONOVAN *enters stage left, crosses right, following* SEYMOUR.)

BOOM BOOM (*to* DONOVAN, *not missing a beat*): —hi-ya, big fella, want a quickie?

(DONOVAN *ignores* BOOM BOOM, *continues right.*)

BOOM BOOM (*calling after* DONOVAN): Yoo-hoo, hump, here I am!

CEIL: Relax your chemise, I already tried.

C.B. (*to* BOOM BOOM): Looks like lover boy's got the hots for Lily Law.

(DONOVAN *exits stage right.*)

JACK (*calling after* DONOVAN): You're making a mistake!

BOOM BOOM (*ditto*): You'll be sorry!

CEIL (*ditto*): We'll visit you in the Tombs!

JACK (*with a look at* C.B.): With our luck, we'll be in the next cell.

C.B. (*to* JACK): You should've let me cripple the bastard when I had the chance.

CEIL: Used to be we were only illegal at election time.

BOOM BOOM (*gleefully*): Remember when they raided the Oak Bar of the Hotel Plaza?

JACK: Wasn't that a riot.

C.B. (*re-creating*): There they sat, some of this country's most prominent piss-elegant pansies—

BOOM BOOM (*ditto*): —blissfully sipping their martinis—

JACK (*ditto*): —oblivious that the boys in blue had infiltrated the potted palms.

CEIL (*to the audience, listing those caught in the raid*): The cops rounded up three senators—

C.B. (*to the audience*): —two governors—

BOOM BOOM (*to the audience*): —an admiral—

JACK (*to the audience*): —a perennial presidential candidate—

C.B. (*to the audience*): —plus a plethora of playwrights—

CEIL (*to the audience*): —a tangle of hairdressers—

JACK (*to the audience*): —sundry Southern novelists—

BOOM BOOM (*to the audience*): —ribbon clerks by the gross—

CEIL (*to the audience*): —the entire panel of a famous television quiz show—

JACK (*to the audience*): —plus the nameless Secretary General—

BOOM BOOM (*to the audience*): —of an equally nameless international organization headquartered on the East River.

CEIL (*to the audience*): Plus call boys—

JACK (*to the audience*): —kept boys—

C.B. (*to the audience*): —tennis pros—

BOOM BOOM (*to the audience*): —and Marines.

CEIL (*to the audience*): Everybody but Gore Vidal.

C.B. (*to the audience*): We all know who's behind the raids.

BOOM BOOM: Cardinal Spellman . . . it's part of his protective covering.*

CEIL: Fanny Spellman? She's far too busy waging her war in Vietnam.*

C.B.: Naw, it's the real estate interests.*

JACK: Sure, they want to clear us queers out of the Village to make room for the high-rises.*

BOOM BOOM: Whoever's behind it, they can't keep shoving it to us.

JACK: Sure they can. Who's going to stop them?

C.B.: We could. Once and for all.

CEIL: "We" who?

BOOM BOOM (*gesturing widely*): Us.

JACK: Ha!

C.B.: There's enough of us.

BOOM BOOM: If we all banded together—

CEIL: Together?

JACK: You can't find two faggots who agree on the recipe for cheese fondue.

BOOM BOOM: But wouldn't it be beautiful?

C.B.: An army of lovers. . . .

CEIL: I can already hear the bitching.

(TIMOTHY *enters stage left, crosses right. He and* JACK *exchange a quick look.*)

*Unsubstantiated street gossip of the period.

BOOM BOOM (*to* TIMOTHY): Find your vice yet?

TIMOTHY: I'm still looking.

CEIL: Losing your inocence ain't all that easy.

TIMOTHY: I'm beginning to realize.

(TIMOTHY *exits stage right.* JACK *watches him.*)

C.B. (*to a distracted* JACK): Jack? *Jack?*

JACK: Huh?

C.B.: You want me to look at that transmission or what?

JACK: Oh . . . yeah . . . sure . . .

(BOOM BOOM, CEIL, JACK, *and* C.B. *ad lib good-byes.*)

JACK (*to* C.B., *as they start left*): . . . and while you're at it, could you check out my fuel injector?

(JACK *and* C.B. *exit stage left.*)

CEIL (*referring to* JACK *and* C.B.): Such a lovely couple.

BOOM BOOM: Made for each other.

CEIL: Pity they're incompatible.

(MURFINO *enters stage left. He is trying to drum up business.*)

MURFINO (*to* BOOM BOOM *and* CEIL): My two most favorite customers!

BOOM BOOM (*to* CEIL): He talking to us?

MURFINO: What are you doing, hanging around out here?

CEIL: Giving the neighborhood a bad name.

MURFINO: The pavement's no place for two classy types like you.

BOOM BOOM: We're engaged in community outreach for the Junior League.

MURFINO: We miss your smiling faces at the Stonewall.

CEIL: You threw us out.

BOOM BOOM: He threw *you* out.

CEIL: Somebody slipped something into my drink.

BOOM BOOM: We suspect it might have been alcohol.

CEIL: Which hardly seems possible, seeing where we were drinking.

MURFINO: You two crack me up.

BOOM BOOM: The feeling's mutual.

MURFINO: How you fixed for cash?

CEIL: Offering a loan?

MURFINO: You got the price of a drink, I might be willing to let bygones be bygones.

BOOM BOOM: Too bad we can't afford your generosity.

CEIL: Sure we can! (*To* MURFINO:) We're rolling in momentary plenty.

BOOM BOOM (*warning*): *Ceil.*

MURFINO: You got dough? (*Opening his arms wide.*) Come home, all is forgiven.

CEIL (*eyeing an angry* BOOM BOOM): Maybe later. . . .

MURFINO: Later? No! *Now.*

BOOM BOOM (*suspicious*): What's the big hurry?

MURFINO (*covering*): Later could be too late. Lately, we're attracting an *early* crowd. Very early. Very attractive. They're all asking for you.

BOOM BOOM: If you've got a crowd, what do you want with us? What's going down?

MURFINO: Are you maligning my magnanimity?

BOOM BOOM: I'm skeptical.

MURFINO: I'm hurt.

CEIL: I'm thirsty.

MURFINO: I'll see you later. Just as long as you're early.

(MURFINO *exits stage right.*)

BOOM BOOM (*to* CEIL): I'm not warning you again.

CEIL: I'm supposed to stand there and let him call you a deadbeat? You heard him, Boom Boom, they're all asking for us.

BOOM BOOM: Fat chance.

CEIL: You know what we need? We need for you to buy me a drink.

BOOM BOOM: I refuse to pay Murfino a door charge for the privilege of sitting in filth and squalor when I get all I want of that at home for free.

CEIL: Filth and squalor, my tush.

BOOM BOOM: Precisely.

CEIL: One little drink.

BOOM BOOM: I'll take you to Danny's.

CEIL (*pouting*): All that corduroy?

BOOM BOOM: The Cherry Lane?

CEIL: I don't have a penny for my loafers.

BOOM BOOM: Carr's?

CEIL: When they push me there in a wheelchair.

BOOM BOOM: Julius's?

CEIL: You got to be kidding.

BOOM BOOM: Why not?

CEIL: They don't allow "ladies" in there.

BOOM BOOM: They can't keep us out.

CEIL: Tell that to Bruno the bouncer.

BOOM BOOM: We've never tried.

CEIL: We're not stupid.

BOOM BOOM: There must be some way . . .

CEIL: Who wants to stand around, watching a bunch of crewcut queens in lettermen's jackets belch beer and dish opera?

BOOM BOOM: . . . some way that you and I can slip in undetected.

CEIL: We'd be in mortal danger. Nobody's more lethal than a sissy who thinks she's passing.

BOOM BOOM (*a solution*): Give me your eyeliner.

CEIL (*digging in her purse*): Why?

BOOM BOOM: You'll see.

CEIL (*giving the "eyeliner" to* BOOM BOOM): It isn't exactly Elizabeth Arden.

BOOM BOOM (*examining the "eyeliner"*): An indelible laundry marker?

CEIL (*defensively*): Yeah, well, I cry a lot.

BOOM BOOM (*brandishing the "eyeliner"*): With this we infiltrate Julius's.

CEIL: How?

BOOM BOOM: We have to butch it up, right?

CEIL: Right.

BOOM BOOM: We draw clefts on our chins, nobody'll notice.

CEIL: I love it!

BOOM BOOM (*returning the "eyeliner" to* CEIL): Here, do me first. (*As* CEIL *complies.*) I said "cleft," not cleavage!

CEIL: Sorry. Habit.

(BOOM BOOM *and* CEIL *are busily butching up their chins as* SEYMOUR *enters stage left.*)

SEYMOUR (*to* BOOM BOOM *and* CEIL): Having fun, girls?

CEIL: Depends on what you got in mind.

SEYMOUR (*flashing his badge*): Vice squad, N.Y.P.D.

CEIL: I'm not up to a squad tonight.

BOOM BOOM: Let's get out of here.

SEYMOUR: Let's see your identification.

BOOM BOOM: I left it in my other purse. (*To* CEIL, *pleading:*) Come *on*, Ceil.

SEYMOUR: I could run you in for impersonating women.

CEIL: You know women who look like this?

BOOM BOOM: *Ceil?*

SEYMOUR (*to* CEIL): Don't give me lip.

CEIL: How do you feel about tongue?

BOOM BOOM (*grabbing* CEIL *by the arm*): That's it, Miss Mouth!

(BOOM BOOM *drags* CEIL *to an exit stage left as* DONOVAN *enters stage left.* SEYMOUR *and* DONOVAN *watch their exit with distaste; they then turn their attention to each other.*)

SEYMOUR (*to* DONOVAN, *taking his standard entrapment stance*): Got a match?

DONOVAN: Got a cigarette?

(SEYMOUR *and* DONOVAN *exchange a cigarette and a light, each careful not to seem to take the initiative.*)

SEYMOUR: Hot tonight.

DONOVAN: Sure am.

SEYMOUR: The weather.

DONOVAN: Oh. Yeah. Muggy.

SEYMOUR: Me, too.

DONOVAN: Muggy?

SEYMOUR: Hot.

(HEATHER *enters stage right carrying a stick of incense and a bouquet of ragtaggle daisies.* SEYMOUR *and* DONOVAN *quickly move apart.*)

HEATHER (*to* DONOVAN): Far out, dig it, and what's happening, man?

DONOVAN: I don't have any spare change.

HEATHER (*handing* DONOVAN *a daisy*): Like if you're not part of the solution, you're part of the problem.

DONOVAN (*tossing* HEATHER *a coin*): Here . . . now go away.

HEATHER (*insulted*): A dime?! Flower Power to you too. (*Crossing to* SEYMOUR.) Far out, dig it, and—

SEYMOUR: You heard him, *go away.*

HEATHER: Tune in, turn on, drop out.

SEYMOUR: Leave.

HEATHER (*handing* SEYMOUR *a daisy*): All you need is love—

SEYMOUR (*sarcastically*): And strawberry fields forever.

HEATHER: Cross my palm with folding money, I'll tell you your horoscope.

SEYMOUR: Make a fast fade.

HEATHER: When were you born? No, let me guess. You're . . . you're a Capricorn.

SEYMOUR (*impressed*): Hey, that's pretty good.

HEATHER: It was easy. You're not what you pretend to be, so you gotta be Capricorn.

SEYMOUR (*with a nervous look toward* DONOVAN): Get out of here.

HEATHER: You don't want to hear your future?

SEYMOUR (*through gritted teeth*): Your scam's endangering my score.

HEATHER (*divining* SEYMOUR's *fortune*): The big plans you have for later tonight?

SEYMOUR (*astonished*): How do you know about—?! (*Pulling* HEATHER *aside.*) Who snitched?

HEATHER (*in all innocence*): The stars know everything.

SEYMOUR: Yeah? So what are they saying about later tonight?

HEATHER: Your expectations of easy success will be adversely thwarted by forces hitherto unforeseen.

SEYMOUR: Beat it. You heard me, *scram.*

HEATHER (*retrieving her daisy*): Give me back my daisy. Your karma would wilt a cactus.

(HEATHER *exits stage left.* DONOVAN *joins* SEYMOUR.)

DONOVAN (*referring to* HEATHER): Kids anymore . . .

SEYMOUR (*worried*): This astrology stuff, anything in it?

DONOVAN: Don't be a chump.

SEYMOUR (*relieved*): Yeah.

DONOVAN (*referring to their previous exchange*): That makes two of us.

SEYMOUR: What?

DONOVAN (*husky voiced*): "Hot."

SEYMOUR (*huskier voiced*): Oh . . . yeah . . . sure seems so.

DONOVAN: Sure does.

SEYMOUR (*an open invitation*): So?

DONOVAN: So?

(MICHAEL *and* DONALD *enter stage left. With increasing frustration,* SEYMOUR *and* DONOVAN *again move apart.*)

MICHAEL (*to* DONALD, *as they cross right*): It's all my mother's fault. Which is all my father's fault. Which was all my mother's fault.

DONALD: Grow up, Michael, forgive and forget.

MICHAEL: I do, Donald. Thanks to my deep and abiding Catholicism, I know that God, in His infinite mercy, will damn my parents to eternal perdition for making me queer.

DONALD (*ironically*): That must be a consolation.

MICHAEL: Why do you refuse to deal with how miserable you are?

DONALD: Because I'm not miserable.

MICHAEL: You're not happy.

DONALD: I'm as happy as the next person.

MICHAEL: That's a very selfish attitude.

DONALD: Why?

MICHAEL: We're all in this together, we should all be equally wretched.

(MICHAEL *and* DONALD *exit stage right.* SEYMOUR *and* DONOVAN *move back together.*)

SEYMOUR (*hand in his pocket*): Am I ever horny.

DONOVAN (*ditto*): I'm intimate with the condition of which you speak.

SEYMOUR: So?

DONOVAN: So?

(JORDAN *and* GORDON *enter stage right. Foiled again,* SEYMOUR *and* DONOVAN *move apart.*)

JORDAN (*to* GORDON, *as they cross left*): No more street cruising, no more bars, no more glory holes. . . .

GORDON: You're taking the fun out of it.

JORDAN: I'm taking the sex out of it—which is a small price to pay for the advancement of mankind.

GORDON: I'm willing to concede that sexual congress, in the wrong hands, can prove contrary to the democratic process, but—

JORDAN: Same-sex affectional preference is strictly a political position—it can never be permitted to degenerate into pleasure.

GORDON: What we probably need is a new set of regulations . . . some clearly defined government guidelines.

JORDAN: Promiscuity is the opiate of the masses.

GORDON: That's not the way I heard it.

JORDAN: They suppressed the original text.

GORDON: They who?

JORDAN: The Mafia bar owners.

GORDON (*nonplussed*): Mafia bar owners?

JORDAN: Who do you think was behind the Kennedy assassination?

GORDON: Isn't that a bit farfetched?

JORDAN (*significantly*): Jack Ruby ran a bar.

(JORDAN *and* GORDON *exit stage left.* SEYMOUR *and* DONOVAN *again move back together.*)

SEYMOUR (*to* DONOVAN): Where were we?

DONOVAN: One of us was about to make a pass.

SEYMOUR: You first.

DONOVAN: You first.

SEYMOUR (*still not wanting to make the first move*): Somebody's gotta do something pretty soon. My seven-inch, thick-headed, blue-veined, throbbing joint's about to shoot its creamy load.

DONOVAN: My gargantuan piece of uncut meat is dripping joy juice all over my huge, hairy balls.

SEYMOUR: So?

DONOVAN: So?

SEYMOUR (*flashing his badge*): So you're under arrest.

DONOVAN (*flashing his badge*): You're under arrest.

SEYMOUR (*astounded*): You mean—?!

DONOVAN (*ditto*): You're a—?!

SEYMOUR: How embarrassing.

DONOVAN: How disconcerting.

SEYMOUR: Is my face ever red.

DONOVAN (*introducing himself*): Donovan, Manhattan South.

SEYMOUR: Seymour, Sixth Precinct.

DONOVAN: You're one hell of a good decoy.

SEYMOUR: You're no slouch yourself. That "gargantuan" bit—a nice touch.

DONOVAN: It's a recent addition to my repertoire.

SEYMOUR: Where'd you pick it up?

DONOVAN: My wife reads.

SEYMOUR: I envy you.

DONOVAN: Use it. She's got plenty more where that came from.

SEYMOUR: You're sure she won't mind?

DONOVAN: Please . . . be my guest.

SEYMOUR: Thanks.

DONOVAN: I was counting on you to make my quota.

SEYMOUR: There's a raid on tonight for the Stonewall. You're welcome to join in.

DONOVAN: Generally I work solo.

SEYMOUR: I favor the individual touch myself.

DONOVAN: It's more personal.

SEYMOUR: I already logged my quota. Down in the subway.

DONOVAN: I can't work the toilets. I'm claustrophobic.

SEYMOUR: The fishing's great. You stick out your rod and reel 'em in. One cock-sucker almost copped my load before I could cuff him.

DONOVAN: You're supposed to let them finish, it's evidence.

SEYMOUR: There's a limit to my stamina.

DONOVAN: I commiserate with you. The wife's starting to complain.

SEYMOUR: Explain to her it's all in the line of duty.

DONOVAN: She claims duty begins at home.

SEYMOUR: Women—they're never satisfied.

(JACK *and* C.B. *enter stage left.* C.B. *is wiping her hands on an oily rag. They don't notice* SEYMOUR *who quickly hides behind* DONOVAN.)

JACK (*to* C.B., *worried*): You're telling me it's terminal.

C.B.: Did I say that?

JACK: What are its chances?

C.B. (*tossing the rag in the garbage can*): First thing tomorrow, bring it by my place.

JACK: I can handle the truth, C.B., really I can.

C.B.: Jack, as your friend and your mechanic, you have to trust me—your Harley will live.

(JACK *and* C.B. *split up.* C.B. *exits stage right,* JACK *exits stage left.*)

SEYMOUR (*referring to* JACK *and* C.B.): Disgusting.

DONOVAN: Revolting.

SEYMOUR: Last week I collared my own nephew.

DONOVAN: Your own nephew?

SEYMOUR: The family was in shock.

DONOVAN: You took him in?

SEYMOUR: What do you think I am? His father paid me not to.

DONOVAN (*taken aback*): You accept gratuities?

SEYMOUR: I figure I earn them.

DONOVAN: This is serious business.

SEYMOUR: This is lucrative business. Take what the mob pays off, add what the old aunties slip you for not incarcerating them, include what their employers give you for reporting their names to the personnel departments, toss in some hustling on the side—a fella can make a decent living.

DONOVAN: You seem not to appreciate that you and I are indispensable to the survival of Western Civilization as we have come to know it.

SEYMOUR: We are?

DONOVAN: We both know what caused the decline and fall of the Roman Empire.

SEYMOUR: I don't get much chance to read the newspapers.

DONOVAN: I'm talking ancient history.

SEYMOUR: We didn't have any of that at St. Sebastian's. The nuns tried to protect us from bad influences.

DONOVAN: If it weren't for us, they'd overrun the whole country.

SEYMOUR: Romans?

DONOVAN: Homos. Everywhere.

SEYMOUR: More money for us. If it weren't for faggots, we could end up assigned to a crime unit. I didn't become a cop to consort with common criminals.

DONOVAN (*quoting verbatim from the F.B.I. Retraining Session for Law Enforcement Officers*): "Homosexuals represent a threat to the community in that when they commit suicide jumping from buildings, they sometimes hit passers-by."

SEYMOUR (*moving away from the buildings*): They do?

DONOVAN: I have that directly from a confederate of mine in the F.B.I.

SEYMOUR: J. Edgar Hoover, he's a fag.

DONOVAN: Who told you that?

SEYMOUR: A cabbie.

DONOVAN: Ah what do the fucking cabbies know. Next they'll be saying Rock Hudson is queer.

(TIMOTHY *enters stage right as* SIDNEY *enters stage left.* TIMOTHY *approaches* SIDNEY *as* SEYMOUR *and* DONOVAN *watch.*)

TIMOTHY (*stopping* SIDNEY): Excuse me, sir—

SIDNEY (*cautious*): Who, me?

TIMOTHY: I was wondering if—

SIDNEY (*reaching for his lighter*): You want a light. I smoke too much. As a bona fide member of the intelligentsia, it's expected of me. You, conversely, are without credentials— (*Lighting his lighter.*) —you shouldn't smoke.

TIMOTHY: I don't.

SIDNEY: You asked me for a light.

TIMOTHY: No, I didn't.

SIDNEY: You didn't? (*Looking at his watch.*) Precisely 11:43.

TIMOTHY: I wasn't asking for the time.

SIDNEY: You weren't?

TIMOTHY: I was wondering if you could—

SIDNEY (*confused*): You don't want a light, you don't want the time . . . what kind of a pickup is this?

TIMOTHY: Pickup?

SIDNEY: Your initial approach leaves much to be desired.

TIMOTHY: I was only—

SIDNEY: There are principles involved here, respected rituals.

TIMOTHY: Sorry.

SIDNEY: "Sorry"? You're "sorry"? You trample all over time-honored tribal customs and you expect me to accept a simple apology?

TIMOTHY: I'm not sure I know what you're talking about.

SIDNEY: You have so much to learn.

TIMOTHY: About what?

SIDNEY: Arousing my prurient interest.

TIMOTHY (*not understanding*): Pardon?

SIDNEY: Dispense with the civilities.

TIMOTHY: Pardon?

SIDNEY: That. Courtesy isn't erotic.

TIMOTHY: Oh.

SIDNEY: And neither is your wardrobe.

TIMOTHY: What's wrong with my clothes?

SIDNEY: Unbutton the top of that shirt.

TIMOTHY: You're treating me like a . . . a . . .

SIDNEY: You're an object.

TIMOTHY: I am not.

SIDNEY: Of desire.

TIMOTHY (*flattered*): I am?

SIDNEY: However transitory.

TIMOTHY: I'm attractive?

SIDNEY: You will be as soon as you comply with my instructions. (As TIMOTHY *unbuttons a button.*) One more button. (TIMOTHY *complies.*) The undershirt is completely unsuitable.

TIMOTHY: I put it on clean this morning.

SIDNEY: What style shorts are you wearing? No, I shudder to think. The sleeves, roll them up.

TIMOTHY (*rolling up his sleeves*): And then may I ask you a question?

SIDNEY (*ignoring*): —tight even rolls, each about three-quarters of an inch.

TIMOTHY: I feel kind of exposed.

SIDNEY (*appreciating the effect*): Yes . . . much better . . . the biceps could stand some nourishment . . . the chest is amusing in its lack of pretension.

TIMOTHY (*irritated*): Look, mister—

SIDNEY: —the trousers are hopeless. Lower them so they rest on your pelvis.

TIMOTHY: My pants stay right where they are.

SIDNEY: That, ultimately, is the prerogative of the dirty old man.

TIMOTHY: Is that what you are?

SIDNEY: Figuratively speaking. Although, when it comes to cleanliness, I'm often accused of compulsion.

TIMOTHY: Do you always wear sunglasses at night?

SIDNEY: I have a penchant for anonymity.

TIMOTHY: Oh.

SIDNEY: I'd introduce myself, but I'm vaguely eminent. . . . I shouldn't want to intimidate you.

TIMOTHY: I'd introduce myself, but my mom warned me not to give my— (*Taking the plunge.*) —my name is Timothy.

SIDNEY: Your name is Tony.

TIMOTHY: No, it isn't.

SIDNEY: They're always called Tony. Or Dean. On occasion, I've even encountered a José.

TIMOTHY: What's wrong with Timothy?

SIDNEY: It lacks the necessary brutishness.

TIMOTHY: It's my name.

SIDNEY: Obstinate, aren't you? I like that. I'm willing to compromise on "Tim"—as long as you're ethnic.

TIMOTHY: I'm part Scandinavian.

SIDNEY: That's not quite what I had in mind.

TIMOTHY: Maybe you should find someone else.

SIDNEY: You talk too much. After exhaustive research in the field, I've come to the conclusion, if they're inarticulate, they do better in bed.

TIMOTHY (*interested*): Whose bed?

SIDNEY: Not so eager. Trade remains passive.

TIMOTHY: Is that what I am? "Trade"?

SIDNEY: Not quite as "rough" as one might hope for.

TIMOTHY: And I remain "passive"?

SIDNEY: Nonreciprocal.

TIMOTHY: That doesn't sound like fun.

SIDNEY: It isn't meant to. Not for you.

TIMOTHY: I was told otherwise.

SIDNEY: You've been misinformed.

TIMOTHY: I don't get anything out of it?

SIDNEY: You're young. No . . . please . . . I'd rather not know "how" young—I'd hate to discover you're too old.

TIMOTHY: Too old for what?

SIDNEY: For us to have a furtive encounter.

TIMOTHY: Furtive?

SIDNEY: *Meaningful.* Which it may well be, in its own shoddy way.

TIMOTHY: I'm not as innocent as you seem to think.

SIDNEY: Do us both a favor.

TIMOTHY: Sure.

SIDNEY: Downplay your sophistication. And while you're at it, you could be a smidgen more surly.

TIMOTHY: Surly?

SIDNEY: Scowl. Curl that hairless upper lip of yours into a sneer.

TIMOTHY (*embarrassed*): Naw. . . .

SIDNEY: The element of danger is essential.

TIMOTHY: I don't know how to sneer.

SIDNEY: You're making this very difficult.

TIMOTHY: I only stopped you to ask a question.

SIDNEY (*answering what he assumes the question will be*): Voraciously "French"—
    receptively "Greek."

TIMOTHY: What?

SIDNEY: The answer to your question.

TIMOTHY: No, it isn't.

SIDNEY (*puzzled*): We seem to be at cross-purposes.

TIMOTHY: That's what I've been trying to tell you.

SIDNEY (*a frightening thought*): You are "out," aren't you?

TIMOTHY: Out where?

SIDNEY: You're uninitiated!

TIMOTHY: I think so.

SIDNEY: Have I been recklessly imprudent?

TIMOTHY (*insinuating*): Are you a . . . a . . . ?

SIDNEY (*closing his closet door*): Certainly not.

TIMOTHY: Where are they, then?

SIDNEY: Who?

TIMOTHY (*exasperated*): The fairies.

SIDNEY: At the bottom of their gardens.

TIMOTHY (*exasperated*): No, you know, the "pansies."

SIDNEY: Make up your mind, are you "in" or "out"?

TIMOTHY: I'm trying to find out where they keep the "sissies."

SIDNEY: First you present yourself as trade, and then you're straight, now suddenly
    the pins start to fly and look who's competition. You're beginning to exhaust
    me.

TIMOTHY: You're pretty hard work yourself.

SIDNEY: Just what is it that you want?

TIMOTHY: I'm looking for a faggot.

SIDNEY: Where did you lose him?

TIMOTHY: I didn't.

SIDNEY: He isn't good enough for you.

TIMOTHY: Who isn't?

SIDNEY: None of them are. Look at yourself, wandering the streets, searching for him. Does he care? He doesn't care. We both know where he is right now.

TIMOTHY: Where?

SIDNEY: He's cheating on you.

TIMOTHY: Who is?

SIDNEY: You can't even remember his name.

TIMOTHY: You've confused me with somebody else.

SIDNEY: You can't remember your lover's name and I'm confused?

TIMOTHY: I don't have a lover.

SIDNEY: That was fast.

TIMOTHY: No, I—

SIDNEY: You needn't explain. I'm conversant with you callow youth.

TIMOTHY: I came here because my . . . because I was under the impression this was where you find the men who molest young boys.

SIDNEY: I never touched you!

TIMOTHY: I never said you did.

SIDNEY (*grabbing* TIMOTHY *by the arm*): That's what you're really after, isn't it? You want to corrupt me!

TIMOTHY: I was hoping for the reverse.

SIDNEY: Everywhere I go, there you are . . . luring me up anonymous alleys with your luridly supple body . . . tempting me into tearoom indiscretions with your taut thighs . . . (*Tightening his grip.*) . . . provoking me with your prepubescent succulence.

TIMOTHY (*trying to ease free*): Maybe you're right . . . maybe I am too old for you.

SIDNEY: If it weren't for you, I'd have a home, faithful pets, the requisite pair of children, a dutiful wife—I could be a normal, useful, productive member of society.

TIMOTHY: What's keeping you?

SIDNEY: You are! Why can't you leave me alone?!

TIMOTHY: Let go of my arm and I will.

SIDNEY: So you can go chasing after him?!

TIMOTHY: Who?

SIDNEY: Why should I care? Get 'em all, morning, noon, and night, seven days a week, fifty-two weeks a year . . . only when you finally do wake up, late some afternoon, ninety percent of the surface of your body covered with hickies, don't come running back to me.

TIMOTHY (*frightened*): I don't even know you.

SIDNEY: You never did. None of you ever tried. Did it ever once occur to you that I might have feelings?

TIMOTHY: *So do I.*

SIDNEY: What has that got to do with anything? My friends all warned me about you. "Sidney," they said, "he's a selfish, self-serving son of a bitch." Why am I wasting my breath? You're not a bartender, this isn't a bar. That's where you'll find what you're looking for. At the bar. They're all sitting there, waiting for you . . . all the sad young men. (*He releases* TIMOTHY.)

TIMOTHY (*at last*): Which bar?

SIDNEY: Any bar.

TIMOTHY: Thanks.

(TIMOTHY *escapes to an exit stage left.*)

SIDNEY (*calling after* TIMOTHY): That's it? That's all you have to say for yourself?

DONOVAN (*to* SEYMOUR): You entrap the closet queen, I'll go after the kid.

(DONOVAN *follows* TIMOTHY, *exits stage left.*)

SEYMOUR (*approaching* SIDNEY): Got a match?

SIDNEY: Aren't you a relief.

SEYMOUR: I am?

SIDNEY (*lighting* SEYMOUR's *cigarette*): It's a pleasure to meet somebody who still cares about the niceties.

SEYMOUR: Hot tonight.

SIDNEY: Yes, you're much more my type. The young man who left so unexpectedly, he wasn't right for me. He never understood me.

SEYMOUR: So?

SIDNEY: So what?

SEYMOUR: So step around the corner, I'll show you my gargantuan piece.

SIDNEY: A provocative proposition.

SEYMOUR: So?

(HEATHER *enters stage right, crosses to* SIDNEY.)

HEATHER (*giving* SIDNEY *a daisy*): Far out, dig it, and what's happening, baby?

SIDNEY (*touched*): For me?

HEATHER: This one's on the house.

SIDNEY: I'd rather have a rose.

HEATHER: Like, man, roses are strictly bourgeois.

SIDNEY (*starting right*): I suppose they are. . . .

SEYMOUR: What about me?

SIDNEY: What about you?

SEYMOUR: Remember? I'm your type.

SIDNEY: So you are. (*Reconsidering.*) —no, it'll never work.

SEYMOUR: What won't?

SIDNEY: Us.

SEYMOUR: Why not?

SIDNEY: You're much too good for me.

SEYMOUR: I can be a real rat.

SIDNEY: You tempt me sorely. No . . . no, it's impossible. I could never relate to someone like you . . . someone I might learn to respect.

SEYMOUR: Give me a chance.

SIDNEY: My dear man, you underestimate my capacity for self-destruction. When the wrong man comes along, I'll know him. (*Continuing stage right, pulling the petals off the daisy.*) I love me, I love me not, I love me, I love me not . . . (Etc.)

BLACKOUT

ACT II

HEATHER, *despondent, sits on the stoop, clutching her stick of incense and her daisies. The incense is unlit. After a moment, C.B. enters stage right. C.B. sees HEATHER, pauses, then joins her.*

C.B. (*to* HEATHER): How ya doing, kid?

HEATHER: Less than mellow.

C.B.: Discouraged?

HEATHER: I'm giving my Inner Peace some rest.

C.B.: Bad day?

HEATHER: Negative vibes.

C.B.: Me, too.

HEATHER: Mars is in conjunction with Saturn.

C.B.: That probably explains it.

HEATHER: What?

C.B.: The Mets. They lost to the Phillies, two to nothing. Agee struck out twice, Clendenon, three times, and Swoboda fanned for four . . .

HEATHER: I empathize.

C.B. (*indicating the hydrant*): You did a nice job on that hydrant.

HEATHER: You like it?

C.B.: It's colorful.

HEATHER: It's a statement.

C.B.: About what?

HEATHER: I couldn't decide.

C.B.: It's . . .

HEATHER: Effective?

C.B.: Yeah.

HEATHER: I'm glad you like it.

C.B.: Your incense is out.

HEATHER: Yeah.

C.B.: Want me to light it for you?

HEATHER: I only burn it a few minutes at a time, otherwise, I have an asthma attack.

C.B. (*referring to the daisies*): Pretty flowers.

HEATHER: They're supposed to be daisies.

C.B.: I thought they looked familiar.

HEATHER: Want to hold them?

C.B. (*shyly*): Me? Naw . . . that's okay . . .

HEATHER (*giving the daisies to* C.B.): Go ahead, hold them. They're friendly.

C.B.: Thanks.

HEATHER: They like to be held.

C.B.: They need water.

HEATHER: I'm not into water, I'm a vegetarian.

C.B.: I always thought vegetarians were—

HEATHER: Have you ever looked at water?

C.B.: Probably.

HEATHER: I mean really *looked* at water. Up close, like through a microscope? I did once.

C.B.: That must have been—

HEATHER: A revelation. Water is alive with hundreds and hundreds of tiny animals, all furry and fuzzy and getting it on and playing it cool and groovin' on the scene—like, man, it's a miniature love-in. Only a cannibal would drink water.

C.B.: Water is vital to plant life.

HEATHER: Which is a myth circulated by the public utilities to enlarge their profits.

C.B.: But you can't just let them dehydrate.

HEATHER: I don't. I keep them in carrot juice.

C.B.: They like that?

HEATHER: Like, man, they really dig it. Especially when I remember the tab of acid.

C.B.: You give them LSD?

HEATHER: On special occasions.

C.B.: No wonder they're wilting.

HEATHER: You think so? Could be they're coming down from a bad trip. (*Hopefully.*) You wouldn't happen to have a Black Beauty on you?

C.B.: Amphetamine?

HEATHER: That'd perk 'em up.

C.B.: I don't use drugs.

HEATHER: What a bummer.

C.B.: Sorry—

HEATHER: Hey, relax, it's nothing you should be embarrassed about—lots of people have hang-ups.

C.B.: I don't.

HEATHER: Sure you do. With your generation, it's chronic.

C.B.: No, see, I've just never felt the need to experiment with chemicals.

HEATHER: You know what your problem is? You're rational.

C.B.: I try to be.

HEATHER: It's a serious limitation.

C.B.: No, see, I've always thought—

HEATHER: Like, you don't have to justify your closed mind to me, I'm tolerant.

C.B.: That's an admirable attribute.

HEATHER: I picked it up from my father.

C.B.: Your father sounds like a—

HEATHER: A real bigot.

C.B.: Is he the reason you left home?

HEATHER: I should, shouldn't I?

C.B.: I wasn't suggesting—

HEATHER: Everybody else my age has already done it.

C.B.: There's no hurry.

HEATHER: I have certain personal considerations which hold me back.

C.B.: Your mother?

HEATHER: My doll collection. I have dolls representing every known country in the Free World. On account of my father, I keep the Iron Curtain countries under my bed.

C.B.: I used to have a doll.

HEATHER: What happened to it?

C.B.: I'm not sure.

HEATHER: Don't you miss it?

C.B.: We weren't really all that close.

HEATHER: Dolls demand a lot of attention.

C.B. (*changing the subject*): So you commute to the Village every night?

HEATHER: All the way from Rego Park. My boyfriend Warren used to come with me, but after a while hanging around down here started getting to him, so he gave up and went gay.

C.B.: That can happen.

HEATHER: I feel kinda guilty.

C.B.: You shouldn't.

HEATHER: About not warning the guys he picks up. Warren lacks scruples.

C.B.: He should go far.

HEATHER: I envy him.

C.B.: How?

HEATHER: Being gay seems to give him a sense of purpose.

C.B.: Disenchanted with the counterculture?

HEATHER: Lately, the anti-establishment's getting overcrowded. I've been checking into alternatives.

C.B.: What would you rather do?

HEATHER: Do you know Boom Boom and Ceil?

C.B.: Sure.

HEATHER: Can you keep a secret?

C.B.: Sure.

HEATHER: They're drag queens.

C.B.: I . . . er . . . may have heard that somewhere.

HEATHER: That's something I could really get into.

C.B.: Being a drag queen?

HEATHER: Why not?

C.B.: I . . . er . . . is there any future in it?

HEATHER: You sound like my father.

C.B.: Forget I said anything.

HEATHER: Another career opportunity has recently come to my attention. These other friends of mine took over a basement and started this neat bomb factory.

C.B.: A "bomb" factory?

HEATHER: Isn't it a great idea? Unfortunately, I had to turn it down.

C.B.: I should hope so. The danger—

HEATHER: The basement. It'd kill my asthma.

C.B. (*indicating the hydrant*): If that hydrant's any example, you have artistic flair.

HEATHER: I know. As long as I can remember, I've shown promise.

C.B.: So why not go to art school?

HEATHER: My father says there aren't any women artists.

C.B.: What does he want you to be?

HEATHER: A nurse. And have babies.

C.B.: Maybe you should run away from home.

HEATHER: What's your gig?

C.B.: I drive a truck. It's my truck. Or it will be when I finish with the payments.

HEATHER: Far out.

C.B.: I picked it up at Fort Dix when they assigned me to the motor pool.

HEATHER (*disapproving*): You were in the Army?

C.B.: I was until they decided to get rid of the undesirables.

HEATHER: I'm a pacifist.

C.B.: It takes all kinds.

HEATHER: I mean I'm not sure how I feel about associating with one of the oppressors.

C.B.: Are you kidding? I didn't even make sergeant.

HEATHER (*undecided*): Still—

C.B.: Look, kid, it was either the WACS or become a gym teacher. I like volleyball— but not as a way of life.

(*An angry* BOOM BOOM *enters stage left, followed by an anxious* CEIL.)

CEIL (*catching up with* BOOM BOOM): —I never meant to say it, Boom Boom, it came out before I could close my mouth.

BOOM BOOM (*turning on* CEIL): *You* came out because you couldn't close that mouth!

CEIL: We were having a party.

BOOM BOOM: *You* were having a party.

CEIL: It's my fault I'm popular?

BOOM BOOM: With my money.

HEATHER (*joining* BOOM BOOM *and* CEIL): Like I detect an aura of disharmony here.

CEIL: I graciously invited Boom Boom to join me at Julius's—

BOOM BOOM: *You* invited *me?*

CEIL (*to* HEATHER *and* C.B.): —and as it was our first time in the establishment, I felt we should make a good impression.

BOOM BOOM (*to* C.B.): So she orders a round for the entire bar and then she points at me and tells the bartender to charge it to "Miss Rich Bitch."

CEIL: They were your friends.

BOOM BOOM: I never saw any of those queens before in my life.

C.B.: Maybe they wanted to be your friends.

BOOM BOOM: Sure they did. As soon as the drinks arrived.

CEIL (*to* HEATHER *and* C.B.): She always has to assume the worst about people.

BOOM BOOM: I have you as a precedent.

C.B.: You two shouldn't fight.

CEIL: Fight? Us? We're sisters.

BOOM BOOM: Not any longer.

HEATHER: You don't mean that.

CEIL (*to* BOOM BOOM): Surely you don't begrudge our raising a glass or two to the memory of Judy?

BOOM BOOM: Judy-schmudy, your single concern was how much free booze you could cadge off of me.

CEIL: May Our Lady of the Ruby Slippers forgive you.

BOOM BOOM: Spare me.

CEIL: Certain people, on their rise to the top, are ruthless to those without whose sacrifices they never would have made it.

BOOM BOOM: Just what did you ever sacrifice for me?

CEIL: Might I remind you who loaned you your first pair of tits?

BOOM BOOM: You're a real drag.

CEIL: At least I'm convincing.

BOOM BOOM: To anyone from New Jersey.

CEIL: You shave twice a day.

BOOM BOOM: You walk like a bowler.

CEIL: Your Peggy Lee is thin.

BOOM BOOM: Your impersonation of Pearl Bailey lacks color.

CEIL (*to* HEATHER *and* C.B.): Listen to her. Her wig's on so tight, she thinks she's a real woman.

BOOM BOOM: I, at least, have never had a strain of V.D. named after me.

CEIL: That is an untruth only partly based on the facts!

BOOM BOOM: Where there's an itch, there's reason to scratch.

CEIL: You and I are through, Rita Reptile!

C.B. (*attempting a reconciliation*): Ladies, ladies . . .

HEATHER (*ditto*): Boom Boom . . . Ceil . . .

CEIL (*ripping off her eyelashes*): Here . . . take back the eyelashes you gave me for my birthday.

BOOM BOOM: Fine with me, Miss Minnie the Moocher. (*Removing her falsies.*) These, as you were so kind as to remind me, are yours.

CEIL: Keep 'em—I shudder to think where they've been!

(CEIL *exits stage right in a huff.*)

BOOM BOOM (*calling after* CEIL): Never again darken my half of this sidewalk.

(BOOM BOOM *exits stage left in an equal huff.*)

HEATHER (*to* C.B.): Shouldn't we go after them?

C.B.: A word to the wise—never mess with a TV on the rag.

(TIMOTHY *enters stage right, followed by* DONOVAN.)

DONOVAN (*catching up with* TIMOTHY): Wait up! What's your hurry?

TIMOTHY: Why are you following me?

DONOVAN: I want to talk.

TIMOTHY: About what?

DONOVAN: Why are you so suspicious?

TIMOTHY: I'm not. I wasn't. Not at first. I'm learning fast.

DONOVAN: Had a bad experience?

TIMOTHY: Not if I can help it.

DONOVAN: You gotta be more trusting.

TIMOTHY: I've met some peculiar people.

DONOVAN: I'm a fairly average guy.

TIMOTHY: So was the last one. Until he went bonkers.

DONOVAN: So why not let me change your luck?

TIMOTHY (*guarded*): How?

DONOVAN: First we talk, get to know each other . . .

TIMOTHY: So talk.

DONOVAN (*going to work*): Hot tonight.

TIMOTHY: I'm not interested in the weather.

DONOVAN: What are you interested in?

TIMOTHY: Depends.

DONOVAN: On what?

TIMOTHY: On what I find.

DONOVAN: What are you looking for?

TIMOTHY: This and that.

DONOVAN: Be more specific.

TIMOTHY: A bar.

DONOVAN (*indicating stage left*): There's a bar up the street, middle of the block.

TIMOTHY: I know, I passed it. A couple of times.

DONOVAN: Want to go there?

TIMOTHY: What kind of a bar is it?

DONOVAN: The kind you're looking for.

TIMOTHY: Which is that?

DONOVAN: You know.

TIMOTHY: Do I?

DONOVAN (*an entrapment classic*): How about I buy you a drink?

TIMOTHY: I can buy my own drinks. (*Unsure of his resources.*) How much do they cost?

DONOVAN: Short of funds?

TIMOTHY: I'm waiting to hear about a job.

DONOVAN (*hoping to compound the charges*): Would you like to make a little cash?

TIMOTHY (*he has a hunch*): Doing what?

DONOVAN (*suggestively*): Use your imagination.

TIMOTHY: Men get paid for that?

DONOVAN: Bundles.

TIMOTHY: Naw . . . I could never do that.

DONOVAN: Why give it away?

TIMOTHY: Who said I was going to?

DONOVAN: Are you interested?

TIMOTHY: Supposing . . . just supposing a person was curious about this line of work, how would this person go about acquiring the necessary job skills?

DONOVAN: Let's discuss the details over that drink.

TIMOTHY: One drink?

DONOVAN: What could be more innocent?

TIMOTHY: I don't guess there's anything wrong with allowing you to buy me a drink.

(SIDNEY *enters stage left, followed by an exasperated* SEYMOUR. TIMOTHY *stops,* DONOVAN *is not at all pleased.*)

SEYMOUR (*calling after* SIDNEY): Wait up!

SIDNEY (*crossing right*): No thank you, not tonight.

SEYMOUR: You can't just walk away.

SIDNEY: I can't afford not to.

TIMOTHY (*to* DONOVAN, *referring to* SIDNEY): That's him . . . that's the nut I told you about.

DONOVAN (*trying to pull* TIMOTHY *off left*): You meet all kinds. . . .

TIMOTHY (*holding back*): No . . . wait . . .

SEYMOUR (*to* SIDNEY): You don't seem to realize how much trouble you're in.

SIDNEY: And you don't seem to realize that when I said I was looking for the wrong man, I had someone much more conventional in mind.

(JORDAN *and* GORDON *enter stage right as* MICHAEL *and* DONALD *enter stage left. They stop to watch.*)

SEYMOUR (*privately to* SIDNEY): You solicited me for immoral purposes.

SIDNEY: You kept following me . . . how else was I going to get rid of you?!

(JACK *enters stage left, joins* C.B. *and* HEATHER.)

SEYMOUR (*privately to* SIDNEY): I'm letting you off easy.

SIDNEY: Fifty dollars?! The last one only cost me ten.

GORDON (*referring to* SIDNEY): Listen to that letch—

JORDAN: —using his vast wealth to sexually exploit that poor laborer.

SEYMOUR (*to* SIDNEY, *increasingly uncomfortable*): Forty—we forget the whole thing.

SIDNEY: This is the third time this month!

DONALD (*to* MICHAEL, *referring to* SIDNEY *and* SEYMOUR): Why can't they keep their domestic problems at home?

MICHAEL (*loudly, for the benefit of* SIDNEY *and* SEYMOUR): It's public displays like this which make it harder for the rest of us.

SEYMOUR (*to* SIDNEY): I categorically deny any complicity in any previous misadventure your abhorrent lifestyle may have led you into.

SIDNEY: You did the leading.

SEYMOUR: So somebody had to start the ball rolling.

SIDNEY: I refuse to be your single source of supplemental income. Once a month, maybe . . . if your financial needs are greater, trot up to the New York Athletic Club and entrap David Rockefeller.

TIMOTHY (*to* DONOVAN): What's he mean "entrap"?

DONOVAN: You wouldn't understand.

SEYMOUR (*to* SIDNEY): Thirty—that's my final offer.

SIDNEY: I intend to report you.

SEYMOUR: Report me?

SIDNEY: To the Better Business Bureau. For falsely advertising your less-than-adequate accoutrements.

SEYMOUR (*wounded*): Less than adequate?!

SIDNEY: Your heard me, Princess Tiny Meat.

SEYMOUR: You vicious queer! (*Collaring* SIDNEY.) I'm taking you in!

SIDNEY (*to the others*): Help!

C.B. (*coming forward*): Let go of him.

SEYMOUR: Stay out of this.

JACK (*coming forward*): Let go of him.

SIDNEY (*to* SEYMOUR): You heard them, unhand my haberdashery.

SEYMOUR (*to* JACK *and* C.B.): He's under arrest.

SIDNEY (*to the others*): He's perpetrating police brutality on my Burberry.

JORDAN (*to* SEYMOUR): What's the charge?

SEYMOUR: Defamation. (*Correcting himself.*) I mean disorderly conduct.

GORDON: Show us your badge.

JORDAN (*to* SEYMOUR): Yeah—

C.B. (*to* SEYMOUR): Identify yourself—

JACK (*to* SEYMOUR): —it's the law.

SEYMOUR: Turn legal on me, I'll run you all in.

JACK: Yeah?

DONALD: Forget it, it's not worth the hassle.

MICHAEL (*to the others*): If he's under arrest, he obviously did something wrong.

C.B.: Bull!

DONOVAN (*to the others*): No, he's right—we shouldn't interfere.

SIDNEY: I'm innocent.

DONOVAN: That's what they all say.

SIDNEY: He wanted me to bribe him.

JACK: Extortion?

SEYMOUR: He's lying.

HEATHER (*coming forward*): I saw everything. The fuzz approached that gentleman there and offered to display his genitalia.

SEYMOUR: Repeat that smut, I bust you for obscenity.

TIMOTHY (*coming forward*): And I heard the cop ask him for money.

DONOVAN: Stay out of it.

TIMOTHY: Remember? (*To the others:*) First he asked for fifty but then he began lowering his price.

C.B. (*to* SEYMOUR): Having a midsummer sale?

SEYMOUR (*to* DONOVAN): Officer in need of assistance.

DONOVAN (*to* TIMOTHY): Time for that drink.

TIMOTHY: I can't leave, I'm a witness.

DONOVAN: I'll catch you later. (*To* SEYMOUR *as he crosses right:*) You're doing fine.

SEYMOUR (*plaintively*): Don't desert me!

DONOVAN (*privately*): Can't jeopardize my cover.

(DONOVAN *exits stage right.*)

TIMOTHY (*to* SEYMOUR): You're in trouble.

HEATHER: Big trouble.

C.B.: The screw's gonna get screwed.

SEYMOUR (*to* TIMOTHY *and* HEATHER): You'll never live to testify.

JACK: Threatening violence?

C.B.: The Review Board takes a dim view of intimidation—

JORDAN: —added to extortion—

GORDON: —entrapment—

HEATHER: —indecent exposure—

SIDNEY: —gross exaggeration.

C.B. (*to* SEYMOUR): You letting him go?

JACK: Or do we bring charges against you?

JORDAN: Yeah, which is it?

TIMOTHY: Yeah?

SIDNEY: Yeah, let the poor miscreant go.

SEYMOUR (*to the others*): You jerks are a joke. All this crap about "Review Boards" and "testifying" . . . you really believe our offender here is eager to expose his degeneracy in court?

SIDNEY (*frightened*): Court? Who mentioned court?

DONALD: They want to make a precedent out of you.

SIDNEY: Me?

JACK: We're keeping you out of jail.

SIDNEY: I've been there before.

C.B.: So this time fight back.

MICHAEL: Fight back?

JACK: He's got a case.

DONALD: Which he won't win.

TIMOTHY (*to* SIDNEY): Fight for your rights.

DONALD (*amused*): Rights?

MICHAEL: People like us don't have rights, we haven't earned them.

JORDAN: Then it's time we began.

SIDNEY (*to the others*): What are you, a bunch of radicals?

C.B.: We're gay—

JACK: —just like you.

SIDNEY: How dare you presume! I'm a practicing heterosexual. Presently on an extended leave of absence. Not that I'm totally inert. I'm acquainted with this perfectly pleasant female whom I escort to dinner twice a month. (*To* SEYMOUR, *pulling money from his wallet:*) Here, take the fifty.

SEYMOUR: Bribery?

SIDNEY: Name your price, I'll write a check.

SEYMOUR: You had your chance.

SIDNEY: Do you take Master Charge?

SEYMOUR (*knocking* SIDNEY'S *money and wallet to the sidewalk*): You nauseate me.

(MURFINO *enters stage right.*)

MURFINO: What's this, a block party?

SEYMOUR: Not any longer.

MURFINO (*picking up* SIDNEY'S *wallet and money*): Seems we have a slight situation here.

SEYMOUR: It's under control.

MURFINO (*hinting*): Sidney there's one of my regulars.

SEYMOUR: He's temporarily out of circulation.

MURFINO (*counting* SIDNEY'S *money*): One of my *best* customers.

SEYMOUR: So?

MURFINO (*offering him a bill*): So couldn't we reach a more amiable solution?

SEYMOUR: We almost did . . . (*glaring at* C.B., JACK, TIMOTHY, *and* HEATHER) . . . until we ran into Nancy Drew and the Hardy Boys.

MURFINO (*flourishing another bill*): Release him into my custody, I'll keep him off the streets.

SEYMOUR (*catching on*): And in your bar?

MURFINO: You got the idea. What harm could he come to?

SEYMOUR (*amused*): Yeah. Why not. (*Remembering.*) But only if he apologizes.

C.B.: Apologizes?

JORDAN: For what?

SEYMOUR: For belittling my manhood.

MURFINO: Tell the nice policeman you're sorry.

JACK: Bullshit!

MURFINO: You people got him into this mess, I'm getting him out. (*To* SIDNEY:) The officer's waiting.

SIDNEY (*to* SEYMOUR, *mumbling*): I'm sorry.

SEYMOUR: Louder.

SIDNEY: I retract my remark.

SEYMOUR: I said *louder.*

JACK (*moving toward* SEYMOUR): You son of a bitch.

GORDON (*blocking* JACK): Forget it—

C.B. (*ditto*): —it's not worth the hassle.

SEYMOUR (*to* SIDNEY): Well?

SIDNEY (*seemingly contrite*): I am heartily sorry for having offended you . . . (*an evil glint in his eye*) . . . with my acute discernment of your overt shortcomings.

MURFINO (*to* SEYMOUR): Satisfied?

SEYMOUR: He's all yours. (*To the others:*) You, I settle with some other time.

(SEYMOUR *exits stage right.*)

MURFINO (*to the others*): Okay, the party's over. Sidney here wants you all to join him for a drink.

SIDNEY: But—

MURFINO (*giving* SIDNEY *his wallet*): You can best express your gratitude to me by drowning your sorrows in premium Scotch.

(MURFINO *pushes* SIDNEY *to an exit stage left.*)

DONALD (*to* MICHAEL, *as he eyes* JACK): Want a drink?

MICHAEL (*as he eyes* GORDON): Well . . .

GORDON (*to* JORDAN, *aware of* MICHAEL): Want to go to the Stonewall?

JORDAN (*as he eyes* DONALD): I . . . er . . . can't. I have an early meeting tomorrow I'm planning to disrupt.

GORDON: I'm chairing that meeting!

JORDAN: Good, I'll see you there.

(JORDAN *exits stage left, hoping* DONALD *will follow.*)

MICHAEL (*to* DONALD): I should go home. Psychoanalysis requires plenty of rest.

DONALD: Okay, Michael, be well—

MICHAEL: We can only hope.

(MICHAEL *exits stage right, hoping* GORDON *will follow.* DONALD *exits stage left, hoping* JACK *will follow.* GORDON *exits stage right, following* MICHAEL.)

JACK (*to* C.B.): The cops can't keep shoving it to us.

C.B. (*amused*): Sure they can.

JACK: We should stop it once and for all.

C.B. (*leading him on*): "We" who?

JACK (*gesturing wildly*): Us!

C.B.: Band together?

JACK (*realizing*): Sounds familiar, doesn't it?

MURFINO: Ah, you can't fight City Hall. Sidney's waiting to buy you that drink.

C.B.: Does he know that?

MURFINO: He will.

HEATHER: I've never been to the Stonewall.

C.B.: Wanta go?

HEATHER: Kinda.

MURFINO: Sure, show the Little Miss a good time.

HEATHER: I don't drink. I wouldn't even know what to order.

TIMOTHY: Do you like milk shakes?

HEATHER: *Do* I.

TIMOTHY: Ask for a Brandy Alexander.

HEATHER (*to* C.B.): Is that alcoholic?

C.B.: Not so you'd notice.

HEATHER: Like, man, why not?

(HEATHER *disposes of her incense and the daisies in the garbage can, exits stage left.* C.B. *rescues the daisies, follows her.*)

MURFINO (*to* JACK): What about you?

JACK: You're allowing me into your bar?

MURFINO: Tonight's a special occasion.

JACK (*moving away from* MURFINO): I'll think it over.

TIMOTHY: I've never been to your bar.

MURFINO: How would you like to be in show business?

TIMOTHY: Me?

MURFINO: From where I stand you got definite talent.

TIMOTHY: You're a producer?

MURFINO: Ever hear of David Merrick?

TIMOTHY: No.

MURFINO: I taught him everything he knows.

TIMOTHY: You really think I have talent?

MURFINO: Can you dance?

TIMOTHY: No.

MURFINO: Can you move to music?

TIMOTHY: I guess.

MURFINO: Congratulations, you got the part.

TIMOTHY (*excited*): I do?

MURFINO: Come with me to my club, we'll see how you look in the costume.

TIMOTHY (*his eye on* JACK): Can I meet you there?

MURFINO: You don't want to pass up an opportunity like this.

TIMOTHY: But I want to say something to someone.

MURFINO: And miss your big break?

TIMOTHY: I'm actually going to be on stage?

MURFINO: With your very own spotlight.

(MURFINO *escorts the dazzled* TIMOTHY *to an exit stage left.* JACK *watches* TIMO-THY *go, is about to follow him, changes his mind, crosses downstage right, leans against the street sign.* DONOVAN *enters stage right, searching for* TIMOTHY.)

DONOVAN (*to* JACK): Where did he go?

JACK: Who?

DONOVAN: The kid I was talking to.

JACK (*nodding stage left*): He went that way. You better hurry, he's on his way to the top.

(DONOVAN *exits stage left.* JORDAN *and* DONALD *enter stage left.*)

JORDAN (*to* DONALD, *as they cross right*): Anal intercourse is fascistic.

DONALD: What's the party line on masturbation?

JORDAN: It's individualistic.

DONALD (*aware of* JACK): Sixty-nine?

JORDAN: Acceptable. But only under certain circumstances. Only if both partici-pants are lying on their sides, and only if the climax is coincidental, and of equal proportions, and only if neither participant in any way at any time moves any part of their anatomy in what might be construed as a forward thrust . . . otherwise you end up with Male Aggression, which, as we all know, is the root of all Third World Oppression.

(JORDAN *and* DONALD, *distracted by* JACK, *exit stage right.* MICHAEL *and* GORDON *enter stage right.*)

MICHAEL (*to* GORDON, *as they cross left*): I disapprove of cruising.

GORDON: As do I.

MICHAEL: I feel a person should get to know the other person first.

GORDON: I feel the same way.

MICHAEL: I hope you didn't think I was trying to pick you up when I asked for the time.

GORDON: It never occurred to me.

MICHAEL: It was pure chance us meeting the way we did.

GORDON: Pure chance.

MICHAEL: Got a place to go?

GORDON (*indicating stage left*): Right around the corner.

MICHAEL: What's keeping us?

GORDON: No time like the present.

MICHAEL (*halting*): No . . . wait . . . I can't.

GORDON: Why not?

MICHAEL: I'm going to Mass on Sunday.

GORDON: We'll be finished by then.

MICHAEL: You don't understand, I've already gone to confession.

GORDON: Reschedule it again for tomorrow.

MICHAEL: Bloomingdale's is having a sale on angora sweaters.

GORDON: If you're worried about committing a sin, we can do it with the lights off.

MICHAEL: Maybe . . . yes . . . *no*, Father Malarkey would never forgive me.

(MICHAEL *exits stage right*.)

GORDON (*calling after* MICHAEL): We'll keep it venial.

(GORDON *exits stage left*. DONALD *enters stage right. Convinced of his self-evident desirability and superior intelligence, a condescending* DONALD *approaches* JACK.)

DONALD (*to* JACK): Am I supposed to be intimidated by you?

JACK: Am I supposed to be turned on by your approach?

DONALD: Who said I'm making one?

JACK: You're standing there.

DONALD: It's a free country.

JACK: I'm in no mood for small talk.

DONALD: You prefer monosyllables?

JACK: You being hostile?

DONALD: Just sociable.

JACK: I'm not.

DONALD: You should smile more.

JACK: I wouldn't want to attract the wrong element.

DONALD: I've never talked to an S&M freak before.

JACK: Lucky me.

DONALD: Isn't it a bit warm for that black leather jacket?

JACK: I hadn't noticed.

DONALD: You own a bike?

JACK: Sure. A Schwinn.

DONALD: Are you being sarcastic?

JACK: To no avail.

DONALD: I wasn't aware that irony was part of the mystique.

JACK: It's germane.

DONALD: Do you often use words like that?

JACK: Indubitably.

DONALD: You're doing that on purpose, aren't you?

JACK: Doing what?

DONALD: Irritating me with your vocabulary.

JACK: Is it working?

DONALD: I can't figure out if you're genuine or not.

JACK: That's twice tonight I've been accused of not being convincing.

DONALD: Maybe you should work on your image.

JACK: I did. Years ago.

(JACK *crosses to downstage left.* CEIL *enters stage right on the arm of a shy* JORDAN *as* BOOM BOOM *enters stage left on the arm of a shy* GORDON. *At first the happy couples don't see each other.*)

JORDAN (*to* CEIL, *as they cross left*): I don't want anyone to see us.

CEIL: Relax.

GORDON (*to* BOOM BOOM, *as they cross right*): Isn't there a less public route?

BOOM BOOM: We meet anyone you know, you introduce me as your sister.

JORDAN (*to* CEIL): You promise? On the grave of Trotsky?

CEIL: Sweetie, a deal's a deal. You buy Ceil a bottle of champagne, she lets you wear her garter belt.

GORDON (*to* BOOM BOOM): What if I don't want to go all the way?

BOOM BOOM: It'll grow back.

JORDAN (*to* CEIL): And your feather boa?

CEIL: I'm not so sure about that.

GORDON (*to* BOOM BOOM, *lewdly*): Straightedged or safety?

BOOM BOOM: Whichever turns you on.

JORDAN (*to* CEIL): Please?

GORDON (*to* BOOM BOOM): Both legs?

BOOM BOOM: Honey, I'll even shave your armpits.

CEIL (*to* JORDAN): Give your little lambkin enough bubbly, she might even let you get into her panties.

GORDON: Jordan!

JORDAN: Gordon!

GORDON: This isn't what it looks like!

JORDAN: You mustn't get the wrong impression.

BOOM BOOM (*to* CEIL): If it isn't Miss Bridge-and-Tunnel.

CEIL (*to* BOOM BOOM): Such a sad case.

BOOM BOOM: Such an unwell woman.

CEIL (*to* JORDAN): Introduce me to your cute friend.

JORDAN: I . . . er . . .

GORDON (*attempting an introduction*): This is—

BOOM BOOM (*glaring at* CEIL): We've met.

CEIL (*to* GORDON): Ditch the bitch and join us for a drinkie.

BOOM BOOM (*holding firm to* GORDON): Warn your friend to watch his wallet.

JORDAN and GORDON (*to* CEIL *and* BOOM BOOM, *pulling free*): Sorry, I changed my mind.

(JORDAN *exits stage left almost as fast as* GORDON *exits stage right.*)

CEIL (*calling after* JORDAN): No—

BOOM BOOM (*calling after* GORDON): —wait—

CEIL (*calling after* JORDAN): —was it something I said?

BOOM BOOM: Good work, Medusa—you managed to repulse two men with a single smile.

CEIL: We are not speaking, Darlene Dynel.

(CEIL, *nose in the air, exits stage right as* TIMOTHY *enters stage left dressed in* SIDNEY's *raincoat and not much else.*)

TIMOTHY (*to* BOOM BOOM): I've been looking for you all over.

BOOM BOOM: That's where I've been.

TIMOTHY: I have great news!

BOOM BOOM: You finally came out?

TIMOTHY (*opening the raincoat to display his costume—a very brief lamé bikini*): I'm a star!

BOOM BOOM (*appreciating*): You're certainly a featured player.

TIMOTHY: I'm a go-go boy.

BOOM BOOM (*she's heard it all before*): At the Stonewall.

TIMOTHY: This big-time producer—

BOOM BOOM: Murfino.

TIMOTHY: —has taken a real interest in—

BOOM BOOM: Cashing in on your buns.

TIMOTHY: I'm about to make my debut and I'd really like you there.

BOOM BOOM: Me?

TIMOTHY: You and the other one.

BOOM BOOM: The other one isn't available.

TIMOTHY: But you can come, can't you? It's my opening night.

BOOM BOOM: Judging from your costume, it isn't formal.

TIMOTHY: You're my only friend. Except for Sidney, who's a lot nicer now that he's had a few drinks. C.B. and Heather are there—Heather has the giggles.

BOOM BOOM: Why not. We can't keep your public waiting.

TIMOTHY: I don't have a public.

BOOM BOOM: Give it time.

(BOOM BOOM *and* TIMOTHY *exit stage left.* DONALD *crosses to* JACK.)

DONALD: I fascinate you, don't I?

JACK: Are you still here?

DONALD: I can see that you're turned on.

JACK: What you see is tension.

DONALD: What do you do?

JACK: You'll never need to know.

DONALD: What do you do for a living?

JACK (*telling the truth*): Illustrate children's books.

DONALD: Now who's being hostile?

JACK: You bring out the brute in me.

DONALD: I find your whole scene pretty funny.

JACK: Glad to be a source of amusement.

DONALD: Come on, admit it, you're comical.

JACK: Not for much longer.

DONALD: Where's your sense of humor?

JACK: In abeyance.

DONALD: I'm really getting to you, aren't I?

JACK: More than you might think.

DONALD: I'm used to it. When you're as attractive as I am, you learn to endure unwanted attention.

JACK: That makes two of us.

DONALD: If we went to your place, what would you do with me?

JACK: Teach you some manners.

DONALD: Is that what you call discipline?

JACK: Public service.

DONALD: Would you spank me? Would you chain me up first? Restraint . . . isn't that what you call it?

JACK: It's what I'm practicing.

DONALD: Subtlety in someone like you is disappointing.

JACK: And obviously ineffective.

DONALD: After you have me in bondage, then what will you do?

JACK: Move to another apartment.

DONALD: Are you rejecting me?

JACK: Fast on the uptake, aren't you?

(SEYMOUR *enters stage left, stands in the shadows unnoticed.*)

DONALD (*stunned*): You can't reject me.

JACK: Why not?

DONALD: Nobody ever rejects me.

JACK: Somebody had to be first.

DONALD: You're sick.

JACK: Because I rejected you?

DONALD: I rejected you. That's why you're into what you're into, you can't make it
    with a normal person.

JACK: Is that what you are?

DONALD: You're sick! And sad! And . . . and pathetic!

(DONALD *exits stage left.*)

SEYMOUR (*sidling up to* JACK): I thought he'd never leave.

JACK (*hostile*): You I also don't need.

SEYMOUR: You helped blow my cover.

JACK (*starting to exit left*): It happens to the best of us.

SEYMOUR (*stopping* JACK): Where you going?

JACK: To the Stonewall. They have a new act I want to catch.

SEYMOUR (*warning*): I'd keep out of there.

JACK: Why?

SEYMOUR: Because . . . (*covering*) . . . it's not your kind of place.

JACK: We've already been through that.

SEYMOUR: I'm off duty.

JACK: Your poor wife.

SEYMOUR: We could have a beer somewhere.

JACK: You never quit, do you?

SEYMOUR: I'm not entrapping you.

JACK: That's what they all say.

SEYMOUR: You invited me to your place, remember?

JACK: What do you mean?

SEYMOUR: We got to keep this confidential. Tell me where you live, I'll meet you there.

JACK: Are you suggesting what I think you're suggesting?

SEYMOUR: I'm not queer or anything, I just like to fool around. (*Producing a nightstick, giving it to* JACK.) I even brought you a present. I figure you know what to do with it.

JACK: You've presented me with a dilemma.

SEYMOUR: Naw, it's just a regulation nightstick.

JACK: With or without lubricant?

SEYMOUR: You're the boss.

JACK: There is a God and he's an evil queen.

SEYMOUR: What's wrong?

JACK: You really don't understand, do you?

SEYMOUR: I'm not inexperienced.

JACK: This isn't happening.

SEYMOUR: Tell me where you live.

JACK: You don't find it difficult reconciling your occupation with your predilection?

SEYMOUR: A job's a job.

JACK: Part of me would like nothing better than to take a cop home and whip the shit out of him—

SEYMOUR: So?

JACK: So a better part of me isn't about to give you the satisfaction.

SEYMOUR: I don't get to hang from your ceiling?

JACK (*returning the nightstick*): I'm damned if I do and damned if I don't.

(DONOVAN *enters stage right.*)

DONOVAN (*to* SEYMOUR): Nice approach, Seymour.

SEYMOUR (*caught*): How long were you standing there?

DONOVAN: Long enough.

SEYMOUR: Convincing, aren't I?

DONOVAN: Too convincing, pansy.

SEYMOUR: It isn't what it looks like.

DONOVAN: We'll let your superior decide.

SEYMOUR: You can't fink on a fellow cop.

JACK: What is this, a convention?

DONOVAN: Stay out of this, faggot, me and your boyfriend have to come to terms.

SEYMOUR: Terms?

DONOVAN: Half your daily take.

SEYMOUR: Half?

DONOVAN: Starting with my cut of what you got off the closet case.

JACK (*to* SEYMOUR, *gleefully*): He's shaking you down!

SEYMOUR: But I work hard for my graft.

DONOVAN: Half.

JACK (*to* SEYMOUR): Maybe if you got down on your knees and begged.

SEYMOUR: But . . . I . . . you . . .

DONOVAN: *Half.*

(C.B. *and* HEATHER *enter stage left, their adrenaline on high.*)

C.B.: Jack—

HEATHER: —like man, it's far out—

C.B.: —they're raiding the Stonewall!

HEATHER: Fuzz all over the place!

JACK (*to* SEYMOUR): That's why you warned me not to go there.

C.B. (*to* SEYMOUR): Look who's still here.

SEYMOUR: Love to stay and chat, but I got business up the block.

(SEYMOUR *exits stage left, nightstick in hand.*)

DONOVAN (*following* SEYMOUR): Wait for me, "partner."

(DONOVAN *exits stage left.*)

C.B. (*to* JACK, *referring to* SEYMOUR): What was that all about?

JACK: If I told you, you'd never believe me.

HEATHER: You should have been with us—

C.B.: —Heather's a hero—

HEATHER: —you're the brave one—

C.B.: —this one cop had me in a hammerlock—

HEATHER: —so I kneed him in the groin—

C.B.: —he sat down on the curb and wept—

HEATHER: —you'd have thought it was the first time he'd ever met with passive resistance.

(*Flashing red lights illuminate the stage, moving from stage right to stage left. They are accompanied by a rise and fall of sirens.* CEIL *enters stage right as* DONALD *enters stage left. They all watch the passing parade.*)

JACK: Reinforcements.

C.B.: They've called out the Tactical Squad.

CEIL: What's happening?

DONOVAN: It's nothing . . . it's just another raid.

(JORDAN *enters stage left as* GORDON *enters stage right.*)

JORDAN (*to* GORDON): Gordon, you almost missed it . . . it's a riot.

(MICHAEL *enters stage left.*)

MICHAEL: It isn't a riot, it's a bunch of hysterical faggots.

DONALD: It's the full moon.

CEIL (*to* C.B.): Boom Boom! Where's Boom Boom?

HEATHER: She had words with this cop at the door—

C.B.: —he took offense—

HEATHER: —they threw her in a paddy wagon.

CEIL: They arrested her?! Quick, somebody, I need money.

C.B. (*giving money to* CEIL): Okay, you guys, let's all toss in for Boom Boom's bail fund.

CEIL (*grabbing* C.B.'s *money*): Who's talking about bail? I gotta go shop.

(CEIL *exits stage right, money in hand.*)

GORDON: They're arresting people?

JACK (*to* C.B.): There's a kid . . . a new go-go dancer—

HEATHER: Tim?

C.B.: He was last seen with Sidney.

HEATHER: We lost them in the scuffle.

MICHAEL: Why can't the authorities concentrate on the blatant ones—

DONALD: —yeah, and leave the rest of us alone.

JACK (*angry, moving toward* DONALD): "Us" who? Us "normal" types?

MICHAEL: The way some of them behave, they're asking for trouble.

JACK: So are you.

DONALD: You're such a big man, why don't you go over there and do something about it?

JACK: Will you come with me?

DONALD: None of this has anything to do with me.

MICHAEL: That's telling him, Donald.

DONALD (*to* JACK): Quite frankly, I wouldn't demean myself.

JACK (*moving at* DONALD): And you called me pathetic.
C.B. (*blocking* JACK): Jack, stop, it's not his fault.

JACK: Whose fault is it?

(SIDNEY *enters stage left. He has lost his hat, coat, and dignity. He clutches his glasses. They are broken.*)

SIDNEY: They took my identification . . . they know where I live . . . where I work . . .

JACK: Where is he? The kid who was with you?

SIDNEY: He's . . . (*Looking around.*) . . . I don't know. Still back there somewhere.

JACK: I'm going after him.

C.B.: Stay here—

MICHAEL: —they'll never let you through.

(JACK *ignores them, exits stage left as* MURFINO *enters stage left.*)

MURFINO: They're wrecking my place.

GORDON: The police?

MURFINO: My customers. They smashed the window . . . you got any idea how much plate glass costs?

DONALD: They're destroying property?

MURFINO: They got the cops barricaded inside—

C.B.: Inside?

MICHAEL: You mean they're winning?

GORDON: *We're* winning!

SIDNEY (*in awe*): Faggots fighting back?

JORDAN: We should be there, fanning the flames.

GORDON: We need to plan a strategy of protest.

JORDAN: Organize opposition.

GORDON: We need a constitution.

JORDAN: A manifesto.

GORDON: A mimeograph machine.

JORDAN: Crowds of demonstrators!

GORDON: We need a leader.

JORDAN: I nominate me.

GORDON: I have the experience. Civil Rights, Ban the Bomb, Planned Parenthood—

JORDAN: At Columbia I singlehandedly set fire to a professor.

GORDON: You're out of order. All those in favor of me? (*His hand flies up.*) One to nothing, I win.

JORDAN: You're manipulating this meeting.

GORDON: You're acting suspiciously like an outside agitator.

JORDAN: Your handling of this organization's funds is highly questionable.

GORDON (*childish*): If you're not going to plan the way I want to plan, I'm going to form my own movement.

JORDAN (*childish*): Not before I form mine. And mine will be national.

C.B.: Whoa!

HEATHER: Hold it.

MURFINO: What the fuck's going on?

SIDNEY: I think what we have here is a flash forward.

MURFINO: If this is the future, maybe you guys are better off where you are.

C.B. (*to* JORDAN *and* GORDON): Let's try to get tonight out of the way first. . . . You political types have years and years ahead of you to screw up the results.

(*Flashing red lights again illuminate the stage, stage right to stage left, again accompanied by a rise and fall of sirens. A triumphant* BOOM BOOM *enters stage left, her hands cuffed. She is followed by a gleeful* TIMOTHY *and a protective* JACK. TIMOTHY *is dressed in his costume and* JACK'S *black leather jacket.*)

BOOM BOOM (*arms above her head*): Look, everyone, I'm engaged!

(JACK *unlocks* BOOM BOOM'S *handcuffs.*)

C.B. (*to* BOOM BOOM): How'd you get free?

BOOM BOOM: While they were shoving us in the doors at the back of the paddy wagon, Miss Marsha was sneaking us out by the driver's side.

MURFINO: Where was the driver?

TIMOTHY: Watching the fun.

JACK: The crowd's getting bigger by the minute.

TIMOTHY: They're tossing pennies at the cops—

JACK: —they upended a VW—

BOOM BOOM: —they're emptying the gas all over the front of the bar—

JACK: —they're lighting matches and flicking them at the door.

MURFINO: My God, my bar!

(MURFINO *exits stage left.*)

BOOM BOOM: —it's wonderful—

(CEIL *enters stage right, carrying a box of Entenmann's.*)

CEIL: Boom Boom!

BOOM BOOM: Ceil!

(BOOM BOOM *and* CEIL *fall into each other's arms.*)

CEIL: They told me you were incarcerated.

BOOM BOOM: I was sprung.

CEIL: I was coming to visit you in jail. I was bringing you this cake, just in case. I even paid money for it. (*Giving the cake box to* BOOM BOOM.)

BOOM BOOM (*opening the cake box*): How thoughtful.

CEIL: Look inside . . . look inside . . .

BOOM BOOM (*removing a nail file*): A nail file?

CEIL: I wanted you should be well groomed.

(SEYMOUR *and* DONOVAN *enter stage left.*)

DONOVAN (*referring to* BOOM BOOM): There she is!

SEYMOUR (*grabbing* BOOM BOOM): You're under arrest for resisting arrest.

DONOVAN (*going for* TIMOTHY): We're taking you also.

JACK (*blocking* DONOVAN): Oh, no you're not.

CEIL (*to* SEYMOUR): Set my sister free!

SEYMOUR: Keep back, you second-rate aberration.

CEIL: Second-rate? I'll have you know I'm the classiest aberration on this block.

BOOM BOOM (*cautioning*): Ceil—

CEIL: He can't talk to me that way.

SEYMOUR: I can talk to you any way I want to.

CEIL: You know what your problem is?! Penis envy!

SEYMOUR: Why you vicious—!

(SEYMOUR *releases* BOOM BOOM, *swings his nightstick at* CEIL, *hitting her in the face.* CEIL *falls to the pavement, the others back away.* JACK *and* C.B. *start forward to help,* CEIL *puts up her hand to stop them.* CEIL *gets up all by herself, turns to face* SEYMOUR. *There is blood trickling from the corners of her mouth.*)

CEIL (*to* SEYMOUR): Satisfied, sweetie? Did you get your rocks off?

BOOM BOOM (*tossing her compact to* CEIL): Miss Ceil, see to your makeup.

CEIL (*catching the compact*): Thanks, hon.

(CEIL, *her eyes on* SEYMOUR, *opens the compact, daintily wipes the corner of her mouth. Tentatively, almost shyly,* JACK *begins to chant at* SEYMOUR *and* DONOVAN, "Who takes the payoffs, you take the payoffs." C.B., BOOM BOOM, TIMOTHY, HEATHER, JORDAN, *and* GORDON *pick up the chant. It is slow, measured, quiet, this being a very new experience for them. The chant is kept up under the following scene.*)

DONOVAN (*backing downstage right, nightstick at ready*): Okay—

SEYMOUR (*backing downstage left, nightstick at ready*): —that's it—

DONOVAN: —move along everybody—

SEYMOUR: —let's disperse—

DONOVAN: —let's break it up—

SEYMOUR: —we don't want no trouble on this street.

CEIL: This street belongs to us.

DONOVAN: Yeah?

BOOM BOOM (*joining* CEIL): Yeah.

CEIL: Me and my friends.

SEYMOUR: Says who?

C.B. (*joining* CEIL): Says me.

JACK (*joining* CEIL): And me.

TIMOTHY (*joining* CEIL): Me, too.

JORDAN and GORDON (*joining* CEIL): That includes us.

HEATHER (*joining* CEIL): Wow, man, like look who's united!

C.B. (*to* MICHAEL, DONALD, *and* SIDNEY): Join us.

(*This new chant, "Join us," replaces "Who takes the payoffs," each new character coming in as cued.*)

MICHAEL: You're only making it harder on the rest of us.

JORDAN (*to* MICHAEL, DONALD, *and* SIDNEY): Join us.

DONALD: Don't be stupid.

JORDAN (*to* MICHAEL): Join us.

MICHAEL: Stop it! You're an impediment to my rapid recovery!

JACK (*to* DONALD): Join us.

DONALD: Sick! And sad! And pathetic!

HEATHER (*to* SIDNEY): Join us.

SIDNEY: I can't . . .

TIMOTHY (*to* SIDNEY): Join us.

SIDNEY: I couldn't . . .

BOOM BOOM (*to* SIDNEY): Join us.

SIDNEY: I have a professional career . . .

THE OTHERS (*to* SIDNEY): Join us.

SIDNEY: Elderly parents . . .

THE OTHERS (*to* SIDNEY): Join us.

SIDNEY: I'd be risking everything . . .

CEIL: Believe me, Miss Thing, you ain't got nothing left to lose.

THE OTHERS: Join us.

SIDNEY (*looking at* MICHAEL *and* DONALD): But . . . ?

THE OTHERS: Join us.

DONALD: Don't listen to them.

THE OTHERS: Join us.

MICHAEL (*to* SIDNEY): They're nothing but a bunch of . . . of degenerates!

THE OTHERS: Join us.

DONALD (*to* JACK): You aren't proving anything!

THE OTHERS: Join us.

DONALD: No! Never! No way!

THE OTHERS: Join us.

DONALD: You faggots are revolting!!

(SIDNEY, *horrified at* DONALD, *makes his decision, tosses his sunglasses in the gutter, joins* CEIL *and the others.*)

SIDNEY (*to* DONALD *and* MICHAEL): You bet your sweet ass we are!

(SIDNEY, CEIL, BOOM BOOM, C.B., HEATHER, JACK, TIMOTHY, JORDAN, *and* GORDON *make a grouping worthy of a statue in Sheridan Square. Again flashing red lights illuminate the stage, again accompanied by sirens.*)

BLACKOUT

BENT

by
Martin Sherman

FOR
Alan Pope and Peter Whitman

Bent was first presented at London's Royal Court Theatre, May 3, 1979. Directed by Robert Chetwyn; designed by Alan Tagg; lighting by Robert Bryan; music by Andy Roberts. The cast was:

MAX	Ian McKellen
RUDY	Jeff Rawle
WOLF	Simon Shepherd
LIEUTENANT	Haydn Wood
2ND LIEUTENANT	Jeremy Arnold
GRETA	Ken Shorter
VICTOR	Roger Dean
FREDDIE	Richard Gale
HORST	Tom Bell
GUARD ON TRAIN	Haydn Wood
OFFICER	Gregory Martyn
CORPORAL	John Francis
CAPTAIN	Peter Cellier

Bent was first presented at New York's New Apollo Theater on December 2, 1979. Directed by Robert Allan Ackerman.

Presented by Jack Schissel and Steven Steinlauf, co-produced by Lee Minskoff and Patty Grubman. The cast was:

MAX	Richard Gere
RUDY	David Marshall Grant
WOLF	James Remar
GUARDS	Kai Wulff, Philip Kraus, and John Snyder
GRETA	Michael Gross
UNCLE FREDDIE	George Hall
OFFICER	Bryan E. Clark
HORST	David Dukes
CAPTAIN	Ron Randell

ACT I

Scene 1

The living room of an apartment. Small. Sparse furniture. A table with plants. A door on left leads to the outside hall. Nearby is an exit to the kitchen. At right, an exit to the bedroom, and nearby an exit to the bathroom.

MAX enters. He is thirty-four. He wears a bathrobe. He is very hung-over. He stares into space.

MAX: Oh God! (*Goes into bathroom—pause—then offstage, from bathroom:*) Oh God!

(*MAX returns to the living room and sits down. RUDY enters. He is thirty. He wears a bathrobe. He also wears glasses. He carries a cup.*)

RUDY: Here. (*Hands MAX the cup; MAX stares and doesn't take it.*) Here. Coffee!

MAX (*takes the cup*): Thanks.

(*They kiss. MAX sips the coffee.*)

RUDY: It's late. It's almost three. We really slept. I missed class. I hate to dance when I miss class. Bad for the muscles. And there's no place to warm up at the club. I hate that nightclub anyhow. The floor's no good. It's cement. You shouldn't dance on cement. It kills my ankle. They've covered it with wood. Last night, before the show, I pounded on the wood—real hard—and I could hear the cement. I'm going to complain. I really am. (*He goes into the kitchen.*)

MAX (*sits in silence and stares*): Oh God.

(*RUDY returns from the kitchen with a pitcher of water and waters the plants.*)

RUDY: The plants are dying. The light's bad in this apartment. I wish we had a decent place. I wish one of your deals would come through again. Oh, listen to me, wanting a bigger place. Rosen's gonna be knocking on our door any minute now, you know that, wanting his rent. We're three weeks overdue. He always comes on a Sunday. He only cares about money. What's three weeks? He can wait. Well, at least I got the new job. I'll get paid on Thursday. If Greta keeps the club open. Business stinks. Well, I guess it means I can't complain about the cement, huh? The thing is, I don't want to dance with a bad ankle. More coffee?

(*MAX shakes his head yes. RUDY goes into the kitchen. MAX stares into space. He puts his hand on his head and takes a deep breath, then closes his eyes.*)

MAX: One. Two. Three. Four. Five. (*Opens his eyes, takes another deep breath.*) Six. Seven. Eight. Nine. Ten.

(RUDY *returns from kitchen and hands* MAX *another cup of coffee.* RUDY *resumes watering the plants.* MAX *watches him for a moment.*)

MAX: Okay. Tell me.

RUDY: What?

MAX: You know.

RUDY: No.

MAX: Come on.

RUDY: I *don't* know. Listen, do you think I should ask Lena for the rent money? She's such a good person. No feeling for music, though. Which is crazy, she's got such a good line. Perfect legs. Teddy wants to do a dance for her in total silence. You think that's a good idea? There's no place to do it, though. There's no work. Lena lost that touring job. So she must be broke. So she can't lend us the money. Want some food?

MAX: Just tell me.

RUDY: What?

MAX: Must really be bad.

RUDY: What must?

MAX: That's why you won't tell me.

RUDY: Tell you what?

MAX: Don't play games.

RUDY: I'm not playing anything.

MAX: I'll hate myself, won't I? (*Silence.*) Won't I?

RUDY: I'll make some breakfast.

MAX: Was I really rotten?

RUDY: Eggs and cheese.

MAX: I don't want eggs.

RUDY: Well, we're lucky to have them. I stole them from the club. They don't need eggs. People go there to drink. And see a terrific show. Oh boy, that's funny, 'cause that show stinks. You know, I'm so embarrassed, I have to think of other things while I'm dancing. I have to think of grocery lists. They can tell, out there, that you're not thinking about straw hats or water lilies—I mean, it really shows; particularly when it's grocery lists. Your face looks real depressed, when you can't afford groceries. . . .

MAX (*rises and puts his hand on* RUDY's *mouth*): Stop it. (RUDY *tries to speak.*) Stop it! (*They struggle; he keeps his hand over* RUDY's *mouth.*) I want to know what I did. (*Releases him.*)

RUDY (*smiles*): I love you. (*Goes into kitchen.*)

MAX: Rudy! Your plants! I'll pull the little bastards out unless you tell me.

(RUDY *comes back in.* MAX *stands over the plants.*)

RUDY: No you won't.

MAX: Like to bet. I did last month.

RUDY: You killed one. That was mean.

MAX: I'll do it again.

RUDY: Don't touch them. You have to be nice to plants. They can hear you and everything. (*To the plants:*) He's sorry. He didn't mean it. He's just hung-over.

MAX: What did I do?

(*Silence*)

RUDY: Nothing much.

MAX: I can't remember a thing. And when I can't remember, it means . . .

RUDY: It doesn't mean anything. You drank a lot. That's all. The usual.

MAX: How'd I get this? (*Pulls his robe off his shoulder, shows a mark on his skin.*)

RUDY: What's that?

MAX: Ouch! Don't touch it.

RUDY: I want to see it.

MAX: So *look*. You don't have to touch.

RUDY: What is it?

MAX: What does it look like? A big black and blue mark. There's another one here. (*Shows a mark on his arm.*)

RUDY: Oh.

MAX: How did I get them?

RUDY: You fell.

MAX: How?

RUDY: Someone pushed you.

MAX: Who?

RUDY: Some guy.

MAX: What guy?

RUDY: Nicky's friend.

MAX: Who's Nicky?

RUDY: One of the waiters at the club.

MAX: Which one?

RUDY: The redhead.

MAX: I don't remember him.

RUDY: He's a little fat.

MAX: Why'd the guy push me?

RUDY: You asked Nicky to come home with us.

MAX: I did?

RUDY: Yeah.

MAX: But he's *fat*.

RUDY: Only a little.

MAX: A threesome with a fat person?

RUDY: Not a threesome. A twelvesome. You asked *all* the waiters. All at the same time, too. You were standing on a table, making a general offer.

MAX: Oh. Then what?

RUDY: Nicky's friend pushed you off the table.

MAX: And . . .

RUDY: You landed on the floor, on top of some guy in leather.

MAX: What was he doing on the floor?

RUDY: I don't know.

MAX: Was Greta mad?

RUDY: Greta wasn't *happy*. (*Pause.*) It was late. Most everyone was gone. And you were very drunk. People like you drunk. (*Pause.*) I'll make some food.

MAX: I don't want food. Why didn't you stop me?

RUDY: How can I stop you?

MAX: Don't let me drink.

RUDY: Oh. Sure. When you're depressed?

MAX: Was I depressed?

RUDY: Of course.

MAX: I don't remember why.

RUDY: Then drinking worked, didn't it? (*Returns to kitchen.*)

(*A blond man, in his early twenties, enters, bleary-eyed, from the bedroom. He is naked.*)

BLOND MAN: Good morning. (*He stumbles into the bathroom.*)

MAX: Rudy!

RUDY (*coming out of kitchen*): What?

MAX: Who was that?

RUDY: Who was what?

MAX: *That!* That person!

RUDY: Oh. Yeah. Him. Blond?

MAX: Yes.

RUDY: And big?

MAX: Yes.

RUDY: That's the one you fell on.

MAX: The guy in leather?

RUDY: Yes. You brought him home. (*Goes into kitchen.*)

MAX: Rudy! Your plants!

RUDY (*returns from kitchen*): You brought him home, that's all. He got you going. All that leather, all those chains. You called him your own little storm trooper. You insulted all his friends. They left. I don't know why they didn't beat you up, but they didn't. They left. And you brought him home.

MAX: And we had a threesome?

RUDY: Maybe the two of you had a threesome. Max, there is no such thing. You pick guys up. You think you're doing it for me, too. You're not. I don't like it. You and the other guy always end up ignoring me anyhow. Besides, last night, you and your own little storm trooper began to get rough with each other, and I know pain is very chic just now, but I don't like it, 'cause pain hurts, so I went to sleep. (*Takes MAX's coffee cup, pours it onto the plants.*) Here, Walter, have some coffee.

MAX: Walter?

RUDY: I'm naming the plants. They're my friends.

(RUDY *goes into the kitchen. The* BLOND MAN *comes out of the bathroom, wearing a towel. He grins at* MAX.)

MAX: Rudy!

RUDY (*returns from kitchen; looks at the* BLOND): Oh. There's a bathrobe in there—in the bedroom.

(*The* BLOND MAN *goes into the bedroom. A pause.*)

MAX: I'm sorry.

RUDY: It's okay.

MAX: I'm a rotten person. Why am I so rotten? Why do I do these things? He's gorgeous, though, isn't he? I don't remember anything. I don't remember what we did in bed. Why don't I ever remember?

RUDY: You were drunk. And high on coke.

MAX: That too?

RUDY: Yeah.

MAX: Whose coke?

RUDY: Anna's.

MAX: I don't remember.

RUDY: You made arrangements to pick up a shipment to sell.

MAX: A *shipment?*

RUDY: Yeah.

MAX: Christ! When?

RUDY: I don't know.

MAX: That can be a lot of rent money.

RUDY: Anna will remember.

MAX: Right. Hey—rent money. Maybe . . . do you think . . .

RUDY: What?

MAX: We can ask him.

RUDY: Who?

MAX: *Him.*

RUDY: You're kidding.

MAX: Why not?

RUDY: We don't know him.

MAX: I slept with him. I think. I wonder what it was like.

RUDY: You picked him up, one night, and you're going to ask him to loan you the rent money?

MAX: Well, you know how I am.

RUDY: Yeah.

MAX: I can talk people into things.

RUDY: *Yeah.*

MAX: I can try.

RUDY: It won't work. He thinks you're rich.

MAX: Rich?

RUDY: You told him you were rich.

MAX: Terrific.

RUDY: And Polish.

MAX: *Polish?*

RUDY: You had an accent.

(RUDY *laughs and returns to the kitchen. The* BLOND MAN *walks out, in a short bathrobe. He stands and looks at* MAX. *An embarrassed silence.*)

MAX: Hi.

MAN: Hi. The robe is short. I look silly.

MAX: You look okay.

MAN: Yes? You too. (*Goes to* MAX *and kisses him, then starts to pull* MAX's *robe off, and bites* MAX *on the chest.*) Ummm . . .

MAX: Hey. Not now.

MAN: Later, then.

MAX: Yes.

MAN: In the country.

MAX: The country?

MAN: Your voice is different.

MAX: Oh?

MAN: You don't have an accent.

MAX: Only when I'm drunk.

MAN: Oh.

MAX: Last night—was it good?

MAN: What do you think?

MAX: I'm asking.

MAN: Do you have to ask?

RUDY (*comes in with a cup of coffee*): Some coffee?

MAN: Yes. Thank you. (RUDY *hands him the cup. A silence.*) This place . . .

MAX: Yes?

MAN: It's really . . . (*Stops—silence.*)

MAX: Small?

MAN: Yes. Exactly.

MAX: I guess it is.

MAN: You people are strange, keeping places like this in town. I don't meet people like you too much. But you interest me, your kind.

MAX: Listen . . .

MAN: Oh, look, it doesn't matter, who you are, who I am. I'm on vacation. *That* matters. The country will be nice.

MAX: What's the country?

MAN: The house. Your house. Your country house.

MAX (*to* RUDY): My country house?

RUDY: Oh. That. I forgot to tell you about that. We're driving there this afternoon.

MAX: To our country house?

RUDY: *Your* country house.

MAX: How do we get there?

RUDY: Car.

MAX: Mine?

RUDY: Right.

MAX: Why don't we stay here?

MAN: Don't make jokes. You promised me two days in the country.

MAX: Your name.

MAN: Yes?

MAX: I forgot your name.

MAN: Wolf.

MAX: Wolf? Good name.

WOLF: I didn't forget yours.

MAX: Look, Wolf, I don't have a car.

WOLF: Sure you do.

MAX: No.

WOLF: You showed me. On the street. Pointed it out.

MAX: Did I? It wasn't mine.

WOLF: Not yours?

MAX: No. I don't have a house in the country, either.

WOLF: Of course you do. You told me all about it.

MAX: I was joking.

WOLF: I don't like jokes. You don't want me with you, is that it? Maybe I'm not good enough for you. Not rich enough. My father made watches. That's not so wonderful. Is it, Baron?

(*Pause.*)

MAX: Baron?

RUDY: Don't look at me. *That* one I didn't know about.

MAX: Baron. (*Begins to laugh.*)

(*There is a loud knock at the front door.*)

RUDY: Rosen!

MAX: Shit!

WOLF: You like to laugh at me, Baron?

(*The knocking continues.*)

MAX: Listen, Wolf darling, you're really very sweet and very pretty and I like you a lot, but you see, I'm not too terrific, because I have a habit of getting drunk and stoned and grand and making things up. Believe me, I'm not a baron. There is no country house. There is no money. I don't have *any* money. Sometimes I do. Sometimes I sell cocaine, sometimes I find people to invest in business deals, sometimes . . . well, I scrounge, see, and I'm good at it, and in a few weeks I will have some money again. But right now, nothing. Rudy and I can't pay our rent. This rent. Right here. This lousy apartment. That's all we have. And that man knocking at our door is our landlord. And he's going to throw us out. Because we can't pay our rent. Out into the streets, Wolf, the streets. Filled with filth, vermin. And lice. And . . . urine. Urine! Unless someone can help us out. Unless someone gives us a hand. *That's* the truth. Look, you don't believe me, I'll show you. Right out there we have, just like in the movies, the greedy landlord. (*Puts his hand on the doorknob.*) Fanfare please.

(RUDY *simulates a trumpet call.*)

MAX: Here he is, the one and only, Abraham Rosen!

(MAX *swings the door open with a flourish. Two men are standing outside—a Gestapo* CAPTAIN *and an* OFFICER *in full Nazi uniform—both holding guns.* MAX *shuts the door.*)

MAX: That's not Rosen!

(*The door is kicked open. The* CAPTAIN *points to* WOLF.)

CAPTAIN: *HIM!*

WOLF: No!

(WOLF *throws the coffee cup at the* CAPTAIN *and runs into the bathroom. The* CAPTAIN *and the* OFFICER *run after him.* RUDY *starts toward the bathroom;* MAX *pulls him back.*)

MAX: Idiot! Run!

(MAX *grabs* RUDY *and they run out the front door. The lights black out on the left side of the stage. A shot rings out in the bathroom.* WOLF *screams. The lights rise on the left side of the stage, as* GRETA *enters.* GRETA *is a man dressed as a woman. He wears a silver dress, high green leather boots, and a top hat, and carries a silver cane. He is both elegant and bizarre.*

The CAPTAIN *watches as the* OFFICER *drags* WOLF *out of the bathroom.* WOLF *is bleeding, but still alive. He looks up at the* CAPTAIN *and crawls slowly toward him.*)

WOLF: Bastard!

CAPTAIN: Wolfgang Granz, we have an order for your arrest. You resisted. Too bad.

(*The* CAPTAIN *grabs* WOLF *by the neck, takes out a knife, and slits his throat.*

GRETA *tugs at a rope above him and pulls down a trapeze. He thrusts himself up onto the trapeze bar and sits there. A projection in the center of the stage reads:*

BERLIN—1934

Lights out on the apartment. Full spotlight on GRETA.)

Scene 2

GRETA *sits on the trapeze. He sings in a smoky, seductive voice.*

GRETA: Streets of Berlin,
      I must leave you soon,
      Ah!
      Will you forget me?
      Was I ever really here?

      Find me a bar
      On the cobblestoned streets
      Where the boys are pretty.
      I cannot love
      For more than one day
      But one day is enough in this city.

      Find me a boy
      With two ocean-blue eyes
      And show him no pity.
      Take out his eyes,
      He never need see
      How they eat you alive in this city.

      Streets of Berlin,
      Will you miss me?
      Streets of Berlin,
      Do you care?
      Streets of Berlin,
      Will you cry out
      If I vanish
      Into thin air?

(*Spotlight dims. Lights rise on* GRETA'S *Club. The stage is to the left.* GRETA'S *dressing room is on the right—a chair facing a mirror, and a screen to change behind.* GRETA *enters the dressing room. The lights fade on the rest of his club.*)

GRETA: My heroes! Where are you?

(MAX *and* RUDY *come from behind the screen. They are dressed in trousers and shirts, pieces of nightclub costumes.* GRETA *looks at them.*)

GRETA: Schmucks!

(MAX *sits on a stool, lost in thought.* GRETA *sits in the chair, adjusting his costume in the mirror.*)

GRETA: I'm getting rid of all the rough songs. Who am I kidding? I'm getting rid of the club. Well—Maybe. Maybe not. I'll turn it into something else. We'll see.

RUDY: Is it safe?

GRETA: What?

RUDY: For us to go home?

GRETA: You fucking queers, don't you have any brains at all? No, it's not safe.

RUDY: I want to go home.

GRETA: You can't. You can't go any place.

RUDY: I have to get my plants.

GRETA: Oh, Jesus! Forget your plants. You can't go home. You certainly can't stay here. And you can't contact friends, so don't try to see Lena, she's a good kid, you'll get her into a lot of trouble. You understand? You have to leave Berlin.

RUDY: Why? I live here, I work here.

GRETA: No, you don't. You're fired.

RUDY: I *don't* understand. What did we do? Why should we leave?

GRETA: Don't leave. Stay. Be *dead* schmucks. Who gives a damn? I don't.

MAX (*looks up*): Who was he?

GRETA: Who was who?

MAX: The blond?

GRETA: Wolfgang Granz.

MAX: What's that mean?

GRETA: He was Karl Ernst's boyfriend.

MAX: Who's Karl Ernst?

GRETA: What kind of world do you live in? Aren't you guys ever curious about what's going on?

MAX: Greta, don't lecture. Who's Karl Ernst?

GRETA: Von Helldorf's deputy. You know Von Helldorf?

MAX: The head of the storm troopers in Berlin.

GRETA: I don't believe it. You've actually *heard* of someone. Right. Second in command at the SA, immediately under Ernst Rohm.

RUDY: Oh. Ernst Rohm. I know him. (MAX *and* GRETA *stare at him.*) He's that fat queen, with those awful scars on his face, a real big shot, friend of Hitler's, runs around with a lot of beautiful boys. Goes to all the clubs; I sat at his table once. He's been *here* too, hasn't he?

MAX: Rudy, shut up.

RUDY: Why?

MAX: Just shut up, okay? (*To* GRETA:) So?

GRETA: So Hitler had Rohm arrested last night.

MAX: You're kidding. He's Hitler's right-hand man.

GRETA: Was. He's dead. Just about anyone who's high up in the SA is dead. Your little scene on top of that table was *not* the big event of the evening. It was a bloody night. The city's in a panic. Didn't you see the soldiers on the streets? The SS? How'd you get here in your bathrobes? Boy, you have dumb luck, that's all. The talk is that Rohm and his storm troopers—Von Helldorf, Ernst, your blond friend, the lot—were planning a coup. I don't believe it. What the hell, let them kill each other, who cares? Except, it's the end of the club. As long as Rohm was around, a queer club was still okay. Anyhow, that's who you had, baby—Wolfgang Granz. I hope he was a good fuck. What's the difference? You picked up the wrong guy, that's all.

RUDY: We can explain to somebody. It's not like we knew him.

GRETA: Sure. Explain it all to the SS. You don't explain. Not anymore. You know, you queers are not very popular anyhow. It was just Rohm keeping you all safe. Now you're like Jews. Unloved, baby, unloved.

RUDY: How about you?

GRETA: *Me?* Everyone knows I'm not queer. I got a wife and kids. Of course, that doesn't mean much these days, does it? But—I still ain't queer! As for this . . . (*fingers his costume*) I go where the money is. Was.

MAX (*gets up*): Money.

GRETA: Right.

MAX: Money. Ah! Greta!

GRETA: What's with you?

MAX: How much?

GRETA: How much what?

MAX: How much did they give you?

GRETA (*laughs*): Oh. (*Takes out a roll of money.*) This much.

MAX: And you told them where Granz was?

GRETA: Told them, hell—I showed them your building.

RUDY: Greta, you didn't.

GRETA: Why not? You don't play games with the SS. Anyhow, it's just what he would do, your big shot here. He's into money, too. He just isn't very good at it. Me, I'm dynamite. Here. I'll do you a favor. Take it. (*Holds out the money.*)

RUDY: No.

GRETA: It will help.

RUDY: We don't want it.

MAX: Shut up, Rudy.

RUDY: Stop telling me to—

MAX: Shut up! It's not enough. We need more.

GRETA: So get more.

MAX: If they catch us, it won't help you.

GRETA: Oh? A threat? (*Pause.*) Tell you what. I'll do you a favor. Take some more. (*Holds out some more money.*) I've made a lot off your kind, so I'm giving a little back. Take it all.

RUDY: Don't take it.

MAX: Okay. (*Takes the money.*)

GRETA: Now get out.

MAX (*to* RUDY): Come on. . . .

RUDY: Where? I'm not leaving Berlin.

MAX: We have to.

RUDY: We don't have to.

MAX: They're looking for us.

RUDY: But I live here.

MAX: Come on. . . .

RUDY: I've paid up for dance class for the next two weeks. I can't leave. And my plants . . .

MAX: Jesus! Come on!

RUDY: If you hadn't gotten so drunk . . .

MAX: Don't.

RUDY: Why'd you have to take him home?

MAX: How do I know? *I don't remember.*

RUDY: You've ruined everything.

MAX: Right. I always do. So you go off on your own, okay? Go back to dance class. They can shoot you in the middle of an arabesque. Take half. (*Holds out some money.*)

RUDY: I don't want it.

MAX: Then fuck it! (*Starts to leave.*)

RUDY: Max!

GRETA: Max. He can't handle it alone. Look at him. Stick together. (MAX *turns back to* RUDY.) Take his hand, schmuck. (RUDY *takes* MAX's *hand.*) That's right.

RUDY: Where are we going to go?

GRETA: *Don't*. Don't say anything in front of me. Get out.

(MAX *stares at* GRETA. *Then he tugs at* RUDY *and pulls him out of the room.* GRETA *removes his wig. He stares at his face in the mirror.*)

BLACKOUT

Scene 3

Lights up on a park in Cologne. A middle-aged man, well dressed (FREDDIE) *sits on a bench. He is reading a newspaper.* MAX *enters. He sees the man and goes to the bench. The man looks up.*

FREDDIE: Sit down.

(MAX *sits.*)

FREDDIE: Pretend we're strangers. Having a little conversation in the park. Perfectly normal. (*Folds the newspaper.*) Do something innocent. Feed the pigeons.

MAX: There aren't any pigeons.

FREDDIE: Here. (*Hands* MAX *an envelope.*)

MAX: You look good.

FREDDIE: You look older.

MAX: What's in this?

FREDDIE: Your papers and a ticket to Amsterdam.

MAX: Just one?

FREDDIE: Yes.

MAX: Shit.

FREDDIE: Keep your voice down. Remember, we're strangers. Just a casual conversation. Perfectly normal.

MAX: One ticket. I told you on the phone—

FREDDIE: *One* ticket. That's all.

MAX: I can't take it. Damn it, I'd kill for this. Here. (*Gives the envelope back.*) Thanks anyway. (*Gets up.*)

FREDDIE: Sit down. It wasn't easy getting new papers for you. If the family finds out . . .

(MAX *sits.*)

FREDDIE: I have to be careful. They've passed a law, you know. We're not allowed to be fluffs anymore. We're not even allowed to kiss or embrace. Or fantasize. They can arrest you for having fluff thoughts.

MAX (*laughs*): Oh, Uncle Freddie.

FREDDIE: It's not funny.

MAX: It is.

FREDDIE: The family takes care of me. But you. Throwing it in everyone's face. No wonder they don't want anything to do with you. Why couldn't you have been quiet about it? Settled down, gotten married, paid for a few boys on the side. No one would have known. Ach! Take this ticket.

MAX: I can't. Stop giving it to me.

(*Silence.*)

FREDDIE: Look over there.

MAX: Where?

FREDDIE: Over there. See him?

MAX: Who?

FREDDIE: With the mustache.

MAX: Yes.

FREDDIE: Cute.

MAX: I guess.

FREDDIE: Think he's a fluff?

MAX: I don't care.

FREDDIE: You've been running for two years now. Haven't you? With that dancer. The family knows all about it. You can't live like that. Take this ticket.

MAX: I need two.

FREDDIE: I can't get two.

MAX: Of course you can.

FREDDIE: Yes. I think he is a fluff. You have to be so careful now. What is it? Do you love him?

MAX: Who?

FREDDIE: The dancer.

MAX: Jesus!

FREDDIE: Do you?

MAX: Don't be stupid. What's love? Bullshit. I'm a grown-up now. I just feel responsible.

FREDDIE: Fluffs can't afford that kind of responsibility. Why are you laughing?

MAX: That word. Fluffs. Look, do you think it's been a holiday? We've tramped right across this country; we settle in somewhere and then suddenly they're checking papers and we have to leave rather quickly; now we're living outside Cologne, in the goddamn forest! In a colony of *tents*—are you ready for that? *Me* in a tent! With hundreds of very boring unemployed people. Except most of them are *just* unemployed; they're not running from the Gestapo. I'm not cut out for this, Uncle Freddie. I was brought up to be comfortable. Like you. Okay. I've been fooling around for too long. You're right. The family and I should make up. So. How about a deal? *Two* tickets to Amsterdam. And two new sets of identity papers. Once we get to Amsterdam, I ditch him. And they can have me back.

FREDDIE: Maybe they don't want you back. It's been ten years.

MAX: They want me. It's good business. I'm an only son. (*Pause.*) Remember that marriage Father wanted to arrange? Her father had button factories, too. I just read about her in the paper; she's an eligible widow, living in Brussels. Make the arrangements again. I'll marry her. Our button factories can sleep with her button factories. It's a good deal. You know it. And eventually, when all this blows over, you can get me back to Germany. If I want a boy, I'll rent him. Like you. I'll be a discreet, quiet . . . fluff. Fair enough? It's what Father always wanted. Just get us *both* out alive.

FREDDIE: I'll have to ask your father.

MAX: Do it. Then ask him.

FREDDIE: I can't do things on my own. Not now. (*Holds out envelope.*) Just this.

MAX: I can't take it.

FREDDIE: He's looking this way. He might be the police. No. He's a fluff. He has fluff eyes. Still. You can't tell. You better leave. Just be casual. Perfectly normal. I'll ask your father.

MAX: Soon?

FREDDIE: Yes. Can I phone you?

MAX: In the *forest?*

FREDDIE: Phone me. On Friday.

(FREDDIE *puts the envelope away.* MAX *gets up.*)

MAX: You look good, Uncle Freddie.

(MAX *leaves.*)

(FREDDIE *picks up his newspaper, glances at it, puts it down, and turns to look again at the man with the mustache.*)

BLACKOUT

Scene 4

The forest. In front of a tent.

RUDY *sits before a fire. He has some apples, cheese, and a knife. He calls back to the tent.*

RUDY: Cheese! Max!

(MAX *comes out of the tent, sits down.*)

MAX: Where'd you get cheese? Steal it?

RUDY: I don't steal. I dug a ditch.

MAX: You *what?*

RUDY: Dug a ditch. Right outside of Cologne. They're building a road. You can sign on each morning if you get there in time. They don't check your papers. It's good exercise too, for your shoulders. I'm getting nice shoulders. But my feet . . . no more dancing feet. Oh, God. Here. Have some.

MAX: I don't want to eat. You shouldn't have to dig ditches. I want some real food, for Christ's sake. (*Takes the cheese.*) Look at this. It's lousy cheese. You don't know anything about cheese. Look at all these tents. There's no one to talk to in any of them. (*Eats a piece of cheese.*) It has no flavor.

RUDY: Then don't eat it. I'll eat it. I have apples, too.

MAX: I hate apples.

RUDY: Then starve. What did you do today, while I was ditch digging?

MAX: Nothing.

RUDY: You weren't here when I got back.

MAX: Went to town.

RUDY: Have fun?

MAX: I'm working on something.

RUDY: Really?

MAX: Yeah. A deal. (*Takes an apple.*)

RUDY: Oh. A deal. Wonderful.

MAX: I might get us new papers and tickets to Amsterdam.

RUDY: You said that in Hamburg.

MAX: It didn't work out in Hamburg.

RUDY: You said that in Stuttgart.

MAX: Are you going to recite the list?

RUDY: Why not? I'm tired of your deals. You're right. This cheese stinks. I don't want to eat it. (*Pushes the food aside.*)

MAX: You have to eat.

RUDY: Throw it out.

MAX: You get sick if you don't eat.

RUDY: So what?

MAX: Okay. Get sick.

RUDY: No. I don't want to get sick. (*Eats a piece of cheese.*) If I get sick, you'll leave me behind. You're just waiting for me to get sick.

MAX: Oh—here we go.

RUDY: You'd love it if I died.

MAX: Rudy! I just want to get us out of here. These awful tents. There's no air. We're *in* the air, but there's still no air. I can't breathe. I've got to get us across the border.

RUDY: Why don't we just cross it?

MAX: What do you mean?

RUDY: This guy on the job today was telling me it's easy to cross the border.

MAX: Oh sure it's simple. You just walk across. Of course, they shoot you.

RUDY: He said he knew spots.

MAX: Spots?

RUDY: Spots to get through. I told him to come talk to you.

MAX: *Here?*

RUDY: Yes.

MAX: I told you we don't want anyone to know we're here, or that we're trying to cross the border. Are you *that* dumb?

RUDY: I'm not dumb.

MAX: He could tell the police.

RUDY: Okay. So I *am* dumb. Why don't we try it anyway?

MAX: Because . . .

RUDY: Why?

MAX: I'm working on a deal.

RUDY: Who with?

MAX: I can't tell you. I can't talk about it before it happens. Then it won't happen. I'm superstitious.

RUDY: Then why'd you bring it up?

MAX: So you'd know that . . .

RUDY: What?

MAX: That I'm trying.

RUDY: This is crazy. We're in the middle of the jungle—

MAX: Forest.

RUDY: Jungle. I'm a dancer, not Robin Hood. I can't dance anymore. I've walked my feet away. But you don't mind. You're working on deals. You worked on deals in Berlin, you work on deals in the jungle.

MAX: Forest.

RUDY: Jungle. I want to get out of here. I could have. I met a man in Frankfurt. You were in town "working on a deal." He gave me a ride. He was an old man, rich too. I could have stayed with him. I could have got him to get me out of the country. He really wanted me, I could tell. But no, I had to think about you. It wasn't fair to *you*. I'm dumb, you're right. You would have grabbed the chance. You're just hanging around, waiting for me to die. I think you've poisoned the cheese.

MAX: It's *your* cheese. Choke on it. Please, choke on it. I can't tell you how much I want you to choke on it. Christ! (*He gets up.*)

RUDY: Where are you going?

MAX: I have to get out of here. I can't breathe. I'm going for a walk.

RUDY: You can't. There's no place to walk. Just tents and jungle.

MAX: I have a fever.

RUDY: What?

MAX: I have a fever! I'm burning up.

RUDY: It's a trick. (*Gets up, goes to him, tries to feel his forehead.*)

MAX (*pulls away*): I know. I'm lying. Get away.

RUDY: Let me feel. (*Feels MAX's forehead.*) You have a fever.

MAX: It's the cheese. *You* poisoned *me.* What the hell. I'll die in the jungle. (*Sits down again.*)

RUDY: Forest. (*Sits.*)

(*Silence.*)

MAX: Remember cocaine?

RUDY: Yes.

MAX: I'd like cocaine.

RUDY: Yes.

MAX: What would you like?

RUDY: New glasses.

MAX: What?

RUDY: My eyes have changed. I need a new prescription. I'd like new glasses.

MAX: In Amsterdam.

RUDY: Sure.

MAX: In *Amsterdam.* Cocaine and new glasses. Trust me. Plants. You'll have plants. Wonderful Dutch plants. And Dutch dance classes. Your feet will come back. And you won't dig ditches. You'll have to give up your new shoulders, though. And you know what? We can buy a Dutch dog. Everyone should have a dog. I don't know why we didn't have a dog in Berlin. We'll have one in Amsterdam. (*Silence.*) Trust me.

(RUDY *looks at* MAX *and smiles. Silence.*)

RUDY: How's your fever?

MAX: Burning.

(RUDY *touches* MAX's *forehead; leaves his hand on the forehead.*)

MAX: Don't.

RUDY: I'm sorry, Max. (*Strokes his forehead.*)

MAX: Don't.

RUDY: I really love you.

MAX: DON'T. (*Pulls* RUDY's *hand away.*) If they see us . . . from the other tents . . . they're always looking . . . they could throw us out . . . for touching . . . we have to be careful . . . we have to be very careful. . . .

RUDY: Okay. (*Pause—starts to sing.*)

Streets of Berlin,
I must leave you soon,
Ah!

MAX: What are you doing?

RUDY: Singing. We're sitting around a campfire, that's when people sing. This must be the way the Hitler Youth does it. They sing old favorites, too. I'm sure they're not allowed to touch either.

MAX: Don't be so sure.

RUDY: Well, it's unfair if they can, and we can't. (*Sings.*)

Streets of Berlin,
I must leave you soon,
Ah!

(MAX *takes* RUDY's *hand, holds it, on the ground where it can't be seen, and smiles.*)

MAX: Shh!

(*They laugh. They both sing.*)

MAX and RUDY:
Will you forget me?
Was I ever really here?

VOICE (*from the darkness*): There! That's them!

(A *bright light shines on* MAX *and* RUDY.)

ANOTHER VOICE (*from darkness*): Maximilian Berber. Rudolf Hennings. Hands high in the air. You are under arrest.

BLACKOUT

Scene 5

A train whistle is heard.

Sound of a train running through the night. A train whistle again.

A circle of light comes up.

It is a prisoner transport train. We see one small corner. Five prisoners are in the light—two men in civilian dress, then RUDY *and* MAX, *then a man, in his twenties, wearing a striped uniform, with a pink triangle sewn onto it.*

A GUARD *walks through the circle of light. He carries a rifle.*

Silence.

RUDY: Where do you think they're taking us?

(*Silence.*
The other prisoners look away.
The GUARD *walks through the circle of light.*
Silence.)

RUDY (*to the* PRISONER *next to him*): Did you have a trial?

(*The* PRISONER *doesn't answer.*)

MAX: Rudy!

(*Silence.*
RUDY *and* MAX *look at each other. They are both terrified.* RUDY *starts to extend his hand, then withdraws it.*
A scream is heard—off, beyond the circle. RUDY *and* MAX *look at each other, then turn away.*
Silence.
The GUARD *walks through the circle of light.*
Silence.
Another scream.
Silence.
The GUARD *walks through the circle of light.*
An SS OFFICER *enters. The circle slightly expands. The* OFFICER *looks at the prisoners one by one. He stops at* RUDY.)

OFFICER: Glasses. (*Silence.*) Give me your glasses. (RUDY *hands the* OFFICER *his glasses. The* OFFICER *examines them.*) Horn-rimmed. Intelligentsia.

RUDY: What?

OFFICER (*smiles*): Stand up. (*Pulls* RUDY *up.*) Step on your glasses. (RUDY *stands— petrified.*) Step on them. (RUDY *steps on the glasses.*) Take him.

RUDY: Max!

(RUDY *looks at* MAX. *The* GUARD *pulls* RUDY *off—out of the circle. The* OFFICER *smiles.*)

OFFICER: Glasses.

(*He kicks the glasses away.*
The OFFICER *leaves the circle of light.*
The light narrows.
MAX *stares ahead.*
The GUARD *walks through the circle of light.*
Silence.
A scream is heard—off, beyond the circle. RUDY's *scream.* MAX *stiffens.*
Silence.
RUDY *screams again.*
MAX *moves, as if to get up.*
The man wearing the pink triangle [HORST] *moves toward* MAX. *He touches him.*)

HORST: Don't.

(*He removes his hand from* MAX *and looks straight ahead.*
The GUARD *walks through the circle of light.*)

HORST: Don't move. You can't help him.

(RUDY *screams.*
Silence.
The GUARD *walks through the circle of light.*)

MAX: This isn't happening.

HORST: It's happening.

MAX: Where are they taking us?

HORST: Dachau.

MAX: How do you know?

HORST: I've been through transport before. They took me to Cologne for a propaganda film. Pink triangle in good health. Now it's back to Dachau.

MAX: Pink triangle? What's that?

HORST: Queer. If you're queer, that's what you wear. If you're a Jew, a yellow star. Political—a red triangle. Criminal—green. Pink's the lowest.

(*He looks straight ahead.*
The GUARD *walks through the circle of light.*
RUDY *screams.*
MAX *starts.*)

MAX: This isn't happening. (*Silence.*) This can't be happening. (*Silence.*)

HORST: Listen to me. If you survive the train, you stand a chance. Here's where they break you. You can do nothing for your friend. Nothing. If you try to help him, they will kill you. If you try to care for his wounds, they will kill you. If you even *see*—see what they do to him, *hear*—hear what they do to him—they will kill you. If you want to stay alive, he cannot exist.

(RUDY *screams.*)

MAX: It isn't happening.

(RUDY *screams.*)

HORST: He hasn't a chance. He wore glasses.

(RUDY *screams.*)

HORST: If you want to stay alive, he cannot exist.

(RUDY *screams.*)

HORST: It *is* happening.

(HORST *moves away.*
The light focuses in on MAX's *face.* RUDY *screams.* MAX *stares ahead, mumbling to himself.*)

MAX: It isn't happening . . . it isn't happening. . . .

(*The light expands.*
The GUARD *drags* RUDY *in.* RUDY *is semiconscious. His body is bloody and muti-lated. The* GUARD *holds him up. The* OFFICER *enters the circle.* MAX *looks away. The* OFFICER *looks at* MAX. MAX *is still mumbling to himself.*)

OFFICER (*to* MAX): Who is this man?

MAX: I don't know. (*Stops mumbling, looks straight ahead.*)

OFFICER: Your friend?

(*Silence.*)

MAX: No.

(RUDY *moans.*)

OFFICER: Look at him. (MAX *stares straight ahead.*) Look! (MAX *looks at* RUDY. *The* OFFICER *hits* RUDY *on the chest.* RUDY *screams.*) Your friend?

MAX: No.

(*The* OFFICER *hits* RUDY *on the chest.* RUDY *screams.*)

OFFICER: Your friend?

MAX: No.

(*Silence.*)

OFFICER: Hit him. (MAX *stares at the* OFFICER.) Like this. (*Hits* RUDY *on the chest.* RUDY *screams.*) Hit him. (MAX *doesn't move.*) Your friend? (MAX *doesn't move.*) Your friend?

MAX: No. (*Closes his eyes. Hits* RUDY *on the chest.* RUDY *screams.*)

OFFICER: Open your eyes. (MAX *opens his eyes.*) Again. (MAX *hits* RUDY *on the chest.*) Again! (MAX *hits* RUDY *again and again and again. . . .*) Enough. (*Pushes* RUDY *down to the ground, at* MAX's *feet.*) Your friend?

MAX: No.

OFFICER (*smiles*): No.

(*The* OFFICER *leaves the circle of light. The* GUARD *follows him.*
The light focuses in—on MAX's *face.*
The train is heard running through the night.
The train whistles.
RUDY *is heard moaning and calling* MAX's *name.*
MAX *stares ahead.*
RUDY *calls* MAX's *name. The name merges with the whistle.*
MAX *takes a deep breath.*)

MAX: One. Two. Three. Four. Five. (*Takes another deep breath.*) Six. Seven. Eight. Nine. Ten.

(RUDY *calls* MAX's *name.*
MAX *stares ahead.*
The lights dim on MAX, *almost to blackout—then, suddenly, they expand and include the three other prisoners. A morning ray of sunlight.*
RUDY *lies at* MAX's *feet.*
The GUARD *walks through the circle of light.*
Silence.
The OFFICER *comes into the circle. He looks at* MAX.)

OFFICER: Stand up. (*Stares at* MAX.) We'll see. (*To* GUARD:) Take him. (*Kicks* RUDY's *body; it rolls over—looks down at it.*) Dead.

(*The* OFFICER *leaves. The* GUARD *pushes* MAX *with his rifle. They walk out of the light. The lights dim on the prisoners.*)

BLACKOUT

Scene 6

*Lights up, on one side of the stage. A large barrel is on the ground. A prisoner-foreman (*KAPO*) stands behind the barrel, with a huge ladle. He stirs it. The* KAPO *wears a green triangle on his prison uniform. Prisoners come up, one by one, with bowls in their hands, to be fed. They all wear prison uniforms.*

A PRISONER *with a yellow star enters. The* KAPO *stirs the soup.*
He fills the PRISONER'S *bowl. The* PRISONER *leaves. A* PRISONER *with a red triangle enters. The* KAPO *stirs the soup.*
He fills the PRISONER'S *bowl. The* PRISONER *leaves.* HORST *enters. The* KAPO *does not stir the soup.*

HORST: Only soup. You skimmed it from the top. There's nothing in it but water. No meat, no vegetables . . . nothing.

KAPO: Take what you get.

HORST (*reaches for the ladle*): Give me some meat.

KAPO (*pushes him back*): Fucking queer! Take what you get!

(*Blackout.*
Lights rise on other side of the stage.
A tight little corner at the end of the barracks.
HORST *crawls in and sits huddled with his bowl. He drinks the soup.*
MAX *enters, crawling in next to* HORST. *He carries a bowl. He wears the prison uniform. On it is a yellow star.*)

MAX: Hi. (HORST *looks at him; says nothing;* MAX *holds up his bowl.*) Here.

HORST: Leave me alone.

MAX: I got extra. Some vegetables. Here. (*Drops some vegetables from his bowl into* HORST'S *bowl.*)

HORST: Thanks. (*They eat in silence.* HORST *looks up. Stares at* MAX'S *uniform.*) Yellow star?

MAX: What?

HORST: Jew?

MAX: Oh. Yeah.

HORST: I wouldn't have figured it. (*Silence.*) I'm sorry about your friend.

MAX: Who?

HORST: Your friend.

MAX: Oh.

(*Silence.*)

HORST: It's not very sociable in these barracks. (*Laughs.*) Is it?

MAX (*points to* HORST's *pink triangle*): How'd you get that?

HORST: I signed a petition.

MAX: And?

HORST: That was it.

MAX: What kind of petition?

HORST: For Magnus Hirschfeld.

MAX: Oh yeah. I remember him. Berlin.

HORST: Berlin.

MAX: He wanted to . . .

HORST: Make queers legal.

MAX: Right. I remember.

HORST: Looked like he would, too, for a while. It was quite a movement. Then the
    Nazis came in. Well. I was a nurse. They said a queer couldn't be a nurse.
    Suppose I had to touch a patient's penis! God forbid. They said rather than be a
    nurse, I should be a prisoner. A more suitable occupation. So. So. That's how I
    got my pink triangle. How'd you get the yellow star?

MAX: I'm Jewish.

HORST: You're not Jewish, you're a queer.

(*Silence.*)

MAX: I didn't want one.

HORST: Didn't want what?

MAX: A pink triangle.

HORST: Didn't *want* one?

MAX: You told me it was the lowest. So I didn't want one.

HORST: So?

MAX: So I worked a deal.

HORST: A deal?

MAX: Sure. I'm good at that.

HORST: With the Gestapo?

MAX: Sure.

HORST: You're full of shit.

(*Silence.*)

MAX: I'm going to work a lot of deals. They can't keep us here forever. Sooner or later they'll release us. I'm only under protective custody, that's what they told me. I'm going to stay alive.

HORST: I don't doubt it.

MAX: Sure. I'm good at that.

HORST: Thanks for the vegetables. (*Starts to crawl away.*)

MAX: Where are you going?

HORST: To sleep. We get up at four in the morning. I'm on stone detail. I chop stones up. It's fun. Excuse me. . . .

MAX: Don't go.

HORST: I'm tired.

MAX: I don't have anyone to talk to.

HORST: Talk to your landsmen.

MAX: I'm not Jewish.

HORST: Then why are you wearing that?

MAX: You told me pink was the lowest.

HORST: It is, but only because the other prisoners hate us so much.

MAX: I got meat in my soup. You didn't.

HORST: Good for you.

MAX: Don't go.

HORST: Look, friendships last about twelve hours in this place. We had ours on the train. Why don't you go and bother someone else.

MAX: You didn't think I'd make it, did you? Off the train?

HORST: I wasn't sure.

MAX: I'm going to stay alive.

HORST: Yes.

MAX: Because of you. You told me how.

HORST: Yes. (*Pause.*) I did. (*Pause.*) I'm sorry.

MAX: About what?

HORST: I don't know. Your friend.

MAX: Oh. (*Silence.*) He wasn't my friend.

(*Silence.*)

HORST: You should be wearing a pink triangle.

MAX: I made a deal.

HORST: You don't make deals here.

MAX: I did. I made a deal.

HORST: Sure. (*Starts to leave again.*)

MAX: They said if I . . . I could . . . they said . . .

HORST: What?

MAX: Nothing. (HORST *crawls past* MAX.) I could prove . . . I don't know how . . .

HORST: What? (*Stops, sits next to* MAX.)

MAX: Nothing.

(*Silence.*)

HORST: Try. (*Silence.*) I think you better. (*Silence.*) Try to tell me.

MAX: Nothing.

(*Silence.*)

HORST: Okay. (*Moves away.*)

MAX: I made . . . They took me . . . into that room. . . .

HORST (*stops*): Where?

MAX: Into that room.

HORST: On the train?

MAX: On the train. And they said . . . prove that you're . . . and I did. . . .

HORST: Prove that you're what?

MAX: Not.

HORST: Not what?

MAX: Queer.

HORST: How?

MAX: Her.

HORST: Her?

MAX: They said, if you . . . and I did. . . .

HORST: Did what?

MAX: Her. Made . . .

HORST: Made what?

MAX: Love.

HORST: Who to?

MAX: Her.

HORST: Who was she?

MAX: Only . . . maybe . . . maybe only thirteen . . . she was maybe . . . she was dead.

HORST: Oh.

MAX: Just. Just dead, minutes . . . bullet . . . in her . . . they said . . . prove that you're . . . and I did . . . prove that you're . . . lots of them, watching . . . laughing . . . drinking . . . he's a bit bent, they said, he can't . . . but I did. . . .

HORST: How?

MAX: I don't . . . I don't . . . know. I wanted . . .

HORST: To stay alive.

MAX: And there was something . . .

HORST: Something . . .

MAX: Exciting . . .

HORST: Oh God.

MAX: I hit him, you know. I kissed her. Dead lips. I killed him. Sweet lips. Angel.

HORST: God.

MAX: She was . . . like an angel . . . to save my life . . . just beginning . . . her breasts . . . just beginning . . . they said he can't . . . he's a bit bent . . . but I did . . . and I proved . . . I proved that I wasn't . . . (*Silence.*) And they enjoyed it.

HORST: Yes.

MAX: And I said, I'm not queer. And they laughed. And I said, give me a yellow star. And they said, sure, make him a Jew. He's not bent. And they laughed. They were having fun. But . . . I . . . got . . . my . . . star. . . .

HORST (*gently*): Oh yes.

MAX: I got my star.

HORST: Yes. (*Reaches out, touches* MAX's *face.*)

MAX: *Don't do that!* (*Pulls away.*) You mustn't do that. For your own sake. You mustn't touch me. I'm a rotten person.

HORST: No. . . .(HORST *touches* MAX *again.* MAX *hits him.*)

MAX: Rotten.

HORST (*stares at* MAX): No. (*Crawls away, and leaves.*)

(MAX *is alone. He takes a deep breath. He closes his eyes. He takes another deep breath. He opens his eyes.*)

MAX: One. Two. Three. Four. Five. (*Takes another deep breath.*) Six. Seven. Eight. Nine. Ten.

BLACKOUT

ACT II

Scene 1

One month later.

A large fence extends across the stage. In front of the fence, on one side, lies a pile of rocks. On the other side—far over—a deep pit.

MAX is moving rocks. He carries one rock from the pile to the other side and starts a new pile. He returns and takes another rock. The rocks are carried one by one. He wears a prison uniform and hat.

A GUARD enters with HORST. HORST also wears a prison uniform and hat. The GUARD is very officious.

GUARD: Here. You will work here.

HORST: Yes sir.

GUARD: He'll explain.

HORST: Yes sir.

GUARD: I'm up there. (*Points off, and up.*)

HORST: Yes sir.

GUARD: I see everything.

HORST: Yes sir.

GUARD: No laying about.

HORST: No sir.

GUARD: I see everything.

HORST: Yes sir.

GUARD (*to* MAX): You.

MAX (*puts down his rock*): Yes sir.

GUARD: Tell him what to do.

MAX: Yes sir.

GUARD: No laying about.

MAX: No sir.

GUARD: I see everything.

MAX: Yes sir.

GUARD (*to* HORST): You.

HORST: Yes sir.

GUARD: Every two hours there is a rest period.

HORST: Yes sir.

GUARD: For three minutes.

HORST: Yes sir.

GUARD: Stand at attention.

HORST: Yes sir.

GUARD: Don't move.

HORST: No sir.

GUARD: Rest.

HORST: Yes sir.

GUARD: Three minutes.

HORST: Yes sir.

GUARD: A bell rings.

HORST: Yes sir.

GUARD (*to* MAX): You.

MAX: Yes sir.

GUARD: Explain it to him.

MAX: Yes sir.

GUARD: No laying about.

MAX: No sir.

GUARD (*to* HORST): You.

HORST: Yes sir.

GUARD: When the bell rings.

HORST: Yes sir.

GUARD: Don't move.

HORST: No sir.

GUARD: Three minutes.

HORST: Yes sir.

GUARD: He'll explain.

HORST: Yes sir.

GUARD (*to* MAX): You.

MAX: Yes sir.

GUARD: You're responsible.

MAX: Yes sir.

GUARD: I'm up there.

MAX: Yes sir.

GUARD (*to* HORST): You.

HORST: Yes sir.

GUARD: I see everything.

HORST: Yes sir.

(*The* GUARD *leaves.* HORST *watches carefully, until he is far gone.*)

HORST: We had a kid like that in school. Used to lead us in Simon Says.

MAX: Okay. I'll explain.

HORST: Okay.

MAX: Hey—we can't stand here. We have to move rocks.

HORST: Yes sir.

MAX: You see those . . .

HORST: Yes sir.

MAX: You take one rock at a time.

HORST: Yes sir.

MAX: And move it over there.

HORST: Yes sir.

MAX: And then when the entire pile is over there, you take one rock at a time, and move it back.

HORST (*looks at* MAX. *Silence*): And move it back?

MAX: Yes.

HORST: We move the rocks from there to there, and then back from there to there?

MAX: Yes sir.

HORST: *Why?*

MAX: Start moving. He's watching.

(MAX *continues to move rocks.* HORST *does the same. They do so in different rhythms, at times passing each other.*)

HORST: Okay.

MAX: It's supposed to drive us crazy.

HORST: These are heavy!

MAX: You get used to it.

HORST: What do you mean, drive us crazy?

MAX: Just that. It makes no sense. It serves no purpose. I figured it out. They do it to drive us crazy.

HORST: They probably know what they're doing.

MAX: But it doesn't work. I figured it out. It's the best job to have. That's why I got you here.

HORST: *What?* (*Puts down his rock.*)

MAX: Don't stop. Keep moving. (HORST *picks up the rock and moves it.*) A couple more things. That fence.

HORST: Yes.

MAX: It's electric. Don't touch it. You fry.

HORST: I won't touch it.

MAX: And over there—that pit.

HORST: Where?

MAX: There.

HORST: Oh yes. It smells awful.

MAX: Bodies.

HORST: In the pit.

MAX: Yes. Sometimes we have to throw them in.

HORST: Oh. Well, it will break the routine. What do you mean you got me here?

MAX: Don't walk so fast.

HORST: Why?

MAX: You'll tire yourself. Pace it. Nice and slow.

HORST: Okay. This better?

MAX: Yeah.

HORST: What do you mean you got me here?

MAX: I worked a deal.

HORST: I don't want to hear. (*Silence.*) Yes, I do. What the hell is this? You *got* me here? What right do you have—

MAX: Careful.

HORST: What?

MAX: You're dropping the rock.

HORST: No I'm not. I'm holding it, I'm holding it. What right do you have—

MAX: You were at the stones?

HORST: Yes.

MAX: Was it harder than this?

HORST: I guess.

MAX: People get sick?

HORST: Yes.

MAX: Die?

HORST: Yes.

MAX: Guards beat you if you didn't work hard enough?

HORST: Yes.

MAX (*proudly*): So?

HORST: So? So what?

MAX: So it was dangerous.

HORST: This isn't?

MAX: No. No one gets sick here. Look at all those guys moving rocks over there. (*Points off.*) They look healthier than most. No one dies. The guards don't beat you, because the work is totally non-essential. All it can do is drive you crazy.

HORST: That's all?

MAX: Yes.

HORST: Then maybe the other was better.

MAX: No, I figured it out! This is the best work in the camp, if you keep your head, if you have someone to talk to.

HORST: Ah! I see! Someone to talk to! Don't you think you should have asked me . . .

MAX: Asked you what?

HORST: If I wanted to move rocks, if I wanted to talk to you. . . .

MAX: Didn't have a chance. They moved you.

HORST: Thank heaven.

MAX: Your new barracks, is it all pink triangles?

HORST: Yes. They're arresting more queers each day; they keep pouring into the camp. Is yours all yellow stars now?

MAX: Yes.

HORST: Good. You might go all religious. There was an old man at the stones. A rabbi. Really kind. It's not easy being kind here. He was. I thought of you.

MAX: Why?

HORST: Maybe if you knew him you could be proud of your star. You should be proud of *something*.

(*Silence.*)

MAX: Don't keep looking at me. As long as they don't see us look at each other they can't tell we're talking.

(*Silence.*)

HORST: Where do the bodies come from?

MAX: What bodies?

HORST: The ones in the pit.

MAX: The fence. The hat trick.

HORST: Oh. What's that?

MAX: Sometimes a guard throws a prisoner's hat against the fence. He orders him to get the hat. If he doesn't get the hat, the guard will shoot him. If he does get the hat, he'll be electrocuted.

HORST: I'm really going to like it here. Thanks a lot.

MAX: I'm really doing you a favor.

HORST: Some favor! You just want someone to talk to so you won't go crazy. And I'm the only one who knows your secret.

MAX: What secret?

HORST: That you're a pink triangle.

MAX: No. I'm a Jew now.

HORST: You are not.

MAX: They think I am.

HORST: But it's a lie.

MAX: It's a smart lie.

HORST: You're crazy.

MAX: I thought you'd be grateful.

HORST: That's why you like this job. It can't drive you crazy. You're already there.

MAX: I spent money getting you here.

HORST: Money?

MAX: Yes. I bribed the guard.

HORST: Where'd you get money?

MAX: My uncle sent me some. First letter I ever got from him. He didn't sign it, but it had money in it.

HORST: And you bribed the guard?

MAX: Yes.

HORST: For me?

MAX: Yes.

HORST: Used *your* money?

MAX: Yes.

HORST: You'll probably never get money again.

MAX: Probably not.

HORST: You are crazy.

MAX: I thought you'd be grateful.

HORST: You should have asked me first.

MAX: How could I ask you? We're in separate barracks. Do you think it's easy to bribe a guard? It's complicated. It's dangerous. He could have turned on me. I took a risk. Do you think I didn't? I took a risk. I thought you'd be grateful.

HORST: I'm *not* grateful. I liked cutting stones. I liked that old rabbi. This is insane. Twelve hours of this a day? I'll be nuts in a week. Like you. Jesus!

MAX: I'm sorry I did it.

HORST: *You're* sorry?

MAX: You haven't figured out this camp, that's all. You don't know what's good for you. This is the best job to have.

HORST: Moving rocks back and forth for no reason. Next to a pit with dead bodies and a fence that can burn you to dust. The *best* job to have?

MAX: *Yes.* You don't understand.

HORST: I don't want to understand. I don't want to talk to you.

MAX: You have to talk to me.

HORST: Why?

MAX: I got you here to talk.

HORST: Well, tough. I don't want to talk. Move your rocks, and I'll move mine. Just don't speak to me.

(*They both move their rocks.*
A long silence.)

MAX: I thought you'd be grateful.

BLACKOUT

Scene 2

The same. Three days later.

MAX *and* HORST *are moving rocks. It is very hot. Their shirts lie on the ground.*

A long silence.

HORST: It's so hot.

MAX: Yes.

HORST: Burning hot.

MAX: Yes.

(*Silence.*)

MAX: You talked to me.

HORST: Weather talk, that's all.

MAX: After three days of silence.

HORST: *Weather* talk. Everyone talks about the weather. (*Silence.*) Anyhow.

(*Silence.*)

MAX: Did you say something?

HORST: No.

(*Silence.*)

HORST: Anyhow.

MAX: Anyhow?

HORST: Anyhow. Anyhow, I'm sorry. (*Stands still.*) Sometimes in this place, I behave like everyone else—bloody awful. Cut off, mean, not human, I'm sorry. You were doing me a favor. This is a good place to be. And the favor won't work unless we talk, will it?

MAX: *Move!*

HORST: What?

MAX: Talk while you're moving. Don't stop. They can see us.

HORST (*starts to move the rock again*): It's hard to talk when you're going one way and I'm going the other. God, it's hot.

(*Silence.*)

HORST: Somebody died last night.

MAX: Where?

HORST: In my barracks. A moslem.

MAX: An Arab?

HORST: No. A moslem. That's what they call a dead person who walks. You know, one of those guys who won't eat anymore, won't talk anymore, just wanders around waiting to really die.

MAX: I've seen them.

HORST: So one really died. In my barracks. (*Silence.*) God, it's hot.

(*Silence.*)

MAX: We'll miss the Olympics.

HORST: The *what?*

MAX: Olympics. Next month in Berlin.

HORST: I knew there was a reason I didn't want to be here.

MAX: Maybe they'll release us.

HORST: For the Olympics?

MAX: As a goodwill gesture. It is possible, don't you think?

HORST: I think it's hot.

(*Silence.*)

MAX: Heard a rumor.

HORST: What?

MAX: We get sardines tonight.

HORST: I don't like sardines.

MAX: It's only a rumor.

(*Silence.*)

HORST: God, it's hot.

(*Silence.*)

MAX: Sure is.

(*Silence.*)

HORST: Sure is what?

(*Silence.*)

MAX: Sure is hot.

(*Silence.*)

HORST: Suppose . . .

(*Silence.*)

MAX: What?

(*Silence.*)

HORST: Suppose after all of this . . . (*Silence.*) We have nothing to talk about.

(A *loud bell rings.*
MAX *and* HORST *put down their rocks and stand at attention, staring straight ahead.*)

HORST: Shit! I'd rather be moving rocks than standing in the sun. Some rest period.

MAX: It's part of their plan.

HORST: What plan?

MAX: To drive us crazy. (*Silence.*) Was I awful to bring you here?

HORST: No.

MAX: I was, wasn't I?

HORST: No.

MAX: I had no right. . . .

HORST: Stop it. Stop thinking how awful you are. Come on, don't get depressed. Smile. (*Silence.*) You're not smiling.

MAX: You can't see me.

HORST: I can feel you.

MAX: I wish we could look at each other.

HORST: I can feel you.

MAX: They hate it if anyone looks at each other.

HORST: I snuck a glance.

MAX: At what?

HORST: At you.

MAX: When?

HORST: Before.

MAX: Yeah?

HORST: A couple of glances. You look sexy.

MAX: Me?

HORST: Without your shirt.

MAX: No.

HORST: Come off it. You know you're sexy.

MAX: No.

HORST: Liar.

MAX (*smiles*): Of course I'm a liar.

HORST: Sure.

MAX: I've always been sexy.

HORST: Uh-huh.

MAX: Since I was a kid.

HORST: Yes?

MAX: Twelve. I got into a lot of trouble when I was . . .

HORST: Twelve?

MAX: Twelve.

HORST: Your body's beautiful.

MAX: I take care of it. I exercise.

HORST: What?

MAX: At night I do push-ups and knee bends in the barracks.

HORST: After twelve hours of moving rocks?

MAX: Sure. I figured it out. You got to keep your entire body strong. By yourself. That's how you survive here. You should do it.

HORST: I don't like to exercise.

MAX: You're a nurse.

HORST: For other people, not myself.

MAX: But you have to think of survival.

HORST: Sleep. I think of sleep. That's how I survive. Or I think of nothing. (*Silence.*) That scares me. When I think of nothing. (*Silence.*)

MAX: Your body's nice, too.

HORST: It's okay. Not great.

MAX: No, it's nice.

HORST: Not as nice as yours.

MAX: No. But it's okay.

HORST: How do you know?

MAX: I looked. I snuck a few glances, too.

HORST: When?

MAX: All day.

HORST: Yes?

MAX: Yes.

(*Silence.*)

HORST: Listen, do you . . .

MAX: What?

HORST: Miss . . .

MAX: What?

HORST: You know.

MAX: No, I don't.

HORST: Everyone misses it.

MAX: No.

HORST: Everyone in the camp.

MAX: No.

HORST: They go crazy missing it.

MAX: No.

HORST: Come on. No one can hear us. You're not a yellow star with me, remember? Do you miss it?

MAX: I don't want . . .

HORST: What?

MAX: To miss it.

HORST: But do you?

(*Silence.*)

MAX: Yes.

HORST: Me too. (*Silence.*) We don't have to.

MAX: What?

HORST: Miss it. (*Silence.*) We're here together. We don't have to miss it.

MAX: We can't look at each other. We can't touch.

HORST: We can feel . . .

MAX: Feel what?

HORST: Each other. Without looking. Without touching. I can feel you right now. Next to me. Can you feel me?

MAX: No.

HORST: Come on. Don't be afraid. No one can hear us. Can you feel me?

MAX: Maybe.

HORST: No one's going to know. It's all right. Feel me.

MAX: Maybe.

HORST: Feel me.

MAX: It's so hot.

HORST: I'm touching you.

MAX: No.

HORST: I'm touching you.

MAX: It's burning.

HORST: I'm kissing you.

MAX: Burning.

HORST: Kissing your eyes.

MAX: Hot.

HORST: Kissing your lips.

MAX: Yes.

HORST: Mouth.

MAX: Yes.

HORST: Inside your mouth.

MAX: Yes.

HORST: Neck.

MAX: Yes.

HORST: Down . . .

MAX: Yes.

HORST: Down . . .

MAX: Yes.

HORST: Chest. My tongue . . .

MAX: Burning.

HORST: Your chest.

MAX: Your mouth.

HORST: I'm kissing your chest.

MAX: Yes.

HORST: Hard.

MAX: Yes.

HORST: Down . . .

MAX: Yes.

HORST: Down . . .

MAX: Yes.

HORST: Your cock.

MAX: Yes.

HORST: Do you feel my mouth?

MAX: Yes. Do you feel my cock?

HORST: Yes. Do you feel . . .

MAX: Do you feel . . .

HORST: Mouth.

MAX: Cock.

HORST: Cock.

MAX: Mouth.

HORST: Do you feel my cock?

MAX: Do you feel my mouth?

HORST: Yes.

MAX: Do you know what I'm doing?

HORST: Yes. Can you taste what I'm doing?

MAX: Yes.

HORST: Taste.

MAX: Feel.

HORST: Together . . .

MAX: Together . . .

HORST: Do you feel me?

MAX: I feel you.

HORST: I see you.

MAX: I feel you.

HORST: I have you.

MAX: I want you.

HORST: Do you feel me inside you?

MAX: I want you inside me.

HORST: Feel . . .

MAX: I have you inside me.

HORST: Inside . . .

MAX: Strong.

HORST: Do you feel me thrust . . .

MAX: Hold.

HORST: Stroke . . .

MAX: Strong . . .

HORST: Oh . . .

MAX: Strong . . .

HORST: Oh . . .

MAX: Strong . . .

HORST: I'm going to . . .

MAX: Strong . . .

HORST: Do you feel . . . I'm going to . . .

MAX: I feel us both.

HORST: Do you . . .

MAX: Oh yes . . .

HORST: Do you . . .

MAX: Yes. Yes.

HORST: Feel . . .

MAX: Yes. Strong . . .

HORST: Feel . . .

MAX: More . . .

HORST: Ohh . . .

MAX: Now . . .

HORST: Yes . . .

MAX: Now! (*Gasps.*) Oh! Oh! My God! (*Has orgasm.*)

HORST: Ohh! . . . Now! Ohh! . . . (*Has orgasm.*)

(*Silence.*)

HORST: Oh.

(*Silence.*)

HORST: Did you?

MAX: Yes. *You?*

HORST: Yes.

(*Silence.*)

MAX: You're a good lay.

HORST: So are you.

(*Silence.*)

MAX: It's awfully sticky.

(*Silence.*)

HORST: Max?

MAX: What?

HORST: We did it. How about that—fucking guards, fucking camp, we did it.

MAX: Don't shout.

HORST: Okay. But I'm shouting inside. We did it. They're not going to kill us. We made love. We were real. We were human. We made love. They're not going to kill us.

(*Silence.*)

MAX: I never . . .

HORST: What?

MAX: Thought we'd . . .

HORST: What?

MAX: Do it in three minutes.

(*They laugh.*
The bell rings.)

BLACKOUT

Scene 3

The same. Two months later.

MAX *and* HORST *are at attention, wearing shirts.*

HORST: I'm going crazy. (*Silence.*) I'm going crazy. (*Silence.*) I'm going crazy. I dream about rocks. I close my eyes and I'm moving rocks. Rocks never end. Never end. (*Silence.*) I'm going crazy.

MAX: Think of something else.

HORST: I can't think. I've been up all night.

MAX: Up all night?

HORST: Come on, didn't you hear? Our barracks had to stand outside all night.

MAX: No.

HORST: Yes. We stood at attention all night long. Punishment.

MAX: What for?

HORST: Someone in our barracks killed himself.

MAX: A moslem?

HORST: Of course not. It doesn't mean anything if a moslem kills himself, but if a person who's still a person commits suicide, well . . . it's a kind of defiance, isn't it? They hate that—it's an act of free will.

MAX: I'm sorry.

HORST: Sure. Yellow star is sorry.

(*Silence.*)

MAX: Heard a rumor.

HORST: What?

MAX: Sardines tonight.

HORST: I hate sardines! I hate all food. Scraps. Sardine scraps. That's all we get anyhow. Not worth eating. Didn't know you could have sardine scraps. (*Silence.*) I'm going crazy.

MAX: Okay. Okay. You're going crazy. I'm sorry. It's my fault.

HORST: What do you mean *your* fault?

MAX: For bringing you here. Because you make me feel so guilty. And you should. This job *is* the worst. I figured it wrong. I'm sorry.

HORST: I'm glad to be here.

MAX: Oh sure.

HORST: I am.

MAX: How can you be?

HORST: That's my secret.

(*Pause. Bell rings.* MAX *starts to move rocks.* HORST *remains still.*)

HORST: Maybe if I closed my eyes . . .

MAX: Heard a rumor.

HORST: What? (*Starts to move rocks.*)

MAX: We may get potatoes.

HORST: When?

MAX: Tomorrow.

HORST: I don't believe it.

MAX: They said so in my barracks.

HORST: Who's they?

MAX: Some guys.

HORST: Are they cute?

MAX: Cut it out.

HORST: You should be with us, where you belong.

MAX: No. But you shouldn't be *here.*

HORST: I want to be here.

MAX: Why would you want to be here—are you crazy?

HORST: Of course I'm crazy. I'm trying to tell you I'm crazy. And I want to be here.

MAX: Why?

HORST: Because. Because I love rocks. (*Pause.*) Because I love you. (*Silence.*) I do. I love you. When I'm not dreaming about rocks. I'm dreaming about you. For the past six weeks, I've dreamed about you. It helps me get up. It helps me make sure my bed is perfectly made so I'm not punished. It helps me eat the stinking food. It helps me put up with the constant fights in the barracks. Knowing I'll see you. At least out of the corner of my eyes. In passing. It's a reason to live. So I'm glad I'm here.

(MAX *is at one pile of rocks, moving them into symmetrical piles.*)

HORST: What are you doing?

MAX: Arranging these neatly. We've gotten sloppy. They can beat you for it. (*Silence.*) Don't love me.

HORST: It makes me happy. It dosen't harm anyone. It's my secret.

MAX: Don't love me.

HORST: It's my secret. And I have a signal. No one knows it. When I rub my left eyebrow at you, like this . . . (*rubs his left eyebrow*) . . . it means I love you. Bet you didn't know that. I can even do it in front of the guards. No one knows. It's my secret. (*Starts to cough.*) It's cold. It was better hot. I don't like it cold.

MAX: Don't love me.

HORST: I can't help it.

MAX: I don't want anybody to love me.

HORST: That's tough.

MAX: I can't love anybody back.

HORST: Who's asking you to?

MAX: Queers aren't meant to love. I know. I thought I loved someone once. He worked in my father's factory. My father paid him to go away. He went. Queers aren't meant to love. They don't want us to. You know who loved me? That boy. That dancer. I don't remember his name. But I killed him. See—queers aren't meant to love. I'll kill you too. Hate me. That's better. Hate me. Don't love me.

(MAX *finishes arranging the rocks. He returns to moving the rocks.*
Silence.
HORST *starts to cough again.*)

MAX: Why are you coughing?

HORST: Because I like to.

MAX: Are you catching cold?

HORST: Probably. Up all night. In the wind.

MAX: Winter's coming.

HORST: I know. (*Silence.*) I just want to close my eyes. . . .

MAX: Heard a rumor.

HORST: I don't care.

MAX: Don't you want to hear it?

HORST: Stuff your rumors. (*Coughs again. Slips. Drops the rock and falls to the ground.*)

MAX: Horst! (*Puts down his rock.*)

HORST: Shit. (MAX *starts toward him.*) *Don't move!* He's watching. The guard. Don't help me. If you help me, they'll kill you. Get back to your rock. Do you hear me, get back! (MAX *returns, picks up his rock, but stands looking at* HORST; HORST *is coughing—looks up at* MAX.) Move! (MAX *moves the rock.*) Right. I'm okay. I'll get up. I'll get up. Don't ever help me. (*Pulls himself up.*) I'm up. It's okay. (*Picks up his rock.*) These bloody things get heavier and heavier. (*Starts to move the rock.*) The guard was watching. He'd kill you if you helped me. Never notice. Never watch. Remember? I love you. But I won't help you if *you* fall. Don't you dare help me. You don't even love me, so why are you going to help? We save *ourselves.* Do you understand? Do you?

MAX: Yes. I understand.

HORST: Promise me. Come on. Promise me. We save ourselves.

MAX: Okay.

HORST: Promise me!

MAX: *YES!*

HORST: You're a fool. I don't love you anymore. It was just a passing fancy. I love myself. Poor you, you don't love anybody. (*Silence.*) It's getting cold. Winter's coming.

(*They walk, moving the rocks, in silence.*)

BLACKOUT

Scene 4

The same. Two months later.

MAX *and* HORST *are moving rocks. They wear jackets.* HORST *is slower than ever, as if dazed. He is holding the rocks with difficulty.*

HORST *has a coughing spell.*

MAX: You have a barracks leader. (HORST's *coughing continues.*) He can get you medicine. (*Coughing continues.*) He can try to get you medicine. (*Coughing continues.*) You have to ask him. (*Coughing continues.*) You have to get help. (*Coughing continues.*) You have to stop coughing—damn it. (*The coughing spell slowly subsides.*)

HORST: It doesn't matter.

MAX: If you're nice to the kapo . . .

HORST: It doesn't matter.

MAX: Some sort of medicine.

HORST: What for? The cough? How about the hands?

MAX: I told you what to do. Exercise.

HORST: They're frostbitten.

MAX: So exercise.

HORST: It doesn't matter.

MAX: Every night, I move my fingers up and down, one at a time, for a half hour. I don't do push-ups anymore. Just fingers.

HORST: It doesn't matter.

MAX: You're losing weight.

HORST: I don't like sardines. (*Starts to cough again. It goes on for a minute, then subsides.*)

MAX: It's getting worse.

HORST: It's getting colder.

MAX: You need medicine.

HORST: Stop nagging me.

MAX: See your kapo.

HORST: He doesn't care.

MAX: Ask him.

HORST: He wants money.

MAX: Are you sure?

HORST: It doesn't matter.

MAX: I thought you cared about yourself.

HORST: You don't know anything.

MAX: I thought you loved yourself.

HORST: It's too cold.

MAX: You know what? (*Silence.*) You know what? You're turning into a moslem. I'm scared.

HORST: Who isn't.

MAX: For you.

HORST: Be scared for yourself.

MAX: Why don't you listen to me?

HORST: Moslems don't listen.

MAX: You're not a moslem.

HORST: You said I was.

MAX: I didn't mean it. You're not a moslem.

HORST: You're not a Jew.

MAX: Can't you ever forget that?

HORST: If I forget that . . . then . . . I am a moslem.

(*The bell rings.*
They both drop their rocks and stand at attention, side by side, looking straight ahead.)

HORST: Look, I'm just cold. My fingers are numb. I can't stop coughing. I hate food. That's all. Nothing special. Don't get upset.

MAX: I want you to care.

HORST: I would. If I was warm.

MAX: I'll warm you.

HORST: You can't.

MAX: I know how.

HORST: No. You don't.

MAX: I do. I'm terrific at it. You said so.

HORST: When?

MAX: I'm next to you.

HORST: Don't start.

MAX: I'll make love to you.

HORST: Not now.

MAX: Yes. Now.

HORST: I have a headache. I can't.

MAX: Don't joke. I'll make love to you.

HORST: No.

MAX: I'll make you warm.

(*Pause.*)

HORST: You can't.

MAX: You'll feel the warm . . .

HORST: I can't.

MAX: You'll *feel* it.

(*Pause.*)

HORST: In my fingers?

MAX: All over.

HORST: I can't.

MAX: I'm kissing your fingers.

HORST: They're numb.

MAX: My mouth is hot.

HORST: They're cold.

MAX: My mouth is on fire.

HORST: My fingers . . .

MAX: Are getting warm.

HORST: Are they?

MAX: They're getting warm.

HORST: I can't tell.

MAX: They're getting warm.

HORST: A little.

MAX: They're getting warm.

HORST: Yes.

MAX: My mouth is on fire. Your fingers are on fire. Your body's on fire.

HORST: Yes.

MAX: My mouth is all over you.

HORST: Yes.

MAX: My mouth is on your chest. . . .

HORST: Yes.

MAX: Kissing your chest.

HORST: Yes.

MAX: Making it warm.

HORST: Yes.

MAX: Biting your nipple.

HORST: Yes.

MAX: Biting . . . into it. . .

HORST: Yes.

MAX: Harder . . . harder . . . harder . . .

HORST: Hold it! That hurts!

MAX: Harder . . .

HORST: No, hold it. I'm serious. You're hurting me.

(A *pause.* MAX *catches his breath.*)

MAX: You pulled away.

HORST: Damn right.

MAX: It was exciting.

HORST: For *you* maybe. I don't try to hurt you.

MAX: I like being hurt. It's exciting.

HORST: It's not. Not when you're rough.

MAX: I'm not being rough.

HORST: Yes you are. Sometimes you are.

MAX: Okay. So what? It's exciting.

HORST: Why'd you have to spoil it? You were making me warm. Why can't you be gentle?

MAX: I am.

HORST: You're not. You try to hurt me. You make me warm, and then you hurt me. I hurt enough. I don't want to feel *more* pain. Why can't you be gentle?

MAX: I am.

HORST: No you're not. You're like them. You're like the Gestapo. You're like the guards. We stopped being gentle. I watched it, when we were on the outside. People made pain and called it love. I don't want to be like that. You don't make love to hurt.

MAX: I wanted to make you warm. That's all I wanted. I can't do anything right. I don't understand you. I used to do things right.

HORST: You still can.

MAX: People liked it when I got rough. Most. Not everybody. He didn't.

HORST: Who?

MAX: The dancer. But everyone else did. Just a little rough.

HORST: Did you like it?

MAX: I don't remember. I could never remember. I was always drunk. There was always coke. Nothing seemed to matter that much.

HORST: Some things do matter.

MAX: Not to you.

HORST: They do.

MAX: I don't understand you. All day long you've been saying nothing matters . . . your cough, your fingers . . .

HORST: They matter.

MAX: I don't understand anything anymore.

HORST: They matter. I'm not a moslem. You're not a Jew. My fingers are cold.

MAX: I want you to be happy.

HORST: Is that true?

MAX: I think so. I don't know. (*Pause.*) Yes.

HORST: Then be gentle with me.

MAX: I don't know how.

HORST: Just hold me.

MAX: I'm afraid to hold you.

HORST: Don't be.

MAX: I'm afraid.

HORST: Don't be.

MAX: I'm going to drown.

HORST: Hold me. Please. Hold me.

MAX: Okay. I'm holding you.

HORST: Are you?

MAX: Yes. You're in my arms.

HORST: Am I?

MAX: You're here in my arms. I promise. I'm holding you. You're here. . . .

HORST: Touch me.

MAX: No.

HORST: Gently. . . .

MAX: Here.

HORST: Are you?

MAX: Yes. Touching. Softly. . . . I'm touching you softly . . . gently. . . . You're safe. . . . I'll keep you safe . . . and warm. . . . You're with me now. . . . You'll never be cold again. . . . I'm holding you now . . . safe . . . and warm. . . . As long as you're here, as long as you're with me, as long as I'm holding you, you're safe. . . .

BLACKOUT

Scene 5

The same. Three days later.

MAX *is moving rocks.* HORST *is putting the rock pile into neat order.*

HORST: The air is fresh today. Clean.

(MAX *hands* HORST *a needle and thread as he passes the rock pile.* HORST *starts to cough—continues coughing—then stops.*)

MAX: It sounds better.

HORST: It does.

MAX: Loosening up.

HORST: It is.

MAX: The medicine is helping.

HORST: Yes. (*Silence.*) Thank you. (*Silence.*) Why don't you tell me.

MAX: Tell you what?

HORST: How you got it.

MAX: Told you. Spoke to my barracks leader. He took me to an officer.

HORST: Which one?

MAX: Some captain. The new one.

HORST: He's rotten.

MAX: You know him?

HORST: I've heard about him. You gave him money?

MAX: Yes.

HORST: I don't believe you.

MAX: Why?

HORST: You don't have any money.

MAX: Why don't you ever believe me?

HORST: Because I can tell when you're lying. You think you're so terrific at it. You're not. Your voice changes.

MAX: It *what?*

HORST: Changes. Sounds different.

MAX: Bullshit.

(*Silence.*)

MAX: Hey . . . Guess who I saw?

HORST: Where?

MAX: In my barracks.

HORST: Marlene Dietrich.

MAX: No. My landlord. From Berlin. Rosen.

HORST: Oh.

MAX: Nice man.

HORST: I thought you hated him.

MAX: Sure, I used to think he was what I was supposed to think he was.

HORST: What was that?

MAX: A lousy Jew.

HORST: He probably thought you were a lousy queer.

MAX: Probably.

HORST: Now he thinks you're not a queer. He must be very confused. It's a shame.

MAX: It's not a shame. Don't start in. (HORST *has a coughing spell.*) You *are* taking the medicine?

HORST (*the coughing subsides*): Of course I am. (*Silence.*) Of course I am. Max. I'm glad you got it.

MAX: So am I.

(*Silence.*)

HORST: Wish I knew how, though.

MAX: I told you.

HORST: You're a liar.

(*Silence.*)

MAX: I never met anyone like you. Can't make you believe anything.

HORST: How'd you get it?

MAX: Won't just be grateful.

HORST: Am I ever?

MAX: Suppose you don't like the answer.

HORST: I'll chance it.

MAX: Then when I tell you, you'll nag me about *that*.

HORST: You chance it.

MAX: I went down on him.

HORST: What?

MAX: I told you you wouldn't like it.

HORST: That SS captain?

MAX: Uh-huh.

HORST: He's the worst bastard in the—

MAX: I know.

HORST: You went down on him?

MAX: I had to. I didn't have any money.

HORST: You touched him?

MAX: No. I just went down on him. That's what he wanted. And I needed the medicine.

HORST: I'd rather cough.

MAX: No you wouldn't.

HORST: Is he queer?

MAX: Who knows? Just horny maybe. Sure, he could be queer. You don't like to think about that, do you? You don't want *them* to be queer.

(*Silence.*)

HORST: I guess not. Well . . . what the hell. There *are* queer Nazis. And queer saints. And queer mediocrities. Just people. I really believe that. That's why I signed Hirschfeld's petition. That's why I ended up here. That's why I'm wearing this triangle. That's why you should be wearing it.

MAX: Do you think that SS bastard would let a queer go down on him? Of course not. He'd kill me if he knew I was queer. My yellow star got your medicine.

HORST: Who needs it?

MAX: Then give it back. Throw it away. Throw it away, why don't you? And die. I'm tired of being told I should have a pink triangle.

HORST: He remember you?

MAX: Who?

HORST: Rosen?

MAX: Yes. He said I owed him rent.

HORST: What's Berlin like? Did he say?

MAX: Worse.

HORST: I miss it.

MAX: Yes. (*Pause.*) Greta's Club?

HORST: No.

MAX: Good. You had taste. The White Mouse?

HORST: Sometimes.

MAX: Surprised you never saw me.

HORST: What were you wearing?

MAX: Things that came off. I was conspicuous.

HORST: Why?

MAX: Because I was always making a fool of myself. Did you sunbathe?

HORST: I loved to sunbathe.

MAX: By the river.

HORST: Sure.

MAX: And you *never* saw me?

HORST: Well, actually, I did. I saw you by the river. You were making a fool of yourself. And I said, someday I'll be at Dachau with that man, moving rocks.

MAX: I didn't like Berlin. Always scared. But I like it now. I miss it.

HORST (*finishes straightening the rocks and resumes moving the rocks*): We'll go back someday.

MAX: When we get out of here?

HORST: Yes.

MAX: We will, won't we?

HORST: We have to. Don't we?

MAX: Yes. Horst?

HORST: What?

MAX: We can go back together.

(*An* SS CAPTAIN *enters. The* GUARD *is with him.* MAX *and* HORST *look up for a second, then continue with their task.*

The CAPTAIN *stares at* MAX *for a long time, then* HORST, *then* MAX *again.*)

CAPTAIN (*to* MAX): You. Jew.

MAX (*stands still*): Yes sir?

CAPTAIN: Feeling better?

MAX: Sir?

CAPTAIN: Your cold?

MAX: Yes sir.

CAPTAIN: Remarkable.

MAX: Yes sir.

CAPTAIN: You seem so strong.

MAX: Yes sir.

CAPTAIN: Not sick at all.

MAX: No sir.

CAPTAIN: No?

MAX: Not now, sir.

CAPTAIN: Carry on.

(MAX *resumes moving rocks. The* CAPTAIN *watches* MAX *and* HORST. *He paces up and down.* MAX *and* HORST *move the rocks. The* CAPTAIN *paces.* HORST *coughs. He catches himself and tries to stifle it.*)

CAPTAIN: Ah. (HORST *stops the cough.*) You. Pervert.

HORST (*stiffens, stands still*): Yes sir?

CAPTAIN: Are you ill?

HORST: No sir.

CAPTAIN: You have a cough.

HORST: No sir.

CAPTAIN: I heard you cough.

HORST: Yes sir.

CAPTAIN: Something caught in your throat?

HORST: Yes sir.

CAPTAIN: From breakfast?

HORST: Yes sir.

CAPTAIN: Ah. Carry on.

(HORST *resumes his work.* MAX *and* HORST *move the rocks. The* CAPTAIN *stands watching them. He takes out a cigarette. The* GUARD *lights it. The* CAPTAIN *smokes the cigarette and watches* MAX *and* HORST.
MAX *and* HORST *continue moving rocks.* HORST *coughs again, attempting to strangle it, but the cough comes through.*)

CAPTAIN: You. Pervert.

HORST (*stands still*): Yes sir.

CAPTAIN: You coughed.

HORST: Yes sir.

CAPTAIN: You're not well.

HORST: I am, sir.

CAPTAIN: I see. (*To* MAX:) You. Jew.

MAX (*stands still*): Yes sir.

CAPTAIN: Watch.

MAX: Watch, sir?

CAPTAIN: Yes. Watch. (*To* HORST:) You.

HORST: Yes sir.

CAPTAIN: Put down that rock.

HORST: Yes sir. (*Puts down the rock.*)

CAPTAIN: Good. Now take off your hat.

(*A long pause.*)

HORST: My hat, sir?

CAPTAIN: Yes. Your hat.

HORST: My hat, sir?

CAPTAIN: Your hat.

HORST: Yes sir.

(HORST *removes his hat.* MAX's *hand moves.* HORST *shoots him a warning stare.*)

CAPTAIN (*to* MAX): You.

MAX: Yes sir.

CAPTAIN: Relax.

MAX: Yes sir.

CAPTAIN: And watch.

MAX: Yes sir.

CAPTAIN (*to* HORST): You.

HORST: Yes sir.

CAPTAIN: Throw your hat away. (HORST *flings his hat on the ground.*) Not there.

HORST: Not there, sir?

CAPTAIN: No. Pick it up.

HORST: Yes sir. (*Picks up his hat.*)

CAPTAIN: Throw it on the fence.

HORST: The fence, sir?

CAPTAIN: The fence. (HORST *starts to cough.*) That's all right. We'll wait. (*The cough subsides.*) Are you better?

HORST: Yes sir.

CAPTAIN: Nasty cough.

HORST: Yes sir.

CAPTAIN: On the fence. Now.

HORST: On the fence. Yes sir.

(HORST *glances at* MAX, *another warning stare, then throws his hat on the fence. The fence sparks.*)

CAPTAIN (*to* MAX): You.

MAX: Yes sir.

CAPTAIN: Are you watching?

MAX: Yes sir.

CAPTAIN: Good. (*To* HORST:) You.

HORST: Yes sir.

CAPTAIN: Get your hat.

(*The* CAPTAIN *motions to the* GUARD. *The* GUARD *points his rifle at* HORST.)

HORST: Now, sir?

CAPTAIN: Now.

HORST: Are you sure, sir?

CAPTAIN: Quite.

HORST: Could I do without my hat, sir?

CAPTAIN: No.

HORST (*is silent for a moment. Feels* MAX *watching and gives him another quick glance, his eyes saying, don't move. Turns to the* CAPTAIN): Yes sir.

(HORST *looks at* MAX. *He takes his hand and rubs his left eyebrow.*
He turns and stares at the CAPTAIN. *The* CAPTAIN *waits. The* GUARD *is pointing his rifle.*
HORST *turns toward the fence. He starts to walk very slowly to his hat. He almost reaches the fence. Suddenly—He turns and rushes at the* CAPTAIN. *He screams in fury.*
The GUARD *shoots* HORST. HORST *continues to lunge at the* CAPTAIN. *His hand is out. He scratches the* CAPTAIN's *face.*
The GUARD *shoots* HORST *in the back. He falls, dead.*
Silence.
The CAPTAIN *holds his face.*)

CAPTAIN: He scratched me. (*To* MAX:) You. Jew. (MAX *is silent.*) You!

MAX: Yes sir.

CAPTAIN: I hope the medicine helped. (*Turns to leave, turns back.*) Get rid of the body.

(*Silence.*)

MAX: Yes sir.

(*The* CAPTAIN *leaves. The* GUARD *points the rifle at* MAX, *lowers it, then walks off, after the* CAPTAIN.
MAX *stares at* HORST.
Silence.
MAX *opens his mouth to cry out. He can't.*
Silence.
MAX *walks to* HORST's *body. He tries to lift it. It is heavy. He manages to pull the body partly up,* HORST's *head resting against* MAX's *chest. He looks away. He takes* HORST, *feet dragging on the ground, toward the pit. The bell rings.*)

MAX: No! (*He looks up—off—at the* GUARD, *then back at* HORST. *He stands at attention.* HORST *starts to fall.* MAX *pulls him up. He stands still, staring in front of him, holding on to* HORST.) It's okay. I won't drop you. I'll hold you. If I stand at attention, I can hold you. They'll let me hold you. I won't let you down. (*Silence.*) I never held you before. (*Silence.*) You don't have to worry about the rocks. I'll do yours, too. I'll move twice as many each day. I'll do yours, too. You don't have to worry about them. (*Silence.*) You know what? (*Silence.*) Horst? (*Silence.*) You know what? (*Silence.*) I think . . . (*Silence.*) I think I love you. (*Silence.*) Shh! Don't tell anyone. I think I loved . . . I can't remember his name. A dancer. I think I loved him, too. Don't be jealous. I think I loved . . . some boy a long time ago. In my father's factory. Hans. That was his name. But the dancer. I don't remember. (*Silence.*) I love you. (*Silence.*) What's wrong with that? (*Silence.*) What's wrong with that?

(*He starts to cry.*
The bell rings.
He drags HORST's *body to the pit. He throws it in the pit.*
He turns and looks at the rocks. He takes a deep breath.
He walks over to the rocks and picks one up. He moves it across to the other side. He takes another deep breath. He stands still.)

MAX: One. Two. Three. Four. Five. (*Takes another deep breath.*) Six. Seven. Eight. Nine. Ten.

(*He picks up a rock. He moves it across to the other side.*
He moves another rock.
He moves another rock.
He moves another rock.
He pauses. He takes a deep breath.
He moves another rock.
He moves another rock.
He stops. He tries to take another deep breath.
He can't. His hand is trembling. He steadies his hand. He picks up another rock and starts to move it.
He stops. He drops the rock. He moves toward the pit.
He jumps into the pit.
He disappears.
A long pause.
MAX *climbs out of the pit.* MAX *holds* HORST's *jacket with the pink triangle on it. Puts the jacket on.*
MAX *turns and looks at the fence.*
MAX *walks into the fence.*
The fence lights up. It grows brighter and brighter, until the light consumes the stage. And blinds the audience.)

EXECUTION OF JUSTICE

by
Emily Mann

FOR
my father, Arthur Mann

Execution of Justice was commissioned by San Francisco's Eureka Theatre in 1982, and developed over the next eighteen months in collaboration with dramaturg Oskar Eustis, artistic director Anthony Taccone, and the company's actors. A co-winner of Actors Theatre of Louisville's 1983 Great American Play Contest, the play received its premiere there the following March, under the direction of Eustis and Taccone.

Acknowledgments

My special thanks to Oskar Eustis, who understood the trial.

Many thanks to the Eureka Theatre and artistic director Tony Taccone, who risked the verdict.

The author also thanks the John Simon Guggenheim Memorial Foundation for its fellowship to research and write the play.

Thanks to the following people for their help and information: Scott Smith and the Harvey Milk Archives, Harry Britt, Rob Epstein and Richard Schmeichen, Supervisor Carol Ruth Silver, Russ Cone, Gene Marine, Corey Busch, Gwenn Craig, Randy Shilts, Mike Weiss, Daniel Nicoletta, Jim Denman, Mel Wax, Marilyn Waller, Warren Hinckle, Bill Bathurst, Edward Mycue, Joseph Freitas, Jim Nicola and New Playwrights' Theatre, Stuart Ross, Bonnie Ayrault, Bill Block, Stephen Wadsworth.

Special thanks to Jon Jory, Julie Crutcher and Actors Theatre of Louisville; Stan Wojewodski and Center Stage; Burke Walker, Tom Cramer, and the Empty Space Theater in Seattle; Doug Wager and Arena Stage; Sharon Ott and Berkeley Repertory Theatre; Liviu Ciulei, Mark Bly, Michael Lupu and The Guthrie Theater; Tom Lynch; Gail Merrifield Papp.

CHARACTERS

DAN WHITE
MARY ANN WHITE, his wife
COP
SISTER BOOM BOOM

CHORUS OF UNCALLED WITNESSES

JIM DENMAN, ex-undersheriff, WHITE's jailer immediately following the shooting
YOUNG MOTHER, late 30s, mother of three
MOSCONE'S FRIEND, old political crony, 50s
MILK'S FRIEND, 30s
GWENN CRAIG, black lesbian leader, 40s
HARRY BRITT, City Supervisor, 40s, MILK's successor
JOSEPH FREITAS, JR., ex-D.A., speaking in 1983

TRIAL CHARACTERS

COURT, the judge
CLERK
DOUGLAS SCHMIDT, defense lawyer
THOMAS F. NORMAN, prosecuting attorney
JOANNA LU, TV reporter
3 PROSPECTIVE JURORS
FOREMAN

WITNESSES FOR THE PEOPLE

STEPHENS, the coroner
RUDY NOTHENBERG, Deputy Mayor
BARBARA TAYLOR, KCBS reporter
OFFICER BYRNE, policewoman in charge of records
WILLIAM MELIA, JR., civil engineer
CYR COPERTINI, appointment secretary to the Mayor
CARL HENRY CARLSON, aide to MILK
RICHARD PABICH, assistant to MILK
FRANK FALZON, Chief Inspector of Homicide
EDWARD ERDELATZ, Inspector

WITNESSES FOR THE DEFENSE

FIRE CHIEF SHERRATT
POLICE OFFICER SULLIVAN
CITY SUPERVISOR LEE DOLSON
FIREMAN FREDIANI
PSYCHIATRISTS JONES, BLINDER, SOLOMON, LUNDE, DELMAN
DENISE APCAR, aide to WHITE

IN REBUTTAL FOR THE PEOPLE

CAROL RUTH SILVER, City Supervisor
DR. LEVY, psychiatrist

CHARACTERS ON TAPE

DIANNE FEINSTEIN, City Supervisor, later Mayor
GEORGE MOSCONE, Mayor
HARVEY MILK, City Supervisor

People of San Francisco, jurors, cameramen, mourners, rioters, riot police

The play can be performed by as few as 18 actors.

TIME

1978 to the present.

PLACE

San Francisco.

ACT ONE: Murder

A bare stage. White screens overhead. Screen: Images of San Francisco, punctuated with images of MILK *and* MOSCONE. *Hot, fast music. People enter. A maelstrom of urban activity.*

Screen: Without warning, documentary footage of DIANNE FEINSTEIN (*almost unable to stand*): As president of the Board of Supervisors, it is my duty to make this announcement: Mayor George Moscone . . . and Supervisor Harvey Milk . . . have been shot . . . and killed. (*Gasps and cries. A long moment.*) The suspect is Supervisor Dan White.

(The crowd in shock. They cannot move. Then they run. In the chaos, MARY ANN WHITE *enters, trying to hail a cab; exits. Screen: A crucifix fades up. Shaft of light. A church window.* DAN WHITE *prays. Audio: Hyperreal sounds of mumbled Hail Marys; of high heels echoing, moving fast; of breathing hard, running.* MARY ANN WHITE *enters, breathless.* WHITE *looks up. She approaches him.)*

WHITE: I shot the Mayor and Harvey.

*(*MARY ANN WHITE *crumples. Lights change.)*

CLERK: This is the matter of the People versus Daniel James White.

(Amplified gavel. Lights change.)

COP (*quiet*): Yeah, I'm wearing a "Free Dan White" T-shirt.
You haven't seen what I've seen—
my nose shoved into what I think stinks.
Against everything I believe in.
There was a time in San Francisco when you knew a guy
by his parish.

*(*SISTER BOOM BOOM *enters. Nun drag; white face, heavily made-up; spike heels.)*

Sometimes I sit in church and I think of those disgusting drag queens dressed
up as nuns and I'm a cop,
and I'm thinkin',
there's gotta be a law, you know,
because they're makin' me think things I don't want to think
and I gotta keep my mouth shut.

*(*BOOM BOOM *puts out cigarette.)*

Take a guy out of his sling—fist-fucked to death—
they say it's mutual consent, it ain't murder,
and I pull this disgusting mess down, take him to the morgue,
I mean, my wife asks me, "Hey, how was your day?"
I can't even tell her.
I wash my hands before I can even look at my kids.

(*The* COP *and* BOOM BOOM *are very aware of each other but never make eye contact.*)

BOOM BOOM: God bless you one. God bless you all.

COP: See, Danny knew—he believes in the rights of minorities. Ya know, he just felt—we are a minority, too.

BOOM BOOM: I would like to open with a reading from the Book of Dan. (*Opens book.*)

COP: We been workin' this job three generations—my father was a cop—
and then they put—Moscone, Jesus, Moscone put this
N-Negro-loving, faggot-loving Chief telling us what to do—
he doesn't even come from the neighborhood,
he doesn't even come from this city!
He's tellin' us what to do in a force that knows what to do.
He makes us paint our cop cars faggot blue—
he called it "lavender gloves" for the queers,
handle 'em, treat 'em with "lavender gloves," he called it.
He's cuttin' off our balls.
The city is stinkin' with degenerates—
I mean, I'm worried about my kids, I worry about my wife,
I worry about me and how I'm feelin' mad all the time.
You gotta understand that I'm not alone—
It's real confusion.

BOOM BOOM: "As he came to his day of reckoning, he feared not for he went unto the lawyers and the doctors and the jurors, and they said, 'Take heart, for in this you will receive not life but three to seven with time off for good behavior.' " (*Closes book reverently.*)

COP: Ya gotta understand—
Take a walk with me sometime.
See what I see every day . . .

BOOM BOOM: Now we are all faced with this cycle.

COP: Like I'm supposed to smile when I see two bald-headed,
shaved-head men with those tight pants and muscles,
chains everywhere, french-kissin' on the street,
putting their hands all over each other's asses,
I'm supposed to smile,
walk by, act as if this is *right*??!!

BOOM BOOM: As gay people and as people of color and as women we all know the cycle of brutality which pervades our culture.

COP: I got nothin' against people doin' what they want, if I don't see it.

BOOM BOOM: And we all know that brutality only begets more brutality.

COP: I mean, I'm not makin' some woman on the streets for everyone to see.

BOOM BOOM: Violence only sows the seed for more violence.

COP: I'm not . . .

BOOM BOOM: And I hope Dan White knows that.

COP: I can't explain it any better.

(*Pause.*)

BOOM BOOM: Because the greatest, most efficient information gathering and dispersal network is the Great Gay Grapevine.

COP: Just take my word for it—

BOOM BOOM: And when he gets out of jail, no matter where Dan White goes, someone will recognize him.

COP: Walk into a leather bar with me some night—
    they—they're—
    there are queers who'd agree with me—it's disgusting.

BOOM BOOM: All over the world, the word will go out. And we will know where Dan
    White is.

COP: The point is: Dan White showed you could fight City Hall.

(*Pause.*)

BOOM BOOM: Now we are all aware, as I said,
    of this cycle of brutality and murder.
    And the only way we can break that horrible cycle is with
    love, understanding, and forgiveness.
    And there are those who were before me here today—gay brothers and sisters—
    who said that we must somehow learn
    to love, understand, and forgive
    the sins that have been committed against us
    and the sins of violence.
    And it sort of grieves me that some of us are not
    understanding and loving and forgiving of Dan White.
    And after he gets out,
    after we find out where he is . . . (*Long, wry look.*)
    I mean, not, y'know,
    with any malice or planning . . . (*Long look.*)
    You know, you get so depressed and your blood sugar goes up
    and you'd be capable of just about *anything!*
    (*Long pause. Smiles.*)
    And some angry faggot or dyke who is not
    understanding, loving, and forgiving—

is going to perform a horrible act of violence and brutality
against Dan White.
And if we can't break the cycle before somebody gets Dan White,
somebody will get Dan White
and when they do,
I beg you all to
love, understand, and *for-give*. (*Laughs.*)

(*Lights fade to black.*)

CLERK: This is the matter of the People versus Daniel James White and the record
will show that the Defendant is present with his counsel and the District
Attorney is present and this is out of presence of the jury.

(*Courtroom being set up. TV lights.*)

JOANNA LU (*on camera*): The list of prospective witnesses that the defense has
presented for the trial of the man who killed the liberal Mayor of San Francisco,
George Moscone, and the first avowedly gay elected official, City Supervisor
Harvey Milk, reads like a Who's Who of City Government . . . (*Looks at list.*)
Judges, congressmen, current and former supervisors, and even a state senator.
The D.A. has charged White with two counts of first-degree murder, invoking
for the first time the clause in the new California capital punishment law that
calls for the gas chamber for any person who has assassinated a public official in
an attempt to prevent him from fulfilling his official duties. Ironically, Harvey
Milk and George Moscone vigorously lobbied against the death penalty while
Dan White vigorously supported it. This is Joanna Lu at the Hall of Justice.

(*Gavel. Spotlight on* CLERK.)

CLERK: Ladies and gentlemen, this is the information in the case now pending
before you: the People of the State of California, Plaintiff, versus Daniel James
White, Defendant. Action Number: 98663, Count One.

(*Gavel. Lights up. Trial in progress. Screen: "Jury Selection."*)

COURT: Mr. Schmidt, you may continue with your jury selection.

SCHMIDT: Thank you, Your Honor.

CLERK: It is alleged that Dan White did willfully, unlawfully and with malice
aforethought murder George R. Moscone, the duly elected Mayor of the City
and County of San Francisco, California.

SCHMIDT: Have you ever supported controversial causes, like homosexual rights, for
instance?

JUROR #1 (*woman*): I have gay friends . . . I, uh . . . once walked with them in a Gay
Freedom Day Parade.

SCHMIDT: Your Honor, I would like to strike the juror.

JUROR #1: I am str . . . I am heterosexual.

COURT: Agreed.

(*Gavel.*)

CLERK: The Defendant Daniel James White is further accused of a crime of felony to wit: that said Defendant Daniel James White did willfully, unlawfully and with malice aforethought, murder Harvey Milk, a duly elected Supervisor of the City and County of San Francisco, California.

SCHMIDT: With whom do you live, sir?

JUROR #2: My roommate.

SCHMIDT: What does he or she do?

JUROR #2: *He* works at the Holiday Inn.

SCHMIDT: Your Honor, I ask the court to strike the juror for cause.

COURT: Agreed.

(*Gavel.*)

CLERK: Special circumstances: it is alleged that Daniel James White in this proceeding has been accused of more than one offense of murder.

JUROR #3: I worked briefly as a San Francisco policeman, but I've spent most of my life since then as a private security guard.

SCHMIDT: As you know, serving as a juror is a high honor and responsibility.

JUROR #3: Yes, sir.

SCHMIDT: The jury serves as the conscience of the community.

JUROR #3: Yes, sir. I know that, sir.

SCHMIDT: Now, sir, as a juror you take an oath that you will apply the laws of the state of California as the judge will instruct you. You'll uphold that oath, won't you?

JUROR #3: Yes, sir.

SCHMIDT: Do you hold any views against the death penalty no matter how heinous the crime?

JUROR #3: No, sir. I support the death penalty.

SCHMIDT: Why do you think Danny White killed Milk and Moscone?

JUROR #3: I have certain opinions. I'd say it was social and political pressures . . .

SCHMIDT: I have my jury.

COURT: Mr. Norman?

(No response. Fine with him. Gavel.)

LU *(on camera)*: The jury has been selected quickly for the Dan White trial. It appears the prosecution and the defense want the same jury. Assistant D.A. Tom Norman exercised only three out of twenty-seven possible peremptory challenges. By all accounts, there are no blacks, no gays, and no Asians. One juror is an ex-policeman, another the wife of the county jailer, four of the seven women are old enough to be Dan White's mother. Most of the jurors are working- and middle-class Catholics. Speculation in the press box is that the prosecution feels it has a law-and-order jury. In any case, Dan White will certainly be judged by a jury of his peers. *(Turns to second camera.)* I have with me this morning District Attorney Joseph Freitas, Jr. *(TV lights on* FREITAS.*)* May we ask sir, the prosecution's strategy in the trial of Dan White?

FREITAS: I think it's a clear case. . . . We'll let the facts speak for themselves. . . .

*(*FALZON *enters, sits at prosecutor's table.)*

CLERK: And the Defendant, Daniel James White, has entered a plea of not guilty to each of the charges and allegations contained in this information.

*(*WHITE *enters.* MARY ANN WHITE *enters with infant in arms, sees him. They sit.)*

COURT: Mr. Norman, do you desire to make an opening statement at this time?

NORMAN: I do, Judge.

COURT: All right. You may proceed.

(Lights change. Screen: "Act One: Murder." Gavel. Screens go to white.)

NORMAN *(opening statement, prosecution)*: Your Honor, members of the jury—and you *(takes in audience)* must be the judges now, counsel for the defense: *(To audience:)*
Ladies and Gentlemen: I am Thomas F. Norman and I am the Assistant District Attorney, and I appear here as trial representative to Joseph Freitas, Jr., District Attorney. Seated with me is Frank Falzon, Chief Inspector of Homicide for San Francisco.
George R. Moscone was the duly elected Mayor of San Francisco. *(Screen: Portrait of* MOSCONE.*)* Harvey Milk was the duly elected Supervisor or City Councilman of District 5 of San Francisco. *(Screen: Portrait of* MILK.*)*
The defendant in this case, Mr. Daniel James White, had been the duly elected Supervisor of District 8 of San Francisco, until for personal reasons of his own he tendered his resignation in writing to the Mayor on or about November the tenth, 1978, which was approximately seventeen days before this tragedy occurred.
Subsequent to tendering his resignation he had the feeling that he wanted to withdraw that resignation, and that he wanted his job back.
George Moscone, it appears, had told the accused that he would give him his

job back or, in other words, appoint him back to the Board if it appeared that there was substantial support in District Number 8 for that appointment.

Material was received by the Mayor in that regard, and in the meantime, Mr. Daniel James White had resorted to the courts in an effort to withdraw his written resignation.

It appears that those efforts were not met with much success.

(Screen: "The Defense, DOUGLAS SCHMIDT.*")*

SCHMIDT: Ladies and Gentlemen, the prosecutor has quite skillfully outlined certain of the facts that he believes will be supportive of his theory of first-degree murder.

I intend to present *all* the facts, including some of the background material that will show, not so much *what* happened on November 27, but *why* those tragedies occurred on November 27.

The evidence will show, and it's not disputed, that Dan White did, indeed, shoot and kill George Moscone and I think the evidence is equally clear that Dan White did shoot and kill Harvey Milk.

Why then should there be a trial?

The issue in this trial is properly to understand *why* that happened.

(Lights. Screen: "Chief Medical Examiner and Coroner for the City and County of San Francisco.")

STEPHENS *(holding photo)*: In my opinion and experience, Counsel, the larger tattoo pattern at the side of the Mayor's head is compatible with a firing distance of about one foot, and the smaller tattoo pattern within the larger tattoo pattern is consistent with a firing distance of a little less than one foot.

That is: The wounds to the head were received within a distance of one foot when the Mayor was already on the floor incapacitated.

*(*NORMAN *looks to jury. Screen: Image of figure shooting man in head from a distance of one foot, leaning down. Lights.)*

SCHMIDT: Why? . . . Good people, fine people, with fine backgrounds, simply don't kill people in cold blood, it just doesn't happen, and obviously some part of them has not been presented thus far. Dan White was a native of San Francisco. He went to school here, went through high school here. He was a noted athlete in high school. He was an army veteran who served in Vietnam, and was honorably discharged from the army. He became a policeman thereafter, and after a brief hiatus developed, again returned to the police force in San Francisco, and later transferred to the fire department.

He was married in December of 1976, and he fathered his son in July 1978.

Dan White was a good policeman and Dan White was a good fireman. In fact, he was decorated for having saved a woman and her child in a very dangerous fire, but the complete picture of Dan White perhaps was not known until some time after these tragedies on November 27. The part that went unrecognized was—for the past ten years Daniel White was suffering from a mental disease. The disease that Daniel White was suffering from is called "depression," sometimes called "manic depression."

(*Lights.*)

NORMAN: Doctor, what kind of wound was that in your opinion?

STEPHENS: These are gunshot wounds of entrance, Counsel.

The cause of death was multiple gunshot wounds . . . particularly the bullet that passed through the base of the Supervisor's brain. This wound would cause instant or almost instant death. I am now holding People's 30 for identification. In order for this wound to be received, Counsel . . . the Supervisor's left arm has to be in close to the body with the palm up. The right arm has to be relatively close to the body with the palm turned away from the body and the thumb in towards the body.

NORMAN: Can you illustrate that for us?

STEPHENS: Yes, Counsel. The left arm has to be in close to the body and slightly forward with the palm up. The right hand has to be palm away with the thumb pointed towards the body and the elbow in slightly to the body with the arm raised. In this position, all of these wounds that I have just described in People's 30 and 29 line up.

(*Freeze. Lights.*)

SCHMIDT (*talking to jury*): Dan White came from a vastly different lifestyle than Harvey Milk, who was a homosexual leader and politician. Dan White was an idealistic young man, a working-class young man. He was deeply endowed with and believed very strongly in the traditional American values, family, and home, like the District he represented. (*Indicates jury.*) Dan White believed people when they said something. He believed that a man's word, essentially, was his bond. He was an honest man, and he was fair, perhaps too fair for politics in San Francisco.

(*Screen:* WHITE *campaigning, American flag behind him. Audio:* ROCKY *theme song, crowd response throughout his speech.*)

WHITE (*to crowd*): Do you like my new campaign song?

CROWD (*Audio: cheering*): Yeah!

WHITE (*to camera; TV lights*): For years, we have witnessed an exodus from San Francisco by many of our family members, friends, and neighbors. Alarmed by the enormous increase in crime, poor educational facilities, and a deteriorating social structure, they have fled to temporary havens. . . . In a few short years these malignancies of society will erupt from our city and engulf our tree-lined, sun-bathed communities that chide us for daring to live in San Francisco. That is, unless we who have remained can transcend the apathy which has caused us to lock our doors while the tumult rages unchecked through our streets.

Individually we are helpless. Yet you must realize there are thousands and thousands of angry frustrated people such as yourselves waiting to unleash a fury that can and will eradicate the malignancies which blight our beautiful city. I am not going to be forced out of San Francisco by splinter groups of radicals, social deviates, and incorrigibles. UNITE AND FIGHT WITH DAN WHITE.

(*Crowd cheers. Lights change. Screens go to white.*)

SCHMIDT: I think Dan White saw the city deteriorating as a place for the average and decent people to live.

COURT: Mr. Nothenberg, please be seated.

SCHMIDT: The irony is . . . that the young man with so much promise in seeking the job on the Board of Supervisors actually was destined to construct his downfall. After Dan White was elected he discovered there was a conflict of interest if he was a fireman and an elected official. His wife, Mary Ann, was a schoolteacher and made a good salary. But after their marriage, it was discovered that the wife of Dan White had become . . . pregnant and had to give up her teaching job. So the family income plummeted from an excess of $30,000 to $9,600 which is what a San Francisco Supervisor is paid. I believe all the stress and the underlying mental illness culminated in his resignation that he turned in to the Mayor on November 10, 1978.

(*Screen:* "MR. NOTHENBERG, *Deputy Mayor.*" *Lights.*)

NORMAN: Would you read that for us?

NOTHENBERG: "Dear Mayor Moscone: I have been proud to represent the people of San Francisco from District 8 for the past ten months, but due to personal responsibilities which I feel must take precedent over my legislative duties, I am resigning my position effective today. I am sure that the next representative to the Board of Supervisors will receive as much support from the People of San Francisco as I have. Sincerely, Dan White." It is so signed.

SCHMIDT (*to jury*): Some days after November the tenth pressure was brought to bear on Dan White to go back to the job that he had worked so hard for, and there was a one-way course that those persons could appeal to Dan White, and that was to appeal to his sense of honor: Basically—Dan you are letting the fire department down, letting the police department down. It worked. That type of pressure worked, because of the kind of man Dan White is.
He asked the Mayor for his job back.

NORMAN: Mr. Nothenberg, on or about Monday the twenty-seventh of November last year, do you know whether Mayor Moscone was going to make an appointment to the Board of Supervisors, particularly for District No. 8?

NOTHENBERG: Yes, he was.

SCHMIDT: The Mayor said: We have political differences, but you are basically a good man, and you worked for the job and I'm not going to take you to fault. The letter was returned to Dan White.

NORMAN: Do you know whom his appointee to District 8 was going to be?

NOTHENBERG: Yes, I do.

NORMAN: Who was that please?

NOTHENBERG: It was going to be a gentleman named Don Horanzey.

SCHMIDT: As I said, Dan White believed a man's word was his bond. (*He moves down to the jury.*)

Mayor Moscone had said: If there was any legal problem he would simply reappoint Dan White. Thereafter it became: Dan White there is no support in District 8 and unless you can show some broad-base support, the job will not be given to you, and finally, the public statement coming from the Mayor's office: It's undecided. But you will be notified, prior to the time that any decision is made. They didn't tell Dan White. But they told Barbara Taylor.

(*Lights change.*)

TAYLOR (*Audio: on phone*): I'm Barbara Taylor from KCBS. I'd like to speak to Dan White.

WHITE (*Audio*): Yuh.

TAYLOR (*Audio*): I have received information from a source within the Mayor's office that you are not getting that job. I am interested in doing an interview to find out your reaction to that. Mr. White?

(*Long pause. Spotlight on* WHITE.)

WHITE (*Audio*): I don't know anything about it.

(*Audio: Click, busy signal. Lights change.*)

TAYLOR (*live*): The Mayor told me: "The only one I've talked to who is in favor of the appointment of Dan White is Dan White."

NORMAN: Thank you, Miss Taylor.

SCHMIDT: After that phone call, Denise Apcar, Dan's aide, told Dan White that there were going to be supporters down at City Hall the next morning to show support to the Mayor's office. In one day they had collected 1100 signatures in District 8 in support of Dan White.

But the next morning, Denise called Dan and told him the Mayor was unwilling to accept the petitioners.

(*Screen:* "DENISE APCAR, *Aide to* DAN WHITE.")

APCAR: Yes. I told Danny—I don't remember my exact words—that the Mayor had "circumvented the people."

NORMAN: Did you believe at that time that the Mayor was going to appoint someone other than Dan White?

APCAR: Oh, yes.

NORMAN: At that time, were your feelings such that you were angry?

APCAR: Definitely. Well the Mayor had told him . . . and Dan always felt that a person was going to be honest when they said something. He believed that up until the end.

NORMAN: You felt and believed that Mr. Milk had been acting to prevent the appointment of Mr. Dan White to his vacated seat on the Board of Supervisors?

APCAR: Yes. I was very much aware of that.

NORMAN: Had you expressed that opinion to Mr. White?

APCAR: Yes.

NORMAN: Did Mr. White ever express that opinion also to you?

APCAR: He wasn't down at City Hall very much that week so I was basically the person that told him these things.

(*Pause.*)

NORMAN: Did you call Mr. White and tell him that you had seen Harvey Milk come out of the Mayor's office after you had been informed the Mayor was not in?

APCAR: Yes, I did. Then he called me back and said, "Denise, come pick me up. I want to see the Mayor."

NORMAN: When you picked him up, did he do anything unusual?

APCAR: Well . . . he didn't look at me and normally he would turn his body a little bit towards the driver and we would talk, you know, in a freeform way, but this time he didn't look at me at all. He was squinting hard. He was very nervous, he was agitated. He was blowing a lot. He was rubbing his hands, blowing into his hands and rubbing them like he was cold, like his hands were cold. He acted very hurt. Yes. He was, he looked like he was going to cry. He was doing everything he could to restrain his emotion.

NORMAN: Did you ever describe him as acting "all fired up"?

APCAR: Yes, yes I—I believe I said that.

NORMAN: Did he mention at that time that he also was going to talk to Harvey Milk?

APCAR: Yes, he did.

NORMAN: Did he ever say he was going to "really lay it on the Mayor"?

APCAR: It's been brought to my attention I said that, yes.

NORMAN: When you were driving Mr. White downtown, was there some discussion relative to a statement you made. "Anger had run pretty high all week towards the Mayor playing pool on us, dirty, you know?"

APCAR: I believe I was describing my anger. At the time I made those statements I was in shock and I spoke freely and I'm sure I've never used those terms before.

NORMAN: When you made those statements it was forty minutes after noon on November 27, was it not?

APCAR: Yes.

NORMAN: Miss Apcar—when you were driving Mr. White to City Hall did you know he was carrying a loaded gun?

APCAR: No. I did not.

NORMAN: Thank you.

(*Lights.*)

SCHMIDT: Dan White went to City Hall and he took a .38 caliber revolver with him, and that was not particularly unusual for Dan White.

Dan White was an ex-policeman, and as a policeman one is required to carry, off-duty, a gun, and as an ex-policeman—well, I think it's common practice.

And additionally, remember, there was the atmosphere created by the Jones-town People's Temple tragedy (*screens flood with Jonestown imagery; music*) which had occurred a few days before November 27, and at that time there were rumors that there were hit lists that had been placed on public officials in San Francisco. Assassination squads. And in hindsight of course we can all realize the fact did not happen, but at the time there were 900 bodies laying in Guyana to indicate that indeed people were bent on murder.

(*Screen:* "OFFICER BYRNE, *Department of Records.*" *Lights.*)

NORMAN: Officer Byrne, do persons who were once on the police force who have resigned their positions, do they have a right to carry a concealed firearm on their person?

SCHMIDT: And I think it will be shown that Jim Jones himself was directly allied to the liberal elements of San Francisco politics and not to the conservative elements.

BYRNE: No, a resigned person would not have that right.

SCHMIDT: And so, it would be important to understand that there were threats directed towards conservative persons like Dan White.

NORMAN: Officer, have you at my instance and request examined those particular records to determine whether there is an official permit issued by the Chief of Police to a Mr. Daniel James White to carry a concealed firearm?

BYRNE: Yes, I have.

NORMAN: What have you found?

BYRNE: I find no permit.

NORMAN: Thank you.

(*Lights.*)

SCHMIDT: Yes, it's a violation of the law to carry a firearm without a permit, but that firearm was *registered* to Dan White.

NORMAN: Mr. Melia, please be seated.

SCHMIDT: Upon approaching the doors on Polk Street White observed a metal-detection machine.

    Knowing that he did not know the man that was on the metal-detection machine, he simply went around to the McAllister Street well, where he expected to meet his aide.

    He did not find Denise Apcar there. She'd gone to put gas in her car. He waited for several moments, but knowing that it was imminent, the talk to the Mayor, he stepped through a window at the Department of Public Works. (*Screen: Slide of windows with man in front demonstrating procedure.*) Which doesn't require any physical prowess, and you can step through those windows, and the evidence will show that though now they are barred, previously it was not uncommon for people to enter and exit there. They are very large windows, and are large, wide sills, (*screen shows windows he stepped through—small, high off the ground, now barred*) and it's quite easy to step into the building through these windows. (*Screen: Slide of man in three-piece suit trying to get leg up.*)

(*Screen: "WILLIAM MELIA, JR., Civil Engineer."*)

MELIA: At approximately 10:35 I heard the window open. I heard someone jump to the floor and then running through the adjoining room. I looked up and caught a glance of a man in a suit running past the doorway of my office into the City Hall hallway.

NORMAN: What did you do?

MELIA: I got up from my desk and called after him: "Hey, wait a second."

NORMAN: Did that person wait or stop?

MELIA: Yes, they did.

NORMAN: Do you see that person here in this courtroom today?

MELIA: Yes, I do.

NORMAN: Where is that person?

MELIA: It's Dan White. (*Pause.*) He said to me: "I had to get in. My aide was supposed to come down and let me in the side door, but never showed up." I had taken exception to the way he had entered our office, and I replied: "And *you are?*" And he replied: "I'm Dan White, the City Supervisor." He said, "Say, I've got to go," and with that, he turned and ran out of the office.

NORMAN: Did you say that he ran?

MELIA: Right.

(Pause.)

NORMAN: Mr. Melia—had you ever seen anyone else enter or exit through that window or those windows along that side?

MELIA: Yes, I had. It was common for individuals that worked in our office to do that.

NORMAN: Were you alarmed when you learned that a Supervisor crawled or walked through that window, or stepped through that window?

MELIA: Was I alarmed?

NORMAN: Yes.

MELIA: Yes. I was . . . alarmed.

(NORMAN *looks to jury.*)

SCHMIDT *(annoyed)*: I think it's significant at this point—also because the fact that he crawled through the window *appears* to be important—it's significant to explain that people *often climb through that window,* and indeed, on the morning of the twenty-seventh, Denise had the key to the McAllister Street well door.

So, Dan White stepped through the window, identified himself, traveled up to the second floor. *(Screen:* "MRS. CYR COPERTINI, *Appointment Secretary to the Mayor.")* And then approached the desk of Cyr Copertini and properly identified himself, and asked to see the Mayor.

(Lights.)

CYR: I am the appointment secretary to Mayor Feinstein.

NORMAN: In November of last year and particularly on November 27 what was your then occupation?

CYR: I was appointment secretary to the elected Mayor of San Francisco, George Moscone. *(She is deeply moved.)*

NORMAN: Mrs. Copertini—were you aware that there was anything that was going to happen that day of November 27 of interest to the citizens of San Francisco, uh . . . I mean, such as some public announcement?

(Pause.)

CYR: . . . There was to be a news conference to announce the new Supervisor for the Eighth District, at 11:30.

NORMAN: Mrs. Copertini, at approximately 10:30 A.M. when you saw Mr. Daniel White, he appeared in front of your desk . . . do you recall what he said?

CYR: He said, "Hello, Cyr. May I see the Mayor?" I said: "He has someone with him, but let me go check with him." I went in to the Mayor and told him that Supervisor White was there to see him. He was a little dismayed. He was a little uncomfortable by it and said: "Oh, all right. Tell him I'll see him, but he will have to wait a coupla minutes."

I asked the Mayor, "Shouldn't I have someone in there with him," and he said: "No, no, I'll see him alone."

I said, "Why don't you let me bring Mel Wax in?" And he said: "No, no, I'll see him alone." And then I went back.

NORMAN: Who was Mel Wax?

CYR: The press secretary.

NORMAN: When you went out to your office, did you then see Mr. Daniel White?

CYR: Yes. I said it will be a few minutes. He asked me how I was and how things were going. Was I having a nice day.

NORMAN: Was there anything unusual about his tone of voice?

CYR: No. I don't think so. He seemed nervous. . . .

I asked him would he like to see the newspaper while he was waiting? He said no, he wouldn't, and I said: "Well, that's all right. There's nothing in it anyway unless you want to read about Caroline Kennedy having turned twenty-one."

And he said: "Twenty-one? Is that right." He said: "Yeah, that's all so long ago. It's even more amazing when you think that John John is now eighteen."

(*Lights change. Funeral Mass: Gregorian chant; boys' choir. Pause.*)

DENMAN: The only comparable situation I ever remember.

CYR: It was about that time he was admitted to the Mayor's office.

(*Pause.*)

DENMAN: was when JFK was killed.

NORMAN: Did you tell Mr. Daniel White that he could go in?

CYR: Yes.

DENMAN: I remember that in my bones, in my body.

NORMAN: Did he respond in any way to that?

DENMAN: Just like this one.

CYR: He said: "Good girl, Cyr."

NORMAN: Good girl, Cyr?

CYR: Right.

DENMAN: When Camelot all of a sudden turned to hell.

NORMAN: Then what did he do?

CYR: Went in.

(*Pause.*)

NORMAN: After he went in there did you hear anything of an unusual nature that was coming from the Mayor's office?

CYR: After a time I heard a . . . commotion.

(*Lights change.*)

YOUNG MOTHER: I heard it on the car radio, I literally gasped.

NORMAN: Explain that to us, please.

YOUNG MOTHER: I wanted to pull over to the side of the road and scream.

CYR: Well, I heard—a series of noises—a group and then one—

YOUNG MOTHER: Just scream.

CYR: I went to the window to see if anything was happening out in the street,

YOUNG MOTHER: Then I thought of my kids.

CYR: and the street was rather extraordinarily calm.

DENMAN: I noticed when I walked outside that there was an unusual quiet.

CYR: For that hour of the day there is usually more—there wasn't really anything out there.

DENMAN: I went to the second floor and started walking toward the Mayor's office.

YOUNG MOTHER: I wanted to get them out of school and take them home,

NORMAN: Could you describe these noises for us?

YOUNG MOTHER: I wanted to take them home and (*makes a hugging gesture*) lock the door.

CYR: Well, they were dull thuds rather like—

DENMAN: And there was this strange combination of panic and silence that you rarely see,

CYR: I thought maybe it was an automobile door that somebody had tried to shut, by, you know, pushing, and then finally succeeding.

DENMAN: it was like a silent slow-motion movie of a disaster.

NORMAN: Do you have any recollection that you can report with any certainty to us as to how many sounds there were?

CYR: No. As I stood there I—I thought I ought to remember—(*She breaks down.*)

DENMAN: There was this hush and aura, people were moving with strange faces, (CYR *sobs*) as if the world had just come to an end.

MOSCONE'S FRIEND: George loved this city, and felt what was wrong could be fixed.

NORMAN: Do you want a glass of water?

(CYR *sobs.*)

DENMAN: And I asked someone what had happened and he said: "The Mayor has been shot."

CYR: I ought to remember that pattern in case it is something, but I—

MOSCONE'S FRIEND: He knew—it was a white racist town. A Catholic town. But he believed in people's basic good will.

(CYR *sobs.*)

COURT: Just a minute. Do you want a recess?

MOSCONE'S FRIEND: He never suspected, I bet, Dan White's psychotic behavior.

NORMAN: Do you want a recess?

MOSCONE'S FRIEND: That son of a bitch killed someone I loved. I mean, I loved the guy.

CYR: No. I'm all right.

COURT: Are you sure you are all right?

CYR: Yes.

YOUNG MOTHER: I just thought of my kids.

(*Long pause.*)

MOSCONE'S FRIEND: I loved his idealism. I loved his hope.

CYR: Then what happened was Rudy Nothenberg left to tell the press that the conference would start a few minutes late.

MOSCONE'S FRIEND: I loved the guy.

CYR: And then he came back to me right away and said: "Oh, I guess we can go ahead. I just saw Dan White leave."

MOSCONE'S FRIEND: I loved his almost naïve faith in people.

CYR: So then he went into the Mayor's office and said: "He isn't here." And I said: "Well, maybe he went into the back room."

MOSCONE'S FRIEND: I loved his ability to go on.

CYR: Then he just gave a shout saying: "Gary, get in here. Call an ambulance. Get the police."

MOSCONE'S FRIEND: See, I got too tired to stay in politics and do it. George and I were together from the beginning. Me, Phil Burton, Willy Brown. Beatin' all the old Irishmen.

DENMAN: I heard right away that Dan White had done it.

MOSCONE'S FRIEND: But George believed, as corny as this sounds, that you do good for the people. I haven't met many of those and George was one of those. Maybe those are the guys that get killed. I don't know.

(Pause. CYR crying.)

NORMAN: All right. All this you told us about occurred in San Francisco, didn't it?

(Pause.)

CYR *(deeply moved)*: Yes.

SCHMIDT: Dan White, as it was quite apparent at that point, had *cracked* because of his underlying mental illness. . . .

(Screen: "CARL HENRY CARLSON, Aide to HARVEY MILK.")

CARLSON: I heard Peter Nardoza, Dianne Feinstein's aide, say "Dianne wants to see you," and Dan White said: "That'll have to wait a couple of minutes, I have something to do first."

NORMAN: I have something to do first?

CARLSON: Yes.

(Pause.)

NORMAN: Do you recall in what manner Mr. White announced himself?

SCHMIDT: There were stress factors due to the fact that he hadn't been notified,

CARLSON: He appeared at the door which was normally left open. Stuck his head in and asked: "Say, Harv, can I see you for a minute?"

SCHMIDT: and the sudden emotional surge that he had in the Mayor's office was simply too much for him—

NORMAN: What did Harvey Milk do at that time if anything?

CARLSON: He turned around.

SCHMIDT: and he cracked.

CARLSON: He turned around

SCHMIDT: The man cracked.

CARLSON: and said "Sure," and got up and went across the hall . . .

SCHMIDT: He shot the Mayor,

CARLSON: to the office designated as Dan White's office on the chart.

SCHMIDT: reloaded his gun, basically on *instinct*, because of his police training,

NORMAN: After they went across the hall to Mr. White's office . . .

SCHMIDT: and was about to leave the building at that point and he looked down the hall,

NORMAN: Would you tell us what next you heard or saw?

SCHMIDT: he saw somebody that he believed to be an aide to Harvey Milk.

CARLSON: A few seconds later, probably ten, fifteen seconds later, I heard a shot, or the sound of gunfire.

SCHMIDT: He went down to the Supervisors' area to *talk* to Harvey Milk.

COURT: Excuse me. Would you speak out. Your voice is fading a bit.

SCHMIDT: At that point, in the same state of rage, emotional upheaval with the stress and mental illness having cracked this man

STEPHENS (*demonstrates as he speaks*): The left arm has to be close to the body and slightly forward with the palm up.

SCHMIDT: *ninety seconds* from the time he shot the Mayor, Dan White shot and killed Harvey Milk.

CARLSON: After the shot, I heard Harvey Milk scream. "Oh, no." And then the first—the first part of the second "no" which was then cut short by the second shot.

STEPHENS: The right hand has to be palm away with the thumb pointed towards the body and the elbow in slightly to the body with the arm raised.

NORMAN: How many sounds of shots did you hear altogether, Mr. Carlson?

CARLSON: Five or six. I really didn't consciously count them.

STEPHENS: In this position all of these wounds that I have just described in People's 29 and 30 line up.

(*Pause.*)

CARLSON: A few moments later the door opened, the door opened and Daniel White walked out, rushed out, and proceeded down the hall.

NORMAN: Now, Mr. Carlson, when Daniel White first appeared at the office of Harvey Milk and he inquired of Harvey Milk, "Say, Harv, can I see you for a minute?" could you describe his tone of voice in any way?

CARLSON: He appeared to be very normal, usual friendly self. I didn't, I didn't feel anything out of the ordinary. It was just very typical Dan White.

(*Lights change.*)

GWENN: I'd like to talk about when people are pushed to the wall.

SCHMIDT: Harvey Milk was against the reappointment of Dan White.

GWENN: In order to understand the riots, I think you have to understand that the Dan White verdict did not occur in a vacuum.

SCHMIDT: Basically, it was a political decision. It was evident there was a liberal wing of the Board of Supervisors, and there was a smaller conservative wing, and Dan White was a conservative politician for San Francisco.

(*Screen:* "RICHARD PABICH, *Legislative Assistant to* HARVEY MILK." *Lights.*)

PABICH: My address is 542–A Castro Street.

GWENN: I don't think I have to say what their presence meant to us, and what their loss meant to us—

NORMAN: What did you do after you saw Dan White put the key in the door of his old office, Room 237?

GWENN: The assassinations of our friends Harvey and George were a crime against us all.

PABICH: Well, I was struck in my head, sort of curious as to why he'd been running.

GWENN: And right here, when I say "us," I don't mean only gay people.

PABICH: And he was—it looked like he was in a hurry. I was aware of the political situation.

GWENN: I mean all people who are getting less than they deserve.

PABICH: I was aware that Harvey was taking the position to the Mayor that Mr. White shouldn't be reappointed. Harvey and I had talked earlier that it would be a significant day.

(*Lights. Subliminal music.*)

MILK'S FRIEND: After Harvey died, I went into a depression that lasted about a year, I guess. They called it depression, anyway. I thought about suicide, well, I more than thought about it.

SCHMIDT: Mr. Pabich, Mr. Milk had suggested a replacement for Dan White, hadn't he?

PABICH: He had, to my understanding, recommended several people, and basically took the position that Dan White should not be reappointed.

MILK'S FRIEND: I lost my job. I stayed in the hospital for, I would guess, two months or so. They put me on some kind of drug that . . . well, it helped, I guess. I mean, I loved him and it was . . .

SCHMIDT: Was he requesting that a homosexual be appointed?

PABICH: No, he was not. (*He stares at* SCHMIDT, *stunned.*)

(*Lights change.*)

MILK'S FRIEND: Well, he was gone and that couldn't change.

SCHMIDT: I have nothing further. Thank you.

MILK'S FRIEND: He'd never be here again, I knew that.

COURT: All right. Any redirect, Mr. Norman?

NORMAN: No. Thank you for coming, Mr. Pabich.

GWENN: It was as if Dan White had given the go-ahead. It was a free-for-all, a license to kill.

MILK'S FRIEND: I had this recurring dream. We were at the opera, Harvey and I.

(PABICH *with* JOANNA LU. *TV lights.*)

PABICH (*on camera*): It's over. Already I can tell it's over. He asked me a question, a clear queer-baiting question, and the jury didn't bat an eye.

MILK'S FRIEND: I was laughing. Harvey was laughing.

PABICH (*on camera*): Dan White's going to get away with murder.

LU (*on camera*): Mr. Pabich . . .

MILK'S FRIEND: Then Harvey leant over and whispered: When you're watching *Tosca*, you know you're alive. That's when I'd wake up.

(PABICH *rushes out, upset.*)

GWENN: I remember the moment I heard Harvey had been shot—(*She breaks down.*)

MILK'S FRIEND: And I'd realize—like for the first time all over again—he was dead.

(*Blackout. Hyperreal sounds of high heels on marble, echoing, moving fast. Mumbled Hail Marys. Light up slowly on* SCHMIDT, NORMAN.)

SCHMIDT: From here I think the evidence will demonstrate that Dan White ran down to Denise's office, screamed at his aide to give him the key to her car.
   And he left, went to a church, called his wife, went into St. Mary's Cathedral, prayed, and his wife got there, and he told her, the best he could, what he remembered he had done, and then they walked together to the Northern Police Station where he turned himself in; asked the officer to look after his wife, asked the officer to take possession of an Irish poster he was carrying . . . (*Screen: Cover of Uris book* Ireland: A Terrible Beauty. *Desolate, haunting.*) and then made a statement, what best he could recall had occurred.

(*Lights.* FALZON *rises from his seat at prosecutor's table.*)

FALZON: Why . . . I feel like hitting you in the fuckin' mouth. . . . How could you be so stupid? How?

WHITE: I . . . I want to tell you about it . . . I want to, to explain.

FALZON: Okay, if you want to talk to me, I'm gonna get my tape recorder and read you your rights and do it right.

NORMAN: The People at this time move the tape-recorded statement into evidence.

(*Screen: "The Confession."*)

FALZON: Today's date is Monday, November 27, 1978. The time is presently 12:05. We're inside the Homicide Detail, Room 454, at the Hall of Justice. Present is Inspector Edward Erdelatz, Inspector Frank Falzon and for the record, sir, your full name?

WHITE: Daniel James White.

(*Lights.*)

FALZON: Would you, normally in a situation like this, ah . . . we ask questions, I'm aware of your past history as a police officer and also as a San Francisco fireman. I would prefer. I'll let you do it in a narrative form as to what happened this morning if you can lead up to the events of the shooting and then backtrack as to why these events took place. (*Looks at* ERDELATZ.)

WHITE: Well, it's just that I've been under an awful lot of pressure lately, financial pressure, because of my job situation, family pressure because of ah . . . not being able to have the time with my family. (*Sob.*)

FALZON: Can you relate these pressures you've been under, Dan, at this time? Can you explain it to Inspector Erdelatz and myself.

WHITE: It's just that I wanted to serve (FALZON *nods*) the people of San Francisco well and I did that. Then when the pressures got too great, I decided to leave. After I left, my family and friends offered their support and said, whatever it would take to allow me to go back into office—well, they would be willing to make that effort. And then it came out that Supervisor Milk and some others were working against me to get my seat back on the Board. He didn't speak to me, he spoke to the City Attorney but I was in the office and I heard the conversation.

I could see the game that was being played, they were going to use me as a *scapegoat*, whether I was a good Supervisor or not, was not the point. This was a political opportunity and they were going to degrade me and my family and the job that I had tried to do an, an more or less *hang me out to dry*. And I saw more and more evidence of this during the week when the papers reported that ah . . . someone else was going to be reappointed. The Mayor told me he was going to call me before he made any decision, he never did that. I was troubled, the pressure, my family again, my, my son's out to a babysitter.

FALZON: Dan, can you tell Inspector Erdelatz and myself, what was your plan this morning? What did you have in mind?

WHITE: I didn't have any devised plan or anything, it's, I was leaving the house to talk, to see the Mayor and I went downstairs, to, to make a phone call and I had my gun down there.

FALZON: Is this your police service revolver, Dan?

WHITE: This is the gun I had when I was a policeman. It's in my room an ah . . . I don't know, I just put it on. I, I don't know why I put it on, it's just . . .

FALZON: You went directly from your residence to the Mayor's office this morning?

WHITE: Yes, my, my aide picked me up but she didn't have any idea ah . . . you know that I had a gun on me or, you know, and I went in to see him an, an he told me he wasn't going to, intending to tell me about it. Then ah . . . I got kind of fuzzy and then just my head didn't feel right and I, then he said: "Let's go into the, the back room and, and have a drink and talk about it."

FALZON: Was this before any threats on your part, Dan?

WHITE: I, I never made any threats.

FALZON: There were no threats at all?

WHITE: I, I . . . oh no.

FALZON: When were you, how, what was the conversation, can you explain to Inspector Erdelatz and myself the conversation that existed between the two of you at this time?

WHITE: It was pretty much just, you know, I asked, was I going to be reappointed. He said, no I am not, no you're not. And I said, why, and he told me, it's a political decision and that's the end of it, and that's it.

FALZON: Is this when you were having a drink in the back room?

WHITE: No, no, it's before I went into the back room and then he could obviously see, see I was obviously distraught an then he said, let's have a drink an I, I'm not even a drinker, you know I don't, once in a while, but I'm not even a drinker. But I just kinda stumbled in the back and he was all, he was talking an nothing was getting through to me. It was just like a roaring in my ears an, an then em . . . it just came to me, you know, he . . .

FALZON: You couldn't hear what he was saying, Dan?

WHITE: Just small talk that, you know, it just wasn't registering. What I was going to do now, you know, and how this would affect my family, you know, an, an just, just all the time knowing he's going to go out an, an lie to the press an, an tell 'em, you know, that I, I wasn't a good Supervisor and that people didn't want me an then that was it. Then I, I just shot him, that was it, it was over.

FALZON: What happened after you left there, Dan?

WHITE: Well, I, I left his office by one of the back doors an, I was going down the stairs and then I saw Harvey Milk's aide an then it struck me about what Harvey had tried to do an I said, well I'll go talk to him. He didn't know I had, I had heard his conversation and he was all smiles and stuff and I went in and, you know, I, I didn't agree with him on a lot of things, but I was always honest, you know, and here they were devious. I started to say you know how hard I worked for it and what it meant to me and my family an then my reputation as, as a hard worker, good honest person and he just kind of smirked at me as if to say, too bad an then, an then, I just got all flushed an, an hot, and I shot him.

FALZON: This occurred inside your room, Dan?

WHITE: Yeah, in my office, yeah.

FALZON: And when you left there did you go back home?

WHITE: No, no, no I drove to the, the Doggie Diner on, on Van Ness and I called my wife and she, she didn't know, she . . .

FALZON: Did you tell her, Dan?

(*Sobbing.*)

WHITE: I called up, I didn't tell her on the phone. I just said she was work . . . see, she was working, son's at a babysitter, shit. I just told her to meet me at the cathedral.

FALZON: St. Mary's?

(*Sobbing.*)

WHITE: She took a cab, yeah. She didn't know. She had knew I'd been upset and I wasn't even talking to her at home because I just couldn't explain how I felt and she had no, nothing to blame about it, she was, she always has been great to me but it was, just the pressure hitting me an just my head's all flushed and expected that my skull's going to crack. Then when she came to the church, I, I told her and she kind of slumped and she, she couldn't say anything.

FALZON: How is she now do you, do you know is she, do you know where she is?

WHITE: I don't know now. She, she came to Northern Station with me. She asked me not to do anything about myself, you know that she, she loved me and she'd stick by me and not to hurt myself.

FALZON: Is there anything else you'd like to add at this time?

WHITE: Just that I've been honest and worked hard, never cheated anybody or, you know, I'm not a crook or anything an I wanted to do a good job, I'm trying to do a good job an I saw this city as it's going, kind of downhill an I was always just a lonely vote on the Board and try to be honest an, an I just couldn't take it anymore an that's it.

FALZON: Inspector Erdelatz?

ERDELATZ: Dan, right now are you under a doctor's care?

WHITE: No.

ERDELATZ: Are you under any medication at all?

WHITE: No.

ERDELATZ: When is the last time you had your gun with you prior to today?

WHITE: I guess it was a few months ago. I, I was afraid of some of the threats that were made an, I, I, just wanted to make sure to protect myself you know this, this city isn't safe you know and there's a lot of people running around an well I don't have to tell you fellows, you guys know that.

ERDELATZ: When you left your home this morning Dan, was it your intention to confront the Mayor, Supervisor Milk, or anyone else with that gun?

WHITE: No, I, I, what I wanted to do was just, talk to him, you know, I, I ah, I didn't even know if I was going to be reappointed or not be reappointed. *Why do we do things, you know, why did I, I don't know.* No, I, I just wanted to talk to him that's all an at least have him be honest with me an tell me why he was doing it, not because I was a bad Supervisor or anything but, you know, I never killed anybody before. I never shot anybody . . .

ERDELATZ: Why did . . .

WHITE: . . . I didn't even, I didn't even know if I wanted to kill him. I just shot him, I don't know.

ERDELATZ: What type of gun is that you were carrying, Dan?

WHITE: It's a .38, a two-inch .38.

ERDELATZ: And do you know how many shots you fired?

WHITE: Uh . . . no I don't, I don't. I, I out of instinct when I, I reloaded the gun ah . . . you know, it's just the training I guess I had, you know.

ERDELATZ: Where did you reload?

WHITE: I reloaded in my office when, when I was I couldn't out in the hall.

(*Pause.*)

ERDELATZ: And how many bullets did you have with you?

WHITE: I, I, I don't know, I ah . . . the gun was loaded an, an, I had some ah . . . extra shots you know, I just, I, 'cause, I kept the gun with, with a box of shells and just grabbed some.

ERDELATZ: Inspector Falzon?

FALZON: No questions. Is there anything you'd like to add, Dan, before we close this statement?

WHITE: Well it's just that, I never really intended to hurt anybody. It's just this past several months, it got to the point I couldn't take it and I never wanted the job for ego or, you know, perpetuate myself or anything like that. I was trying to do a good job for the city.

FALZON: Inspector Erdelatz and I ah . . . appreciate your cooperation and the truthfulness of your statement.

(*Lights change.* WHITE *sobbing.* MARY ANN WHITE *sobbing, jurors sobbing.* FALZON *moved.*)

NORMAN: I think that is all. You may examine.

COURT: Do you want to take a recess at this time?

SCHMIDT: Why don't we take a brief recess?

COURT: Let me admonish you ladies and gentlemen of the jury, not to discuss this case among yourselves nor with anyone else, nor allow anyone to speak to you about the case, nor are you to form or express an opinion until the matter has been submitted to you.

(*House lights up. Screen: "Recess."*)

ACT TWO: In Defense of Murder

As audience enters, documentary images of MILK *and* MOSCONE *on screen.*

*MOSCONE (*on video*): My late father was a guard at San Quentin, and who I was visiting one day, and who showed to me, and then explained the function of, the uh, the uh death chamber. And it just seemed inconceivable to me, though I was pretty young at the time, that in this society that I had been trained to believe was the most effective and efficient of all societies, that the only way we could deal with violent crime would be to do the ultimate ourselves, and that's to governmentally sanction the taking of another person's life.

*MILK (*on video*): Two days after I was elected I got a phone call—the voice was quite young. It was from Altoona, Pennsylvania. And the person said, "Thanks." And you've got to elect gay people so that that young child, and the thousands upon thousands like that child, know that there's hope for a better world. There's hope for a better tomorrow. Without hope, they'll only gaze at those blacks, the Asians, the disabled, the seniors, the us'es, the us'es. Without hope, the us'es give up. I know that you cannot live on hope alone. But without it, life is not worth living. And you, and you, and you, gotta give 'em hope. Thank you very much.

(Lights up. Courtroom. FALZON *on witness stand.* DAN WHITE *at defense table sobbing.* MARY ANN WHITE *behind him sobbing. Five jurors sobbing.)*

WHITE (*audio*): Well, it's just that I never really intended to hurt anybody. It's just this past several months, it got to the point I couldn't take it and I never wanted the job for ego or, you know, perpetuate myself or anything like that. I was just trying to do a good job for the city.

FALZON (*audio*): Inspector Erdelatz and I ah . . . appreciate your cooperation and the truthfulness of your statement.

*(*FALZON *switches tape off.)*

NORMAN: I think that is all. You may examine.

*(Lights change. Screen: "*INSPECTOR FRANK FALZON, *Witness for the Prosecution." Screen: "Act Two: In Defense of Murder.")*

SCHMIDT: Inspector Falzon, you mentioned that you had known Dan White in the past, prior to November 27, 1978?

FALZON: Yes, sir, quite well.

SCHMIDT: About how long have you known him?

*Monologues by Milk and Moscone excerpted from *The Times of Harvey Milk*, a film by Robert Epstein and Richard Schmeichen.

181

FALZON: According to Dan, it goes way back to the days
    we attended St. Elizabeth's Grammar School together, but
    we went to different high schools.
    I attended St. Ignatius, and he attended Riordan.
    He walked up to me one day at the Jackson Playground,
    with spikes over his shoulders, glove in his hand,
    and asked if he could play on my team.
    I told him it was the police team,
    and he stated that he was a new recruit at Northern Station,
    wanted to play on the police softball team,
    and since that day Dan White and I
    have been very good friends.

SCHMIDT: You knew him fairly well then, that is fair?

FALZON: As well as I know anybody, I believed.

SCHMIDT: Can you tell me, when you saw him first on November 27, 1978, how
    did he appear physically to you?

FALZON: Destroyed. This was not the Dan White I had known, not at all.
    That day I saw a shattered individual,
    both mentally and physically in appearance,
    who appeared to me to be shattered.

    Dan White, the man I knew
    prior to Monday, the twenty-seventh of November, 1978,
    was a man among men.

SCHMIDT: Knowing, with regard to the shootings of Mayor Moscone and Harvey
    Milk, knowing Dan White as you did, is he the type of man that could have
    premeditatedly and deliberately shot those people?

NORMAN: Objection as calling for an opinion and conclusion.

COURT: Sustained.

SCHMIDT: Knowing him as you do, have you ever seen anything in his past that
    would lead you to believe he was capable of cold-bloodedly shooting some-
    body?

NORMAN: Same objection.

COURT: Sustained.

SCHMIDT: Your Honor, at this point I have anticipated that maybe there would be
    some argument with regard to opinions not only as to Inspector Falzon, but
    with a number of other witnesses that I intend to call, and accordingly I have
    prepared a memorandum of what I believe to be the appropriate law. (*Shows
    memo.*)

COURT: I have no quarrel with your authorities, but I think the form of the questions that you asked were objectionable.

SCHMIDT: The questions were calculated to bring out an opinion on the state of mind and—I believe that a lay person, if he is an intimate acquaintance, surely can hazard such an opinion. I believe that Inspector Falzon, as a police officer, has an opinion.

COURT: Get the facts from this witness. I will let you get those facts, whatever they are.

SCHMIDT: All right, we will try that. Inspector Falzon, again, you mentioned that you were quite familiar with Dan White; can you tell me something about the man's character, as to the man that you knew prior to the—prior to November 27, 1978?

NORMAN: Objection as being irrelevant and vague.

COURT: Overruled. (*To* FALZON:) Do you understand the question?

FALZON: I do, basically, Your Honor.

COURT: All right, you may answer it.

NORMAN: Well, Your Honor, character for what?

COURT: Overruled. (*To* FALZON:) You may answer it.

FALZON: The Dan White that I knew prior to Monday, November 27, 1978,
        was a man who seemed to excel in pressure situations,
        and it seemed that the greater the pressure, the more enjoyment that Dan had,
        exceeding at what he was trying to do.

Examples would be in his sports life,
that I can relate to,
and for the first time in the history of the State of Califoirnia,
there was a law enforcement softball tournament held in 1971.

The San Francisco Police Department entered
that softball tournament along with other major departments,
Los Angeles included,
and Dan White was not only named on the All-Star Team
at the end of the tournament,
but named the most valuable player.

He was just outstanding under pressure situations,
when men would be on base and that clutch hit was needed.

At the end of the tournament, a dinner was held,
the umpires were invited,
and one individual had umpired baseball games for over thirty years,
made the comment that Dan White

was the best ballplayer he had ever seen participate
in any tournament in South Lake Tahoe.

Another example of Dan White's attitude toward pressure
was that when he decided to run for the District 8 Supervisor's seat,
and I can still vividly remember the morning
he walked into the Homicide Detail and sat down to—
announced that he was going to run for City Supervisor,

I said: "How are you going to do it, Dan?
Nobody heard of Dan White. How are you going to go out there,
win this election?"

He said: "I'm going to do it the way the people want it to be done,
knock on their doors, go inside, shake their hands,
let them know what Dan White stands for."

And he said: "Dan White is going to represent them.
There will be a voice in City Hall, you watch, I'll make it."

He did what he said he was going to do,
he ran, won the election.

SCHMIDT: Given these things that you mentioned about Dan White, was there anything in his character that you saw of him, prior to those tragedies of the twenty-seventh of November, that would have led you to believe that he would ever kill somebody cold-bloodedly?

NORMAN: Objection, irrelevant.

COURT: Overruled.

NORMAN: Let me state my grounds for the record.

COURT: Overruled.

NORMAN: Thank you, Judge. It's irrelevant and called for his opinion and speculation.

COURT: Overruled. (*To* FALZON:) You may answer that.

FALZON: Yes, your honor.

I'm aware—I'm hesitating only because
there was something I saw in Dan's personality
that didn't become relevant to me
until I was assigned this case.

He had a tendency to run, occasionally,
from situations.
I saw this flaw, and I asked him about it,
and his response was that his ultimate goal
was to purchase a boat, just travel around the world,

get away from everybody,
and yet the Dan White that I was talking to
was trying to be involved with people,
constantly being a fireman,
being a policeman, being a Supervisor.
He wanted to be helpful to people,
and yet he wanted to run away from them.
That did not make sense to me.

Today, this is the only flaw in Dan White's character
that I can cite up here, and testify about.

Otherwise, to me, Dan White was an exemplary individual,
a man that I was proud to know and be associated with.

SCHMIDT: Do you think he cracked? Do you think there was something wrong with him on November 27?

NORMAN: Objection as calling for an opinion and speculation.

COURT: Sustained.

SCHMIDT: I have nothing further. (*Turns back.*) Inspector, I have one last question. Did you ever see him act out of revenge the whole time you have known him?

NORMAN: Objection. That calls for speculation.

COURT: No, overruled, and this is as to his observations and contacts. Overruled.

FALZON: The only time Dan White could have acted out in revenge
is when he took the opposite procedure
in hurting himself,
by quitting the San Francisco Police Department.

SCHMIDT: Nothing further. Thank you, sir.

NORMAN: Inspector Falzon, you regard yourself as a close friend to Mr. Daniel White, don't you?

FALZON: Yes, sir.

NORMAN: Do you regard yourself as a *very* close friend of Mr. Daniel White?

FALZON: I would consider myself a close friend of yours, if that can relate to you my closeness with Dan White.

(*Pause.* NORMAN *uncomfortable.*)

NORMAN: Of course, you haven't known me as long as you have known Mr. Daniel White, have you, Inspector?

FALZON: Just about the same length of time, Counsel.

(*Long pause.*)

NORMAN: Inspector Falzon, while you've expressed some shock at these tragedies, would you subscribe to the proposition that there's a first time for everything?

FALZON: It's obvious in this case; yes, sir.

NORMAN: Thank you. (*He sits.* FALZON *leaves the witness stand and takes his seat beside him at the prosecutor's table.*) The Prosecution rests.

(*Lights change. Screen: "The Prosecution Rests." Commotion in court.*)

COURT: Order.

(*Gavel. Lights.* FREITAS *alone.*)

FREITAS: I was the D.A.
  Obviously in some respects, the trial ruined me.
  This trial . . .

(*Screen: Pictures of* WHITE *as fire hero. Screen: "The Defense." Subliminal music. Lights up. Four character witnesses dressed as fire chief, police officer, fireman, City Supervisor (suit).*)

SHERRATT (*fire chief*): Dan White was an excellent firefighter. In fact, he was commended for a rescue at Geneva Towers. The award hasn't been given to him as yet, uh . . .

FREDIANI (*fireman*): Dan White was the valedictorian of the fire department class. He was voted so by members of the class.

(*Screen: Still of* WHITE *as valedictorian.*)

MILK'S FRIEND: When I was in the hospital, what galled me most was the picture of Dan White as the All-American Boy.

SHERRATT: but a meritorious advisory board and fire commission were going to present Mr. White with a Class C medal.

(*Screen: Still of* WHITE *as fire hero.*)

FREDIANI: Everybody liked Dan.

SCHMIDT: Did you work with Dan as a policeman?

SULLIVAN (*policeman*): Yes, I did.

MILK'S FRIEND: Maybe as a gay man, I understand the tyranny of the All-American Boy.

(*Screen: Still of* WHITE *as police officer.*)

FREDIANI: He loved sports and I loved sports.

(*Screen: Still of* WHITE *as Golden Gloves boxer.*)

SULLIVAN: Dan White as a police officer, was a very fair police officer on the street.

MILK'S FRIEND: Maybe because I am so often his victim.

GWENN: I followed the trial in the papers.

SCHMIDT: Having had the experience of being a police officer, is it unusual for persons that have been police officers to carry guns?

SULLIVAN: Uh, pardon me, Mr. Schmidt?

GWENN: I thought then something was wrong with this picture.

SCHMIDT: I say, is it uncommon that ex-police officers would carry guns?

GWENN: Something was wrong, we thought, when the Chief Inspector of Homicide became the chief character witness for the defense.

SULLIVAN: No, it is a common thing that former police officers will carry guns.

GWENN: Why didn't the Chief Inspector of Homicide ask Dan White how he got into City Hall with a loaded gun?

SCHMIDT: Without a permit?

SULLIVAN: Yes.

GWENN: White reloaded after shooting the Mayor. If it was "reflex," police training, why didn't he reload again after shooting Harvey Milk?

SCHMIDT: Is there anything in his character that would have led you to believe he was capable of shooting two persons?

NORMAN: Objection.

COURT: Overruled.

SULLIVAN: No, nothing whatever.

GWENN: And what can explain the coup de grace shots
White fired into the backs of their heads as they lay there
helpless on the floor?

DOLSON (*Supervisor*): Dan in my opinion was a person who *saved* lives.

GWENN: Where is the prosecution?

(*Pause.*)

FREITAS: I mean, I would have remained in politics. Except for this. I was voted out of office.

SCHMIDT (*to* DOLSON): Supervisor Dolson, you saw him on November 27, 1978, did you not?

DOLSON: I did.

FREITAS: In hindsight, you know, I would have changed a lot of things.

SCHMIDT: What did you see?

FREITAS: But hindsight is always perfect vision.

(*Screen: Still of* WHITE *as City Supervisor outside City Hall.*)

DOLSON: What I saw made me want to cry . . .
    Dan was always so neat.
    Looked like a marine on parade;
    and he made me feel ashamed of the way I usually looked,
    and here he was, this kid, who was badly disheveled,
    looking like he had been crying.

GWENN: What pressures were you under *indeed?*

DOLSON: and he had his hands cuffed behind him,
    which was something I never expected to see.
    He looked crushed, looked like he was absolutely *devastated*. (*Sobs.*)

GWENN: As the *"victim"* sat in the courtroom
    shielded by bulletproof glass,
    we heard of policemen and firemen sporting
    "Free Dan White" T-shirts
    as they raised 100,000 dollars for Dan White's defense fund,
    and the same message began appearing
    in spray paint on walls around the city.
    FREE DAN WHITE.

DOLSON: I put my arm around him, told him that everything
    was going to be all right,
    but how everything was going to be all right,
    I don't know. (*He is deeply moved.*)

(MARY ANN WHITE *sobs.*)

GWENN: And the trial was still happening,

SCHMIDT (*deeply moved*): Thank you. I have nothing further.

(DOLSON *sobs.*)

GWENN: but the tears at the Hall of Justice are all for Dan White.

(*All exit. Lights change.* FREITAS *alone in empty courtroom, nervous, fidgeting.*)

FREITAS: I was voted out of office.
    (*Screen:* "JOSEPH FREITAS, JR., *Former D.A.*")
    Well, I'm out of politics and I don't know whether
    I'll get back into politics
    because it certainly did set back my personal ah . . .
    aspirations as a public figure dramatically.
    I don't know . . .

    You know, there was an attempt to not allow our office to prosecute the case
    because I was close to Moscone myself.

And we fought against that.
I was confident—(*Laughs.*)
I chose Tom Norman because he was the senior homicide prosecutor
for twenty years and he was quite successful at it.
I don't know . . .

There was a great division in the city then, you know.
The city was divided all during that period.
George was a liberal Democrat and Dick Hongisto.
I was considered a liberal Democrat
and George as you'll remember was elected
Mayor over John Barbagelata who was the leader
of what was considered the Right in town.
And it was a narrow victory.
So, after his election, Barbagelata persisted in attacking them
and keeping
I thought—
keeping the city divided.
It divided on emerging constituencies like
the gay constituency.
That's the one that was used to cause the most divisive
emotions more than any other.
So the divisiveness in the city was there.

I mean that was the whole point of this political fight
between Dan White
and Moscone and Milk:
The fight was over who controlled the city.

The Right couldn't afford to lose Dan.
He was their swing vote on the Board of Supervisors.
He could block the Milk/Moscone agenda.
That was why Milk didn't want Dan White on the Board.
So, it was political, the murders.

Maybe I should have,
again in hindsight, possibly Tom,
even though his attempts to do that may have been ruled inadmissable,
possibly Tom should have been a little stronger in that area.
But again, at the time . . . I mean,
even the press was shocked at the outcome . . .

But—
Well, I think that what the jury had already bought
was White's background—
Now that's what was really on trial.
Dan White sat there and waved his little American flag
and they acquitted him.

They convicted George and Harvey.
Now if this had been a poor black or a poor Chicano
or a poor white janitor who'd been fired,
or the husband of an alleged girlfriend of Moscone's
I don't think they would have bought the diminished capacity defense.

But whereas they have a guy who was a member of a
county Board of Supervisors who left the police department,
who had served in the army, who was a fireman,
who played baseball—
I think that's what they were caught up in—
that kind of person *must* have been crazy to do this.
I would have interpreted it differently.
Not to be held to a higher standard, but uh . . .
that he had all the tools to be responsible.

One of the things people said was:
"Why didn't you talk more about George's background, his family life, etc.?"
Well . . .
One of the reasons is that Tom Norman did know that,
had he opened up that area,
they were prepared,
yeah—
they were prepared to smear George—
bring up the incident in Sacramento.
With the woman—
(And other things.)
It would be at best a wash,
so why get into it?
If you know they're going to bring out things
that aren't positive.
We wanted to let the city heal. We—
And after Jonestown . . .
Well—it would have been the
city on trial.

If the jury had stuck to the facts alone,
I mean, the confession alone was enough to convict him . . .
I mean, look at this kid that shot Reagan,
it was the same thing. All the way through that,
they said, my friends—
"Well, Christ, look at what the prosecutors went through on this one, Joe—
It's tragic that this has to be the kind of experience
that will make you feel better.

And then about White being anti-gay
well . . .

White inside himself may have been anti-gay, but
that Milk was his target . . .
As I say—*Malice was there.*
Milk led the fight to keep White off the Board,
which makes the murder all the more rational.
I know the gay community thinks the murder was anti-gay:
political in that sense. But
I think, they're wrong.

Ya know, some people—in the gay community—
ah—even said I threw the trial.
Before this, I was considered a great friend
to the gay community.
Why would I want to throw the trial,
this trial—
in an election year?

Oh, there were accusations you wouldn't believe . . .

At the trial, a woman . . . it may have been one of the jurors—
I can't remember . . .
Actually said—
"But what would Mary Ann White do without her husband?"
And I remember my outrage.
She never thought,
"What will Gina Moscone do without George?"
I must tell you that it's hard for me to talk about a lot
of these things,
all of this is just the—just
the tip of the iceberg . . .

We thought—Tommy and I—Tom Norman and I—
We thought it was an open-and-shut case
of first-degree murder.

(*Lights.*)

NORMAN: It wasn't just an automatic reaction when he fired those last two shots into George Moscone's *brains* was it, Doctor?

COURT: Let's move on, Mr. Norman. You are just arguing with the witnesses now.

NORMAN: Your Honor—

COURT: Let's move on.

(*Screen: "The Psychiatric Defense." Lights up. Psychiatrists, conservative dress, in either separate witness stands or a multiple stand unit.*)

SOLOMON: I think he was out of control and in an unreasonable stage. And I think if the gun had held, you know, maybe more bullets, maybe he would have shot more bullets. I don't know.

LUNDE: This wasn't just some mild case of the blues.

SOLOMON: I think that, you know, maybe Mr. Moscone would have been just as dead with one bullet. I don't know.

JONES: I think he was out of control.

DELMAN: Yes.

NORMAN: George Moscone was shot four times, Doctor. The gun had five cartridges in it. Does that change your opinion in any way?

SOLOMON: No. I think he just kept shooting for awhile.

(NORMAN *throws his notes down.*)

SCHMIDT: Now, there is another legal term we deal with in the courtroom, and that is variously called "malice" or "malice aforethought." And this must be present in order to convict for murder in the first degree.

JONES: Okay, let me preface this by saying I am not sure how malice is defined. I'll give you what my understanding is.
    In order to have malice, you would have to be able to do certain things: to be able to be intent to kill somebody unlawfully. You would have to be able to do something for a base and antisocial purpose. You would have to be aware of the duty imposed on you not to do that, not to unlawfully kill somebody or do something for a base, antisocial purpose, that involved a risk of death, and you would have to be able to act, despite having that awareness of that, that you are not supposed to do that, and so you would have to know that you are not supposed to do it, and then also act despite—keeping in mind that you are not supposed to do it.
    Is that your answer—your question?

SCHMIDT: I think so.

(*Pause.*)

JONES (*laughs*): I felt that he had the capacity to do the first three:
    that he had the capacity to intend to kill,
    but that doesn't take much, you know,
    to try to kill somebody,
    it's not a highfalutin' mental state.

    I think he had the capacity to do something for a base and antisocial purpose.
    I think he had the capacity to know that there was a duty
    imposed on him not to do that,
    but *I don't think he had the capacity to hold that notion
    in his mind while he was acting;*

so that I think that the depression,
plus the moment, the tremendous emotion of the moment,
with the depression,
reduced his capacity for conforming conduct.
(*Pause.*)
As ridiculous as this sounds, even to the point of instituting
to kill the Mayor,
what he describes is more simply—
is striking out, not intending to kill,
well, obviously, if you have a gun in your hand,
and you are striking out,
you know you are going to cause at least great bodily harm,
if not death,
but as near as I can come to the state of mind at that time,
he was just, you know, striking out.
(*Pause.*)
In fact, I asked him:
"Why didn't you hit them?"
And he was flabbergasted that I asked such a thing,
because it was contrary to his code of behavior,
you know, he was taken aback, kind of—
hit them seemed ridiculous to him—
because it would have been so unfair,
since he could have defeated them so easily
in a fistfight.

SCHMIDT: Thank you. (*He sits; to* NORMAN:) You may examine.

NORMAN: Doctor Jones, when let off at City Hall the accused was let off at the Polk Street entrance and then walked a block and a half to Van Ness Avenue. Why wouldn't he just enter City Hall through the main entrance?

JONES: He got towards the top of the stairs, then looked up, saw the metal detector and thought: "Oh, my goodness, I got that gun."

(*Pause.*)

NORMAN: Doctor, why would he care whether there was a metal detector there, and that a gun would have been discovered upon his person?

JONES: Well, I would presume that would mean some degree of hassle. I mean, I presume that the metal detector would see if somebody is trying to bring a weapon in.

NORMAN: That is usually why they have it. (*Pause.*) Did he realize at that time that he was unlawfully carrying a concealable firearm?

JONES: I presume so.

NORMAN: Dr. Jones, if it's a fact that Dan White shot George Moscone twice in the body, and that when George Moscone fell to the floor disabled, he shot twice more into the right side of George Moscone's head at a distance of between 12 and 18 inches, he made a decision at that time, didn't he, to either discharge the gun into the head of George Moscone, or not discharge the gun into the head of George Moscone?

JONES: If decision means he behaved in that way, then, yes.

NORMAN: Well, didn't he have to make some kind of choice based upon some reasoning process?

JONES: Oh, no, not based on reasoning necessarily. I think—I don't think that I— you know, great emotional turmoil in context of major mood disorder—he was enraged and anxious and frustrated in addition to the underlying depression, I think that after Moscone says "How's your family?" or "What's your wife going to do?" at that point, I think that it's—it's over.

NORMAN: It's over for George Moscone.

SOLOMON: I think that if you look at the gun as a transitional object, you can see that transitional objects are clung to in—in situations of great—of anxiety and insecurity, as one sees with children—

NORMAN: Doctor, are you telling us that a person who has lived an otherwise law-abiding life and an otherwise moral life could not premeditate and deliberate as is contemplated by the definition of first-degree murder?!

SOLOMON: I'm not saying that absolutely. Obviously, it's more difficult for a person who lives a highly moral life. And this individual, Dan White, had, if you want—a hypertrophy complex. Hypertrophy meaning overdeveloped. Rigidly. Morally. Overdeveloped—
But I would say in general, yes.
I don't think you'd even kill Mr. Schmidt if you lost this case.

NORMAN: It's unlikely.

SOLOMON: You may be very angry, but I don't think you will do it because I think you are probably a very moral and law-abiding citizen, and I think if you did it, I would certainly recommend a psychiatric examination, because I think there would be a serious possibility that you had flipped. (*Pause.*) It's most interesting to me how split off his feelings were at this time.

LUNDE: Dan White had classical symptoms that are described in diagnostic manuals for depression and, of course, he had characteristics of compulsive personality, which happens to be kind of a bad combination in those sorts of people.

NORMAN (*frustrated*): You are aware that he took a gun with him when he determined to see George Moscone, a loaded gun?

SOLOMON: Yes.

NORMAN: Why did he take that gun, in your opinion, Dr. Solomon?

SOLOMON: I might say that I think there are symbolic aspects to this.

COURT: Let's move on to another question.

NORMAN: Well, Your Honor . . .

COURT: Let's move on.

NORMAN (*frustrated*): All right. Dr. Delman, after he went in the building armed with a gun through a window and went up to see George Moscone, at the time he came in to see George Moscone, do you feel that he was angry with George Moscone?

DELMAN: Yes.

NORMAN: When George Moscone told him that he wasn't going to appoint him, do you think that that brought about and increased any more anger?

DELMAN: Yes.

NORMAN: All right. Now there was some point in there when he shot George Moscone, isn't that true?

DELMAN: Yes.

NORMAN: Do you know how many times he shot him?

DELMAN: I believe it's four.

NORMAN: Well, Doctor, do you put any significance upon the circumstances that he shot George Moscone twice in the head?

DELMAN: The question is, "Do I put any significance in it?"

NORMAN: Yes.

DELMAN: I really have no idea why that happened.

NORMAN: Well, Doctor, do you think he knew that if you shot a man twice in the head that it was likely to surely kill him?

DELMAN: I'm sure that he knew that shooting a man in the head would kill him, Mr. Norman.

NORMAN: Thank you! (*He sits.*)

SCHMIDT: But, it is your conclusion, Doctor, that Dan White could not premeditate or deliberate, within the meaning we have discussed here, on November 27, 1978?

DELMAN: That is correct.

(NORMAN *slaps hand to head. Lights.*)

BLINDER: I teach forensic psychiatry.
I teach about the uses and abuses of psychiatry in the judicial system.
The courts tend to place psychiatry in a position

where it doesn't belong. Where it becomes the sole arbiter
between guilt and innocence.
There is also a tendency in the stresses of the adversary system
to polarize a psychiatric statement so that a psychiatrist finds himself trying to
    put labels on normal stressful behavior,
and *everything* becomes a mental illness.
And I think that is an abuse.
(*Refers to his notes.*)
Dan White found City Hall rife of corruption.
With the possible exceptions of Dianne Feinstein and Harvey Milk,
the Supervisors seemed to make their judgments, their votes,
on the basis of what was good for them,
rather than what was good for the city.
And this was a very frustrating thing for Mr. White:
to want to do a good job for his constituents and find he
was continually defeated.

In addition to these stresses, there were
attacks by the press
and there were threats of literal attacks on Supervisors.
He told me a number of Supervisors like himself
carried a gun to scheduled meetings.
Never any relief from these tensions.

Whenever he felt things were not going right,
he would abandon his usual program of exercise and good nutrition
and start gorging himself on junk foods:
Twinkies, Coca-Cola.

Soon Mr. White was just sitting in front of the TV.
Ordinarily, he reads. (Mr. White has always been an identifiable Jack London
    adventurer.)

But now, getting very depressed about the fact he would not be reappointed,
he just sat there before the TV
binging on Twinkies.
(*Screen: "The Twinkie Defense."*)
He couldn't sleep.
He was tossing and turning on the couch in the living room
so he wouldn't disturb his wife on the bed.

Virtually no sexual contact at this time.
He was dazed, confused, had crying spells,
became increasingly ill,
and wanted to be left alone.

He told his wife:
"Don't bother cooking any food for me.
I will just munch on these potato chips."

Mr. White stopped shaving
and refused to go out of the house
to help Denise rally support.
He started to receive information that he would not be reappointed
from unlikely sources.
This was very stressing to him.

Again, it got to be cupcakes, candy bars.
He watched the sun come up on Monday morning.

Finally, at 9:00 Denise called.
He decides to go down to City Hall.
He shaves and puts on his suit.
He sees his gun—lying on the table.
Ammunition.
He simultaneously puts these in his pocket.
Denise picks him up.
He's feeling anxious about a variety of things.
He's sitting in the car hyperventilating,
blowing on his hands, repeating:
"Let him tell me to my face why he won't reappoint me.
Did he think I can't take it?
I am a man.
I can take it."

He goes down to City Hall, and I sense that time is short
so let me bridge this by saying that as I believe
it has been testified to,
he circumvents the mental *[sic]* detector,
goes to the side window,
gets an appointment with the Mayor.
The Mayor almost directly tells him,
"I am not going to reappoint you."

The Mayor puts his arm around him saying:
"Let's have a drink.
What are you going to do now, Dan?
Can you get back into the Fire Department?
What about your family?
Can your wife get her job back?
What's going to happen to them now?"

(*Pause. Lights up low on* MARY ANN WHITE.)

Somehow this inquiry directed to his family struck a nerve.
The Mayor's voice started to fade out and Mr. White felt
"As if I were in a dream."

He started to leave and then inexplicably turned around
and like a reflex
drew his revolver.
He had no idea how many shots he fired.

The similar event occurred
in Supervisor Milk's office. *[sic]*

He remembers being shocked by the sound of the gun
going off for the second time like a cannon.
He tells me that he was aware that he engaged in a lethal act,
but tells me he gave no thought to his wrongfulness.
As he put it to me:
"I had no chance to even think about it."

He remembers running out of the building,
driving, I think, to church,
making arrangements to meet his wife,
and then going from the church
to the Police Department.

(*Pause.* BLINDER *exhausted.*)

SCHMIDT: Doctor, you have mentioned the ingestion of sugar and sweets and that sort of thing. There are certain theories with regard to sugar and sweets and the ingestion thereof, and I'd like to just touch on that briefly with the jury. Does that have any significance, or could it possibly have any significance?

BLINDER (*turns to jury*): First, there is a substantial body of evidence that in susceptible individuals, large quantities of what we call junk food, high-sugar-content food with lots of preservatives, can precipitate antisocial and even violent behavior.

There have been studies, for example, where they have taken so-called career criminals and taken them off all their junk food and put them on meat and potatoes and their criminal records immediately evaporate. (*Pause.*) It's contradictory and ironic, but the way it works is that for such a person, the American Dream is a Nightmare. For somebody like Dan White.

SCHMIDT: Thank you, Doctor.

(*Lights fade on psychiatrists. Pause. Blazing white lights up on* MARY ANN WHITE. *She is almost blinded. She comes forward.*)

SCHMIDT: You are married to this man, is that correct?

MARY ANN: Yes.

SCHMIDT: When did you first meet him?

MARY ANN: I met him—(*Sobbing.*)

SCHMIDT: If you want to take any time//just let us know.

Note: // = overlap; next speaker starts, first speaker continues.

MARY ANN (*pulling herself together*): I met him in April, 1976 . . .

SCHMIDT: And you were married//and you took a trip?

MARY ANN: Yes. Yes, we went to Ireland on our honeymoon
  because Danny just had this feeling that Ireland was like a place
  that was just peaceful.

  He just really likes—loves—everything about Ireland and so we—(*Sobbing.*)

SCHMIDT: Excuse me.

MARY ANN: —so we went there//for about five wee—

SCHMIDT: During that period did you notice anything//unusual about his behavior?

MARY ANN: Yes, I mean, you know, when we went I thought—went thinking
  it was going to be kind of romantic,
  and when we got there, it was all of a sudden,
  he went into almost like a two-week-long mood,
  like I had seen before, but I had never seen one, I guess,
  all the way through,
  because when we were going out, I might see him for a day,
  and being a fireman, he would work a day,
  and then I wouldn't see him,
  and when we got to Ireland . . .

  I mean, I was just newly married and I thought:
  "What did I do?"

SCHMIDT: After he was on the Board, did you notice these moods//become more
  frequent?

MARY ANN: Yes, he had talked to me about how hard the job was on him.
  You know, from June he started to talk about how it was.
  Obviously you can sense when you are not sleeping together,
  and you are not really growing together,
  and he would say,
  "Well, I can't—I can't really think of anyone else
  when I don't even like myself."
  And I said, "It's just him.
  He's not satisfied with what I'm doing
  and I don't like myself//and so I can't . . ."

SCHMIDT: Did you see him on the morning of . . . November 27.

MARY ANN: Yes//I did.

SCHMIDT: And at that time did he indicate what he was going to do//that day?

MARY ANN: It was just, he was going to stay *home*.
  (*With uncharacteristic force.*) He wasn't leaving the house.

(*Beat.* SCHMIDT *looks to jury.*)

SCHMIDT: Later that morning, did you receive a call//to meet him somewhere?

MARY ANN: Yes. I did. Yes, I went to St. Mary's Cathedral.
  I went
  and I saw him
  and he walked over toward me and I—
  I could see that he had been crying,
  and I, I just kind of looked at him
  and he just looked at me
  and he said,
  he said,
  "I shot the Mayor and Harvey."

SCHMIDT: Thank you.

(DAN WHITE *sobs.* SCHMIDT *puts hand on* WHITE'S *shoulder.* MARY ANN WHITE *stumbles off the stand to her husband.* WHITE *shields his eyes. She looks as if she will embrace him.*)

SCHMIDT: The defense is prepared to rest at this time.

(MARY ANN WHITE *sobs. Hyperreal sound of high heels echoing on marble. Mumbled Hail Marys.*)

COURT: Let me admonish you ladies and gentlemen of the jury,
  not to discuss this case among yourselves nor with anyone else,
  nor to allow anyone to speak to you about the case,
  nor are you to form or express an opinion until the matter has been
    submitted to you.

(*All exit. Screen: "The Defense Rests."*)

*MILK'S FRIEND (*enters alone*):
  We got back from the airport the night of the twenty-seventh
  And my roommate said:
  There's going to be a candlelight march.
  By now, we thought it had to have reached City Hall.
  So we went directly there. From the airport to City Hall.
  And there were maybe seventy-five people there.
  And I remember thinking:
  My God is this all anybody . . . cared?

  Somebody said: No, the march hasn't gotten here yet.

  So we then walked over to Market Street,

---

*Dialogue from *The Times of Harvey Milk*, a film by Robert Epstein and Richard Schmeichen.

which was two or three blocks away.
And looked down it.
And Market Street runs in a straight line out to the Castro area.
And as we turned the corner,
there were people as wide as this wide street
As far as you could see.

(*Screens flooded with the lights of candles. Documentary footage of the march. We see what* MILK'S FRIEND *describes. Music: Barber Adagio. The entire company enters holding candles.*)

*YOUNG MOTHER (*after a long while*):
Thousands and thousands of people,
And that feeling of such loss.

(*Music continues.*)

*GWENN: It was one of the most eloquent expressions of a
community's response to violence
that I have ever seen . . .

A MOURNER (*black armband*): I'd like to read from the transcript of Harvey
Milk's political will.

(*Reads:*) This is Harvey Milk speaking on Friday, November 18.
This tape is to be played only in the event of my death
by assassination.

(*Screen: Pictures of* MILK.)

I've given long and considerable thought to this,
and not just since the election.
I've been thinking about this for some time prior to the election
and certainly over the years.
I fully realize that a person who stands for what I stand for—
a gay activist—
becomes a target for a person who is insecure, terrified,
afraid or very disturbed themselves.

(WHITE *enters, stops.*)

Knowing that I could be assassinated at any moment
or any time,
I feel it's important that some people should understand
my thoughts.
So the following are my thoughts, my wishes, my desires,
whatever.

*Dialogue from *The Times of Harvey Milk*, a film by Robert Epstein and Richard
Schmeichen.

I'd like to pass them on and played for the appropriate people.
The first and most obvious concern is that
if I was to be shot and killed,
the Mayor has the power,
George Moscone,

(*Screen: Pictures of* MOSCONE, *the funeral, the mourners, the widow.*)

of appointing my successor . . .
to the Board of Supervisors.
I cannot prevent some people
from feeling angry and frustrated and mad,
but I hope that they would not demonstrate violently.
If a bullet should enter my brain,
let that bullet destroy every closet door.

(*Gavel. All mourners blow out candles.* WHITE *sits. Blackout. Screen: "The People's Rebuttal." Screen: "*DR. LEVY, *Psychiatrist for the Prosecution." Lights up.*)

LEVY: I interviewed the defendant several hours after the shootings of November 27.
    In my opinion, one can get a more accurate diagnosis the closer one examines the suspect after a crime has been committed.
    At that time, it appeared to me that Dan White had no remorse for the death of George Moscone.
    It appeared to me, he had no remorse for the death of Harvey Milk.
    There was nothing in my interview which would suggest to me there was any mental disorder.
    I had the feeling that there was some depression but it was not depression that I would consider as a diagnosis.
    In fact, I found him to be less depressed than I would have expected him to be.
    At that time I saw him, it seemed that he felt himself to be quite justified. (*Looks to notes.*)
    I felt he had the capacity to form malice.
    I felt he had the capacity to premeditate. And . . .
    I felt he had the capacity to deliberate,
    to arrive at a course of conduct weighing considerations.

NORMAN: Did you review the transcript of the proceeding wherein the testimonies of Drs. Jones, Blinder, Solomon, Delman, and Lunde were given?

LEVY: Yes. (*Pause.*) I found nothing in them that would cause me to revise my opinion.

NORMAN: Thank you, Dr. Levy. (*Sits.*)

SCHMIDT (*stands*): Dr. Levy, are you a full professor at the University of California?

LEVY: No. I am an associate clinical professor.

(SCHMIDT *smiles, looks to jury.*)

SCHMIDT: May I inquire of your age, sir?

LEVY: I am fifty-five.

SCHMIDT: Huh. (*Picking up papers.*) Doctor, your report is dated November 27, 1978, is it not?

LEVY: Yes.

SCHMIDT: And yet the report was not written on November 27, 1978?

LEVY: No. It would have been within several days//of that time.

SCHMIDT: And then it was dated November 27, 1978?

LEVY: Yes.

SCHMIDT: Well, regardless of the backdating, or whatever, when did you come to your forensic conclusions?

LEVY: I'd say the conclusions would have been on November 27.

SCHMIDT: And that was after a two-hour talk with Dan White?

LEVY: Yes.

SCHMIDT: Doctor, would it be fair to say that you made some snap decisions?

LEVY: I don't believe//I did.

SCHMIDT: Did you consult with any other doctors?

LEVY: No.

SCHMIDT: Did you review any of the witnesses' statements?

LEVY: No.

SCHMIDT: Did you consult any of the material that was available to you, save and except for the tape of Dan White on the same date?

LEVY: No. That was all that was made available to me//at that time.

SCHMIDT: Now I don't mean to be facetious, but this is a fairly important case, is that fair?

LEVY: I would certainly think so,//yes.

SCHMIDT: But you didn't talk further with Mr. White?

LEVY: No. I was not requested to.

SCHMIDT: And you didn't request to talk to him further?

LEVY: No. I was not going to do a complete assessment.

SCHMIDT: Well, in fact, you didn't do a complete assessment, is that fair?

LEVY: I was not asked to do a complete assessment.

COURT: Doctor, you are fading away.

LEVY: *I was not asked to do a complete assessment.*

SCHMIDT: Thank you. (*Blackout. Commotion in court.*) She wants to tell the story so it's not responsive to the questions.

(*Lights up. Screen:* "SUPERVISOR CAROL RUTH SILVER, *Witness for the Prosecution.*")

SILVER (*very agitated, speaking fast, heated*): He asked in what other case did a dispute between Dan White and Harvey Milk arise! And it was the Polk Street closing was another occasion when Harvey requested that Polk Street, which is a heavily gay area in San Francisco, I am sure everybody knows, and on Halloween had traditionally had a huge number of people in costumes and so forth down there and has//traditionally been recommended for closure by the Police Department and—

SCHMIDT: I am going to object to this, Your Honor.

SILVER: It was recommended—

COURT: Just ask the next question.

SILVER: I am sorry.

NORMAN: Did Mr. Milk and Mr. White take positions that were opposite to each other?

SILVER: Yes.

NORMAN: Was there anything that became, well, rather loud and perhaps hostile in connection or consisting between the two?

SILVER: Not loud but very hostile. You have to first understand that this street closure was recommended by the Police Chief and had been done customarily in the years past//and is, was—came up as an uncontested issue practically.

SCHMIDT: Your Honor, I again—

COURT: Please, just make your objection.

SCHMIDT: I'd like to.

COURT: Without going through contortions.

SCHMIDT: There is an objection.

COURT: All right. Sustained.

NORMAN: Miss Silver, did you know, or did you ever see Mr. White to appear to be depressed or to be withdrawn?

SILVER: No.

NORMAN: Thank you. (*Sits.*)

(SILVER *flabbergasted, upset.*)

COURT: All right. Any questions, Mr. Schmidt?

SCHMIDT: Is it *Miss* Silver?

SILVER: Yes.

(SCHMIDT *looks to jury, smiles. Lights up on* MOSCONE'S FRIEND.)

SCHMIDT: Miss Silver, you never had lunch with Dan White, did you?

SILVER: Did I ever have lunch?

MOSCONE'S FRIEND: George was socially brilliant in that he could find the injustice.

SCHMIDT: I mean the two of you?

SILVER: I don't recall having done so//but I—

MOSCONE'S FRIEND: His mind went immediately to what can we do?

SCHMIDT: Did you socialize frequently?

MOSCONE'S FRIEND: What can we practically do?

SILVER: No, when his son was born//I went to a party at his house and that kind of thing.

SCHMIDT: Did Mr. Norman contact you last week, or did you contact him?

MOSCONE'S FRIEND: Rather like the image of Robert Kennedy in Mississippi in 1964.

SILVER: On Friday morning I called his office to—

MOSCONE'S FRIEND: Y'know, he'd never seen that kind of despair before

SILVER: because I was reading the newspaper—

SCHMIDT: Yes.

MOSCONE'S FRIEND: but when he saw it//he said,

SILVER: And it appeared to me that—

COURT: Don't tell us!

MOSCONE'S FRIEND: "This is *intolerable.*"

SILVER: I am sorry.

MOSCONE'S FRIEND: And then he did something about it.

(*Beat.*)

COURT: The jurors are told not to read the newspaper, and I am hoping that they haven't//read the newspapers.

SILVER: I apologize.

COURT: Okay.

SCHMIDT: Miss Silver—

COURT: I am sorry, I didn't want to cut her off—

SILVER: No, I understand.

COURT: from any other answer.

SCHMIDT: I think she did complete the answer, Judge. In any event, you contacted Mr. Norman, did you not?

SILVER: Yes, I did.

SCHMIDT: And at that time, you offered to Mr. Norman to round up people who could say that Dan White never looked depressed at City Hall, is that fair?

SILVER: That's right. Well, I offered to testify to that effect and I suggested that there were other people//who could similarly testify to that fact.

SCHMIDT: In fact, you expressed it though you haven't sat here and listened to the testimony in this courtroom?

SILVER: No, I have never been here before Friday when I was subpoenaed//and spent some time in the jury room.

SCHMIDT: But to use your words, after having read what was in the paper, you said that the defense sounded like (*as if he were spitting on his mother's grave*) "bullshit" to you?

SILVER: That's correct.

(*Subliminal music.*)

DENMAN: I thought I would be a chief witness for the prosecution.

SCHMIDT: Would that suggest then that perhaps you have a bias in this case?

DENMAN: What was left unsaid was what the trial should have been about.

SILVER: I certainly have a bias.

SCHMIDT: You are a political enemy of Dan White's, is that fair?

SILVER: No, that's not true.

DENMAN: Before, y'know, there was a lot of talk about assassinating the Mayor among thuggish elements of the//Police Officers Association.

SCHMIDT: Did you have any training in psychology or psychiatry?

DENMAN: And those were the cops Dan White was closest to.

SILVER: No more than some of the kind of C.E.B. courses lawyer's psychology for lawyers//kind of training.

DENMAN: I think he knew a lot of guys would think he did the right thing and yeah they would make him a hero.

SCHMIDT: I mean, would you be able to diagnose, say, *manic depression depressed type*, or could you distinguish that from *unipolar depression*?

SILVER: No.

(*Pause.*)

DENMAN: I was Dan White's jailer for seventy-two hours after the assassinations.

SCHMIDT: Did you ever talk to him about his dietary habits or anything like that?

DENMAN: There were no tears.

SILVER: I remember a conversation about nutrition or something like that, but I can't remember//the substance of it.

SCHMIDT: I don't have anything further.

DENMAN: There was no shame.

COURT: Any redirect, Mr. Norman?

NORMAN: Yes.

DENMAN: You got the feeling that he knew exactly what he was doing and there was no remorse.

(*Pause.*)

NORMAN: Miss Silver, you were asked if you had a bias in this case. You knew Harvey Milk very well and you liked him, didn't you?

SILVER: I did; and also George Moscone.

NORMAN: Miss Silver, speaking of a bias, had you ever heard the defendant say anything about getting people of whom Harvey Milk numbered himself?

(*Lights up on* MILK'S FRIEND.)

SILVER: In the Polk Street debate—

MILK'S FRIEND: The night Harvey was elected,
    I went to bed early
    because it was more happiness than I had been taught
    to deal with.

SILVER: Dan White got up and gave—
    a long diatribe—

MILK'S FRIEND: Next morning we put up signs saying "Thank You."

SILVER: Just a—a very unexpected and very uncharacteristic of Dan,
    long hostile speech about how gays and their lifestyles
    had to be contained and we can't//
    encourage this kind of thing and—

SCHMIDT: I am going to object to this, Your Honor.

COURT: Sustained, okay.

MILK'S FRIEND: During that, Harvey came over and told me
    that he had made a political will
    because he expected he'd be killed.
    And then in the same breath, he said (I'll never forget it):
    "It works, it works . . ."

NORMAN: All right . . . that's all.

MILK'S FRIEND: The system works// . . .

NORMAN: Thank you.

(*Pause.*)

DENMAN: When White was being booked, it all seemed fraternal.
    One officer gave Dan a pat on the behind when he was booked,
    sort of a "Hey, catch you later, Dan" pat.

COURT: Any recross?

DENMAN: Some of the officers and deputies were standing around with half-smirks
    on their faces. Some were actually laughing.

SCHMIDT: Just a couple.

DENMAN: The joke they kept telling was,
    "Dan White's mother says to him when he comes home,
    'No, dummy, I said milk and baloney, not Moscone!'"

(*Pause.*)

SCHMIDT: Miss Silver, you are a part of the gay community also, are you?

SILVER: Myself?

SCHMIDT: Yes.

SILVER: You mean, am I gay?

SCHMIDT: Yes.

SILVER: No, I'm not.

SCHMIDT: I have nothing further.

MOSCONE'S FRIEND: George would have said, "This is intolerable," and he'd have done something about it.

COURT: All right. . . . You may leave as soon as the bailiff takes the microphone off.

(SILVER *sits for awhile, shaken.*)

COURT: Next witness, please.

DENMAN: I don't know . . .
All I can say is, if Dan White was as depressed
as the defense psychiatrists said he was before he went to City Hall,
then shooting these people sure seemed to clear up his mind . . .

(SILVER *exits toward door.* LU *with TV lights.*)

LU (*on camera*): Miss Silver, Supervisor Silver, would you like to elaborate on Mr. White's anti-gay feelings or hostility to Harvey Milk or George Moscone?

SILVER: No comment, right now.

(SILVER *distraught, pushes through crowd, rushes past.*)

LU (*on camera*): Did you feel you were baited, did you have your say?

SILVER (*blows up*): I said I have no comment at this time!!! (*Exits.*)

COURT: Mr. Norman? Next witness?

NORMAN: Nothing further. Those are all the witnesses we have to present.

COURT: The People rest?

NORMAN: Yes.

COURT: Does the Defense have any witnesses?

SCHMIDT (*surprised*): Well, we can discuss it, Your Honor. I am not sure there is anything to rebut.

(*Lights. Commotion in court. Screen: "The People Rest." Lights up on* SCHMIDT *at a lectern, a parish priest at a pulpit. Screen: "Summations."*)

SCHMIDT (*in a sweat, going for the home stretch*):
I'm nervous. I'm very nervous.
I sure hope I say all the right things.

I can't marshall words the way Mr. Norman can—
But—I believe strongly in things.

Lord God! I don't say to you to forgive Dan White.
I don't say to you to just
let Dan White walk out of here a free man.
He is guilty.
But the degree of responsibility is the issue here.
The state of mind is the issue here.
It's not who was killed; it's why.
It's not who killed them; but why.
The state of mind is the issue here.

Lord God! The pressures.
Nobody can say that the things that happened to him
days or weeks preceding
wouldn't make a reasonable and ordinary man
at least mad,
angry in some way.

Surely—surely, that had to have arisen, not to kill,
not to kill, just to be mad, to act irrationally,
because if you kill, when you are angry, or under the heat of passion,
if you kill, then the law will punish you,
and you will be punished by God—
God will punish you,
but the law will also punish you.

Heat of passion fogs judgment, makes one act irrationally,
in the very least,
and my God,
that is what happened at the very least.

Forget about the mental illness,
forget about all the rest of the factors that came into play
at the same time:
Surely he acted irrationally, impulsively—out of some passion.

Now . . . you will recall at the close of the prosecution's case,
it was suggested to you this was a calm, cool, deliberating,
terrible terrible person
that had committed two crimes like these,
and these are terrible crimes,
and that he was emotionally stable at that time
and there wasn't anything wrong with him.

He didn't have any diminished capacity.
Then we played these tapes he made directly after

he turned himself in at Northern Station.
My God,
that was not a person that was calm and collected and cool
and able to weigh things out.
It just wasn't.

The tape just totally fogged me up the first time I heard it.
It was a man that was, as Frank Falzon said, broken.
Shattered.
This was not the Dan White that everybody had known.

Something happened to him and he snapped.
That's the word I used in my opening statement.
Something snapped here.

The pot had boiled over here,
and people that boil over in that fashion,
they tell the truth.

Have the tape played again, if you can't remember what was said.
He said in no uncertain terms,

"My God,
why did I do these things?
What made me do this?
How on earth could I have done this?
I didn't intend to do this.
I didn't intend to hurt anybody.
My God,
what happened to me?
Why?"

Play the tape.
If everybody says that tape is truthful, play the tape.
I'd agree it's truthful.

With regard to the reloading and some of these little
discrepancies that appeared to come up.
I am not even sure of the discrepancies, but if there were
discrepancies,
listen to it in context.
(*Picks up transcript, reads.*)
"Where did you reload?"
"I reloaded in my office, I think."
"And then did you leave the Mayor's office?"
"Yes, then I left the Mayor's office."

That doesn't mean anything to me at all.
It doesn't mean anything to me at all.

And I don't care where the reloading took place!

But listen to the tape.
It says in no uncertain terms,
"I didn't intend to hurt anybody.
I didn't intend to do this.
Why do we do things?"
I don't know.
It was a man desperately trying to grab at something . . .

"What happened to me?
How could I have done this?"

If the District Attorney concedes
that what is on that tape is truthful,
and I believe that's the insinuation we have here,
then, by golly,
there is voluntary manslaughter,
nothing more and nothing less.

Now, I don't know what more I can say.
He's got to be punished
and he will be punished.
He's going to have to live with this for the rest of his life.
His child will live with it
and his family will live with it,
and God will punish him,
and the law will punish him,
and they will punish him severely.

But please, please.
Just justice.
That's all.
Just justice here.
(*He appears to break for a moment.*)
Now I am going to sit down and very soon,
and that's it for me.

And this is the type of case where, I suppose,
I don't think Mr. Norman is going to do it,
but you can make up a picture of a dead man,
or two of them for that matter,
and you can wave them around and say
somebody is going to pay for this
and somebody *is* going to pay for this.

Dan White is going to pay for this.
But it's not an emotional type thing.

I get emotional about it, but
you can't because you have to be objective about the facts . . .

I get one argument.
I have made it.
And if I could get up and argue again,
God,
we'd go on all night.

I just hope that—
I just hope that you'll come to the same conclusion
that I have come to.
And thank you for listening to me.

(SCHMIDT *holds the lectern, then sits.*)

NORMAN: Ladies and gentlemen of the jury, having the burden of proof,
I am given an opportunity a second time to address you.

I listened very carefully to the summation just given you.
It appears to me, members of the jury,
to be a very facile explanation and rationalization
as to premeditation and deliberation.
The evidence that has been laid before you
screams for murder in the first degree.

What counsel for the defense has done is suggest to you
to *excuse* this kind of conduct and call it something that it isn't,
to call it voluntary manslaughter.

Members of the jury, you are the triers of fact here.
You have been asked to hear this tape recording again.
The tape recording has been aptly described
as something very moving. We all feel a sense of sympathy,
a sense of empathy for our fellow man, but you are not to let
sympathy influence you in your judgment.

To reduce the charge of murder to something less—
to reduce it to voluntary manslaughter—
means you are saying that this was not murder.
That this was an intentional killing of a human being
upon a quarrel, or heat of passion.
But ladies and gentlemen,
that quarrel must have been so extreme
at the time
that the defendant could not—
was incapable of forming
those qualities of thought which are
malice, premeditation, and deliberation.

But the evidence in this case doesn't suggest that at all.
Not at all.

If the defendant had picked up a vase or something
that happened to be in the Mayor's office
and hit the Mayor over the head and killed him
you know,
you know that argument for voluntary manslaughter
might be one which you could say the evidence admits
a reasonable doubt. But—

Ladies and gentlemen:
The facts are:
It was *he*—Dan White—who brought the gun to City Hall.
The gun was not there.
It was *he* who brought the extra cartridges for the gun;
they were not found there.

He went to City Hall and when he got there
he went to the Polk Street door.

There was a metal detector there.
He knew he was carrying a gun.
He knew that he had extra cartridges for it.

Instead of going through the metal detector,
he *decided* to go around the corner.
He was capable at that time of expressing anger.
He was capable of, according to the doctor—
well, parenthetically, members of the jury,
I don't know how they can look in your head and tell you
what you are able to do. But—
They even said that he was capable of knowing at that time
that if you pointed a gun at somebody and you fired that gun
that you would surely kill a person.
He went around the corner,
and climbed through a window into City Hall.

He went up to the Mayor's office.
He appeared, according to witnesses,
to act calmly in his approach, in his speech.

He chatted with Cyr Copertini;
he was capable of carrying on a conversation
to the extent that he was able to ask her how she was,
after having asked to see the Mayor.
(*Looks to audience.*)
He stepped into the Mayor's office.

After some conversation,
he shot the Mayor twice in the body.
Then he shot the Mayor in the head twice
while the Mayor was disabled on the floor.
The evidence suggests that in order to shoot the Mayor
twice in the head
he had to *lean down* to do it.
(*He demonstrates, looks to jury.*)
Deliberation is premeditation.
It has malice.
I feel stultified to even bring this up.
This is the *definition* of murder.

He reloaded the gun.
Wherever he reloaded the gun,
it was *he* who reloaded it!

He did see Supervisor Milk
whom he knew was acting against his appointment
and he was capable of expressing anger in that regard.

He entered the Supervisors' area
(a block from the Mayor's office across City Hall)
and was told, "Dianne wants to see you."
He said, "That is going to have to wait a moment,
I have something to do first."

Then he walked to Harvey Milk's office,
put his head in the door and said,
"Can I see you a moment, Harv?"
The reply was, "Yes."

He went across the hall and put three bullets
into Harvey Milk's body,
one of which hit Harvey directly in the back.
When he fell to the floor disabled,
two more were delivered to the back of his head.

Now what do you call that but premeditation and deliberation?
What do you call that realistically
but a cold-blooded killing?
Two *cold-blooded executions.*
It occurs to me that if you don't call them that,
then you are ignoring the objective evidence
and the objective facts here.

Members of the jury, there are circumstances here
which no doubt bring about anger,

maybe even rage, I don't know,
but the manner in which that anger was felt
and was handled
is *socially something that cannot be approved.*

Ladies and gentlemen,
the quality of your service is reflected in your verdict.

(NORMAN *sits.* JOANNA LU, *at door, stops* SCHMIDT. *TV lights.*)

LU (*on camera*): Mr. Schmidt, do you—

SCHMIDT: Yes.

LU (*on camera*): Do you feel society would feel justice is served if the jury returns two manslaughter verdicts?

SCHMIDT (*wry smile*): Society doesn't have anything to do with it. Only those twelve people in the jury box.

COURT: Ladies and gentlemen of the jury,
Now that you have heard the evidence,
we come to that part of the trial where you are instructed
on the applicable law.

In the crime of murder of the first degree
the necessary concurrent mental states are:
Malice aforethought, premeditation, and deliberation.

In the crime of murder of the second degree,
the necessary concurrent mental state is:
Malice aforethought.

In the crime of voluntary manslaughter,
the necessary mental state is:
An intent to kill.

Involuntary manslaughter is an unlawful killing without malice aforethought
and without intent to kill.

The law does not undertake to limit or define the kinds of passion
which may cause a person to act rashly.
Such passions as desperation, humiliation, resentment,
anger, fear, or rage,
or any other high-wrought emotion . . .
can be sufficient to reduce the killings to manslaughter
so long as they are sufficient to obscure the reason
and render the average man likely to act rashly.

There is no malice aforethought
if the killing occurred upon a sudden quarrel
or heat of passion.

There is no malice aforethought
if the evidence shows that due to diminished capacity
caused by illness, mental defect, or intoxication,
the defendant did not have the capacity
to form the mental state constituting malice aforethought,
even though the killing was intentional,
voluntary, premeditated, and unprovoked.

(*A siren begins. Screen: Images of the riot at City Hall—broken glass, cop cars burning, riot police, angry faces. Audio: Explosions.*)

GWENN (*on video*): In order to understand the riots, I think you have to understand that the Dan White verdict did not occur in a vacuum—

COURT: Mr. Foreman, has the jury reached verdicts//in this case?

GWENN: that there were and are other factors which contribute to a legitimate rage that was demonstrated dramatically at our symbol of Who's Responsible, City Hall.

(*Screen: Images of City Hall being stormed. Line of police in riot gear in front.*)

FOREMAN: Yes, it has, Your Honor.

GWENN: The verdict came down and the people rioted.

COURT: Please read the verdicts.

GWENN: The people stormed City Hall, burned police cars.

(SCREEN: *Image of City Hall. Line of police cars in flames.*)

FOREMAN (*reading*): The jury finds the defendant Daniel James White guilty of violating Section 192.1 of the penal code.

GWENN: Then the police came into our neighborhood. And the police rioted.

FOREMAN: Voluntary manslaughter, for the slaying of Mayor George Moscone.

(MARY ANN WHITE *gasps.* DAN WHITE *puts head in hands. Explosion.* RIOT POLICE *enter.*)

GWENN: The police came into the Castro and assaulted gays.
They stormed the Elephant Walk Bar.
One kid had an epileptic seizure and was almost killed for it.
A cop drove a motorcycle up against a phone booth
where a lesbian woman was on the phone,
blocked her exit
and began beating her up.

COURT: Is this a unanimous verdict of the jury?

FOREMAN: Yes, it is, Judge.

Gwenn (*off video*): I want to talk about when people are pushed to the wall.

COURT: Will each juror say "yea"//or "nay"?

(*Violence on stage.*)

YOUNG MOTHER: What about the children?

MOSCONE'S FRIEND: I know who George offended.
I know who Harvey offended.

JURORS (*on tape*): Yea, yea, yea//yea, yea, yea.

MOSCONE'S FRIEND: I understand the offense.

YOUNG MOTHER: What do I tell my kids?

GWENN: Were the ones who are responsible seeing these things?

YOUNG MOTHER: That in this country you serve more time for robbing a bank than
for killing two people?

JURORS (*on tape*): Yea, yea, yea//yea, yea, yea.

GWENN: Hearing these things?

MILK'S FRIEND: I understand the offense.

GWENN: Do they understand about people being pushed to the wall?

YOUNG MOTHER: Accountability?

(*Yea's end.*)

MILK'S FRIEND: Assassination.
I've grown up with it.
I forget it hasn't always been this way.

YOUNG MOTHER: What do I say?
That two lives are worth seven years and eight months//in jail?

MILK'S FRIEND: I remember coming home from school in sixth grade—
JFK was killed—
six years later, Martin Luther King.
It's a frame of reference.

(*Explosion.*)

COURT: Will the foreman please read the verdict for the second count?

DENMAN: It's a divided city.

MOSCONE'S FRIEND: The resentment of change is similar. I can understand that.
It's my hometown. (*Irish accent.*) They're changin' it, y'know?

DENMAN: The people were getting caught up in the change
and didn't know.

MOSCONE'S FRIEND: You grew up in old Irish Catholic//San Francisco . . .

DENMAN: They didn't know why it was—
    like Armageddon.

MOSCONE'S FRIEND: and Bill Malone ran the town and "these guys"
    are disruptin' everything.

FOREMAN: The jury finds the defendant Daniel James White guilty of Section 192.1
    of the penal code, voluntary manslaughter, in the slaying of Supervisor Harvey
    Milk.

(DAN WHITE *gasps.* MARY ANN WHITE *sobs.* NORMAN, *flushed, head in hands.*
Explosions. Violence ends. RIOT POLICE *control the crowd.* TV *lights.*)

BRITT (*on camera*): No—I'm optimistic about San Francisco.

COURT: Is this a unanimous decision by the jury?

FOREMAN: Yes, Your Honor.

BRITT: I'm Harry Britt. I was Harvey Milk's successor.

CARLSON: If he'd just killed the Mayor, he'd be in jail today.

YOUNG MOTHER: To this jury, Dan White was their son.

MILK'S FRIEND: Harvey Milk lit up my universe.

YOUNG MOTHER: What are we teaching our sons?

(WHITE *raises his hands to his eyes, cries.* MARY ANN WHITE, *several jurors sob.*)

BRITT: Now, this is an example I don't use often because
    people will misunderstand it.
    But when a prophet is killed . . .
    It's up to those who are left
    to build the community or the church.

MOSCONE'S FRIEND: Dan White believed in the death penalty;
    he should have gotten the death penalty.

YOUNG MOTHER: How do you explain//the difference?

BRITT: But I have hope and as Harvey said,
    "You can't live without hope."

MOSCONE'S FRIEND: I mean, that son of a bitch//killed somebody I loved.

MILK'S FRIEND: It was an effective//assassination.

MOSCONE'S FRIEND: I loved the guy.

(*Pause.*)

MILK'S FRIEND: They always are.

GWENN (*quiet*): Do they know about Stonewall?

BRITT: Our revenge is never to forget.

(*The* FOREMAN *walks to the defense table, gives* SCHMIDT *a handshake.* NORMAN *turns away.*)

LU (*on camera*): Dan White was examined by the psychiatrist at the state prison. They decided against therapy. Dan White had no apparent signs of mental disorder. . . . Dan White's parole date was January 6, 1984. When Dan White left Soledad prison on January 6, 1984, it was five years, one month, and eight days since he turned himself in at Northern Station after the assassinations of Mayor George Moscone and Supervisor Harvey Milk. Mayor Dianne Feinstein, the current mayor of San Francisco, has tried to keep Dan White out of San Francisco during his parole for fear he will be killed.

(*The* COP *enters.* SISTER BOOM BOOM *enters.*)

BOOM BOOM: Dan White! It's 1984 and Big Sister is watching you.

LU (*on camera*): Dan White reportedly plans to move to Ireland after his release.

MOSCONE'S FRIEND: What do you do with your feelings of revenge?
    With your need for retribution?

BRITT: We will never forget.

(*Screen: Riot images freeze. A shaft of light from church window.*)

BOOM BOOM: I would like to close with a reading from the Book of Dan. (*Opens book.*) Take of this and eat, for this is my defense. (*Raises a Twinkie. Eats it. Exits.*)

LU (*on camera*): Dan White was found dead of carbon monoxide poisoning on October 21, 1985 at his wife's home in San Francisco, California.

(*Lights change.* DAN WHITE *faces the* COURT.)

COURT: Mr. White, you are sentenced to seven years and eight months, the maximum sentence for these two counts of voluntary manslaughter. The Court feels that these sentences for the taking of life is completely inappropriate but that was the decision of the legislature.

Again, let me repeat for the record:
Seven years and eight months is the maximum sentence
for voluntary manslaughter, and this is the law.

(*Gavel. Long pause.* WHITE *turns to the audience/jury.*)

WHITE: I was always just a lonely vote on the Board.
    I was just trying to do a good job for the city.

(*Long pause. Audio: Hyperreal sounds of high heels on marble. Mumbled Hail Marys. Rustle of an embrace.* SISTER BOOM BOOM *enters. Taunts* POLICE. POLICE *raise riot shields. Blackout. Screen: "Execution of Justice." Gavel echoes.*)

THE WELL OF HORNINESS

by
Holly Hughes

FOR
my sister

AUTHOR'S NOTE

Let me just say I never had any aspirations of a thespian nature; this script was somewhat of an accident. What led to the writing was this: economic desperation, and too many Bloody Marys. I seem to remember someone daring me to write a lesbian porno screenplay. All of a sudden there was a producer on the scene, plus all of those hangers-on associated with the cinema: directors, best boys, and would-be gaffers. And they were drinking Bloody Marys, too. We drank a toast to a project that we hoped would be the cinematic equivalent of the Pet Rock. In other words, a scam to keep us in cheeseburgers 'til we took that final bow. There was to be no "art" involved. Instead, what I came up with was *The Well of Horniness*. Gone were the producers, etc., and hopes of the big score. Now I'm older, no wiser, but infinitely more pretentious. The moral: Never drink and type.

The Well of Horniness was first staged at the WOW Café. The stage was linguini-shaped, with the narrowest part of the noodle facing downstage. The narrator, dressed as a cub reporter and sweating profusely, was downstage left throughout the piece. Other actors entered and exited through a window that led into the adjacent kitchen or into the broken piano we neglected to remove from the stage. This sounds more interesting than it actually was. Staging was early sixties soap opera. All of the actors screamed on "the Well . . ." This is the best part of the play, so I advise all future productions to exploit it to the fullest. All of the performers were, and still are as far as I know, women. I'm pretty tough about this part. No men in *The Well*, okay? I don't care if you're doing a staged reading in Crib Death, Iowa—no men. And don't think I won't know about it. My spies are everywhere. But there's a plus: academic types just love this kind of stuff—cross-dressing, women playing men. It's your entree into avant-garde circles, if you don't mind walking in circles.

The Well of Horniness had another life as a live radio show produced by Janee Pipik for WBAI radio in New York City. After that, I began to present the show as a radio play, with actors performing all of the sound effects live. This seemed to be quite popular with the audience, as well as relieving the cast of the odious task of learning lines. Occasionally the cast should break into frenetic sexual activity, such as the spaghetti dinner scene, or major catfights, as in the beginning of "In the Realm of the Senseless." I have presented this play with as many as ten performers and as few as three. I would not recommend it as a one-woman show, unless of course that one woman happens to be Sally Field.

The Well of Horniness was originally presented on March 3, 1983, at the WOW Café, New York City. It was directed by the author. The acting coach was Lois Weaver. The cast was:

NARRATOR	Peggy Shaw
GEORGETTE/DINETTE/AL DENTE	Alina Troyano
ROD/MARGARET DUMONT	Maureen Angelos
VICKI	Holly Hughes
BABS	Helen Frankenthal

WAITRESS/RANGER   Sally White

GARNET MCCLIT   Sharon Jane Smith

This show went through many permutations (not to mention casts), in the process exploiting the following people: Susan Young, Reno, Rebecca High, Janee Pipik, Laura Lanfranchi, Mindy Mitchell, Robin Epstein, Claire Moed, Ela Troyano, Uzi Parnes, Lisa Kron, Deborah Margolin, and many more.

PART ONE

NARRATOR: Finally, the story they said couldn't be told shatters the airwaves! Brought to you by House of Shag 'N' Stuff, where tomorrow's carpets are here today, and by Clams A-Go-Go of Passaic, where our motto is: "Shellfish is a swell dish!" Happy housewives know that when it comes to eating out, nine out of ten men think of one thing:

MAN #1: Give me fish!

MAN #2: I want filet!

NARRATOR: And remember! We deliver! When you're thinking of sending something special to that special someone, why not say it with fish!

(Knock, door opening.)

WOMAN: Yes?

DELIVERY BOY: Three shrimp dinners!

WOMAN: I didn't order any shrimp dinners. . . . This must be somebody's idea of a sick joke! *(Door slam.)*

NARRATOR: Yes! That's exactly right! It's the Well—

(Cast screams.)

NARRATOR: —of Horniness! The continuing saga of one woman's sojourn in the septic tank *(toilet flush)* of the soul!

LOUISE: Harold! Come over here! Right this minute!

HAROLD: What is it, Louise?

LOUISE: It's those two new girls on the block, Harold, something about the way they walk, something about the way they talk . . . something about the way they look . . . at each other. . . . Harold, I could swear they're Lebanese! *(Theme from "Twilight Zone.")*

HAROLD: You're just imagining things, Louise. They're just a couple of sorority girls.

NARRATOR: Have we got news for you, Harold. Those two girls are members of the Tridelta Tribads, an alleged sorority, but in reality just a thinly veiled entrance to the Well *(scream)* of Horniness! The setting, a peaceful New England town, just a town like many others, a town that clasped American values to her bosom! *(Baby crying.)* An American town—where every winter day is a white Christmas *(humming "White Christmas")* and every Wednesday night is Prince Spaghetti Night! *(Female voice calls: "Anthony!")* Just a town, a town like many

*NOTE: Stage directions throughout refer to sound effects unless otherwise indicated.

others with its local pubs and taverns. (*Cork pop.* WAITER's *voice:* "Monsieur, ze Blue Nun, ze 1979!") And dinner theatres where tone deaf emcees flourish and where the citizens can go to meet or cheat that someone special. But beneath the apparently serene breast of new-fallen snow, a whirlpool rages. . . . (*sucking noises*) sucking the weak, the infirm, the original, and all others who don't wear beige down . . . down, down. As carrots in the Cuisinart . . . (*blender*) so are souls in the Well (*scream*) of Horniness! Meet Georgette. (*Phone dialing.*)

GEORGETTE: Hello, White Casa? The usual. You know the way I like it—extra hot.

NARRATOR: Coming from one of the town's most established families, her pedigree was unblemished except for a drop of Catholic blood on her mother's side of the family. But underneath the cloak of respectability, evil budded in her bosom. By the time she had pledged her college sorority, Georgette had already fallen into the Well (*scream*) of Horniness! And Vicki, the town's leading Excedrin consumer:

VICKI: Darn these childproof tops!

NARRATOR: A recent emigrée to this town like many others, she came to this quiet hamlet to forget. By day she clips coupons (*scissors*) and attends Aquacise classes. By night she prays for amnesia. Few would guess this well-groomed word-processing trainee was once of the sisterhood of sin. The memories gnaw at her mind like starving hamsters in a Kleenex box. (*Scratching.*) Is there any hope for Vicki? Is there any hope for anyone once they've fallen into the Well (*scream*) of Horniness? And here's Rod:

ROD: Honey, I'm home! Hey, hey, hey, whatcha got for me? (*Glasses clinking.*)

VICKI: I made some Harvey Wallbangers!

NARRATOR: Vicki's fiancée, Georgette's brother Rod, once had dreams of becoming a golf pro. But like many young men of his milieu, his youthful idealism was trampled by his drive for success. The punch bowl from his graduation open-house was barely drained when he became a VP in the family business—a chain of discount carpet warehouses. Rod and Vicki—on the surface just a couple of lovebirds (*kiss*) about to tie the knot! (*Choking sounds.*) Then our happy couple makes a date with destiny. (*Theme from "Jeopardy."*)

ROD: Hey, Vick, whaddya say to a little R'N'R?

VICKI: Uh, okay.

ROD: Why don't I give my sister Georgette a ring? I been dying for the two of you to meet.

VICKI: Oh, Rod, I really don't feel up to a crowd.

ROD: What's a crowd? She's family. Besides, you'll love her and (*snaps his fingers*) come to think of it . . . you two were in different chapters of the same sorority!

VICKI: What did you say, dear?

ROD: The same sorority . . . the Tridelta Tribads. Come on, Vick, I remember how you loved that club and those gals!

VICKI: You don't understand, I can never see those women again.

ROD: So who says you have to mention the sorority at all . . . you'll be gabbing about color swatches and floor buffers. Why in no time at all you'll be bosom buddies. (*Rod picks up telephone.*)

VICKI: Now I'll never be able to keep the secret of my past from him—those so-called sorority sisters!

NARRATOR: Vicki—a would-be word-processor with a past she can't outrun!

VICKI: I can't believe his sister is one of *them!* They are . . . everywhere!

NARRATOR: Later that night, Rod and Vicki arrive at the fabulous new dinner theater, The Vixen's Den, where Georgette is already waiting.

BABS: Miss, you're gonna have to check that—oh, haven't seen you in a while.

GEORGETTE: Oh, hi, how ya doing.

BABS: Since when do you care? Oh, sorry . . . it's just that . . . I thought . . . I mean . . . after we spent . . . together . . . it was special . . .

GEORGETTE: Can it, Babs. I'm here to meet my family. Hey, Babs—who's that foxy lady over by the palms? Whatsa scoop on her?

WAITRESS: Miss, would you like a drink while you're waiting?

VICKI: Uh, I'd like a Harvey Wallbanger. Uh, miss, make it a double.

BABS: I don't know and I don't care!

GEORGETTE: Yeah, well I *do.* See ya around, Babs. . . .

BABS: Ah, okay, Georgette. Call me or I'll call you, okay Georgette, okay? If I said anything mean about the way we were, I didn't mean it. . . .

NARRATOR: Georgette cuts through the dining room as surely as a honey bee picks out the last wildflower in a field of crab grass. And where is our hero? There he is, threading his way through the salad bar. . . . (*Dishes scraping.*)

ROD: Pardon me, ma'am, but somebody else might want some croutons, too.

NARRATOR: Will Rod return in time to save his beloved from the predatory clutches of his own flesh and blood . . . ? We'll find out after this word from our sponsor. . . .

ROD: High cost of wall-to-wall keeping you awake at night? Like to cover up the cement floor in the master bedroom with a little snazzy something or other, but can't shell out an arm or a leg? Then visit New England's chain of carpet warehouses—House of Shag'N'Stuff. We're open twenty-four hours to serve you better! Take a look at these beauties! Oh, sorry, we're on the radio. Just listen to these colors! You wouldn't believe how loud they are: *Green! Red! Orange! Yellow! Hot Pink!* Yes siree, this week, and this week *only*, we're running a chainwide special on these polytrilon, one-hundred-percent washable throwrugs in designer colors! Throw 'em anywhere, the kitchen, living room, throw 'em at the kids . . . heh-heh! Dads! Tired of mowing that big green expanse of nothingness? Got a fortune sunk in weed killer? Pave the whole thing over and just toss around a few of these babies for accent! They'll never notice and I'll never tell! Once you see our low, low prices and easy terms you'll be bitten by the bug, too! *Shag Fever!* So hurry on down to any one of our convenient locations or come by our main branch and showroom right off Route 17 in this town, a town like many others!

(VICKI *and* GEORGETTE *stand frozen during the monologue, in near-embrace.*)

ROD: Vicki, hon, this is my sister Georgette. Hey, I'm so glad the two of you, my two favorite gals, are finally meeting.

GEORGETTE: So lovely. (*She kisses* VICKI's *hand.*)

VICKI: Enchantée, I'm sure.

WAITRESS: The Pasta Arrivederci . . . coming in for a landing. (GEORGETTE *starts slurping on noodles.*)

ROD: Georgette! For Chrissakes, this isn't a hamburger joint!

NARRATOR: Despite her resolve, Vicki finds she cannot resist the way Georgette plays with her food.

GEORGETTE: Whatsamatter honey? You sit in a puddle, or you just glad to see me?

WAITRESS: Excuse me, Miss, are you gonna order anything or are you just gonna eat hers?

ROD: Noodles all around, Garçonette, and while you're at it, how's about a little fruit of the vine to wash this slop down?

WINE STEWARD: Very well, Monsieur! (STEWARD *pours wine all over* GEORGETTE's *blouse.*) Oh, pardon! How clumsy of me.

ROD: Will ya get a load of that! What is it with you guys? Run a Wet T-Shirt contest on the side?

VICKI: Let me try! Usually if you get it while it's still damp . . .

ROD: Well, whaddya know? It's another testimonial to the miracle of synthetics!

(*Fork falls.*)

NARRATOR: As Vicki's fork clatters to the ground, something darker than etiquette draws Vicki down.

VICKI: Excuse me.

NARRATOR: What began innocently enough, takes a turn for the worse underneath the table. Vicki finds no cutlery, but Georgette's legs, two succulent rainbows leading to the same pot of gold.

ROD: I suppose I should wait until after dinner, but I really want to pick your brains on some of the places I've been looking into as possible honeymoon hideaways. (ROD *pulls a bunch of brochures out of his jacket pocket.*) I'm looking for something that has a lot to offer, particularly a good golf course. I bought Vick a set of clubs for her last birthday and darn it all if she doesn't have a better putt than I do! Well, that's neither here nor there. I just mean you can't spend all your time in bed, hah-hah. Right? This South Seas plantation offers a lot— twenty minutes from the Tampa-St. Pete Airport, and ninety minutes from Disney World and Busch Gardens. And Georgette, get a load of this private beach. It's pretty reasonable, too, if we take the American plan. The breakfast, the greens' fees and happy hour are thrown in. Although I must say I'm a bit wary of these all-inclusive deals! There's always hidden charges that amount to no savings at all. You gotta be careful, these damned travel agents see the rock on her finger and the stars in my eyes and they'll soak ya every time, I swear to God, and they'll laugh all the way to the bank, am I right? Well, here's some of the brochures—they all look great on paper. You can take a gander at them after dinner and Vicki wanted to . . . hey, hey, Vick, what's up? You find that fork yet?

VICKI: I see it but I can't quite reach it.

ROD: Well for Chrissakes, let's get the waitress. Vick—whatsa matter? You come up too soon?

VICKI: I feel a little hot, Rod. Maybe I'd better go freshen up.

ROD: You do. (VICKI *exits.*) Georgette, I'm a bit concerned with Vicki lately.

GEORGETTE: Yeah?

ROD: Something's fishy, I can't quite put my finger on it, can you?

GEORGETTE: I'm working on it. Maybe I'd better go check on her. (GEORGETTE *exits.*)

ROD: Great, I'd hate for her to miss the floor show.

NARRATOR: But their romantic powder-room rendezvous is cut short! (*Gun shot.*)

WAITRESS: Omigod! She's been shot!

NARRATOR: As Georgette's perforated remains cool by the powder room, Vicki gives the maître d' the slip.

VICKI (*hands waitress a slip*): Could you wrap this for me?

NARRATOR: And is swallowed by the silent orifice (*swallowing sounds*) of the night.

NEWSBOY: Extra, extra! Read all about it! Future carpet queen slays sister-in-law during floor show!

NARRATOR: Vicki—ruthless killer, or just a girl with a lot of luck, all of it bad? We'll find out, after this word from our sponsor!

ROD: That's right . . . House of Shag'N'Stuff is expanding! We've opened a whole new floor with plenty of eager beaver sales people to serve you better! Here's one of them now. Come up here, little lady, and tell us all about it.

SALES LADY: Attention, Art Mart shoppers! We have a blue light special in the Generic Modernist department. In order to make room for the new '84s (*slash*) Art Mart is slashing prices to the stretcher bars on these late-model master-pieces. Schnabel, Salle, Haring: we've got the brand names you want at prices you won't believe! What's the secret of Art Mart's everyday low, low prices? We buy directly from the artists as they're being thrown out into the streets and pass the savings to you, the art consumer. And all Art Mart paintings come with our exclusive guarantee: one-hundred-percent avant-garde or your money back! Remember: today's kitsch is tomorrow's collectible. Want something that will shock the neighbors for years to come? Let our home decorating department help you select that very special work-in-progress for any room in the house. And while you're Art Marting, visit the deli and check out the new weiner wonder, "Pesto Pup" (*pup barking*)—cuisine on a stick. Thank you for Art Marting!

NARRATOR: But what really happened that fateful night at the salad bar? Was it something in the vinaigrette? Was there someone else who could have pulled the trigger? To many, the flight of the ex-muff-diver, future mop-squeezer, Vicki, was as good as a confession. What else but terrible guilt could make a woman in heels sprint? For in the cramped quarters of the gay-girl ghetto, blowing your girlfriend to kingdom come could be written off as taking your space! And what about Babs, the hat-check girl? Their one-night-stand left Babs stranded high on the bunny slope of love.

BABS: One night? One night? It was a whole ski weekend at Stowed Finger Lodge!

NARRATOR: Who killed Georgette? And who cares? And what will become of Vicki? Could it be she faces a brighter future in a prison rehab program than in today's saturated word-processing field? And then there's Rod . . . whose entire life soured between the salad bar and the powder-room. For answers to these and even more trivial questions, watch for the next episode of the Well (*scream*) of Horniness.

BLACKOUT

PART TWO: Victim Victoria

NARRATOR: The Well (*scream*) of Horniness! Part Two, "Victim Victoria." The setting, a peaceful New England town. A town like many others where murder and depravity offer a welcome respite from the tedious convenience of one-stop shopping. Just a town, a town like many others . . . with a gorgeous gendarme who loves girls almost as much as she loves murder.

GARNET: Garnet McClit, lady dick. (*Typewriters, police station office. Enter* AL DENTE.)

NARRATOR: It was another spit-colored Manhattan morning. Al Dente found the usual cornucopia of crimes cluttered his desk at the New York precinct. The police chief was a cop's cop: tough and stringy as a pot roast with a face to match. (*Office intercom buzzing.*)

AL: Yeah?

SECRETARY (*through intercom*): Got a make on that DOA, chief.

AL: Okay. Send in Garnet McClit. Looks like this is her baby.

(GARNET *enters.* GARNET *and* AL *size each other up.*)

NARRATOR: Enter Garnet McClit, lady dick. An inspired Irish rookie from the concrete backwaters of the Garden State. Being an Irish tomboy left her with two options: the convent or the beat. She went with the latter, with no regrets. Once in a while, though, she dreamed of heading someplace more romantic, like Milwaukee, where being a cop and being Irish still meant something.

GARNET: Whatsa scoop, Chief?

AL: Your lucky day, McClit. You play it smart and this'll get you outta parking violations and into the big leagues. You know that new Amazon watering hole?

GARNET: The Vixen's Den?

AL: Yeah. Well, the boys just paid it a little visit.

GARNET: Snazzy joint. Food any good?

AL: They couldn't stick around to find out so they just got something to go. A stiff. Here, read all about it. Didn't take long for those nutty dames to start making pesto of each other.

GARNET: Georgette, that's bad.

AL: Big wheel, huh? Well, she's stopped turning.

GARNET: There's going to be trouble, Chief. Those tribads gotta short fuse. When the *New York Pest* gets a hold of this . . .

AL: Forget the *Pest*. When our boys get through rounding up their head honchas, those bra burners won't be able to get together a softball game, let alone a rumble. Gotta line on the suspect?

GARNET: Vicki, yeah. I know her. Who doesn't? Heard she defected a few years back. Word was she'd turned a real Breck girl. Gotta job, boyfriend, the works.

AL: She gave the maître d' the slip. We'll bag her soon enough, though. She can't go too far too fast in those heels. Tell me, how do those tribads feel towards a girl once she's had a change of heart?

GARNET: I've been sniffing around this scene a long time. I seen a lotta these broads make a beeline for the straight and narrow. But I'm telling you, none of them has made it to the altar yet.

AL: So they take it kinda personal when one of the flock goes AWOL?

GARNET: Let's just say the tribads are not exactly pro-family.

AL: Are these dames ditzy enough to frame Vicki?

GARNET: No way, Chief. Vicki's a lotta things, but she's just not suitable for framing.

AL: Any way you slice it, it's our chance to bust up this daisy chain for keeps.

GARNET: Maybe so. Still these muff-divers have been spoiling for a rumble and now they've got an excuse. There's gonna be one helluva crackdown.

AL: You mean . . . ?

GARNET: What I'm saying is this: until you get that word-processor on ice, there's not a bisexual between here and Scranton that'll be safe.

(*Blackout. Lights up in forest scene.* VICKI *running in circles.*)

NARRATOR: Vicki ran and ran. Without direction, though not without purpose. But why did she run, if she were, indeed, innocent? Perhaps in her heart of hearts, there was something she longed for more fervently than justice or even her own freedom. A sequel, perhaps? As the Zen masters have said: what is the sound of one hand clapping? Or as the TV moguls restated: what is the use of one great pilot without a thirteen-week run? And so Vicki ran until the wilderness lay all around her. Vicki knew she was lost. Alone with the elements.

DISEMBODIED VOICE OF GOD OR CARL SAGAN DOING GOD: Oxygen, helium, hydrogen and whiskey sours, these elements form the building blocks of life as we know it.

(*Twig snaps. Animal sounds.*)

NARRATOR: Or was she alone? Her soul called out to the heavens (*phone being dialed*) . . . but as usual got a busy signal. (*Phone busy signal. Ominous bird calls.*) Overhead, three bald scavengers circled with the deadly precision of a lazy Susan laden with tainted hors d'oeuvres.

VICKI: Who's there? Yoo hoo, here I am.

NARRATOR: Somewhere in the uncharted recesses of her mind, Vicki knew she was the heroine and could not be killed off. Not with a series in the offing.

(*Dream sequence music, with typing sounds.*)

NARRATOR: Perhaps her old college chum, the writer, might construct a few close calls. She might have to run down a few blind alleys, in orthopedically hazardous footgear, bullets of myopic snipers snagging her nylons.

(*During this narration,* VICKI *acts out her fantasy of landing a guest spot on a TV dectective show. She shifts into a more operatic mode.*)

NARRATOR: Or perhaps it would be a gothic affair. She might be compelled to run across the moors, in a flimsy peignoir, nipples baying at the north star. But this much was certain: she would be rescued.

(*Footsteps. A shadow approaches and eclipses* VICKI.)

VICKI: Oh, no, no, no, God, no. You're not William Shatner.

NARRATOR: William Shatner? Is he in this?

(*Blackout. Lights up on street scene with* GARNET.)

NARRATOR: For Garnet McClit, seasoned sapphic flatfoot, Al Dente's theories were as meaningless as pork fried rice without the duck sauce. Who pulled the trigger and why? Vicki's guilt was another stale assumption she wouldn't buy and couldn't swallow. Pass the mayo, please. No, to Garnet, the field was wide open. So that left just . . . everybody. Only problem was—everybody seemed to have an alibi as airtight as a Tupperware cakesaver. Only person Garnet hadn't checked out was Babs, the hat-check girl. Sure, she knew Georgette had had a fling with her. So what? Tribads were known to change partners more times than Masons in a three-legged relay. Would Georgette have jeopardized a promising career in dental hygiene for a few moments of empty ecstasy with a hat-check girl? A woman whose phony accent fooled no one about her bridge-and-tunnel origins? Garnet didn't think so. Still . . . what about their affair? Just a Sunday drive—or a joy ride thru the Well (*scream; sound of falling body and splash*) of Horniness. Georgette was six feet under. Her side of the story died with her. But if she could have talked, what would she say?

GEORGETTE (*voiceover that comes out of nowhere, or more exactly, through an offstage reverb mike*): Just in case you really want to know, Babs was the best-looking thing I ever saw. I got steamed up watching her cross the street. Whatever a broad's supposed to have on the ball, she's got it. My tongue felt a foot thick when we talked and if she'd asked me to jump, I'd a said, "How high?" So why'd I dump her? I'll tell you this. And you can tuck it away if it means anything to you. I don't like her and I don't know why.

GARNET: I wished I'd gotten the specs on the hat-check hussy. I wouldn't know her if she got in bed with me.

(Blackout. Ominous organ stab. Lights up in coffee shop with ROD *and* AL.*)*

ROD: When that deal on the linoleum mine comes through, I'll have the entire home-decorating industry painted into a corner.

AL: Don't get me wrong, Rod, my boy, idealism is great, especially in an election year. But you gotta remember you're talking about South America, you're talking about a lotta Catholics. . . .

ROD: What are you driving at, my man?

AL: I'm talking about Catholics—whole different ball game.

ROD: Is it as bad as all that? I mean they're still human.

AL: Human, yes, but they're afraid of patent leather. They do it in the middle of the day and eat macaroni and cheese after. They think God is made out of plastic and glows in the dark. Human, I wonder . . .

ROD: I know what you're trying to do, Al, but I gotta dream. Something to keep me going. I'm not going to give it up . . . it's all I got . . . now. I still think we got the right to a few things. To a roof over our head. To a nice piece of shag under your feet.

AL: Don't go too far, my boy, it's not just the Catholic thing here. . . . Some of these people aren't even white and put that in your pipe and smoke it. Shag, Rod, you're gonna give 'em shag? These people live in paper sacks and eat what the dog wouldn't touch. And why? Because they're lazy. Too damn lazy to go shopping. And frankly I just don't see how giving away throw rugs to Salvador is going to change all that.

ROD: Well, it won't. At least, not overnight.

(Pinteresque pause. Audience gets nervous, thinking the show has taken a bad turn.)

AL: Take a tip from me, all that linoleum ain't going to keep you warm at night.

ROD: Whatcha got for me?

AL: I gotta very classy dame for you . . . very low mileage . . . and she don't take tips. . . .

ROD: Can that fish, Al, I'm through with the lousy broads you dig up. The last one was so skinny I coulda sliced semolina on her hip bones.

(Blackout on ROD *and* AL. *Lights up on street scene.)*

NARRATOR: Garnet McClit took a long drag on her cigarette and leaned against the tenement doorway. She studied the glowing butt. And flicked it into the gutter. It was 11:30 P.M. on the Lower East Side. Most of the natives were just getting up. Then Garnet saw her.

(Enter BABS.*)*

NARRATOR: Something strangely exotic about the eyes, the way they seemed to float in her face like two wontons in a hot and sour soup. Her full figure stood out in sharp contrast to the clusters of anorexic clubgoers beginning to fill the street. Someone or something in Garnet's brain sent a wake-up call to her crotch.

GARNET: What're you doing out at this hour, hon? Pretty girl like you oughta be home, watching the funny car races.

BABS: It's curtains for me and my gal. Like she just didn't meet my needs. Besides, she was just a runt.

GARNET: You like big girls, huh?

NARRATOR: In the harsh light of the ghetto street lamp, the woman's eyes glittered like a tape measure. Garnet seemed to make the grade.

BABS: That's right. Real big. Like you.

GARNET: Too bad I'm a career girl.

BABS: Oh, I really go for girls with Blue Cross. You don't work around the clock, now, do you, Ms. Officer?

GARNET: I go home. Alone. To sleep.

BABS: Oh, that's too bad. Guess I gotta go sit on that tar beach all by my lonesome.

GARNET: What tar beach is that?

BABS: Just down the street. Sometimes I get real lonesome up there, just me and my Walkman.

NARRATOR: Watching her turn and walk away made the insides of Garnet's thighs feel like butter left out on a hot stove. But she was too much of a cop to cave in to simple lust. Just a fleshy little trashpasser—oh, excuse me, that's flashy little trespasser—Garnet thought, as she followed her into the building.

(*As* GARNET *enters the building,* BABS *clubs her.* BABS *grabs* GARNET'*s gun.*)

BABS: Ooh, picking up a bargain like this puts a girl in a mood for a real shopping spree. Something in the home improvement line. I gotta feeling a certain carpet salesman might feel like doing some private price slashing.

NARRATOR: Can she be stopped? (*Organ stab.*) Can a clerical worker who's tasted blood ever hope to break into middle management? (*Organ stab.*) Can anyone be satisfied once they've dipped into the Well (*scream*) of Horniness? Even as Babs weaves her wicked web, our hero is engaging in some innocent male bonding in another part of town.

(*Blackout. Lights up in coffee shop with* ROD *and* AL.)

ROD: Hey, buddy, do you see a waitress?

AL: I see this woman in white. But I don't think she's a waitress.

ROD: Why not?

AL: 'Cause she looks like we're sick. What do you think about that?

ROD: I think we are sick and she's the cure. Hey nurse, nurse, me and my buddy are dying of hunger.

(WAITRESS *enters. Maxwell House jingle is played.* WAITRESS *sets coffee cups down on table.*)

ROD: Miss, is this decaf?

WAITRESS: But you said coffee.

ROD: But I meant Sanka brand coffee.

WAITRESS: Why didn't you tell me you didn't want real coffee?

ROD: Well now, Miss, Sanka brand *is* real coffee, isn't that right, Al?

AL: Sure is, Rob. Howsabout joining us for a cup, Miss?

(*Exit* WAITRESS.)

AL: You're still thinking about her, aren't ya?

(ROD *sighs.*)

AL: I'm going to say something and I don't think you're gonna be able to hear it, but Vicki was a cheap little poodle of a woman. She flunked outta community college and probably killed your sister.

ROD: Lies! Lies! I will not hear it! Vicki went away to school!

AL: Yeah, away to the Hoboken bilingual keypunch school. Hardly the Seven Sisters, now is it?

ROD: But I still love her!

AL: Rod, my friend, someday you're gonna find you got off easy. The woman had no depth. Taking the plunge with her woulda been like highdiving off the shallow end.

NARRATOR: Rod felt he could forgive Vicki everything, even her fried chicken, if only he could have her back. Suddenly, he felt protective towards her, the way sauteed onions must feel towards calves' liver.

(*Lights down on coffee shop, up on the forest.* VICKI *is softly giggling with an unseen admirer.*)

NARRATOR: Even as Rod finds himself knee-deep in thought, our finely wrought fiction is unraveling in another area.

(*Theme music up under following, probably "America the Beautiful" would be the most appropriate.*)

NARRATOR: To the north lay the majestic Catatonics. To the work-weary masses, these are the promised lands . . . where God's chosen people have chosen to spend forty days and forty nights in the wilderness, on the American plan. But the granite cleavage did not contain happy memories for Rod. For it was there during a family vacation, that his other sister, Dinette, was snatched from their campsite by ravenous raccoons. The family was left stunned, and . . . bitter! No more Sierra Club calendars for them! Even with the family in the carpet trade, it was the kind of scandal you couldn't sweep under the rug.

RANGER: They finally found that little tyke. What was left of her, anyway.

DEPUTY: Born with a silver spoon in her mouth.

RANGER: That's probably why they killed her.

NARRATOR: There was no way they could know their daughter lived, nor that the carcass found outside the Winnebago was not Dinette, but, in fact . . . a London Broil! (*Sizzle.*) Dinette remembered none of this. Not her brother Rod, twin Georgette, nor the split-level mediterranean mansion. Suckled by her ring-tailed abductors, she became like them—forced to hunt and prowl by night like the hideous half-human apparitions that haunt late-night TV. Roots, berries, and an occasional Eskimo Pie—on these she thrived. The forest provided her with all she needed; that is, except for the one thing she craved the most—entrance to the Well (*scream*) of Horniness. But now she had Vicki. She had hit rock bottom! Happy at last! It was a muggy summer night in the mountains. The clouds rested like soggy cotton balls upon the brow of the mountain. It was a night made just for lovers. Somewhere a loon cried.

OFFSTAGE VOICE: Madge, what'd you do with the keys to the Buick?

NARRATOR: From their seclusion in the Christmas tree farm, the wild lovers watched the last rounds of a sudden-death golf tournament. How could they know the danger that surrounded them?

(*Sound effects of faraway police sirens, drawing nearer. Offstage voice yells "Fore!" Golf balls start pelting* VICKI.)

NARRATOR: Omigod! She's been hit! And from what I can see, quite badly! Her eyeliner's running down the street!

(*Footsteps.* VICKI *slumps into* DINETTE's *arms, who starts to carry her offstage when we hear footsteps running closer. Flashlight on lovers.*)

RANGER: There she is! Bag that she-devil! Don't let that varmint escape! Somebody call an ambulance!

(DINETTE *drops* VICKI *and exits.*)

NARRATOR: Yes, yes, of course. (*Dialing sounds.*) Is there a doctor in the house?

(DOCTOR *enters from audience.*)

DOCTOR: Here I am.

NARRATOR: You're too young to be a doctor!

DOCTOR: I'm a resident. I can do anything a real doctor can do except play mixed doubles. Bring her to my office!

NARRATOR: And so an ambulance bears Vicki away.

(*Blackout.*)

NARRATOR: At the hospital a dedicated team of professionals try to work Vicki in.

(*Lights up in hospital.* DOCTOR *and* VICKI *with* NURSE, *who is* BABS, *acting very bored.*)

BABS: No appointment, well dear . . . Ah, you're in luck! A cancellation!

DOCTOR: We're here to help you. But you must try to help yourself. Any small detail you can recall is important. Concentrate, how did you get from the nightclub to the mountains?

VICKI: I don't remember.

DOCTOR: What did you do there?

VICKI: I don't remember.

DOCTOR: Who were you with?

VICKI (*hesitates*): I don't know . . .

DOCTOR: Are you sure?

VICKI: Yes, I'm quite sure. I've just had a terrible shock, you know.

DOCTOR: Yes, kidnapping and loss of memory are terrible, indeed, but nothing compared to the shock you'll get when you pay the bill. Now, dear, I just want you to relax and try to forget this nasty amnesia. That's right! Relax and try to breathe normally. Nurse, will you fix a cup of coffee to calm down the patient.

NURSE: Certainly, doctor. All right honey, how do you like it?

VICKI: I don't remember. Oh, doctor, doctor, it's terrible!

DOCTOR: Vicki, what is it?

VICKI: All I can remember is that I left my clothes at the laundry and lost the ticket. Now I don't remember what the bag looked like. Gone, all gone, my favorite socks, everything I ever loved . . . gone!

DOCTOR: Just relax and watch this crystal. You have box seats at a Ping-Pong tournament. Your eyes never leave the ball. You are getting sleepy, sleepy, sleepy. . . . (DOCTOR *falls asleep and starts snoring.*)

BABS: Doctor, wake up.

DOCTOR: Ah, Vicki, what do you remember?

VICKI: It's no good, my mind's a blank. . . .

DOCTOR: Yes, we know that. (*To* NURSE:) I'm confident I can restore the patient's true identity.

BABS: You can, but why?

DOCTOR: Prepare 28cc of phenobarbothanx.

NURSE: Phenobarbothanx . . . pheno, as an antibiotic?

DOCTOR: Right.

NURSE: And barbo . . . as a sedative?

DOCTOR: Right.

NURSE: And thanx?

DOCTOR: And thanx for the memories!

(*Organ stab.*)

NARRATOR: Can the doctor restore Vicki's true identity? Can anyone save Vicki from the vegetable patch? Can . . . wait a minute. Haven't I seen that nurse before . . .? That's no nurse, that's *her*! Omigod! It's the proverbial hat-check girl in white-collar clothing. Tune in next week for the startling conclusion of the Well (*scream*) of Horniness!

(*Organ theme song up. Blackout.*)

PART THREE: In the Realm of the Senseless

NARRATOR: The Well (*scream*) of Horniness! Part Three, "In the Realm of the Senseless." The setting, a peaceful New England town, just a town like many others, where men are men—

OFFSTAGE VOICE: And so are the women!

NARRATOR: The play that puts lesbians on the map . . . and possibly the menu!

MARGARET DUMONT: Do tell, how are the lesbians today?

BABS: Hot! Mmmmmmmmm . . .

GARNET: Steaming . . . (*Slurping sounds.*)

GEORGETTE: Served in their own juices! (*Lip smacking.*)

NARRATOR: Tonight's episode. (*Organ stab.*) In our last episode we left Vicki (VICKI *giggles.*)—our heroine—

BABS: Our heroine! Our heroine! What am I? Chopped liver?

NARRATOR:—the plucky pervert who gave up security and a half share in the Hamptons—all because her love for women was greater than her love for self. At last, dialogue that reveals the way women—

VICKI: Listen, sister . . .

NARRATOR: —really talk to each other.

VICKI: A little piece of advice: you could be put on pre-recorded tape.

NARRATOR: This is the play women who love women have been waiting to see!

BABS: Can that chowder! Who wants to see an uptight WASP from the Midwest stumble around in a polyester dress? I'm the one they come to see.

THE ACTRESS WHO PLAYED GEORGETTE: Who's gonna see you on the radio?

NARRATOR: A collaborative effort—

BABS: This is my big moment! I got my teeth capped for this part!

NARRATOR: Unlike traditional theater . . .

ROD: Hey, hey, girls, come on—remember, there are no small parts—

GARNET: There are only small minds, Rod.

BABS: You should know, you've got one of the smallest!

NARRATOR: A proverbial filling up and spilling over of sapphic sentiment!

VICKI: Good things come in small actresses!

240

BABS: Tell me about it, I came in several small actresses.

NARRATOR: Yes, ladies and genders, our show is another fine example of women working together.

THE ACTRESS WHO PLAYED GEORGETTE: Where's my lipstick! Which one of you took my lipstick!

NARRATOR: A testimonial to women's love for one another!

BABS: I wouldn't touch anything of yours!

NARRATOR: Of their ability to surmount the limitations of their own egos, to work collectively!

BABS: I'm the star! I'm the star! I'm the star!

NARRATOR: In this, our final episode—

ROD: Thank God, I can't take another minute with these dizzy dames.

NARRATOR: —we find Vicki (*sound of panting, shoes running*) on the lam, in the picturesque Catatonic Mountains. She seems hopelessly lost—

ROD: Well, if it's hopeless I say let's just put on the laugh track and break out some brews!

NARRATOR: I said *seems* hopelessly lost, Rod.

ROD: Just checking there, buddy.

BABS: She's hopeless, all right.

VICKI: Now just a minute, Babs, you two-bit thespian!

BABS: Who are you calling a thespian? I'm a normal woman! I'm no introvert—not like the rest of you.

NARRATOR: Vicki is wandering in a daze.

(*Sound of golf course up.*)

VICKI: A daze! Oh, don't you think I should wear something that shows off my figure?

BABS: Not unless you're wearing a cast-iron girdle under it!

NARRATOR: We last saw Vicki, prostrate on a Lazy Boy (VICKI *snores*) about to get an injection to restore her memory.

BABS: Shall I call you at the hospital, Doctor?

DOCTOR: Why? I'll be at the golf course. I thought I could get in nine holes before "The Cosby Show."

NARRATOR: As the doctor exits, the nurse readies the needle . . . wait a minute— that's no nurse, that's *her*.

(BABS *steps forward to acknowledge the hissing from the rest of the cast that increasingly greets her villainous appearances. She loves it.*)

NARRATOR: Poor Vicki, nobody is there to hold her hand as she gets the prick. What's really in the needle? A regular Florence Nightshade, aren't we, Babs? And how did you penetrate the brotherhood of healing?

BABS: I'm a Kelly girl!

NARRATOR: Babs administers the heinous hypo, only to send Vicki down (*organ stab*) DOWN (*organ stab*) DOWN (*organ stab*) DOWN, into the Well (*scream*) of Horniness. Can nothing stop the testy temp worker? She callously climbs over Vicki (*sound of Babs grunting with physical effort*) who was as limp as a closet case on her wedding night. Babs begins dialing. . . .

(*Dialing phone.*)

BABS: Hello, I'd like to speak to Police Chief Al Dente. . . . No? Well, give him a message. . . . Tell him he can pick up that touch typist he's been trailing.

(*Sound of phone hanging up. Blackout.*)

(*Lights up on Police Office.*)

NARRATOR: Meanwhile, down at headquarters, Al Dente was feeling very excited. The feds had been on the case for weeks. Finally, after combing the area, they had turned up something.

OFFICER (*holds up a ratty-looking wig*): Looks like human hair, Chief.

AL: Yes it does, but that's the beauty of dynel, my boy.

NARRATOR: Just as he thought, the word-processor had wigged out and run. The chief had seen it a million times before: when the chips were down, the chicks left town. They just couldn't take the heat, and if the heat didn't get them, it was the humidity. The chief was getting pretty steamed up himself.

AL: I'd have the supper-club sniper in the slammer if it wasn't for stupidity.

OFFICER: Sorry, Chief, I . . .

AL: *My* stupidity. I should have never assigned the androgyne to the case.

OFFICER: You mean Garnet?

AL: Sending her out by herself to sniff out a girl was like sending a blind man out without a cane.

OFFICER: I don't get it, Chief—

AL: They'd both disappear into the first manhole they'd uncover.

OFFICER: I still don't get it.

AL: That's the last tribad on the force, you hear me? They've got no ambition.

OFFICER: But Garnet seemed like such an eager beaver.

AL: Even on the ballfield—they don't care if they live or die in the bush leagues.

OFFICER: Chief, I got something on my mind.

AL: So spit it out.

OFFICER (*spits*): I can't help but think, well . . .

AL: Well?

OFFICER: Well, maybe you're wrong about Vicki.

AL: Phooey.

OFFICER: I think she's innocent.

AL: If she's innocent, I'll eat her.

OFFICER: But Chief, YECH!

AL: You want me to believe the femme was framed? And not only framed, but fingered? But by who?

(*Organ stab.*)

NARRATOR: And how many?

(*Organ stab. Phone rings.*)

AL (*picking up the phone*): Police morgue. You stab it, we slab it. Is this a takeout or a delivery?

CALLER: I gotta little massage for Garnet McClit.

AL: What?

CALLER: Tell her I got her clues, she can pick 'em up anytime.

(*Dial tone and organ stab.* GARNET'S *theme up.*)

NARRATOR: The cryptic call sheds no light on the case at hand. But it did remind the Chief that the lady dick had not been spotted since the last commercial. While the Chief mused, Garnet was still struggling to regain consciousness. Bab's blow had taken the edge off the sapphic sleuth's ordinarily sharp senses. Even the simplest thing—standing up—seemed as difficult as putting on a girdle under water. (*Gurgle and snap.*) Garnet didn't know who or what had hit her. And what of the mysterious woman she had met? Now, she was a knockout, thought the leggy gumshoe as she stumbled home. (*Key in door.*) The detective declined to disrobe but immediately fell into a stupor. (*Thud.*) It wasn't as comfortable as a futon, but it was about all she could afford on her salary. (GARNET *lights a cigarette.*) As for the case, it went on the back burner. But in the morning (*rooster*) all Garnet's theories were still half-baked. She'd have to scrape something together for the Chief. (GARNET'S *theme out.*) While we wait for the punchline, Rod is back at the ranch-style poring over some new carpet commercials. (*Water pouring.*)

(*Ding-Dong!*)

BABS: Avon calling!

NARRATOR: But when he opened the door . . . This was no saleslady.

ROD: Hey, hey!

NARRATOR: From her careless capri pants to her skimpy halter top, Rod's eyes swept over her hills and valleys like two pilots on a search-and-destroy mission, missing only one thing: (*organ stab*) the Redhead was packing a rod! (*Trigger clicks.*)

BABS: Okay, Mr. Carpet King, don't try anything funny. Not that that's a danger in this show. I'll make a sister outta you real fast!

(*Hospital ambience music.*)

NARRATOR: Back at the hospital, a bevy of blonds arrive to frisk our friend Vicki.

BLOND A: The chief said they're gonna pin this caper on you.

VICKI: What! And leave a mark in my dress? Just let him try. . . .

BLOND B: He said to find something . . .

BLOND A: Anything . . .

BLOND B: And make it stick. . . .

(*Organ.*)

NARRATOR: Vicki was almost at the breaking point. She had been pursued all over the state, from hotel to motel. She had lost her curling iron and was—*gasp*— almost out of Sweet 'N Low. Would this torture never end? Once again she called out to the heavens . . .

(*Dialing, ringing, recording up.*)

ROD AS GOD: Hi! Thanks for calling. I'm not able to come to the phone right now, but leave your name, number, and religious persuasion after the beep and I'll get back to you. (*BEEP!*)

NARRATOR: Then she heard the most vicious vixen bark out:

BLOND A: Spread 'em, sister!

NARRATOR: The command seemed strangely familiar to Vicki. As she complied she thought . . .

VICKI: PRISON!!

NARRATOR: She would have prayed for amnesia, but she didn't know if her insurance would cover a relapse. In desperation, she thought of England. But that was worse than prison!

VICKI: At least in prison they had central heating and decent coffee!

NARRATOR: She felt a hand run the length of her leg. (*Feet running.*)

VICKI: Find anything you like?

BLOND B: Just browsing.

VICKI: Well, if you don't see it, just ask for it. Maybe I have it in the back.

BLOND A: She's clean.

VICKI: Maybe you should get a second opinion.

(*Hospital out.*)

(*Car doors opening, slamming; typing. Police office up.*)

NARRATOR: Vicki is escorted downtown for the arraignment while Al Dente waits for Rod and Garnet. There has been no answer at Rod's residence.

(*Ringing phone.*)

AL: Maybe he's on his way. Or maybe he just got tied up. (*Ominous organ stab.*)

GARNET: Whatsa scoop, Chief?

AL: I got the housewife on the hotseat.

GARNET: So why the long face?

AL: It's not that I care about that crummy little clerical worker. The broad's a brat. But Rod is my buddy.

NARRATOR: At the mention of his friend's name, the chief was choked with feeling.

(*Gagging.*)

GARNET (*on reverb or voice over*): This must be that male bonding I've heard so much about.

(*Office sound effects fade to courtroom ambience.*)

NARRATOR: For his friend's sake, Al decides to spare Rod and spoil the child, Vicki.

JUDGE: Order! Order in the court!

(*Various voices are heard ordering:* "BLT!" "Two eggs whole wheat toast!" "Whiskey down!" "More Fire!" "Russian dressing!" *ad nauseam.*)

JUDGE: Okay, Vicki, let's make a deal! (*Game show theme music up.*) Do you want the sentence I just offered you? Or will you take the cell Carol Merrill is standing in front of? Or how about I give you five bucks for the phone number of every woman you ever slept with?

NARRATOR: Vicki passes up the chair, the sofa bed, and the Judge's generous offer of amnesty in exchange for a date, in order to take an all-expense-paid trip for one (*cheers and applause*) UP THE RIVER! (*Groans.*)

(*Cell door closing.*)

(*Jail ambience up.*)

BABS: No more word-processing for you, honey! It's license plates from now on! (*Cackle, cackle.*)

NARRATOR: Can Vicki survive her stint in the slammer? (*Organ keys.*) Is it the end of the line for this lezzie? (*Organ keys.*) We'll find out after this word from our sponsor!

(*Disco music up.*)

ROD: It's Saturday night in hipcity and you're a loose woman on the loose—you want to move and groove to the latest beat, you want to go (*singing*) "Where the boys . . ." Aren't!

BABS: That's where *we'll* be!

ROD: If you're like us.

BABS: And we know you are or you wouldn't be listening.

ROD: You want to cut the rug at your favorite Amazon watering hole. And in this town, a town like many others, the place to go for girls is . . . the Vixen's Den! And this month . . . we're having a sale! We've slashed our already low, low prices on wine, women and song!

GARNET: That's right, the girls are really coming out for this one!

ROD: We want you to come and come again! So hurry on down to the Vixen's Den, right off Route 17 in this town, a town like many others!

BABS: Oh, and tell 'em Babs sent ya.

(*Disco music out.*)

NARRATOR: Vicki was very upset. She didn't realize the prison uniforms would have *horizontal* stripes!

VICKI: Oh God, I'm all *hips*!

INMATE A: Oh, yoo-hoo.

INMATE B: How ya doing, Goldilocks?

INMATE A (*in a stage whisper*): We haven't had a blond in a while.

VICKI: Oh, hello, I'm sorry I'm . . . I've never been behind bars before.

INMATE C: Whatsa matter, don't you drink?

INMATE A: Don't mind her, my little turnover.

INMATE B: Whatcha get sent up for anyway? Mugging an Avon lady?

INMATE C: Scratch somebody's eyes out at the sale table?

INMATE A (*in mock sympathy*): Shoplifting at Bonwit's again, tsk, tsk.

INMATE C: Ah, let up girls, she's taking it kinda hard.

INMATE B (*lecherously*): That's not all she's gonna be taking kinda hard when we get through with her.

INMATE A: Relax, Goldilocks . . .

INMATE C: We're just trying—

INMATE A: —to make you—

INMATE B: —feel—

INMATE A: —welcome. Right, girls?

(*Unison sounds of affirmation.*)

INMATE B: We wish we could make you feel really welcome, but they locked the broom closet.

INMATE A: Shush, you gotta give her something to look forward to . . .

NARRATOR: In desperation, Vicki buries her head in her skirt. (*Mumbling from* VICKI.)

INMATE C: You might as well get used to it.

INMATE B: Goldiwet.

INMATE C: Honeydung.

INMATE B: Little Miss Pussytwat. You're one of us now.

INMATE A: After all—

INMATE C: —we're *all*—

INMATE A: —sisters—

INMATE B: —under the skin, aren't we, girls?

INMATE C: You could learn to like it . . .

INMATE A: We could teach you . . .

NARRATOR: Vicki began to wail.

INMATE B: Come on, save the wails.

INMATE C: Oh, go on and scream. It'll break the monotony.

VICKI: Let me out! I'm not supposed to be in jail! I'm white and I can work if I have to!

INMATE B: Oh, leaving so soon? Tsk, tsk, don't let *us* keep you.

VICKI: I don't belong here! This must be a misprint, a typo, I don't like this anymore! And you . . . all of you . . . I don't like you either!

INMATE A: *Ouch!*

INMATE B: *Ooh!* She really knows how to hurt a girl!

INMATE A: Come to think of it, you may be right.

INMATE C: Maybe you don't like us, —

INMATE B: —but—

INMATE C: —you are *like* us—

INMATE B: —dearie.

INMATE A: And you do belong here with us.

NARRATOR: Vicki knew they were baiting her. But she didn't go for it.

VICKI: No thanks, I ate a heavy lunch.

(*Blackout. Organ.*)

INMATE A: What happened?

INMATE B: Who turned out the lights?

INMATE C: Damn it all, I told you if you put too many vibrators in one socket this'll happen every time.

(*Organ. Lights up.* GARNET *theme up.*)

NARRATOR: While Vicki had been incarcerated, Garnet was at home piecing together the evidence until she got a clear picture of the villainess . . . *Babs!*

(*Hiss. Sound of car.*)

GARNET: I gotta get to the bottom of this.

(*Car speeds up.*)

NARRATOR: Immediately she rushed to the prison, the crime of the scene. Little did our gamey gumshoe know there was no bottom to the Well (*scream*) of Horniness! (*Organ to prison sounds.*) During all the confusion, Garnet entered the prison and grabbed Vicki in the dark.

VICKI: That's not the dark.

GARNET: And you're not a real blond.

VICKI: Bye, girls, *hee hee.*

INMATE B: Don't kid yourself, honey, there's no bi-girls here.

INMATE A: You'll be back, too—

INMATE C: —Goldilocks.

INMATE B: Sooner than you—

INMATE A: —think.

GARNET: Come on, let's make tracks.

VICKI: But won't that make it easier for them to follow us?

GARNET: Good point. We'll go in my car.

(*Car doors open/close—running car.*)

NARRATOR: Vicki instinctively put her trust in Garnet. But she was taken aback by the brunette's casual attitude.

VICKI: Darn, I shoulda asked for a receipt.

NARRATOR: Her fate was in Garnet's hands.

VICKI: That isn't all I've thought of putting in Garnet's hands.

NARRATOR: But for now, Vicki was content. She hated sex in cars.

VICKI: It reminds me of an unhappy affair I had with a geologist that left me between a rock and a hard place.

NARRATOR: Garnet, a dyed-in-the-wool tribad from the word come, studied her companion. Vicki was just her type. Garnet, cursed with the kind of carnal appetite that no *single* girl could satisfy, had, in desperation, turned to married women.

GARNET: This Vicki is made of pretty tough stuff.

NARRATOR: All this running around could ruin a girl's hairdo.

GARNET: But not hers, no sir. No listless locks on this lezzie.

NARRATOR: When did that busy, busy gal, our heroine, find the time to tend her tresses?

(*Organ stab.*)

NARRATOR: Finally, Garnet could not stand the silent meeting of the mutual admiration society.

VICKI: They have me convicted already.

GARNET: You've been holding up fine so far. I know it's been a lengthy exposition and you're tired. But don't go to pieces on me now.

VICKI: I can't help it. I can't go on much longer like this. You don't know what it's like, always on the go. Living outta a suitcase. If I don't get a chance to go to bed soon, I don't know what will become of me . . . or the show. But *you* probably don't understand. You're not a blond.

GARNET: No, I'm a brunette, but I have feelings, too.

(*Car swerves to roadside.*)

VICKIE: What's the matter? Why are we slowing down? Are we out of material?

NARRATOR: Vicki's eyes met Garnet's. Their gazes locked. (*Click.*)

VICKI: Garnet . . . I . . . I'm a wanted woman in seven states.

GARNET: Make it eight, baby. You're wanted by me in the state I'm in.

NARRATOR: For too long the lady dick had been tortured by the woman sitting next to her. . . . But the sight of her breasts jiggling—her thighs whispering together—was too much. Garnet traced the outline of Vicki's body with her lips. Vicki's passion stirred. Something in her oven of love began to rise. She threw her head back on the car seat. She felt just like a pair of French doors awaiting Loretta Young's entrance. (*Radio being tuned.*) Garnet played Vicki as expertly as a teenager plays a transistor. When she felt she had had some pretty good reception, Garnet moved in on some fine tuning. (*Radio: "One Adam 12, One Adam 12, come in please."*) A call from the car radio mangles the mood.

GARNET: Roger, I read you.

DISPATCHER: Roger's off tonight. It's Friday.

GARNET: Right. Whatsa scoop?

DISPATCHER: We have a 411 underway at the carpet warehouse off Route 17.

VICKI: *Rod!*

(*Car moves off.*)

NARRATOR: As Garnet and Vicki speed to the scene of the crime . . . (*Organ.*) Omigod, that's no radio dispatcher. . . . (*Organ.*) That's *her.* . . . (*Organ. Hiss.*) You Kelly girls really get around, don't you? And what have you done with Rod? (ROD *gagged and mumbling.* BABS *laughs.*) Bound and gagged in his own office! And why drag our heroine into this wholesale horror? (*Organ.*)

BABS: Well, you wanted to see her again, didn't you? Better make it a good look, because it'll be your last. (*Hiss.*)

(*Door creaks open. Echoed footsteps.*)

NARRATOR: Garnet and Vicki enter the warehouse . . .

VICKI: It's kinda quiet in here for a shootout, doncha think?

GARNET: Vicki, a cop doesn't think in a crisis.

BABS: Hold it right there! If it isn't Van Dyke and Van Dick! Well, well, Garnet, we meet again. What took you so long?

GARNET: Search me.

BABS: An excellent suggestion, sucker. We'll start with Ms. Twinkie Tits over here.

GARNET: *Babs!*

VICKI: Is there something funny about my breasts, honey?

GARNET: Not a thing, dear. . . . Now see here, this is no way to treat a lady. Where are your manners?

BABS: This is no comedy of manners, dick, despite rumors to the contrary. This is just business as usual for tribads.

(Organ; mumbling sounds from Rod.)

VICKI: Rod! Here I am!

(Dream music starts.)

BABS: You can't go back to him, sister. If it was him you wanted, you shoulda figured that out a long time ago.

(Gunshot.)

(BABS *laughs.*)

(Dream music up.)

ROD: Honey, Vick, it's just a bad dream, wake up. You're with me now, you're safe.

VICKI: I can go back! I will! You'll see . . . I'm gonna be a good wife!

ROD: Wake up. Of course you'll be the best little wifeypoo a man could ever want.

VICKI: *Rod!* Omigod . . . You're not tied up . . .

ROD: Right you are. I got the night off so I could take you out to dinner. You musta dozed off while I was on the phone.

VICKI: But . . . I . . . was . . .

ROD: Honey, you were dreaming.

VICKI: But everything seemed so real.

ROD: You know how dreams are. But darling, I'll tell you what's real . . . you and I. . . . Why don't you freshen up while I go start the car?

(Music up.)

NARRATOR: As carrots in the Cuisinart so are the souls in the Well *(scream)* of Horniness. Goodnight and have a nice life.

A WEEKEND NEAR MADISON

by
Kathleen Tolan

A *Weekend Near Madison* was presented by Actors Theatre of Louisville (The State Theatre of Kentucky), Jon Jory, producing director, with the generous assistance of Humana Inc. at the seventh annual Humana Festival of New American Plays, February 23 through April 3, 1983. The cast was as follows:

JIM	Randle Mell
DOE	Robin Groves
DAVID	William Mesnik
NESSA	Mary McDonnell
SAMANTHA	Holly Hunter

Directed by Emily Mann; stage manager: Wendy Chapin; asst. stage manager: Richard A. Cunningham.

The Actors Theatre of Louisville production of *A Weekend Near Madison* was subsequently presented Off Broadway by Dasha Epstein at the Astor Place Theater in New York City.

CHARACTERS

DAVID, in his mid-thirties
DOE (DOROTHY, DODY), early thirties
JIM, early thirties
NESSA (VANESSA), early thirties
SAMANTHA (SAMMY), about twenty-three
BUTCH, a big dog who never gets seen

David and Doe are married.
David and Jim are brothers.

TIME

Early autumn, 1979.

SETTING

Wisconsin.

Scene 1

The set is the kitchen and living room area of a house built by David and Dorothy. It is open, airy, "lived in," "home made"; it doesn't seem professionally designed or decorated. Windows (unseen) are down front, stage right, and, possibly, a skylight.

Upstage is a small hall area where there is a closet, the door to the outside, and an exit offstage to the rest of the house. The kitchen area is upstage left, living room area with bookshelves and a couch upstage right, both opening up into one living/dining area downstage. A big wooden dining table is down left, a stereo down right.

The middle of the night. Rain, lightning, thunder in the distance. JIM *and* DOROTHY *stand together in the kitchen, talking quietly. She is wearing a robe and holds a bottle of milk and a pan. His clothes are wet and muddy; his knapsack is at his feet. They are deeply involved in their conversation; it is in full swing.*

JIM: Well, that's what's so devastating about it.

DOE: Yes.

JIM: I mean, I've had experience with—well, with Munch—

DOE: Yes.

JIM:—and some of Van Gogh's—like his self-portraits—

DOE: Right.

JIM: —where you glimpse the torment—

DOE: Uh-huh.

JIM: —and the decision to put it out—

DOE: Yes.

JIM: But with cultural art there's always that decision, you know?

(DOE *nods.*)

JIM: Here, you never have the feeling that a decision has been made. It's that they can't *not* do it.

DOE: And it has nothing to do with the public.

JIM: Right. Right. It just had to be done. It's so . . . well, it really is raw. Not raw like not cooked or not finished, but raw like without skin, you know?

DOE: Yes. (*Pause.*) Yes. (*Pause.*) On the edge.

JIM: Yeah. Except most of them were over the edge.

DOE: And . . . but . . . you were saying . . . about trying not to hang on to old patterns, or have expectations that come from past . . .

JIM: Oh, yeah. Right. Well, it's the immediacy of the work—it's exactly what you

257

were saying—the daring to give up the past and the future and let the present completely take over. Of course it can be pretty terrifying . . .

DOE: Yes.

(*Pause. They stand, lost in thought. Lightning, thunder, Butch barks.*)

DOE: Do you ever . . . sometimes it seems that if I stopped—didn't in some way hang on to what I've just done or plan to do—not even that. If I gave up the sense of myself—myself in the world—the sense of the space I occupy—I would disappear.

JIM: Wow. (*Beat.*) I know what you mean.

DOE: And yet . . . for the work to be what it could be . . .

JIM: How has it been . . . ?

DOE: Oh, scratching away. I haven't been able to finish anything.

(*Pause.*)

JIM: There was this Yugoslavian sculptor—?

DOE: Yes.

JIM: —who did these incredible, weird creatures in wood—

DOE: Uh-huh.

JIM: —and someone asked him how he thought them up, and he said, "Oh, they're hidden in the tree trunk—they live there. I just set them free. I release them from the matter that keeps them hidden."

DOE: Mmm.

(*Phone rings.* DOROTHY *picks it up, listens, hangs up.*)

DOE: David's got it. We should tell him you're here.

JIM: Yeah. (*Beat.*) Hi, Dody.

DOE: Hi, Jimmy. Do you want to change?

JIM: Oh, yeah. (*He gets clothes from pack, takes off wet boots, etc.*) God. I can't believe I'm here.

DOE: We've missed you.

JIM: Yeah, me too. I've really been needing to connect up again. Oh—are Vanessa and . . .

DOE: They're staying in our almost finished guest quarters in the barn.

JIM: No kidding.

DOE: We met them after their concert and all drove back together.

JIM: How is she?

DOE: Fine. She's just like Vanessa.

JIM: Right. How was the concert?

DOE: Well . . . have you heard her latest album?

JIM: No.

DOE: Well . . . it was an amazing celebration of "Women." . . . Those of us who weren't "Women" sat in varied degrees of discomfort.

JIM: Uh-huh.

DOE: Some of the songs were very "We Shall Overcome."

JIM: Yeah.

DOE: Her energy and . . . generosity are still very much there . . . the way she opens herself up to the music and people. . . . She is an incredible performer.

JIM: Yeah.

DOE: She seems very happy.

JIM: Huh.

DAVID (*enters*): Dorothy? I'm sorry about that—Jimmy!

JIM: Hey, bro.

(*They shake hands, embrace.*)

DAVID: Baby bro. Jesus Christ. How was the hitch?

JIM: Good.

DAVID: Far out. Good to see you, man. You look . . . weathered.

JIM: Yeah.

DAVID: How's the real world these days? Life on the road? Do you feel back in touch with "America"?

JIM: Uh-huh.

DAVID: Far out. Far out. Sorry you didn't make it in time for the concert. Your old girlfriend was hot.

JIM: Uh-huh.

DAVID: And Samantha's a little Zoot Sims. That girl can cook.

JIM: I'm sorry I didn't make it.

DAVID: Yeah! It was great! You did have to check your cock at the door, but I figured that was cool, considering man's atrocities against women—especially at concerts.

JIM: Uh-huh.

DAVID: Uh-huh. Dody's nervous.

DOE: What?

DAVID (*to* DOE): It's okay, honey. (*To* JIM:) She thinks they're going to try to win her over.

DOE: David.

DAVID: I understand, honey—Jimbo and I are already won over, right, Jimmy?

JIM: Right, Dave.

DAVID: So. What've you been up to, man?

JIM: Oh, I don't know. Going to work, coming home, sitting on the couch until it's time to go to bed. That's about it. Stopping in the kitchen long enough to make a peanut butter sandwich or put a chicken pot pie in the oven. Typical wild, fast-paced city life.

DAVID: Uh-huh. Great. (*To* DOE *and* JIM:) The two of you will have a lot to talk about.

DOE: Yes.

(*Lightning, crack of thunder, heavy rain.*)

DAVID: Shit. I better check the roof on the barn. They may be having some very wet dreams.

DOE: Oh.

JIM: I think I'll clean up a little . . .

DAVID: Go for it, man. Anything you need?

JIM: No, I'll just . . . (*He goes into inner part of house with his dry clothes.*)

DAVID (*cuddles* DOE *and sings a chorus to her of Sam Cooke's "Bring It On Home To Me," after which there is a pause as he holds her*): Oh, baby, baby, baby, baby.

DOE: What's the matter?

DAVID: Oh, baby. (*Pause, then he steps away and moves to the door.*) That was Tilly Edwards on the phone.

DOE: I know.

DAVID: What? (*Pause*).

DOE: Why don't you get some help?

DAVID: Dorothy, this is my responsibility.

DOE: Why are you doing this? (*Beat.*)

DAVID: My job?

(*Pause, during which* JIM *enters, notices the tension.*)

JIM: Hi.

DAVID: Dorothy's mad at me.

DOE: David.

DAVID (*heated*): It's a very delicate stage of the therapy. It's taken a long time to develop the trust that's essential for anything to work. She needs me, now, to be available to her. (*Beat.*) It's a complicated issue, constantly debated: Where's the line—when is it too personal? Most of these guys won't even look at it—they hide behind some conventional image of the respected doctor or scientist—as if science were some kind of monolithic, unequivocal truth. Science—science is a living, breathing process—I mean, Christ! The human psyche! Christ! As if knowledge were finite!

(*Lightning, thunder.* DAVID *opens door;* Butch *barks.*)

DAVID: Why didn't they take their dog into the barn?

DOE: Scared of chickens.

DAVID: They're not sleeping with the chickens.

DOE: And ladders.

DAVID (*he leaves. Off*): No. No. Down! Get down! Butch! No! Down!

JIM: What . . . ?

DOE: This child has taken over our life.

JIM: One of his patients?

DOE: Yes.

(*Big crack of thunder,* Butch *howls.*)

DOE: Poor Butch. (*She goes to the door, opens it, speaks into the night.*) Hi, Butch.

(*Butch responds.*)

DOE: Hi. Yes, it's okay. Good dog. (*She comes back in.*) I wish I could let him in.

JIM: David still gets asthma?

DOE: Yes. Do you think he'd like some warm milk?

JIM: David?

DOE: Butch.

JIM: Oh. I don't know.

DOE: David hates it.

NESSA (*off*): Land! Oh, my God—sailors—land ho!

(DAVID, SAM, *and* NESSA *burst in, carrying instruments, fishing gear, and bundles wrapped in sleeping bags and blankets. Butch is barking.*)

SAM (*as they enter, to* DAVID): I wrapped the sleeping bag around it. It's by the door.

DAVID: That's all?

SAM: I can go.

DAVID: I got it.

NESSA (*entering, calling back to Butch*): Butch, stay. Under the roof. Under the roof. Good dog! (*She's in.*) Jimmy—! Oh, my God—fabulous!

(*They hug.*)

NESSA: You got here! How're you doing? You look great—oh, God, I got you wet.

JIM: That's okay.

(*Butch has been whining.*)

SAM: Nessa, do you have the biscuits in your pack?

NESSA: Oh, yeah, good idea. Oh—Jimmy, this is Sammy.

JIM: Hi.

SAM: Hi.

NESSA: This is Jim. (*To* JIM:) I've just been telling Sammy all about you— (*she takes biscuit from* SAM) oh, great. I couldn't believe it when Dody said you were going to try to make it out here for the weekend—oh, wait a sec. (*She goes out the door.*) Here ya go, Butch. Yes. Yes. Now lie down. Come on, lie down. Atta boy. Now stay. Stay. (*She comes back in.*) This is so fantastic! Jimmy! What are you up to? How long has it—oh—how is the woman you were living with—are you still—?

JIM: Sarah. Yeah. We broke up.

NESSA: Oh—I'm sorry.

JIM: Yeah.

NESSA: And are you—what are you . . .

JIM: I still work in a gallery. Set up exhibits, write the catalog, stuff like that.

NESSA: Huh. No kidding. That's great.

JIM: Yeah. So how's it been going?

NESSA: Oh, it's been fabulous. God. You wouldn't believe all the women, all over the country, who are just coming out. It's like—winter's over, and everybody's just celebrating the spring.

JIM: Wow.

NESSA: Yeah. We've talked to so many different women—one who had been married for *thirty years*, do you believe it?—and—where was this?—Butte, Montana, wasn't it?

SAM: Yeah.

NESSA: And she woke up one day and said to her husband, "That's enough." And she packed her bags and moved into this women's collective that'd been happening for about two years just outside of town. I guess she'd been running into them at the store and stuff. Anyway, it's so incredible. It's like wildfire.

JIM: God.

DOE: Would you like something dry to put on?

NESSA: Oh, yeah, that'd be great.

(*They gather up some of their stuff and begin to follow* DOE *off.*)

DAVID (*comes back in from outside*): Shit. That fucking roof. I'm really sorry.

NESSA: Listen, man, it was refreshing to be awakened by a rush of fresh Wisconsin rainwater.

DAVID: Right. Far out. That's really beautiful.

(*The women go off.*)

DAVID (*to* JIM): So, how're ya doing, Shlamazal? (*He gets beers for* JIM *and himself.*)

JIM: Okay.

DAVID: How does she seem to you?

JIM: Vanessa?

DAVID: No. Doe.

JIM: Oh. Great. I mean, how is she?

DAVID: Great. Sick of me, but great. How are you? You've finally come out of hiding, eh?

JIM: Why is she sick of you?

DAVID: Who wouldn't be after seven years, living outside of nowhere?

JIM: Yeah, you have a point.

DAVID: Thanks. (*Beat.*) She hasn't published anything in two years.

JIM: Why's that?

DAVID: I don't know. What are you doing?

JIM: What do you mean?

DAVID: What happened with Sarah?

JIM: Oh. Well . . . I don't know. She didn't think I was "realizing my potential."

DAVID: Uh-huh.

JIM: Yeah. You'd've been on her side. She passed the bar and got hired by this hot-shot firm and has all these great, new, "upward mobile" friends.

DAVID: Uh-huh.

JIM: Last year we broke up about five times.

DAVID: Great.

JIM: Yeah, and then one of us would get lonely enough and drunk enough to end up on the other's doorstep and we'd be together for a week or two and then we'd have to start breaking up again.

DAVID: Uh-huh.

JIM: I haven't seen her in about four months. She's having an affair with a lawyer at the firm. Last week I threw away her toothbrush.

DAVID: Good going.

JIM: Thanks. There're still big gaps on the shelves where her books used to be . . . I keep meaning to push my books together or buy some more books or something . . .

DAVID: And this isn't salt in the wound?

JIM: What do you mean?

DAVID: Seeing Vanessa.

JIM: I wanted to see her. I wanted to see how she is now. I wanted us all to have the chance to be together. . . .

DAVID: Uh-huh. Are you painting?

JIM: David, I'm doing fine.

DAVID: I know.

(*The women come back in.* SAM *and* NESSA *wear big flannel nightshirts.*)

DOE: My father's wife. David didn't have the heart to tell her he never wears them, so now he gets a new one every Christmas.

DAVID (*whistles*): Oh, boy, you two look pretty damn cute.

NESSA: "Cute"? Did you say "cute"?

DAVID: That's right, baby, I never seen you look so cute. I think this should be the new outfit for The Awakening.

JIM: What's The Awakening?

NESSA: That's the name of our group.

JIM: Oh. (*Beat.*) I'm sorry I didn't make it in time for the concert.

NESSA: We have another one tonight.

SAM: Yeah, but it's for women only.

NESSA: Oh, yeah.

SAM (*to* JIM): Maybe you could go in drag. Whatta ya think, Nessa?

NESSA: Sure.

JIM: I'll think about it.

NESSA: Great—what could you wear?

JIM: Oh, I don't know. I guess jeans and a T-shirt.

SAM: Yeah, that'd be good.

NESSA (*has been looking around. She sings three or four lines of* "*Natural Woman*" *à la Aretha Franklin*): God—you guys have done so much. I haven't been here since the wedding.

DOE: It wasn't much more than a frame then.

NESSA: Oh, wow, what a fabulous stove—where did you get this?

DAVID: Oh, wow, yeah, isn't it neat?

NESSA: No, really, it's an industrial stove—Sammy, this is what I was talking about.

SAM: Yeah, it's really nice.

DOE: The Western Wisconsin Wrecking Company has an auction every spring.

SAM: You have a lot of books.

DAVID: That's nothing. You should see her study.

SAM (*to* DOE): Have you read most of them?

DOE: No.

DAVID: Yes.

SAM: Books are great. They can be good friends. (*Pause.*) Are there any good places to fish around here?

NESSA: Oh, yeah, Dorothy, I remember your father fishing—oh God, remember?

DOE: I remember us forging through the swamps in a desperate search, and you doing a belly dive in the mud of the river bank in your beautiful dress.

NESSA (*laughing, to* SAM): On the morning of their wedding, Dorothy's father went fishing!

DOE: Good old Dad. He is eccentric.

DAVID: Avoiding his only daughter's wedding ain't eccentric, it's classic.

DOE: Well . . .

NESSA: How're Herb and Jenny?

DAVID: Speaking of eccentric?

NESSA (*smiles*): Yeah.

JIM: Dad died.

NESSA: You're kidding.

DAVID: No. Dad died almost two years ago.

NESSA: Oh, you guys, I'm so sorry.

JIM: Yeah.

NESSA: He was such a wonderful guy. How did he die?

DAVID: Cancer. Not too original.

SAM: Somebody was telling me the other day that one out of five people will get cancer sometime in their life.

NESSA: How's Jenny? (*Pause.*)

DAVID: Mom's fine. She's living, happily, still, right Jimmy?

JIM: Yeah. I brought a letter from her.

DAVID: —in an ashram in India.

NESSA: What?!

DAVID: Well, she didn't want to stay on Long Island, she said she'd go crazy there, and most of her friends spend half the year in Florida, which she hates, and she refused to "impose" on us out here in the wilderness, and Jimbo's pad in Philadelphia was not what she'd had in mind for "passing through the golden years," as she put it—

NESSA: I love her. She is so great.

DAVID: So, she'd been going to this yoga center a couple of times a week for years— even dragged Dad along on a yoga retreat one summer. And she liked the "kids" at the center, and they told her about this ashram in Kashmir—

NESSA: Incredible.

DAVID: —so she decided to check it out. She liked it. She thought the swami was a "nice man"—

NESSA: God. It's like Jenny's come out, in her own way.

DAVID: What do you mean?

NESSA: It's like she's taken over her own life, d'you know?

DAVID: When she and Dad were together she wasn't living her own life?

NESSA (*protesting*): No, no, David. I thought they were fabulous together. It's just that at the time she married, what choices did she have?

DAVID: It's possible that she was in love with the guy.

NESSA: Yeah, I know. I just think it's such an exciting time. You look around and see all these women making these incredible choices that completely blow your mind, d'you know? That's all I'm saying.

DAVID: Yeah. Well, my mind is blown, I'll agree to that. And as far as I'm concerned, Mommy's mind is blown.

JIM: What do you mean?

DAVID: She couldn't take the grief. She couldn't take life, or any life that resembled the life she'd had with Dad.

NESSA: Oh . . .

JIM: Are you serious?

SAM: Why is that bad?

DOE: Why is what bad?

SAM (*to* DAVID): Well, you said she went to India because she felt too much sorrow here; she wanted a fresh start?

DAVID (*to* NESSA): I mean, what the hell does her life have to do with Eastern mysticism? And how can you of all people approve of a life given up to the worship of some man?

NESSA: Well . . .

JIM: It's not that.

DAVID: This need so many people feel to give their life to someone, it's very common, and it's very dangerous. I know because it happens with me all the time. And, in fact, the therapy isn't always effective if it doesn't happen, that submission, and even worship, as a stage, so anyone who puts himself into that position is taking on a fucking big moral responsibility.

DOE: You don't have any reason to believe that Swami Visada has ignored that responsibility—

JIM: Life in the ashram shouldn't be compared to psychotherapy. It isn't the same thing.

DAVID: But it's fake.

DOE: David.

DAVID: It's fake. When a person cuts himself off, so totally, from his roots—

DOE: Honey, how is this your roots? This is as much an idea. This American pioneer setting is hardly representative—

NESSA: What's wrong with making a conscious choice? What's wrong with an idea?

JIM: Why does how you are living have to reflect how you have lived?

DAVID: What gets me—what really gets me, is these fucking criminals, who call themselves spiritual leaders, leading masses of lost, white, middle-class "young people"—the disillusioned children of the foolish liberal parents who didn't give them any fucking moral and religious structure that they could then adjust or reject—. So these mindless, morally starved kids—

JIM: Do you exclude yourself?

DAVID: What?

JIM: I mean I think it's human, because of our make-up, and maybe society's barrenness, that we all crave some kind of higher order . . .

NESSA: Nobody's denying that there are a lot of assholes in the world.

SAM (*pause; looking at the floor*): Look at the footprint in the tile!

DOE: Oh, yeah, isn't that neat?

SAM: Yeah. Where did they come from?

DOE: The tiles were made in Mexico. There's another footprint over there.

SAM: Wow. Nessa, look at this. (*To* DOE:) Do you think it was a raccoon? Do they have raccoons in Mexico?

DOE: I don't know.

NESSA: Oh, yeah, that's great.

SAM: I bet he never thought his footprint would be on somebody's tile floor in Wisconsin. And we'd all be looking at it. And talking about it. In English.

(*Phone rings.* DAVID *answers it.*)

DAVID: Hello. Yes, Tilly . . . I hear you. I thought we'd said you'd stay with Jennifer. . . . What are you going to do now? . . . And if she's not home? . . . Do you promise? All right. I'll see you Monday at two o'clock. . . . Yes. Get some sleep. . . . You know I do. Goodbye. (*He hangs up. Beat. He speaks to the group.*) Sorry. She's a patient, going through a rugged time.

SAM: Is there anything we can do?

DAVID: Ah . . .

SAM: Do you want to invite her to our concert tonight?

DAVID: To your concert?

SAM: Or anything. But, I mean, sometimes it's really a trip, all these women giving each other all this energy.

DAVID: Yes, well . . .

NESSA: Has she been in touch with any of the women's groups at the university? They know about the concert. And anyway, it'd be a good thing for her to do. There're some very solid collectives in Madison.

DAVID: Uh-huh.

NESSA: What does that mean?

DAVID: Uh-huh, great, I'll send her over.

NESSA: Uh-huh.

DAVID: Although I have been included in the very small group of male shrinks which the Midwest Feminist Alliance has deemed "non-sexist," I happen to find certain aspects of the women's movement a real turn-off, to put it crudely.

NESSA: Oh, great. You know why? 'Cause you can't control it, man.

DAVID: Uh-huh. Uh-huh, that's probably it. Gee, it's all coming back! Those wonderful nights we all spent together, sitting around the kitchen table, solving the problems of the world—

NESSA: Oh, yeah! Oh, yeah! Oh, David, I forgot how fucking *crazy* you used to make me!

DAVID: *I? I?* I eyeiyeiyei.

JIM (*laughing, muttering to himself*): Ah-ha. This is great. This is great.

DAVID: What are you muttering about?

JIM: Oh, God, remember on Cranberry Hill—

DAVID (*to* JIM): I can't believe you.

JIM: —when Vanessa got us all to be macrobiotic.

DAVID: Ah, yes. And the secret midnight cruises over to the A&W for burgers and shakes—oh, God, remember the group sessions we'd spend on Dorothy's refusal to give up coffee? (*To* NESSA:) You'd go into those long philosophical harangues about yin and yang—

NESSA: Wow, you're really on my case, aren't you?

DAVID: And everybody else had accepted this—

DOE: I accepted it. It sounded great to me. I just knew I wasn't evolved enough to give up my morning coffee. And *I* wasn't interested in sneaking it, like at least one hypocrite I knew.

DAVID: Ouch! Well, you were very impressive on that issue, challenging the "dictatorship," threatening to leave if there continued to be even an "atmosphere of disapproval" of your coffee drinking. That was definitely one of your great moments.

DOE: Thank you.

NESSA (*to* DAVID): D'you know—. (*She laughs.*) Oh, man. You're dying for me to bite, aren't you?

DAVID: What are you talking about?

NESSA: You're making it hard, man, you're really making it hard.

DAVID: What?

NESSA: This is not a fad.

DAVID: What exactly—

NESSA: So what if "certain aspects" turn you off—

DAVID: Ah-ha!

NESSA: So what if there are things that aren't, like, "tasteful." And any movement is gonna attract fucked up people as well as strong, healthy, intelligent people, and some who would've been sympathetic are turned off. Well so fucking what. They'll be part of the second wave. I mean, you know this, David, any movement is going to alienate people who are too lazy to look at the main intentions of the movement. And I'll tell you something. I came out because I was sick and tired of being a goddamn "sympathizer." (*Pause.*) It's the only way. I really believe that. Women have been oppressed for so long that nothing is going to change if we keep sleeping with our oppressors. I'm sorry, but it's true. Okay, just look at sex. Men fuck you, and the only way, this is true, think about it, the only way to really get off is to submit, I mean there has to be an element of that, of letting go, d'you know, to have it work. So if you're letting go with the people who are keeping you down—. And if it's one of those rare cases where the guy isn't an asshole, and he really cares about who you are, it's even harder. Because if the guy is that sensitive he's gotta be really fucked up. (*Beat.*) Think about it. We have all been so programmed in so many ways to think of the woman as serving the man. The only way to change that is for women to return to the source. To each other. It's the only way.

(*Silence.*)

JIM: Boy, do I feel insignificant.

NESSA: Oh, Jimmy, I'm sorry—I mean, you shouldn't take it personally.

JIM: What?

DOE: There are men in the world as well as women.

NESSA: Dody, I know that. I know that.

DOE: Vanessa . . .

NESSA: What? Do you think this is a personal attack?

DOE: How can I not take it personally?

NESSA: Dorothy, how can you? God, you know me better than that. I love you guys. I would never judge you. I believe in you.

DAVID: The fucking contradictions—

NESSA: So what. So I don't sit around making safe, rational statements, being sure that what I say doesn't contradict anything else I've said. So fucking what. I love you guys. That's true. I support whatever you're trying to do. *And* I believe that sexism is so built into the system that there is no way we can fix it if we accept the foundation that's there.

DOE: It's so limited. It's so limited.

NESSA: Now wait a minute, Dody—

DOE: It's so much easier to fit everything into a nice little ideological mold. It may be more difficult to live with the awareness of—of the ambiguity of everything . . .

DAVID: Do you think men don't have to submit to make it work?

NESSA: David, I wasn't saying—

DOE: We're all oppressed. We're all the oppressors and we're all oppressed. I mean, we all have these fears . . . these fears of each other and ourselves and . . . unless you see that, unless you see that, Vanessa, there's no hope—for any of us. I mean, life is more complicated—it's more complicated than you want to admit.

(*Pause.*)

DAVID (*to* NESSA): So you think Tilly should become a lesbian.

NESSA: Damnit, David, I was just—it's just that a lot of women feel more connected and happy when they realize they're not alone.

DOE: Unless they realize they are alone.

NESSA: (*Beat.*) You're not alone, Dody. You're not alone, d'you know? You need to know that.

JIM (*gets up, looks among his things, finds letter*): Um. Can I read you guys this letter Mom wrote?

DAVID: What?

JIM: I mean, this might be a terrible time, but it might be a good time.

(*Pause; silent consent.*)

JIM: David?

DAVID: Go ahead.

JIM: Okay. Let's see. She says, "My darling, all of my darlings, it's difficult to write words and thoughts, when they all flow into the ocean of love. My pen wants to write love, love, love, a thousand times. That is all there is, my darlings. It's infinite, it's overflowing. It's as if I'd been living in little boxes, hundreds of little boxes, and they all went up in flames. How frightening it was at first, because it meant giving up, giving up ways you thought you needed, and then it is wonderful, because everything, everything is inevitable. The other day I found a copy of *Brothers Karamazov* in the ashram library. Remember your father reading it aloud to us after supper when you boys were in high school? It was his favorite. Remember Father Zossima's words to Alyosha? 'When you are left alone, pray. Throw yourself on the earth and kiss it. Kiss the earth and love it with an unceasing, consuming love. Love all men, love everything. Seek that rapture and ecstasy, prize it, for it is a gift of God, and a great one; it is not given to many but only to the elect.' " Then she says, "We are all just drops in the sea, my darlings, drops in the great big ocean of love. Om shanti, shanti, shanti. Mom."

SAM: Wow.

NESSA: Incredible.

DAVID (*laughing*): Jesus Christ. Let me see that.

(DOE *has gone to the door.*)

DAVID: Where are you going?

DOE: For a walk.

DAVID: It's raining.

DOE: It stopped. (*She leaves.*)

NESSA: May I take a shower?

DAVID: Yeah.

NESSA: Sammy, wanna take a shower?

SAM: No thanks, not now.

NESSA: Okay. (*She goes out.*)

DAVID: That woman can drive me crazy. Up the wall. (*To* SAM:) How can you put up with her?

SAM: We do pretty well.

(DAVID *has gone into the kitchen area, gotten out cheese, sausage, whiskey.*)

JIM: Is that food over there?

DAVID: Yeah.

JIM: Samantha, are you hungry?

(SAM *nods.*)

DAVID: I'll put it on the table.

JIM (*to* SAM): You want whiskey, beer, or warm milk?

SAM (*smiles*): Whiskey.

JIM: Me too.

SAM: Wow, look at the moon.

JIM: Oh, yeah.

(SAM *and* JIM *sit at the table, drink, look at the moon.* DAVID *remains apart.*)

DAVID: (*Pause, outburst, to* JIM.) Serving the man. What a laugh. What a laugh. I have been serving, serving, serving the woman all my fucking life and I'm sick of this bullshit. Do you know what? I am getting—and it's not just me—it's happening all over the country—more and more straight men who think they're homosexual—who have become so fucking intimidated by these women, they don't know how to behave, or which of their impulses are "good" or "appropriate" or "evolved." I mean, Christ, they just don't want to bother anymore.

(*Pause. Butch barks.* SAM *stands up.*)

SAM (*to* JIM): Did Nessa give Butch another biscuit?

JIM: I don't know.

SAM: I'll go ask her. (*She goes and gets a biscuit, turns and addresses* DAVID.) I love her.

DAVID (*looks at* SAM): Uh-huh. (*Beat.*) I apologize.

SAM: Thank you. (*She leaves.*)

(JIM *and* DAVID *look at each other. Possibly they laugh.* DAVID *goes to the stereo and puts on Paul Winter's "Winter Consort.")*

DAVID: Did she ask you to come out here?

JIM: Who?

DAVID: Doe.

JIM: What? No. What do you mean?

DAVID: You haven't been out here in three years.

JIM: I know.

DAVID (*he sees* DOE *out side window*): What's she doing out there?

JIM: I wanted to come out. To spend time. And then when you said Vanessa'd be here . . . maybe it was stupid, but I've been missing that time. I thought, if I could touch that time again, when we were . . . when there was so much hope . . .

DAVID (*he has been staring out the window*): Here she comes. Oh, no—it's the maple. The maple's been hit. Oh, no.

JIM: What?

DAVID: Looks like lightning got our tree.

(DOE *comes in from outside with a few maple leaves.*)

DAVID: Honey.

DOE: The maple's down.

DAVID: I know.

(*She goes to him, they look out the window.*)

DOE: It was just beginning to turn.

(JIM *stays seated at table, music plays,* DAVID *and* DOE *look out window, phone rings.* DAVID *goes and answers it.*)

DAVID: Hello . . . Yes, Jennifer . . . yes. Where is she now? You're looking at her? Good. I'll meet you at the hospital. (*He hangs up, picks it back up, dials.*) Christ.

DOE: Is it . . .

DAVID: Tilly slashed herself up.

DOE: Oh, no.

DAVID: (*Into phone.*) Hi, this is Dr. Rabinowitz. Who's on tonight? Good. Yes . . . Sid? Tilly Edwards is on the way in with lacerations of the arms and chest, possibly severe. . . . White, nineteen . . . ambulance. Thanks, I'll meet you there. . . . Right. (*He hangs up.*) I'll get ready. (*He leaves.*)

JIM: (*Pause.*) Want some whiskey?

DOE (*staring out window*): Mmm. Do you know that poem . . . uh . . . "In the slight ripple the mind perceives the heart"?

JIM: (*Pause.*) At the Waldon Psychiatric Clinic in Bern, there is a large collection of artwork, done by some of the schizophrenics who have been there. Do you know what most of the pieces are? Means of escape: model guns, daggers, keys, airplanes, parachutes, enormous shoes and socks. (*Beat.*)

DAVID (*he comes in with change of clothes, papers, etc.*): See you later.

DOE: All right, honey.

DAVID: I have some morning sessions, so I'll probably crash at the office.

DOE: Okay.

JIM: 'Night.

DAVID: 'Night, Jimmy. (*He leaves.*)

(*Butch barks,* NESSA *comes in.*)

NESSA: The biscuit got soggy. (*She gets another biscuit.*) Poor Butch. (*She goes outside. Off:*) Come here, Butch. David, where are you going?

DAVID (*off*): Hospital.

NESSA (*off*): Oh, wow, is it serious?

DAVID (*off*): I don't know.

(*Car starts up, leaves, as Butch barks.* SAM *comes in. She has been in the shower, too. She sips her whiskey.*)

NESSA (*off*): Yes, yes, good boy, Butch.

(SAM *opens the door, stands in the doorway.*)

NESSA (*off*): Good boy. Sammy—look at the sky!

SAM: The air smells so fresh. (*She goes outside.*)

(*We hear their laughter, calls to Butch.*)

DOE: Sometimes I want so much to live in a run-down tenement in New York City, and only eat food that comes in cardboard and cellophane wrappers, and not be able to sleep at night because of the bottles crashing outside the window, and the sirens wailing and the cats screaming. And the music blaring and people yelling at each other in languages I don't understand. And the rattle of the fan in the summer and the clatter of the pipes in the winter. And, no matter where I look, *not* be able to see the horizon.

Scene 2

Afternoon. JIM *stands, holding a book he's been reading, looking out side window.* NESSA *and* SAM *enter from outside.* SAM *gets together her fishing gear.*

NESSA (*entering*): Jimmy—great—I'm glad you're here.

JIM: Hi.

NESSA: Hi.

SAM: Hi.

NESSA: Listen, would you have some time now? I'd like to talk to you about something.

JIM: Sure.

NESSA: Where's Doe?

JIM: Upstairs.

SAM: I'm going.

JIM: You going fishing? Where?

SAM: Dorothy said there's a path behind the barn that leads through the woods down to the river.

JIM: I might check it out later.

NESSA: Great!

SAM: Okay.

NESSA (*to* SAM): Are you sure you don't want to stay here, honey?

SAM: Yup. See you later.

JIM: Good luck.

SAM: Thanks. Bye.

NESSA: Bye, honey.

(SAM *leaves.*)

NESSA (*voice lowered*): Jimmy, how do they seem to you?

JIM: Who?

NESSA: Dody and David.

JIM: Oh. They seem okay.

NESSA: Do you think so?

JIM: Sure. Why?

276

NESSA: Well, I couldn't tell.

JIM: You've only been here one day.

NESSA: Well, that's true. That's true.

JIM: And us being here keeps it from being one of their typical days.

NESSA: Yeah. Yeah, that's true. So you think they're okay.

JIM: I don't know. I really don't know, Vanessa. David has been pretty involved with his patient.

NESSA: Oh, yeah. Yeah. (*Pause.*) And Dody seems okay to you?

JIM: What do you mean?

NESSA: She seemed so upset . . .

JIM: You've always managed to touch a nerve with Dody.

NESSA: Oh, yeah, well . . . but I mean even before that. I mean, I don't feel like we've really connected.

JIM: I don't know, Nessa. Dorothy isn't always completely here.

NESSA: Now that's true. That's really true. Dody. This morning she was standing at the counter with half an orange in one hand and one of those juicers—not the automatic kind—the glass—this. (*She has found juicer on counter.*)

JIM: Yeah.

NESSA: And she was just standing there, holding the orange in the air, and finally she said, "You know, sometimes I forget how to do this." And we laughed, and then she made the juice. But she was serious.

JIM: Yeah.

NESSA: I guess she's always been like that.

JIM: Yeah.

NESSA: But you think they're happy?

JIM: I don't know, Vanessa.

NESSA: (*Pause.*) It seems weird that they don't have kids.

JIM: Why is that?

NESSA: Well, they've been married five years, and were together a long time before that.

(*Silence.*)

NESSA: Well, Sammy and I want to have a baby.

JIM: Oh.

NESSA: She doesn't want to have it and I do. We talked about artificial insemination, but that seemed so . . . artificial, d'you know? Something didn't feel right about it. Not theoretically, but the actual experience. And we thought about just going out and picking up some guy, but you don't know anything about him, you know? He might be diseased, or a maniac, or something, and the point would be to not get to know him well enough to find any of that out. (*Beat.*) And we thought of asking a gay man, but the gay men we know would either love a child themselves and would want partial rights, which we decided we wouldn't want to do, or else they really don't like women, so that wouldn't work. (*Pause.*) So I thought of asking David.

JIM: You're kidding.

NESSA: It seemed like a really good idea before we got here. David and Dody and I have a past together. We've had a wonderful friendship that's meant a lot to all of us. And it seemed like it'd be better to conceive a child with a friend. And the fact that he and Doe have been so solid for so long and will probably have their own kids if they want kids, so he wouldn't feel possessive. And being a shrink would make it easier for him to see the whole situation objectively, to remove himself, I mean in a good way. . . . And since he and I were never lovers—

JIM: Since when?

NESSA: Oh, that. I forgot about that. That was just a couple of drunken nights. I mean we were never, you know, involved.

JIM: Right.

(*Silence.*)

NESSA: I'm sorry . . . I'm sorry I brought this up.

JIM: Why?

NESSA: Well, you seem pissed off. (*Pause.*) Jimmy, this may sound really, you know, ridiculous to you—I mean, two women want to have a baby—now that's really funny. But it's not a joke—it's my life. I don't know how to do this. (*Pause.*) I— deeply—deeply—want a child. We've looked into adopting one—politically, that seemed like a better choice, but being a gay couple is an enormous handicap—I mean, the agencies just don't want to consider that you could really have a happy, stable home—I mean, that's just too threatening—I mean, that you could be a good parent and everything. And—but—but also I feel . . . to have the capacity to grow a child, to be a part of that cycle, to continue it . . . to feel it grow inside me, and bear it and nurse it and . . . to care for another life . . . I know it sounds corny, but it's real . . .

JIM: (*Pause.*) Okay.

NESSA: Okay, what?

JIM: Okay, I accept what you're saying. I'm sorry I was defensive.

NESSA: Oh.

JIM: But I can't say that I think David is going to be open to this plan.

NESSA: Yeah. Both of us thought . . . we don't feel as sure as we did before about asking him.

JIM: Yeah.

NESSA: In fact, we both feel a lot better about asking you.

JIM: What? (*Pause.*) Asking me? But—you were saying—you were saying that one of the important things is that David's married. And that you and he hadn't—hadn't been involved.

NESSA: I know. I know, but now I don't think that's important, if it's okay with you.

JIM: You don't?

NESSA: No. Samantha and I talked it out and she agrees. She really likes you.

JIM: Oh. Well, I like her too.

NESSA: And we both feel we could trust you. (*Pause.*) Jimmy, I don't want to bulldoze you—I really don't. I know I always do that and I don't mean to—I don't want to do that . . . but if you did—if you felt okay about it . . .

JIM: Vanessa. (*Pause.*) I don't know. I don't think . . . I mean . . . I mean, I'd really like to help you out, but . . .

NESSA: It's okay. It's okay. I understand.

JIM: No, no—I mean, I'd like to be of help . . .

NESSA: Listen, Jimmy, I mean, it's okay. Don't feel bad.

JIM (*pause*): I'll think about it, okay?

NESSA: Really?

JIM: I mean, I think it's a very bad idea, but I'll think about it.

NESSA: Okay. Right. Well, here's the thing—I mean, just so you know, while you're thinking about it. We'll be leaving tomorrow for Beloit. You could come with us, or we could meet up in Milwaukee in three days if you—or even if you just want to hang out and talk about it some more—I mean, depending on your job in Philadelphia, but we could work that out. I'd like to get started right away if you decide yes, because I think I'll be ovulating sometime in the next week or so.

JIM: Uh-huh.

NESSA: (*Pause.*) But, Jimmy?

JIM: Huh?

NESSA: Well, I just want to say that you're a part of my life. I mean, that's just there, d'you know, whatever happens, that'll just always be there.

JIM: Uh-huh.

NESSA: But—. I'll just let you think about it. I know it's heavy. I mean, this wasn't one of the possibilities we were told about when we were kids. So . . . but I'll just go find Sammy. If you want to come down, Dody said there were a couple of extra rods in the front closet. . . . So I'll see you later, okay?

JIM: Okay.

NESSA: Or maybe I should just hang out here, in case things come up—d'you know? I mean if you have any thoughts?

JIM: No, why don't we talk about it more later.

NESSA: Yeah. Right. That seems good. Okay then. I'll just be down at the river.

(DOE *comes in.*)

JIM (*to* NESSA): Okay. (*To* DOE:) Hi.

NESSA: Oh, hi, Dody, how's it going?

DOE: Clunk, clunk, clunk. Anybody want some tea?

NESSA: No thanks, Dody. I'm gonna go find Sammy. I'll see you guys later, okay?

DOE: Okay.

NESSA: Bye-bye.

JIM: Bye.

(NESSA *leaves.*)

JIM: Clunk, clunk, clunk?

DOE: Mmm. They do say that it's rare for a writer to feel that what he's writing is any good, or, if he's having a hard time writing at all, that he'll ever write again. So, though it *seems* that I can't write, well, it's impossible to know until it's finished. So I just don't finish anything.

JIM: Very clever.

DOE: Yes. Would you like some tea?

JIM: Yeah—how about some warm milk?

DOE: Really?

(JIM *nods.*)

DOE: Sure. Let's see. Is that what I want? That's the important question: What about me!?

JIM: This one incredible artist, she was about sixty-five when Dubuffet visited her in this psychiatric hospital.

DOE: Yes.

JIM: She'd been committed twenty-five years before and was known to be completely incoherent.

DOE: Uh-huh.

JIM: So she's babbling away, making no sense at all, and then, suddenly, when for a moment she and Dubuffet are alone, she turns to him, looks him straight in the eye, and says, "You see, my dear, I don't care to be grown up."

DOE: Mmm. Is that how you're feeling?

JIM: Yeah. I wanna be a baby.

DOE: You are a baby. You're a grown up baby.

JIM: It's just that choosing to not be responsible allowed her to be in a world of complete creative freedom.

DOE: Have you been painting at all?

JIM: Yeah.

DOE: And how has it been?

JIM: Pretty clunky.

(*They laugh.*)

DOE (*she sets cups, etc. on table*): Nutmeg? Cinnamon? Honey?

JIM: Yeah.

(*Door flies open.* SAM *appears, calls back to* NESSA. *Butch barks.*)

SAM: I forgot my knife! (*She enters, her pant legs soaking wet and goes to her pack.*)

NESSA (*off*): Eeeek! It's moving! Sammy!

(*Butch barks.*)

SAM (*rummaging through pack*): I know it's here.

DOE: What happened?

SAM: I caught a trout!

JIM: Fantastic!

DOE: How great!

SAM: A rainbow. He's gotta be over two pounds. It's incredible. I haven't caught anything in over two years. Maybe we should fry him up right now. Is anybody hungry? They really taste best just caught. God. I never used the Irresistible before. No—wait a sec. Did I use the Irresistible or the Near Enough? I usually use the Blue Dun Spider or the Brown Bivisible. I tried the Fanwing Royal Coachman further upstream. (*Looking over the flies on her vest.*) Here's the Pink Lady. . . . Oh, my God—I think it was the Muddler! God! (*She calls out the door.*) Nessa! It was the Muddler!

NESSA (*off*): Great!

SAM (*to* DOE *and* JIM): God, it was so beautiful. I'd never gotten a drag-free drift on a first cast like that. Maybe I should see if I can catch another one so there'd be enough for dinner. God. What time is it?

NESSA (*off*): Six o'clock.

SAM: Oh, no. Hey—! I left my gear down there—!

NESSA (*off*): I've got it.

SAM: Oh. (*Back in.*) Damn. We have to have a rehearsal at six. Roxy called this morning and said she thought we were shaky with a couple of the new songs last night. Oh, damn. Maybe we could have a late supper tonight after the concert. Everybody could just have a taste? (*Back to the doorway.*) Van? Are we going to come back here before the performance?

NESSA (*enters*): No, we won't have time. Honey, if you want to clean it before we go, you'd better do it now. Dody, is there any newspaper we could use?

DOE: Piled up on the floor of the closet.

(NESSA *goes into closet.*)

SAM (*to* NESSA): So I guess we'll just grab a sandwich in town?

DOE: Why don't you make some to take with you?

SAM: Oh, that's an idea, Van?

NESSA (*emerges from closet with newspapers*): I think we're all going to eat at somebody's house in Madison. Come on, honey. (*She goes outside.*)

SAM: Okay. Well, I'll just go clean it and put it in the icebox. (*She goes out.*)

(*We hear car sounds, horn blows; Butch barks.*)

NESSA (*off*): Hey, Davidio!

DOE: David's back. He called this morning and said he'd gotten two hours of sleep.

JIM: And his patient's okay?

DOE: Yes. She'll be fine.

NESSA (*off*): David, look!

DAVID (*off*): Hey, chickies, whatcha doing?

NESSA (*off*): Hey, cocky, Sammy caught a fish!

DAVID (*appearing in doorway*): Far out. I'm starving.

SAM (*appears too*): Well, we thought that maybe we'd wait until after the concert because we have to go rehearse.

DAVID: What? Oh, no, it really should be eaten right away. Listen, it's okay. After you finish cleaning it, just give it to me and you can go. We know how to cook it.

SAM: Oh, well . . .

(DAVID, SAM, *and* NESSA *all come in.*)

NESSA: Go to hell, Rabinowitz. Don't listen to this bastard, Samantha. Here's the fish. I'll put it in the fridge. (*She does so.*) And if you dare touch it, Rabinowitz, I'll kill you.

DAVID: Ooooo.

SAM (*with newspapers, etc.*): Where should I toss these?

DAVID (*indicating*): Here. Well, good going, Samantha!

SAM: Thanks. I'm really happy.

NESSA: Sammy, we should get ready. Susan'll be here any minute.

SAM: Okay.

(NESSA *and* SAM *rummage through their packs.*)

DAVID (*arms around* DOE): Hi, honey.

DOE: How're you feeling?

DAVID: I'm feeling pursued by several very determined psyches. I wasn't able to shake them doing eighty on the road, so I think I'll go for a run. See if that works.

SAM: Is your patient okay? Tilly?

DAVID: She's fine. She's not going to be able to make the concert tonight, but other than that, it looks like the worst is over.

NESSA: You know, I bet you're usually a pretty good shrink, even though you're such a fucked up guy in your personal life.

DAVID: Oh, yeah! Well, fuck you, baby.

(SAM *goes out to change.*)

NESSA: Oh, yeah! And those comebacks! I'd forgotten about that razor edge wit—

DAVID: Oh, boy, am I gonna get you.

(DAVID *chases and eventually corners* NESSA.)

NESSA: Eeek! You better watch out, Rabinowitz—my hands have been registered as deadly weapons with the San Francisco police!

DAVID: Carmichael, I have been responsible and full of integrity all day long, got it? When I've finished teaching my little class at the university, and attending various neurotics in my office, and advising the young, earnest interns at the hospital, I get into my sadly abused Volvo and crawl out beyond the city limits and a change takes place. I welcome this change as my healthy need to balance the pressure and demands of my profession. So you better watch out, girlie! (*He attacks her and tickles her relentlessly.*)

NESSA (*she fights back*): Hi—! Ho—! Engowa!

(*They are weak with laughter.* DAVID *grabs her—a rough pinch or squeeze on ass or breast; we may not even see it.*)

NESSA: Hey—fuck you, David. Watch it.

DAVID: Oh, yeah, wow.

(*They collapse, separately, on floor.* SAM *comes back in dressed for the concert, goes to fridge, opens, stands, closes, goes to her instruments, inspects.*)

DAVID (*to* NESSA): Do you have to use our room to "fix yourself up," or can I go change into my macho jogging outfit?

NESSA: Oh, go ahead. I don't want to miss this embarrassing display.

DAVID: I'll be out in thirty seconds, if I can find my jockstrap.

NESSA: Oh, wow, far out.

(DAVID *goes.*)

SAM: Should we bring back some white wine?

DOE: Sure, if you'd like. That'd be nice.

NESSA: Jimbo, do you want us to try to sneak you in?

JIM: No. I don't think I can handle being a woman tonight.

NESSA: Okay.

(*We hear car sounds, a horn blowing, Butch barking.*)

SAM (*opens door, waves*): They're here. (*She calls out the door.*) We'll be right out! (*Back in.*) Come on, Nessa. (*She gets her stuff, goes out.*)

NESSA: I can't move.

JIM: Come on, Nessa. The women of the world await you.

NESSA: Yes, yes. That's true. The women of the world await. (*She jumps up, gets her clothes.*)

(DAVID *enters.*)

NESSA (*to* DAVID): Hey, wow, am I glad I got to stay around for this!

(SAM *comes back in.*)

DAVID (*to* NESSA): Eat your heart out, baby. (*He goes outside.*)

NESSA (*sings*): MACHO-MAN! (*She sees* SAM *standing, looking at her.*) I'm ready. Let's go.

SAM: Okay. (*To* DOE *and* JIM:) See you later.

DAVID (*re-enters*): Where's the cattail?

DOE: I don't know.

DAVID: Shit. (*He goes back out.*)

SAM: Oh. Was it leaning against the shed? I think Butch ate it.

DOE: It's okay.

JIM: What does he do with a cattail?

DOE: Keeps the bees away.

JIM: Oh.

NESSA: Okay, you guys, see you later.

DOE: Have a good show.

NESSA: Thanks. Bye, Jimmy.

JIM: See you later.

SAM: We'll probably be back around eleven or eleven-thirty.

DOE: Okay. Whatever. We'll leave the door unlocked.

NESSA: Come on, honey.

SAM: Bye.

DOE: Bye.

JIM: Bye.

(SAM *and* NESSA *leave.*)

DAVID (*re-enters*): It's not there. I'll take the tennis racket. (*He goes into hall closet, re-appears with racket.*) Be right back.

DOE: Bye.

(*He's gone.*)

DOE: Whew. (*Beat.*) Hi.

(JIM *looks at her.*)

DOE: Are you okay?

JIM: Well . . . I guess I'm kind of overwhelmed by . . . well, you know. Modern Life.

DOE: Ah, yes.

JIM: And all this talk about women.

DOE: Yes.

JIM: I mean, it just makes me feel, well, not being a woman . . .

DOE: Uh-huh.

JIM: I have this memory of this one day when we were all living together.

DOE: Yes.

JIM: It was a Saturday afternoon in October. Everyone else had gone into Boston for the weekend, so it was just Nessa and you and David and me.

DOE: Uh-huh.

JIM: Chad Jackson had gotten a big load of wood earlier in the week, and we'd agreed to divide it between the two houses and help each other split the logs on Saturday.

DOE: I remember that weekend.

JIM: Uh-huh. I'd been inside all week, bent over some overdue research paper . . .

DOE: Uh-huh.

JIM: That afternoon David retrieved me from my little cell and we walked down the road to Chad's. It was this incredible day—bright and windy and it smelled like snow—in fact they were forecasting the first storm, so Chad and David and I got into this kind of frenzy to beat the snow.

DOE: Uh-huh.

JIM: We were splitting and stacking and yelling and cursing and telling stories, and then the work itself—the physical labor—together with being out in that day— kind of overtook us. And we just kept going, lifting and splitting and lifting and splitting, in silence. Just our breath and the chopping and throwing and the sounds of the woods. . . . And when we'd done half of it, we hopped into the truck and drove the rest up to our place and went at it there. And I was panting and aching and soaked with sweat—I had no idea where the strength was coming from to lift the ax. At one point I straightened up and just stood there.

The light was fading, the sky was a pale yellow, cut with a thin string of charcoal clouds. A patch of the yard was washed with a golden light from the kitchen window. I looked up, and you and Nessa were standing there, looking out at us. And I waved. And you both waved. And, I felt this fullness. . . . I've never felt so full . . . of life . . . as I did at that moment. (*Pause.*) And I felt like a man. A man. In some deep, ancient sense. (*Pause.*) I don't know. I mean, if I were honest, I guess I'd say that's all I really want. That kind of romantic, traditional thing. I mean, it did feel like we were continuing something . . . the men outside, splitting wood for the long winter, the women in the kitchen cooking dinner. I mean, I mean, everything else seems so insignificant when I think of that moment.

DOE (*moves to* JIM): Come here.

(*They embrace, hold each other. Pause.*)

DOE: Do you miss her?

JIM: Vanessa?

DOE: Mm-hm. Have you been in love like that since then?

JIM: I . . . I don't know. I miss her. I miss you. I miss David. I miss everything.

(*They laugh, still in embrace.*)

JIM: Sometimes I'm just walking down the street, and I get gripped with this intense desire to fall on my knees at the feet of whatever strange woman I happen to be passing and grab the hem of her coat and beg her to take me home with her.

(*They laugh.*)

DOE: Oh, Jimmy.

JIM: (*Beat.*) Do you ever think of having children?

DOE: I can't.

JIM: You can't? I didn't realize that.

DOE: I had an abortion about a year ago and there were complications.

JIM: What do you mean?

DOE: We waited until the last possible moment, which made the operation more difficult. They poked a hole in my uterus and I got an infection which made me sterile.

JIM: Oh my God.

DOE: Yes. There you have it. Another example of Modern Life.

JIM: Why did you have the abortion?

DOE: I don't know. I mean . . . we weren't "ready," or something. We decided it wasn't a "good time." David had just been appointed to be a consultant to all the psychiatric wards in the region. I'd just signed with a publisher for a collection of my short stories.

JIM: Huh.

DOE: (*Pause.*) We were afraid of . . . something. Something in us or between us . . . I don't know. We haven't been able to really face each other since it happened. (*Pause.*) It's strange, to be barren, to be a barren woman. I've never felt so defined before, so mortal. That, more than anything else. It—it's terrifying to feel so—so mortal.

JIM: (*Pause.*) If there's anything I can do, I'll do it. I mean, anything—anything you want me to do . . .

(*Butch barks.*)

DAVID (*off*): Hey, Butch! Yeah! Atta boy! Down! Down! (*He enters.*) Hola, muchachos, que pasa?!

JIM: Hola.

DAVID (*looks at* JIM *and* DOE): Oh-oh, this looks like a heavy. No more heavies, guys, please, no more heavies today. (*Opens fridge, drinks from bottle of juice.*)

JIM: Heavy? Who's heavy?

DAVID (*goes and kisses* DOE): My little honey. Are you going to leave me? Are you going to run away with the lesbians and leave me?

DOE: No, dear.

DAVID: You're not?

JIM: I may, but she's not.

DAVID (*cuddling* DOE): You're not? Are you going to run off and live in New York?

DOE: I don't think so, darling.

DAVID: You're not? Promise me you won't leave me.

DOE: I won't leave you.

DAVID: At least not until after dinner.

DOE: Okay.

DAVID: Oh, God, thank you, baby. (*He goes to change, stops. To* JIM:) How long can you stay?

JIM: You mean here?

DAVID: Yeah. When do you have to be back in Philly?

JIM: Couple of weeks. I don't know. I might go to Beloit with Nessa and Samantha, and go from there.

DOE: But they're leaving tomorrow.

DAVID: What?! Jimmy, you can't go following those girls around. It's no good. You've gotta try to make a life of your own.

JIM: Yes, David, I know.

DAVID: You're not serious.

JIM: She wants to spend some time with me and I'm thinking about it.

DAVID: Oh, Jimmy, Jimmy, Jimmy. What's going on?

JIM: Nothing. Nothing's going on.

(*Phone rings.* DAVID *answers.*)

DAVID: Hello. Yes. Yes. . . . You're kidding. Uh-huh. Right. All right. Right. (*He hangs up. Beat.*) Fuck.

DOE: What happened?

DAVID: Tilly's dead.

DOE: What?

DAVID: She killed herself.

DOE: Oh, no.

JIM: God.

DAVID: Fuck. (*Pause.*) I'll go change. (*He doesn't move.*)

DOE: Do you need to go to the hospital?

DAVID: Yeah.

DOE: Would you like some company?

DAVID: No. (*Beat.*) Thanks. (*Beat.*) Or yes. It would be good of you to come along.

DOE: All right.

DAVID: You don't mind? You hate hospitals—don't feel you have to.

DOE: No, I'd like to.

DAVID: Okay.

JIM: How did she . . . ?

DAVID: O.D.'d on some pills right there under everybody's noses. They don't seem to know where she got them or quite how she took them with her hands and arms completely bandaged. (*Pause.*) I'll get dressed.

(DOE *gets ready.* DAVID *returns, dressing.*)

DAVID (*to* DOE): Okay?

DOE: Yes. Jimmy, if you want to go anywhere, just take the jeep.

JIM: Okay. I'm sorry about this.

DAVID: Yeah. Me too. Thanks.

DOE: Bye.

JIM: Bye.

(*They leave.* JIM *is alone. Blackout.*)

Scene 3

Night. JIM *alone. Butch is barking.*

SAM (*off, lowered voice*): Butch, shh! Good boy.

NESSA (*off*): Hey, Butch.

(*Door opens.*)

NESSA: Yes, yes.

SAM (*entering quietly*): I'll get him a biscuit, okay?

NESSA (*entering*): Yeah. (*She walks around, sees* JIM.) Hi, Jimmy.

JIM: Hi.

SAM (*walks around*): Hi.

JIM: Hi.

NESSA: Are Dody and David sleeping?

JIM: No, they're at the hospital.

NESSA: What happened?

JIM: David's patient died.

NESSA: Oh, no.

SAM: God.

NESSA: How terrible.

JIM: Yeah.

NESSA: God. Should we do something? I mean, is there anything . . .

JIM: I don't think so. (*Pause.*) How was the concert?

NESSA: Great.

SAM: Yeah. (*She goes to the fridge, opens it.*) You didn't eat the fish.

JIM: Nope.

SAM: Maybe we could cook it up for breakfast, when everybody's here. Do you think?

NESSA: Sure, honey, that'd be great. I'm not hungry now.

SAM (*to* JIM): We ate at Ho-Jo's.

JIM: What'd you have?

SAM: Clamburgers.

JIM: Mmmm.

NESSA: Jimmy, do you feel like talking tonight—?

JIM: I'm not sure I have much to say. I haven't been able to think very clearly about it.

(SAM *has gotten biscuit and gone to the door.*)

NESSA: Sammy, why don't you stay?

SAM: I want to let Butch run a little and then I'll come back. (*She goes out.*)

JIM: (*Pause.*) So what do you imagine would happen?

NESSA: What do you mean?

JIM: Well, tell me how you think this would work out.

NESSA: Well . . .

JIM: I mean, I'd join your tour, and—?

NESSA: Oh. Yeah. After Milwaukee. (*She takes schedule from her pocket.*) Let's see. Um. Beloit, Milwaukee, Appleton, Green Bay. Then Minneapolis, Iowa City, Grinnel, Omaha, and . . . I guess that's it. Then home. Then we'll be in San Francisco for about three weeks and then we'll play some festivals up the coast . . .

JIM: Uh-huh.

NESSA: And you could just be with us, whatever, as long as you wanted, until . . . I mean, maybe it'd happen right away. . . .

JIM: So, say I came with you tomorrow. You and Sammy and Butch and I would stay with friends, or . . . ?

NESSA: Oh, um. (*Refers to her schedule.*) Let's see. Beloit. We'll be staying in a lesbian collective.

JIM: I see. What would I do? Pitch a tent in the yard?

NESSA: (*Laughs.*) Oh, Jimmy, God, I don't know. Maybe we could stay in a motel if we can't work something out with the collective. That would be okay. I'd pay for it, and everything.

JIM: Uh-huh.

NESSA: But I'm sure the women will be supportive of what we're doing.

JIM: Uh-huh. So we'd share the details of this project with the various lesbian collectives as we traveled across the country.

NESSA: Jimmy, you don't have to make it sound that way. If you want to do it, we'll find a way to work it out that we both feel good about.

JIM: Okay. Say we work it out. So we do it. Then what?

NESSA: What?

JIM: Well, then you go sleep with Samantha?

NESSA: Oh, well, yeah, I guess so. I mean, I think it'd be better if we didn't become lovers, d'you know? I mean, Sammy and I have agreed on a monogamous relationship. Also, I really consider myself gay, d'you know? So I think it would be better to have sessions that were really clearly about making me pregnant and not then, well, you know, continue it, like sleeping together. I don't think that would be a good idea.

JIM: Do you remember me, Vanessa?

NESSA: What?

JIM: Do you remember me?

NESSA: Of course. Of course I remember you. What are you talking about?

JIM: (*Beat.*) So we'd check into a motel, and "make it"?

NESSA: Jimmy . . .

JIM: How're we going to do it? Reading magazines?

NESSA: What?

JIM: Watching TV? Watching our color set in our acrylic motel room? (*Pause.*) Maybe I'm old-fashioned, but I've never been able to just turn a part of myself off and "make it." I can't, well, I can't, you know, "perform"—

NESSA (*laughs*): Oh, Jimmy—

JIM: Vanessa, for Christ's sake will you listen to me? I'm taking this—I'm trying to take this whole thing very seriously. I'm trying to be open and honest and respect your situation. But. I've never used sex as a sport. I know a lot of people do, and I guess that's fine. I mean, sex is sex, I know that. And the fact that people chain sex to love and commitment may be wrong or unrealistic or debilitating. I mean, I've had some flings over the years, but I guess there was always the hope that it might become something deeper. . . .

NESSA (*goes to him, puts her arms around him*): Jimmy.

JIM (*removing himself*): There! See? What the hell was that?

NESSA: What?

JIM: What was that? How do you think I can hold back my feelings, Vanessa?

NESSA: What are you talking about? What do you think I'm doing?

JIM: I—

NESSA: Do you think I'm doing some kind of cheap—

JIM: No—

NESSA: —seduction? Jesus Christ, Jimmy.

JIM: I just said that—

NESSA: What's wrong with feelings? I mean—

JIM: Right.

NESSA: (*Beat.*) Why do you cubbyhole everything?

JIM: What? Me cubbyhole everything? I mean—fuck—really. You're the lesbian feminist in a monogamous relationship who wants to get planted by a straight male who you trust and respect and who's a friend but who won't be included in the results of the planting. I mean, maybe you better look at that, at what kind of importance you put on the source of your child. Maybe you should look at that, Vanessa.

(*Silence.* SAMMY *enters, is noticed.*)

JIM: I just don't ever trust separating things in the world. It doesn't seem right. (*Pause.*) And. To know there was a child in the world that I'd helped make, who might even resemble me . . . I don't know. Maybe it's just vanity and possessiveness. (*Pause.*) And then I do wonder how good it would be for a child to be brought up just by women. I mean, men are important too, damnit. You should have a little more respect.

NESSA: Jimmy—

JIM: No, really. You should show a little more sensitivity. We're people too. We have thoughts and feelings, passions and concerns about life and art and—. I mean, I am a man. I'm a man, damnit. What do you women want? What do you want? (*Beat.*) Christ.

(*Silence.*)

SAM: I don't think you want to do it. (*Pause.*) It's okay, don't feel bad. I wouldn't want to do it if I were you. I think it's a hard time to be a guy. (*Pause.*) I think the most important thing about bringing up kids is that they're really wanted and they get a lot of love and support. And the people bringing them up love and support each other.

JIM: Yeah.

SAM: (*Pause.*) So we'll try to do that. I don't know. Hopefully it'll work out. We want it to be a good thing, right, Nessa?

NESSA: Right.

(*Silence.*)

SAM: So anybody wanna get stoned? This woman at the concert laid this stuff on me. She said it was really good.

(JIM *and* NESSA *gesture no thanks.*)

NESSA: No thanks, honey.

SAM (*lights and smokes a joint, puts on a record*): Is this okay (*the music*)?

(JIM *and* NESSA *gesture it's fine.*)

NESSA: It's fine, honey.

SAM: So. (*To* JIM:) Is this a good visit for you?

JIM: What do you mean?

SAM: I mean, is it good for you to get away, to see your brother and everything?

JIM: Well, I don't know. I don't know. I haven't really seen my brother. I mean, we've never really . . . never really been able to be close . . . in a way.

SAM: Oh. (*Pause.*) Do you like Philadelphia? I went there once when I was little— the whole family drove out there, you know, the Liberty Bell and everything. I thought that was really weird that the Liberty Bell was cracked. I never got to know how—how come it's cracked? I mean, did that happen in a war or something?

JIM: I don't know.

(*Pause.*)

NESSA (*to* JIM): Do you remember those paintings you did of me?

JIM: Of course. "Abstractions on the Theme." "Her Breast, 1 through 12," "Her Thigh, 1 through 8," "Her Earlobe, 1 through 6" . . .

NESSA: Oh, God. The weeks and weeks we spent in the root cellar.

JIM: Somebody actually bought "Her Earlobe #6."

NESSA: No kidding. Well, I thought they were brilliant. People just didn't get them. They were too advanced.

JIM: Yeah, well, actually it was my landlord. Oh, and this friend of a friend bought "Inner Arm #7." That was one of your favorites.

NESSA: It was? Which one was it?

JIM: Reds and browns.

NESSA: Oh, the really hot one? Really intense?

JIM: Yeah. Anyway, the rest are molding in the basement of my apartment building.

NESSA: You're kidding. God, I'll buy some of them.

JIM: (*Pause.*) Listen . . . um . . . why don't we just do it?

NESSA: What?

JIM: We'll do it. You want to get pregnant, you ask a friend to help you out. Fuck it. We'll just do it.

SAM: Are you sure—

JIM: You know, let's not even talk about it any more. I mean, all I do is sift and weigh and sift and weigh and try to balance my profound life in view of all the artistic and philosophical theories I've read and studied. I'm sick of it.

NESSA: Well, Jimmy—

SAM: Do you want—

JIM: I'll make you pregnant. Let's not have any more talk. We'll just do it. (*He grabs a sleeping bag.*)

SAM: You want to start now?

JIM: We'll just go up to the study, okay?

NESSA: Well . . .

SAM: It's okay with me.

NESSA: Are you sure . . . You think it's the best . . . ?

JIM: You've both really thought it out, right?

SAM: Right.

NESSA: Right. (*Pause.*) Well . . .

SAM: Go on, Nessa. I think it's good.

NESSA: Okay. (*To* JIM:) Okay, let's do it.

JIM: Okay.

(*Pause.*)

NESSA (*to* SAM): Are you okay down here? Do you want to come along, or . . . ?

SAM: No. I'm okay.

NESSA (*to* JIM): You go ahead. I'll be right there, okay?

JIM: Yeah. (*He leaves.*)

NESSA (*to* SAM): Are you sure about this?

SAM: Yup.

NESSA: You don't feel weird about it?

SAM: Yeah, I feel weird about it, but I still think it's a good idea.

NESSA: Right.

SAM: (*Slight pause.*) Do you feel weird about it?

NESSA: Well, I guess it's a little strange, but I think we'll be glad.

SAM: Me too.

NESSA: Okay, well, I'll be down in a little bit.

SAM: Okay.

(NESSA *begins to leave.*)

SAM: Nessa?

NESSA: Yeah?

SAM: C'm'ere.

(*They come together, embrace.*)

NESSA (*quietly*): I love you, my darling. I love you so much.

SAM: See you later. (NESSA *leaves.* SAM *stands there for a while, then goes to records, finds Harry Belafonte's "Calypso," and puts it on. She then goes to the phone, dials. Into phone:*) I'd like to charge this to my phone in San Francisco, 415–332–3510. Hi, Mom. Did I wake you up? I'm sorry. Fine. Yeah, it's going really well. Uh-huh. Thanks for the sweater. I got it just before we left. Yeah, I've been wearing it a lot. Uh-huh. How's Dad? And Winky? . . . Well, sorry to wake you up. Go back to sleep. I think we'll be in Omaha on the 28th. Yeah. I'll send a postcard. Uh-huh. Okay, say hi to everyone. Me too. Bye. (*She hangs up. Stands still for a beat. Picks up receiver again and dials. Into phone:*) Could you charge this to 415–332–3510? Samantha Harris. Yeah. Hi, is Eliza there? Oh, yeah? Okay, could you just tell her Sammy called? Okay. And just tell her, we're doing it. Yeah. Thanks. Bye. (*She hangs up, goes to the stereo, turns the volume up, then goes to the fridge, opens, gets out fish, stands looking at it for a while, puts it down on the counter, looks around the kitchen, finds a shelf of cookbooks, takes them all down and begins to look through them.*)

(*Butch begins to bark.*)

DAVID (*off*): Down! Get down! Down! Goddamn dog.

(SAM *goes toward door, meets* DAVID *and* DOE *in doorway.*)

DAVID: Hi.

SAM: Hi. Sorry. (*Calls out.*) It's okay, Butch.

(*Butch is yowling.* SAM *goes out.* DAVID *and* DOE *come in.*)

DAVID: What's going on? What time is it?

(DOE *goes and sits in living room area, stares out downstage window.* DAVID *looks at the clock.*)

DAVID: Jesus. Where is everybody?

DOE: Why don't you go to bed?

DAVID (*he sees the fish*): Is she cooking her fish now? How long are they staying?

DOE: They're leaving in the morning.

DAVID: Oh. (*Beat.*) Are you hungry?

DOE: Am I angry?

DAVID: Hungry.

DOE: Oh. Yes.

DAVID: Me too. (*Beat.*) Are you angry?

DOE: No.

DAVID: (*Pause.*) You shouldn't have come.

DOE: I forgot how you are there.

DAVID: What do you mean?

DOE (*slowly*): In the midst of all those victims of whatever decay or violence, whatever act of rage or chaos, you glow. You look like a knight in a storybook.

DAVID: Things are clearer there. It's life and death. It makes more sense.

DOE: Yes.

DAVID: Don't leave me, baby.

DOE: David.

DAVID: What?

DOE: Don't.

DAVID: What?

DOE: That's such a cozy thing to say.

DAVID: What? What does that mean?

DOE: Let's not talk about it now.

DAVID: What do you want me to say? I'll say it—anything. (*Beat.*) Okay, how about, "I'm an asshole." (*Beat.*) How about, "I fucked up—it's my fault, all of it, everything's my fault."

DOE: Don't.

DAVID: Not enough? How about, "I killed her. I got too involved, I lost perspective, I killed her. I killed Tilly." Is that it? Done.

DOE: Oh, David.

DAVID: Slashing herself up—that's not a suicidal act, it's a plea for help, damnit. (*Beat.*) Maybe when she woke, in the hospital, the feeling of . . . futility.

DOE: Yes.

DAVID: What? (*Beat.*) What?

DOE: Do you want me to leave you?

DAVID: What?

DOE: I never suggested I leave you. This is your idea.

DAVID: What are you talking about?

DOE: Do you want me to leave? Is that what you want?

DAVID: Doe.

DOE: Let's face it.

DAVID: Face what?

DOE: You don't love me anymore.

DAVID: What?! I don't love you? What, are you crazy? I live and breathe you, for Christ's sake. What do you want?

DOE: I want to mourn the death of our child.

DAVID (*audible or inaudible*): Oh, God.

DOE: We've been so careless. How careless we've been.

DAVID: Oh, honey.

DOE: I want to stop feeling I've had my womanhood wrenched from me. I want you to stop hating me for not being able to bear you a child.

DAVID (*not protesting; a fact*): Oh, honey, no.

DOE: I want no more substitutes dragged through our life, dead or alive.

DAVID: *(Pause.)* I thought you'd had enough of me, that there was nothing I could give you, that I'd helped destroy the only thing you could . . . you could need me for, and . . . I didn't think you needed me.

DOE: I need you. I really need you. *(They hold each other. Pause.)* I want . . . I want to go back into this.

DAVID: Uh-huh.

DOE: You're the only person I've known who would go there with me, with whom I didn't see the limits, where anything was possible. Do you think we got scared of it, of how big it was?

DAVID: Uh-huh. *(Beat.)* Doe?

DOE: Hmm?

DAVID: I love you.

DOE: I know.

DAVID: I just *love* you. I've never loved anyone else, ever—you're the only one. I love you so much.

DOE: I know, my darling, I know.

(They continue to hold each other. Pause. Then Butch barks, SAMMY comes in as they relax apart.)

DAVID *(to SAM)*: Hi.

SAM: Hi. Are you . . . do you want me to . . .

DAVID: No, come on in. Are you cooking your fish?

SAM: Yeah.

DAVID: Where are Jim and Nessa?

SAM: What? Oh. They're upstairs.

DAVID: Oh.

SAM: They should be down in a little while.

DAVID: Is anything wrong?

SAM: No.

DAVID: Oh.

SAM: I'm sorry about your patient.

DAVID: Thank you.

SAM: Was it the woman you talked to last night? Tilly?

DAVID: Yes.

SAM: Oh. I'm sorry. (*Beat.*) I had a friend who killed herself.

DAVID: You did?

SAM: Yeah. We were in high school together, except half the time she wasn't there 'cause she'd have to go cool out in the hospital. I used to visit her a lot. We'd play music and stuff. She used to hate the food they'd make her eat, so once I put my mom's waffle iron and all this stuff into my guitar case, and smuggled it past the nurses and we had this great meal—waffles and we cooked the bacon on the waffle iron and it came out checkered. I just remember sitting around, laughing, eating checkered bacon. (*Pause.*) I still can't get over that she killed herself. I guess some people just don't want to live. (*Pause.*) Do you believe in heaven or anything?

DAVID: I don't know.

SAM: Oh, you should—it's great. I really believe Annie is up there, looking down on us, laughing, having a great time. She was a wonderful musician. She played the oboe. So I figure she's sitting up there in the clouds, doing these incredible riffs on her oboe.

(*They smile.*)

SAM: Did Tilly play an instrument?

DAVID: I don't know. She may have played the piano. I think she did.

SAM: Wow. That's great. So maybe she and Annie are doing some really beautiful music up there.

(*They laugh gently.*)

DAVID: Yeah, maybe.

(*Silence.*)

SAM: Are you hungry?

DAVID: Yeah. (*He goes over to the fish.*) Are you going to cook this?

SAM: Yeah. I got all your cookbooks out. I'm sorry—I'll put them back. I was reading all the different recipes. There are a lot of different ideas. But I think with fresh fish it's best to keep it simple because it's so good.

DAVID: Yeah.

DOE: How was the concert tonight?

SAM: Oh, it was incredible. One of those nights that everything connects. Everything just took off.

DOE: Great.

SAM: Yeah, it's a rare thing, when all you can do is just keep relaxing and telling yourself to trust it? Not to shy away or hold back? And you just ride it. You're not doing anything, it's doing it all, like with fishing. Lug, lug, lug, trudge, trudge, trudge, cast, reel, cast, reel, water, water, water, trees, sky, rain, clouds, sun, standing, waiting, wading, back and forth and back and forth, upstream, downstream, and then—! Everything stops. And it's there. And it's just you and the fish, in the wilderness, just the two of you. And everything else is like the back up.

DAVID: Huh. That's great.

(NESSA *appears.*)

DAVID (*sees* NESSA): Hi.

NESSA: Hi.

DAVID: Where's Jim?

NESSA: He's upstairs.

DAVID: What's he doing?

NESSA: I think he fell asleep. I'll be right back—I'm just going to hop through the shower.

SAM: We're cooking the fish.

NESSA: Oh, that's great, honey. I'll be right back. (*She goes.*)

DAVID: What's going on?

SAM: What's going on? Well, what do you mean?

DAVID: Did something happen? Is something going on?

SAM: Oh. (*Pause.*) Well, it's the kind of thing where in some ways you could say so. I mean, old friends meeting and important things being said. And . . . where everybody is in their life. I . . . I'm glad I got to come here and be here, even though it's been sad and difficult, but that's not always so bad.

DAVID: (*Pause.*) Uh-huh. (*Pause.*) I think I'll go change. Then I'll help you with the fish, okay?

SAM: Okay, great, thanks a lot.

DAVID (*looks over at* DOE *who has curled up on the couch*): Dody? (*Beat.*) She's asleep.

SAM: Yeah.

(DAVID *starts to go,* JIM *appears.*)

DAVID: Hi.

JIM: Hi.

DAVID: (*Pause.*) I'll be right back. (*He leaves.*)

JIM: I can't find my shoe. (*He looks around.*) Did I leave my shoe down here?

SAM: I don't know.

JIM: Damnit.

NESSA (*she comes in*): Hi. Where's David?

SAM: He'll be right back.

(JIM *is rummaging through his stuff.*)

NESSA: (*Beat.*) What are you doing, Jimmy?

JIM: I can't find my shoe.

NESSA: Did you leave it upstairs?

JIM: No.

NESSA: Are you sure? Do you want me to run up and look?

JIM: It's not up there.

NESSA: Okay. Did you look under the couch?

JIM: Vanessa, don't worry about it, okay?

NESSA: Okay. Okay. (*Pause.*) Sammy, we didn't do it.

JIM: What are you saying?

NESSA: I said we didn't do it.

JIM: Oh.

NESSA: I mean, we started to, but . . .

JIM: I wanted to. I wanted to be able to do it. It's difficult, one's limits—what a person is able to do.

SAM (*beat*): Uh-huh. (*Beat.*) Are you going to try again?

NESSA: Well . . . we should, that's true. We should give it another try. This wasn't the best . . .

JIM: Right.

NESSA: What?

JIM: But it was funny. It was entertaining.

NESSA: What? Jimmy, I laughed because I was feeling—

JIM (*overlapping*): You laughed? You couldn't stop laughing.

NESSA: But then I did stop.

JIM: I can't manage it, Vanessa, get it?

NESSA: Yes. Right. I get it. Okay. Okay, Jimmy. (*Beat.*) So. It'll be okay, though. We'll just have to rethink things. It'll work out, right, Sammy?

SAM: Yeah.

NESSA: Maybe the artificial thing. I don't know. (*Pause.*) Maybe I have been attached to . . . to the tradition. Maybe that's true. Maybe I did want you to be the father—I mean, know that it came from you, because I would trust that . . . but then not have to give you anything back. (*Beat.*) And the traditional way of conception, the man and the woman, how that happens—maybe I have been attached to that. (*Beat.*) I mean, I don't think the artificial thing is great, but . . . maybe it is the thing for us to do. (*Pause.*) I guess all I could think of was this life that was going to begin . . . here . . . and I didn't think. (*Beat. To* SAM *and* JIM:) I'm sorry. (*To* JIM:) I do remember you, Jimmy.

JIM: Thank you.

DAVID (*he comes in*): Hey—what's happening—Dody?—honey, do you just want to sleep?

(DOE *has been lying with her eyes open.* DAVID *comes and sits with her.*)

DOE: Look at the sky.

(*Pause as all look out whichever windows or skylight at the sky.* JIM *moves apart,* NESSA *moves to* SAMMY, DAVID *is with* DOE.)

SAM: Hey . . . does anybody feel like going for a ride? Drive around, find a lookout and watch the sunrise?

NESSA: Yeah.

SAM: Go to an all-night diner, watch the burnouts nodding off their stools, get some eggs and toast, o.j., coffee, sausage, a stack of cakes, you know, a little something?

DAVID: What about the fish?

SAM: Oh. Hell, you can have the fish—eat it, stuff it, frame it, I don't care.

DAVID: We'll save some for you.

NESSA: Don't you want to come?

DAVID: No. Take the jeep. (*He throws* NESSA *keys.*)

DOE: I recommend the Dodgeville Diner deep-fried french toast.

NESSA: Mmmm. You sure you don't want to come?

DOE: Yeah.

NESSA: Jimmy?

JIM: I think I need to crash.

NESSA: You do? Are you sure?

JIM: Yeah.

NESSA: Okay. Will you guys be up before we go?

DAVID: Yeah.

(JIM *and* DOE *nod.*)

NESSA: Okay, see you later.

SAM: Bye.

(JIM, DOE, *and* DAVID *each say or nod* "Bye." SAM *and* NESSA *leave. Butch barks.*)

NESSA (*off*): Hi, Butch! Wanna come for a ride?

(*Barks, jeep starts, honks. Silence.*)

DAVID: So.

JIM: I'm going back.

DAVID: You're what? To Philly? You mean today?

(JIM *nods.*)

DAVID: Why?

JIM: Well, I don't know. I feel like I should go back, live my own life and all that. (*Pause.*) I miss Dad.

DAVID: Yeah.

JIM: I wish we'd known he was going to die. I mean, I always assumed he'd be around for a long time. And I think about moments we shared . . . if I'd concentrated harder, noticed and appreciated things more. So much of it seems so hazy.

DAVID: Yeah.

JIM: (*Beat.*) I really want to spend time with Mom.

DAVID: Uh-huh.

JIM: Do you think you might want to come?

DAVID: I don't know. We'll talk about it. Maybe in the spring.

JIM: Okay.

DAVID: Listen, why don't you stick around for a few more days?

JIM: Um. Okay.

DAVID: Good.

(DAVID *moves to turn off the lights.* DOE *goes to* JIM, *touches his shoulder or cheek.*)

DOE: 'Night, Jimmy.

JIM: 'Night.

DOE: Will you sleep now?

JIM: Uh-huh.

DOE: Okay.

DAVID: 'Night, Jimbo.

JIM: 'Night.

(DAVID *and* DOE *leave for bed.* JIM *goes to the fish, looks at it, gets milk and graham crackers, sits at the table, watches the sunrise out the window as he dunks the crackers in the milk and eats. Lights fade out.*)

REMEDIAL ENGLISH

by

Evan Smith

Remedial English was presented as part of the fifth annual Young Playwrights Festival held at Playwrights Horizons in New York City from September 16 through October 12, 1986. It was directed by Ron Lagomarsino. The set was designed by Rick Dennis, costumes by Michael Krass, and lighting by Ann G. Wrightson. The cast was as follows:

VINCENT	Greg Germann
SISTER BEATRICE	Anne Pitoniak
ROB	Nicholas Kallsen
COACH	Shawn Elliott
CHRIS	Jim Fyfe
DAVID	Adam Redfield

CHARACTERS

VINCENT
SISTER BEATRICE
ROB
COACH
CHRIS
DAVID

TIME

One day of school, and that evening.

SETTING

Cabrini Catholic Academy—a private high school for boys in a medium-sized southern city—and VINCENT's home.

Scene 1

VINCENT *and* SISTER BEATRICE *are alone on stage,* VINCENT *seated right and* SISTER BEATRICE *seated behind a desk, left.* VINCENT *is wearing the Cabrini Catholic Academy uniform, a blue-knit sport shirt with the school crest over the left breast, khaki slacks, a black belt, and black penny loafers. He is in the waiting room of the office of* SISTER BEATRICE, *a teaching nun—a post-Vatican II nun, wearing not a flowing black habit and wimple, but a navy blue skirt, a white blouse buttoned to the neck, nurses' shoes, and a shapeless polyester blazer of white and light-blue stripes. On the jacket lapel is a simple stainless steel cross. At present, she is fully occupied grading test papers, and* VINCENT *is fully occupied waiting. In fact, we see from the expression on his face at rise that he has been waiting for quite some time.*

VINCENT *leans forward in his chair as if to look through a half-open door into* SISTER BEATRICE'S *office. He sees only* SISTER *gleefully wielding a red pen. He leans back, stretches, and then addresses her. She cannot hear what is essentially an interior monologue.*

VINCENT: Sister, I think it's very rude of you to keep me waiting like this. It's been fifteen minutes since you said, "I'll be finished in a minute," and unless I'm doing worse in algebra than I thought, you're off by fourteen minutes. Fourteen minutes may not seem like much to you—time moves pretty quickly after your hundredth birthday—but this is *supposed* to be my study hall. I have many important things to do during my study hall. I am developing a fascinating abstract pattern to fill the margins of my chemistry book, I'm right in the middle of *Lake Wobegon Days*, and I have almost finished my project of inserting the complete works of Judith Krantz into the library's card catalog. This is a school, after all, Sister. You of all people shouldn't want to see me wasting my time.

What did I do to merit such treatment? Is it because of that little tiff we had in English yesterday? Sister, we all say things in the heat of argument which we later regret. I'm sorry I called T. S. Eliot a "social-climbing Yankee papist." I don't even remember what I *meant* by that!

Have you forgotten all the good times we have had together? Don't you remember Dramatic Literature when I was a sophomore? We read aloud to the class . . . I was Jean . . . you were Miss Julie . . .

Oh, good grief, *please* don't tell me you found the Sister Beatrice Virgin Vote! God, how could I ever explain that? But if you *did* find it, you should at least be pleased with the results! Fifty-eight percent of my music class said that they thought you were a virgin. Sister, you've got to understand, such a large part of my life is spent in your company, and yet I hardly know anything about you! You've got to expect a certain amount of healthy curiosity and speculation. Do you ever wish you hadn't become a nun? What would you have done instead? Do you have any regrets? *Are* you a . . . ? Never any answers from this woman of mystery. Oh, well, you take your time, Sister, I don't mind waiting.

(SISTER *appears to be finishing her work. She shuffles her papers into order, looks at her watch, and goes to the unseen door.*)

SISTER: There. I thought I'd never finish these. Thank you for waiting so patiently.

VINCENT: You know what a patient disposition I have, Sister. But I must admit, I am rather shocked to see you spending your mornings hurriedly finishing up work from the night before. I was always told to do my homework at home.

SISTER: I expect you to do as I say, not as I do. Besides, this is a Monday morning, my least favorite of the week, and these are from D-Group. You'll notice I used up three red pens.

VINCENT: Ah, D-Group. That's the class that laughs every time you mention a dangling participle.

SISTER: Perhaps, perhaps. But they have their good points, too. For example, they never contradict me, unlike certain young men. There is something very charming about a class that believes everything you say.

VINCENT: Now that wouldn't be any fun. Your mind would rot.

SISTER: Speaking of mind-rot, I've been looking over your transcript.

VINCENT: Sister, it's a perfectly respectable transcript.

SISTER: Well, well, let's see. Shall we examine it more closely?

VINCENT: Do we have to?

SISTER: Now, your standardized test scores put you in the ninety-ninth percentile.

VINCENT: That's good.

SISTER: Yes, that's very good. It would lead one to believe that you were an intelligent young man.

VINCENT (*Mr. Humility*): Well . . .

SISTER: But we know better.

VINCENT: We do?

SISTER: Of course. Because we come down here and we see that your grade point average is a C.

VINCENT: A very high C! Five one-hundredths from a B.

SISTER: It was enough to keep you out of the Honor Society.

VINCENT: I know.

SISTER: Vincent, there is no excuse for a student of your ability to be making such grades.

VINCENT: I have an A in your class, Sister.

SISTER: And what about Algebra? And History? And Christian Morality?

VINCENT: Now, sometimes I pay a lot of attention in that class.

SISTER: I'm not talking about waking up long enough to proclaim the death of God and then going back to sleep! Getting attention from you in class is like drawing blood from a stone. You're a million miles away every day. You have a mind! Why don't you use it?

VINCENT: I do! Remember all those Beetle Baileys I translated into Latin?

SISTER: That's very admirable.

VINCENT: Thank you.

SISTER: I am the last person to throw cold water on a young man's creativity. But the point I am trying to make is that you don't give everything equal access to that mind of yours. And so, Mr. Ryan, we come to the purpose of this little chat.

VINCENT: You mean there's more?

SISTER: Oh, yes! As you know, I have a class of D-Group students, all of whom are bright and eager to learn.

VINCENT: Despite the fact that they haven't quite gotten the knack of their opposable thumbs.

SISTER (*after giving him a short, disapproving smile*): As it turns out, some of them want so desperately to learn that I have decided they should have personal tutors.

VINCENT: Are they failing that badly?

SISTER: Worse. But they need Senior English to graduate, and the last thing I want is Mommy calling me up to ask why I am keeping her little Johnny from graduating with his friends.

VINCENT: What has this got to do with me? I'm not failing anything.

SISTER: It occurred to me that the best way to bring you down from your little cloud would be to give you a student of your own. You are going to be an English tutor.

VINCENT: You're going to make a problem student a tutor?

SISTER: I want you to know what it's like to talk yourself blue in the face to a blank wall. So, for one hour, every day, some time after school, you will teach English to one of my D-Group students. Now, I was thinking of giving you Bubba Thompson . . .

VINCENT: Uh, Bubba Thompson. Gee, I don't think so . . .

SISTER: What do you mean?

VINCENT: Well, we had cross words once, and I don't think we would get along very well.

SISTER: You had cross words with Bubba Thompson?

VINCENT: Well, I had cross words, and he just furrowed his brow and tried to understand what I was saying.

SISTER: I see. Well, who have we got?

VINCENT (*with hesitation*): What about, umm, Rob Andrews?

(ROB *enters from left and goes to his locker. A young man of* VINCENT's *age,* ROB *is drop-dead beautiful. He is wearing old shorts, shoes, and shirt for P.E. He opens his locker, which contains his school uniform, and takes off his shirt.*)

VINCENT: He's in that class, isn't he?

SISTER (*checking her list*): Yes, he is. And he isn't doing any better than anyone else. Why? Would you rather tutor him?

VINCENT (*thinking quickly*): Oh, well, it's just that I kind of know him from P.E. Our lockers are across from each other.

(ROB *has taken off his shoes and socks, and he now takes off his shorts, revealing white cotton briefs. He stretches, and is apparently reluctant to put his uniform on.*)

VINCENT: We've become pretty good friends.

SISTER: Oh, well, that will never do. I can't have you tutoring your best friend; you wouldn't get anything done.

VINCENT: Oh, no, no, no! We're not *best* friends. We're more like nodding acquaintances. You know, we just sort of know each other. We only have one real class together, History, and so we kind of know who the other person is; that way, we wouldn't be going into this as strangers. We could get right to work.

(ROB *has gotten his uniform out of his locker and put on his shirt.*)

SISTER: Well, then, that's fine with me. You will be paid five dollars an hour.

VINCENT: Great.

SISTER: And I'll tell Mr. Andrews.

VINCENT: Fine.

SISTER: Now you've really got to make an effort to teach him.

VINCENT: Oh, I will.

SISTER: Because he needs to pass to graduate.

VINCENT: I understand.

(ROB *has got his pants on.*)

SISTER: So if that is all—

(SISTER *freezes for* VINCENT's *next speech.*)

VINCENT: Uh, Sister, I do think I should tell you that the only reason I finagled my way into tutoring Rob Andrews is because he is the best-looking boy I have ever seen in my life, and I have been obsessed by him ever since we were freshmen. And the only way I know him from P.E. is that I watch him change his clothes every chance I get. In actuality, I know him about as well as I know Mary Tyler Moore.

(ROB *has now got his school shoes on and his P.E. clothes put away.* SISTER *returns to normal.*)

SISTER: You've got a class shortly.

VINCENT: That's right.

SISTER: And this is your first day of tutoring.

VINCENT: Oh, really? I didn't realize.

SISTER: Yes, today. Don't forget.

VINCENT: I won't. Bye.

SISTER: Good-bye now.

VINCENT: Uh, Sister, if you don't mind my asking, what did you do before you became a nun?

SISTER: I became a novice right after I graduated from high school. Why?

VINCENT: Just curious. Thank you. Bye.

SISTER: Good-bye.

(VINCENT *leaves her office, then stops center stage.*)

VINCENT: Virgin.

(*The lights fade on* SISTER.)

Scene 2

ROB *finishes dressing and moves center.* ROB *and* VINCENT *meet.*

VINCENT: Looks like I'm going to be your tutor.

ROB: Yep.

VINCENT: So, like, when do you want to meet? After school?

ROB: Can't. Gotta work. How about eight?

VINCENT: Fine.

ROB: Where?

VINCENT: Uh—my house?

ROB: Okay. But I gotta leave by nine.

VINCENT: Perfect.

ROB: Yeah.

VINCENT: So I'll see you at eight, then . . .

ROB: Sure.

VINCENT: Hey, have we got History next?

ROB: Uh, yeah, we do.

VINCENT: I guess I'd better get my book then!

ROB: Yeah.

VINCENT: Well, I'll be seeing you . . .

ROB: Sure.

(ROB *exits, and* VINCENT *watches him. After he is gone,* VINCENT *stands a moment, then collapses in a heap.*)

Scene 3

Lights come up on the History classroom. There are five desks. They contain VIN-CENT, CHRIS, DAVID, *and* ROB *and one is empty. The* COACH *sits behind his desk.*

COACH (*disinterested and poorly informed*): And so, gentlemen, the uh, Greeks wound up going from pretty much Athens in the west, to uh, pretty much Persia and, uh, almost India in the east, which was pretty darn big in those days. And all of this was pretty much the fault of Alexander the Great.

(CHRIS *raises his hand.*)

COACH: Uh, yes, Christopher, what may I do for you, sir?

CHRIS: Wasn't Alexander the Great a homosexual?

(*The class laughs, except* VINCENT *and* CHRIS. CHRIS *knows he can get away with this by playing it straight.*)

COACH: Well, Chris, are you looking for a role model, or something?

CHRIS: No, no. I'm just trying to find out the whole story. I'm really into history, you know?

COACH: Yeah, I know. You're trying to be a jackass is what.

CHRIS: No, really, Coach, isn't that true? Wasn't Alexander the Great a little light in the loafers?

COACH: I'll be perfectly honest with you, I haven't got the slightest idea. But we are not here to discuss the, uh, questionable personal habits of historical figures. Now if you'll be so kind as to let me continue?

CHRIS: Oh, sure, Coach.

COACH: Thank you.

CHRIS: Any time.

(COACH *gives him a look that says, "Shut up," and* CHRIS *laughs.*)

COACH: As I was saying, the Greek Empire went from Athens to Persia, and the Greeks kind of spread their culture all over that area in between. It was called, I believe, Hellenic culture, and you might want to write that down, gentlemen. I don't think your memories are all that good, especially going by your last tests. . . .

(*The* COACH's *voice fades and the lights dim except those on* VINCENT.)

VINCENT: Rob is really the most beautiful boy I have ever seen in real life. And when you think about it, being beautiful is as good as being smart, or athletic, or a really great singer. All of those things you're born with, so what makes being born smart better than being born beautiful? Everybody is born with a most: most beautiful, most talented, or, for that matter, most obnoxious. Good God, I hope my most is a good one.

(*The lights come back up and we again hear the* COACH.)

COACH: So, Mr. Ryan, what do you suppose the answer to that question might be?

VINCENT (*taken by surprise*): Well, Coach, I've been giving that one some thought, and you know, I'm really stumped. That's a tough one.

COACH: Yeah, it is. The answer, gentlemen, is Sparta, the most militant of the Greek city-states. Now if you guys think that this school is strict, you would've wet your pants in Sparta. . . .

CHRIS: Coach, if the Greeks were so tough, how did the Romans kick their ass?

COACH: That's a good question, Chris.

(*Once again, the* COACH *becomes silent as the lights focus on* VINCENT.)

VINCENT: Chris is just bubbling over with mosts. I mean, he's just a great guy. He plays both football and basketball very well, and if his plays don't always make the team win, boy, do they make him look good. He's handsome, too. If you don't believe me, just ask him. And he's so smart! Gets straight A's. He spends every night before a test studying his voluminous notes, and sometimes he changes those voluminous notes into little, tiny notes. And sometimes he keeps on studying those little, tiny notes right up to and during the test! What dedication!

DAVID: Coach, how could the Romans and the Greeks both have Asia Minor in their empires? I thought they were enemies.

CHRIS: Because they didn't have them at the same time! Look at the dates on the maps, you idiot!

(CHRIS *leans far over in his desk to bop* DAVID *on the head with his book.*)

DAVID: Ow!

CHRIS: Sorry about that, Coach. You've gotta discipline him or he'll never learn.

VINCENT: David here is smart, but he tries too hard. If he would only calm down long enough to use his brain, he would have something to offer the world. He and Chris became friends in kindergarten over twelve years ago, and they've forgotten how not to be. They are best friends out of habit. In the same way, David is part of the group, out of habit. But if he were to walk into class today, not knowing a soul, I wouldn't give him one semester. On the other hand, he could surprise you. He has a very resilient ego. (*He goes over to* ROB's *desk and kneels beside it.*) And then there is Rob, who is . . . beautiful. (*He becomes lost in reverie.*)

COACH: Mr. Ryan.

(*Slowly* VINCENT *returns to his desk.*)

COACH: Mr. Ryan.

(VINCENT *sits.*)

COACH: Vincent, are you there, sir?

(*The lights return to normal.* VINCENT *looks up as the class laughs.*)

COACH: Uh, would you like to tell us what was going on in there, Mr. Ryan? Or should I just mark you absent today?

VINCENT: Oh, you don't have to do that, Coach.

COACH: I don't. I feel like I should thank you or something. If you don't start paying more attention, I'll thank you with this stapler upside your head. Now, Chris, why don't you tell us what was so all-fired special about the way the Greeks ran their outer provinces.

CHRIS: Sure, Coach. Well, the Greeks didn't like to bring in a bunch of their own guys to run a conquered territory, so they just kept the local people and pretty much let them keep their own laws, too, not like the Romans who . . .

(*As* CHRIS's *voice fades, so do the lights.* VINCENT *is still staring at* ROB.)

Scene 4

Lights come up on VINCENT *alone, center stage.*

VINCENT: The Cabrini Catholic Academy handbook is very clear on what is considered proper behavior in the halls. A student has exactly three minutes to get from class to class, during which time he is to conduct himself in a manner befitting an institution of learning; ergo, there is to be no running, no eating, no talking, and no rough-housing. However, if you want to talk, go ahead, that one is never enforced. Or better yet, sing. At the top of your lungs. Only one song, however, is considered proper for hall-singing. (*He sings:*)

There she was,
Just a-walkin' down the street,
Singin'
Doo-wah-diddy
Diddy-dum
Diddy-doo!

Under no circumstances should you be caught singing "Over the Rainbow." As a general rule of thumb, any Judy Garland tune is out. If you find the official Cabrini bookbag too cumbersome, there is a world of variety in the way you can carry your books. There is this—(*in his right hand*) and there is this (*in his left hand*). Never carry your books like this—(*across his chest*).

All of these rules, of course, are widely disregarded. But you never know who is watching. (*He looks carefully to the left, then to the right, then sings:*)

If happy little bluebirds fly
Beyond the rainbow
Why, oh, why, can't—

(VINCENT *is transported to Carnegie Hall. He bows as the lights fade.*)

Scene 5

Lights come up on the English room. VINCENT, DAVID, *and* CHRIS *are sitting with expressions of mixed amusement, morbid curiosity, and disbelief;* SISTER BEATRICE *is reciting.*

SISTER: Hear the sledges with the bells—
Silver bells!
What a world of merriment their melody foretells!
How they tinkle, tinkle, tinkle
In the icy air of night
While the stars that oversprinkle
All the heavens seem to twinkle

With a crystalline delight;
Keeping time, time, time,
In a sort of Runic rhyme,
To the tintinnabulation that so musically wells
From the bells, bells, bells, bells,
Bells, bells, bells,
From the jingling and the tinkling of the bells!

Hear the loud alarum bells—
Brazen bells!
What a tale of terror, now, their turbulency tells!
In the startled ear of night
How they scream out their affright!
Too much horrified to speak
They can only shriek, shriek,
Out of tune,
In a clamorous appealing to the mercy of the fire,
In a mad expostulation with the deaf and frantic fire,
By the sinking or the swelling in the anger of the bells—
Of the bells, bells, bells, bells,
Bells, bells, bells—
In the clamor and the clangor of the bells!
Hear the tolling of the bells—
Iron bells!
What a world of solemn thought their monody compels!
In the silence of the night,
How we shiver with affright,
At the melancholy menace of their tone!
For every sound that floats
From the rust within their throats
Is a groan.
To the tolling of the bells,
Of the bells, bells, bells, bells—
Bells, bells, bells—
To the moaning and the groaning of the bells.

(*She throws herself into a deep curtsey, then bounces up, very pleased with her performance.*)

SISTER: That was "The Bells" by Edgar Allan Poe. David, suppose you tell us what the chief poetic device of this poem is.

DAVID: Huh?! Well, uh . . . (*He immediately becomes flustered, and searches vainly through his book for the answer.*) I've got the answer right here . . .

SISTER: Christopher, why don't you help him out.

CHRIS: Well—

DAVID: No, I know this one. I know it! (*His search continues fruitlessly.*)

SISTER: Christopher?

CHRIS: As I was saying, *personification* is—

DAVID (*having finally found the answer*): Personification! (*He gives up disgustedly.*)

CHRIS: —the chief poetic device of this poem, "The Bells" by Edgar Allan Poe. A very fine poem, I might add.

SISTER: I'm glad you think so, Christopher. Why don't you tell us what it says to you.

(CHRIS *does far better with one-word answers. He pauses. He has never, however, been one to let ignorance keep him from voicing an opinion, so he forges ahead.*)

CHRIS: Well, this poem told me a lot about bells. I felt I really got to know the different kinds and their individual qualities. . . . I especially enjoyed the part about the alarum bells. I could really feel the danger in the air.

SISTER: Very good, Christopher. Mr. Ryan, what did you think of "The Bells"?

VINCENT: Um, it had some interesting images . . .

SISTER: Interesting images . . .

VINCENT: Some nice wordplay . . .

SISTER: Wordplay . . .

VINCENT: Very evocative descriptions . . .

SISTER: Good descriptions. What else?

VINCENT: To be perfectly honest—

SISTER: What?

VINCENT: —it is the silliest poem I have ever read.

SISTER: Since you are so enthusiastic about "The Bells," class, why don't you write a simple thousand-word essay discussing the author's purpose in writing it.

CHRIS: But Sister! I *do* like it!

SISTER: Then you shouldn't mind writing about it.

CHRIS (*more to* VINCENT *than to* SISTER): I didn't say it was silly . . .

SISTER: Right now we will go on to our next poem, since we're almost out of time. On page 232, you will find "A Noiseless, Patient Spider" by Walt Whitman.

DAVID: Wasn't he a homo?

SISTER: Be quiet, David.

(*She takes a deep breath, opens her mouth, and is about to speak when the class-change bell rings.* CHRIS *and* DAVID *fly out, leaving* VINCENT *and a disappointed* SISTER BEATRICE.)

VINCENT: Hear the lunchbell, joyful bell.

SISTER: Never make fun of a woman when she's down.

VINCENT: Are you down?

SISTER: Have you ever felt that you're spending your entire life trying to make a point that nobody gets?

VINCENT: You would be surprised, Sister.

SISTER: Your day is coming, young man. Have you spoken to Mr. Andrews?

VINCENT: Yes, this morning.

SISTER: You will soon know exactly what I'm talking about.

VINCENT: Oh, you are too smart for me, Sister.

SISTER: You have to get up pretty early, Mr. Ryan. Pretty early.

VINCENT: Sister knows best.

SISTER (*having collected her papers, about to leave*): And by the way, when you are tutoring Mr. Andrews, keep your mind on English.

VINCENT: I beg your pardon?

SISTER: Your mind is so susceptible to wandering. . . . Keep it on English, understand? Bye.

(SISTER *exits, and* VINCENT *looks after her thoughtfully.*)

Scene 6

Lights come up on the lunchroom. At a table sit CHRIS, VINCENT, *and* DAVID. *They are eating their lunches.*

CHRIS: Jesus, David, sometimes you are such an idiot! The tangent wave begins at negative one-half pi, not zero; when you are drawing the phase shift, you start at negative one-half pi, not zero. When you draw the phase shift for sine or cosine, then you begin at zero. Jesus!

DAVID: But I thought Mrs. Allen said—

CHRIS: Will you forget what you thought Mrs. Allen said, you never think right anyway. For God's sake, you're usually fuckin' asleep in that class anyway, no wonder you're failing.

DAVID: I'm not failing.

CHRIS: Oh, Jesus, excuse me, you've got a fucking D-minus, that's such a big difference!

DAVID: Well, it's not failing.

CHRIS: You will be failing after the test tomorrow; I can see you getting a twelve.

DAVID: The only reason you're passing is because you cheat all the time.

CHRIS: *You* cheat! But you still fail! You're the only person I know who can cheat on a test and still get a forty-four. (*To* VINCENT:) You know what he did? He had all the answers to the multiple choice in code on his pencil, but this idiot starts at the wrong end of his pencil and fills them all in backwards! You're just lucky Mrs. Allen didn't realize that if she had graded your paper backwards, you would have had a hundred. Jesus, you're stupid!

DAVID: Vincent, what did you get?

VINCENT: What?

DAVID: In Algebra and Trig?

VINCENT: Oh, an eighty-two.

CHRIS: I got a ninety-eight.

VINCENT: Yeah, but I got an honest eighty-two. An eighty-two to be proud of. An eighty-two that says, "Hey, I learned eighty-two percent of this chapter." Your ninety-eight says, "Chris can cheat without getting caught."

CHRIS: That's an accomplishment, too.

VINCENT: I thought we were in school to learn.

CHRIS: Learn? Here? Ha! We're in high school to get practice in faking our way through life.

DAVID: And to party.

CHRIS: And to party! *Party!* I think I can safely say I have fully learned the art of partying. All you need is three kegs and a hundred people.

DAVID: And a good band.

CHRIS: Right. Aw, shit. You know what I heard? They're gonna get the same band for the prom this year that they had last year. That sucks.

DAVID: Yeah, well . . . Who are you taking?

CHRIS: Patricia, who are you taking?

DAVID: You know who I'm taking.

CHRIS: Sharon?! You're actually taking Sharon?

DAVID: What's wrong with that? I like Sharon.

CHRIS: Why? Does she fetch? Can she play dead?

DAVID: Very funny.

CHRIS: Does she have a sister? Or should I say a litter? We could fix Vincent up—

VINCENT: Leave David alone. He should be able to attend the prom with the date of his choice, free from harassment.

CHRIS: Who are you taking?

VINCENT: Me?

CHRIS: Yeah, who?

VINCENT (*after a pause*): I don't dance.

CHRIS: You can't get a date?

DAVID: You don't have to dance.

VINCENT: I can get a date.

CHRIS: Who are you gonna ask?

VINCENT: I don't know.

CHRIS: Yeah.

(*The lights focus on* VINCENT.)

CHRIS: Sharon. David, you are a jerk.

VINCENT: Actually, Chris, I was thinking of asking Rob Andrews.

DAVID: Would you just forget it?

VINCENT: I think we would look pretty sharp together, in evening wear.

CHRIS: How can I? I have to be seen with you.

VINCENT: I can't dance, though. Of course, he could lead . . .

DAVID: You don't even know her!

VINCENT: I've never asked someone for a date before; I don't know how . . .

CHRIS: I hope to keep it that way.

VINCENT: Rob in a tuxedo . . .

DAVID: There's more to a girl than just being pretty.

VINCENT: We'd go to dinner afterwards. I guess I'd have to pay.

CHRIS: I've noticed. That's what makes them such bitches.

VINCENT: I'd say good-bye to him on his front porch . . .

DAVID: Jesus, Chris, you've got to have a better reason for wanting to spend time with a girl than just she's good-looking. Don't you agree, Vincent?

(*Lights snap back to normal.*)

VINCENT: Yeah! What?

DAVID: Shouldn't you have a better reason for going with a girl than just she's beautiful?

VINCENT: Absolutely.

CHRIS: What would you know?

VINCENT: What I lack in experience I make up in moral fortitude. A girl's physical attractions should be the last of her qualities put under consideration.

(*As* VINCENT *is finishing that little pontification,* ROB *enters from the right and crosses to the left.* VINCENT *sees him, feels terribly hypocritical, puts his head on the table and covers his face.*)

VINCENT: Oh, Jesus.

CHRIS (*stopping* ROB): Rob, what time is it?

ROB: Five after one.

CHRIS: Yo, wait up. The bell is about to ring; wake up, guy. You'll be late.

VINCENT (*sheepishly picks up his head; to* ROB): Hello.

ROB: Hi.

VINCENT: Haven't forgotten about tonight?

ROB: Nope. Eight.

VINCENT: Eight.

(ROB *and* DAVID *exit.*)

CHRIS: What's at eight?

VINCENT: I'm going to tutor Rob in English.

CHRIS: You're going to tutor Rob Andrews?!

VINCENT: Yeah.

CHRIS: Ha! Good luck!

VINCENT: Why thank you, Chris. Maybe I will get lucky.

Scene 7

Lights come up in the locker room. VINCENT *has his P.E. clothes in a bag.*

VINCENT: It is interesting to note, I believe, that fidelity is responsible for the making of more saints than the apparition of Mary and the Stigmata combined, and among favorite plot devices in opera, fidelity is second only to the intercepted letter and is way ahead of the babe kidnapped at birth. It is my belief, however, that both Bernadette and Butterfly would break under the weight of maintaining fidelity of thought in the Cabrini locker room; especially to a jock who had difficulty remembering their names. Nonetheless, I am the picture of nonchalance and self-control in the locker room. The jock of my dreams is wearing nothing more than a towel as he walks by me? I'd rather hear about David Gray's sister's braces, very complex orthodontal tools, those. The finest ass in the school is walking back from the shower stark naked? I wouldn't notice such a thing, I'm too busy trying to repair a badly frayed shoelace. (*He pulls out a tennis shoe.*) You can't let these things go on too long. You could wind up with serious sneaker damage.

(DAVID *enters and sits down on the bench in front of the locker next to* VINCENT. ROB *enters left and exits right, gym bag in hand.* DAVID *and* VINCENT *begin to change for P.E., starting with their shoes and socks.*)

DAVID: I'm not failing, and he knows I'm not. I've got a seventy-four, and if I get anything higher than an eighty-nine on this next test, it will be a seventy-five, and that's a C. Of course, if I get anything lower than a forty, I'll have a sixty-nine, which *is* failing, but I'm not worried about that. The only reason I got that forty-four was because of the term paper in Global Perspectives—I didn't have any time to study. I'll probably wind up with a C, or if I really work, I could have a B. But I'm not failing. Chris is the one who had better watch out about failing. One of these days, he's gonna get caught cheating, and then see if he's president of the Math Club!

VINCENT: Why are you telling me all this? Tell Chris. You shouldn't let him talk to you the way he does.

DAVID: Nah, then I'd never hear the end of it. (*Pause.*) You know, Miz Culbert caught him cheating once, but she didn't do anything. She just took his test. If I got caught cheating, I would be put on suspension so fast it wouldn't even be funny.

VINCENT: No, you wouldn't and neither would I. We're too well-liked by the faculty.

DAVID: You know, Miz Culbert would be pretty, but her tits are too small.

VINCENT: What?

DAVID: Miz Culbert's tits are too small. She would be pretty, but she's got no chest.

VINCENT: Are you serious?

DAVID: Yeah, haven't you ever noticed?

VINCENT: No, I can't say that I have.

DAVID: Really? How could you help it?

VINCENT: I just don't notice that kind of thing.

DAVID: That's weird, man.

VINCENT: It's not weird. Why is that weird?

DAVID: I don't know. That's all I think about in music. What about Miss Sanders? Have you ever noticed her chest?

VINCENT (*exasperated*): Christ, David, you've known me for three years, can't you—

(*There is an awkward pause.* VINCENT *is afraid to finish what he has begun, and* DAVID *doesn't often see* VINCENT *upset. Then, from offstage, we hear* CHRIS's *voice, followed shortly by* CHRIS.)

CHRIS (*off*):

There she was,
Just a-walkin' down the street

(*He appears.*)

Singin'
Doo-wah-diddy
Diddy-dum

(*On "dum," he hits* DAVID *on the head with a football.*)

Diddy-doo!

(*To* DAVID:) Come on, man, you're on my team today. Vincent, *think fast!*

(*He throws the football at* VINCENT *and exits.*)

DAVID: Are you going to play today?

VINCENT: I don't think so.

(DAVID *exits. Lights up on* VINCENT, *center, tossing the football in one hand.*)

VINCENT: I've grown to like P.E. I'm not much into sports, but then the coaches aren't much into getting me into sports. So I just pretend like I'm participating, and they pretend like they don't know I'm pretending. It works out very nicely; they can concentrate on coaching the guys who are actually interested in football, and I can concentrate on the guys. Well, really, one guy in particular. It's a purely academic interest, mind you—after all, I have only a scant five hours to prepare for an evening tutorial.

Scene 8

The lights come up on the living room of VINCENT's *house. There is a sofa, center.* VINCENT *tries on clothes to find the right look. Suddenly, he hears a silent doorbell* ring. *He goes to the door, and opens it, revealing* ROB. *They fall into a passionate kiss. Then* VINCENT, *still embraced by* ROB, *pulls his head back and looks at the other boy.*

VINCENT: Sure you're gonna do that.

(*He pushes* ROB *out the door. He starts to pace, occasionally looking at his watch. Then he sits down. The doorbell really rings.* VINCENT *opens the door, and* ROB *enters, dressed in a tank-top T-shirt and jeans. He carries a textbook, a notebook, and pen.*)

VINCENT: Well, hello. Come in.

ROB: Hi.

VINCENT: Did you just get off work?

ROB: No, I had to go home and shower, first.

VINCENT: Oh, I see.

ROB: Why, am I late?

VINCENT: Only about forty minutes. I hadn't really noticed until now.

ROB: I'm sorry.

VINCENT: Don't worry about it, but we don't have a whole lot of time left. Didn't you say you had to be somewhere at nine?

ROB: Yeah.

VINCENT: So . . . have a seat. (*He notices that* ROB *is already seated.*) How are you doing in English? Sister Beatrice made it sound like you were having some trouble.

ROB: I guess you could say that.

VINCENT: What are your grades like?

ROB: Mostly failing. But I did get a C the other day.

VINCENT: Well, that's . . . average, at least.

ROB: Yeah.

(*There is a pause.*)

VINCENT: What are y'all studying right now?

ROB: English.

VINCENT: Yes, but, uh, what aspect of English?

ROB: Oh, we're in poetry right now.

VINCENT: Yeah, she's got my class on the same thing. Does she read to y'all?

ROB: Yeah.

VINCENT: She's quite a character, sometimes.

ROB: Yeah.

(*Pause.*)

VINCENT: Is that your book?

ROB: Yeah, it is. Here. (*He hands the book to* VINCENT.)

VINCENT: What page are y'all on?

ROB: 547.

VINCENT (*finds the page*): Ah, "There Is No Frigate Like a Book." Have you read this?

ROB: Maybe, I don't remember.

VINCENT: Oh. Okay. I'll read it.

> There is no frigate like a book
>   To take us lands away,
> Nor any coursers like a page
>   Of prancing poetry.
> This traverse may the poorest take
>   Without oppress of toll;
> How frugal is the chariot
>   That bears the human soul!

Um, did you notice how the words she chose enhanced the meaning of the poem?

ROB: What was the meaning?

VINCENT: Well, what do you think?

ROB: I don't know, we haven't gone over that one yet. Sometimes she gives us stuff to read and never does tell us what it means.

VINCENT: Yeah, she does that to us, too.

ROB: But she expects us to know it for a test.

VINCENT: Oh, well, that's her way . . .

ROB: She's a bitch, that's all.

VINCENT: Well, be that as it may, when Emily Dickinson wrote "There Is No—"

ROB: What was her name?

VINCENT: Emily Dickinson.

(ROB *gets out his pen and starts to write in his notebook.*)

ROB: Dick—in—son . . . Wasn't she the bitch who lived locked away in her house all her life?

VINCENT: Uh, yes, but I wouldn't exactly call her a bitch.

ROB: You know what I mean. It doesn't sound like she was completely normal.

VINCENT: Nobody is.

ROB: Whatever. So what does it mean? (*He is poised to take notes.*)

VINCENT: She is just saying that books are a way of traveling around the world in your mind, that doesn't cost anything and—

ROB: Wait!

(ROB *is writing laboriously.* VINCENT *is amazed to find that he is taking down his every word.*)

ROB: . . . doesn't . . . cost . . . anything. And. What now?

VINCENT: I guess that pretty much says it.

ROB: Great. What's next? (*He smiles; apparently poetry is going to be easier than he thought.*)

VINCENT: Uh, well, let's see. (*He looks at the next page.*) It's "On Going to the Wars," by Richard Lovelace.

ROB: Like in Linda?

VINCENT: I suppose so, yeah. It goes like this:

> "Tell me not, sweet, I am unkind
> That from the nunnery
> Of thy chaste breast and quiet mind,
> To war and arms I fly.
>
> True, a new mistress now I chase,
> The first foe in the field;
> And with a stronger faith embrace
> A sword, a horse, a shield.
>
> Yet this inconstancy is such
> As you, too, shall adore;
> I could not love thee, Dear, so much
> Loved I not honor more."

This poem always gets on my nerves . . . (ROB *starts to write this.*) No, no, you don't have to write that. I'll tell you when you should write something down. I was just going to say that my personal opinion of the poem is that it is highly irritating, not to mention philosophically unsound.

ROB: Why's that?

VINCENT: Well, here's this guy telling his girlfriend he's going to risk his life for honor; that's stupid; he's probably fighting over hunting rights in some royal forest, and he'll probably come out without a scratch while a couple of hundred of his serfs will be hacked to death—in the name of honor. Wars aren't fought for noble reasons; they're fought over money. I can't think of any war worth fighting.

ROB: Well, what if the Russians invaded us, what then?

VINCENT: If they want the country that badly, let them have it.

ROB: That's stupid.

VINCENT: No, think. Communism and dictatorship will never take hold in America. Russia's known nothing but tyranny for the past thousand years. We've had freedom since the 1600s. We'd never stand for it; it just wouldn't work.

ROB: So we would have to fight them.

VINCENT: No, we could use peaceful methods like civil disobedience or passive resistance—haven't you ever heard of Gandhi?

ROB: The guy in the movie?

VINCENT: Yeah, he freed India from the English without fighting a war.

ROB: Oh.

VINCENT: Yeah!

ROB: Well, I still think we should nuke 'em off the face of the earth.

VINCENT: That is the most asinine statement I have ever heard in my life.

ROB: Oh? What does asinine mean?

VINCENT (*thinking more of belly buttons than ideology*): Asinine means . . . interesting; that is the most . . . interesting statement I have ever heard in my life. That brings us to "Oh Who Is That Young Sinner" by A. E. Houseman.

ROB: Hey, are we almost done? 'Cause I've got to meet my girlfriend soon.

(*Pause.*)

VINCENT: Girlfriend?

ROB: Yeah.

(*Pause.*)

VINCENT: Oh, who is it—she! Who is she?

ROB: Joan McNamara.

VINCENT: Oh, I know Joan! Does she still drive that pink Volkswagen?

ROB: No, she totaled it.

VINCENT: Wow, was she hurt?

ROB: No. But her father had to re-lay the foundation of their pool.

VINCENT: Oh . . . heh, that sounds like Joan. Y'all are supposed to go out tonight?

ROB: Yeah.

VINCENT: Gonna get something to eat?

ROB: Maybe. Might just hang out at her house. But, hey, don't think I won't have any time to study.

VINCENT: No, no. I wasn't even thinking about that. Just being nosy, I guess. I don't go out much. (*There is a pause.*) But anyway. Our next poem is "The Garden of Love" by William Blake.

ROB: Sounds like a porno flick.

VINCENT:

> I went to the Garden of Love
> And saw what I never had seen.
> A chapel was built in the midst,
> Where I used to play on the green.
>
> And the gates of the chapel were shut,
> And "Thou Shalt Not" writ over the door;
> So I turned to the Garden of Love
> That so many sweet flowers bore;
>
> And I saw it was filled with graves
> And tombstones where flowers should be;
> And priests in black gowns were walking their rounds
> And binding with briars my joys and desires.

So you see that the Garden of Love is really a metaphor for organized religion. He is saying that the "Thou Shalt Not" approach to religion takes most of the innocent fun out of life. It's binding with briars his joys and desires. (*He takes a deep breath.*) And I really doubt he was thinking of this when he wrote the poem, but I can't help but associate that last line with—homosexuality.

ROB: You mean this poem is about fags?

VINCENT: No! I mean . . . it could be, if you wanted to see it that way. I mean, uh, it fits in with the general idea, in that homosexuals don't really hurt anyone, and yet most of organized religion is screaming at them that they are sinners, when all they are doing is having sex, and what's so awful about that?

ROB: When it's two guys? That's sick.

VINCENT: Maybe to you, but not to them, so why is it your business? Why is it the Church's business?

ROB: It's in the Bible.

VINCENT: A lot of things are in the Bible! In the Old Testament it says not to eat ham, do you follow that? In the New Testament, it says to forgive your enemies, to turn the other cheek, an idea the Old Testament totally contradicts. Do you know that in grade school the nuns told me it was all right to kill during a war? That God wouldn't mind?

ROB: That's true, it's okay when there's a war on.

VINCENT: Not if you follow the teachings of Christ. And I have yet to meet a Christian who does.

ROB: You're a Christian.

VINCENT: Not really. I'm an atheist.

ROB: You are not.

VINCENT: Yes, I am. Is that hard to believe?

ROB: You're really an atheist?

VINCENT: Sure. My belief about God is that there is none. Jews don't accept Christ, well, I don't accept any of it.

ROB: You've got some strange ideas, man.

VINCENT: What, that I think that if two people love each other, they should be able to have sex, be it man-man, woman-woman, or even man-woman? That it's wrong to kill people wholescale over something stupid like oil lanes, or land, or worse still, politics? That Christ should be taken at His meaning, not His word? Those ideas aren't strange at all. In fact, the poets have been screaming all of that at the pig-headed human race ever since time began! If you ask me, to believe anything else is not only strange, but dangerous!

(*There is a short pause as* VINCENT *exults in self-righteousness.*)

ROB: Should I be takin' notes or something?

(*That takes all the wind out of* VINCENT. *He slumps down onto the sofa.*)

VINCENT: No.

ROB: Okay. (*He looks at his watch.*) Hey, I've gotta be going. (*He gathers his books.*) It's been real interesting.

VINCENT: Really interesting. It's been really interesting.

ROB: Oh. Sure. So, uh, will I see you tomorrow night, same time?

(ROB *freezes.*)

VINCENT: Tomorrow night, same time? You mean forty minutes late?! Good Lord, what nerve! Sister Beatrice meant this to be a challenge, but, Jesus, I'm not up to it! He calls Emily Dickinson a bitch, can't figure out "There Is No Frigate Like a Book," and is a war-monger, to boot! I don't care how beautiful he is, if he tries to walk through that door tomorrow night, I'll clobber him with the family Bible!

ROB (*back to normal*): Will I see you tomorrow night, same time?

VINCENT: Sure.

ROB: Great. Well, I've gotta be going. See ya. (*He heads for the door.*)

VINCENT: Wait! (*And then lightly:*) Do you feel like you've learned anything tonight?

ROB (*enthusiastically*): Yeah! I've got that Dickinson bitch down cold.

VINCENT: Oh. Well, that's great.

ROB: See ya.

(ROB *exits.* VINCENT *stands a moment in thought. He then crosses back to the mirror he looked in at the beginning of the scene, and looks again. He looks away, then crosses to the sofa, where he picks up* ROB's *English book and distractedly thumbs through the pages. Then he remembers something. He looks up a certain page in the book and reads aloud!*)

VINCENT:

Oh, life is a glorious cycle of song,
A medley of extemporanea;
And love is a thing that can never go wrong:
And I am Marie of Romania.

FORGET HIM

A play in one act

by
Harvey Fierstein

Forget Him was first produced at the Fine Arts Theatre of Southampton College in New York by the East End Gay Organization as part of its second annual playwrights' gala on September 4, 1982. The production was directed by Eric Concklin with setting by Bill Stabile. The cast was:

MICHAEL   Phillip Astor
EUGENE   James A. Harris
MARLOWE   Nancy Heikin

The play was also perfomed at Town Hall in New York City as part of an evening celebrating the sixth anniversary of The Glines. The production was directed by Herb Voegler, with setting by Bill Stabile. The cast was:

MICHAEL   Harvey Fierstein
EUGENE   Court Miller
MARLOWE   Estelle Getty

CHARACTERS

MICHAEL: A pleasant-looking young man in his late twenties.

EUGENE: A bit older than Michael. The handsomest of the three.

CLYDELLE MARLOWE: The oldest of the group. He looks out of place.

The stage is bare but for a long fuchsia-colored fainting bed (chaise longue). Sitting on it, stage left to right, are MICHAEL, EUGENE, *and* MARLOWE. *All three are dressed in white;* MICHAEL *and* EUGENE *are casual,* MARLOWE *wears a suit.*

The lights rise on them sharply. They stare blankly straight ahead, unmoving. Suddenly MICHAEL *lets out a loud yell. He recovers his composure, turns to look at* EUGENE *only to find no reaction.* MICHAEL *faces front again.*

Pause.

MICHAEL *lets out another yell, a louder one at that. He once again turns to find no reaction on* EUGENE's *face.* MICHAEL *looks forward again.* MARLOWE *moves now for the first time, leaning over slightly to look at* EUGENE. *He sees that* EUGENE *is unmoved and faces front again.*

Pause.

MICHAEL *screams again, stops quickly and turns to* EUGENE *hoping to find some reaction. There is none.* MARLOWE *turns to* EUGENE *as well, sees the frozen expression and turns back.* MICHAEL *faces front again.*

Pause.

Taking a deep breath, MICHAEL *lets loose a series of loud screams and yells. Exhausted, he searches* EUGENE's *face. No reaction.* MICHAEL *and* MARLOWE *turn simultaneously toward each other. They stare into each other's faces. They turn to face forward again.*

Pause.

MARLOWE (*with philosophic abandon*): The best of us forgets himself.

MICHAEL (*quiet determination*): I want my money back.

MARLOWE: Forget it.

MICHAEL: I want my money back!

MARLOWE: You got what you paid for.

MICHAEL: I paid for the best.

MARLOWE: And I'm the best.

MICHAEL: And him?

MARLOWE: You picked him.

MICHAEL: You picked him.

MARLOWE: For you.

MICHAEL: I'll sue.

MARLOWE: You'll lose.

(*Pause. Stalemate. They face forward in silence.* MICHAEL *screams again, stops, checks* EUGENE, *and faces forward.*)

MARLOWE: I too loved . . . once.

MICHAEL (*pleading his case to the audience*): You wouldn't believe how much he charged me.

MARLOWE: I lost money. But what's money, we're talking happiness.

MICHAEL: I'm not happy!

MARLOWE: That's my fault?

MICHAEL: *Yes!*

MARLOWE: So, sue.

MICHAEL: I will.

MARLOWE: You'll lose.

(MICHAEL *is about to scream again.* MARLOWE *covers his ears.* MICHAEL *decides not to scream, but continues pleading his case.*)

MICHAEL: I saw his ad in the paper and called.

MARLOWE: My fault, I'm sure.

MICHAEL: He took my check on the spot.

MARLOWE: With a gun to his head.

MICHAEL: Twelve weeks—not a word.

MARLOWE: Three weeks for the check to clear.

MICHAEL: Four weeks' salary.

MARLOWE: Nine weeks' work.

MICHAEL: Finally I got a call.

MARLOWE: No charge for the toll.

MICHAEL: He had found "Him."

MARLOWE: A challenge. But I rose.

MICHAEL: I was to meet them at such and such place, at such and such time.

MARLOWE: *If* it was convenient.

MICHAEL: *If* it was convenient.

MARLOWE: Such a man he wants to sue.

MICHAEL: We met in a rented hall.

MARLOWE: Public viewings preclude private displays.

MICHAEL: It was the Gay Synagogue's Annual Purim Party.

MARLOWE: A choice affair.

(*The lights fade to romantic party twinklings as* MICHAEL *gets carried further into the mood, reliving the experience.*)

MICHAEL: I held great expectations.

MARLOWE: You're a pip.

MICHAEL: It was spring. A cool clear spring evening. I wore a white yarmulke.

MARLOWE: There was magic in the air.

MICHAEL: There was a fine crowd dancing, talking, drinking the Purim punch.

MARLOWE: A rented hall, a Purim punch, and thou.

MICHAEL: I mingled lightly, watching nervously for Mr. Marlowe. I didn't see him. The unmistakable strains of "The Monster Mash" wafted gently from the dance floor as I surveyed the assemblage wondering, Is that "Him"? Could this be "He"? I toyed with the lady finger sandwiches but was too tense to swallow. I waited.

MARLOWE: They also starve who only stand and wait.

MICHAEL: My throat was parched with anticipation. With trembling hands I was ladling a cup of Purim punch when, across the crowded room, our eyes met. I didn't need Marlowe to tell me who he was. He was "Him." He was beautiful. He was smiling. I was squinting as I hadn't worn my glasses. Our eyes locked, or so it seemed. The record on the dance floor changed to who knows what. My soul played another tune. As I stared across at the beautiful stranger, my ears heard nought but Ezio Pinza singing "The Love Ballet" from *West Side Story.*

(MARLOWE *sings the romantic break from the gym scene dance music as* MICHAEL, *with outstretched arms, performs the all-too-familiar choreography replete with finger snapping.*)

MICHAEL (*truly transformed*): And in that moment I lost all sense of who or what or where I was. For all I knew I was Natalie Wood and he was Richard Beymer. Or he was Natalie Wood and I, Richard Beymer. What did it matter? We'd work that out later. My sense and senses stripped, I started slowly across the dance floor toward my destiny . . .

MARLOWE (*shattering the mood completely*): My cue.

(*The lights return, the music stops.*)

MICHAEL: He stepped between us, bringing me back to the rented room and Purim punch.

MARLOWE: To everything, turn, turn, turn . . .

MICHAEL: And demanded final payment.

MARLOWE: And a time to every purpose . . .

MICHAEL: In cash.

MARLOWE: *If* all was satisfactory.

MICHAEL: *If* all was satisfactory. I paid.

MARLOWE: What else?

MICHAEL: But "He" was gone.

MARLOWE: The Purim feast had served its purpose. Private pairs want private parts.

MICHAEL: I was handed a piece of paper. A name and address imprinted there.

MARLOWE: Seek and ye shall find.

MICHAEL: Eugene Sloane.

MARLOWE: Michael and Eugene.

MICHAEL: On the Upper West Side.

MARLOWE: Sloane and DeLosa. Magic!

(*The lights fade once again, but this time to romantic blues with white twinkling stars.*)

MICHAEL: Marlowe gone, thoughts of Mr. Sloane bubbled in my brain. Tears of expectation rose in my throat. I hailed a cab.

MARLOWE: Yellow Cab: the wings of love.

MICHAEL: I arrived at a luxury condo, doorman and all.

MARLOWE (*offering out a business card*): All included in the one low price.

MICHAEL: I was escorted to a duplex penthouse. I was fainting.

MARLOWE: Tax and tip included.

MICHAEL: I stood before the door. I tested my breath, pinched a blush into my cheek and gave a stylish rake to my yarmulke. I rang.

(*He reaches out and mimes ringing the bell. We hear a doorbell chime, "Be My Love,"* from Romeo and Juliet.)

MARLOWE: I give group rates.

MICHAEL: The door was opened by Eugene's personal secretary and gentleman's gentleman, Beulah.

MARLOWE: Senior citizen discounts available.

MICHAEL: He led me to a fuchsia fainting bed and handed me a cocktail. Silently he lowered the lights, started the music and stole away.

MARLOWE: A fuchsia chaise, a Yukon Jack, and how.

MICHAEL: I was alone. I waited. The blood coursed through my breast, the booze through my brain—when suddenly, in the doorway, parting pink satin drapes and gold tasseled teasers, he appeared.

MARLOWE: Oh, rapture!

MICHAEL (*yelling*): I want my money back!

(*The mood is broken. The lights restore.*)

MARLOWE: Now don't be hasty.

MICHAEL: Four hours is hasty, Mr. Marlowe. Four days may be rushing things. But four years?

MARLOWE: Frankly, Mr. DeLosa, I can see you're unhappy. And far be it from me to add to your unhaptitude, but after four years this is none of my concern.

(MICHAEL *screams again.*)

MARLOWE: Please, Mr. DeLosa. You're frightening no one but yourself.

(MICHAEL *stares to the front as* EUGENE *moves for the first time. He reaches out and pats* MICHAEL'S *knee comfortingly. His hand rests there on the knee. Pause.* MAR-LOWE *and* MICHAEL *turn simultaneously and study* EUGENE'S *hand. Pause. They face forward once again.*)

MARLOWE: You certainly can't claim he's unresponsive.

MICHAEL: You, Mr. Marlowe, are a fraud!

MARLOWE: Mr. DeLosa, you forget yourself. And me! I am hardly one of those fly by night, astro-illogically charted, macho-magic computer data-based dating services. I am Clydelle Marlowe of "Marlowe's Social Intro's Inc." My family has been adjoining loving pairs for six generations. I can produce any number of affidavits from any combination of individuals which will attest to my competence and downright dexterity at Cupid's art. And so, for you to sling five-letter words at me when I have come from the goodness of my heart to hear your frivolous complaints, sans obligation (which guarantee expired three years and four months ago; see paragraph thirty-nine, mini-contract B), well . . . I'm wounded. Deeply and profoundly wounded.

MICHAEL: Are you finished?

(MARLOWE *nods.*)

MICHAEL (*yelling again*): I want my money back!

MARLOWE: You got what you paid for.

MICHAEL: I paid for the best.

MARLOWE: Which is more than you deserve.

MICHAEL: Which is less than you gave.

MARLOWE: I gave what you asked for.

MICHAEL: This is not what I asked for.

MARLOWE: This *is* what you asked for and I've got the documents to prove it.

MICHAEL: I'll call your bluff.

MARLOWE: I'll smack your face.

MICHAEL: You say you can prove it; prove it.

MARLOWE: You're on.

(MARLOWE *defiantly whips out a packet of papers from his jacket pocket. He slips a pair of reading glasses on.*)

MARLOWE: I have your full application.

MICHAEL (*imitating him*): You have my full attention.

MARLOWE (*unfolds and studies the papers*): Now, according to this document, you called upon my unique services because, and I quote, "I am tired of the bars, bathrooms, backrooms, and balconies that compose the sad sex-nests and brooding grounds of our 'Wham-bam-thank-you-Ma'am-see-you-later-when-my-Jones-is-comin'-down-saturated subculture.'"

MICHAEL: I never said that!

MARLOWE: No, I did. What you said was, "I want someone to love me," but I find that a bit naked, don't you? I admire the honesty, but I loathe the desperation.

MICHAEL: I was only trying to make myself clear.

MARLOWE: Water is clear. Love wants wine. N'est-ce pas? (*Point made, he returns to the papers.*) Let us now review your checklist of specifically requested requirements. Sex? Male. You'll have to grant me that one. Height? Five ten or over. Right again. Hair? (*Actor's coloring.*) Batting a thousand. Eyes? (*Actor's coloring.*) Money back indeed. Build? Athletic. No extra charge. Personal equipment? You didn't check a box.

MICHAEL (*a bit embarrassed*): I know.

MARLOWE: You have to check a box.

MICHAEL: Frankly I found that question . . . questionable.

MARLOWE: Questionable?

MICHAEL: Crude.

MARLOWE (*offering the paper and a pen*): What's crude to the goose is food for the gander. Check a box.

MICHAEL (*looking at the boxes*): Is there one for optional?

MARLOWE: These are human organs, Mr. DeLosa, not bucket seats.

MICHAEL (*checking a box*): Hasn't anyone ever told you that size doesn't count?

MARLOWE (*takes back the paper*): Anyone who says size doesn't count, doesn't know how to count. (*Looks at the answer.*) Is this what you wanted or received?

MICHAEL: Received.

MARLOWE: Mr. DeLosa, you give me pause. (*He clears his throat and gets on.*) Well, then there's hobbies, interests, positional preferences . . .

MICHAEL: It's none of those.

MARLOWE: Well, if the problem isn't with him, it must be with you. (*He glares accusingly.*) Let's review *your* self-description, shall we? Sex? Male. Height? (*Actor's height.*) Hair? Yes. (*He looks at* MICHAEL *and shakes his head.*) Eyes? (*Actor's coloring.*) Build? Slim. (*He looks at* MICHAEL *again.* MICHAEL *glares back.*) Personal equipment?

(MARLOWE *holds the paper and pen out to* MICHAEL. MICHAEL *takes it, reads it, starts to check a box, then stops and considers. He thinks. He scratches. He finally checks a box and hands the paper back.* MARLOWE *looks at it.*)

MARLOWE: If you say so. Well, the rest is pretty standard. . . . Wait, what's this penciled in here?

MICHAEL: There wasn't a box for it.

MARLOWE: That's probably the mix-up right there. You can't go around giving answers to which there are no questions.

MICHAEL: I felt it was relevant.

MARLOWE: If it was relevant there'd be a box. What does it say?

MICHAEL (*under his breath*): Virgin.

MARLOWE: Pardon?

MICHAEL (*slightly clearer*): Virgin.

MARLOWE: Once more with feeling.

MICHAEL: It says I was a virgin!

MARLOWE: Virgin?

MICHAEL: Virgin.

MARLOWE: Virgin.

MICHAEL: *Virgin!*

MARLOWE: En masse or parcel?

MICHAEL: Wholly.

(*Pause. And then* MARLOWE *lets out a huge scream of laughter.*)

MICHAEL: Something bothering you?

MARLOWE: A wholly virgin homosexual? (*Laughs again but sees* MICHAEL *is not amused.*) You've got to admit it's different.

(MICHAEL *stands, clears his throat, poses himself in a lecturing posture and delivers his speech with practiced conviction.*)

MICHAEL: I have never made an attempt to be contrary either in my sexual preference or the non-performance thereof. I am simply the seed sown and grown of the nourishment provided. While heterosexuals may unquestionably enter their marriage beds in any condition they see fit, it seems that me and mine are disallowed such a choice. Why? I ask you, why? Were we not all raised in the same homes, with the same parents, rules, and examples? Were we not all privy to the same pubescent jokings, auto-erotic fussings, familially doled en-guilt-ments? Why then should we not be *expected* to exercise the same choices? In my opinion it is because our ethnicity is defined by our sexual preference. That preference misnomered to identify only a particle of our social and political activities. And in so naming, such misunderstanding leads to the creation of fear and myth. There is, in the majority's ruled mind, no such thing as a "homo-ual." If there is no sex, there is no such being. A homosexual who chooses to await his matrimonial pairing becomes, in this mythic misunderstanding, an object of jeers and fears while a heterosexual man in my position might seem foolish but would be admired for his restraint. Well, I am here to state proudly that I have exercised the choice not openly offered. I have denied the old-wives'-tale mentality one more shining example of their lack of wisdom. I am a homo-ual. I believe in the sanctity of commitment, entering such in the pure state to which I was born, untainted, untouched, and untasted. I thank you.

(*He bows and seats himself with finality.*)

MARLOWE: A prepared statement?

MICHAEL: I get asked a lot.

MARLOWE: Have you thought of selling transcripts?

MICHAEL: I want my money back!

MARLOWE: Mr. DeLosa, while hoping not to inspire another prepared statement, I must admit that I still haven't caught the gist of your complaint.

MICHAEL: I'm unsatisfied. Isn't that enough?

MARLOWE: For washers, dryers, and magazine subscriptions maybe. But I need to understand. Finish your story.

MICHAEL: What story?

MARLOWE: Same old story. "He'd just entered the room . . ."

MICHAEL: Do I have to?

MARLOWE: You want your money back?

MICHAEL: He'd just entered the room . . .

(*The lights fade back again to blues.*)

MICHAEL: I was reclining on the fuchsia chaise, semi-sipped demijohn in hand, tête to toes tingling toward revelation when he appeared. He appeared more perfect than before, now draped in a gently clinging kaftan, relaxed and at home at home. He leaned softly against the drapes and smiled. I was frightened by his confidence. He was more than I had bargained for. I felt unworthy. The only thought that kept me from bolting for the door was that he too had seen me at the Purim Fest and had parted with great sums to bring me to his fainting couch. The idea made me blush. I struggled to speak. "Eugene?" I croaked. He raised his arm and lowered the lights 'til we glowed a candle's breath from darkness.

(*The lights lower to a golden glow. As* MICHAEL *speaks,* EUGENE *comes to life acting out the scene with him.*)

MICHAEL: He approached the chaise and I. He sat beside me. I could barely breathe. He touched me. (*A crescendo of romantic music swells up.*) Softly he caressed my cheek. Slowly, sensuously, he ran his fingers over my face, through my hair and from there down across my ears and around my neck. I shivered with arousal. Arousal hitherto the realm of Brontë, Genet, and Barbara Cartland. Still I could not speak, but raised my hand to stay his advancement. He kissed each finger as his searching palms inflamed my shoulders and found my heaving breast. He was now fully prone and I halfway as my conscience battled for control. "Not so fast. This is forever. You've waited this long, be certain now." But the moment was too perfect, his loving too adept, and I too ripe to stop.

(EUGENE's *head is now buried in* MICHAEL's *neck as he writhes in ecstasy.*)

MICHAEL: I gave myself fully to the union of our bodies, casting aside the years of chaste vigilance, as my heart cried forth, "This is the time. Now is the moment. Here is the bonding you've long awaited. This is 'Him.' Your lover and your life. And even if he's not, you've got a money back guarantee!"

(*They reach their height and* EUGENE *collapses onto* MICHAEL's *chest.* MICHAEL *strokes his hair softly.*)

MICHAEL: And so we spent our night and half the following day: napping, loving, holding together. My dreams were alive with the years to come. Years of Eugene and I lying in perfect contentment as one forever on a fuchsia chaise.

(MARLOWE *snaps the mood and the lights return to normal.*)

MARLOWE: I'm certain that in a thousand words or less I could never express how much your sharing this experience has meant to me, but I'm a busy man with a weak constitution who would appreciate greatly your getting to the point: What's your problem?

(MICHAEL *sits up forcefully, pushing* EUGENE *off of him. As they sit up,* MICHAEL *is now placed in the center of the couch surrounded by the others.*)

MARLOWE: Well?

(MICHAEL *points at* EUGENE.)

MARLOWE: So?

(MICHAEL *gestures toward* EUGENE *again.*)

MARLOWE: Yeah, so?

(MICHAEL *shakes a violent finger at* EUGENE.)

MARLOWE: What? He doesn't play charades?

(MICHAEL *screams at the top of his lungs.* MARLOWE *covers his ears.*)

MARLOWE: Please, Mr. DeLosa, I'm not deaf!

MICHAEL (*at long last*): Well, he is!

MARLOWE: I can see that, Mr. DeLosa, I'm not blind.

MICHAEL: Well, he is!!!

MARLOWE: That's right. I forgot.

MICHAEL: Well, I didn't!

MARLOWE: But you knew.

MICHAEL: No I didn't.

MARLOWE: Well, I knew.

MICHAEL: You could have told me.

MARLOWE: Funny, I thought I had.

MICHAEL: Funnier, you hadn't.

MARLOWE: Either way, I was sure you'd notice.

MICHAEL: Well, I didn't. Not until well into the next day. And by then it was too late. The deed was done. The die cast. The untrodden road taken, the apartment sublet . . .

MARLOWE: You work fast.

MICHAEL: And he's no shirker.

MARLOWE: So this is your big complaint? You think this is grounds for incompatability; that he's deaf and blind and you're not?

MICHAEL: You make it sound so petty.

MARLOWE: I don't judge.

MICHAEL: You don't understand either.

MARLOWE: I wouldn't necessarily say that. I can imagine how trying it must be to lead someone around everywhere he wants to go.

MICHAEL: I don't lead him around. Beulah takes him out, or the chauffeur. Unless, of course, we're going out together and then . . . it's kinda nice having him on my arm.

MARLOWE: But having to speak in sign language always must be frustrating.

MICHAEL: I figure we miss about fifty percent of what the other one's saying. I'd call that better than average for most couples.

MARLOWE: But you must have to read the newspapers to him . . .

MICHAEL: Beulah does that.

MARLOWE: But you do all the shopping . . .

MICHAEL: Beulah.

MARLOWE: The cleaning.

MICHAEL: Beulah.

MARLOWE: The cooking and bill paying . . .

MICHAEL: Beulah's work is never done. And on Beulah's day off, Eugene cooks. He's a gourmet chef. Certified. French and Greek.

MARLOWE: But living on a physically challenged man's pension . . .

MICHAEL: What pension? Look at this joint. He's loaded.

MARLOWE: Then what is he, stupid?

MICHAEL: Third ranking mathematician in the world.

MARLOWE: He beats you?

MICHAEL: Wouldn't flick a fly.

MARLOWE: Insensitive.

MICHAEL: A saint.

MARLOWE: Unfaithful.

MICHAEL: I'd kill him.

MARLOWE: Booze and dope!

MICHAEL: Milk and cookies!

MARLOWE: Then *what?*

MICHAEL: He's deaf and blind. Don't you listen?

MARLOWE: But you just said . . .

MICHAEL: Can you imagine what it's like to have to remove your gloves in twelve
    degree weather just to tell him to put his gloves on? Or what it's like to be in a
    crowd of people who figure that you're deaf too so they can say whatever they
    want about you? Or how it feels when kids drop coins behind you to test if
    you're really deaf? Better yet, when people hand you coins. Have you any idea
    how thoughtless thoughtful people can be? Like the ones who scream and wave
    their arms thinking he'll hear them better. Or the ones who help you across
    streets that you don't want to cross. Let me tell you about the restaurants that
    make you sit in the back. The store clerks who serve you in the stockrooms. Cab
    drivers pretend not to see us. Muggers can't wait to greet us. Religious people
    cross themselves.
        And does he make it any easier? God forbid. When I first moved in he threw
    a party for me to meet all of his friends, most of whom are deaf, the rest blind.
    Two hundred and fifty people in this room. Two hundred and fifty laughing,
    talking, partying people and I could still hear the cat walk across the floor. You
    know how creepy that is? And you wouldn't believe what they talk about. You
    think "Dead Baby" jokes are sick? You should hear the ones they tell about
    people who can hear and see! And how can you argue? Everytime there's a
    disagreement it turns into a wrist slapping contest. I've never been good with
    languages. His colleagues think I'm a dope, his friends say we have nothing in
    common and his mother thinks he married below him. . . . It hasn't been easy,
    Mr. Marlowe, let me tell you.

MARLOWE: If you're so unhappy why didn't you leave before this?

MICHAEL: I already told you; I have my principles.

MARLOWE: But after four years, why leave now?

MICHAEL: Enough is enough.

(EUGENE *waves his hand in front of* MICHAEL *to get his attention. When they
"speak" the one "listening" puts his hand over the hand of the other. Words are spelled
out this way.* MICHAEL *will speak aloud as he spells.* EUGENE, *of course, speaks
silently.*)

MICHAEL (*taking his hand*): What?

(EUGENE *spells.*)

MICHAEL: We're not finished yet.

(EUGENE *spells.*)

MICHAEL: We'll eat later.

(EUGENE *spells.*)

MICHAEL: If you're hungry go eat.

(EUGENE *pouts.*)

MARLOWE: That's the most beautiful thing I've ever seen. "And hand in hand, By the edge of the sand, They danced by the light of the moon."

MICHAEL (*incredulously*): What?

MARLOWE: "The Owl and the Pussycat." Norman Lear. I'm sorry, but I find that extraordinarily romantic.

MICHAEL: It's *not* romantic.

MARLOWE: It is if you don't speak the language.

MICHAEL: Romantic is dancing together to a record you call "Our Song." Romantic is chasing each other through a snowy park. Romantic is a teasing wink across a crowded room, a scribbled note under the bathroom door, hearing "Hi, Hon, I'm home" instead of . . . (*He fingerspells wildly.*)

(EUGENE *waves for attention.* MICHAEL *grabs his hand.*)

MICHAEL (*annoyed*): What?

(EUGENE *spells.*)

MICHAEL: I'm telling him about you.

(EUGENE *spells.*)

MICHAEL: Yes, he knows you're deaf.

(EUGENE *spells.*)

MICHAEL: Yes, he knows you're blind.

(EUGENE *spells.*)

MICHAEL: Yes, he knows you're hungry.

MARLOWE: So romantic.

MICHAEL: Mr. Marlowe, will you help me?

MARLOWE: What can I do?

MICHAEL: Admit that you were wrong. Say you made a mistake and that we never should have been matched up.

MARLOWE: You're not getting a refund.

MICHAEL: Forget the money.

MARLOWE: Forgotten.

MICHAEL: Say you were wrong.

MARLOWE: But I'm not.

MICHAEL: Say it anyway.

MARLOWE: What do you want from me? If you're unhappy, leave.

MICHAEL: I can't just leave Eugene. He's the most wonderful man I've ever met. And he loves me.

MARLOWE: So?

MICHAEL: What if he's not "Him"? What if my "Him" is wandering the streets out there waiting for me, his perfect "Him" to come along? And here I am, trapped by my convictions, held captive by a less than perfect love, never to know whether I truly belong here or if my destiny drifts further and further away from me. But if it was all a mistake . . . ? Your mistake?

MARLOWE: Is that what this is all about? Shame on you, pointing an odious finger at me when all you want is to pass the buck and walk blamelessly away. I'm sorry. Forget it.

MICHAEL: You got me into this.

MARLOWE: And you can get yourself out. I'm sorry.

(EUGENE *waves and then spells.*)

MICHAEL (*to* EUGENE): He said he's sorry.

(EUGENE *looks puzzled.*)

MARLOWE: I'll take my coat now.

MICHAEL: You can't just leave me like this.

MARLOWE: With a word of advice then: Forget him.

MICHAEL: I can't just forget him

MARLOWE: Not him, Mr. DeLosa, "Him." (*Shaking the application.*) This "Him" who scribbles bathroom notes and sings "Your Song." Forget "Him."

MICHAEL: But I love "Him."

MARLOWE: You don't even know if he exists. What's not to love?

MICHAEL: Please, Mr. Marlowe, say you were wrong.

MARLOWE: And what if I wasn't? What if he's "Him" after all?

MICHAEL: Then I'll come back.

MARLOWE: What if he won't take you back?

MICHAEL: Of course he'd take me back. He loves me.

(EUGENE *waves and then spells.*)

MICHAEL (*to* EUGENE): He asked if you'd take me back.

(EUGENE *spells.*)

MICHAEL: I told him you love me.

(EUGENE *spells.*)

MARLOWE: What'd he say?

MICHAEL (*not missing a beat*): That he doesn't love me. (*Suddenly realizing what's been said. Spelling to* EUGENE.) What do you mean you don't love me?

(EUGENE *shrugs, "Sorry."*)

MARLOWE: Interesting.

MICHAEL (*to* EUGENE): How can you say you don't love me?

(EUGENE *spells.*)

MARLOWE: What'd he say?

MICHAEL: He said he's sorry.

MARLOWE: Me too.

MICHAEL (*vehemently to* EUGENE): You love me!

(EUGENE *spells.*)

MARLOWE: What? What?

MICHAEL: He says he likes me.

MARLOWE: Could've been worse.

MICHAEL (*spelling desperately*): It's not fair. I have to do everything around here. I have to use sign language, I have to read braille. The least you can do is love me.

(EUGENE *spells.*)

MICHAEL (*spelling desperately*): Aha! You're just saying these things to make it easier for me to leave. (*To* MARLOWE:) He's just saying these things to make it easier for me to leave. (*To himself:*) But he wouldn't be saying these things to make it easier for me to leave if he didn't want me to leave. (*To* EUGENE:) You want me to leave?

(EUGENE *spells and shakes his head.*)

MICHAEL: Then you *do* love me!

(EUGENE *shakes his head and then shrugs "Sorry." All three face forward as in the opening. Pause.*)

MICHAEL (*to* EUGENE): Are you sure?

(EUGENE *nods his head and then shrugs, "Sorry."*)

MARLOWE: Is he sure?

(MICHAEL *nods to* MARLOWE.)

MARLOWE: Kinda blows your big exit, huh?

MICHAEL (*grabbing* EUGENE'S *hand*): Prove it.

(EUGENE *looks puzzled.*)

MARLOWE: Forget him.

MICHAEL (*ignores* MARLOWE *and pleads*): I never ask you for anything. I do whatever has to be done and I don't complain because I figure you're doing all you can to make this thing work. But you've got to love me. I depend on that. Every day, every hour, I depend on you loving me. You can't all of a sudden just say you don't. I don't believe you. You've got to prove it.

(EUGENE *spells.*)

MARLOWE: What'd he say?

MICHAEL (*blankly to* MARLOWE): After dinner.

(MARLOWE *nods and shrugs.*)

MICHAEL (*grabs* EUGENE'S *hand*): You want me to leave?

(EUGENE *shrugs.*)

MICHAEL (*threatening him*): I'm leaving.

MARLOWE: Me too. May I have my coat?

MICHAEL (*to* EUGENE): You really don't care whether I stay or go?

(EUGENE *spells.*)

MARLOWE: Well?

MICHAEL: He does care, he doesn't love me.

MARLOWE: Could be worse.

MICHAEL (*to* EUGENE): Prove it!

(EUGENE *spells.*)

MARLOWE (*translating simultaneously*): After dinner?

(MICHAEL *nods to* MARLOWE.)

MARLOWE: Love to, but I really must be off.

MICHAEL (*to* EUGENE): You'd better have proof and it better be good, Buster.

MARLOWE: So, you'll be staying after all?

MICHAEL: We'll see.

MARLOWE: Either way I hope you'll take my advice and forget him.

MICHAEL (*screeching*): Who? Forget who?

MARLOWE (*thinks for a moment*): Either one.

(MICHAEL *lets out one last scream and then freezes.* MARLOWE *stands and walks off. Pause as* MICHAEL *and* EUGENE *sit silently next to each other.* MICHAEL, *pouting, spells into* EUGENE's *hand.*)

MICHAEL: You love me.

(EUGENE *shrugs playfully.*)

MICHAEL: I'll see to dinner.

(MICHAEL *starts to get up but* EUGENE *stops him gently and spells into his hand.*)

MICHAEL: Forget dinner? But you're hungry.

(EUGENE *spells and as he does he moves romantically in on* MICHAEL.)

MICHAEL: Forget hunger?

(EUGENE *spells and buries his face in* MICHAEL's *neck.*)

MICHAEL: Forget everything . . . but us?

(MICHAEL *smiles and succumbs to* EUGENE *as they both fall over the back of the chaise onto the floor. From behind the fuchsia chaise appears* MICHAEL's *hand fingerspelling into the air and his voice in ecstasy.*)

MICHAEL: Oh, Eugene, you *do* love me!

(*The hand "faints" and drops from sight as the lights fade and the music swells.*)

THE LISBON TRAVIATA

by
Terrence McNally

The Lisbon Traviata was first produced at Theatre Off Park, in New York. It was produced by Sherwin M. Goldman, Westport Productions, and Theatre Off Park Inc. It opened on June 4, 1985, with the following cast:

STEPHEN	Benjamin Hendrickson
MENDY	Seth Allen
MIKE	Stephen Schnetzer
PAUL	Steven Culp

Directed by John Tillinger; set design by Philipp Jung; lighting design by Michael Orriss Watson; costume design by C. L. Hundley; sound design by Gary Harris; production stage manager John M. Atherlay; stage manager Charlie Eisenberg.

CHARACTERS

MENDY: Middle-aged, attractive, takes care of himself. Wears good clothes well. Intelligent. His manner can be excessive (it often is) and may take some getting used to.

STEPHEN: Ten years younger than Mendy but looks even younger. Good looking. Fair. In trim shape. Somewhat closed and guarded in his manner.

MIKE: Several years younger than Stephen. Handsome, sexual. Dark coloring. Moves well. Direct manner.

PAUL: Mid-twenties. Good looking. Appealing, friendly, open manner. Likes himself.

TIME

The recent past.

SETTING

New York City.

Mendy's apartment is warm, romantic, crowded with good antiques. One would be hard pressed to imagine a lovelier cocoon. The windows are heavily draped. There is a fire in the fireplace.

Stephen and Mike's apartment is unfurnished/unfinished looking. You will be surprised to learn that they have lived there for several years. And whereas Mendy's apartment is cluttered, Stephen and Mike's is downright messy.

Mendy's apartment is in a brownstone. Stephen and Mike's is in a high-rise.

The one thing both apartments have in common are lots and lots of phonograph records, cassettes, and reel to reel tapes and the elaborate equipment necessary for playing them. Mendy's records and tapes are strewn all over the place. Those in Stephen and Mike's place are alphabetically arranged in a large, hi-tech cabinet and many built-in shelves. Mendy's hi-fi equipment is probably out of date. Stephen and Mike's is the latest thing.

ACT I

MENDY'S. *After dinner. There are dessert plates and coffee cups about. Records are strewn everywhere.* STEPHEN *is seated on the end of a chaise, not lying back in it. His shoes are off.* MENDY *is at the hi-fi, trying to find a certain groove on a well-worn record. He has the volume on the amplifier up quite high, so that the noises he is making on the record with the phonograph needle are quite loud and painful.*

STEPHEN: Jesus, Mendy!

MENDY: Dammit!

STEPHEN: Be careful!

MENDY: I can't wait till you hear this.

STEPHEN: I wish you'd let me do it.

MENDY: I've been playing it all day.

STEPHEN: Just start at the beginning of the record.

MENDY: Here we are!

STEPHEN: I don't—.

MENDY: Ssshh! (*The needle has found the groove* MENDY *was looking for and begun to track the record. Unfortunately, and almost at once, we hear a steady clunk, clunk, clunk. Not only is the record badly scratched but the needle is stuck.*)

STEPHEN: I don't believe you.

MENDY: I just bought it!

STEPHEN: All it takes you is one playing to ruin a record: the first!

MENDY: Ssshh! Now listen to this. (*He handles the tone arm none too gently.*)

STEPHEN: I told you to put everything on cassettes.

MENDY: Ssshh!

STEPHEN: Though God knows you'd find a way to scratch them, too!

MENDY: Ascolta! (*The needle is tracking now. We will hear the music that follows over the steady clunk, clunk, clunk of the nick in the record. What we are listening to is a pirated recording of Maria Callas. The sound is appropriately dim and distant and decidedly low-fidelity. The music is Violetta's opening recitative "E strano . . . è strano" from* La Traviata.) It's to die.

STEPHEN (*almost at once*): La Traviata, London, June 20, 1958, with Valletti, Zanasi; Nicola Rescigno conducting.

MENDY: You've heard it?

STEPHEN: I have it. Just turn it off. That scratch is worse than chalk on a blackboard.

MENDY: When did you buy it?

STEPHEN: I don't know. A month ago, six weeks.

MENDY: They told me it just came out.

STEPHEN: Where was that?

MENDY: Music Masters.

STEPHEN: Music Masters! They haven't even gotten in the Lisbon *Traviata* yet. I told you to go to Discophile.

MENDY: What Lisbon *Traviata*?

STEPHEN: The Lisbon *Traviata*. What do you mean "What Lisbon *Traviata*?"

MENDY: There's a Lisbon *Traviata*?

STEPHEN: Kraus is the Alfredo.

MENDY: Alfredo Kraus is the Alfredo?

STEPHEN: No, Lily Kraus. Do you have Nilsson's *Frau* from Munich?

MENDY: How is she?

STEPHEN: Loud, louder, loudest. But Rysanek is spectacular.

MENDY: How is she?

STEPHEN: Who she? What she?

MENDY: Maria!

STEPHEN: Oh that she!

MENDY: The Lisbon *Traviata*!

STEPHEN: She's fantastic. Did you get the new *Masked Ball* on Philips?

MENDY: Didn't you bring it?

STEPHEN: I assumed you had it. Caballé and Carreras have their moments but Colin Davis's conducting is so non-echt-Italian, you know?

MENDY: Stephen, I'm talking about the Lisbon *Traviata*.

STEPHEN: So was I. Then I changed the subject to the new *Masked Ball*.

MENDY: Fuck the new *Masked Ball*.

STEPHEN: I don't know why you hate Caballé so much.

MENDY: She can't sing.

STEPHEN: Oh, come on, Mendy. She has a beautiful voice.

MENDY: It's not enough.

STEPHEN: You've got to admit she's trying. I mean, she has improved.

MENDY: Not enough. Is Discophile still open?

STEPHEN: Mendy!

MENDY: What's their number?

STEPHEN: What am I supposed to do while you run down there?

MENDY: You haven't heard Sutherland's *Merry Widow,* have you?

STEPHEN: I hate Sutherland. So do you. You'd buy anything.

MENDY: What's their number?

STEPHEN: It's after nine.

MENDY: What is their number, will you?

STEPHEN: How should I know?

MENDY: Be that way! (*He goes to phone and punch dials Information.*)

STEPHEN: It's not that good.

MENDY: You just said it was fantastic.

STEPHEN: Well it is, but not that fantastic.

MENDY (*into phone*): Information?

STEPHEN: You know they charge you for that?

MENDY (*into phone*): Do you have the number for a Discophile on West 8th Street?

STEPHEN: It's your quarter.

MENDY (*into phone*): Yes, it's in Manhattan. (*Covers phone, groans.*) Oy!

STEPHEN: If you think I'm going to sit here all by myself while you—.

MENDY (*back into phone*): Discophile! That's "D" as in . . . as in . . . you've got me so rattled . . .!

STEPHEN: "D" as in David.

MENDY: De Los Angeles. Not the town. The singer. Victoria De Los Angeles. All right, Information, have it your way: "D" as in David then. (*Covers phone.*) Do you believe this?

STEPHEN: WAtkins 9-8818.

MENDY: What?

STEPHEN: WAtkins 9-8818.

MENDY: Never mind, Information. And don't charge me for this! (*He hangs up and punch dials another number.*) WAtkins 9-8818, was it?

STEPHEN: Have you heard Sills's last *Thais*?

MENDY: Unfortunately, I heard her first *Thais*.

STEPHEN: Anyone who didn't hear her early Manons never heard Sills.

MENDY: I heard her Manon.

STEPHEN: You heard her middle and late Manons. I said her first Manons.

MENDY: I heard her Manon in '71 at The New York State Theatre and it was one big wobble.

STEPHEN: 1971 was already her middle Manons. I'm talking about '68/69.

MENDY (*into phone*): Hello? Discophile? You don't sound familiar. Do you have a copy of the Callas Lisbon *Traviata*? The Callas Lisbon *Traviata*. It's a pirate. Thank you. (*Covers phone.*) No wonder he doesn't sound familiar. They're playing Janet Baker.

STEPHEN: Who else?

MENDY: The *Nuits d'Eté*.

STEPHEN: They'll never beat Eleanor Steber's.

MENDY: No, wait. It's not Baker, it's Crespin. Or is it? (*He listens hard.*)

STEPHEN (*trying to take the phone*): Here, let me.

MENDY (*pulling away with phone*): Just a minute. Did Christa Ludwig ever record it?

STEPHEN: I hope not. Will you let me?

MENDY: Don't grab! (STEPHEN *takes the phone from* MENDY *and listens.*)

STEPHEN: Number one, it's not *Nuits d'Eté*. It's *L'Invitation Au Voyage*. Number two, it's Jessye Norman.

MENDY: Number three, fuck you.

STEPHEN (*into phone*): Hello? (*He covers phone.*) They're out of the Lisbon *Traviata*. Thay have Dallas and London and he thinks La Scala if you want him to check.

MENDY: Give me that! (*He takes the phone.*) You're sure you don't have the Lisbon? Did you try the shelf under the Angel and RCA cut-outs? Sometimes Franz puts them there. He isn't around by any chance? When do you expect it back in again? How many have you sold so far? Thirty? You've sold thirty Lisbon *Traviatas*? (*To* STEPHEN:) They've sold thirty Lisbon *Traviatas*! (*Back into phone.*) You wouldn't by any chance know off-hand who you might have sold some of them to? Couldn't you look? I mean, you must keep receipts, some sort of record. It's kind of an emergency. I'm calling for Mme. Scotto, I'm her secretary and she asked me to track down a copy before she leaves town in the morning. Renata Scotto, who else?

STEPHEN: You're incredible!

MENDY: She's doing her first Violetta in years and everybody's told her to listen to the Callas Lisbon *Traviata* first. She never sings anything without listening to Callas first. I know she'd really appreciate it if you could make some effort to track one down. Yes, tonight. I told you, she's leaving in the morning, first thing. But couldn't you at least—? We've tried Music Masters. They're the ones who stuck me with this *Traviata* everybody seems to have already heard! Besides, they're closed. I don't think I've communicated the urgency of this call to you. Thanks for nothing. (*He hangs up.*) Stephen?

STEPHEN: No. I'd love to hear this.

MENDY: You don't even know what I was going to say.

STEPHEN: Mendy, I always know what you're going to say.

MENDY: Please.

STEPHEN: I said no.

MENDY: It's only eight blocks.

STEPHEN: I'm not going eight blocks and back in this weather for a record album.

MENDY: Who said anything about back? We'll go there and stay. This was a dinner invitation, not a slumber party. I'll pay for the cab.

STEPHEN: No!

MENDY: You're going to have to go home eventually. We'll just do it now.

STEPHEN: I'm not going home tonight.

MENDY: Where are you going?

STEPHEN: None of your business.

MENDY: Are you tricking with that guy I saw you at *Parsifal* with?

STEPHEN: Don't be ridiculous.

MENDY: He lives just down the street. I've seen him walking his dog.

STEPHEN: You think everyone's a trick.

MENDY: Larry Daimlett had him at the Pines last summer.

STEPHEN: So?

MENDY: He's very into drugs.

STEPHEN: He is not.

MENDY: Larry thinks he took cash from his wallet. Close to a hundred dollars. He knows he took his lime green cashmere cable-knit sweater from Andre Oliver.

STEPHEN: I don't believe you.

MENDY: The question is: do you believe Larry Daimlett?

STEPHEN: I believe Larry Daimlett would have liked to sleep with Hal at the Pines last summer.

MENDY: Hal? Is that his name? Hal what?

STEPHEN: Koerner.

MENDY: That's the one. He's a writer and he waits tables at the Headless Horseman.

STEPHEN: Just two nights a week.

MENDY: But not enough to keep him in cashmere sweaters and out of other peoples' wallets.

STEPHEN: That's really a vicious story.

MENDY: Don't say I didn't warn you.

STEPHEN: I thought you had some new things to play me.

MENDY: I'm sure you've already heard them. Listen, why don't you put something on, make yourself comfortable and let me run over to your place and get it?

STEPHEN: Mike's there.

MENDY: I'll just be a second. All he has to do is hand it to me.

STEPHEN: He's got someone.

MENDY: A trick?

STEPHEN: I didn't ask.

MENDY: Well, if it's not a trick I'm sure he wouldn't mind if I just popped over and—.

STEPHEN: I'll bring it over tomorrow.

MENDY: I want to hear it tonight.

STEPHEN: I'm sorry! How's this Pavarotti *Tosca*?

MENDY: Terrible.

STEPHEN: Why did you buy it then?

MENDY: Because I didn't know it was terrible until I had listened to it. Couldn't you just call him and ask if it would be okay?

STEPHEN: I can tell you: it wouldn't be. What's this Kabaivanska recital like?

MENDY: Ghastly.

STEPHEN: I wish Maria had recorded these. Kabaivanska's too bland. Maria should have recorded everything. Callas sings Mussorgsky. Callas sings the George and Ira Gershwin Song Book. Callas sings the Beatles.

MENDY: Maybe I could call him.

STEPHEN: It's just a record.

MENDY: That's easy for you to say. You've already heard it. Is it good?

STEPHEN: I told you, it's fantastic.

MENDY: "Not that fantastic" is what you said.

STEPHEN: It's just another *Traviata*.

MENDY: Maria never sang "just another *Traviata*." She wasn't capable of "just another *Traviata*." The whole point of Maria is that she never sang just another anything.

STEPHEN: What about those last La Scala *Medeas*?

MENDY: That was different. She was sick. She had a temperature, her blood pressure had fallen alarmingly. Her doctors told her not to appear. And if you'd listen to those recordings carefully you'd hear that she brought a lot of new insights to it.

STEPHEN: New insights but no voice.

MENDY: What about the way she does *"Lontan! Lontan! Serpenti, via da me!"*?

STEPHEN: Well, certain phrases, maybe.

MENDY: And what about the C at the end of the second act?

STEPHEN: It's not a C. It's a B flat and it's a fluke. She only took the C in the Dallas performances.

MENDY: Are you sure it's not a C?

STEPHEN: Have you got it?

MENDY: Somewhere. I always thought she took the C in the last La Scala performances, too.

STEPHEN: The last time she took the C at the end of the second act of *Medea* was in Epidaurus in 1962.

MENDY: There's no recording of those two *Medeas* in Epidaurus.

STEPHEN: I was there.

MENDY: You never told me that.

STEPHEN: Well, I was.

MENDY: You heard Maria sing *Medea* in the ancient Greek theater at Epidaurus?

STEPHEN: And the *Normas* there, two years later.

MENDY: I don't believe you.

STEPHEN: Why not?

MENDY: Well how come you never mentioned it?

STEPHEN: I don't know. It's not exactly the kind of thing you go around mentioning all the time. "Hi, I'm Steve. I heard Maria Callas sing *Medea* in Epidaurus, Greece. How about you?"

MENDY: You think you would have mentioned it to me at least.

STEPHEN: You heard her concert at the Acropolis in 1957.

MENDY: August 5th.

STEPHEN: Well, if you heard her in Athens in 1957 why can't I have heard her in Epidaurus in 1964?

MENDY: Who was the Pollione?

STEPHEN: Jon Vickers.

MENDY: Vickers never sang *Norma* with her. It was one of the tragedies of his career and hers.

STEPHEN: Well, it was someone like Vickers.

MENDY: The day Flaviano Labò is anything like Jon Vickers is the day Joan Sutherland does her first *Lulu*.

STEPHEN: Flaviano Labò, my God, that's right.

MENDY: The Adalgisa was what's-her-face . . .?

STEPHEN: The Greek mezzo with hair on her chest. What's her name? Paleo-something . . .!

MENDY: Lithic! Who sang Clotilde?

STEPHEN: I don't remember who sang Clotilde. Nobody ever remembers who sang Clotilde. I doubt if Maria would remember who sang Clotilde with her in Epidaurus.

MENDY: I bet she remembered who sang Clotilde with her in London on November 8, 1952.

STEPHEN: The whole world remembers who sang Clotilde with her in London in 1952: Big Joan herself. The Beast From Down Under.

MENDY: Maria said Sutherland didn't have the legato to sing a good Clotilde.

STEPHEN: The rhythm to sing it is what Maria said.

MENDY: I read "legato."

STEPHEN: Well, you read wrong. Besides, Sutherland has legato. Even I would grant her that. But she always sings behind the beat. That's why Maria said she didn't have the rhythm to sing even a decent Clotilde. God knows what Maria thought of her Norma.

MENDY: You're too butch to know so much about opera.

STEPHEN: I'm not butch. Risë Stevens is butch. Are you still looking for that *Medea*?

MENDY: Here's Dallas, the first La Scalas with Lenny, Covent Garden, but where's the last La Scalas?

STEPHEN: Mendy, I don't want to hear *Medea*. Any of them. I hate *Medea*. I loathe *Medea*. I despise *Medea*.

MENDY: I just can't believe you were there.

STEPHEN: We didn't speak to one another for five years, remember. It was probably during that period. Didn't I send you a card from Epidaurus?

MENDY: No.

STEPHEN: I must have been really mad at you.

MENDY: It was mutual.

STEPHEN: Do you remember what it was about?

MENDY: Perfectly.

STEPHEN: You take Peter Wingate to a performance of *Tristan* I would have given my right tit to see just because I met Michael at your annual Callas birthday party.

MENDY: Not met, left with.

STEPHEN: Mendy, Michael wasn't interested in you.

MENDY: That's no excuse. He should have been.

STEPHEN: I could have killed you. They never sang *Tristan* together again. The coupling of the century.

MENDY: I thought that was you and Mike.

STEPHEN: I guess we were sort of the Liz and Dick of Off Broadway.

MENDY: I was so in love with you.

STEPHEN: You just thought you were in love with me.

MENDY: That's not true. When you two left together—I remember I was standing right over there listening to Bobby Staub hold forth about his dinner with Susan Sontag—(thank God, they never made a movie out of that; p.s. Bobby has shingles)—and when I saw that door close on you two and I knew you'd be making love within the hour . . .

STEPHEN: It was more like ten minutes.

MENDY: I felt like a combination of the Marschallin—all gentle resignation, *"ja, ja,"* age deferring to beauty and all that rot—and the second act of *Tosca*—stab the son of a bitch in the heart—*"Questo è il baccio di Tosca."*

STEPHEN: You want to hear something funny?

MENDY: I thought I just had.

STEPHEN: That first time I saw Mike, I wasn't even sure he was gay.

MENDY: On these premises? Darling, I've been raided.

STEPHEN: He was so . . . I want to say masculine but that's not the word. There's something beyond masculine.

MENDY: I know: me.

STEPHEN: Even before he'd seen me, before we were introduced, I knew he was going to be the one. It was like the first act of *Carmen*. Don José is thrown the acacia flower and his fate is sealed.

MENDY: *Carmen* isn't gay.

STEPHEN: That depends on who's singing her. You know what I feel like? The Rosa Ponselle *Vestale* arias.

MENDY: The way you feel about *Medea* is the way I feel about *Vestale*. And anyway, they're in the country.

STEPHEN: What do you want to hear then?

MENDY: The Lisbon *Traviata*.

STEPHEN: You're obsessed with the Lisbon *Traviata*.

MENDY: You knew I would be.

STEPHEN: I thought you had it.

MENDY: I don't care what they're doing over there. I just want them to give me the record. Tell them I'll wear a ski mask. I'll go blindfolded. They can throw it down to me in the street out the window.

STEPHEN: Call them yourself. I'm not doing it.

MENDY: I should have told that cretin at Discophile I worked for Birgit Nilsson. I'm sure she has much more clout than Renata Scotto.

STEPHEN: Can I put on this Olivero/Domingo *Fanciulla*?

MENDY: No! (*Into phone.*) Hello, Mike? Who is this? (*Covers phone.*) "A friend of his." I bet! (*Into phone.*) Would you ask him to call Stephen when he gets back?

STEPHEN: Mendy!

MENDY: Tell him I'm at Mendy's. He has the number. Thank you. (*He hangs up.*) Mike's out getting pizza. They're listening to *Sweeney Todd*.

STEPHEN: Why did you do that, Mendy? He's going to think I was calling to check up on him. I'm going to tell him it was you. And then you're going to tell him it was you.

MENDY: The trick sounded cute.

STEPHEN: You reduce everything to tricks.

MENDY: Maybe that's because I haven't had one since 1901.

STEPHEN: All great beauties are finally alone. Look at Maria.

MENDY: Stephen, tell me something: why can't I find anyone to love?

STEPHEN: Don't start, Mendy. Please!

MENDY: Is he?

STEPHEN: Is who what?

MENDY: The trick cute?

STEPHEN: He's all right.

MENDY: I thought you didn't know him.

STEPHEN: I said I didn't know if he was a trick.

MENDY: You just said he was.

STEPHEN: Maybe he is. Why don't you call him and ask him? You would, too!

MENDY: All I asked was, was he cute?

STEPHEN: I said he was all right.

MENDY: You've met?

STEPHEN: No. I saw him. In our lobby. He was going up. I was coming down.

MENDY: Then how did you know it was him?

STEPHEN: I just did. What is this? The riddle scene from *Turandot*? Could we put something on?

MENDY: What's his name?

STEPHEN: I don't know. Paul.

MENDY: Just Paul?

STEPHEN: Paul Della Rovere.

MENDY: Paul Della Rovere! If that's not a trick's name, I'd like to know what is.

STEPHEN: He's a social worker, so I doubt it. You know what they're like: serious and looking for a real commitment. Has anyone ever said anything to you about your scotch?

MENDY: No, why?

STEPHEN: It's terrible.

MENDY: I don't drink.

STEPHEN: Well, your guests do and it's terrible.

MENDY: Tell me a good brand and I'll buy it. So what's going to happen?

STEPHEN: With Mike and I? Nothing.

MENDY: Mike and me. What if he and this number get serious?

STEPHEN: They won't.

MENDY: Why not?

STEPHEN: We have an agreement.

MENDY: So did you and Jimmy Marks when you met Mike.

STEPHEN: Jimmy and I weren't serious in the first place. We were each other's Pinkerton pretending to be each other's Butterfly. No one got hurt.

MENDY: That's not how I remember it.

STEPHEN: He got over it. I see him and Donald together and I can't believe we were ever lovers. It's like it never happened.

MENDY: As if it never happened.

STEPHEN: Shut up, Mendy!

MENDY: Bad grammar is a knife, right here.

STEPHEN: You just need to get laid.

MENDY: You're right.

STEPHEN: What happened to you and that curator anyway?

MENDY: I took him to *Pelléas and Melisande* and he fell asleep.

STEPHEN: *Pelléas*? Give the guy a break. Try *Bohème*, *Trovatore*. Something with balls. Something with *music*.

MENDY: Debussy has balls. He just doesn't wear them on his sleeve.

STEPHEN: You'd rather listen to opera than fuck.

MENDY: Opera doesn't reject me. The real world does.

STEPHEN: The "real" world is here. . . . (*He points to his forehead.*) . . . and here . . .
(*He points to his crotch.*) It's a very short journey.

MENDY: I don't understand love. *"Non capisco amore."*

STEPHEN: I don't think I understand anything but.

MENDY: I don't understand agreements either. I never thought the two of you would
last. And when it did, I was a little envious. And now that it's over. . . .

STEPHEN: It's not over.

MENDY: I feel a little sad.

STEPHEN: I said it's not over. It's different.

MENDY: That's obvious. If he's with someone else, it sounds like the first act of
Carmen is turning into the last. The final duet.

STEPHEN: *"Frappe-moi donc ou laisse-moi passer."*

MENDY: More chest. Maria does it with more chest. *"Frappe-moi donc ou laisse-moi
passer."* Do you think he'll move out?

STEPHEN: Basta! What about Marilyn Horne's *Tancredi* from Dallas last year?

MENDY: Which one?

STEPHEN: The November 3rd. She flats too much on the one from the 7th and the
one on the 5th wasn't recorded.

MENDY: That's the one I have.

STEPHEN: You would.

MENDY: It's in the country.

STEPHEN: Everything good you have is in the country.

MENDY: Everything good you have, like the Lisbon *Traviata*, is only eight blocks
from here.

STEPHEN: What's the November 5th *Tancredi* like?

MENDY: Terrible. She's sharp.

STEPHEN: Marilyn Horne doesn't sharp. She flats.

MENDY: Well she sure as shit sharped November 5 in Dallas, Texas.

STEPHEN: Really? I'll have to hear it sometime.

MENDY: You'll have to come to Connecticut.

STEPHEN: I wouldn't cross the street to hear Marilyn Horne sing on pitch. She sings like a truck driver.

MENDY: What do you expect? Marilyn Horne was a truck driver. She was discovered singing the Habanera in a Los Angeles gravel pit.

STEPHEN: Now that's vicious.

MENDY: What's vicious is you not getting the goddamn Lisbon *Traviata*. How long does it take to get a pizza anyway?

STEPHEN: Maria flats on the Lisbon *Traviata*.

MENDY: Where?

STEPHEN: Twice in "*Ah, fors'e lui,*" once in "*Sempre Libera*" and practically the entire "*Dite alla giovine*" is a quarter tone down.

MENDY: I don't believe you.

STEPHEN: It's on the record.

MENDY: Maria never flatted in her entire life. Sharped, yes; flatted, never.

STEPHEN: Maybe it was something she ate, a rancid paella or something, I don't know, Mendy, but she flatted in Lisbon just like Marilyn Horne sharped in Dallas.

MENDY: Fuck Marilyn Horne; we were talking about Maria.

STEPHEN: I can't help it if I was born with perfect pitch.

MENDY: And fuck your perfect pitch. It's Maria's pitch that you're impugning.

STEPHEN: Who's impugning? I'm stating facts. On the night of March 27, 1958, Maria Callas sang flat in a performance of *La Traviata* at the Teatro San Marco in Lisbon, Portugal. Nobody's perfect.

MENDY: Maria is.

STEPHEN: Was.

MENDY: And always will be. (*He is dialing a number.*)

STEPHEN: Mendy, leave them alone!

MENDY: I may not have your ear but I have a pitch pipe I bought in Salzburg at that music shop three doors down from the house Mozart was born in. Von Karajan was there buying batons.

STEPHEN: What does that have to do with it?

MENDY: Herbert Von Karajan would hardly be seen buying batons in a music shop that didn't sell excellent pitch pipes. We'll see how flat Maria was. (*Into phone.*) Is he back yet? What's-his-name? Your friend whose apartment you're at who's out buying pizza. They've got me so rattled over here I can't even remember his name.

STEPHEN: It's Michael.

MENDY: Thank you. (*Covers phone.*) I love this one's voice. Della—what was it?

STEPHEN: Rovere.

MENDY: He could be the first hump tenor with that name.

STEPHEN: I thought you thought Corelli was a hump.

MENDY: I never said I thought Franco Corelli was a hump. I said I liked his legs in *Turandot*.

STEPHEN: Mike is going to kill you for this.

MENDY: They're playing *Sweeney Todd* so loud over there I don't know how they can even think. (*Into phone.*) Mike? It's Mendy.

STEPHEN: Tell him that wasn't me who called before.

MENDY: I wonder if I could ask you a favor?

STEPHEN: Tell him it wasn't me.

MENDY: Stephen's telling me to tell you it wasn't him, whatever that means. Listen—.

STEPHEN: Let me talk to him when you're finished.

MENDY: You've got a record over there, it's Stephen's actually, the Lisbon *Traviata*.

STEPHEN: He won't have a clue what you're talking about.

MENDY: The Lisbon *Traviata*! If you could perhaps turn Mme. Lansbury down for just a moment . . . ? Thank you. (*Covers phone.*) He called him "Babe." What's-his-name? The Italian Hump. Mike called him "Babe."

STEPHEN: So?

MENDY: I bet *Sweeney Todd*'s not all they're playing.

STEPHEN: Anyway, he's Portuguese.

MENDY: The Italian Hump is Portuguese? Maybe he was there.

STEPHEN: Maybe he was where?

MENDY: The Lisbon *Traviata*! (*Into phone.*) Can you hear me now? Yes, perfectly. Listen, Mike, there's a favor I'd like to ask you. Well, it's two favors actually. (*To* STEPHEN:) Would you stop snooping at my desk?

STEPHEN: I'm not snooping. I was looking for *Opera News*.

MENDY (*into phone*): Stephen left a record album there I specifically asked him to bring over with him tonight. I was wondering if I stopped by I might pick it up?

STEPHEN: Are these your tickets for *Elektra*? I got fourth row on the aisle.

MENDY: How soon? I could come right now. Couldn't you wait a couple of minutes until I got there? It's only a couple of blocks.

STEPHEN: Eight blocks, Mendy.

MENDY: What if I took a cab? You'll be passing right by here. I could meet you halfway.

STEPHEN: Who's the postcard from?

MENDY: I don't want to be a pest about it, Michael, but really, it's terribly important.

STEPHEN: It looks like Rio.

MENDY: If you just got back with the pizza I don't understand why you have to go rushing out again to the movies. If you'd called when I asked you to call, as soon as you got back with it, I could have been there and gone by now. This is all really very inconsiderate of you, Michael. As a matter of fact to me it is a matter of life and death. I'm sorry I feel this way, too.

STEPHEN: Why didn't you tell me Lester was sick?

MENDY: Never mind the second favor. I'm sorry I asked you the first.

STEPHEN: Don't hang up.

MENDY: The next time you're offered a pair of free tickets to the Met, they won't be from me. That's not the point. I offered them. Whether or not you used them is immaterial.

STEPHEN: Don't hang up.

MENDY: You're a selfish, inconsiderate, self-centered, stereotypical, aging, immature queen. No wonder you don't have any friends. Yes, all that just because you won't bring a goddamn record album over here or let me come over there and get it! Besides, the Maria Callas Lisbon *Traviata* is not just another goddamn record album. Right now, at this particular moment in my not so terrific life, it's probably the most goddamn important thing in the world to me but I wouldn't expect an insensitive faggot whose idea of a good time is sitting around listening to Angela Lansbury shrieking on about "The Worst Pies in London," like yourself, to understand what I'm talking about. I'm not surprised you don't like opera. People like you don't like life.

STEPHEN: I want to talk to him when you're through.

MENDY: Not a moment too soon! (*Back into phone.*) Your ex-lover would like a word with you, Michael, though for the life of me, I can't imagine why. Although after tonight I can understand why you're his ex. There's not one person in this entire city who thought it would last, including David Minton. I will simply never, never understand how he got that way with you in the first place. (*Hands phone to* STEPHEN.) Here.

STEPHEN: You could've been over there by now. (*Into phone.*) Mike? Hi.

MENDY: Tell him his friend Mr. Della Rovere used to work standing room at the old Met.

STEPHEN: I don't know. Some Callas record.

MENDY: I had him halfway through Flagstad's farewell *Isolde*.

STEPHEN: That's okay.

MENDY: I know some people who had him during her first.

STEPHEN: Did you know Lester Cantwell has been in a hospital in Rio de Janeiro for the past five weeks with a ruptured spleen?

MENDY: I refuse not to be taken seriously like this!

STEPHEN: Mendy got a card from him.

MENDY: Doesn't he think I meant any of it?

STEPHEN: I don't know. (*To* MENDY:) How long ago did you get it?

MENDY: After what I just said to him and he has the nerve to ask me about Lester Cantwell's ruptured spleen?

STEPHEN: Mendy, he's one of our best friends and we'd like to know.

MENDY: If he's one of your best friends then why don't you just call him? He's been back for at least three weeks.

STEPHEN (*into phone*): Did you hear that? How is he?

MENDY: Like he always is: hysterical. The spleen business was months ago if you'd just looked at the postmark and I thought I asked you not to snoop around my desk in the first place anyway!

STEPHEN (*back into phone*): I guess it has been a while since we spoke to him. What are you two up to anyway?

MENDY: Would you mind not monopolizing that thing? I'm expecting a call.

STEPHEN: It's a dumb movie but the special effects are fantastic. You're seeing it with Dolby-ized sound, I hope. It wouldn't be anything without it.

MENDY: I thought they were in such a hurry.

STEPHEN: We're just listening to records. I might have something on later. I'm waiting for a call.

MENDY: What am I? Stage door canteen? Some pit stop? Some place to kill time while you wait for a late date to call? Fuck you, too, Stephen.

STEPHEN: The guy I told you about. The writer.

MENDY: What writer? He's a waiter at a second-rate, over-priced gay restaurant.

STEPHEN: He wasn't sure if he'd be free after work.

MENDY: His kind never is. Stephen, I told you I was expecting a call.

STEPHEN: I was going to ask you to walk Sammy! Sometimes I completely forget. Two years and I still . . .! Oh, listen, I think we might be out of bread.

MENDY: Listen to you two. You'd think you were married.

STEPHEN: Why can't the two of you go to his place? I told you it wasn't definite. Forget it. I took a change with me.

MENDY: No wonder she forgot the record. She's carrying tomorrow's wardrobe in there.

STEPHEN: As long as he's out by eight. Well, I guess you'd better tell him about that loose floorboard on my side of the bed. We don't want a lawsuit on our hands. (*He laughs at something, then extends phone to* MENDY.) He wants to talk to you.

MENDY: Well, I don't want to talk to him.

STEPHEN: Just in case, he wants to know what the other favor was.

MENDY: In case of what?

STEPHEN: In case he might be able to do it.

MENDY: You really don't take me seriously, either one of you!

STEPHEN: Oh, come on.

MENDY: I was only going to ask him, not that it matters now and I certainly wouldn't want to put him out or anything, even if he did spend three summers with me on Fire Island as a permanent, non-paying, non-dishwashing, non-anything but hanging around on the Meat Rack guest, if his little Portuguese friend had maybe heard Maria's *Traviata* in Lisbon but if he's so heavily into Stephen Sondheim I would seriously doubt it.

STEPHEN (*into phone*): Did you hear that? (*To* MENDY:) He's asking him.

MENDY: He's just wasting his time. Six times over and back I could've been.

STEPHEN: Why don't you put on the Berlin *Lucia*?

MENDY: I'm sick of it. Besides, I lent it to Elaine.

STEPHEN: I thought Elaine hated opera.

MENDY: She likes the Berlin *Lucia*. She was over the other night and loved it.

STEPHEN: You still see her?

MENDY: What do you think? We had more than a kid together.

STEPHEN: Is she seeing anyone?

MENDY: Some broker but Jason can't stand him.

STEPHEN: He must be ten or so by now.

MENDY: Thirteen. What's happening?

STEPHEN: I guess he's still asking. Thirteen! He's one thing I envy you. Remember the time we—

MENDY: What loose board?

STEPHEN: —took him to?—Hunh?

MENDY: You said something about a loose board on your side?

STEPHEN: Oh, there's a loose floorboard on my side of the bed, my ex-side of the bed, and if you don't know about it, you could step on it wrong and it could pop up and you could hurt yourself. I should have let Mr. Della Rovere find out for himself.

MENDY: Then they are sleeping together?

STEPHEN: It would seem so.

MENDY: I knew it. And you're sleeping with Marcel Proust-manqué.

STEPHEN: Whenever I can. It beats that day couch in our alcove.

MENDY: The minute I saw you two at *Parsifal* I said to myself, "He's with a trick."

STEPHEN: Knowing you, you probably said it to the people you were with.

MENDY: Well, Stephen, it was kind of obvious.

STEPHEN: What's so obvious about two men going to *Parsifal* together?

MENDY: Face it, darling, ice hockey at the Garden it's not. (*Indicating telephone.*) What are those two doing over there?

STEPHEN: Is there anyone or anything you don't reduce to sex?

MENDY: My son, Jason, my station wagon, and Maria Callas.

STEPHEN: You talk about not having a lover but have you ever listened to yourself?

MENDY: I have an analyst for that.

STEPHEN: What does he say?

MENDY: He can't find a thing wrong with me.

STEPHEN: How long has it been? Ever since I met you, right?

MENDY: Ten years, six analysts. Elaine says I go through them like Kleenex.

STEPHEN: She should—. (*Into phone.*) Hello?

MENDY: Know or talk?

STEPHEN: It's Paul.

MENDY: For me?

STEPHEN: He doesn't have all night.

MENDY (*into phone*): Paul? This is Mendy. Did Mike tell you what I—? Well, that's what I was wondering but if you're not sure then I'm sure you weren't. Well of course someone sang it. Someone usually does. Otherwise there's no performance. (*Makes face at* STEPHEN.)

STEPHEN: You're wasting your time.

MENDY (*covers phone*): Pick up! (*He motions to extension phone; then back into phone.*) This would have been in '56 or 7.

STEPHEN: It was 1958. March 25th and 27th.

MENDY: Stephen says it was 1958.

STEPHEN: March 25th and 27th.

MENDY: You were how old then? (*Covers phone, to* STEPHEN:) Don't pick up. (*Back into phone.*) But you remember your grandparents taking you to an opera? No, the one with bulls in it is *Carmen. Traviata's* about a courtesan dying of consumption. A courtesan: what Stephen was before he started writing plays and an avocation to which he will soon be returning if he doesn't write another one. No, horses and camels are *Aida.* I wish you could remember the singers as well as you do the animals. It begins at a party. Everyone is drinking champagne and being very gay. I'll ignore that. And then the tenor's father, the baritone, comes in and ruins everything, as fathers will. And then there's a gambling scene and in the last act she reads a letter, "Teneste la promessa," and dies. You remember that much? Then you definitely remember *Traviata.* Now try to describe the soprano who was singing Violetta. Violetta is the heroine. You're making me feel like Milton Cross. Skip it. Just tell me about the soprano. Other than the fact that you didn't like her, what can you tell me about her? "Lousy" is a strong word, Paul. So is "stunk." I don't care about your opinion. It's her name I'm after. I think you heard Maria Callas. That's a good question. I just loved her so much. I still do. Everything about her. Anything. I take crumbs when it comes to Maria. She's given me so much pleasure, ecstasy, a certain solace I suppose, memories that don't stop. We'll never see her likes again. How do you describe a miracle to someone who wasn't there? Do yourself a favor. Put on one of her records sometime. If what you hear doesn't get to you, really talk to you, touch you someplace here, I'm talking about the heart, move you, the truth of it, the intensity . . . well, I can't imagine such a thing. I don't think we could be friends. There's a reason we called her La Divina. But if you don't even remember who sang *Traviata* that night, then there's no point in going on with this even if you did hear Callas. For people like you, it might as well have been Milanov. Skip that one, too. Listen, thank you for your trouble. Enjoy the movie. I don't care what your grandparents thought of her either! The three of you heard the greatest singer who ever lived and you don't even remember it. Yes, she's dead; thanks to people like you. Murderer! I hope you hate the movie. (*He hangs up.*) God, I loathe the Portuguese.

STEPHEN: Half an hour ago you were in love with the sound of his voice. (*He hangs up the extension.*)

MENDY: Half an hour ago I didn't know he was at the Lisbon *Traviata* and doesn't even remember her.

STEPHEN: He remembers the *Traviata.* It's Callas he doesn't remember.

MENDY: They're the same thing. And stop calling her that! Callas! It makes her sound faraway, formidable.

STEPHEN: She was and is. Now, what do you want to hear?

MENDY: Anything! *Einstein on the Beach.*

STEPHEN: The whole thing?

MENDY: Oh, I forgot: you're in a rush.

STEPHEN: I'm not in a rush now. He doesn't get off until after midnight. It's a tentative date anyway. What about this *Andrea Chenier?*

MENDY: I'm not in the mood for verismo.

STEPHEN: I just want to hear what Marton does with it.

MENDY: She does what she does with everything: screams her way through it.

STEPHEN: I like her *Tosca.*

MENDY: There is only one *Tosca.*

STEPHEN: That's ridiculous. You can't listen to Maria all the time.

MENDY: Why not?

STEPHEN: It's not . . . I was going to say "normal."

MENDY: You? Normal? Your whole life is a mockery of the word.

STEPHEN: It's limiting.

MENDY: There are no limits as far as she is concerned. Maria Callas is opera.

STEPHEN: You don't have to convert me, Mendy. If you'll remember, I was into her several years before you.

MENDY: You didn't discover Callas. We both did. It's like Columbus and the Vikings. They both discovered America, only not at the same time. The point is they both got there.

STEPHEN: Well, in this case I'm the Viking and you're Columbus.

MENDY: It's not a contest.

STEPHEN: No, but it's a fact.

MENDY: Have it your way. You usually do.

STEPHEN: What is that supposed to mean?

MENDY: Nothing. I thought you were going to put something on.

STEPHEN: Everything means something.

MENDY: Well, don't you?

STEPHEN: You know I don't.

MENDY: I wasn't talking about Mike.

STEPHEN: Well, then don't make a remark like that.

MENDY: I was talking about . . . I don't know what I was talking about.

STEPHEN: You usually don't.

MENDY: Thanks a lot.

STEPHEN: What about this *Forza* from Venice?

MENDY: It's dreadful. What I meant was, you've always had someone.

STEPHEN: I've always wanted someone. How's Di Stefano?

MENDY: I said it was dreadful. You think I don't want someone?

STEPHEN: You're always looking too hard. It doesn't happen that way.

MENDY: How does it happen?

STEPHEN: I don't know. It just happens. But if you try making it happen, somehow it never does.

MENDY: In other words, I frighten people off with my needs?

STEPHEN: I didn't say that.

MENDY: That's what Elaine thinks.

STEPHEN: I guess I'm only attracted to people who are attracted to my needs.

MENDY: And I guess your needs are more attractive than mine.

STEPHEN: I don't find any needs particularly attractive, especially my own.

MENDY: That sounds ominous.

STEPHEN: It is. What about this *Nabucco*?

MENDY: The last thing I'm in the mood for tonight is a chorus of Hebrews.

STEPHEN: I just want to hear Scotto do the big aria.

MENDY: You can take it home with you.

STEPHEN: I told you: I'm not going home.

MENDY: Doesn't what's-his-name have a phonograph?

STEPHEN: I told you: it's not definite.

MENDY: Just anything but *Nabucco*. I've got the new *Adriana* with Caballé and Carreras.

STEPHEN: So do I. It's atrocious.

MENDY: Well what do you expect from those two? The Spanish Fric 'n' Frac.

STEPHEN: Nine thousand fucking records and I can't find one.

MENDY: What about *Der Fliegende Holländer*?

STEPHEN: You know how you feel about a chorus of Hebrews? That's how I feel about Flying Dutchmen.

MENDY: There's always Maria.

STEPHEN: I'm sick of Maria. I'm sick of Supervia. I'm sick of Schwarzkopf. I'm sick of life.

MENDY: I'd hate to be your date tonight.

STEPHEN: You read the last play.

MENDY: You asked me what I thought.

STEPHEN: You didn't tell me anything I didn't already know.

MENDY: That's no reason to stop writing.

STEPHEN: Movies that don't get made and pilots that don't sell are writing.

MENDY: That's not writing, that's typing. I'm talking about your immortal soul.

STEPHEN: I haven't got one. I lost it to Maria Callas.

MENDY: No, you lost it to Michael Deller. Right over there. Eight years ago.

STEPHEN: Nobody was supposed to notice that. May I have more scotch?

MENDY: I thought you didn't like it.

STEPHEN: When did that stop me? Could we put on something by Leyla Gencer? She's good for when you're really fucked. The only thing I care about right now is that phone ringing.

MENDY: I don't believe that.

STEPHEN: You'd better. My fate for the next couple of hours is in the hands of a wildly attractive young man I'm not even sure I approve of. I certainly don't his prose style. Michael would rip him apart.

MENDY: What are we going to do about you?

STEPHEN: I just want to feel his arms around me for the next couple of hours. Somebody's arms. Anybody's. What about *Wozzeck*?

MENDY: No! I hate twentieth-century opera. You do, too. Give me bel canto or give me death.

STEPHEN: You hate the twentieth century.

MENDY: What about some chamber music and we'll talk?

STEPHEN: I hate chamber music. Nobody dies in it. I need story. Do you have Merman's closing night in *Gypsy*?

MENDY: No, but I have her opening night in *Norma*.

STEPHEN: Dame Clara Butt! You really would buy anything.

MENDY: Stephen, when you were talking about needs?

STEPHEN: Yeah?

MENDY: You said you didn't particularly like your own.

STEPHEN: I don't, some of them.

MENDY: Why should our needs be so difficult to live with?

STEPHEN: I don't know. They just are. Where did you get this? (*He has picked up a magazine.*)

MENDY: What?

STEPHEN: The new *Blueboy*.

MENDY: I don't know. I think Tom Ewing must have left it here.

STEPHEN: I still only have last month's.

MENDY: You actually read those things?

STEPHEN: No one reads them, Mendy. God, he's gorgeous.

MENDY: He's all right.

STEPHEN: You wouldn't kick him out of bed.

MENDY: He's too beefy.

STEPHEN: They're called muscles.

MENDY: Thirty pounds heavier he'd look like Jon Vickers in *Peter Grimes*.

STEPHEN: Will you look at those legs!

MENDY: My needs are different.

STEPHEN: They're perfect.

MENDY: They're urgent.

STEPHEN: I love legs like that.

MENDY: If I don't get back into a relationship soon, I don't know what I'm going to do.

STEPHEN: I told you: don't fret it. Just lay back and let it happen.

MENDY: You make it sound like something obscene.

STEPHEN: With a little luck, it is. We've all seen him.

MENDY: That one?

STEPHEN: His name is Curt. He's a hustler.

MENDY: You mean you actually know that person?

STEPHEN: He runs an ad in *The Native* every week. He does anything. Grant Eberstadt had him.

MENDY: Grant Eberstadt had that?

STEPHEN: I said he'd do anything.

MENDY: But Grant Eberstadt! What's the matter?

STEPHEN: For a minute I thought it was Hal.

MENDY: Your waiter friend?

STEPHEN: I wish you'd stop calling him that. He's a writer.

MENDY: He looks like that?

STEPHEN: A little.

MENDY: No wonder you're hoping he'll call.

STEPHEN: I thought you'd seen him walking his dog.

MENDY: I have, but if he'd been dressed like that, believe me, I would never have noticed the dog. This one is beautiful.

STEPHEN: So's Hal. (*Short pause.*)

MENDY: He really looks like that?

STEPHEN: Don't you think so? (*Short pause.*)

MENDY: If this is what you go for, no wonder you never saw anything in me.

STEPHEN: I'm going to turn the page, all right?

MENDY: Why is it that whenever I say anything serious, you let it pass?

STEPHEN: The only thing we ever saw in one another, Mendy, was Maria Callas.

MENDY: That's not true.

STEPHEN: Think about it. I'm going to turn the page, all right?

MENDY: Like I said: have it your way.

STEPHEN: Like you said: I usually do.

MENDY: That was a very hurtful thing you just said.

STEPHEN: It's true. (*He turns the page.*) If it weren't for Maria, I doubt if we'd even be friends. Well, maybe we'd be friends but we wouldn't be—. (*He turns the page.*)

MENDY: Wouldn't be what?

STEPHEN: Friends like this.

MENDY: I always thought we should have been lovers.

STEPHEN: Oh, come on! That one has a sexy neck.

MENDY: We could have been, too, if . . .

STEPHEN: Nice and thick.

MENDY: . . . if this had been the best of all possible worlds.

STEPHEN: You know whose neck I'm in love with? Alan Bates's.

MENDY: You were so cute then.

STEPHEN: Thanks a lot.

MENDY: I had my good points, too.

STEPHEN: You still do.

MENDY: Well then?

STEPHEN: Can you see the two of us in bed together? First we'd get the giggles and then we'd quarrel over which *Puritani* to play.

MENDY: There is only one *Puritani* to play.

STEPHEN: The Mexico City, May 11, 1952 one.

MENDY: Over her 1954 Chicago performances?

STEPHEN: You see? Besides they were in '55.

MENDY: What are those? They look like the want ads.

STEPHEN: They're the classifieds. Here's one for you. He's into rare Tebaldi tapes.

MENDY: Let me see that. Oh my God, he is!

STEPHEN: Why don't you give him a call? Maybe he's nice.

MENDY: If he likes Tebaldi, I doubt it. It was a Tebaldi fan who threw those radishes at Maria at the Saturday matinée *Norma*. Tebaldi fans were like that.

STEPHEN: You never seem to run into them anymore.

MENDY: It's true. After she stopped singing, it was as if they vanished from the face of the earth. We, on the other hand, are still everywhere. Maria lives through us. We've kept her alive or maybe it's vice-versa. We're some kind of survivors.

STEPHEN: She's the only one who didn't.

MENDY: You didn't tell me: how does she do the letter on it?

STEPHEN: What letter?

MENDY: Maria on the Lisbon *Traviata*.

STEPHEN: Great.

MENDY: Better than Dallas?

STEPHEN: Different. More like Covent Garden.

MENDY: It couldn't be better than Dallas. Nothing will ever be better than Dallas. *"Teneste la promessa. La disfida ebbe luogo, il Barone fu ferito, pero migliora."* (*The telephone has started to ring.* MENDY *picks it up.*) *"Curatevi: mertate un avvenir migliore.* Giorgio Germont." Heartbreak House. Just a moment. (*To* STEPHEN:) It's for you.

STEPHEN: So soon?

MENDY: Ask him to drop by if he'd like.

STEPHEN (*into the phone*): Hi. How's it going? Mendy. He was just camping.

MENDY: That's not true. I was doing Maria. I wasn't camping. I never camp.

STEPHEN: We're just sitting around, playing a few records.

MENDY: And looking at his picture in *Blueboy*!

STEPHEN (*dead serious*): Mendy!

MENDY: Ask him over.

STEPHEN (*into phone*): Listen, are you going to be free later tonight or what?

MENDY: He can come here first. There's food, tell him.

STEPHEN: Oh. I understand.

MENDY: He's standing you up? How dare he? Let me speak to that—!

STEPHEN (*to* MENDY): If you don't shut up I am going to break your face open! (*Into phone.*) Nothing. I could meet you after if it wouldn't be too late. I guess you're right. I was just hoping to see you tonight. I know it wasn't definite. I'm sorry, too. What about tomorrow night?

MENDY: You're supposed to be going to *Meistersinger* with me.

STEPHEN (*into phone*): That's right. I forgot. You know we have seats for Ashkenazy/Perlman next Sunday?

MENDY: You're not going to the Albanese recital in Hoboken?

STEPHEN: Do you think you'll have any free time before then?

MENDY: She's doing two arias from *Rondine*!

STEPHEN: Like I said, I just want to see you sometime. You'd better get back there then. That's one mean maître d'. That's okay. I'll probably just head home; I've got the new Muriel Spark. I like her, too. Well, okay, then. Call when you can. (*He hangs up.*)

MENDY: What's the problem?

STEPHEN: Something came up.

MENDY: I'm sorry.

STEPHEN: Well, it wasn't definite. He said this might happen.

MENDY: Join the club. I loathe the younger generation. What do you want me to put on?

STEPHEN: I knew this would happen.

MENDY: I bet you haven't heard the tapes of the television documentary.

STEPHEN: Shit.

MENDY: It just came out.

STEPHEN: I think I'm going to take off.

MENDY: Don't you want to hear it? They're all on it. Scotto, Caballé, Tebaldi, Gobbi, all of them. They all talk about how much she meant to them and how she changed the face of opera. Zeffirelli narrates.

STEPHEN: Some other time.

MENDY: It's very moving.

STEPHEN: I saw the program.

MENDY: You know you don't want to go.

STEPHEN: I don't know what I want to do.

MENDY: Then stay. You want some ice cream?

STEPHEN: I'll get the Lisbon *Traviata* to you.

MENDY: Why don't you want to hear the documentary? It brings her all back. It's like she was in the room with you. You'll cry when you hear parts of it. I do every time.

STEPHEN: I already have it. Thanks for dinner.

MENDY: You already have it? Where are you going?

STEPHEN: I'll probably do the bars first and see if anything is happening.

MENDY: You want me to come with you?

STEPHEN: We tried that.

MENDY: It wasn't my fault.

STEPHEN: Mendy, I was doing fine with that one guy until you came over and burst into the second act of *Tosca*.

MENDY: No one has a sense of humor in those places.

STEPHEN: Including me.

MENDY: I thought he looked like a wizened lizard anyway.

STEPHEN: That's your opinion.

MENDY: I'll be good.

STEPHEN: For the last time, no. I do better on my own. So would you.

MENDY: Are you going to be walking by your place?

STEPHEN: I don't know. Why?

MENDY: I thought I might pop up and get the record.

STEPHEN: I said I'd get it to you.

MENDY: What's wrong with right now?

STEPHEN: You're impossible.

MENDY: Just let me play the last side of the documentary for you.

STEPHEN: I'd like to but I've just got to get out of here and go someplace.

MENDY: Just the last side.

STEPHEN: All right, but as soon as it's finished—!

MENDY: I promise. Just sit down.

STEPHEN: I mean it, too.

MENDY: Okay, okay. (STEPHEN *sits and starts idly flipping through the issue of* Blueboy.) You're not listening.

STEPHEN: I will, I will! (*He will continue to flip through the pages as we hear the sound of the phonograph needle trying to find the leading groove again. After several attempts, it makes it. The record is badly scratched. Clunk, clunk, clunk. We hear the end of the PBS television documentary on the life of Maria Callas. Franco Zeffirelli is telling us about the life and legend of Maria Callas.*)

ZEFFIRELLI: On the morning of September 16, 1977, shortly after awakening, Maria Callas died of a heart attack in her Paris apartment. She was fifty-four years old.

MENDY: You're not listening.

STEPHEN: Yes, I am. (*He turns another page.*)

ZEFFIRELLI: There has been perhaps only one faithful companion to Maria throughout her life, her loneliness. The price sometimes one has to pay for the glory and the success. It's also the price of being God's instrument. It really seems to me that God used Maria's talent to communicate to us his planet of beauty. To enrich our souls, to make us better men. Maria Callas, the glory of opera. (*Callas begins to sing* "Ah, non credea mirarti" *from* La Sonnambula.)

MENDY: Stephen!

STEPHEN: I'm listening, I'm listening. (STEPHEN *continues to turn more pages.* MENDY *is silent. The voice of Maria Callas on the soundtrack is beginning to fade. So are the lights. Blackout.*)

ACT II

STEPHEN *and* MIKE's. *Early morning. Pale, gray light from the windows. The room is in much disarray. We notice a box of pizza. There is a pair of pants on the floor. The needle on the phonograph is endlessly tracking the run-off groove at the end of a record side. The light on the telephone answering machine is blinking, indicating that a message has been received. The door to the bedroom is closed.*

A key is heard in the door. STEPHEN *enters. He is in the same clothes as the evening before, only now he wears a windbreaker over his sweater. He carries a small duffel bag, a copy of the* New York Times, *and a brown paper bag with coffee and Danishes.*

STEPHEN: Hello! It's me! (*He is no sooner through the door than he is aware of the phonograph needle tracking the end of the record. He puts down his things and goes to the phonograph. He takes the arm off the record, stops the turntable and removes the record, being careful to hold it by the edges and perhaps blowing off any dust that might have collected.*) Where . . .? (*He is clearly looking for the record's protective inner-sleeve and outer album cover.*) Dammit! (*He has seen them on the coffee table under the box of pizza. Some of the pizza has gotten onto them.* STEPHEN *is not amused. He returns the record to its sleeve and jacket and then goes back to the stereo unit and switches it to an FM station. Rock music is heard. It is unbearably loud. Clearly, whoever was playing the stereo last was running it at full volume.* STEPHEN *quickly lowers the volume and carefully tunes in a classical music station. As he does so, his annoyance is again apparent. The Schubert "Wanderer" Fantasie is being played.* STEPHEN *satisfies himself with the volume and the reception. Next, he kicks off his shoes and unzips his windbreaker. At the same time, he moves to the answering machine and rewinds the messages. He takes off his windbreaker and hangs it up in the hall closet as the following messages are played back.*)

MENDY'S VOICE (*on the answering machine*): Mike? It's Mendy again. You want to pick up? Hello? Don't tell me you're not back yet? What did you two go see? *Berlin Alexanderplatz?* All right, I guess you're not there. Call me just as soon as you come in. It doesn't matter how late. I'll be up all night. Really. 4, 5 A.M. How could I sleep knowing there's a new Maria? (*He sings.*) "Nessun dorma!" (*He stops.*) Hello? (*The machine disconnects. A new message is heard.*) Mike, it's me. Hello? I thought I heard you pick up and we were cut off. Hello! Hello! I guess not. Please, Mike, just as soon as you come in. I really would appreciate it. How are you, anyway? No one ever sees you anymore. Call sometime. I mean, call as soon as you get this but call some other time, too. You know what I mean! Ciao. (*He hangs up. Another message is heard.*)

MAN'S VOICE: Hello. I'd like to leave a message for Mike. This is Gary Adler. We met at Kenny Horton's. You said to give you a ring sometime. My number is 909-1389. I'd like to hear from you. I hate these things. (*He hangs up. Another message is heard.*)

STEPHEN'S VOICE: Mike? It's Stephen. Please pick up. I really need to speak to you. Listen, I'm kind of stuck out here. I don't . . . Uh, forget it. (*He hangs up. Another message is heard.*)

WOMAN'S VOICE (*somewhat slurred*): Hello, Stephen. It's your mother. Nothing important. Just calling. You don't have to call back. If you don't want to. Love you. (*Short pause.*) It's your mother. Say hello to Mike. Hello, Mike. I hate these things. (*She hangs up. Another message is heard.*)

MAN'S VOICE: This is a message for Stephen Riddick. My name is Todd Newman. David Minton gave me your number. I'm directing a workshop production of *On the Other Hand* and I'd like to speak to you before we go into rehearsal. I thought the original production was all wrong. David said you did, too, so I thought maybe we could talk. I really love your work, Mr. Riddick. My number is 681-1100. Thank you. Best time is nights. (*He hangs up. Another message is heard.*)

MAN'S VOICE: Mike? It's Allan Weeks. From Boston. I was in your neighborhood. Sorry I missed you. I'll try you next trip. (*He hangs up. There are no more messages.* STEPHEN *goes to machine and turns it off. The bedroom door opens.* PAUL *starts into the living room. He is naked.*)

PAUL: Oh!

STEPHEN: Hi.

PAUL: Hello. Excuse me. (*He goes back into the bedroom and closes the door.* STEPHEN *sits with the coffee and a Danish and opens the* Times. *He reads for a few moments, then lowers paper, turns and looks towards bedroom a beat. Then he raises paper and reads again. Bedroom door opens and* MIKE *comes out. He holds the bedclothes around his middle. He goes to the clothes scattered around the room and begins picking them up.*)

MIKE: Sorry.

STEPHEN: It's all right.

MIKE: You been here long?

STEPHEN: Just got here.

MIKE: We'll be out of your way.

STEPHEN: What makes you think you're in it? (*Beat.* STEPHEN *reads.* MIKE *looks for and picks up clothing.*)

MIKE: How was your evening?

STEPHEN: All right.

MIKE: Did you see your friend?

STEPHEN: Something came up.

MIKE: I'm sorry.

STEPHEN: How was yours?

MIKE: Fine.

STEPHEN: You left the phonograph on all night.

MIKE: Not again!

STEPHEN: That clunk, clunk would drive me crazy.

MIKE: I was better off with my old record player. Maybe it wasn't high fidelity but at least it turned itself off. I'm sorry. From now on I'll stick to the radio.

STEPHEN: That's not what I said. (*He lowers paper.*) What are you looking for?

MIKE: It's all right.

STEPHEN: I think there's something over there. (*He motions with his head.*)

MIKE: Where? (STEPHEN *repeats the motion.* MIKE *crosses and picks up a jockstrap.*) Thank you. So what did you do?

STEPHEN: The bars.

MIKE: Was anybody there?

STEPHEN: Are you speaking society or numbers?

MIKE: I'm asking a question.

STEPHEN: I got coffee.

MIKE: Thanks. (*He's finished gathering the clothes and starts going to the bedroom.*) He's got to get to work.

STEPHEN: Where's that?

MIKE: Somewhere uptown. East 70s, I think.

STEPHEN: It's getting cold. (MIKE *goes to paper bag with the coffee in it and sees that there are two more containers in it.*)

MIKE: They gave you three?

STEPHEN: I asked for three. The Danish are just from Smilers. Jon Vie wasn't open yet.

MIKE: That's okay. (*He starts for the bedroom carrying the clothes and the two containers of coffee. His hands are full. He is trying to keep the bedclothes around him, carry the clothes he picked up off the floor and balance two containers of coffee at the same time. He stops outside the bedroom door and kicks it.* STEPHEN *lowers the paper and watches.*) Paul! I can't . . .! (*At one point the bedclothes drop and we get a view of his backside. He quickly gets the bedclothes back up around his middle and turns to see if* STEPHEN *has seen this. Their eyes meet and hold a beat.* PAUL *opens the bedroom door from within.*) Quick! Grab these! (*He goes into the bedroom. The door closes.* STEPHEN *resumes reading the* Times *but a moment later he lets the paper fall and stares in front of him.*)

STEPHEN: They liked the new Stoppard. (MIKE *comes out of the bedroom. He has put a bathrobe on.*)

MIKE: What's it like out?

STEPHEN: Okay.

MIKE: They said more rain. (*He has gone to a closet and taken out a clean towel.*)

STEPHEN: I thought he was . . .!

MIKE: What?

STEPHEN: Nothing.

MIKE: What?

STEPHEN: Nothing. Do you have to use that towel? Use one of the old ones. I thought he was so late for work!

MIKE (*evenly*): Stephen.

STEPHEN: Those are our best towels. They're a set. I'm sorry but I see no reason to take one of them when you have a whole closetful of old unmatched ones to choose from. I'm just being practical.

MIKE (*wearily*): Yeah. (*He exchanges the towel for another one.*)

STEPHEN: Only you would take a towel from a perfectly good set instead of a single one.

MIKE: Yes, Mother.

STEPHEN: It's common sense for Christ's sake! (MIKE *goes back into the bedroom and closes the door.* STEPHEN *is clearly annoyed with himself.*) Shit! (*He goes to bedroom door, starts to knock, then thinks better of it. He crosses to window and looks out. He goes back to sofa and sits. He looks at* Times, *puts it aside.*) I'll make more coffee! (*No response from the other room. He doesn't move. The recording of the Schubert "Wanderer" Fantasie being played by the FM station has gotten stuck. The same phrase is repeated over and over and over.* STEPHEN *smiles and shakes his head.* MIKE *comes out of the bedroom. This time we can hear the sound of the shower running in the bathroom adjacent to the bedroom.*)

MIKE: Did you say something?

STEPHEN: NCN is fucking up. Listen to that. You'd think they'd—Hello? (*Someone at the station bumps the needle and the record resumes playing properly.*) It's about time. If I ran a station, heads would roll if that ever happened. (*He gets up.*) I said I'd make more coffee.

MIKE: Not for us. (*He sits and works on a Danish.*)

STEPHEN (*moving to kitchen area and preparing coffee*): You know with CDs, stuck records, scratches, that sort of thing is going to be a thing of the past.

MIKE: I said not for us, thank you.

STEPHEN: I heard you. Though actually I was in Tower Records and there was this guy returning a CD he claimed was defective. The Beethoven Third. "What's the matter with it?" the salesman sort of sniffed. CDs are supposed to be indestructible. "I can't get access to the third movement," the guy said. Do you believe it? "I can't get access to the third movement." Welcome to the future. You sure?

MIKE: He doesn't drink it.

STEPHEN: Another health nut. I can understand not smoking but this other shit! Will he take de-caf?

MIKE: We're fine.

STEPHEN: What time does he have to be at work anyway? What is he, a milkman?

MIKE: We're going by his place first.

STEPHEN: The two of you?

MIKE: I said I'd drive him.

STEPHEN: Where does he live?

MIKE: 106th Street and Amsterdam.

STEPHEN: In our car? Lots of luck. So long hubcaps. So long tape deck. So long motor.

MIKE: It's Columbia.

STEPHEN: Fuck you it's Columbia. It's fucking Harlem. I ought to know. I went there.

MIKE: It's changed.

STEPHEN: They were saying that when Lou Gehrig went there. Look what happened to him.

MIKE: The car will be fine.

STEPHEN: What does he have to go home for anyway?

MIKE: To change.

STEPHEN: Into what? Another jockstrap?

MIKE (*rising*): Okay.

STEPHEN: What's the matter? What did I say?

MIKE: I'm sorry you're home earlier than I thought we'd agreed.

STEPHEN: I'm sorry I got tired playing Orphan Annie in the fucking rain but do you hear me complaining? You're gonna need your sense of humor if we're gonna get through this and so far I've been working mine for all it's worth. I just want to know what you and Joe College have against the 7th Ave.-Broadway I.R.T.

MIKE: I said I'd drive him.

STEPHEN: The subway's faster.

MIKE: I want to drive him. I like him.

STEPHEN: Why didn't you say so? That's all you had to say. Like I understand. I can relate to like. Like is lovely. Like is nice. Like is human. Like is likable. (*During this* MIKE *will cross to the radio and change stations till he picks up mellow-rock-type music. He will also lower the volume.*)

MIKE: Do you mind? That stuff was making me nuts. His name is Paul.

STEPHEN: I know.

MIKE: He's not a college student. He's a graduate student.

STEPHEN: Social work.

MIKE: You know all this.

STEPHEN: He looks like a . . .

MIKE: I'm not interested.

STEPHEN: . . . something in the rodent family.

MIKE: That's your opinion.

STEPHEN: I'm glad you see something in him. It must be his charm or his brain. God knows it's not his meat.

MIKE: This is hopeless.

STEPHEN: So move.

MIKE: Maybe I should. Did you get your messages?

STEPHEN: All two of them. So who's Gary Adler? "We met at Kenny Horton's. You said to give you a ring sometime. Little Gary would like to hear from you big Mike." (*It's an accurate, deadly imitation.*)

MIKE: He's an editor at Dodd Mead with terminal bad breath for Christ's sake.

STEPHEN: What's keeping you? Little Gary sounds like a real winner.

MIKE: 106th and Amsterdam will be just fine.

STEPHEN: I'm sorry about the towels.

PAUL (*off*): Mike!

STEPHEN: I mean it.

PAUL (*off*): I'm out!

STEPHEN: Go on, I'll be nice.

PAUL (*off*): She's all yours! (MIKE *turns and exits into the bedroom. After a moment,* STEPHEN *crosses to bedroom and knocks.*)

STEPHEN: Guys? Can I get in here a second? Thanks. (*He goes into bedroom leaving the door open. Sound of the shower is louder. We can hear voices but nothing distinct. A few beats later and* PAUL *will come into the room where he will finish dressing.*)

PAUL (*over his shoulder*): That's all right. I think I've got everything. (*He moves across room to window and looks out, checking the weather. A beat later and* STEPHEN *comes back into the room, closing the bedroom door behind him. It should be clear, even to* PAUL, *that* STEPHEN *is trying to keep him out here.*)

STEPHEN: I couldn't find it.

PAUL: Oh. I'm sorry.

STEPHEN: It's not your fault.

PAUL: What were you looking for?

STEPHEN (*dismissing it as unimportant*): Something I thought you might get a kick out of.

PAUL: What's that?

STEPHEN: Mike would kill me. (*Gesturing to* PAUL *that he's free to return to the bedroom and* MIKE.) Don't let me keep you.

PAUL: This is fine. I'm sorry about . . . (*His gestures recall the awkwardness of their first meeting.*)

STEPHEN: It's perfectly all right.

PAUL: We just didn't hear you.

STEPHEN: Please! It's Jim, right?

PAUL: Paul.

STEPHEN: Paul, of course! Jim's fairer. Coffee?

PAUL: I don't drink it.

STEPHEN: Good thinking. De-caf?

PAUL: That's all right.

STEPHEN: I'm Stephen.

PAUL: I know. We spoke on the phone last night.

STEPHEN: You broke my friend Mendy's heart.

PAUL: I didn't even know what he was talking about.

STEPHEN: The Lisbon *Traviata*.

PAUL: It sounds like a murder mystery. "The Lisbon Traviata."

STEPHEN: You think so?

PAUL: Well, a mystery anyway. "The Maltese Falcon."

STEPHEN: Those are nice pants.

PAUL: Thank you. They're from Barney's.

STEPHEN: Why don't you put something on?

PAUL: I am.

STEPHEN: The stereo. I'll get your coffee.

PAUL: I told you, I don't drink it—.

STEPHEN: It's de-caf, cross my heart. Go ahead, put something on.

PAUL: I wouldn't know where to begin.

STEPHEN: They're all in alphabetical order by composer, title, or performer. If they're not, we know who to blame.

PAUL: I didn't know they made this many records.

STEPHEN: What would you say to a little Lisbon *Traviata*?

PAUL: I'd say "Hello, little Lisbon Traviata." (*He laughs.*) I don't think so. Opera's kind of . . .

STEPHEN: I like the fit.

PAUL: I guess if I understood what they were singing about . . .

STEPHEN: Love and death. That's all they're ever singing about. Boy meets girl, boy gets girl, boy and girl croak. That's all you need to know, from *Aida* to *Zaide*.

PAUL: I'd be over my head.

STEPHEN: It's very simple. What do all those people sitting around the Met think those operas are about? Opera is about life and death passions, not sitting on your butt listening to some fat canary sing. Maria understood that. That's where her voice came from, the guts.

PAUL: Maria?

STEPHEN: Callas, Greek-American soprano, 1923–1977, famous for the dramatic intensity she brought to her characterizations. Where did you two meet?

PAUL: Me and Mike?

STEPHEN: Mike and I. Mendy introduced us. My friend you were on the phone with last night. *La Dame Aux Camélias.* He insisted he was madly in love with me and then made sure I met Michael. I believe that's called self-destructive.

PAUL: I met Mike where I used to work.

STEPHEN: Where was that? A gym?

PAUL: No. I never worked in a gym.

STEPHEN: You have a beautiful body.

PAUL: It was a restaurant. Vanessa's. In the Village.

STEPHEN: I know Vanessa's. It used to be wonderful. Still, I'm impressed.

PAUL: I was a waiter, part-time. I couldn't afford to eat there.

STEPHEN: Lucky for you Mike could.

PAUL: No, lucky for me he got my table. Now I'm working in a light gallery part-time, Upper East Side. I'm a graduate student at Columbia working for an M.S.W.

STEPHEN: Master of Social Work.

PAUL: Right!

STEPHEN: What's a light gallery?

PAUL: A showroom for lights. Lighting fixtures. One of these.

STEPHEN: Are they twill?

PAUL: I think so.

STEPHEN: A social worker? I thought about being a priest.

PAUL: Really?

STEPHEN: For about exactly five minutes. Then I thought about joining the Peace Corps, for exactly one.

PAUL: I spent two years in Zaire with the Peace Corps.

STEPHEN: Really?

PAUL: It was no picnic.

STEPHEN: I'll bet. I admire people who devote themselves to public service.

PAUL: That's probably why we do it!

STEPHEN: Twill wouldn't fit like that.

PAUL: I'm sorry?

STEPHEN: You're very sweet when you smile like that. I can see what Mike sees in you. Now I'm sorry. We're even. I went to Columbia.

PAUL: I know.

STEPHEN: I hated it, so I transferred to Yale. I hated Yale more, so I transferred back. Then I discovered other gay men, Greenwich Village, and the American Theater in roughly that descending order and somehow never made it back to Morningside Heights. I'm still six points short of my B.A.

PAUL: Mike says you're a playwright. A very good one.

STEPHEN: He's right.

PAUL: I'm not much of a theatergoer. I'd like to go more but on my budget . . . I just saw *Cats*.

STEPHEN: You can die a happy man.

PAUL: Am I nuts, but I hated it? I'd rather see *Bambi*.

STEPHEN: I like your taste in theater, animals, and extremely sexy pants. (*This time their eyes meet and hold. The sound of the shower has stopped.*)

MIKE (*off*): Paul!

STEPHEN: We're in here! (*To* PAUL:) Saved by the shower.

MIKE (*off*): Paul!

PAUL: Yoh!

STEPHEN: What did you expect?

PAUL: From Mike's description of you? Not this. (*The tea kettle has started to whistle.*)

STEPHEN: Your water's boiling.

MIKE (*off*): Stephen!

STEPHEN (*on his way to the bedroom*): It's about time! (*He opens door and goes in.*)

MIKE (*off*): Paul!

STEPHEN (*off*): Put some clothes on. (*The bedroom door closes. Silence.* PAUL *stands, undetermined what to do. The kettle is still whistling. A beat later and* MIKE *comes out of the bedroom, a towel around him, wet from the shower.*)

MIKE: What's going on?

PAUL: Nothing.

MIKE: Are you all right?

PAUL: I'm fine.

MIKE: He's not . . .?

PAUL: I can handle it. Hurry up.

MIKE: Shit.

PAUL: I thought he knew.

MIKE: He does know.

PAUL: I didn't want to meet him like this.

MIKE: You think I did? I'm sorry.

PAUL: It's not anybody's fault. (MIKE *is aware of kettle whistling. He goes and turns down flame as* STEPHEN *comes out of the bedroom.*)

STEPHEN: I thought you were in such a hurry. (*To* MIKE:) I'll do that.

PAUL: Really, nothing for me.

MIKE: Why don't you come in and keep me company while I dress?

PAUL: I'm fine.

MIKE: I think it might be better if you—.

PAUL: Really! Hurry up. (MIKE *goes. He doesn't like it but he goes.*)

STEPHEN: I found what I was looking for. (*He hands* PAUL *an envelope which* PAUL *will open while* STEPHEN *goes to stereo unit and puts in a cassette. It is Alban Berg's* Wozzeck. *Next* STEPHEN *crosses to bedroom door, which* MIKE *has left open and pops his head in.*) Excuse us. (*He closes it.*) Mike hates opera. That should've told me right away we weren't fated to last. After eight years, it gets pretty hard to relate to someone who isn't into *The Flying Dutchman,* you know?

PAUL: Why did you give me these?

STEPHEN: Because I'm a shit. (*He hits cassette "play" button. It is quite loud.*) I mean, how many times can you make love before *Parsifal* comes up? (*No reaction to this from* PAUL *who continues to look at what are clearly a collection of Polaroid photos that were in the envelope* STEPHEN *gave him. At the same time,* MIKE *opens the bedroom door. He is in his socks and underwear and clearly annoyed at the deafening volume of the* Wozzeck *cassette.*)

MIKE: Stephen!

STEPHEN: He requested it! I swear to God. "I don't suppose you have the Boulez recording of *Wozzeck*, Steve?" "As a matter of fact, I do, young man." You could have knocked me over with a feather.

MIKE: Turn it down.

STEPHEN: Just a second. The big hit tune's coming right here.

MIKE: I'm sorry, Paul. (*He crosses the living room to cassette player.*)

STEPHEN: Why no one's made a disco arrangement of this! (MIKE *turns off cassette.*)

MIKE: You shit.

STEPHEN: That's just what I told him. Now what would you say to a little *Pirata* Mad Scene with Maria herself? Pirated from Carnegie Hall, January 27, 1959. Pirated *Pirata*! Get it? The high E alone is guaranteed to clear your sinuses. (*He is busily looking for another cassette.*)

MIKE: Cut it out, Stephen.

STEPHEN: Okay, we'll stick with *Wozzeck*. (*He pushes the "play" button on the cassette deck.* MIKE *hits him.* STEPHEN *goes down.* MIKE *turns off the cassette.*)

MIKE: Do it again and I'll break your fucking head open. (STEPHEN *is getting to his feet.*)

PAUL: Hey, come on you two, don't. I'll go.

STEPHEN: Your friend's talking to you.

MIKE: I mean it.

STEPHEN: Maybe you want him to see this side of you.

MIKE: Don't you dare turn that on. Don't Stephen. Don't make me do this.

STEPHEN: The only thing that makes you do anything is your cock and your sick, deluded idea that if you stick it in enough places maybe you'll forget what a miserable, fucked-up, phony faggot you are in the first place. (*He punches the "play" button again.* MIKE *hits him again. Again* STEPHEN *goes down. This time there is blood.* MIKE *turns off the cassette.*)

MIKE: I haven't hit anyone since the fifth grade. What are you doing to me? Christ! (*To* PAUL:) I told you to come in there with me.

PAUL: I'm sorry. I'm going.

MIKE: I'm sorry, I—! (*To* STEPHEN:) Get up!

PAUL: I'll call you.

MIKE: I'm taking you.

PAUL: I'm late. (MIKE *sees the Polaroid pictures that* STEPHEN *has given* PAUL *to look at.*)

MIKE: What are—? Give me those.

PAUL: I don't care.

MIKE: Where did you—?

PAUL: I said I don't care.

MIKE: They were his idea.

PAUL: It's okay. Mike, call me. I'm late.

MIKE: I was gonna take you.

PAUL: Make sure he's okay.

MIKE: I can be ready in a minute.

PAUL: I can't.

MIKE: Wait! (*He kisses* PAUL *who pulls away.*)

PAUL: I'll call you.

MIKE: Hey! (*He kisses* PAUL *again. There is desperation in it. We can see that* PAUL *never really responds or relaxes into it.*) I love you, Paul.

PAUL: Me, too. I gotta go. (*He goes to door. He has some trouble with the different locks.* MIKE *just stands watching him. We should get the feeling that* PAUL *and* MIKE *will never see each other again.*) Making a graceful exit from a New York City apartment is just about impossible unless you're some sort of Houdini. Everybody's got a different arrangement.

MIKE (*seeing* PAUL's *almost got it*): There you go.

PAUL: Thanks.

STEPHEN: Don't be a stranger. (PAUL *goes.* MIKE *crosses to apartment door, opens it and sticks his head out into the hallway.*)

MIKE: Push the "Up" button, too. Sometimes it doesn't register if you just hit "Down." Can you hear it? Your hair's still wet. You want to use a dryer? I hear it. Here it comes. Good morning, Mrs. Di Marco. I'll call you, Paul. Or you can call me. I'm home. All day. I've got a deadline. What I said back there. . . . (*He gestures with his head back towards the living room.*) I meant it. I do. If I see him, I will, Mrs. Di Marco. You're welcome. So long, Paul. (*Pause. He closes door and turns back into the room. He looks at* STEPHEN *who is still on the floor. Their eyes meet.*) You're pathetic.

STEPHEN: You want to fuck me?

MIKE: Look at you.

STEPHEN: You want me to fuck you?

MIKE: You just did. (*He will try to rip up the Polaroids. It is close to impossible.*)

STEPHEN: How much do you want to bet he's never read Proust?

MIKE: With a little luck, he's never even heard of him.

STEPHEN: You'll need a scissors. (MIKE *is still trying to rip up the Polaroids.*)

MIKE: I asked you to destroy these.

STEPHEN: I know.

MIKE: You said you had.

STEPHEN: I lied. (MIKE *gives up trying to rip up the Polaroids.*) I told you.

MIKE: Get up, will you?

STEPHEN: I like it down here.

MIKE: At least . . . Here! (*He tosses him a towel from the kitchen.*) Wipe your mouth.

STEPHEN: I'd forgotten how funny blood tastes.

MIKE: Here. (*He points to a place on his chin where* STEPHEN *is not wiping.*)

STEPHEN: It's us. We're tasting ourselves.

MIKE: You're still . . .! (*He goes to* STEPHEN, *takes towel and wipes the blood off a spot on his chin.*)

STEPHEN: Ow!

MIKE: Shut up!

STEPHEN: Why don't you want to fuck me?

MIKE: Stephen!

STEPHEN: You used to love my ass.

MIKE: Stop.

STEPHEN: You're the only person I ever let fuck me. A lot of guys wanted to but I wouldn't let them. I guess I was saving myself for you.

MIKE: Suit yourself. (*He throws towel down, gets up and goes to bedroom.*)

STEPHEN: You know, I never really liked fucking you. You said "ouch" too much. (MIKE *slams bedroom door.*) Well, not "ouch" exactly. It was more like a whining moan of general discomfort. "Are you okay, Mike?" "Unh-hunh." That "unh-hunh" was a real wet blanket. Well, all that's in the past and dead and buried. Let's talk about who gets the Sutherland-Pavarotti *Porgy and Bess.* (*Beat.*) He doesn't want to talk about who gets the Sutherland-Pavarotti *Porgy and Bess.* (*He is getting to his feet.*) I'm up! You had your chance and blew it. (*He is heading towards the phonograph.*) I'm going to put something on. Don't worry, something nice. I can't stand it without music. I'll put on something you'll like. Trust me. (MIKE *comes out of the bedroom. He is dressed in jeans and undershirt. He will pick up the container of coffee* STEPHEN *brought him and take it back into the bedroom during the following exchange.*) What deadline?

MIKE: A review.

STEPHEN: What review?

MIKE: Just a review. What do you care?

STEPHEN: Isn't that cold? (MIKE *goes into bedroom and closes door.*) I'll make some fresh! I wasn't planning on going in today either. (*He has taken out a record and put it on the turntable. The music is the beginning to* Lohengrin. *He sets it at a low, very "easy listening" level.*) I'm not going to tell you what this is. You should be able to guess. We saw it together. (MIKE *comes out of the bedroom with the container of coffee.*) Are you listening? (*He indicates the music.* MIKE *pours container of coffee down the sink.*) I told you. (MIKE *will start to make fresh-perked coffee.*) I said I'd do that. (MIKE *continues to make coffee.*) I'll give you three guesses and one hint: it's not *La Bohème*.

MIKE: Are you crazy?

STEPHEN: You used to like this game.

MIKE: I used to like a lot of things.

STEPHEN: Starting with me. (*At once.*) That's not de-caf!

MIKE: I don't want de-caf.

STEPHEN: I'll give you another hint: it's German.

MIKE: Stark raving mad.

STEPHEN: Don't you wish. Stark raving clarity is what it's called.

MIKE: I like him, Stephen. We have a nice thing going.

STEPHEN: I heard you say you loved him. Funny, he doesn't seem that hung to me.

MIKE: Wouldn't you like to know?

STEPHEN: I groped him and what I felt was strictly minimal. (*With an explosive gesture* MIKE *sweeps several glasses, plates, and kitchen items from off the counter. They make a lot of noise and mess.*) All right, we'll change the subject.

MIKE: We don't have another subject.

STEPHEN: Where's your sense of humor?

MIKE: I wouldn't put it past you.

STEPHEN: What is that supposed to mean?

MIKE: Anybody who would . . . (*He has taken up the Polaroids and will next find a scissors and begin to methodically cut them into little pieces.*) . . . show these to someone else . . .

STEPHEN: Is what? Is sick? Is crazy?

MIKE: You said it, I didn't.

STEPHEN: Try angry!

MIKE: What were you thinking?

STEPHEN: I wasn't thinking. It's not about that.

MIKE: This was deliberate.

STEPHEN: No kidding. I'll tell you something else it was: hostile.

MIKE: What did you hope to accomplish?

STEPHEN: I don't know. (*He suddenly doesn't.*)

MIKE: Other than embarrassing me? But I'll tell you something: I'll get over it.

STEPHEN: But will Joe Jockstrap? There's the rub.

MIKE: Is that what this was all about? I thought we had an agreement.

STEPHEN: I thought he should know what a hot number he was getting involved with.

MIKE: He found that out a long time ago.

STEPHEN: You don't just come between that and someone else and expect to get away with it.

MIKE: There's nothing to come between.

STEPHEN: Don't say that.

MIKE: What do you expect me to say when you pull a stunt like this?

STEPHEN: You knew where they were.

MIKE: I must have been nuts to let you take these.

STEPHEN: We both were.

MIKE: Really nuts.

STEPHEN: It's called in love.

MIKE: This isn't love.

STEPHEN: I said in love.

MIKE: And I said "nuts."

STEPHEN: How about wild, passionate sexual abandon, and a hell of a lot of fun?

MIKE: I trusted you.

STEPHEN: He hasn't seen your pee-pee yet?

MIKE: These weren't for other people.

STEPHEN: You can tell him the real tragedy is neither one of us is ever going to look that good again. (MIKE *continues to destroy the Polaroids as* STEPHEN *stands behind him and watches over his shoulder.*) You remember where we took those?

MIKE: No.

STEPHEN: Look again.

MIKE: The Cape?

STEPHEN: There's Sammy.

MIKE: Where?

STEPHEN: See, just the top of his head? That dog never gave us any privacy. No matter what we were doing, he'd just get right into the act. Talk about having a twenty-three pound fly on your wall! That was one shameless cocker spaniel.

MIKE: He thought you were attacking me.

STEPHEN: He was right. I was. God, I miss him.

MIKE: Me, too.

STEPHEN: Funny we never got another one.

MIKE: Just as well.

STEPHEN: You give up? (*He gestures towards the phonograph.*) *Lohengrin.* That's too bad. First prize was a trip to Positano to hear Leontyne Price in *Gypsy.* Why not? Birgit Nilsson's doing it in Stockholm, Joan Sutherland in Sydney, Kiri at Guadalcanal, Jessye Norman turned it down. I think she was right. (*He has taken off the* Lohengrin *record and turns on a rock-and-roll radio station.*) I'm not in the mood for this. Are you in the mood for this? (*He is already turning off the rock-and-roll station.*)

MIKE: Could we have no music for a change?

STEPHEN: I'll keep it low.

MIKE: What's wrong with quiet?

STEPHEN: You have to listen to yourself think. I dare you not to like this. (*He puts Villa-Lobos's* Bachianas Brasileiras #5 *on the record player.*)

MIKE: Stephen, we better talk.

STEPHEN: We are talking. I've done nothing but. You're the silent one. What's the matter? Cat got your tongue? (*This last has been almost sung, swayed to the music as he comes back over to his spot behind* MIKE *who is still sitting and destroying the Polaroids.*) Is that the last one? Can I have it?

MIKE: No.

STEPHEN: Why not? I have seen your pee-pee.

MIKE: This isn't a way I care to think of myself.

STEPHEN: That's funny. I find the man in that picture very attractive.

MIKE: I'm not talking about attractive.

STEPHEN: I am. (*He indicates the last picture.*) Look at those proportions. They're perfect. To me they're perfect. My kind of perfect. The only one I care about. (*They are both looking at this last Polaroid;* STEPHEN *over* MIKE'*s shoulder.*) Wonderful full lips. Generous. I like that. Thick neck. I like that, too. Or did I already tell you that? I told someone. Deep, burning, really-nail-you eyes. Right at the camera. Right through it. Where am I going to find that again? And see that line there? Defining the pelvis. There's some wonderful name for it, somebody's girdle, Achilles's or Hercules's or Atlas's or something. His is perfection. The thighs. Everything. It's everything I ever wanted. I can look at that picture and get hard. I used to look at them and masturbate when you weren't around. Even when you were sometimes. Once, I remember this so clearly, you were out here reading a new Updike, one of the Rabbits, and I was looking at those and jacking off.

MIKE: Jesus.

STEPHEN: Don't give me Jesus. Give me the picture.

MIKE: No, I said. (*He will start to cut up the final Polaroid.*)

STEPHEN: I want the picture, Mike. Listen to me! This isn't easy for me to say. Let me have that much. Something! (MIKE *gets up and disposes of the pieces of Polaroid.* STEPHEN *stays where he was.* MIKE *turns off stereo. There is a long silence.*) I guess I blew it, hunh? Shit. Eight hundred years of analysis and I still say exactly what's on my mind.

MIKE (*suddenly aware of the silence*): I see what you mean.

STEPHEN: Now what about this deadline?

MIKE: Stephen, this arrangement isn't working for either one of us. I think we should end it.

STEPHEN: The arrangement's fine. It's me. I saw those records, the mess, and just went crazy.

MIKE: That's how I am, Stephen. I always was. You just didn't notice it. I scratch records, I eat pizza, I use the wrong towel.

STEPHEN: I said I was sorry.

MIKE: You can't have it both ways.

STEPHEN: I don't want it both ways. I want it this way. Just try to be careful next time.

MIKE: There will be a next time, Stephen.

STEPHEN: I know.

MIKE: I like him.

STEPHEN: Fine.

MIKE: I really like him.

STEPHEN: Don't touch the phonograph and you can bring John Simon up here.

MIKE: I don't want another morning like this.

STEPHEN: It's settled. It won't ever happen again.

MIKE: It's not a threat, Stephen. Maybe we should live alone.

STEPHEN: Believe me, I have and it's not all it's cracked up to be.

MIKE: I'm serious.

STEPHEN: On your income? Hello, Astoria. Quit stalling. Now what about this deadline?

MIKE: They want at least a thousand words on the new Mailer.

STEPHEN: God, he cranks them out.

MIKE: That's what they used to say about you.

STEPHEN: They got too much of a good thing, so they turned. Look at us. Just kidding, kidding. A sense of humor never was your strong point. Hey, let go. I have.

MIKE: They grow 'em stubborn in Arkansas.

STEPHEN: I thought you had a piece on Saul Bellow to do.

MIKE: I did and it's done and it was Joyce Carol Oates.

STEPHEN: They're the same person. One has hair, the other doesn't. They both write the same book. You want me to look at it before you turn it in?

MIKE: I already have.

STEPHEN: And?

MIKE: Anderson loved it. Three years there and I finally get an "A" from that son of a bitch. What's on your agenda?

STEPHEN: I wasn't going to do anything but go to the shrink and punch her out, then come back here and listen to the complete *Ring* cycle and watch *Heaven's Gate* on our lovely VCR. That should take me to 2 A.M. and bedtime.

MIKE: What about work?

STEPHEN: What's that?

MIKE: It's killing me, Stephen. Watching you let it all slip away. How do you think it makes me feel?

STEPHEN: One writer in the family is enough.

MIKE: It's your life. Excuse me while I get on with mine. (*He goes to desk and shuffles papers, not sitting at it. He writes on a page with a pencil.*)

STEPHEN: I wonder what Norman Mailer would think about a big fruit like you reviewing his book?

MIKE: As long as it's favorable, I don't think he'd give much of a shit.

STEPHEN: I'm going to send your editor an anonymous letter: "Michael D. sucks cock" and sign it "Mary McCarthy."

MIKE: They know.

STEPHEN: The horror? They couldn't possibly.

MIKE: Shut up and listen to this and tell me what you think.

STEPHEN: Shut up? He's being firm with me. The brute.

MIKE: I may be going out on a stylistic and critical limb here. "Norman Mailer's bark is worse than his bite. For all his macho posturing and ball scratching, he remains, *au fond*,"—I love that *au fond*, don't you love the way I worked that *au fond* in there?—". . . he remains *au fond* a Sentimentalist in the great American tradition of Hawthorne, Melville, Twain, and Hemingway. His new book has the spikey, tough shell of a sea urchin. Inside, the meat is a sweet chocolate goo." (*Pause.*) Well?

STEPHEN: You've gone mad.

MIKE: You don't like it?

STEPHEN: You begin with a cliché (that bark), stoop to an obscenity (those balls), drop a little French (*au fond* yourself), get your facts wrong (I told you Twain wasn't a Sentimentalist), and end with a stomach-turning metaphor.

MIKE (*laughing*): And that's just my first paragraph!

STEPHEN (*uncertain*): God knows what you've been turning in!

MIKE: This might be more like it. (MIKE *offers the paper to* STEPHEN.)

STEPHEN (*reading what* MIKE *has actually written*): "Dear Stephen. Write. Be happy. Know that I love you, Mike."

MIKE: Better? (*Pause. They look at each other. We feel the chance for physical intimacy between them rise, hover about them and pass.*)

STEPHEN: What about Mailer?

MIKE: What about you?

STEPHEN: I want to write. I think about it. Some days I sit there, turn the typewriter on, put the paper in and listen to it hum.

MIKE: What happens?

STEPHEN: Nothing. It hums. My mind goes blank. My fingers just stay on the keys. They don't move. Nothing moves. So I put a record on, usually Callas, sometimes not, and make another cassette. I'm taping my own records. Records of recordings. Why? I don't even hear the music anymore. I have her memorized, frozen right here. *"Vissi d'arte," "Casta Diva,"* every nuance, memorized. I've tried to wean myself off her—listen to a Beethoven Quartet, a Haydn Trio—but I keep coming back . . . I'm stuck in grand opera, mired in Callas.

MIKE: I wish I could help you.

STEPHEN: You used to. I remember when these fingers went clickety-click-click! Maria would be on in the background and you'd be loving me the way I wanted to be loved (you used to come up behind me while I was working and just put your hands on my shoulders!) and I hoped I was loving you the way you wanted to be loved and the words came pouring out and the words turned into plays and the plays were plays that got done, plays that people seemed to like. And then it all changed. March 11, three years ago, 4:27 A.M. when I realized you actually weren't coming home. Sorry. Ever since, I've sat here, listening to Callas, and wondering why you don't love me anymore.

MIKE: It's not my fault you're not writing, Stephen.

STEPHEN: I know.

MIKE: You wrote those plays. I didn't.

STEPHEN: I wrote them for you.

MIKE: You hardly knew me.

STEPHEN: They were what attracted you to me. They were my siren song for all the world to hear. Sooner or later I knew the right one would hear it. *Der Richtige.* The right one. *Arabella.* I thought he was you. It could have been. It should have been. For a couple of years, it was.

MIKE: Your plays weren't your siren song. You were. I thought you were the most terrific looking, acting, everything human being I'd ever met. After you, the lights went out on everybody else.

STEPHEN: So what happened?

MIKE: I don't know. But to take your talent, abuse it, waste it—!

STEPHEN: We're not talking about my talent.

MIKE: I am. You stopped writing.

STEPHEN: I didn't stop writing. I stopped feeling that what I had to say was important, that anyone wanted to hear it.

MIKE: Stephen, you stopped writing. Everything else is bullshit.

STEPHEN: Thanks.

MIKE: I've spent the past three years just trying to get you to go from here to there. (*He is pointing to the typewriter.*) I can't anymore.

STEPHEN: Don't give up on me.

MIKE: You've given up on yourself. Writers write.

STEPHEN: I'm not just a writer.

MIKE: You're not much of anything right now.

STEPHEN: Fuck you, fuck est, fuck everybody.

MIKE: It's yourself you're fucking.

STEPHEN: Only metaphorically. You're the one with his dick up somebody else's ass. I just got it, my next play! A man comes home and finds the one person he loved, he trusted, he needed . . . and I need you very much, Goddamn you! . . . he finds that person, that Judas, that prick in bed with a social working electrician from Zaire who's wearing a twill truss. It's a comedy.

MIKE: I have a better idea. Write about this. Start with love at first sight and end with behavior that is making me physically ill. Honest to God, Stephen, I feel like I'm going to vomit.

STEPHEN: Go ahead. It's your mother's carpet.

MIKE: What we've come to!

STEPHEN: I can't believe I would still harp on est! That was . . . what? . . . five years ago we did the training?

MIKE: Stephen!

STEPHEN: Did we get it?

MIKE: I'll tell you something else you've stopped: feeling.

STEPHEN: No, I've stopped feeling good. There's a big difference. I'm feeling all over the place. Come on, Michael, chow down for old times' sake. (MIKE *has gone to the phone.*) What do you think you're doing?

MIKE: I'm sorry, Stephen, but I can't help the pain you're in.

STEPHEN: You were supposed to change all that.

MIKE: How, for Christ's sake?

STEPHEN: By loving me. (STEPHEN *breaks the phone connection.* MIKE *re-dials without a pause.*)

MIKE: I did love you.

STEPHEN: Not enough.

MIKE: There is no "enough" for you.

STEPHEN: I can't help that.

MIKE: You'd better. You're never going to meet anyone who can.

STEPHEN: I'm sorry, but I thought I had. (*Again* STEPHEN *breaks the phone connection. Again* MIKE *re-dials without a pause.*)

MIKE: I still love you.

STEPHEN: Good, then you can tell what's-his-face that it's all off.

MIKE: I just don't want to be in this kind of relationship with you or anyone else.

STEPHEN: If I hear that asshole word one more time . . .!

MIKE: I don't know what other word to use to describe this nightmare.

STEPHEN: Try lovers.

MIKE: I did.

STEPHEN: We're lovers, baby. Fuck all this other shit: we're lovers.

MIKE: Were, Stephen. (STEPHEN *goes to phonograph and starts looking for another record.*)

STEPHEN: I'm sorry but I need something. Wear earplugs. Get lost. Drop dead. (MIKE's *patience for the party to answer is wearing thin.*) Look, I'm sorry I behaved that way. I'll apologize to him.

MIKE: Shit! (*He hangs up and dials another number.*)

STEPHEN: I doubt if he's there yet.

MIKE: I wasn't calling him!

STEPHEN: I told you: I had a lousy night with Mendy, my date stood me up, the bars are filled with your potential assassin. I spent most of the night at a porno flick. I let somebody give me a hand job. So much for gay pride. (*He puts on a new record. It is Beverly Sills singing the soprano aria from Mozart's* Zaide.)

MIKE (*into phone*): May I speak to Mr. Deller, please? . . . His brother . . . Thank you.

STEPHEN: You want to take a guess at the composer? (*Dismissing this suggestion at once.*) Anyone would know this was Mozart. But you'll never guess the music. It's an aria from *Zaide*. He wrote it when he was two or something. It's hardly ever done. *"Ruhe sanft, mein holdes Leben"* which I would translate roughly as "Rest softly, my dearest love."

MIKE: Bob! Hi, listen, can I stay with you two for a while? It's really gotten impossible here.

STEPHEN: He knows?

MIKE: I hope Ginny won't mind. I called her first but there was no answer. Thanks. I'll be at my office if there's a hitch . . . I don't know how he is. I haven't talked to Mom since Sunday. I'm sure she'd call if there were any change. Okay. Thanks. Yeah. (*He hangs up.*)

STEPHEN: You told them?

MIKE: It was pretty obvious.

STEPHEN: You should have made things more obvious to me. How is your father?

MIKE: The same, I guess. One of us would've heard. Do you know where that overnight bag is?

STEPHEN: We left it in St. Bart's. It was falling apart.

MIKE: The blue one?

STEPHEN: Oh, you mean the tote! If it's not here, it's out in Sag. What about the house anyway?

MIKE: What about it?

STEPHEN: If anything happens to me, it's yours. So's this.

MIKE: Don't worry. I won't want either one.

STEPHEN: Who's worried? I'll be dead. It's you I'm thinking about. I guess I'll have to change my will and everything. God knows what that will cost!

MIKE: This is difficult enough. Don't make it worse.

STEPHEN: You're the one who got me to change my will in the first place.

MIKE: Changing your will? That's all you can talk about? I'm sorry I ended up being such an inconvenience to you.

STEPHEN: You know what I mean!

MIKE: I'm not blithely walking out of here. I'm running for my life. I disappear in this relationship. You gobble me up. You're a killer: an obsessive, possessive murderer.

STEPHEN: Has it ever occurred to you it's because I love you?

MIKE: And it frightens the hell out of me.

STEPHEN: He's just a trick.

MIKE: Maybe. Maybe that's all I want right now. Maybe that's all I ever wanted. A warm body, a little support, and a giggle. At least he's not trying to kill me.

STEPHEN: Spare me the accolades. I saw what you two are all about. K-Y and poppers.

MIKE: It's the best sex I've had in three years.

STEPHEN: That wasn't just my fault. People go through phases.

MIKE: The pity is they stay in them. Let's both be grateful we're getting out. I meant it, Stephen, we do deserve better. Maybe I'll stop going around with this knot in my gut twenty-four hours a day. Maybe you'll write something.

STEPHEN: Don't count on it.

MIKE: One line in a diary would be better than this.

STEPHEN: I just want to know what I'm supposed to tell that lawyer.

MIKE: Tell him you want to leave everything to build a memorial statue to Maria Callas.

STEPHEN: You know, that's not a bad idea.

MIKE: Why not? She's dead. It's the living you have trouble with. (*He will go into the bedroom, this time leaving the door ajar.*)

STEPHEN: It's on the top shelf in my closet. The blue tote. Behind the tennis balls. (*He goes to phonograph and turns off Beverly Sills singing the Mozart aria from* Zaide.) Nice try, Bubbles. (*He is looking for something new to play. Calling off.*) What do you want to hear? What about Tebaldi? You always liked her. That should have been a tipoff! (*The telephone begins to ring.* STEPHEN *mimics an answering machine announcement.*) "Hi, this is Stephen. Neither Mike nor I is here to answer your call. I'm lifting weights. Mike is watching the Knicks game. This is my butch answering machine voice. Do you like it?" (MIKE *comes out of bedroom during this to see who is calling.*)

MENDY'S VOICE (*on the answering machine monitor*): This is ridiculous! (*At the sound of* MENDY'S VOICE, MIKE *will go back into the bedroom.*) I know you're there. You have to be there. I'm not getting off until you pick up. Hello? Stephen, this isn't funny!

STEPHEN: What should I play, Mendy? I'm standing in front of the largest record collection in the Western World, my lover is leaving me, and I don't know what to play.

MENDY'S VOICE: All right for you, Stephen! You can take your Lisbon *Traviata* and shove it.

STEPHEN: The Lisbon *Traviata*! (*He will take out the recording and put it on the turntable during the following. And again it is a careful, fastidious ritual.*)

MENDY'S VOICE: One day they will find Maria's Venice *Walküre* and her Genoa *Tristan* and her Chicago *Trovatore* with Jussi Björling and Ebe Stignani to refresh your feeble, febrile, fetid, fart of a memory and I will make it my life's work to see that no one, anywhere on this earth, this entire planet, allows you to hear those tapes. I hope I've made myself clear. Don't bother to call back! (*He smashes down the phone.*)

STEPHEN: It's funny but after all these years I still don't know whether I even like Mendy. Sometimes I don't know who I like. Anyone. Slowly but surely I'm coming to the conclusion that analysis sucks. (*The Prelude to* La Traviata *is heard.* STEPHEN *sits and really seems to be listening to it.*) I'll never forget the night she did this at the Old Met. The excitement in the air. Lenny Bernstein was in a box with Jackie Kennedy. No, that was the return as Tosca seven years later when she was Jackie Onassis and she was with Adlai Stevenson. Fuck it. Who cares? God, that woman's fucked up my life! Not Jackie, Maria. Piano legs. The myopic cunt. Medea re-born at Flower of Fifth Hospital. La Divina. I miss you, Madame Callas. All right, have it your way, "Maria," you usually do. I could have saved you. You would still be singing. Can I ask you something? Who were you singing for? Me, too; me, too. Can I ask you a favor? Sing "Melancholy Baby." (MIKE *enters from the bedroom with an overnight bag and a small suitcase.*) I just hope you know that what you're doing is stupid, ridiculous, and utterly meaningless. It's also rash.

MIKE: Will you be going out to the house this weekend?

STEPHEN: What do you care?

MIKE: Yes or no?

STEPHEN: If Caballé cancels, yes. If she deigns to put in an appearance, no.

MIKE: When will you know?

STEPHEN (*shrugging*): With Montsy it's right down to the wire. (*At an annoyed sigh from* MIKE.) Why don't you call her? She's staying at Burger King.

MIKE: I think it will be easier to get my things out if you aren't here.

STEPHEN: All this because you've got a hard-on for a social worker with a nice body?

MIKE: I thought you'd noticed.

STEPHEN: I notice everything.

MIKE: Then how come you missed what we've turned into?

STEPHEN: How could I miss that? I didn't know how to deal with it. I was hoping it would go away or one of us would get used to it or both of us would or a new soprano would come along or I could see one of your tricks and not be ripped with jealousy or I could not mind so desperately being stood up by a cute waiter who's too young for me and for that reason alone could show some respect—I am someone, after all—but at his age and given half a choice, I wouldn't want to sleep with this either—or I could castrate myself or I could castrate you or we could just get heavily into saltpeter together or we could just pretend that none of this mattered—none of it, none of it—and gracefully grow old together.

MIKE: I don't know what to say, Stephen.

STEPHEN: Sure you do. (*At once, nodding towards the phonograph.*) Sometimes I think this is the most beautiful music ever written. (*A pause. La Traviata fills the room.*)

MIKE: I do love you, you know.

STEPHEN: Other times it's the Good Friday Music from *Parsifal.* Or *The Magic Flute*, Pamina's aria. Or *Fidelio*, the entire second act.

MIKE: Stephen.

STEPHEN: I heard you. You just don't want to suck my cock.

MIKE: I just want to be away from you.

STEPHEN: So you can suck someone else's cock.

MIKE: You have my brother's number. (*He looks to* STEPHEN *for some indication of what is really going on with him.*)

STEPHEN (*cocking his head towards the music*): Do you think Maria is wobbling right there or would you call that an expressive vibrato?

MIKE: Stephen, to me she was always one big wobble. I just got tired pretending.

STEPHEN: A man who would lie about liking Maria Callas would lie about anything.

MIKE: If you could be in touch with your feelings the way you are with her.

STEPHEN: She is my feelings. She doesn't abandon me.

MIKE: That's the pity.

STEPHEN: What?

MIKE: Skip it.

STEPHEN: For someone who is causing me a lot of pain—a lot of it—you're very concerned about my feelings.

MIKE: I don't want to hurt you.

STEPHEN: Then don't do this.

MIKE: You'll be fine without me.

STEPHEN: I won't make it without you.

MIKE: You just think you won't.

STEPHEN: Don't tell me what I think. I'll tell you what I think and what I think is this: You're leaving me at a wonderful moment in our long, happy history of queerness to seek a new mate to snuggle up with. Right at the height of our very own bubonic plague.

MIKE: You'll find someone.

STEPHEN: I don't want someone. No, thank you. I'll stay right here. Those are dark, mean, and extremely dangerous streets right now. You can say all you want against Maria, no one's ever accused her of causing AIDS. Renata Scotto, yes; Maria, no.

MIKE: Why can't you be serious?

STEPHEN: It hurts too much, okay? Asshole. Self-centered, smug, shit-kicking, all-his-eggs-in-one-basket, stupid asshole. (*He goes to the phonograph.*)

MIKE: That's not going to make it hurt any less.

STEPHEN: Shut up! Shut up and listen to this. The least you can do is sit there with me and listen to one last "*Sempre Libera.*"

MIKE: I don't want to.

STEPHEN: It's the by-now almost-legendary Lisbon *Traviata.*

MIKE: Stephen, I don't care if it's the Hoboken One.

STEPHEN: Mendy would kill to hear Maria sing this. (*He has begun to play Callas singing "Sempre Libera".*)

MIKE: I'm not Mendy. Stephen, I've spent the past half-hour trying to get through to you; I've spent the past eight years. You live in *Tosca.* You live in *Turandot.* You live in some opera no one's ever heard of. It's hard loving someone like that.

STEPHEN: Maria does this phrase better than anyone.

MIKE: Listen to me. Turn that down and listen.

STEPHEN: I heard you: It's hard loving someone like me. (*He turns up the volume to a painfully loud level. Callas is all we can hear.* MIKE *goes.* STEPHEN *stands listening to Callas and "Sempre Libera." The music is very loud.* STEPHEN *picks up the scissors* MIKE *used to destroy the Polaroids. The apartment door opens.* MIKE *comes angrily back into the apartment. He has forgotten something. He sees* STEPHEN *still lost in the music.*)

MIKE: Look at you! I just didn't want to hurt you. Hurt you? Fat chance. Who could compete with Maria Callas? (*He comes up to* STEPHEN *who stands with his back to him. As he reaches out to put his hands on* STEPHEN's *shoulders,*

STEPHEN *whirls around and stabs* MIKE *in the stomach with the scissors.*) Jesus.

STEPHEN: This part. Listen. No one does it like Maria.

MIKE: Jesus, Stephen, Jesus.

STEPHEN: Listen to that. Brava La Divina.

MIKE: This is real, Stephen.

STEPHEN: I know! (*He moves away from* MIKE *who drops to his knees.* MIKE *is in shock. The blood is beginning to spill from his mid-section. There will be a lot of it. We will see the life oozing from him.*)

MIKE: I'm hurt. I'm really hurt. I'm scared to look.

STEPHEN: It's the music. It's not the right music. (*He goes to phonograph. He will take off the Callas and put on the "Humming Chorus" from* Madama Butterfly *during the following.*)

MIKE: Stephen, please, you gotta call somebody. We can't handle this.

STEPHEN: Sometimes Maria doesn't work for me. She was never soothing, you know. Sometimes you want a nice tit like this to suck on.

MIKE: Stephen, please!

STEPHEN: Sometimes I think this is the most beautiful music ever written. Christ knows, it's the most banal. (*The "Humming Chorus" from* Madama Butterfly *begins here.*)

MIKE: I'm dying.

STEPHEN: I know. Me, too.

MIKE (*in growing terror and disbelief*): You fucking killed me.

STEPHEN: We fucking killed each other. I'm not mad. My feelings have led me towards an act of utter logic. I'm surprised more people don't stab their lovers. Instead, they yak, yak, yak. Where does that get them? Nowhere. But look at us. The final duet.

MIKE: Please get help.

STEPHEN: It's okay. I'm here. Your lover's here. Didn't José stab his Carmen? Wozzeck his Marie?

MIKE: Don't let me die, Stephen.

STEPHEN: People don't die from these. They die from what you were doing to me. They die from loss.

MIKE: I'm sorry. I said I was sorry. Please, get help. (*The phone begins to ring.*)

STEPHEN: Here! This is beautiful. Listen. If music be the food of love, play on. Give me excess of it.

MENDY'S VOICE (*on the answering machine*): The only reason I called back, Stephen, is to tell you that Albert Benedetti has just come by with a copy of the Lisbon *Traviata* and we have just put it on and so there!

MIKE (*weakly*): Mendy!

MENDY'S VOICE: He also brought over Sutherland's *Adriana* from San Diego if you really want to laugh.

MIKE: Mendy.

MENDY'S VOICE: He also said to tell you, since he's the only one still speaking to you, that Vickers has cancelled all his *Parsifals*. Such is life. You're still a cunt but I'll probably forgive you, though I can't for the life of me see how Mike puts up with you. It's begun. She just said "*Flora, amici.*" Divine woman! What would we do without her? (*He hangs up. The "Humming Chorus" is still playing on the phonograph.* STEPHEN *drops to floor and cradles* MIKE *in his arms.*)

STEPHEN: I'm sorry.

MIKE: Please, call someone, before it's too late.

STEPHEN: Sshh. When the music's over. Listen. It'll soothe you.

MIKE: Hurry.

STEPHEN: When the music's over. (STEPHEN *looks at* MIKE. *Their eyes have met and held. The life continues to ebb from him. Slow fade to blackout.*)

THE FAIRY GARDEN

by
Harry Kondoleon

The Fairy Garden was first produced Off Off Broadway at the Double Image Theater in New York City in June, 1982. It was directed by Max Mayer; the costume design was by Nan Cibula; the lighting design was by Robert Jared; and the stage manager was Shannon J. Sumpter. The cast, in order of appearance, was as follows:

DAGNY	Janet Kirby
ROMAN	Robert Dean
MIMI	David Marshall Grant
THE FAIRY	Lizzie Miller
BORIS	Drew Eliot
THE MECHANIC	Ken Olin

The Fairy Garden was subsequently presented by the Second Stage (in association with Tony Kiser), in New York City, in June 1984. It was directed by Carole Rothman; the set design was by Andrew Jackness; the lighting design was by Frances Aronson; the costume design was by Mimi Maxman; the sound design was by Gary Harris; and the production stage manager was Robin Rumpf. The cast, in order of appearance, was as follows:

DAGNY	Ann Lange
ROMAN	John Glover
MIMI	Mark Soper
THE FAIRY	Carol Kane
BORIS	Robert Weil
THE MECHANIC	Rick J. Porter

The music for the song in *The Fairy Garden* and permission for its use in performance of the play can be obtained directly from the composer: Gary S. Fagin, 274 Water Street, New York, N.Y. 10038.

CHARACTERS

DAGNY, a thirty-year-old woman, a blonde.
ROMAN, Dagny's friend, in his thirties, dark-haired.
MIMI, Roman's lover, in his thirties, light-haired.
THE FAIRY
BORIS, Dagny's husband, about fifty.
THE MECHANIC

TIME

A summer afternoon.

SETTING

The garden behind a large expensive Tudor style house. Garden furniture to include three chairs and a table covered with plates of food, sweets, glasses, decanters, and cut flowers. Behind the table and chairs are many beautiful flowers.

A stage curtain should open to surprise and please with the pretty picture revealed. Something about the curtain should be old-fashioned and homemade-ornate, reminiscent perhaps of children's theater from the last century.

DAGNY, ROMAN, *and* MIMI *are dressed studiedly casual, chic, and modern. When the curtain parts they are revealed languishing. They look as though they are to be photographed together.* DAGNY, *drinking, swallows and speaks.*

DAGNY: I'm not getting the kind of help I need.

ROMAN: I told you what to do but you won't listen.

MIMI: Dagny, take this dish of marzipan away from me or I will consume every last bit and surely burst.

ROMAN: Exercise self-control, it will do your tired soul some good.

MIMI: My soul's not nearly as tired as my belt buckle.

ROMAN: That we knew.

DAGNY: Boys, please, help me with this, I really am in a spot.

MIMI: Outline it for us, just outline it.

DAGNY: There's nothing to outline. If I divorce Boris, he won't give me any alimony. If I stay married to him, I can't go away with my new boyfriend.

ROMAN: Well, Dag, if you can't even refer to the new boyfriend by his first name, stay with the husband with the money. That's the solution.

DAGNY: Darling, but I'm unhappy.

ROMAN: Well, me too.

DAGNY: I never used to be unhappy with Boris. He's never hit me.

ROMAN: What about last Christmas when you went to Capri? You were unhappy then.

DAGNY: You only remind me of that because I forgot to buy you something.

ROMAN: No you didn't, you got me that scarf.

DAGNY: That scarf was from Saks and you knew it.

ROMAN: But I like it and tell everyone it's from Capri.

MIMI: Why don't you keep Boris and the boyfriend?

DAGNY: Because, darling, Boris discovered my diary last night and hit the roof.

ROMAN: Could it have been his really first encounter with the truly explicit?

DAGNY: Joke now, but if I don't have any money, no more parties for us.

ROMAN: And be banished from the fairy garden forever? I'd first forsake an eye.

DAGNY: You may have to. Boris said that it was the influence of my loose, immoral friends—meaning you two, darling—that I had become unfaithful and he had a mind to come right out here and give you each a sock in the eye.

MIMI: A sock in the eye each, that would make a pair.

ROMAN: Before he comes out have him bring a tray of soda water, this has gone the way of all flat things.

DAGNY: Someone talk me into staying married. Give me the pros and the cons. Mimi, you're good at this, give them to me, the pros and the cons.

MIMI: I'm not good at this at all.

ROMAN: The pros are Boris is rich and has a nice house and he works nearly all day every day which makes him delightfully absent and when he is around, bless his toad heart, he sits silently in his study, at worst occasionally making small croaking noises into his dictaphone. At Christmas time not only does he purchase large precious jewels to adorn whatever spaces happen to be available on your person but he has been known to give your good friends—Mimi and me, for example—gold trinkets and high-priced bric-a-brac.

MIMI: These are the pros.

ROMAN: They certainly are. The cons aren't even worth listing; you get penniless overnight: right back where you started from.

MIMI: But you won't have to deal with smelly Boris anymore.

ROMAN: Is he smelly?

DAGNY: A little.

MIMI: And then you get your new boyfriend.

DAGNY: New is always good.

ROMAN: But poor? New and poor? What's better, new and poor or old and loaded?

DAGNY: That's a hard question.

ROMAN: A question that I am sure plagued the ancients. Another is why is there never any ice in the ice bucket.

DAGNY: Did I forget to put ice in there?

ROMAN: You always do.

MIMI: Dagny, what does your boyfriend do?

DAGNY: Do? What do you mean do? He loves me.

ROMAN: Dagny, what Mimi here is trying to say in his Mimi way is what exactly does the boyfriend do to collect his meager existence?

DAGNY: It's not meager.

ROMAN: We know, darling, your diary said so, but I mean employment, darling, employment, cast your mind back to when you were a wee little receptionist in big Boris's company and you carried home a check so tiny it flew away when you passed a magazine stand.

DAGNY: Boris is not big.

ROMAN: Big money, darling, is big enough for me; it's always been a handy measuring stick.

DAGNY: He's the mechanic, I think.

MIMI: A mechanic, well, that's good. Mechanics make a lot of money, don't they?

ROMAN: No, they do not, Mimi.

DAGNY: He lives over a garage.

ROMAN: Oh Dagny, what were you thinking of?!

DAGNY (*slightly defensive*): He's very cute in a boyish, innocent kind of way. He said I looked like a princess.

ROMAN: Were you wearing that hat with the points and rhinestones?

DAGNY: Yes and you can't borrow it.

MIMI: Hire him as a chauffeur and put him over your garage, that's what Sarah Miles did.

DAGNY: In real life?

MIMI: Not in real life, in a film.

ROMAN: That's your trouble, Dag, you think you're in a film and you're not.

DAGNY: Well, I ought to be. If I were in a film, my unhappiness wouldn't be so unhappy because people would be watching it and it wouldn't all seem like such a silly waste.

ROMAN: One more depressing crack like that and I'm going home.

DAGNY: Don't go! I'm desperate. I know I don't look it but I am. I can't go on like this. Boris makes my skin crawl. I wake up sick next to him. I'm in love with the mechanic: it's that simple. I'll live with him at any price. I'll do anything to get what I want: I always have and I always will. I love him, I love him! I don't care what it sounds like, I'd even kill for love. I would!

ROMAN: Well, then do it. Go in the house and kill Boris and then come out here and get your Academy Award.

MIMI: Do it, Dagny. If you love him, do it. Do it for love.

ROMAN (*holding up the ice bucket*): Yes and while you're inside, fill this up with ice, would you, dear? (DAGNY *exits to the house with the ice bucket.*) Your humor is all very top drawer this afternoon, isn't it, Little Mimi?

MIMI: I don't know what you mean.

ROMAN: You know exactly what I mean, I mean undercutting every word, every vowel I've uttered this afternoon—that's what I mean. Did you think I wouldn't notice? Oh-so-subtly fingering this, clattering that, making wry observations and askew references anywhere so long as it's interrupting or undermining me in some way. But this is nothing new, you're always trying to exclude me in your own personal passive weak way!

MIMI: You love to hear yourself use this shrewish voice.

ROMAN: And you just love yourself, *yourself* and no one else—not me, that's for certain. I once—*briefly*—talked myself into believing you did love me but that was an invention of self-pity. I couldn't believe I could be that big a jerk or you that big an ice cube. Meanwhile, everyone thinks you're so sweet—the warm one. I'm the warm one! You sit there smugly as if Dagny were your friend and I was some stupid intruder that happened to pop in on you two chatting. Could it be so easy for you to forget Dagny was first my friend? That she's still more my friend even now? And yet you insist on using that little conspiratorial voice. Why? Because you know it irks me, that's why.

MIMI: Be nice to me: when you're in the Hopeless Ward, I'll be the only one who'll come and visit.

ROMAN: I don't want you to visit! I'd only flee to such a hostelry to escape you!

MIMI: Oh get off my fucking back for five minutes won't you? I've got the whole night to push you away, must it start midday? Can't you relax? Can't you—if for no other reason than the sparkling change of pace it would bring—call off your sour marching band? Yes, I am better looking. Yes, I am more desirable—and that means just *that*: more people *desire* me, want me, fantasize about me, etcetera, than you. You aren't bad looking, Roman, and I've told you so and I've told you so and I've told you so. I've complimented you, I've repeated compliments I've overheard or thought I overheard, I've even invented compliments just to please you but *really* I don't care. I do not care that you are insecure, paranoid, nervous, or whatever you're calling your disease these days. I don't care that you think I'm performing sex acts with every man *you* find attractive. If you were more on the ball instead of constantly under it you might have noticed I have stopped all sex acts with you and anyone: I've had enough. I got too bored and expert, too distanced, too detached and deterred but you're too plain demented to understand. I want to wake up with my own hands on my own shoulders, so do not touch me, not as a joke, not as a jest, not as an anything, not now, not ever.

ROMAN: Well, it's good to know you can still articulate.

MIMI: Good to know also that maybe it's time to say auf Wiedersehen or Toot-Toot-Tootsie Good-bye or whatever droll distortion will suit the occasion. Be practical, Roman, it's over, over, and *really* out. You want the apartment? Keep it. You don't want the apartment? I'll keep it. Furniture? Mementos? Objects of art, clutter, or sentiment? We'll draw straws, we'll roll dice, we'll throw them against the wall: I don't give a fuck!

ROMAN: Oh, now I see. Now I see what the whole afternoon has been leading up to. This. Divorce. How inevitable everything seems when the ax finally falls. Okay, I'll bite, who is it? Who's the new fool? Come on, tell me.

MIMI: Call your therapist, Roman. He gets paid to listen to your prattle, I only get fatigued.

ROMAN: It's what's-his-name, isn't it? Isn't it? It is.

MIMI: Oh shut up! Be adult, won't you? I say it's over, let's get away from it, but no, not you, you won't let go, not until you've played out every paroxysm of cheap sentiment and soap opera.

ROMAN: You really hate me.

MIMI: I do not hate you.

ROMAN: You really hate me. That's okay. Everything's okay.

MIMI: Roman—

ROMAN: No! Don't talk! I said everythinig's okay. I'm no dope. I can see the sun setting just like everybody else. You're right, we'll split everything up even, uneven—whatever—and what we can't split we'll, as you say, throw them against the wall. It's a smart plan. I'll see my travel agent in the morning and make arrangements. A long trip out to sea. The salt water will do me good. I've been on land too long. The cold black sea swallowing me will be an enduring pleasure compared to what I've had to put up with on earth.

MIMI: Oh, brother.

ROMAN: The ice water will be a warm retreat compared to the years of drowning in the thankless cesspool I called love.

MIMI: Roman, call your therapist.

ROMAN: Oh call your own! I will not call my therapist! I will not call another living soul! Auf Wiedersehen indeed! Auf Wiedersehen to you! Auf Wiedersehen to me! Auf Wiedersehen to everything! (DAGNY *enters with the ice bucket dripping and nearly overflowing with blood. There is blood on the front of her dress.*)

DAGNY: Look, I've spoiled my dress.

ROMAN: Oh my God! Is that blood? That's tomato juice, isn't it?

DAGNY: It's blood.

MIMI: That's blood?!

DAGNY: Boris's blood. (MIMI *looks into the ice bucket, lets out a cry of horror and revulsion, then a dry heave.* ROMAN *slaps* MIMI *twice across the face.*)

ROMAN: Calm down! Dagny, you don't mean you killed Boris, that you really killed him.

DAGNY: I do mean it, I did.

ROMAN: You killed Boris?

DAGNY: Yes. I went inside and I told Boris. I said, "My diary told the truth, I'm in love and I'm not in love with you!"

ROMAN: What did he say?

DAGNY: He started to cry and said he knew. He said he knew I didn't love him, then he got on his knees and, crying, he started kissing my feet. He said that he loved me, that he would love me always and couldn't live without me and wanted to die if I left him.

ROMAN: Yes?!

DAGNY: Then he picked up his letter opener—you know, the one shaped like a sword—handed it to me and said I had cut up his heart and I should finish the job and take what was mine.

ROMAN: That's when you did it!

DAGNY: No. I said, "No."

MIMI: You said no.

DAGNY: That's right. Then he started punching me, screaming, "Slut! Slut!"

ROMAN: Then you plunged the letter opener into his heart!

DAGNY: No.

MIMI: You didn't do it.

DAGNY: Not then.

ROMAN: When then?

DAGNY: He drew his face up very close to mine and said my mechanic was dead, that he had hired a thug to arrange an accident, that while he was under one of those cars suspended in the air, it fell and crushed him to death. He said he died slowly, writhing agonized for hours under the smashed car until the ambulance arrived to deliver his dead body to the morgue.

MIMI: That can't be true!

ROMAN: Why not?! It is true, I'm sure, Dagny. So you killed Boris—you ripped out his heart for having ripped out yours!

DAGNY: No. This isn't a heart in here. (*Putting her hand into the bucket and bringing up the wet, dripping head by its hair.* MIMI *and* ROMAN *scream.*)

MIMI: Put it back! Put it back!

DAGNY: I can't put it back, it took a long time to get it off.

MIMI: Oh my God! Dagny, Dagny, how could you do such a thing—is it possible?

DAGNY: It took a lot of sawing.

ROMAN: We've got to hide it, Dagny, hide it from the law.

MIMI: What are you talking about—there's a body, too.

ROMAN: That's right, we have to do something with that, too.

DAGNY: I'm going to have to go to the electric chair now, aren't I? Perhaps everything in my life was leading up to this. Everytime I thought I was outsmarting fate, there was the electric chair waiting just around the corner for me. They still have electric chairs, don't they?

ROMAN: Well, if they don't, they have something else.

MIMI: I can't imagine you, Dagny, in prison. I'll go. I'll say I did it. I'll take the blame. I'll say Boris made me irritable and I cut off his head.

ROMAN: Oh that's plausible!

MIMI: What difference does it make what I say? I'll say I went out of my mind.

ROMAN: And the blood on Dagny's dress?

MIMI: She tried to stop me, tried to save her husband.

ROMAN: And where was I?

MIMI: Asleep. Asleep out here.

DAGNY: You would lie for me, Mimi, lie and go to jail?

MIMI: Yes, I would.

ROMAN: I think we'd be better off burying it, burying it some place so obvious no one would think to look there—right here in the garden!

MIMI: What about the body?

ROMAN: We should bury the head and then think about the body.

DAGNY: There's some fertilizer and soft earth just here behind these flowers.

ROMAN: Perfect. Everyone take a spoon and start digging. Don't discuss it, just dig. (*Spoons in hand, on their knees,* DAGNY, ROMAN, *and* MIMI *dig behind the upstage flowers.* THE FAIRY *enters.* THE FAIRY *should be played by an extremely short woman.* THE FAIRY's *dress should conform to traditional notions of what a fairy must wear: a white tulle dress, shimmering and iridescent with small diamonds and pearls, a full skirt of mid-calf length, a bodice with decolletage and a small glittering tiara. A very short pixie haircut would be nice.* THE FAIRY *walks mostly on her toes.* DAGNY, ROMAN, *and* MIMI *hear* THE FAIRY *hum-*

ming and see THE FAIRY *idly dancing around the garden. They, among the flowers, look up facing the audience and stare at* THE FAIRY *with disbelief.*) Who in hell are you?

THE FAIRY: Why, I'm just a little fairy.

ROMAN: What?

THE FAIRY: A fairy, a fairy, can't you hear?

DAGNY: What are you doing here?

THE FAIRY: This is my garden.

DAGNY: But I live here.

THE FAIRY: Good for you. I've been coming here for a hundred years now. I love it. I used to come with friends but I find as I get older I seem to want to hog the things I love.

MIMI: You're not a real fairy, I mean not really, not a fairy-fairy?

THE FAIRY: But of course I am, darling, what do you think. Now button your lips and hear my fairy song. Flute please. (*She is accompanied by an invisible flutist. She sings "The Fairy Song."*)

> Dogs in the park
> Cats in the river
> Drink till it's dark
> And ruin my liver.
> Oh life told me so
> Life told me so.
>
> Making and taking
> Moving and staying
> All alone tonight
> All alone tomorrow
> I see what you see
> I see what you see.
>
> Birds in the ocean
> Fish in the sky
> Keep it in motion
> Then lay down and die.
> Oh life told me so
> Life told me so.
>
> World turn, world turn
> Uphill and downhill
> Who's alone tonight?

Who's alone tomorrow?
I see what you see
Come kiss and hold me.
Oh life told me so
Life told me so.

DAGNY: Why did you sing that song?

THE FAIRY: Because fairies like to take a little time everyday to sing a song. You should, too.

DAGNY: But that song, I know it. I remember it from somewhere.

THE FAIRY: It's my own composition.

ROMAN: Why have you come here?

THE FAIRY: I told you, I come here all the time. There used to be a wishing well here—oh, I'd say about fifty years ago, a great big wishing well—oh, what a busy place! Do you remember it?

ROMAN: None of us were alive fifty years ago so we didn't need a wishing well. But I suppose you were kept quite busy flitting about it.

THE FAIRY: I *was* a busy little bee, in a manner of speaking. Every time I came to visit, I granted a wish.

DAGNY: That's why you've come here today, isn't it? To grant us all our wishes.

THE FAIRY: Not exactly, darling. Don't jump ahead of my story. I grant one wish per visit.

ROMAN: Only one? And you call yourself busy?

THE FAIRY: How do you think I stay so fresh?

MIMI: And you've chosen us, to grant us a wish.

THE FAIRY: Yes, I have, as a matter of fact. Now, rather than waste a lot of time, I'll tell you what you wish for.

DAGNY: Please.

THE FAIRY: You wish Boris's head were out of the ice bucket and back on his head. Am I right?

DAGNY: I do?

ROMAN: How did you know her husband's name was Boris?

THE FAIRY: Oh how do I know this and how do I know that!

DAGNY: Leave her alone, Roman.

THE FAIRY: Women do understand women, isn't that so, Dagny?

DAGNY: Yes.

THE FAIRY: Yes, well.

MIMI: How do you know Dagny wants Boris's head reattached? Maybe that's not her wish at all. Maybe she wishes her mechanic were here to take her in his arms and kiss her, to drive away with her and love her endlessly in some out-of-the-way garage.

THE FAIRY: He was crushed, I've been told, by a falling vehicle and, I imagine, no longer able to take much of anything in his arms.

ROMAN: But if you're half the fairy you say you are, you could bring him back in a snap, arms and all.

MIMI: Shut up, Roman, you're going to alienate her.

ROMAN: Can't you see she's a fake? She's no fairy! This is a practical joke!

THE FAIRY (*to* DAGNY): Wish for anything you like. Wish for the mechanic, he's very handsome I'm sure. Yes I know, I know, I've heard. A fairy is sensitive to all kinds of engines.

ROMAN: I don't have a wish!

THE FAIRY: Wish for someone to love. That's all you've ever wished for anyway, isn't it? Wish for that.

MIMI: I wish I were dead.

THE FAIRY: I've granted some of those wishes but ever so rarely and I always end up regretting it. People are jewels, pity to put them in a box before they have a chance to shine. Don't you agree? Wish instead for peace with yourself, to look in the mirror and say, "Hello there," to look again in the afternoon and say, "Hello again," and then again at night, "Hello. Hello. Hello."

DAGNY: But we only have one wish.

THE FAIRY: Right you are, darling, one and only.

MIMI: But there are three of us.

THE FAIRY: One two three, it's all the same to me.

DAGNY (*to* ROMAN *and* MIMI): What should we do?

THE FAIRY: Be prudent.

MIMI: We have nothing to lose—we can wish for the world.

THE FAIRY: The world? What will you do with the world? The world will call you gangsters. The world will say three greedy things sat in a garden and planned to behead their benefactor. "Jail! Jail!" the world will cry and the three will go off to cement dungeons, expelled from everything pretty on this planet. How sad never to smell new lilacs, to see the amaryllis and touch the rose in bloom. Think me silly, think me dumb, a world without the flower is a place to run from, place to run from, a place to run from willy-nilly, willy-nilly it's a place to run from.

DAGNY: I wish Boris's head was back on.

THE FAIRY: Good show!

ROMAN: Well, I would have at least liked the opportunity to forfeit my vote.

MIMI: I vote for Boris, too.

THE FAIRY: Good Boris! We'll get a head on his shoulders yet.

DAGNY (*picking up the ice bucket and handing it to* THE FAIRY): Here.

THE FAIRY (*ignoring the bucket*): Forgive me for staring but I can't help but admire your earrings. I love diamonds and those are wonderfully large.

DAGNY: They were a wedding gift from Boris.

THE FAIRY: Really! What good taste he had.

ROMAN: I picked them out.

THE FAIRY: More credit to you! May I have them?

DAGNY: What?

THE FAIRY: The earrings, darling, may I have them?

ROMAN: I knew there was something to this.

DAGNY: I can't give you these earrings.

THE FAIRY: But you must. What I mean is, you have to. I need diamonds from everyone if the wish is to come true.

MIMI: You mean you take pay? You don't do the wishes for free?

THE FAIRY: Free? Darling, you've got to be kidding. As my mother used to say, nothing is for free. Hand over the earrings. (*Taking the earrings.*) Come on, come on, I haven't all afternoon, I've got to get in the house and work on the head. Now, what else have we? (*To* MIMI:) You have an earring, too! Just one, but oh so bright and sparkling, what a perfect little diamond. Do give it to me.

MIMI: Take it.

ROMAN: It's out of style anyway.

THE FAIRY: Style's a very relative thing, but you must know that.

ROMAN: I'm afraid I don't have diamonds for you.

THE FAIRY (*circling* ROMAN, *searching*): I doubt that. Everyone has some kind of diamond, maybe little, maybe hidden, but a diamond hunter will surely find it, yes, surely find it in the end! A diamond in your tooth, what a clever filling! Just a tiny baby diamond hiding out in the womb. Come out! Come out! (THE FAIRY *sticks her hands in* ROMAN'S *mouth to get the diamond.*)

ROMAN: Kindly remove your hands from my mouth!

THE FAIRY (*she has extracted the diamond*): Got it. Oh, how I do love getting paid for what I do! People who aren't properly paid for their work believe they're working in vain and lo and behold they soon lose all pride in what they're doing and become shoddy practitioners where once they were magicians. (THE FAIRY *picks up the bucket of blood and, with a swift gesture, removes the front panel of* DAGNY'S *dress thus removing all traces of blood and in no way changing the look of the dress.*) I'm going inside for a while. Here are some Wash'n'Drys— everyone freshen up and relax. Bye. (*After having given each a packet of those pre-moistened towelettes you get on airplanes,* THE FAIRY *exits with the blood-ied dress panel and the bucket containing Boris's head.* DAGNY *and* MIMI *open their Wash'n'Drys, sit in their seats and wash their hands and faces.*)

ROMAN: What an afternoon!

MIMI: I wonder if what Boris said was true, whether he really had the mechanic killed or whether he was only making it up to get back at you.

DAGNY: I was thinking the same thing. But in a strange way it doesn't really seem to matter anymore, do you know?

MIMI: Yes, I do.

DAGNY: Today reminds me of something. I can't quite place it but some other time. Maybe of when I was little, when I believed in things, I don't know. But I know I'm thinking of everything differently now. I'm not so anxious and I'm sensing things around me more acutely. Oh, Mimi, look at the flock of birds!

MIMI: I love you, Dagny.

DAGNY: Do you, do you love me?

MIMI: Yes, I do.

DAGNY: And I love you.

ROMAN: What is going on here?

DAGNY: I've felt this for some time, this other love between us but I've been afraid to touch it. I know you're not one of those confusing bisexual people, so, tell me, how do you love me?

MIMI: I love you, that's all. I don't want to make babies or build houses, I just love you. I want you to lean on me and I want to lean on you.

ROMAN: What are you saying? You don't love-love each other!

DAGNY: We do, Roman—I'm certain of it. It's been unendurable—knowing and not knowing—loving Mimi always and never admitting it to myself.

ROMAN: No! No! You're not taking Mimi from me!

MIMI: Roman, we're through.

ROMAN: No, we're not!

DAGNY: But, Roman, you and Mimi weren't happy together, you're not in love anymore, you'll be better apart.

ROMAN: No, I won't.

MIMI: You'll just get used to it, Roman, you've lived alone before, you can do it again, you'll meet someone else. Dagny—don't take this to heart, we were breaking up anyway. It's been over for some time.

ROMAN: Stop saying that!

MIMI: But it's true—what's left between us?

ROMAN: Something. Whatever it is, it's something and I don't want nothing, I'm afraid of nothing, I'm afraid, I'm afraid!

MIMI: I'm sorry, Roman, but Dagny and I are in love—

ROMAN: Oh, *love*! *Love*! You love *Can-Can*, marzipan, and Tarzan, that's what you love! Tell her—tell her, Mimi, tell her what sort of merchandise you are, lift your shirt and show her where you're stamped DEFECTIVE.

DAGNY: Roman, darling, we love you, we don't want to hurt you, not ever.

ROMAN: Monsters! Monsters! Don't touch me!

MIMI: Oh stop it, Roman!

ROMAN: Well, Dag, you've turned out to be quite the little friend, a classic of sorts. And I've played my role brilliantly—admit it—the grand buffoon, the cuckold. Where's my citation?

MIMI: The best thing is to ignore him when he gets this way.

ROMAN: Yes! Ignore him! Ignore the whole thing! After all, what is it? Two silly queers breaking up—you can't call it a marriage so I guess it's hardly a break-up at all. There's no children to fight over, just some peculiar plants and tropical fish—they'd toss it all out of court. Stick the plants back in the earth and throw the fish in the river, that's natural. Yes, ignore it, that's best.

MIMI: Roman—

ROMAN: Yes, best! Best best best, let's do what's best. I'll cut off my head and you can bury that—the official fairy of the day can come out and help dig or just throw it in the garbage pail. Haven't you heard? The sanitation workers are all sorcerers!

MIMI (*shaking* ROMAN *violently, shouting, out of control*): Shut up! I can't stand to hear your voice anymore! Shut up! I'll kill you if you say another word, I swear to God I'll kill you!

ROMAN (*on the ground, hands over his face*): Kill me—I don't want to be alone—I'd rather be dead. Kill me now, save me the trouble later.

MIMI: All right, stand up, Roman. Come on, get on your feet.

ROMAN: No, I can't, I can't, don't make me, I can't get up, leave me, go, go. (*Enter* BORIS *and* THE FAIRY, *arm-in-arm*. THE FAIRY *is now smartly dressed as a contemporary woman. Her dress has a blood-red print on it. She wears a diamond necklace.* BORIS *is a rosy-cheeked, runtish, middle-aged man in an elegant suit. The couple is ebullient.*)

BORIS: Nobody move. I've got a big surprise. Meet my fiancée: Chantal Ringold!

THE FAIRY: Hello, everybody.

DAGNY: Fiancée? But, Boris, we're married.

BORIS: I know but, Dagny, I've fallen in love—all my life I'm a bachelor and then twice in the last two years I find true love. Forgive me, Dagny, can you ever?

DAGNY: Boris! Your head! You've got your head on!

BORIS: Yes, for the first time in my life I feel as though I have my head screwed on correctly. All these years I had it buried in ledgers and financial reports—what an unreal world. I made you part of that stunted way of life and you sought refuge with your friends Roman and Mimi and I thank you both for taking care of her. I'm going away with Chantal. My lawyer will handle the divorce, Dagny—I've instructed him to perform every detail of the operation in your favor: you'll lack nothing. All I ask is that you set me free.

DAGNY: Set you free?

BORIS: That's right.

DAGNY (*waving her hand vaguely*): Yes, you're free.

BORIS (*kissing* DAGNY): Thank you, darling. (*To* THE FAIRY:) We're free, darling, isn't it wonderful?!

THE FAIRY: Fabulous.

BORIS: But this means you're free, too, now, Dagny. You can go marry your boyfriend—what's his name?

DAGNY: The mechanic—you killed him.

BORIS: Killed him? What are you saying?

DAGNY: You mean you didn't kill him? You told me you did.

BORIS: I would never say such a thing. What's wrong with you? Are you acting like this because you're angry? You'll forgive me in the future, you'll see.

MIMI: Boris, your head doesn't hurt?

BORIS: No, why? Actually I've never felt better.

MIMI: That's good.

THE FAIRY: We're off to Capri!

BORIS: Chantal summered there as a child with her Italian nanny. She's fluent in Italian.

THE FAIRY (*bubbling*): Che bello vedervi, amici miei!

BORIS: It's made her a capricious little bunny, hasn't it! (BORIS *and* THE FAIRY, *glued to one another, giggle and kiss.*)

ROMAN: Don't you see who she is?! Look at her! She's the Fairy!

BORIS: Does Chantal remind you of someone you used to know?

ROMAN: What's her last name?

BORIS: Ringold.

ROMAN: That's a made-up name if I ever heard one! Look at her! She's not who she says she is. She's deceiving you!

THE FAIRY: Have we met before?

ROMAN: Oh we've met all right, you fairy!

BORIS: Roman!

ROMAN: She's the Fairy! Dagny! Mimi! Tell Boris.

BORIS: What's wrong with him? Roman, stop it, what's happening to you?

ROMAN (*to* THE FAIRY): Tell him! Admit you're a fairy! Fairy! Fairy! Fairy!

BORIS: Roman, I'm going to have to ask you to please refrain from insulting my fiancée, it's offending me. The name calling is highly inappropriate—strange coming from you, to say nothing of in bad taste.

THE FAIRY: It must be the bright afternoon sun and the cassis—I love cassis, do you, Roman?

ROMAN: How did you know we were drinking cassis?

THE FAIRY: Isn't that what this is?

MIMI: Roman has been drinking and it's hot out and he's upset.

DAGNY: Yes, excuse our bad manners, Chantal. We've been terrible hosts. Won't you sit down? Can I pour you a drink?

THE FAIRY: Oh no, we've just been having champagne in the house, Boris and I, and I'm quite tipsy as it is!

BORIS: My tipsy-doodle!

THE FAIRY: Oh, Boris! He's too much, how did you put up with him?

DAGNY: Funny, Chantal, I didn't see you when I went into the house to talk to Boris.

BORIS: You came in the house?

DAGNY: Didn't I?

BORIS: Well, it's true I heard you filling the ice bucket earlier, but then you left it on the table. I'm afraid the ice is sitting there now, melting.

DAGNY: Oh yes, I'm always forgetting the ice. Chantal, forgive me for staring but I can't help but admire your necklace. I love diamonds and those are wonderfully large.

THE FAIRY: They are a bit hard to miss aren't they?! An engagement present from my little Boris here. I can't stop kissing him! I'm making such a display of myself—can you ever forgive me?!

MIMI: Hard to believe so many stones on one chain.

THE FAIRY: I told Boris it was too extravagant but he wouldn't listen. Well, you know. (*She laughs.*)

BORIS: I'm getting very embarrassed.

DAGNY: You two think you're the only ones with news? Mimi and I have news, too.

MIMI: Dagny and I are in love and we're going away together.

BORIS: Dagny, is this true? How wonderful! I've always thought there was something between you two. God bless us all, what a wonderful day! But Roman. Mimi, what about Roman?

ROMAN: I'm not here anymore. I've turned into a vase.

DAGNY: Roman and Mimi have broken up.

THE FAIRY: Oh, I'm sorry to hear that.

BORIS: No hard feelings I hope. Friendship is so fragile and the contingencies of life so harsh.

THE FAIRY: What a good opportunity, Roman, for you to turn a new leaf. The chance is there for all of us.

ROMAN: Liar! Liar!

BORIS: Perhaps it's time Chantal and I ran off. We're going away until everything legal can be arranged. Mimi, Dagny, use the house if you need to, you know.

DAGNY: We're leaving now, too.

MIMI: Yes, we are. It's best to leave quickly without pausing.

THE FAIRY: Well, I'm ready. Hold me close, Boris—love has made me so excited I feel I could fly.

BORIS: I'll never let go!

THE FAIRY (*waving as she runs off with* BORIS): Arrivederci!

MIMI: Good-bye! Come on, Dagny.

ROMAN: No good-bye?

MIMI: Good-bye.

ROMAN: Go to hell!

MIMI: Come on, Dagny, let's go before we can't go.

DAGNY: Wait for me in front, please—I want to say something to Roman—just wait in the driveway. (MIMI *exits.*) Roman, do me a favor, take my hand. Take my hand, take it! I know all this is killing you and that I seem fickle and insane but believe me, Roman, I do love Mimi, I do! Love is like that, Roman, you wake up from a long sad dream where you've been walking around without your head or hands and then suddenly it's light outside and you can get up and live your life. When I worked in Boris's office, I had to connect voice to voice all day. I wanted to interrupt calls and ask, are you the one for me, are you the one I've been looking for? Then I gave up hope and decided to nab Boris.

ROMAN: And now, in an equally illogical turn of mind, you've decided to nab Mimi.

DAGNY: What's logical? Tell me.

ROMAN: Why do you want Mimi? Because you say you do—just like that? Hot-cold, on-off—no rhyme, no reasons.

DAGNY: That's right.

ROMAN: Has everyone taken some pill, some pill I don't know about which lets you forget everything from one minute to the next?

DAGNY: You really hate me.

ROMAN: Yes I do! Everything's so easy for you, Dagny, floating like some fireproof cherry blossom from one catastrophe to the next. Don't you think I would like to do that—to have one blessed moment of unmindfulness?!

DAGNY: That's the rhythm of life; when you fall out of sync with it, you get left behind.

ROMAN: You're so right, bye!

DAGNY: You know my mother and my father and what they did to me—

ROMAN: Okay, Dagny! I've heard this story, I know it. We cried together over it— what your mother and father did to you, what my mother and father did to me, what everyone's mother and father did to them. I told my sad story and you told me yours, let's just shake hands and say good-bye.

DAGNY: You think I'm callous. I am. But I'm not the only one. Everyone is. Everyone in the world is.

ROMAN: Well at least you'll never lack company.

DAGNY: I'll always be your friend.

ROMAN: Stick it in your diary.

DAGNY: You'll forgive me in the future, you'll see.

ROMAN: That's right, bye. I know the rules, everything must happen quickly—a kiss on both cheeks and a knife in the back, it's a familiar stage direction. I just lost my timing back there for a minute but I'm okay now. Bye. (*Shrieked.*) *Just go!* (DAGNY *runs out.* ROMAN *sits crying for a moment.* THE MECHANIC *enters. He is what you would expect, with young, blunt, good looks. He wears a car mechanic's uniform with a cap.*)

THE MECHANIC: Is this where Dagny lives? Wow! What a set-up! Took me ten minutes just to get up the driveway.

ROMAN: I take it by your costume you're the mechanic. Well, why not, everyone else has been here. Step right up. It can be assumed by your looks you were not crushed under the weight of a falling automobile, am I right?

THE MECHANIC (*amused*): What? Hell no.

ROMAN: No, well, it wouldn't figure. Maybe I was hit by a falling automobile; it would explain the headache I've developed over the course of the afternoon. So, you're Dagny's mechanic.

THE MECHANIC: Hey, right, Dagny mention me?

ROMAN: Yes. Briefly.

THE MECHANIC: She is hot for me.

ROMAN: You don't say.

THE MECHANIC: Well, I am for her, too.

ROMAN: Yes, of course. Well, be that as it may, I guess you're wondering where she is.

THE MECHANIC: Hey, do you want to see me dance?

ROMAN: Dance. You dance?

THE MECHANIC: I'm a dancer.

ROMAN: We were told you live over a garage.

THE MECHANIC: I do.

ROMAN: Well, don't you fix cars when you come downstairs?

THE MECHANIC: Hell no.

ROMAN: You're not a mechanic?

THE MECHANIC: I'm The Mechanic.

ROMAN: Is that symbolic and I'm not getting it?

THE MECHANIC: That's my role—my get-up: I'm a dancer at a club. A stripper.

ROMAN: A stripper.

THE MECHANIC: That's right, a good one.

ROMAN: And that's your costume.

THE MECHANIC: You got it. That's how I met Dagny. She went crazy over me, big tipper.

ROMAN: Big tips, hey?

THE MECHANIC: Oh yeah, the women more than the guys.

ROMAN: There are men where you strip?

THE MECHANIC: You know, the gays. At first the managers said no gays! Ladies only! But then they figured they'd bring in more money and the ladies and the gays get along so well.

ROMAN: Makes sense.

THE MECHANIC (*picking up a marzipan fruit from the table*): What's this?

ROMAN: A marzipan. It's almond paste shaped like a fruit.

THE MECHANIC: Yeah? What for?

ROMAN: I haven't the smallest clue.

THE MECHANIC: You're a gay, aren't you?

ROMAN: You ask as if you were picking kiwi.

THE MECHANIC: Yeah? What's that?

ROMAN: A kiwi? It's a fruit.

THE MECHANIC: Yeah? Where does it come from?

ROMAN: Who can say?

THE MECHANIC (*takes out a joint and lights it*): Mind if I get high?

ROMAN: Be my guest.

THE MECHANIC: Want some?

ROMAN: No thanks.

THE MECHANIC: Want to see me dance?

ROMAN: Not really.

THE MECHANIC: I'm wearing my costume. I wear it all the time now. It solves everything. You wouldn't believe how I used to fuss getting dressed. I mean getting dressed just regular. I was worse than a girl. I took forever. You wouldn't believe it.

ROMAN: I believe it.

THE MECHANIC: Now I just put this on.

ROMAN: And take it off.

THE MECHANIC: Yeah, and take it off. How come you don't want to see me dance?

ROMAN: I just don't. How come you don't want to know where Dagny is?

THE MECHANIC: I came here to tell her I don't want to go away with her. We had a good thing but it was just a thing.

ROMAN: Right. Well, she went away with someone else.

THE MECHANIC (*eating the marzipans*): Yeah? I guess she just needed to get away.

ROMAN: That must have been it. A lot of people needed to get away today.

THE MECHANIC: Yeah? How did he take it, her husband, Borloff?

ROMAN: Boris? He ran off with a fairy.

THE MECHANIC: No kidding! Yeah? A gay? He's a gay too?

ROMAN: In a way. I guess so.

THE MECHANIC: So you're sitting here all by yourself, aren't you feeling down? Don't you need cheering up?

ROMAN: Look, you're very nice and all that but I really don't want to see you strip.

THE MECHANIC (*he follows his own stage directions*): Oh come on, I'm so good. You just sit there very still and I'll show you my routine. I don't have my music here but you can imagine it. Don't talk, just watch. Okay, first—you know, when the music just starts—I jump out and circle around like I'm looking at this really big car that needs a lot of work. You get it? Then I take my hat off and I wipe my brow, all the time a little bit swaying like this—subtle, you know, nothing faggy. Then I lift the imaginary hood and take out my wrench and start tightening things, like this. By this time, it's as if I'm getting a little sweaty, so I unbutton my shirt a little bit, take my hat off again and wipe my brow, real sexy. Then I take out my imaginary pump and start pumping up the car. This pumping really gets them in the audience—they go crazy—pumping my hips like this.

Then suddenly, instead of doing it real slow, I whip off my shirt and throw it over my head—throwing it over my head prevents the really horny ones in the audience from ripping it to pieces—keeps my overhead down if I don't have to replace my costume. Then I dance around a bit—this part doesn't relate to the car very much, but the bold ones all start running up to stick tips in my pocket around now. They love me—I guess they're all pent up and lonely or something. I don't know, someone should do a study. Anyway, then, as if I'm on one of those thingie's on wheels, I get on the floor and act as if I'm sliding under the car to play with the carburetor or something.

ROMAN: The carburetor's on top, under the hood.

THE MECHANIC: What? Oh yeah? Well then, the muffler, whatever, I'm down there and I'm undoing my belt and yanking off my trousers, meanwhile they're all screaming like the house is on fire. I leap up—I'm wearing my jockstrap, my undershirt and athletic socks and work boots—and I start shadow boxing fast and then slow. Now I'm building up a real sweat and the girls and the gays are throwing tens and twenties like nobody's business and I'm really going strong—the music's really loud here and I walk it around for a second so everyone can get a load of me. Then I turn around real sudden like I heard someone call my name and real slow peel off my undershirt which is good and wet: this I throw into the audience. (*The undershirt should be thrown on stage not into the actual audience.*) Everyone screams, glasses fall and I do some more of this sort of shadow boxing, get more bills stuffed this time into my jock, quickly tighten up the screws on the tires, take the ignition key, stick the key in, gas it, accelerate and Pow! Lights out. (*He collapses into a chair, using a linen napkin to wipe his sweat.*) Well, how did you like it?

ROMAN: I didn't.

THE MECHANIC: Yeah? Why not?

ROMAN: I guess I'm frigid.

THE MECHANIC: Yeah? For real? How about if I let you kiss me?

ROMAN: Thanks just the same. Don't you ever take a day off?

THE MECHANIC: Maybe I just feel sorry for you sitting here all by yourself.

ROMAN: Don't bother.

THE MECHANIC: Maybe I'll just kiss you.

ROMAN: Are you feeling a little "gay" this afternoon too or is this the equinox and everyone's changing into something else?

THE MECHANIC: You don't live in that house, do you?

ROMAN: No, I do not.

MECHANIC: I was just thinking it's such a big house and you say everyone's gone off—maybe you and I could live in the house together. From the looks of it, lots of room, we wouldn't get in each other's way.

ROMAN: I'll pass.

THE MECHANIC: What have you got better to do?

ROMAN: I'm waiting for Father Christmas. If I start today, I have less than four months to draw up the list of the things I really want. I perform this task in monastic seclusion. So won't you please go?

THE MECHANIC: You're one of the nervous ones, aren't you? Dagny said you were fun.

ROMAN: Dagny? Who's Dagny?

THE MECHANIC: Never heard of her. I get it. How about having a little fun?

ROMAN: Get away from me.

THE MECHANIC: I think you want to play and you just don't know it.

ROMAN: I'm sure you're wrong.

THE MECHANIC: Drop all the attitude, what's it ever going to get you? Don't you even know what you want? If you don't know what you want you can't get what you want.

ROMAN: I don't want you—I'm trying to make that message clear.

THE MECHANIC: Trying to make that message queer? What message? Do you have a message? Are you the messenger boy? Now how about you laying a little tip on me for doing my routine?

ROMAN: A tip. For your routine.

THE MECHANIC: That's right. I didn't go through all that for nothing.

ROMAN: I asked you not to bother.

THE MECHANIC: You begged me to do it.

ROMAN: You really look too dumb to play a predator so why not go back now to your imaginary garage or strip-tease den or wherever you feel most comfortable. That's good advice, a tip.

THE MECHANIC: Maybe I'll give you a tip, the tip of my fist in your funny face— maybe that's your bag, a little roughhouse.

ROMAN (*suddenly picking up a knife, holding it up, exploding violently*): Go now! Go! Go! Or I swear to God I'll cut your head off myself—I'll cut it right off! (THE MECHANIC, *collecting quickly what clothes he can, runs out. ROMAN puts the knife back down on the table, picks up a glass of wine and drinks. Offstage we can hear* THE FAIRY *humming "The Fairy Song."* THE FAIRY *enters as she appeared first, in fairy regalia.*)

THE FAIRY: Hello, Roman.

ROMAN: Oh, it's you. What happened, was Capri closed?

THE FAIRY: You don't approve of me, do you?

ROMAN: Speaking English again? How quaint.

THE FAIRY: Don't be bitter with me; we're so alike, you and I.

ROMAN: No we're not. For one thing I'm a lot taller.

THE FAIRY: I could be tall too if I wanted to be. Everyone can be anything they want to be.

ROMAN: It must be so tiring to be so wise, to change costumes so quickly, all the time playing with people's lives and laughing.

THE FAIRY: You paint a very unpleasant portrait of me.

ROMAN: You posed for it, go hang it. (*She slaps him across the face. He slaps her back. She slaps him again. He slaps her again.*)

THE FAIRY: It's a myth that fairies enjoy pain so why don't we stop this.

ROMAN: It's worth the pain just to get a swing at you.

THE FAIRY: I could turn you into a toad.

ROMAN: I am a toad. There's nothing you can do to me. That's the great comfort of sitting at the bottom of a well.

THE FAIRY (*looking at one of the silver platters on the table*): Are these really cucumber sandwiches?

ROMAN: What else would they be? Why did you want Boris?

THE FAIRY: I thought Boris was kind of cute in a boyish innocent kind of way, and he'd be fun to kiss and hold for a few minutes.

ROMAN: And Dagny and Mimi? How long will that last?

THE FAIRY: A week, two weeks, maybe even a month.

ROMAN: It's all pinball to you, isn't it?

THE FAIRY: I tried to make it up to you.

ROMAN: The stripper?

THE FAIRY: I thought you'd like him. He wasn't your cup of tea?

ROMAN: I've lost my taste for tea.

THE FAIRY: You'll forgive me in the future, you'll see.

ROMAN: I've heard that before.

THE FAIRY: When you've lived as long as I have you become a great mimic.

ROMAN: How old are you anyway?

THE FAIRY: I'll be a hundred and twenty in March.

ROMAN: How is it you live so long?

THE FAIRY: Every diamond I get I throw up into the sky and I get an extra ten years to stick around. So you see it's to my advantage sometimes to grant wishes. But I imagine I'll wake up very tired one morning and just throw my necklace over a bridge.

ROMAN: Well, you look, as they say, very well preserved.

THE FAIRY: Thank you, darling, you look very good yourself, better than you think.

ROMAN: Thanks. Tell me, where is poor Boris now? Did you abandon him mid-Atlantic?

THE FAIRY: I'm with him now; we're laughing in the airport: he's wild about me, says I'm his dreamboat.

ROMAN: How do you do it? Trick photography?

THE FAIRY: I'm everywhere I've ever been and everywhere I'm ever going. It's the same for you. You're with Mimi and Dagny right now laughing in these chairs. Don't you see yourself, where you've been and where you're going?

ROMAN: No, I don't.

THE FAIRY: Don't you see him, little Roman picking mushrooms, petting ponies at the animal shelter, counting to ten?

ROMAN: Please, I don't even have the energy to become a figure in a glass ball.

THE FAIRY: You wanted a house with doors that opened onto water, tiny grandchildren running by your side. Look into yourself and see it. A lake and a boat out on it, rippling along, no fish biting, no fish caught, everything still, quiet, easy, all things true and all things coming true. (*Very lightly and imperceptibly, it has begun to snow.*)

ROMAN: Is it very late?

THE FAIRY: Oh yes, we've been talking for a long time.

ROMAN: Where did the time go?

THE FAIRY: It just goes.

ROMAN: And you? What do you get out of it?

THE FAIRY: Me? (*She laughs.*) I'm going to grant you a free wish, Roman. Wish for anything.

ROMAN: I wish everything rotten would disappear. That's what I wish for. Make everything rotten go away, just keep the pure parts.

THE FAIRY: You want the world to disappear.

ROMAN: That's what I want, I want the world to disappear.

THE FAIRY: Close your eyes and kneel down. Do as I say. (ROMAN *closes his eyes and kneels down.*) Now think of a memory, a good one, focus on it, describe it out loud.

ROMAN (*after a moment*): I'm six or seven years old and I'm not wearing shoes—I've gone out in my pajamas. It's late night or early morning, there's light everywhere from the moon and the coming sun. The grass under my feet is wet. Seconds ago it rained and everything is glittering. My parents are asleep inside upstairs. The house is dark and looks far away like a ship. I am holding bunches of violets and daffodils. All things beautiful and cruel circle me, the bees and the dragonflies. In the hedges between the silver leaves there's a sudden movement. Tiny fairies are dancing from leaf to leaf with garlands they've constructed of dew, tossing opalescent wreaths, doing cartwheels and somersaults—(THE FAIRY *has sat herself on* ROMAN's *shoulders and undone her skirt belt which lets down from the thick tulle skirt a much longer tulle skirt which, as* ROMAN *stands on the cue "somersaults," covers completely* ROMAN's *body so that the effect is* ROMAN *disappearing and* THE FAIRY *extremely tall in a beautiful long dress.*)

THE FAIRY: —somersaults and they are making words rhyme effortlessly, giving gifts of robin eggs, candy stores, seasons, soft kisses in the dark, fir trees, marble, glass, silk, candlelight, limes, cinnamon, train whistles, rocket ships, gondolas. They are laughing and dancing and exchanging phone numbers. "Oh we will never be this young or this happy again!" the fairies say to one another, "Oh no not ever as here in the garden!" (*The snowfall has thickened a bit. A flute plays "The Fairy's Song" and the giant fairy dances about. Delighted, she throws her head back and laughs and then, taking a small curtsy, she bows her head humbly. Fade out. Curtain.*)

JERKER

OR

THE HELPING HAND

A Pornographic Elegy
with
Redeeming Social Value
and
A Hymn to the Queer Men
of
San Francisco
in
Twenty Telephone Calls,
Many of Them Dirty

by

Robert Chesley

Jerker, or The Helping Hand was first presented by Celebration Theatre in Los Angeles, on July 18, 1986. The production was directed by Michael Kearns, with scenic design by Craig Gereau, lighting design by Michael Johnson, and stage management by Susan Bell. The cast was:

J.R.   David Stebbins
BERT   Joe Fraser

This production was subsequently presented by Southeastern Arts Media and Education Project, Inc., at New Moves in Atlanta, Georgia, in November of 1986.

Jerker, or The Helping Hand opened on December 19, 1986 at the Sanford Meisner Theater, New York City, presented by Helping Hand Productions, Gene Paul Rickard, executive producer. The production was directed by Nicholas Deutsch, with scenic and lighting design by John Wright Stevens, and stage management by Maude Brickner. The cast was:

J.R.   Jay Corcoran
BERT   John Finch
ANOTHER MAN   Jay Berkow

The Snowdrop

Now—now, as low I stooped, thought I,
　　I will see what this snowdrop is;
So shall I put much argument by,
　　And solve a lifetime's mysteries.

A northern wind had frozen the grass;
　　Its blades were hoar with crystal rime,
Aglint like light-dissecting glass
　　At beam of morning prime.

From hidden bulb the flower reared up
　　Its angled, slender, cold, dark stem,
Whence dangled an inverted cup
　　For tri-leaved diadem.

Beneath these ice-pure sepals lay
　　A triplet of green-pencilled snow,
Which in the chill-aired gloom of day
　　Stirred softly to and fro.

Mind fixed, but else made vacant, I,
　　Lost to my body called my soul
To don that frail solemnity,
　　Its inmost self my goal.

And though in vain—no mortal mind
　　Across that threshold yet hath fared!—
In this collusion I divined
　　Some consciousness we shared.

Strange roads (while suns, a myriad, set)
　　Led us through infinity;
And where they crossed, there then had met
　　Not two of us, but three.

　　　　　　　—WALTER DE LA MARE

CHARACTERS

BERT: a San Francisco faggot, aged anywhere from thirty to fifty or so; possibly older, though if he is, he is essentially youthful in appearance.

J.R.: a San Francisco faggot in his mid-thirties or early forties.

ANOTHER SAN FRANCISCO FAGGOT

(N.B. San Francisco faggots are beautiful, loving, sexy men. They have facial hair, fairly often in the extravagant, fanciful styles of the Old West. Their eyes are alive, and their voices are relaxed and gentle. Their beauty transcends any considerations of age, race, body type, or traditional "good looks.")

TIME

1985.

SETTING

San Francisco.

Scene 1

There are two playing areas: BERT's *bed and* J.R.'s *bed. Each area has some sort of bedside lighting and a telephone; in addition,* BERT's *area can be lit by night-city light coming in his window, and his telephone has an answering machine. By* J.R.'s *bed, propped against the wall, is a pair of Canadian crutches.*

Lights up on J.R., *in bed, wearing only jockey shorts, playing with his erection with one hand while dialing a number on his phone. When* BERT's *phone rings, the window light comes up in his area, and we see him sleeping in bed, and then, startled awake, answering his phone sleepily. He does not turn on his bedside light.*

BERT: Hello? (*Pause.*) Hello?

J.R. (*low*): Hi.

BERT: Who is this? Hello?

J.R. (*stroking his cock under the covers*): How're you doing? I'm feeling pretty good.

BERT: Just going to sleep.

J.R.: You hard?

BERT (*realizing what kind of a call this is, and deciding to go along with it*): Yeah. (*Lies back.*) I'm hard, sort of.
J.R.: You touching yourself?

BERT: No.

J.R.: I am. Feels good.

BERT: Yeah?

J.R.: Yeah. Why don't you put your hand on your cock?

BERT (*doing so; aroused*): Okay. (*Pause.*) Feels good.

J.R.: Good. Ya wearing anything?

BERT: No. I don't, in bed.

J.R.: Never wear pajamas?

BERT: Nope.

J.R.: Underwear?

BERT: Nope.

J.R.: Just skin, huh?

BERT: Yup.

455

J.R.: Feelin' your cock?

BERT: Yup.

J.R.: What's it like?

BERT: Gettin' hard.

J.R.: What's it *look* like? How big?

BERT: 'Bout seven inches.

J.R.: Yeah?

BERT: Yeah.

J.R.: Thick?

BERT: Pretty thick. And straight.

J.R.: You cut?

BERT: Yeah. You?

J.R.: Nope: sliding that foreskin up and back, up and back.

BERT: Sounds good.

J.R.: Feels good. Peelin' my head.

BERT: Yeah.

J.R.: So tell me about that cock of yours. Big head?

BERT: In proportion.

J.R.: Where's it feel best?

BERT: Right under the head.

J.R.: You hard?

BERT: Yup. Real hard.

J.R.: Okay. I want you to lick your finger and then just tickle that part of your cock for me: just that part, right under the head.

(BERT *licks his finger and puts it back under the covers, continues to play with himself.*)

J.R.: You just touching that part?

BERT: Yup.

J.R.: What's your other hand doing?

BERT: Holding my balls.

J.R.: Feel good?

BERT: Yup.

J.R.: I like thinking about your cock.

BERT: Yeah?

J.R.: I like thinking about you jerking it.

BERT: Yeah?

J.R.: Making it feel good.

BERT: Yeah. Yeah.

J.R.: How do you do it? Jack off.

BERT: How?

J.R.: I want you to tell me exactly what you're doing to yourself.

BERT: I'm lying back, halfway. Got my hands under the covers, and I'm holding the phone with my chin, against my pillow.

J.R.: Your legs straight out?

BERT: Yeah, straight out, but apart. Feet about two feet apart.

J.R.: Yeah?

BERT: Yeah. Got my balls in my left hand, and I'm pushin' them down between my legs, so's to pull my cockskin tight from the base. (*Licks finger again.*) And my right hand's doin' just what you told me to do, just stroking that place under the head of my cock, real light.

J.R.: Yeah? Well, I want you to jerk it now, and I want you to tell me just exactly what you're doing, just how you do it.

BERT: Easing on my balls, now, still got 'em cupped in my hand, but I'm hooking my thumb over the base of my cock, and holding it there, firm 'n hard; and I'm pressing the base, the root, you know? And now I got my other fingers on my cock—my right hand, I mean; four fingers on the underside of the shaft, thumb on top, near the head, and I'm pulling up and down, up and down, stretching my legs out and tensing, gonna shoot a load onto my belly—

(*During the end of the above speech, J.R. cums quietly but not silently, and then drops the phone receiver back in the cradle. Blackout.*)

Scene 2

Lights up on both areas. J.R. is dialing; BERT is reading in bed with his bedside light on when his phone rings.

BERT (*answering his phone*): Hello?

J.R. (*low and sexy*): You feelin' horny?

BERT: I could.

J.R.: What'ya doin'? Not asleep?

BERT: Reading.

J.R.: In bed?

BERT: Yeah.

J.R.: Not wearing anything?

BERT: Nope.

J.R.: You got any jockey shorts?

BERT: In my drawer.

J.R.: No dirty ones?

BERT: Nope.

J.R.: In the laundry?

BERT: Sorry.

J.R.: So'm I. (*Slight pause.*) But the clean ones'll do.

BERT: What d'ya want me to do?

J.R.: I want ya to go get 'em. Will you do that?

BERT: Sure.

J.R.: Wait: just get 'em. Don't put 'em on yet.

BERT: Okay. Hold a sec. (*Puts receiver down, gets out of bed and goes off; returns with a pair of jockey shorts, gets into bed again and picks up the receiver.*) Okay.

J.R.: You got your jockey shorts?

BERT: Yeah.

J.R.: I want you to smell them. (BERT *does so.*) You smellin' them?

BERT: Yeah.

J.R.: What's it like?

BERT: Smells clean, soft.

J.R.: Ya like it?

BERT: Yeah.

J.R.: Okay. You in bed again?

BERT: Yeah.

J.R.: Under the covers?

BERT: Yeah.

J.R.: I want you to pull your jockeys on. Under the covers. Slowly. You do that for me? I'll tell you just how.

BERT: Okay. (*Starts doing so, with a bit of awkwardness, as he's also holding the phone receiver with his chin. As he does it:*)

J.R.: First the right foot . . . then the left . . .

BERT: Yeah.

J.R.: Okay, now pull them up slowly, over the calves, up to your knees. Okay?

BERT: Okay.

J.R.: Leave 'em there. How's your cock doin'?

BERT: Gettin' hard.

J.R.: Good. Play with it a bit. (BERT *does so.*) Feel good?

BERT: Yeah.

J.R.: Good. Yeah. Now I want you to pull your jockey shorts up all the way, over your butt, over your cock. (BERT *does so.*) You like the feel of that?

BERT: Yeah.

J.R.: You feeling your cock through your jockey shorts?

BERT: Yeah. Feels good.

J.R.: Real hard, huh? Pressed in there?

BERT: Yeah. Got a wet spot at the tip.

J.R.: Well, good! Just like a horny kid, huh? Ever wear your jockeys to bed when you were a kid, huh?

BERT: Yeah.

J.R.: Like the feel of getting hard in your jockeys, all snug and soft?

BERT: Yeah.

J.R.: Cock pressed tight? Wanna burst out?

BERT: Yeah.

J.R.: Let's say we're two kids in bed together, feelin' good.

BERT: Okay.

J.R.: Feelin' our hard-ons, in our jockeys. Snuggling.

BERT: Yeah. Good.

J.R.: Think you can bring yourself off? In your jockeys?

BERT: Yeah.

J.R.: Wanna do that for me?

BERT: Sure.

J.R.: I'll do mine too. I wanna listen to you.

(BERT *props the phone receiver under his chin to use both hands under the covers.*)

BERT: Two kids, huh? Two horny kids playing in bed, huh? Huh?

J.R.: Yeah.

BERT: Feelin' *so* good, so damn good, playin' with our cocks. Yeah, yeah. You're my little brother, huh? You're my little brother, and I'm gonna teach you how to feel good, how to feel *real* good. But we gotta be quiet, real quiet, 'cause we don't wanna get caught. Two horny brothers, gettin' it on in bed together, yeah. Yeah. (*Louder.*) Hey! You my little brother? (*On the verge of cumming.*) Huh? Huh?

J.R. (*also about to cum*): Yeah, yeah! You're my big brother, look *up* to you!

(*They cum, both rather quietly.* BERT *pants a bit;* J.R. *giggles.*)

J.R.: I liked that.

BERT (*giggling too*): Never had a brother, 'til now.

J.R.: Didn't either. Always wanted one. Always.

BERT: Me too.

J.R.: You shoot your load into your jockeys, or did you cheat?

BERT: Cheat?

J.R.: Take your dick out.

BERT: No—I shot in my jockeys.

J.R.: Good. Now you've got a dirty pair. I want you to save 'em. For me. (*Hangs up. Blackout.*)

Scene 3

Lights up on J.R. *dialing and on* BERT's *bed, which is empty, lit by the window light.* BERT's *phone rings two times, and is then answered by his answering machine.*

BERT (*voice on answering machine, with a bit of Sylvester in the background*): Hi, this is Bert. I can't come to the phone right now, but if you leave your name, your number, and the date and time of the call, I'll call you back as soon as I can. Please wait 'til you hear the beep, and please talk slowly and clearly, 'cause this machine's not doing so well, and isn't expected to make it through the summer. (*We hear a bit more Sylvester, and then the beep.* J.R. *hangs up. No blackout.*)

Scene 4

Immediately following. J.R. *is playing with himself. Then he smiles to himself—an idea has occurred to him—and lies back with his eyes closed and brings himself to the point of cumming. He sits up and re-dials, still on the verge of cumming.* BERT's *phone rings twice and then is answered by his machine.*

BERT (*as before*): Hi, this is Bert. I can't come to the phone right now, but if you leave your name, your number, and the date and time of the call, I'll call you back as soon as I can. Please wait 'til you hear the beep, and please talk slowly and clearly, 'cause this machine's not doing so well, and isn't expected to make it through the summer.

(J.R.'s *timing is beautiful: just after the beep he pants two or three times, then holds for a second, and then cums with a gratifying "Ah—! Ah—!" into the receiver. He lies there for a few seconds more, then gives a low chuckle, kisses the receiver silently and sweetly, and hangs up quietly. Blackout.*)

Scene 5

Lights up on J.R. *dialing and on* BERT's *empty bed, lit by his bedside light.* BERT's *phone rings a few times, and then he enters, naked and toweling himself off. He answers the phone.*

BERT: Hello?

J.R.: Hi there.

BERT: Hi.

J.R.: You want some action?

BERT: Hold a sec. Just got out of the shower. Can you call back in a minute or so?

J.R.: I'd rather wait.

BERT (*smiling*): Okay. I'll just be a minute.

J.R.: I'm waiting. (*And, of course, he is playing with himself.*)

(BERT *puts the phone receiver on his pillow and exits. When he comes back, he has dried off, and his hair is combed. He stands for a bit, looking at the telephone receiver and playing with his cock lightly. He climbs into bed and picks up the receiver.*)

BERT: You still there?

J.R.: Waitin' for you, Bert.

BERT (*smiles*): Okay, little brother. I've been planning this one.

J.R.: What?

BERT: Thinking about you last night, waitin' to see if you'd call—

J.R.: Oh?

BERT: Yeah, and I got sort of carried away, planning a little outing for you, for my little brother.

J.R.: Yeah?

BERT: Yeah. Wanna go? Ready?

J.R.: Sure.

BERT (*settling down*): Thought we'd do a little exploring, ya know. See what the woods are like, back of our house. Maybe pretend we're scouts or something, or maybe Indians. Just for fun, just a boy's game.

J.R. (*into it*): Yeah?

BERT: Yeah. How'd you like that, huh? Going down that trail into the woods, you following me. D'ya think I know where I'm going?

J.R.: Hope so. I like following you. Where ya going to take me, Bert?

BERT: Oh, a place I know. 'Bout a fifteen- or twenty-minute walk, pretty deep in the woods.

J.R.: Yeah?

BERT: Yeah. Don't want anyone to discover us, see? I got a special game I wanna play with you, scout. Gonna put you to the test.

J.R.: Yeah? What kind of test?

BERT: A little endurance test. Just wait. You'll see. Now: you see that tree over there?

J.R.: Yeah?

BERT: Big tree, at the edge of the clearing?

J.R.: Yeah?

BERT: You know what I'm going to do to you?

J.R.: No.

BERT: Wanna guess?

J.R. (*faking a little panic in his voice; enjoying the game immensely*): What'ya gonna do to me?

BERT: Take a look at that tree, buddy. What do you see, in the grass there? Lying in the grass by the tree?

J.R.: I dunno. Can't make it out.

BERT: Step closer, then. Get a better look. If you dare.

J.R.: Is it—rope?

BERT: Good guess, buddy. Now: guess who's gonna get tied to that tree.

J.R.: You're gonna tie me to that tree, huh?

BERT: Yeah. You'd like that. Put you to the test. See how much you can take. How d'you feel about that? Think you're up to it?

J.R. (*with a rush*): Sort of scared inside.

BERT: You're not gonna chicken out on me?

J.R.: No, sir.

BERT: Good. First we're gonna blindfold you—that's why I brought my bandana. Turn around.

J.R. (*softly*): Yeah?

BERT: Yeah. There. Blindfold you so you can't see.

J.R. (*closing his eyes; playing with himself furiously*): Thank you, sir.

BERT: Okay, now. Turn back around. Back up against the tree. Don't stumble.

J.R.: Yessir.

BERT: Gotta tie you up! *Uh!* Tie you up tight and secure, so you can't get away! *Uh!* So you can't even squirm much! *Uh!* You like the feel of that, tied to a tree in the middle of the woods?

J.R.: I'm scared. What'ya gonna do to me?

BERT: Yeah—I can see you're trembling, all right: don't know what's gonna happen to you, do you? Might be anything. Might be you're pretty helpless right now, all tied up. Might be you've let yourself in for a little torture test, see if you can stand it. You like standing there, all tied up to that tree and blindfolded, waiting and wondering what's gonna happen to you? You like that?

J.R.: Yessir.

BERT: Supposing I loosen your belt, huh? What you gonna do if I pull your jeans down? Supposin' I unbutton your jeans, huh? Not much you can do about it, is there, huh?

J.R.: Don't do that, sir. Please don't.

BERT: Don't do what, boy?

J.R.: Don't pull my jeans down, sir. Please don't.

BERT: Supposin' I *want* to do it, boy?

J.R.: Please don't, sir. Please.

BERT: Too bad, boy. Gonna yank your jeans down, down to your knees. *Huh!* Can't go further than that, 'count of the rope around your boots—

J.R.: No, sir! Please don't!

BERT: There you stand, yellin' like a yellow kid, tied up there against that tree, blindfolded, and standing in your jockey shorts, right out there in the woods. You know what I'm gonna do to you?

J.R.: Please don't, sir. Let me go, sir!

BERT: You can't tell what I'm gonna do, 'cause you can't see. But I'll tell you this much: I like the look of your hard-on, pressing against the cotton of your jockey shorts, *straining* to get out. Keeps *trying* to get out, doesn't know how . . .

J.R. (*breathless*): Yeah . . . yeah . . .

BERT: Hey—don't you cum yet, buddy. You hear me?

J.R. (*as before*): Yeah.

BERT: Good boy. Man, you look hot like that, tied up against that tree. I could shoot my load all over you. But I'm not gonna —yet. Gonna put you to the test, first: gonna see how much you like ball games, boy. Gonna see how much your balls can take.

J.R. (*pulling his balls as he jerks himself*): Yessir?

BERT: That's right, boy. Now, you can't see what I'm gonna do to you right now, but you know *somethin's* gonna happen when you feel me grab your jockeys and yank 'em *up.*

J.R.: What'ya gonna do to me? Hey, no!

BERT: Gonna cut you free from your jockeys, boy. That's why I brought my Bowie. Cut *right up* through the leg-hole—

J.R.: Hey, no! No! Please, no—!

BERT: —right up—*Uh!*—through the waistband—*Uh!* There! Your jockeys are half off, and your cock's nearly free, standing up at attention with your jockeys at half mast.

J.R.: Yeah?

BERT: Could leave 'em that way, one leg on . . .

J.R.: Yeah?

BERT: But I've got another use for 'em. Gonna cut off the other side. *Uh!* There!

You're free. Or at least your cock is free, standing out there in the fresh air real nice and hard. Gonna spit in my palm and play with its head a bit, appreciate that nice foreskin, make you squirm. But don't you cum, boy, you hear me?

J.R. (*breathless*): Yessir. I won't, sir.

BERT: Gonna take the head of that cock in my palm and *squeeze* it, let it slide into that foreskin, knead it, yank on it real gentle, drive you mad 'cause I told you: don't cum yet, little brother.

J.R. (*as before*): Yeah, yeah . . .

BERT: Okay, boy. You feel that? Know what that is? It's your jockey shorts, or what's left of 'em. Gonna tie you up, gonna tie you up *special*: gonna tie your jockeys around your cock and balls, right at the root of your cock, gonna yank it *tight!*—make you wince! You like that?

J.R. (*as before*): Yessir. I do, sir.

BERT: Okay, gotta squat down here, now, so's to get at your balls.

J.R.: Yessir!

BERT: Pull 'em out, stretch 'em. Nice balls for a boy. Didn't know my little brother was growing into such a hot man. I like pulling your balls. Feel good?

J.R.: Yes it does, sir.

BERT: Good—'cause now I'm gonna tie 'em up too, with your jockey rag, you understand? Tied tight around your big balls, stretch 'em out. There. Now I got something to yank your balls by. Hold 'em down *firm*, make 'em *ache*.

J.R. (*pleading*): No! No, sir!

BERT: But there isn't a thing you can do about it, 'cause you're tied to that tree and you're helpless. Can't even squirm much, but you sure wish you could squirm away somehow!

J.R. (*beating furiously again, knowing the climax of the game is near*): Please don't, sir! Please!

BERT: Don't you like a little ball torture, boy?

J.R.: I—I can't take it, sir!

BERT: *Sure* you can, boy! I'm gonna yank a little harder, just to show you!

J.R.: I—please!—stop!

BERT: Don't you cum yet, you little *bastard!*

J.R.: Please—! Please—!

BERT: *Yah!* that hurt'ya? That hurt'ya?

J.R.: Stop! Stop! No!

BERT: I'm not lettin' go!

J.R.: No! I'm—I'm about to—!

BERT: *Hold* it, man! You feel me pressin' up against you?

J.R.: Yeah!

BERT: Ya know what I'm gonna do?

J.R.: No—no—I—

BERT: Huh? Gonna scrape my cheek against your face—feel the stubble, huh? That's your brother, man! Gonna force your mouth open with my tongue, huh? Gonna make you *kiss* me, huh? Gonna kiss you 'cause you're so fuckin' beautiful—

J.R. (*cumming*): Hahhh!

BERT: *Kiss* you, huh? *Kiss* you, huh? (*Cumming.*) *Huh! Huh! Huh!*

(*They both lie there for a bit, panting happily.*)

J.R.: Heyyy—!

BERT: Shall I untie you now, huh?

J.R. (*laughing*): Thanks. That was great.

BERT (*little laugh*): Enjoyed it myself. Shot all over the goddamned place.

J.R. (*dabbing up with his cum towel*): You're hot.

BERT: Got a hot little brother. Bet you know more than you let on, don't you? Playin' innocent with me.

(J.R. *laughs softly.*)

BERT: You been playin' around?

J.R. (*going along with the protogame*): I—I don't know what you mean . . .

BERT: Don't lie to me. Bet you been playin' around *somewhere*, boy—a horny kid like you? Bet I could make you fess up to a *lot*, a lot of messin' around.

J.R.: Yeah?

BERT: Yeah. Next time.

J.R.: Huh.

BERT: Yeah. Right now it's bedtime for you. Gonna tuck you in, give you a little kiss, ruffle your hair a bit, and put out the light.

J.R.: Hey: thanks. Good night.

BERT: Good night, boy. Sweet dreams. (*Hangs up. Blackout.*)

Scene 6

Lights up on J.R., *dialing. When* BERT'S *phone rings, the window light comes up on him, lying in bed, awake.* BERT *answers his phone.*

BERT: Hello?

J.R. (*low*): Hi.

(*Pause.*)

BERT: That my little brother?

J.R.: Yup. Wanna play?

(*Pause.*)

BERT: Not tonight.

J.R. (*sensing that* BERT *is troubled*): You okay?

BERT: Yeah—just had a heavy evening, that's all.

J.R. (*gently*): Yeah?

BERT: Just—talking with a friend who's . . . in bad shape.

J.R. (*half muttered*): Yeah, yeah. Sorry.

BERT: But it's okay you called. Don't be sorry.

J.R.: Okay. I'm not sorry. Just the sound of your voice turns me on.

BERT (*little laugh*): Yeah?

J.R.: Yeah. I got a beautiful brother. I'll beat off thinking of that.

BERT (*little laugh*): Okay. But call back? Another time? Promise?

J.R.: You bet. Good night.

BERT: Good night.

(*Pause.* J.R. *hangs up first, regretfully; the lights go off in his area.* BERT *holds onto the receiver, lost in his thoughts, until it begins beeping at him.*)

BERT: Shit. (*Hangs up. Blackout.*)

Scene 7

As before. When the lights come up this time, BERT *has been watching television in bed, and drinking beer; he switches the television off with a remote control device, and answers his phone.*

BERT: Hello?

J.R.: Hi. How're you doin'?

BERT: Okay.

J.R.: Good. (*Suggestive tone.*) Been thinkin' 'bout you.

BERT: Yeah?

J.R. (*deciding to go ahead*): Yeah. Did my laundry today, ya know?

BERT: Yeah?

J.R.: Waitin' for it to dry I, uh, leaned over the dryer for a bit, ya know, pressing against it 'cause it's warm? And I got hard, thinking of you, picturing my big brother, Bert. Felt good, pressin' my hard-on against the machine, the warmth.

BERT (*chuckles*): How'd you picture your brother?

(*Pause.*)

J.R.: Oh, I *know* what you look like, Bert.

BERT: Yeah? You do?

J.R.: Yeah. We met.

BERT: We did?

J.R.: Didn't think you remembered. How'd you think I got your number?

BERT: I gave it to you?

J.R.: You sure did. I don't find a brother like you by just picking a name out of the phone book.

BERT: Where?

J.R. (*laughs*): You really wanna know?

BERT: Sure.

J.R.: How often do you give your phone number out?

BERT: Not usually, nowadays.

J.R.: Okay. It was at Badlands.

BERT: Oh?

J.R. (*chuckling*): You gonna tell me you never go there? Gonna tell me you *never* stand by the men's room so's you can watch the guys piss? I've seen you there since, you know. That's a bad habit you have: it's not nice to watch guys piss.

BERT (*laughs*): So? *I* think it's nice.

J.R.: Y'know what you deserve?

BERT: No.

J.R.: Next time you're a bad boy?

BERT: What?

J.R.: Hmm. Maybe we should.

BERT: What?

J.R.: Grab you and shove you into that urinal trough and piss all over you. Spread the word in the bar that the party's in the men's room: the pig's wallowing in piss, come 'n give 'm a load of hot, steaming piss. Think you'd like that?

BERT (*laughs*): Yeah. (*Wistfully.*) Once, once upon a time, days gone by.

J.R.: Oh, it's safe to get pissed *on*, Bert. Probably.

BERT (*seriously*): Don't know if I could control myself.

J.R. (*black English*): Shut yo mouth, chile. (*Own voice.*) Pun intended.

BERT: Hmm.

(*Pause.*)

J.R. (*resuming the game*): But you *deserve* it, for being naughty. For public *lewdness*.

(*They both laugh; both are playing with themselves.*)

BERT: So I gave you my number.

J.R.: And don't remember doing it.

BERT: Remind me.

J.R.: *Just* the number, on a scrap of paper.

BERT: I *don't* usually do that.

J.R.: You seemed to be feeling especially good that evening.

BERT: You remember when?

J.R.: Yup.

BERT: Well?

J.R.: February. Your birthday.

BERT (*recalling getting wrecked that evening; nodding his head*): Ooooh . . .

J.R.: February 14th, to be exact, in case you don't remember.

BERT (*laughs*): You gettin' fresh with me, boy?

J.R.: Nossir. Just wanna be courteous, friendly, helpful, and obedient.

BERT (*laughs*): So remind me who you are.

J.R.: I was the one wearing jockey shorts.

BERT: That's a big help. What d'you look like?

J.R.: Real stunner. Absolutely unforgettable.

BERT: Shut up. Tell me.

J.R.: Oh, sort of average, not bad looking. Dark hair, regulation moustache. Stand a bit under six feet tall, body in pretty good shape. The standard man-of-your-dreams type, just like thousands of others, Bert, baby. *

BERT: Must've been *something* special. I don't usually give out my number like that.

J.R.: So you keep saying. Hell, you'd need a social secretary! (*Camping.*) "I'm sorry, Bert has his hands *full* right now. Can I put you on *hold?*"

BERT (*laughs*): So's that all the information you're gonna give me?

J.R.: That's all you'll ever know.

BERT: What about a name? I've gotta call my little brother something.

J.R.: You can call me J.R.

BERT: J.R.

J.R.: Yeah.

(*Pause.*)

BERT (*switching gears; erotic*): So what'ya been up to, J.R.? My little brother been gettin' into trouble?

J.R. (*immediately picking up on* BERT's *tone*): I didn't do nothin'.

BERT: Yeah? What's that sticky stuff on your jockey shorts, then?

J.R. (*guilty*): I dunno.

BERT: You been playin' with yourself?

J.R. (*he is, of course*): No . . .

BERT: That's good, 'cause if I ever catch you doin' that, I'm gonna have to take you out to the woodshed, you understand?

J.R.: I . . . I . . . it's nothin'. Okay? Just forget about it.

BERT: You sound guilty as all hell, boy. Maybe I'd better take a closer look. Pull your jeans down, J.R.

* J.R.'s description of himself may or may not be true in part or whole. Some of the audience will pick up on the fact that he is omitting mention of what must be the most obvious aspect of his appearance. If J.R. is played by a black or Asian actor, an additional problematic irony will arise, in the play as in our community. N.B.: Badlands is a racially mixed bar.

J.R.: No, I—I don' wanna.

BERT: 'Cause if I find you've been *lying* to me—

J.R.: Hey! Leggo-a-me! *Leggo!*

BERT: Lyin' to me about playing with yourself—

J.R.: I *didn't!* I *didn't!*

BERT: Yeah? Well, what's *that,* then, huh? Sticky and cold, huh? Smells like cum, boy, smells like boy-cum—

J.R.: No!

BERT: You shot your cum in your jockey shorts 'cause you were playin' with yourself, and then you *lied* to me about it.

J.R.: No!

BERT: Gonna *tan* your *ass,* J.R.

J.R. (*really excited*): No! I didn't mean to!

BERT: Didn't mean to *lie* to me? Don't sass me, boy! Don't you tell me no!

J.R.: I'm sorry, sir.

BERT: Not as sorry as you're *gonna* be, boy! I'll give you ten counts to get to that woodshed and get your pants down to your ankles. You understand?

J.R.: Yessir!

BERT: One! . . . Two! . . .

J.R.: I'm trying, sir! Please don't!

BERT: Three! . . . Four! . . .

J.R.: Please!

BERT: Five! . . . Six! . . . You gettin' *ready,* boy?

J.R.: Please don't, sir!

BERT: Seven!

J.R.: I said I was sorry!

BERT: Eight!

J.R. (*close*): Please! Please!

BERT: Nine!
J.R. (*cumming*): No! Nooo!

BERT (*over* J.R.'s *"Nooo!"*): Ten! You *ready,* boy?

(J.R. *doesn't answer; he is panting.*)

BERT: Hey, boy! You *ready?*

J.R. (*chuckling; panting*): Hey—uh—Bert, I—uh—shot. (*Laughs.*)

BERT: You *what?*

J.R.: I shot.

(*Pause.*)

BERT: Bad boy.

J.R.: It's *your* fault. You *made* me do it. (*Chuckles; dabs himself with his cum towel.*)

BERT: I've half a mind to beat your ass anyway, boy. (*Sexy.*) Yeah: you deserve that.

J.R. (*picking up on the possibility that* BERT *is near cumming himself*): Yeah? But—I'm sorry . . . I didn't mean to . . .

BERT (*bringing himself off intensely*): Yeah? Strap you up and whip your ass, boy. Gonna make you holler! Tan your ass so good you won't be able to sit down for a *week!*

J.R. (*into it; protesting, almost whimpering*): No! No!

BERT (*cumming*): Ah—yeah! Yeah! Ahhh . . . (*Pause. He chuckles.*)

J.R. (*chuckles*): Heyyy . . .

BERT: Yeah?

J.R.: Nothin'. (*Longish pause. Affectionately.*) Good night, Bert.

BERT (*chuckles*): Good night, J.R. You be a good boy, now, you hear?

J.R.: Yessir.

(*Pause. They both are smiling, feeling their connection. They hang up. Blackout.*)

Scene 8

As before. When the lights come up, BERT's *area is lit by the window light, and he is in bed, crying. When his phone rings, he sits up and turns on the light, and pauses, looking at the telephone. After four rings, his machine clicks on and begins its spiel, but* BERT *changes his mind suddenly and answers.*

BERT (*over the spiel*): Wait a moment—I'm here. (*Turns off machine.*) That you, J.R.?

J.R.: Yeah. Hi. Wanna play?

(*Pause.*)

BERT: Not tonight. Okay?

J.R.: Okay. (*Pause.*) You okay, brother?

BERT: Yeah. Well, not really. But I'll be okay.

J.R.: You sure?

BERT: Yeah, thanks.

(*Pause.*)

J.R.: Well . . . good night, then. I want you to know I really like my big brother.

BERT (*smiles*): I like you too, J.R. Good night.

J.R.: 'Night.

(*Pause.* J.R. *hangs up and sits thinking.* BERT *turns off his light and lies down. No blackout.*)

Scene 9

Immediately following. J.R. *re-dials and* BERT's *phone rings.* BERT *answers his phone, but does not turn on his light.*

J.R.: Hey . . . you wanna talk? I mean, just talk?

(*Pause.*)

BERT: Yeah. (*Pause.*) Yeah, I do.

J.R.: What is it, huh?

BERT (*bursting into tears silently*): It's . . . I . . . a friend, he's in the . . . (*choking*) in the hospital, and . . .

(*Pause.*)

J.R.: Is it . . . ?

(*Pause.*)

BERT (*tense sigh*): Yeah. (*Pause.*) They . . . got him on the . . . on the respirator . . .

J.R.: Oh. Yeah.

BERT: And he's . . . not gonna make it.

J.R.: I'm sorry.

BERT (*shaking with sobs*): He's . . . I've never . . . I've never seen anything so . . . he's . . . he's . . . Shit! He's so thin I didn't recognize him, and that fucking machine, it's like pumping him up and down, it's . . . *obscene.* He's . . . awful, he's sweating, his skin's . . . like *clay* . . .

J.R.: Yeah. (*Bites his lip.*) Yeah, yeah. I know.

BERT (*collecting himself a bit*): I've never . . . (*Sighs tensely.*) He's such a beautiful guy . . . he *was* . . . oh shit, *shit!*

J.R.: I wish I could hold you, put my arms around you, you know?

BERT: Yeah, I wish you could, too.

J.R.: Let you nestle your head into my arms, against my chest.

BERT: Yeah.

J.R.: Let you cry.

BERT: I'd . . . like that.

J.R.: It's so fucking hard, so fucking hard.

(*Pause.*)

BERT: Look . . . I want to tell you, okay? I want to tell you about this guy, I mean: I mean the way he *was*, 'cause he was a beautiful guy. Is that okay?

J.R.: Sure. I'd like to hear. Tell me.

BERT: He's . . . okay, well his name is David, and I guess all I really have to say about him is . . . he's a *decent guy.* And beautiful, too, you know—not because he was any movie-idol type, not because he was a muscle builder or anything, but . . . because it was like there was a light inside him which made him strong, gentle . . . kind. *That* kind of beauty, you know: sexy, sure—sexy as anything, but *more*, too, and *all together.*

J.R.: Yeah?

BERT: Yeah, and . . . well, like I said: decent. *Nobody* deserves what—what he's going through, I know, nobody. But . . . ! It just makes me *sick*, inside, because it's so fucking *unfair!* He came to San Francisco—you really want to hear this?

J.R.: Sure. If you want to tell me.

(*Pause.*)

BERT: I do. He . . . well, like a *lot* of other guys, he left the Midwest. I know it's a joke, people put down the Castro for being Midwest, but it *isn't*, really: it *isn't a joke.* Okay, so David cuts hair, and I know that's a joke, too, a cliché—but he set himself up in business and he did well enough for himself, and that's not a joke either: he had to fight to have his own life the way he wanted it. That's how I knew him first, see, he cut my hair, and, well, sure . . . he *did* a lot of his customers, of course, right there in the barber's chair. He was a hot guy, and . . . lots of fun and . . . sweet, beautiful. And horny. (*Nearly in tears.*) And fuck it all, *there's nothing wrong with that!*

J.R.: I didn't say there was.

BERT: Yeah, I know—no, you didn't. But, you know, everyone's putting it down nowadays. (*Mimicking.*) "The party's over! The party's over!" (*Own voice.*) Well, fuck it all, *no! That wasn't just a party!* It was more: a *lot* more, at least to some of us, and it was *connected* to other parts of our lives, *deep* parts, *deep* connections. I'm not gonna deny that drugs were part of it, and I *know* for some guys it was—or it turned out to be—hell. But that's not the whole story. For me, for a *lot* of guys, it was . . . *living*; and it was *loving.* Yeah: *It was loving*, even if you didn't know whose cock it was in the dark, or whose asshole you were sucking. And *I don't regret a single moment of it: not one.*

(*Pause.*)

J.R.: Yeah.

(*Pause.*)

BERT: I'm not sorry.

(*Pause.*)

J.R.: Bert?

BERT: Yeah?

(*Pause.*)

J.R.: I was in Vietnam. I don't want to talk about that now, except to say I nearly died there. And for what? What would have been the purpose? Greed, stupidity: that's what I gave . . . a part of my life for. And some of the things I saw there: I still see them sometimes when I close my eyes: like they were so terrible, so *evil*, they burned into my eyes and I'll see them as long as I live. I'm not going to tell you about them. I don't tell anyone. But take my word.

BERT: Yeah.

J.R.: I just wanna say: I know, I *saw* what . . . "immoral" means, I learned what "immoral" means. And that's why nobody but nobody tells me I'm immoral if I love a man, if I love a hundred men in one night: if I love sucking ass, if I love licking boots, if I love taking piss from a guy's cock, or if I have a quickie blow job in the Union Square men's room: all that is *good*—really, truly, *basically* good. Something in me *knows* that, knows that it's just the exact opposite of the evil I've seen.

(*Pause.*)

BERT: Yeah.

J.R.: But now I'm scared.

BERT: Yeah.

J.R.: And you're scared.

BERT: Yeah. Yeah, I am.

(*Pause.*)

J.R.: A friend was telling me yesterday: when he beats off? He fantasizes it's four or five years ago, *before* . . . He can't even *fantasize* he's doing what he wants to do with another man unless it's before . . . all this.

BERT: Yeah. I understand.

J.R.: He's scared, too.

BERT: Yeah.

J.R.: So what does that leave us, huh? Not much.

BERT: No.

(*Pause.*)

J.R.: Not much, except what's maybe best, and what *can't* be destroyed: caring for each other. Even if we're . . . (*long pause*) doomed. Loving can't be killed: it's stronger. That's why even if I *can't* hold you in my arms, just telling you I want to . . .

BERT: Helps. It helps me.

J.R.: Helps me, too.

(*Pause.*)
BERT: You're a beautiful guy.

(*Pause.*)

J.R.: Maybe we're the lucky ones.

BERT: Maybe.

(*Pause.*)

J.R.: You all right now?

BERT: Better. Thanks.

(*Pause.*)

J.R.: Thank you for telling me about David.

BERT: Yeah.

J.R.: Good night, brother.

BERT: Good night. (*Slight pause.* BERT *hangs up, and the lights in his area go out as he snuggles down into bed.*)

J.R. (*eyes closed, head raised, clutching the telephone receiver; bitterly*): Yeah. I'm beautiful. I'm one of the lucky ones. I didn't have my face blasted away.

(*Pause.* J.R. *hangs up. Blackout.*)

Scene 10

As before. Window light on BERT's *area; another man is with him in bed, dozing.* BERT *answers his phone immediately, and talks quietly.*

BERT: J.R.?

J.R.: Yeah. Hi.

BERT: Hi.

J.R.: How're you doing?

BERT: I'm okay.

(*Pause.*)

J.R.: And . . . David?

BERT: He's okay, too. Now.

(*Pause.*)

J.R.: Yeah.

(*Pause.*)

BERT: Thanks for calling. Thanks for asking.

J.R.: I'm sorry.

BERT: We're all in this together. No use being sorry.

J.R.: Yeah. I know.

BERT: But . . . it's good to hear your voice. Thanks, really.

J.R.: Kisses and hugs. (*Kisses the receiver silently.*)

BERT: Same to you, buddy.

J.R.: Good night.

BERT: Gimme a call tomorrow, okay? Can you?

J.R.: Sure.

BERT: Thanks.

(J.R. *kisses the receiver again and hangs up. Blackout.*)

Scene 11

As before. BERT *is reading a porn magazine in bed and playing with himself. When the phone rings, he takes a final toke on the joint he has been smoking, and then answers the phone; as he talks he holds the receiver by his chin while he pinches out the end of the roach.*

BERT: 'Lo—J.R.?

J.R.: Yeah. How're you doing?

BERT: 'Ts okay.

J.R.: Wanna play?

BERT: Wanna talk. For a bit. 'Ts okay? Then maybe play.

J.R.: Sure.

BERT: Don't mean heavy talk. Just I like hearing your voice, and I want to feel good, talk about good stuff.

J.R. (*laughs*): What do you mean?

BERT: I wanna know more about you.

J.R.: You sure?

BERT: Yeah.

J.R.: Like what?

BERT: Like what does the J.R. stand for?

J.R.: James Reilly.

BERT: That your whole name?

J.R.: No. First and middle.

BERT: You're not going to tell me more?

J.R.: No.

BERT: Why not?

J.R.: I like anonymous encounters.

BERT: This is getting to be more than an encounter, J.R.

J.R. (*laughs*): A friend of mine, you know—I kid you not—he's had an ongoing anonymous encounter with a guy for *fifteen years* now. A long-term relationship, see, but a relationship between strangers. A guy he cruised on the tram— the old green blimps? Well, he'd been cruising this guy, mornings and evenings, to and from work, for months and months, maybe even a year. Until the inevitable happened: MUNI broke down in the tunnel, the car was jam-packed, this guy was standing pressed against my friend, who was seated, you see, and, well, you can imagine the rest. The next week the guy followed my friend home, got his address and name from the mailbox—so I guess it isn't *entirely* anonymous after all, not *quite*—and called him up, asked if he could come over. My friend said sure. And they've been going at it for fifteen years now. But they've never said a word to each other, *not a word*, except over the phone, and that's just the bare minimum: yes or no.

BERT (*amused*): Ha!

J.R.: An anonymous relationship. They don't know anything about each other.

BERT: I love it. It's—San Francisco.

J.R. (*laughs*): Yup. And *nobody* can say it's without meaning: just that both parties have voluntarily chosen to limit the *medium* for meaning—limit it to what's good, limit it to sex. At least I think we can *assume* it's good, after fifteen years.

BERT (*laughs*): I guess so. So you're not telling me your last name?

J.R.: Why should I? What's it to you?

BERT: Well, tell me just a bit more about yourself.

J.R. (*calculatingly*): I will, if *you* tell me a story.

BERT: A story?

J.R.: About San Francisco. And anonymous love. I'm writing a history, a history of love among strangers.

BERT (*laughs*): I gotta think. But you tell me first.

J.R.: I just did.

BERT: No, I mean more—about you. Who are you?

J.R.: What the hell do you mean?

BERT: You know.

J.R.: Well, I'm your little brother, for one thing.

BERT: I already know *that*. What . . . well, what do you do?

J.R.: About what?

BERT: Stop teasing. Who *are* you? What . . . work do you do?

J.R.: Are you a New Yorker? Don't answer.

BERT: Why?

J.R.: Well, just the very *idea* that a person *is* his job.

BERT: Oh, come on.

J.R.: All right. I'll tell you. This might surprise you, but I'm a—historian. And a liar, which is the same thing. Now that I've told you what I "am," you're free to believe what you want. I admit I've told you some lies.

BERT: But I know some things about you anyway.

J.R.: So tell me.

BERT: What I do?

J.R.: No! I don't want to know! I already know more than I want to know about *that.*

BERT: Oh? How?

J.R.: Well, I have the advantage—or disadvantage—of knowing, and remembering, what you look like. And so, I am sorry to say, I've seen you in a three-piece suit, coming out of the MUNI station and walking down Castro Street with that beautiful horde of guys, all obviously on their way home from nine-to-five jobs downtown. I don't want to know anything more about *that.* I prefer to think of you in your Badlands drag, or your Ambush drag—'cause I've seen you there, too.

BERT: Oh?

J.R.: Yeah. We pissed together there a couple of weeks ago. I thought it was a hoot. Nice dick you got.

BERT: I don't remember.

J.R.: Your dick? Well, it's—

BERT: No, *you.*

J.R.: Typical, typical.

BERT: No, I don't remember who I piss with.

J.R.: Just their dicks, huh? You didn't exactly look me in the face.

BERT: Well, next time say hello.

J.R.: Not on your life. Tell me a story.

BERT: Oh . . . yeah.

J.R.: Yeah?

BERT: Well . . . okay. I know. This is a true story.

J.R.: I'll put it into my history of San Francisco. And that's the truth.

BERT: Okay.

J.R.: Just make it hot.

BERT: It's not kinky, just . . . nice.

J.R.: Okay. Go on. Just remember I'm playing with myself. (*He is.*)

BERT: Okay. It was quite a few years ago, I guess, because I was still living on O'Farrell Street, you know: the edge of the Tenderloin. And because I remember it was the first time I ever saw anyone wearing a Walkman. Maybe it was 1979, or around then. But anyway: it was one of our pretty, pretty afternoons— sunny, breezy, air *so* clear, you know—and I was walking down Hyde Street from the CALA at California, carrying my groceries home, and there in front of me, walking down the hill too, was a gorgeous guy, bopping to the music he was listening to on his Walkman. *Pretty* guy: smiling eyes, full of energy and . . . happiness. Nice beard. Nice, hairy legs—he was wearing shorts. So I caught up with him at the corner, waiting to cross, and he caught my eye and smiled at me and took off his headphones and didn't say anything but put the headphones on me so I could hear. And we walked down the hill that way, hand-in-hand in fact, and connected by the wire from the headphones. And we were both turning on—just out of happiness, or it seems like that's what it was, now. You still with me?

J.R.: Yes, I am. Tell me more.

BERT: Well, I smoked a bit before you called, and I know I can get talking more than *anyone* wants to listen.

J.R.: This one wants to listen. Go on.

BERT: Okay. Where was I?

J.R.: On Hyde Street, hand-in-hand with a hunk and his Walkman.

BERT: Yeah, yeah, yeah. So . . . we got to O'Farrell and I turned to him and took off the headphones to hand them to him, but he said just: "Take me home. I'll give you the gentlest fuck west of the Mississippi." Just that.

J.R.: So? Did you? Did he?

BERT: Are you kidding? This was 1979. And I was *hard*. And so was he.

J.R.: And?

BERT: And I took him up to my apartment and I didn't even put the groceries away: we went straight to the bedroom and stripped, and I pulled down the Murphy bed and we cuddled and played around for a bit before he started working on my ass. (BERT *starts playing with himself.*) He rolled me over onto my stomach and told me just to relax, and he started with a backrub, which was just heaven; then he worked his way down, of course. He was kneeling between my legs, and he worked my asshole with Lube for the longest time, getting it to relax so there was just no tightness, no fear, just letting go so that I almost dozed off, even though I was hard—like a morning dream when you don't have to wake up and get out of bed, but can just lie there and feel good. Let's see: then he lowered

himself onto me and slid his cock in all the way, but so gently and smoothly—
and I was so relaxed—that there was not even a bit of pain. I don't think my ass
has ever felt so sensitive. His cock felt *warm* in me, and *full*, so nice and full.

(J.R. *is close to cumming, but he is quiet about his panting as he listens.*)

BERT: So he began sliding in and out of me, in and out, so gently!—so gently! And
he kissed me behind my ear and he sucked my shoulder, and we both sort of
giggled because we were feeling so good together. He was right, absolutely right:
I've never had such a gentle, *sensitive* fuck, before or after, and he must have
gone at it twenty minutes at the *very* least, just sliding his cock back and forth so
steadily inside my ass, and both of us on the edge of cumming, but not tensing
up to it, but relaxing instead, you know, and letting the feeling, the tingle, go
through all of our bodies, and feeling so good to be so close, body to body. And
then he whispered in my ear: "You're gonna feel me cum inside you"—and I
did: I felt his cum pulse up his shaft inside my ass, I could count the pulses—

(J.R. *cums silently.*)

BERT: —and it felt warm and good, one of the most wonderful things I think I've ever
felt, one of the most wonderful *connections* I think I've ever had with another
person, one of the most beautiful acts of love I think I have ever known. And
then we rolled over onto our sides, and he was still in me, and we just lay there
for a bit. And that was all: we kissed and hugged and said goodbye, and for the
rest of the day and all that evening I *glowed*, I just *glowed*, like he was still
making love to me.

J.R.: Woooo . . . that was *nice*. (*Dabs himself off.*)

BERT: You liked that?

J.R.: I came.

BERT (*laughs*): Really?

J.R.: Would I lie to you? Of *course* I did.

BERT: Well, I know it's possible to get a good fuck anywhere in the world—I guess it
is, or used to be. But there was something about the . . . *happiness* of this guy,
the happiness, and the . . . easy, open, clean *naturalness* of the whole thing,
that makes the story—San Francisco, for me.

J.R.: I agree. Absolutely.

BERT: *And it was love*, even if it was only for a few hours.

J.R.: Which is frequently best.

BERT: Yup. (*Laughs. Pause.*) Hey, thanks.

J.R.: For what?

BERT: For reminding me.

J.R.: Of what?

BERT: No: for getting me to remember—that it was love. And . . . a virus can't change that: can't change that fact.

(*Pause.*)

J.R.: No, it can't.

(*Pause.*)

BERT: Thanks. Really.

J.R.: Kisses and hugs, brother.

BERT (*little laugh*): Same to you. (*Softly.*) Hey . . . good night.

J.R.: Thanks for the story, Bert. (*Pause.*) Good night. (*Kisses the telephone receiver silently and hangs up. Blackout.*)

Scene 12

As before. BERT *is lit by window light, but puts his bedside light on when he answers his phone.*

BERT: 'Lo. That you, J.R.?

J.R.: Yeah. What's up? Pun intended.

BERT: Not doin' so well.

J.R.: Oh?

BERT: Flu or something. Been in bed all day, feeling rotten. (*He coughs into his pillow.*)

J.R.: I'm sorry. You gonna be okay?

BERT: Oh yeah, yeah. I never get sick for long.

J.R.: Good. (*Pause.*) Wanna talk?

BERT: Yeah. Can't get to sleep anyway, feeling sorry for myself. I'm a bad patient, I complain, so—(*Breaks off to cough into his pillow.*)

J.R.: You sure you're okay?

BERT: Yeah. Get my mind off it, I'll be okay. More than okay. Tell me a story.

J.R.: A story?

BERT: Yeah. A bedtime story.

J.R.: Like a fairy tale?

BERT: Yeah, but just the happy ending, okay?

J.R.: Hmmm.

BERT: Will you?

J.R.: I'm thinking. Give me a bit.

BERT: Okay. I—(*Coughs into his pillow.*)

J.R.: What?

(*Pause, while* BERT *coughs. Then:*)

BERT: Nothin', it's nothing. I was just going to say it doesn't have to be a dirty story . . .

J.R.: Pigs in mud?

BERT: You know. Just a bedtime story, not a playtime story. I just wanna lie here and listen to you, 'cause I've been alone all day.

J.R.: Okay. I know. This is a fantasy I used to have—to enjoy, love it—when I was a kid. For years it was my favorite fantasy, and maybe it was my first fantasy, or maybe it was a dream I had to begin with. Okay?

BERT: Sure.

J.R.: I've never told it to anyone before.

BERT: Yeah? Good. Then it'll be *our* fantasy, just ours.

J.R.: Okay, sounds good to me. So . . . (*an idea*) yeah! We'll do it *together,* so that at the end there'll be not just two of us, but *three.*

BERT: What?

J.R.: You'll see . . . yeah. It'll work. But—uh.

BERT: Yeah?

J.R.: Okay, I'll just say this: when I was a kid, I didn't know what men *did* together—I mean sexually. I *really, really* wanted to *touch* men, *be* with them, smell them, be in bed together. . . . I guess it was the *affection* I wanted. And you know? I think that's still basically it, still what I want the most.

BERT: Yeah?

J.R.: Yeah, well, we *are* being intimate here, *aren't* we? What I'm trying to say is that when I was a kid that's as far as I got in my fantasies: just into bed, because I didn't *know* there was sex, didn't know it consciously. So this is an *affectional* fantasy, but not exactly a *sexual* fantasy. See?

BERT: That's okay. That's fine with me.

J.R.: Okay. Here goes then. Let's see. How to start. (*Pause. A change of lighting and perhaps a music cue indicate that "real" time and space have dissolved, and what we now see is fantasy. J.R. puts his phone receiver down, and stands by his bed—without his crutches. During the rest of this sequence he talks directly to* BERT, *though* BERT *continues to talk only to his phone receiver; as he tells his story, J.R., "invisible" to* BERT, *eventually moves into* BERT'S *area, and sits on* BERT'S *bed, like an adult telling a child a bedtime story.*) Let's pretend I'm standing by your bed, okay?

BERT: Okay.

J.R.: And I put out my hand to you, and you take it, and you get out of bed.

BERT: Yeah.

J.R.: And then I undress you.

BERT: I *am* undressed.

J.R.: Pretend you're wearing pajamas, okay? I want to undress you.

BERT: Okay.

J.R.: So . . . I unbutton your pajama jacket and let it slip to the floor, and I pull down your pajama bottoms and you step out of them so you're standing naked.

BERT: Yeah, okay.

J.R.: Then I get undressed, too, so we're both naked. And I tell you not to be afraid: don't be afraid of anything.

BERT: Okay.

J.R.: 'Cause I'm taking you to your front door, okay? And we're going to go out, naked, okay? Don't be afraid. I'm holding your hand.

BERT: Okay.

J.R.: So: I—no, *you:* you open the door, and there, in front of us, is a beautiful, enchanted forest. Uh—this isn't your standard *Drummer* fantasy, you understand.

BERT: Go ahead. I love it.

(*Two or three times during the course of the ensuing story* BERT *coughs into his pillow.*)

J.R.: Okay. So . . . well, okay, when I was a kid I called this forest the Forbidden Forest. It's filled with terrible perils and frightful things. But we're going to go to the end of the story: all the adventures and battles and scary things are over now, done with. We're—*two* young princes, fairy-tale princes, brothers, and we're walking through the beautiful forest. It's near nightfall. The last bit of the sun hits the top of the trees, and a sudden cool breeze comes through the forest, touches our faces and combs through our hair. We're weary, terribly weary, but we have only a little bit further to go. And then there, in front of us, in the very middle of the Forbidden Forest, stands a beautiful palace, all made of smooth black marble, polished like mirror. It's very dim and looming in the dusk. The gates of the palace open magically when we approach, and we walk first through a luxuriant garden. The grand doors of the palace open before us, and we enter a great hall, lit by torches. As we walk in, torches set in the walls light up before us and are extinguished as we pass. We are being led up a black marble staircase and then down a high, gloomy hall to a chamber where a large, steaming bath has been prepared for us. We take off our clothes, and—

BERT: I thought we were naked.

J.R.: Oh—no, no. When we became princes we got princes' clothing, like Prince Charming. I always was more interested in *him* than in the fairy-tale princesses—Snow White, Cinderella, whatever. *I* identified with Sleeping *Beauty*: *I* wanted that kiss.

(BERT *laughs.*)

J.R.: You enjoying this?

BERT (*perhaps a bit surprised that he is; nodding*): Yeah.

J.R.: Okay. I'll go on. We . . . take off our clothes and bathe. We wash each other. And the water takes away our weariness and leaves us . . . light, and content. And when we get out of the bath, there are fresh clothes put out for us, and we dress each other. And then a strange, distant music—very sweet, very pure— calls us back down the high, gloomy hall and down the black marble stairs to the banquet hall. It, too, is lit by torchlight, and there are three places set at the huge, old table—set for a plain supper of clear, steaming broth and fresh bread, and red wine in golden goblets. We take our seats across from each other, knowing we are to wait for the appearance of our host, and it turns out that he has been the music we have heard: the sweet, gentle music . . . coalesces, comes together and becomes visible at the head of the table, and there he stands, a beautiful man, without age, smiling. And when we see him, the last bit of fear we had in all our wonder just melts away, and we know we are safe at last, and that his magic is good. And as we take our supper we tell him of all the adventures and perils and . . . *bitter* sorrows we had journeying through the Forbidden Forest, to find his palace; and he questions us about each adventure, peril, and sorrow, and from the answers he brings forth from us we understand that each one, even the most terrible, was a lesson on our journey to the palace; and we understand that we ourselves were lessons for others whose paths crossed ours in the Forest. And when all is over and all is told, it is late, and we, the three of us, rise from the table and ascend a spiral staircase, round and round, up a tower. He leads us, holding a torch. And at the top of the tower is the bedchamber, with a large, old royal bed. The three of us undress and part the bedcurtains and lie down together in each others' arms—we three beautiful men, two princely brothers and a man made of magic and music. We hold each other and we kiss (J.R. *leans over* BERT *and kisses him;* BERT *still relates only to* his telephone receiver), and we drift off to sleep. (*Long pause.*) And that's all. (J.R. *returns to his bed and picks up his telephone receiver; the lighting indicates a return to "real" time and space.*) That's the happy ending.

BERT: Sleep?

J.R.: Yeah.

BERT: Sounds good to me.

J.R. (*lightening*): Oh, in the morning we get up and run through the woods naked, bathe in the crystal spring, pluck golden pears in the magic garden—that sort of thing.

BERT (*laughs*): Sounds great. (*Pause.*) It's been such a *long* time since anyone told me a bedtime story. Not since I was a kid. (*Coughs into his pillow.*) Thank you.

J.R.: Not too unbutch for you?

BERT: No. I loved it.

J.R.: Good. (*Little laugh. Pause.*) Think you'll be able to get to sleep now?

BERT: Yeah. I think so. (*Coughs into his pillow.*) Call again soon, huh?

(*Pause.*)

J.R. (*regretfully*): I'm going to be out of town for a week or so.

BERT (*disappointed*): Yeah?

J.R.: Yeah. Sorry. Work. New York.

BERT: Ugh.

J.R.: Well, I'll give you a call, just to see how you're doing.

BERT: Thanks. I'm not an invalid, you know.

J.R.: I didn't mean that. Maybe I'll call just because I'm horny for you, okay?

BERT (*laughs*): Okay.

J.R.: And I can tell you, you better get yourself ready for some brother-to-brother, sweaty, down-and-dirty *pig* sex, you understand?

BERT: Yeah?

J.R.: Enough of this nicey-nice-lovey-dovey stuff: I'm gonna make you eat ass and suck my balls and drink my piss like you never have before, you get me?

BERT: Hot, throbbing cocks? Hard, pounding muscles?

J.R.: You got it. Meanwhile, you can work on those jockey shorts you started for me: get 'em real stiff and crusty for me, okay? I wanna dream about you doin' that when I'm in New York.

BERT: Okay.

J.R.: Okay. Good night. (*Kisses the receiver silently.*)

BERT: Good night.

(*They hang up. Blackout.*)

Scene 13

BERT's *phone rings. The window light comes up in his area;* J.R.'s *area remains in darkness.* BERT's *bed is empty. We hear his machine answer the call: mellow music, and then* BERT's *voice, sounding a bit drunk and/or stoned, saying* "Good evening— or good whatever time of day it is you're calling, though it's evening now as I record this message for you, and a beautiful evening it is. An especially good evening to my little brother, if it's you calling; I'm really sorry to miss your call, if it's you 'cause I miss you and I want you to know—" *and then a click and the beep. We then hear, coming over the machine,* J.R. *laughing and saying:* "I miss you, too. Sorry you're out. But I'll be home Wednesday, so sit by your phone with your cock in your hand ready, okay? Kisses and hugs." *And then we hear him hang up, and the machine clicks off.*

Scene 14

Lights up on J.R. *in bed, playing with himself and dialing; the window light comes up on* BERT's *area, but his bed is still empty. We hear his machine answer the call.*

BERT'S ANSWERING MACHINE (*Judy Garland singing*):

> You really shouldn't have done it,
> You hadn't any right.
> I really shouldn't have let you
> Kiss me.
> And although it was wrong
> I never was strong,
> So as long as you've begun it,
> And you know you shouldn't have done it . . .
> Oh, do it again—

BERT (*voice on the answering machine*): Please leave me a message. I'll get back to you as soon as I can. Thanks.

J.R.: Hold on, brother. I'll call you back in a minute. (*Hangs up. Lights out in* BERT's *area only.* J.R. *continues to play with himself. No blackout.*)

Scene 15

Immediately following. J.R. is playing with himself.

J.R.: Gonna crawl into bed with my brother. Gonna snuggle next to him, huh? Gonna feel his body next to me, gonna slide my legs right down next to his, under the sheets, huh? Gonna feel *warm* and *cozy*, next to him . . . yeah. (*Long, low.*) Hey . . . I'm gettin' hard. I like being next to you, Bert, I like your warmth, huh? I like your smell, next to me, huh? Hey! What'ya doin'? Wrestlin'? (*Laughs.*) Yeah! Yeah! Hey, you got me *pinned down* under you! (*Starts dialing his phone, panting.*) Hey—you're not gonna . . . ? Hey, no, you leave my jockey shorts *on*! Leggo! Leggo! You're not supposed to . . . !

(*The lights do not come up on* BERT's *area. Over the speaker system we hear a phone ring three or four times.*)

J.R.: Hey! Hey! *Stop* that! It feels too good! *Stop* it! *Stop* it!

(*We hear a woman's voice answer the phone:* "Hello? Hello? Who *is* this?" *Simultaneously:*)

J.R.: You're suckin' your brother's cock! You're gonna make me shoot! I'm gonna shoot my load right down your hot—(*Suddenly realizing he has misdialed; breaking into laughter and cumming accidentally.*) Oh no! Oh shit!

(*Shaking with laughter, he hangs up; still laughing, he dabs himself off with his cum towel. No blackout.*)

Scene 16

Immediately following. J.R., still shaking with laughter, re-dials. Lights up in BERT's *area; his bed is empty, as before.*

BERT'S ANSWERING MACHINE (*Judy Garland singing*):
> You really shouldn't have done it,
> You hadn't any right.
> I really shouldn't have let you
> Kiss me.
> And although it was wrong
> I never was strong,
> So as long as you've begun it,
> And you know you shouldn't have done it . . .
> Oh, do it again—

BERT (*voice on the answering machine*): Please leave me a message. I'll get back to you as soon as I can. Thanks.

J.R. (*so convulsed with laughter it's difficult to get it out*): Shit, Bert, you're never gonna *believe* this, but (*breaks down into giggles*) I—I—no, I'll tell you later. I fucked it up. Good night, sweetheart. (*Hangs up. Blackout.*)

Scene 17

Lights up on J.R. *dialing. The window light comes up on* BERT's *area, but his bed is empty, as before.*

BERT'S ANSWERING MACHINE (*Judy Garland singing*):

>You really shouldn't have done it,
>You hadn't any right.
>I really shouldn't have let you
>Kiss me.
>And although it was wrong
>I never was strong,
>So as long as you've begun it,
>And you know you shouldn't have done it . . .
>Oh, do it again—

BERT (*voice on the answering machine*): Please leave me a message. I'll get back to you as soon as I can. Thanks.

J.R.: Just your little brother, wondering where you are. (*Hangs up; grimaces in comic puzzlement as the lights fade.*)

Scene 18

Lights up on J.R. *dialing. The window light comes up on* BERT's *area, but his bed is empty, as before.*

BERT'S ANSWERING MACHINE (*Judy Garland singing*):
>You really shouldn't have done it,
>You hadn't any right.
>I really shouldn't have let you
>Kiss me.
>And although it was wrong
>I never was strong,
>So as long as you've begun it,
>And you know you shouldn't have done it . . .
>Oh, do it again—

BERT (*voice on the answering machine*): Please leave me a message. I'll get back to you as soon as I can. Thanks.

J.R.: Hey, Bert—where are you? I asked Hank at the Badlands whether he'd seen you, and he said you hadn't been around for weeks. Can you—please give me a call? My number is 771–0725. (*Pause.*) Thanks. (*Hangs up and sits thinking as the lights fade.*)

Scene 19

Lights up on J.R. dialing. The window light comes up on BERT's *area, but his bed is empty as before.*

BERT'S ANSWERING MACHINE (*Judy Garland singing*):

You really shouldn't have done it,
You hadn't any right.
I really shouldn't have let you
Kiss me.
And although it was wrong
I never was strong,
So as long as you've begun it,
And you know you shouldn't have done it . . .
Oh, do it again—

BERT (*voice on the answering machine*): Please leave me a message. I'll get back to you as soon as I can. Thanks.

J.R.: Bert, it's J.R. Look, maybe it's stupid, but I'm worried about you. Would you—please give me a call—my number is 771–0725. Okay? I just wanna know you're okay. Thanks. I . . . love you. Please call. (*Hangs up. Sighs tensely and chews his thumbnail and fights back tears as the lights fade.*)

Scene 20

Lights up on J.R. dialing. The lights do not come up on BERT's *area. Over the speaker system we hear two rings, and then a mechanical voice:* "We're sorry. The number you have reached. Two. Six. Eight. Five. Four. Oh. Nine. Has been disconnected. Please check that you have dialed correctly. Two. Six. Eight—" J.R. *hangs up, stunned. He sobs convulsively as the lights fade out.*

J.R.: Oh no. Oh no. Oh no . . .

AS IS

by

William M. Hoffman

IN MEMORY OF:

R.A.

S.A.

Fortunato Arico

M.B.

Michael Baseleon

Francis Brady

Stephen Buker

Phil Carey

Gregory Y. Connell

Daniel Corcoran

Wilfredo Davilla

Arthur Ellenbogen

Bill Elliot

Tom Ellis

Timothy Farrell

Christian Fincke

Neil Flanagan

George Harris

Mark Johnson

Charles Ludlam

Ed Lynch

André Mathis

J. J. Mitchell

John Murphy

Pierre Murue

Arthur Naftal

Stephen Pender

Glenn Person

Russell Redmond

L.S.

Tony Serchio

Giulio Sorrentino

Larry Stanton

David Summers

Rick Wadsworth

Larry Waurin

Stuart White

SPECIAL THANKS

Jerry Vezzuso, Beth Allen, Nestor Almendros, John Bishop, George Boyd, Victor Bumbalo, John Corigliano, David Courier, Penny Dashinger, Barry Davidson, East End Gay Organization, Gay Men's Health Crisis, Barbara Grandé-LeVine, Jay Harris, Stephen Harvey, Joel Honig, Reed Jones, Daniel Irvine, David Kapihe, Robert Kubera, Rodger McFarlane, Terrence McNally, Barbara Myers, Claris Nelson, Constance Mary O'Toole, Kent Paul, Candida Scott Piel, David Richardson, Luis Sanjurjo, Mary Scarborough, June Stein, Paul Theobald, Dr. Kenneth Unger, Tobin Wheeler, Lanford Wilson, the New York Foundation for the Arts, Albert Poland, and Marshall W. Mason.

As It Was

"It must be the combination of quiche and leather," I think I joked to a friend over the phone the first time I heard about the mysterious new disease attacking gay men. It was 1980, '81, I'm not sure. I think it was early spring and I was sitting in my office, drinking my first decaffeinated espresso of the morning. I had just finished reading the previous day's New York Times. I like to have my news a little stale so I don't get too alarmed at the state of the world. I told my friend the article was absurd: a disease capable of distinguishing between homo- and heterosexual men? Come on.

At the time, I was in the midst of writing Act One of the libretto to A Figaro for Antonia, which the Metropolitan Opera had commissioned, and when I wasn't writing I was jogging. So, for a period, I was totally immersed in work. When I came back up for air it registered that my roommate's best friend, Tim, was dying in a hospital in San Francisco. He had a pneumonia that antibiotics couldn't touch, and wild viral infections of the brain. He finally fell into a coma and succumbed.

But was it really surprising, I asked myself, that Tim would get ill? A terrific person, generous, funny, warm, but definitely in the fast lane. And when Freddy went into the hospital I told myself that he had been looking for trouble: I mean, he practically lived at the gay bathhouses. People like me were not going to come down with AIDS. I wasn't going to the baths. I didn't drink or take drugs. And I was running twenty to thirty miles a week. I felt invulnerable.

And then Larry took sick: mild ailments that wouldn't clear up, not bothersome enough to stop him from running the marathon faster than I could conceive of doing. Larry was younger than I, and he didn't drink or take drugs. A few months later he died.

And then Brian, who lived over in the East Village. And then George, the kid from the early Caffe Cino days of Off Off Broadway. And then Freddy the cellist. And then that guy who ran the flower shop on Sixth—what was his name?

I was busy writing a comic opera as daily the news got worse. My close friend Stephen came down with a chronic case of swollen glands, which was labeled an "AIDS-related complex." It seemed as if the disease was closing in on me personally. I was reminded of the pre-Salk-vaccine polio epidemic of my childhood, when you avoided movie theaters and swimming pools. I remembered Wally, the boy

496

upstairs who liked to bully me, until infantile paralysis made him weak and stupid, and I remembered classmates who suddenly stopped coming to school.

But during the polio epidemic, as during the Tylenol and Legionnaire's Disease scares, the media and the government committed themselves wholeheartedly to the side of the victims. In the early eighties, with few exceptions, the main concern of people outside the gay community was reassuring themselves that it was only happening to "them," and not to "us." I felt isolated from society in a way I never had before.

As the mortality figures mounted, and as I heard stories of people with AIDS being abandoned by friends and families, mistreated by health workers, and evicted from apartments (in one case being thrown from a window), stories of the Holocaust came to my mind. Most of my family in Europe had perished during the war. As far as I know they never made it to the concentration camps, but were murdered on the street by their Polish and Latvian neighbors. I knew intellectually that the epidemic was *not* the Holocaust, but I had no other experience of mass death and public indifference and brutality to compare it with.

I was writing about the rebellion of Figaro and the tragedy of Marie Antoinette when I learned that my favorite uncle, Wolf, had cancer. And my father was not recovering from his stroke as fully as I had hoped. All around me there was illness and death. I fell into a depression.

So, sometime in 1982, as a sort of a therapy, I started to express my feelings on paper. I decided to write a play about a man named Rich—a writer and runner—who comes down with AIDS; his former lover, Saul; and their friends and families.

I did my research. I visited friends who had the disease; I talked with a hospice worker; I went to support groups; I attended lectures; I made field trips to the Gay Men's Health Crisis (the most important organization dealing with the disease in New York City); I spent hours eavesdropping in gay bars, taking the public pulse.

I was willing to go to any lengths for my play, except to imagine myself having AIDS. I was not afraid of contracting the disease through casual physical contact with those who had it. I was well aware that AIDS is transmitted only by an exchange of body fluids. But on a deep irrational level, I was terrified of catching it by identifying with those who had it.

Consequently, for a long period, my central characters, Rich and Saul, were shadowy and undeveloped, compared with the background figures. But one day I realized the depth of my fear and asked God to protect me as I wrote the play. He did.

All along my characters cracked jokes, which I tried to suppress. People were in the process of expiring, and here I was laughing. I mean, this was supposed to be a *serious* play. Well, I had to do something to keep my spirits up, I rationalized.

Half hoping to depress myself, I'd call up my uncle, and to my chagrin he'd make me smile with some reminiscence of the Yiddish theater. (He was a playwright and poet, like me.) And my father was always eager for a joke, the dirtier the better—and he was in his eighties.

I was having dinner with my friend Constance Mary O'Toole, who was a hospice worker at St. Vincent's Hospital in Greenwich Village, in the heart of New York's gay community, when it finally dawned on me that maybe humor was a key to my play.

She said, "We tell a lot of jokes in my line of work." I also began to realize that among the people with AIDS that I was meeting, those with a sense of humor were doing better than those without.

I permitted the play to be funny. I found that audiences at the Circle Repertory Company, where I was workshopping sections of the piece as I wrote them, responded to the humor. It enabled them to accept the pain of the sadder material.

Encouraged by my director Marshall W. Mason and producer John Glines, I also allowed the spirit of A *Figaro for Antonia* to infiltrate *As Is*. I asked myself, "Why should I write a totally realistic play, when I take extravagant liberties with time and space in musical theater? Why can't I allow my characters to speak eloquently, when I'm planning to let them do that at the Met?"

By the time we moved from our Off Broadway home at the Circle Rep to the Lyceum Theater on Broadway, the good humor and the good spirits of some of the people with AIDS that I had met, their lovers and families, people like Connie O'Toole, and my family (my father and uncle died in 1984) had completely subverted the depression that prompted the writing of the play.

Facing my own worst fears has made me feel . . . What do I feel now? Sad at the loss of friends. Frustrated by my powerlessness over a force of nature. Angry at those who have the power to help and won't. But I'm pretty comfortable with people who have AIDS. I'm sane on the subject of my own health. And when I'm frightened in this time of trouble, I'm loving to myself.

—*William M. Hoffman*

As Is was developed in the Circle Repertory Company playwrighting and directing workshops under the leadership of Daniel Irvine. It was directed by George Boyd.

The present script is of the June 1987 revival at the Circle Repertory Company, directed by Michael Warren Powell.

As Is was first presented by the Circle Repertory Company and The Glines, at the Circle Repertory Company, New York City, March 10, 1985.

The play opened at the Lyceum Theatre, May 1, 1985. It was produced by John Glines/Lawrence Lane, Lucille Lortel, and The Shubert Organization (associate producer Paul A. Kaplan). Directed by Marshall W. Mason; settings by David Potts; lighting by Dennis Parichy; costumes by Michael Warren Powell; sound by Chuck London Media/Stewart Warner; production stage manager Fred Reinglas.

The cast, in order of appearance, for both productions:

HOSPICE WORKER	Claris Erickson
RICH	Jonathan Hogan
SAUL	Jonathan Hadary
CHET	Steven Gregan
LILY	Lily Knight
BROTHER	Ken Kliban
BUSINESS PARTNER	Claris Erickson
PICKUP 1	Ken Kliban
PICKUP 2	Lou Liberatore
CLONE 1	Mark Myers
CLONE 2	Lou Liberatore
CLONE 3	Steven Gregan
BARTENDER	Ken Kliban
MARTY	Mark Myers
VINNIE	Steven Gregan
PWA 1	Mark Myers
PWA 2	Lily Knight
PWA 3	Ken Kliban
PWA 4	Lou Liberatore
PAT	Lou Liberatore
BARNEY	Ken Kliban
NURSE	Claris Erickson
HOSPITAL WORKER	Lou Liberatore

Also: Doctors, TV Commentator (Prerecorded), Average People, Drug Dealers and Customers

PRODUCTION NOTE

In approaching the original production of *As Is*, I felt it was important to find a visual stage life for the play that permitted the freedom of time and place that the text suggests. David Potts, the designer, and I came up with an open stage that suggested simultaneously the stature of the classical Greek theater and the frankness of Brecht, and still allowed the audience, with a little imagination, to see the realistic studio/apartment of a New York photographer. I feel it is important that the actors remain on stage as much as possible, to witness as a community the events of the play in which they do not participate as characters. The audience must be kept from feeling "safe" from this subject, so the actors of the "chorus" must act as a bridge between the fictional characters and the real theater event, and also as an unconventional kind of "threat"—keeping the audience aware that entertaining as the play may be, the subject is deadly. The desired effect is to assist the audience in a catharsis, as they are required to contemplate our common mortality.

—*Marshall W. Mason*

The "Red Death" had long devastated the country. No pestilence had ever been so fatal, or so hideous. . . . The scarlet stains upon the body . . . were the pest ban which shut the victim out from the sympathy of his fellow-men. . . . But the Prince Prospero was happy and dauntless and sagacious. When his dominions were half depopulated, he summoned to his presence a thousand hale and light-hearted friends . . . and with these retired to the deep seclusion of one of his castellated abbeys. . . . A strong and lofty wall girdled it in. The wall had gates of iron. The courtiers brought furnaces and massy hammers and welded the bolts. . . . With such precautions the courtiers might bid defiance to contagion. In the meantime it was folly to grieve, or to think. The Prince had provided all the appliances of pleasure. There were buffoons, there were improvisatori, there were ballet-dancers, there were musicians, there was Beauty, there was wine. All these and security were within. Without was the "Red Death."

—EDGAR ALLAN POE, *The Masque of the Red Death*

My tale was heard, and yet it was not told;
My fruit is fallen, and yet my leaves are green;
My youth is spent, and yet I am not old;
I saw the world, and yet I was not seen;
My thread is cut, and yet is is not spun;
And now I live, and now my life is done.

—CHIDIOCK TICHBORNE, "Elegy"

CHARACTERS

SAUL
RICH

Depending on the budget and the skills and aptitudes of the performers, at least four other men and two women play the following:

HOSPICE WORKER
CHET
BROTHER
BUSINESS PARTNER
LILY
TV ANNOUNCER (Prerecorded)
DOCTORS (5)
BARTENDER
PICKUPS (2)
MARTY
VINNIE
CLONES (3)
PEOPLE WITH AIDS (4)
AVERAGE PEOPLE (6)
HOTLINE COUNSELORS (2)
NURSE
HOSPITAL WORKER
DRUG DEALERS AND CUSTOMERS (5)

Except for short exits, the actors remain onstage for the whole play. There is no intermission.

TIME

The present.

SETTING

New York City.

Stage right is SAUL's *fashionable loft space, suggested by a sofa, Barcelona chair, bench, and area rug. Upstage center is a bar; stage left, a bench.*

The HOSPICE WORKER, *a dowdy middle-aged woman, walks downstage center and addresses the audience.*

HOSPICE WORKER: Mother Superior always used to say, "Watch out for the religious cranks, Sister Veronica." When I started working for the hospice I had a touch of the crank about me. I think maybe that's why they gave me the old heave-ho from the convent. But I've kept my vow of chastity and I've made a pilgrimage to Lourdes.

My job is to ease the way for those who are dying. I've done this for the last couple of years. I work mainly here at St. Vincent's. During the day I have a boring secretarial job, which is how I support my career as a saint.

I was much more idealistic when I started. I had just left the convent. I guess I thought working with the dying would give me spiritual gold stars. I thought I'd be able to impart my great wisdom to those in need of improvement. I wanted to bear witness to dramatic deathbed conversions, see shafts of light emanating from heaven, multicolored auras hovering above the heads of those in the process of expiring. I always imagined they would go out expressing their gratitude for all I had done.

A quick joke: Did you hear about the man who lost his left side? . . . He's all *right* now. All right now. (*She laughs.*) We tell a lot of jokes in my line of work.

(*She takes her seat. Lights come up on two casually dressed men in their thirties seated in the living area.*)

RICH: You take Henry.

SAUL: Cut him in half.

RICH: You can keep him.

SAUL: What are we going to do about him?

RICH: I said he's yours.

SAUL: You found him.

RICH: I don't want him.

SAUL: Chet doesn't like cats?

RICH: I knew this would happen. Don't start in.

SAUL: We gotta get things settled.

RICH: Then let's. How 'bout if we simplify things: sell everything and split the cash.

SAUL: Even the cobalt glass?

RICH: Yes.

SAUL: And Aunt Billie's hooked rug? Say, how's she doing?

RICH: She's on medication. Sell the rug.

SAUL: I will not sell the manikin heads. I don't care what you say.

RICH: Then take them.

SAUL: And the chromium lamp? I love that lamp.

RICH: Take it.

SAUL: And the Barcelona chair?

RICH: The Barcelona chair is *mine!* (*Beat.*) Fuck it. Take it. Take everything. I won't be Jewish about it. (*He rises to go.*)

SAUL: Why didn't you warn me we were going to play Christians and Jews today? I would have worn my yellow star.

RICH: I've gotta go. (RICH *is leaving.*)

SAUL: Where're you going?

RICH: I'm not feeling so hot. Let's make it another day.

SAUL (*blocking his way*): Sit down.

RICH (*pushing his hand away*): Don't push me.

SAUL: Sorry. I don't like this any more than you, but we gotta do it. It's been six months. (*Lightening things up.*) A divorce is not final until the property settlement.

RICH: Saul . . .? (*He's about to say something important.*)

SAUL: What, Rich? (*He waits expectantly.*) What?

RICH: Never mind.

SAUL: What? . . . What? . . . You always do that!

RICH: I want the chair.

SAUL: You can have the fucking Barcelona chair if Chet wants it so bad! . . . What about the paintings? Do you want to sell the Paul Cadmus?

RICH: Yes.

SAUL: You love the Cadmus. (*Silence.*) And who's going to buy the Burgess drawings? Did you hear that Kenny had a heart attack?

RICH: We'll donate them to the Metropolitan.

SAUL: Just what they always wanted: the world's largest collection of Magic Marker hustler portraits. (RICH *nods.*)

RICH: They're yours.

SAUL: But you commissioned them. We'll split them up: I get the blonds and you get the blacks—or vice versa.

RICH: All yours.

SAUL: Then you get the Mickey Mouse collection.

RICH: Sell it.

SAUL: You don't sell collectibles. Not right now. What's with this money mania? Between the book and the catering, I thought you were doing well.

RICH: I want to build a swimming pool.

SAUL: You don't swim.

RICH: I want a Mercedes.

SAUL: You don't drive. It's Chet—he'll bankrupt you! (*Beat.*) I don't believe I said that . . . (*Sincerely.*) Your book is beautiful.

RICH: I never thanked you for the cover photograph.

SAUL (*shrugging off the compliment*): How's it selling?

RICH: Not bad—for short stories. Everyone mentions your photo. Ed White said—

SAUL: Your book is terrific. Really.

RICH: I'm glad you like it.

SAUL: One minor thing.

RICH: What's that?

SAUL: I thought the dedication was a bit much.

RICH: Why are you doing this?

SAUL: Don't you think quoting Cavafy in Greek is a little coy?

RICH: Please!

SAUL: Why didn't you just say, "To Chet, whose beautiful buns inspired these tales"?

RICH: Jesus Christ!

SAUL: I'm sorry!

(*Silence.*)

RICH: I sold the IBM stock. You were right about it. You have always been right about money. (*He hands* SAUL *a check.*) This includes the thousand I borrowed for the periodontist.

SAUL: You sure?

RICH: Take it.

SAUL: I'm not desperate for it.

RICH: It's yours.

SAUL: I don't want it.

RICH: Damn it!

SAUL (*taking the check*): Okay.

RICH: That makes us even now.

SAUL (*examining the check*): Clouds and trees.

RICH: Let's get on with this.

SAUL: Is he waiting for you downstairs? You could have told him to come up.

RICH: Shit. No! Can it. (*Beat.*) I won't be wanting the copper pots.

SAUL: Why not? When you and Chet move to your space you'll want to cook again.

RICH: I just don't want them! People change. (*Silence.*) I'm eating out a lot.

SAUL: Chet can't cook?

RICH (*deciding not to respond with a bitchy comment*): You keep the rowing machine.

SAUL: Have you lost weight?

RICH: And the trampoline.

SAUL: There's some Black Forest cake in the fridge. (SAUL *goes toward the kitchen to get the cake.*)

RICH: Stop it.

SAUL: Stop what?

RICH: Just stop.

SAUL: I can't.

RICH: We're almost through.

SAUL: I have feelings.

RICH: You have only one feeling.

SAUL: He won't make you happy.

RICH: Here we go again. (RICH *gets up to go.*)

SAUL: Don't!

RICH: Keep everything.

SAUL: I'm not myself.

RICH: Nothing is worth this.

SAUL: I've been upset.

RICH: I mean it.

SAUL: Don't go. Please. (RICH *sits. Long pause.*) I visited Teddy today at St. Vincent's. It's very depressing . . . He's lying there in bed, out of it. He's been out of it since the time we saw him. He's not in any pain, snorting his imaginary cocaine, doing his poppers. Sometimes he's washing his mother's floor, and he's speaking to her in Spanish. Sometimes he's having sex. You can see him having sex right in front of you. He doesn't even know you're there. (*Pause. Both men look down at their feet.*) Jimmy died, as you must have heard. I went out to San Francisco to be with him the last few weeks. You must have heard that, too. He was in a coma for a month. Everybody wanted to pull the plug, but they were afraid of legal complications. I held his hand. He couldn't talk, but I could see his eyelids flutter. I swear he knew I was with him. (*Pause.*) Harry has K.S., and Matt has the swollen glands. He went for tests today . . . I haven't slept well for weeks. Every morning I examine my body for swellings, marks. I'm terrified of every pimple, every rash. If I cough I think of Teddy. I wish he would die. He *is* dead. He might as well be. Why can't he die? I feel the disease closing in on me. All my activities are life and death. Keep up my Blue Cross. Up my reps. Eat my vegetables.

Sometimes I'm so scared I go back on my resolutions: I drink too much, and I smoke a joint, and I find myself at the bars and clubs, where I stand around and watch. They remind me of accounts of Europe during the Black Plague: coupling in the dark, dancing till you drop. The New Wave is the corpse look. I'm very frightened and I miss you. Say something, damn it. (*Beat.*)

RICH: I have it.

(*Immediately the lights come up on the left side of the stage.*)

CHET (*a handsome, boyish man in his early twenties*): You what?

LILY (*a beautiful woman, thirtyish*): You have what?

BROTHER (*to his wife, whom we don't see*): He has AIDS.

SAUL: I don't think that's funny.

PARTNER: Don't be ridiculous.

RICH: That's the bad news.

PARTNER: You ran the goddamned marathon.   LILY: Darling!

RICH: The good news is that I have only the swollen glands.

(*Two doctors appear in white gowns.*)

DOCTOR 1: We call it a "Pre-AIDS
Condition."

DOCTOR 2: "AIDS-related Complex."

RICH: And I've lost some weight.

SAUL: I'm in a state of shock.

LILY: Move in with me. Chet doesn't
know how to take care of you.

RICH: I tire easily. My temperature
goes up and down.

DOCTOR 1: Your suppressor cells outnumber your helper cells.

BROTHER: I don't care what he has, Betty, he's my brother.

CHET: You're my lover.

LILY: You're my buddy.

PARTNER: Rich and I started the business about a year ago. But now
word got out that Rich has this
disease. I tried to explain: he
doesn't touch the food; I do all
the cooking. But they won't listen.

BROTHER: I'm not in the habit of kissing my brother. I touched him
on the back when I arrived and
when I left.

PARTNER: Why would they? I wonder if I'd use a caterer who had AIDS.

SAUL: Doctors make mistakes all the time.

DOCTOR 2: There are a number of
highly experimental treatments.

DOCTOR 1: Of highly experimental
treatments.

LILY: I got this job.

CHET: If you don't mind, I'll sleep on the couch tonight. You've been sweating a lot.

LILY: I can't turn it down. The work is
pure dreck, and who wants to
tour Canada in January, but
they're paying a fortune. I'll be
back in four weeks.

BROTHER: When he offered me a cup
of coffee I told him I'd have a can
of beer.

PARTNER: I can understand what he's
going through. Myself, I've been
wrestling with cancer for a while.

SAUL: Remember when they told my
niece she had skin cancer?

It turned out to be dry skin.

PARTNER: I'm winning.

CHET: I hope you don't mind, but I'll use the red soap dish and you'll use the blue.

RICH: Christ! I've been putting the blocks to you nightly for months and now you're worried about sharing the fucking soap dish?

BROTHER: Christ, I didn't even use the bathroom, even though I had to take a leak so bad I could taste it. Now, that's paranoid.

PARTNER: I wonder if it's safe to use the same telephone, or whether I'm being paranoid.

CHET: I know I'm being paranoid.

LILY: They're flying me out to the Coast.
I hate that place.

RICH: Chet, you've been out every night this week. Do you have to go out again?

BROTHER: I know you're scared, Betty, but I will not tell my own brother he's not welcome in my house.

CHET: Need something from outside?

BROTHER: He's spent every Christmas with us since we got married, and this year will be no exception.

RICH: Forget I said anything: just don't wake me up when you get in.

BROTHER: You're forcing me to choose between you and my brother.

CHET: See you later.

LILY: I've been dating this guy Mick —can you imagine *me* dating? Well, he's very nice, and he's got a lot of money, and he's not impressed with my life in the theater and he's straight—and that's why I haven't been up to see you. Rich?

CHET: You know I'd do anything for you.

RICH: You're walking out on me.

BROTHER: We're going to Betty's mother's for Christmas.

CHET: I need more space to get my head together.

SAUL: What did you expect?

RICH: Chet, please, I need you!

(RICH *tries to put his arms around* CHET. *Everyone except* SAUL *pulls back terrified.*)

CHET, BROTHER, LILY, PARTNER, DOCTORS: Don't touch me! (*Beat.*)

LILY: Please forgive me!

CHET: This thing has me blown away.

BROTHER: If it weren't for the kids.

PARTNER: I don't know what the hell we're going to do.

SAUL: Bastards!

(CHET, BROTHER, PARTNER, *and* LILY *put on white gowns and become doctors.*)

RICH (*to* DOCTOR 1): Doctor, tell me the truth. What are my chances?

DOCTOR 1: I don't know.

RICH (*to* DOCTOR 2): Doctor, tell me the truth. What are my chances?

DOCTOR 2: I don't know.

RICH (*to* DOCTOR 3): What are my chances?

DOCTOR 3: I just don't know.

RICH (*to* DOCTORS 4 *and* 5): Am I going to make it, doctors, yes or no?!

DOCTORS 4 and 5: I'm sorry, we just don't know.

SAUL: Rich?

DOCTORS: We don't know.

TV COMMENTATOR (*prerecorded*): Since 1981, nearly 32,000 Americans have been diagnosed with AIDS [use current fatality figures] and about sixty percent of them have died. Scientists project that by 1991, some 54,000 people will be dead. So far, nine out of ten patients have been homosexual or bisexual men or intravenous drug users. Experts estimate that from four to seven percent of all adult patients were infected through heterosexual intercourse. When will science conquer this dreaded plague? We don't know. We don't know. We simply don't know. Don't know. (Etc.)

SAUL: And for three months you kept this from me.

(*The doctors exit. We're back in* SAUL'S *apartment.*)

RICH: I don't want your pity.

SAUL: You're my friend. You'll stay with me till you feel better.

Rich: Aren't you afraid I'll infect you?

SAUL: Maybe you already have.

RICH: And maybe I haven't.

SAUL: Maybe I gave it to you.

RICH: Maybe you did.

SAUL: We'll take precautions.

RICH: Paper plates, Lysol, face masks—no, I'd prefer to live alone, thank you.

SAUL: You need me.

RICH: Besides, if I live with you, where am I going to bring my tricks?

SAUL: You pick up people?

RICH (*standing at the bar*): I go to bars . . . I pick up guys . . . but I give them a medical report before we leave . . . (*Without a pause, we're in a bar.* RICH *is talking to a stranger.*) I should tell you something.

PICKUP 1: You like something kinky. Whips? Golden showers? Fist?

RICH: It's not like that.

PICKUP 1: I once picked up a guy who liked to be yelled at in German. The only German I know is the "Ode to Joy" from Beethoven's Ninth. (*Yelling like an enraged Nazi.*) "O Freude, schöner Götterfunken, Schweinehund, Tochter aus Elysium, Dummkopf!"

RICH: I have a very mild case of lymphadenopathy.

PICKUP 1: What's that?

RICH: An AIDS-related condition.

PICKUP 1: Oh, shit.

RICH: Just the swollen glands—

PICKUP 1: No way. Uh-uh . . . Good luck . . . Oh, man . . .

(PICKUP 1 *exits. We're back with* RICH *and* SAUL.)

RICH: So I stopped telling them.

SAUL: You mean you take them home and don't tell them?

RICH: We do it there in the bar.

SAUL: How can you?

RICH: I lurk in dark corners where they can't see my lumps. I'm like a shark or a barracuda, and I snap them up and infect them.

SAUL: How can you joke about this?

RICH: I don't care. I'm going to die! I'll take as many as I can with me. And I've pissed in the Croton Reservoir. I'm going to infect the whole fucking city! Wheeeee!

SAUL: No fucking around, give me a straight answer. Do you still pick up people?

RICH: Maybe I ought to wear a sign around my neck and ring a bell: "AIDS, I've got AIDS, stand clear!" Would that make you happy? Or maybe I should dig a hole in the ground, douse myself with kerosene, and have a final cigarette. No muss, no fuss. Is that what you want?

SAUL: Forgive me for not trusting you. It's just that I'm frightened of it. I don't know what I'm saying half the time.

RICH: How the fuck do you think I feel? My lover leaves me; my family won't let me near them; I lose my business; I can't pay my rent. How the fuck do you think I feel?

SAUL: You'll stay here with me.

RICH: Till death do us part.

SAUL: I love you.

RICH: I don't want your love!

SAUL: Take what you can . . . [get]! I didn't mean that. I love you. I always have. You have nowhere to go. You've got to stay with me.

RICH: Shit shit shit.

SAUL: You were kidding about picking up people.

RICH: What do you think? What would you do in my place?

SAUL: I wouldn't . . . I'd . . . Therapy! . . . I don't know what I'd do.

(*We're back in the bar.*)

PICKUP 2: Jesus, I've told you all about myself. I've really spilled my guts to you. I *needed* to do that. Maybe I shouldn't say this, but, Christ, you know something? I like you very much. Even though you *are* a writer . . . Would you like to come home with me?

RICH: I'd like to very much . . . (*he checks his watch*) but I have an appointment.

PICKUP 2: Then tomorrow, how about tomorrow? I don't want to lose track of you. I don't know when I've had such a good time. I can *talk* to you.

RICH: I've enjoyed myself, too.

PICKUP 2: Then maybe we'll have dinner, maybe go to the movies. Do you like movies? There's an Alfred Hitchcock festival at the Regency. Or maybe we could see the new Mark Morris—

RICH: Thanks, but I have to tell you something. I have—

PICKUP 2: You have a lover. I knew it. You're too nice to be unattached.

RICH: I have . . . I have . . . I have a lover.

(*We're back with* SAUL.)

SAUL: You have a lover.

RICH: I don't even know where he is.

SAUL: I don't mean Chet. I mean me. (RICH *turns away. He's back in the bar with another stranger,* CLONE 1, *who is wearing a leather jacket and reflecting aviator glasses.* SAUL *continues to plead to* RICH'S *back.*) What about me? (RICH *tries in vain to get* CLONE 1's *attention.*)

RICH: Pardon me.

SAUL: What about me?

RICH: Yo. Yoo-hoo. Hello.

SAUL: What about *me*?!

RICH (*to* CLONE 1): What about me?!

CLONE 1: What about you?

RICH: I'm a very interesting guy. You look like a very interesting guy. Let's talk. And if you don't want to talk, let's go back there and let's . . . (RICH *stares* CLONE 1 *straight in the face.*) I'll do anything you want. Anything.

CLONE 1: I want you to get the fuck out of my face. Can't you see I'm cruising that dude over there? (*We notice for the first time an identically dressed man standing across the room.*)

RICH: Well, fuck you.

CLONE 1: What's that, buddy?

(RICH *turns his back on* CLONE 1 *and starts talking loudly to the bartender.*)

RICH: Gimme a Jack Daniels straight up—*no* ice—make it a double, and a Heineken chaser.

BARTENDER: Double Jack up, Heinie back.

(CLONE 2 *has moseyed on over to* CLONE 1. *They stand side by side, facing the audience, feigning indifference to each other.*)

CLONE 2: Your name Chip?

RICH: No ice!

BARTENDER: No ice.

CLONE 1: Chuck.

RICH: Hate ice.

CLONE 2 (*extending his hand*): Chad. (*The clones shake hands.*)

RICH (*to the bartender*): Put 'er there, Chet—I mean Chump. You come here often? (*He downs the shot and beer as quickly as he can.*)

CLONE 2: Thought you were this guy, Chip, I met here on Jockstrap Night.

CLONE 1: Haven't been here since the Slave Auction.

CLONE 2: Look familiar. (*With synchronized actions the clones turn to look at each other, then turn away.*)

CLONE 1: Go to the Spike?

CLONE 2: Been there.

RICH (*to the bartender*): Quiet for a Friday . . .

CLONE 1: I know where.

RICH: Not much action.

CLONE 2: Palladium?

RICH (*offering his glass*): Same . . .

CLONE 1: Nah.

RICH: Probably's this disease thing.

CLONE 1: Bookstore on Christopher. Ever go there?

CLONE 2: Stopped going since this disease thing.

CLONE 1: Gotta be real careful.

RICH: No use getting hysterical.

CLONE 2: Right. Me, I'm HIV negative.

CLONE 1: Can you prove it? (*He punches* CLONE 2 *on the arm.*) Kidding.

CLONE 2: Gotta be real careful. Run six miles a day.

RICH: My philosophy is: you've got it, you've got it. Nothing you can do about it. (*He offers his glass.*) Same.

CLONE 1 (*tweaking* CLONE 2's *nipple*): So what're you up for?

CLONE 2: Come right to the point, don't you?

(*The clones perform a macho mating ritual of arm wrestling, punching, and ass grabbing to determine who is the "top man."*)

RICH: Poor bastards that got it: cancer, pneumonia, herpes all over. I mean, I'd kill myself if I had to go through all that shit. Get a gun and perform fellatio on it . . .

CLONE 2: What're you up for, Daddy?

RICH: Slash my wrists *with* the grain . . .

CLONE 1: Me top.

RICH: Subway tracks?

CLONE 1: Got some beautiful . . . (*He snorts deeply to indicate cocaine.*)

CLONE 2: Ever do opium?

CLONE 1: I have a water pipe. We'll smoke it through some Southern Comfort.

RICH: Or maybe I'd mix myself a Judy Garland: forty reds and a quart of vodka. (*He hands his glass to the bartender.*) Fuck the beer!

CLONE 1: We're roommates now. What about you?

RICH (*the ecstatic drunken poet*): "Glory be to God for dappled things . . ."

CLONE 2: I'm free, white, and twenty-four.

RICH: "For skies of couple-colour as a brinded cow . . ."

SAUL: I know it sounds stupid, but take care of your health.

RICH: "For rose-moles all in stipple upon trout that swim . . ."

CLONE 2: In bed, I mean.

RICH: I don't care what anybody says, I believe that somewhere, you know, *deep* down. (*He holds out his glass.*)

CLONE 1: I'll do anything you want.

RICH: Beyond all this incredible pain and confusion, anxiety, fear, terror . . . (*He holds out his glass.*)

BARTENDER: No ice.

CLONE 2: Anything?

RICH: I believe that there might be . . . (*searching for words to describe the Supreme Being*) that there could be . . . that there is—

CLONE 1: Safe sex!

SAUL: You're drinking too much.

RICH: I believe in a perfect . . . (*He is having a booze-fueled vision of the Godhead.*)

CLONE 2: Mirrors . . .

RICH: Shining . . .

CLONE 1: Chains . . .

RICH: Powerful . . .

SAUL: Vitamins . . .

RICH: Pure . . .

(*A third clone appears.*)

CLONE 3: Condom . . .

CLONE 1: Dildo . . .

SAUL: Diet . . .

RICH: Free . . .

CLONE 2: Dungeon . . .

SAUL: Acupuncture . . .

RICH: Truthful . . .

CLONE 3: Ten inches . . .

SAUL: AZT . . .

RICH: Beautiful . . .

CLONE 3 (*approaching the bar, to the* BARTENDER): Beer! (*He accidentally spills beer on* RICH.)

CLONE 2: Watersports.

RICH (*raging drunkenly*): Asshole!

CLONE 1: Hey!

RICH: I'll kill ya, faggot!

SAUL (*intervening*): Hey! . . . He's been drinking.

BARTENDER: Get that jerk outta here!

RICH: What's a matter, can't you fight like a man?

SAUL (*gently but firmly*): Rich.

RICH: Fuck all that shit!

SAUL: Rich.

RICH: Let Him cure me!

SAUL (*trying to distract him*): Did you hear the one about the faggot, the black, and the Jew?

RICH (*to God in the sky, shaking his fist*): You hear me, motherfucker?

SAUL: How did that go?

RICH: Cure me!

(*They are out on the street by now.*)

SAUL: C'mon, keep moving.

RICH: I'm a very bad person.

SAUL: You're an asshole.

RICH: I wanted to go to bed with that guy.

SAUL: I practically beg you to move in—

RICH: I wasn't going to tell him about me or anything.

SAUL: And what do you do?

RICH: But you want to know something?

SAUL: You disappear for two weeks.

RICH: I wouldn't do that. I would *never* do that.

SAUL: I almost called the cops.

RICH: You believe me?

SAUL: Believe what?

RICH: I never never never would ever do that.

SAUL: Do you remember the one about the Polish Lesbian?

RICH: Never.

SAUL: She liked men. (*The joke pretty much sobers* RICH *up.*)

RICH: You asshole.

SAUL: You schmuck.

RICH: You prick.

SAUL: God, I miss talking dirty.

RICH: Talking dirty makes it feel like spring. (*He is the superstud.*) Suck my dick, faggot.

SAUL (*superstud*): Kiss my ass, cocksucker.

RICH: Sit on it, punk.

SAUL: Lick boot, fruit.

RICH: God, how I used to love sleaze: the whining self-pity of a rainy Monday night in a leather bar in early spring; five o'clock in the morning in the Mineshaft, with the bathtubs full of men dying to get pissed on and whipped; a subway john full of horny high school students; Morocco—getting raped on a tomb-stone in Marrakesh. God, how I miss it.

SAUL: I miss my filthy old ripped-up, patched button-fly jeans that I sun-bleached on myself our first weekend on the Island. Remember? It was Labor Day—

RICH: Memorial Day.

SAUL: And we did blotter acid. Remember acid before they put the speed in it? And we drank muscadet when we got thirsty.

RICH: Which we did a lot.

SAUL: Remember?

RICH: Remember Sunday afternoons blitzed on beer?

SAUL: And suddenly it's Sunday night and you're getting fucked in the second-floor window of the Hotel Christopher and you're being cheered on by a mob of hundreds of men.

RICH: And suddenly it's Friday a week later, and he's moved in, sleeping next to you, and you want him to go because you've met his brother Rod or Lance—

SAUL *(practically sighing)*: Miles.

RICH: —late of the merchant marines, who's even humpier.

SAUL: Orgies at the baths—

RICH: Afternoons at the Columbus Avenue bookstore. *(They are in the back room of a gay porno shop, or "bookstore." They play their favorite bookstore habitués.)* More! *Give* it to me!

SAUL: Give it to *you*? Give it to *me*! Get out of my way, he's mine!

RICH: No, he's mine! Keep your hands off my wallet!

SAUL *(a black queen)*: Sistuhs, theyuh's plenty heah fo' ivrybody.

RICH *(a tough New York queen)*: Hey, Mary, the line forms at the rear.

SAUL: And whose rear might that be, sugar?

(Two other men appear in the bookstore.)

MARTY: Hey, Vinnie?

VINNIE: Marty?

MARTY: What are you doing here? You said you were gonna buy the papers.

VINNIE: You said you were gonna walk the dogs.

MARTY: You trash! *(They exit, bickering.)*

SAUL: I always knew when you were fucking around.

RICH: You did your share.

SAUL: *Moi?*

RICH: I knew why Grand Union wouldn't deliver to our house. *(They have returned to the loft.)*

SAUL: God, I used to love promiscuous sex.

RICH: Not "promiscuous," Saul, nondirective, noncommitted, nonauthoritarian—

SAUL: Free, wild, rampant—

RICH: Hot, sweaty, steamy, smelly—

SAUL: Juicy, funky, hunky—

RICH: Sex.

SAUL: Sex. God, I miss it. (RICH *lowers his eyes.* SAUL *nods and goes to* RICH. *He takes* RICH'S *face in both hands and tries to kiss him square on the mouth.* RICH *pulls away frantically.*)

RICH: NO!

SAUL: It's safe!

RICH: You don't know what you're doing!

SAUL: It's my decision!

RICH (*shaking his head*): No. Uh-uh. NO! (SAUL *sits on the sofa.* RICH *tries to take* SAUL'S *hand, but* SAUL *pulls it away. Beat.*) The best times for me were going out with you on shoots.

SAUL: I thought you found them boring.

RICH: I enjoyed them.

SAUL: I was always afraid of boring you.

RICH: Remember staying up all night shooting the harvest moon at Jake's place?

SAUL: My fingers got so cold I could barely change film.

RICH: It was almost as bright as daylight. Remember the apple tree stuck out in the middle of the pasture, how the moonlight drained it of color?

SAUL: I remember the smell of the blanket we took from the barn.

RICH: Remember, I bet you I could find five constellations?

SAUL: You found six . . . I never wanted us to break up.

RICH: Passive aggression.

SAUL: I wanted things to always remain the same. I'm still like that. I even like eating the same things day after day.

RICH: Pork chops, French fries—

SAUL: No change. I used to love our routine together. I'd go to work and then you'd be there when I got home, writing—

RICH: Drinking.

SAUL: I'd do this and you'd do that, and then we'd . . . (*he makes a graceful gesture to indicate making love*) for a while—while *Mission Impossible*'d be on low in the background.

RICH: And then *Star Trek*.

SAUL: I never got tired of the same—

RICH: We were stagnating.

SAUL: —day after day the same, so we'd have a structure to fall back on when life dealt us its wild cards or curve balls. I want to be just half awake, like at the seashore, watching the waves roll in late in the afternoon, hypnotized by the glare of the sun, smelling the sea breeze and suntan lotion. (*Beat.*)

Mom is what? She's lying there next to Dad on the Navaho blanket, with white gunk on her nose, and my baby sister has finally stopped screaming and is sucking on the ear of her dollie. And Aunt Ellie—the one who said she thought I had good taste when she met you—is snoring next to husband number three. Her bazooms are going up and down, up and down, almost popping out of her bathing suit. It's so peaceful. (*Long pause.*)

I was at the St. Mark's baths soaking in the hot tub when I first heard about AIDS. It was how many years ago? My friend Brian—remember him?—was soaking, too, and he told me about a mutual friend who had died the week before. It was "bizarre," he said . . .

(*A group enters, quietly talking.*)

1ST MAN: The first person I knew who had AIDS was George. I had just seen him at the movies—*Mommie Dearest*—and we had a big laugh together. I remember he had a little cough. I ran into his mother it couldn't have been a week later and she told me he had died. It was absurd. I had just seen George.

1ST WOMAN: The first time it really hit me was when my boss got ill. When Roger got out of the hospital I didn't know what to say. I said, "You look so much taller." He said, "Well, I've lost about forty-five pounds."

It hit home after that.

2ND WOMAN: The first time I heard about it I was standing in my kitchen. I was about to go out shopping for my youngest's birthday party. The phone rang. It was this doctor calling me about my son Bernard. He used all these words I can't pronounce. And then he said, "Do you understand what I've told you?" I said yes. Right before he hung up he said, "So you know he has AIDS." That's the first time I heard that word.

1ST MAN: Do you understand what I've told you?

1ST WOMAN: So you know he has AIDS.

JOHN: The first time I heard about AIDS was in 1980. I was on the seven A.M. shuttle to Boston, trying to make a nine o'clock appointment in Cambridge. I was looking over the shoulder of the man next to me, at his newspaper, and I caught the words "cancer," "promiscuous," "homosexual."

I turned white.

3RD MAN (a cop): The word never really registered in my mind until they transferred this guy with AIDS to our unit. Maybe I thought AIDS was like Legionnaire's Disease

or Toxic Shock Syndrome—one of those rare diseases you read about in the papers. Anyway, the guys on the job were up in arms that they were going to expose us to it. I didn't know what to think. I got used to Bobby though. He wanted to keep working very badly.

I think he had a lot of courage.

1ST and 2ND MEN: I think he had a lot of courage.

2ND WOMAN: He was in the theater.

3RD MAN: I couldn't figure it out.

4TH MAN: The first memorial service I went to was on the set of *Oh Calcutta!* It was for Bill. He was in the theater. They filled the house. He had hidden the fact that he was ill for a year. A while before he asked me if I wanted his dog—a beautiful huskie. I couldn't figure it out. He loved that dog. . . . Since that time I've been to how many memorial services? Seth . . . Robby . . .

1ST WOMAN: . . . Fortunato

3RD MAN: . . . Stephen . . .

4TH MAN: . . . Phil . . .

1ST WOMAN: . . . Arthur . . .

2ND WOMAN: . . . Neil . . .

1ST WOMAN: . . . John . . .

2ND WOMAN: . . . Julie . . .

3RD MAN: . . . Luis . . . Larry and his lover Danny . . . Stuart . . . J.J. . . . Maria . . . Jamal . . .

2ND WOMAN: . . . David . . . Stuart . . . J.J. . . . Maria . . . Jamal . . .

2ND WOMAN: . . . Francis . . .

2ND MAN: . . . Greg . . .

2ND WOMAN: . . . Freddie . . .

1ST MAN: . . . Tom . . .

2ND MAN: . . . André . . .

3RD MAN: . . . Glen . . .

1ST and 4TH MAN and 1ST WOMAN: . . . Russell . . . Luis . . . Larry and his lover Danny . . . David . . . Stuart . . . J.J. . . . Maria . . . Jamal . . .

2ND MAN: . . . Larry . . . David . . . Stuart . . . J.J. . . . Maria . . . Jamal . . . Charles . . .

(The group exits.)

SAUL: . . . and he told me about a mutual friend who had died the week before. It was "bizarre," he said. Brian died last week of the same thing. And he and I once soaked in the same hot tub, making a kind of human soup. . . . That's all I ever wanted to do was relax. *(Long pause.)* You'll stay with me. I won't bother you.

RICH: Just until I feel better.

SAUL: I understand: you're not coming back to be my lover.

RICH: Right. Is that okay?

SAUL: Schmuck. *(Mimicking him.)* Is that okay? Is that okay? It's *okay!* Asshole. Who the fuck wants you anyhow? And when I have guests stay the night, you disappear into your room. Right?

RICH: Right. Understood. (*Offhand.*) You seeing somebody?

SAUL: I said when I have guests.

RICH: You planning an orgy?

SAUL: Just so we understand each other.

RICH: I should mention one thing.

SAUL: No, you do not have to spend Passover with the tribe.

RICH: I miss your father.

SAUL: Then go live with him. He *likes* you. The two of you could be very happy together.

RICH: One thing.

SAUL: He's never really liked me.

RICH: Saul.

SAUL: He's always been polite but—

RICH: Are you finished?

SAUL: No, I will not bring you coffee in bed. I only do that for lovers. Besides, I broke your blue mug.

RICH: Saul, please.

SAUL: On purpose.

RICH: One thing. I'm embarrassed. I'm just about broke. The doctors. Tests.

SAUL: I thought you were insured.

RICH: They're pulling a fast one.

SAUL: We'll sue. I'll call Craig. He'll know what—

RICH: Craig told me not to have high hopes.

SAUL: We'll get by. You'll see.

RICH: I'll keep track of every cent you spend on me. You'll get it all back when I can work. I swear.

SAUL: Not to worry, I'll take it out in trade.

RICH: Saul, I'm frightened! (SAUL *takes him in his arms.*)

SAUL: We'll be okay, we'll be okay . . .

(*They hold each other.* LILY *walks into the scene with* CHET. *She's dressed in evening wear and is carrying a number of accessories, including a mirror and a shawl.* CHET *is dressed in cutoffs and a sweatshirt. We are in a flashback.*)

LILY: Rich, congratulations! It's fantastic that they're going to publish your book.

(SAUL *tries to break from the clinch, but* RICH *holds him back.*)

RICH: No autographs, please.

LILY: It's wonderful, it really is, but can you guys celebrate later?

SAUL (*to* RICH): Let me go. (*To* CHET:) How do you do? I'm Saul.

LILY: Shit. Saul, Rich—my cousin Chet.

SAUL (*trying to shake hands*): Hi, Chet. (*To* RICH:) You're strangling me.

CHET: Hi.

RICH (*to* SAUL): It's your last chance to kiss the author before he becomes famous and goes straight.

SAUL: Straight to the bars. (*To* CHET:) So how do you like New York?

CHET: I only got here yesterday. Lily's taking me to a show tonight.

RICH: Do you think success will change me?

SAUL: God, I hope so.

LILY: I know I'm being a pig, but I need head shots by six o'clock. (*She lowers a roller of colored background paper.*) It's a dazzling role for me and (*to* SAUL) you're such an artist.

SAUL: Rich is the "artiste" in the family.

LILY: Chet, be an angel and bring Saul his camera. It's by the bar. (CHET *looks for the camera.*)

SAUL (*to* CHET): Don't let your cousin push you around the way she does me.

LILY: Come on, Saul, make click-click.

SAUL: Unless you like that sort of thing.

RICH: That's all I get?

LILY (*to* RICH, *about* SAUL): Leave the boy alone.

RICH: A hug and a bitchy remark?

SAUL (*to* RICH): That and a subway token.

RICH (*to* SAUL): No "Gee, Rich, I'm so proud of you"?

SAUL (*smiling falsely*): Gee, Rich, I'm so proud of you.

RICH: I finally have some good news and he's annoyed.

CHET (*to* LILY, *holding the camera*): What should I do with this?

SAUL: Well, your brother called, while you were out guzzling lunch with your agent, Dr. Mengele. Call him back.

RICH: What'd he have to say?

SAUL: Call him and ask him. I'm not your secretary.

RICH (*imitating him*): I'm not your—

SAUL: He forgot my fucking name again. How long we been together?

RICH: Too long. Forget my brother. It's my first fucking book. Let's celebrate.

SAUL: You celebrate.

LILY: I'll throw a party.

RICH: What'll you serve, organic cabbage juice?

SAUL (*to* LILY): His brother's a scumbag.

RICH: He likes you, too.

CHET (*to* SAUL, *still holding the camera*): Do you want this?

SAUL (*to* CHET): Thanks, Chuck.

CHET: Chet. (SAUL *accepts the camera from* CHET, *but ignores the correction.*)

LILY (*fondly, to* RICH): You're such a lush.

RICH: Whatever happened to my old drinking buddy?

LILY: Did you know they have gay A.A. meetings? (RICH *makes a face.*)

SAUL (*to* RICH, *trying to be nice*): It's great news, babes, really.

RICH: You really don't give a fuck.

SAUL: Just how many copies you think a book of "fairy tales" will sell?

LILY: I picked a fine day to have my picture taken.

SAUL: If you only knew how much I love doing head shots.

RICH (*to* SAUL): Ah, fuck it, I guess I'm being childish.

SAUL: I shouldn't have said that. I'm thoughtless. (RICH *shrugs.*)

LILY: And I'm Sneezy. No, really, I'm selfish. But I want that role so bad. I play the ghost of Marie Antoinette. (*To* SAUL, *throwing the scarf around her neck and taking a tits-and-ass pose:*) How do you like this, hon? "Let them eat . . ." (*She drops the pose immediately as* SAUL *starts to photograph her.*)

SAUL: Move your head a little to the . . . (*She moves her head.*) Good. (SAUL *snaps her.*)

RICH (*going to the living area, followed by* CHET): I'm going running. (RICH *changes into jogging clothes.*)

CHET: How far do you run?

RICH: Depends. I'm in training for the marathon.

CHET: The marathon! Hey, that's great. I run, too.

RICH: Oh, yeah? (LILY *and* SAUL *are busy taking pictures in the other side of the loft. hey can see* RICH *and* CHET, *but they can't easily hear them.*)

LILY: How's this?

CHET: Congratulations on the book.

RICH: Thanks.

SAUL: That's right.

LILY: I forget the director's name. He's Lithuanian.

CHET: That poem of yours that Lily has hung up in her kitchen, I read it. I think it's great.

SAUL: Great.

RICH: You don't much look like the poetry type.

LILY: Bulgarian.

CHET: I'm not. I just love your poem.

RICH: Are you a student?

CHET: Just graduated from San Francisco State.

LILY: Everybody in the play is dead.

SAUL: Your cousin's hot. Is he gay?

LILY: I don't know. I'll ask him. (*Yelling to* CHET.) Chet, are you gay?

SAUL: Christ.

RICH: That's what I call tact.

LILY: Well?

CHET (*loud, to* LILY): Yes.

LILY: Thanks, hon.

SAUL: Give us a little more cheek . . .

CHET: There's a line of your poem I don't understand.

RICH: Only one? I have no idea what any of it means.

CHET: "The final waning moon . . ."

SAUL: Don't smile.

RICH: "And the coming of the light."

CHET: I love the way it sounds.

SAUL: Smile.

CHET: "The final waning moon/And the coming of the light."

SAUL (*indicating to* LILY *that he wants a sexy pose*): He loves you.

CHET: Oh, I get it.

RICH: Lily tells me you're looking for a place to stay.

CHET: New York is so expensive.

SAUL: He lusts for you.

RICH: A friend of mine wants someone to take care of his loft while he's in L.A.

SAUL: He wants to ravage you.

CHET: I'll do it.

RICH: He has eight cats.

CHET: Eight tigers, I don't care.

LILY: I love that play.

RICH: It's in Tribeca.

SAUL (*yelling to* RICH): I apologize about the book.

(RICH *and* CHET *ignore* SAUL.)

CHET: Where's Tribeca?

SAUL: Did you hear me?

RICH: On the isle of Manhattan.

CHET: We're on the isle of Manhattan.

RICH: We are.

LILY: The main characters are all ghosts.

CHET: I know that.

SAUL: I'll throw him a party.

RICH: That's about all you have to know.

SAUL: A big bash.

CHET: Is it?

LILY: We'll do it together.

RICH: I'll tell you a few more things.

CHET: Will you?

SAUL: I'll even invite his brother.

RICH: You bet your ass I will.

SAUL (*snapping up the roller of background paper*): Finished.

(LILY, RICH, and CHET *leave.* SAUL *goes to the sofa. The* HOSPICE WORKER *comes forward.*)

HOSPICE WORKER: A woman is told by her doctor that she has cancer and has only a month to live. "Now wait just one minute," she tells the doctor. "I'll be wanting a second opinion." To which the doctor replies, "Okay, you're ugly, too."

    David told me that one. He was an old Jewish man who had survived the Lodz ghetto in World War II. He'd seen everything in his life, and when the time came for him to go, he accepted it. The doctors wanted to go to obscene lengths to keep his body alive, but he refused. I loved him.

    But most of my people are more like Margaret. She was in her nineties. She half accepted the fact that she was dying. One moment she'd be talking to you about which nephew she was definitely going to cross out of her will, and the next she'd be telling you about the summer vacation she was planning in Skibbereen. She had terminal cancer! But I always go along with what they have to say. My job is not to bring enlightenment, only comfort.

    Which reminds me: Margaret's family saw her as some kind of prophet. The whole clan was in the room waiting to hear her last words. She had developed a distinct dislike for her family, so I was sitting closest to her when she went, and therefore I could hear what the poor soul was whispering. After it was all over, they asked me what prayer she had been uttering. I told them the Lord's Prayer. I didn't have the heart to tell them that what she was saying was "Oh, shit, oh, shit, oh, shit."

    I've worked with thirty-five people altogether. About a third of them had AIDS. It *is* the Village.

(*She exits. Lights come up on left area. An AIDS support group is in session.*

PERSON WITH AIDS 1: Funny thing is, I wasn't at all promiscuous.

PWA 2: Oh, please.

PWA 1: I swear. And I never drank much—once in a while a beer with Mexican food—and I don't smoke, and drugs, forget . . . I met Jerry in my sophomore year—we shared the same dorm room at Hofstra—and we fell in love, and that was it for me. When the sex revolution thing happened, I remember I felt retarded. Everybody was doing all those wild things. Me, I was going to the opera a lot. As far as I know, Jerry didn't screw around. He swore he didn't. But then . . . he's not around for me to cross-examine. He left me.

RICH: Well, I . . .

PWA 3: What?

RICH: No.

PWA 4 (*a young housewife, eight months pregnant*): At least when I come here I don't have to lie. Like "Bernie's doing better. I'm fine." I can even crack up if I want to. Don't worry, I won't do it two weeks in a row. I mean, who's there to talk to in Brewster? These things don't happen in Brewster. Police officers don't shoot up heroin, cops don't come down with the "gay plague"—that's what they call it in Brewster. I can't talk to Bernie. I'll never forgive him. Have a chat with the minister? "Well, Reverend Miller, I have this little problem. My husband has AIDS, and I have AIDS, and I'm eight months pregnant, and I . . ." You guys know what I mean. You're the only people in this world who know what I mean.

PWA 5: I know what you guys are going to tell me: I'm suffering from the homophobia that an oppressive society blah blah blah. I never felt good about being gay.

PWA 2: Oh, Mary.

PWA 5: Gay was grim. It was something I did because I had to. Like a dope fiend needs his fix. It always left me feeling like shit afterward. And that's the truth. I felt guilty. I still feel that way.

(PWA 4 *leans over to put a consoling hand on him. He pulls away.*)

PWA 2: I was part of a team trying to teach robots how to use language. (*He moves and talks like a robot.*) "I'm Harris, your android model 3135X. I can vacuum the floors, cook cheeseburgers, play the piano." It's much harder to teach robots to understand. (*Instructing a backward robot.*) "Joke." (*The robot responds dutifully.*) "Noun: a clash of values or levels of reality, producing laughter. Example: Have you heard about the disease attacking Jewish American princesses? It's called MAIDS. You die if you *don't* get it. Ha. Ha." My co-workers asked me to leave. They were afraid of contracting AIDS through the air, or by my looking at them. You see, they are scientists. My last act before I left was programming one final robot. (*He behaves like a robot again.*) "Good morning. This is Jack—(*he suddenly becomes a flamboyantly gay robot*) but you can call me Jackie—your *fabulous* new android model 1069. If you wish to use me— and I *love* being used—press one of those cunning little buttons on my pecs. Go on, press one—(*he switches from a campy tone to an almost angry, accusatory one*) or are you afraid of me, too?" That was my stab at immortality.

RICH: I'm not sure I have it anymore. I feel guilty saying this, like somehow I'm being disloyal to the group. I'm getting better, I know it. I just have these lumps, which for some reason won't go away, and a loss of weight, which has made me lighter than I've been for years.

PWA 3: Lose weight the AYDS way!

RICH: But anyway, I feel great. I feel the disease disappearing in me. Only a small percentage of those with the swollen glands come down with the rest. I'm going to *not* come here next week. I'm sorry.

PWA 3: Rich?

SAUL (*calling to* RICH *as if he were in the next room, while feeling the glands in his neck and armpits*): Rich?

RICH (*still to group*): Why do I keep on apologizing?

SAUL: Rich?

RICH: If I *really* thought that I was coming down with it . . . We all have *options*.

PWA 2: Rich?

SAUL: Rich.

RICH (*entering* SAUL'S *area*): What?

SAUL: Here, feel my glands.

RICH: You are such a hypochondriac.

SAUL: Do you think they're swollen?

RICH (*placing his hands around* SAUL'S *neck*): They feel okay to me. (*Transylvanian accent.*) But your neck—eet is grotesquely meesshapen. (*Suddenly mock-strangling* SAUL.) Here, let me feex it. (*They start wrestling on sofa.*)

SAUL: Not fair!

RICH: You're such a hypochondriac.

SAUL: Ow! *I'm* such a hypochondriac. You and your vitamins!

RICH: You and your yoga!

SAUL: You and your yoghurt!

RICH: It's working. My ratio's up.

SAUL: All right! (*To the tune of* "*New York, New York.*")
T-cells up,
The suppressors are down.
New York, New York . . .

RICH: Hey, I love you! You know that?

SAUL: If you love me, get off my chest!

RICH: I don't dare. You'd try and get even. You're that way.

SAUL: We'll call a truce. One, two, three . . .

RICH and SAUL: Truce. (*As* RICH *climbs off* SAUL'S *chest,* SAUL *pulls him down, lifting his shirt, and gets him in a hammerlock.*)

SAUL: You were right. You never should have trusted me.

RICH: Unfair . . . foul . . . most unfair!

SAUL: Fuck fair. The winner gets his way with the loser. (*They tussle until* RICH *gives up.*) Having vanquished the good ship *Socrates*, the savage pirate chief Bigmeat takes the first mate as his captive.

RICH (*in falsetto*): No, Captain Bigmeat, no!

SAUL: I've had me eye on ye since that time we met in Bangalore. Ye can't escape me now, matey. I shall ravish ye fer sure. (SAUL *tickles* RICH.)

RICH: No! . . . I'm pure of blood and noble born! (*Gradually their play turns more and more sexual, which* RICH *resists at first.*) No! . . . No! . . . (*Relents.*) Perhaps . . . Please!

SAUL: Now I got ye, boy-o . . . boy-o . . . boy-o . . . Oh, boy! (*Finally* RICH *stops struggling.* RICH *and* SAUL *are close together, panting, exhausted.* SAUL *is about to make love to* RICH *when he notices a mark on his back.*)

RICH: What? (SAUL *ignores him and looks at the mark carefully.*) What? You seduce me, you finally succeed in getting me hot and bothered, and what do you do as I lie here panting? You look at my birthmark.

(SAUL *looks at* RICH's *back. He touches some marks.*)

RICH: What is it?

SAUL: Nothing.

RICH: What is it? Tell me!

SAUL: I'm sure it's nothing!

RICH: What! WHAT! WHAT! . . .

(*Immediately, the* HOSPICE WORKER *draws a curtain that surrounds the entire living area of* SAUL's *loft, hiding it from view. Overlapping the closing of the curtain, we hear the ringing of two telephones. Lights up on two men sitting side by side, answering multiline telephones.*)

PAT: Hotline, Pat speaking.

BARNEY: Hotline. This is Barney. (*To* PAT, *covering the phone:*) Oh, no, it's her again.

PAT: Are you a gay man?

BARNEY: Didn't we speak a few days ago? (*To* PAT, *covering the phone:*) She doesn't stop.

PAT: We're all worried.

BARNEY: Is he bisexual?

PAT: Calm down, first of all. (*The third line rings.*)

BARNEY: Is he an IV drug user?

PAT: It's not all that easy to get it—*if* you take a few precautions. (*To* BARNEY, *covering the phone*:) Okay, I'll get it. (*He speaks into the phone.*) Please hold on. (*He presses a button.*)

BARNEY: It wasn't my intention to insult you.

PAT: Hotline . . . Shit. (*To* BARNEY, *pressing a button*:) Lost him. Fucking phone.

BARNEY: So what makes you think he has AIDS?

PAT (*to phone*): Hello.

BARNEY: He is what?

PAT: The disease is spread through the blood and the semen.

BARNEY: American Indians are *not* a risk group. (*To* PAT, *covering the phone*:) American Indians?

PAT: So wear a condom.

BARNEY: There's half a zillion diseases he has symptoms of.

PAT: Make *him* wear a condom. (*The phone rings.*)

BARNEY: Please hold. (*He presses a button.*)

PAT: Kissing is acceptable.

BARNEY: Hotline . . . (*In response to a hate call.*) And your mother eats turds in hell! . . . Thank you. (*He presses a button.*)

PAT: Myself, I don't do it on the first date.

BARNEY: I would definitely check it out with a physician.

BARNEY: Spots? I'm not a doctor. . . .   PAT: Stroking, holding, rubbing, mir-
 Go to a doctor.   rors, whips, chains, jacking off,
                                                              porno—use your imagination.

BARNEY: I'm sorry you're lonely.

PAT: Our motto is: "On me, not in me."

BARNEY: Madam, we're busy here. I can't stay on the line with you all day.

PAT: You have a nice voice, too, but I'm seeing someone.

BARNEY: Hello?

PAT: Thanks.

BARNEY (*to* PAT): Thank God.

PAT: Good luck. (*They hang up at the same time.*)

BARNEY: Spots. I love it.

PAT (*to himself*): I am not seeing anyone.

BARNEY: What are you talking about?

PAT: I was saying how much I love being celibate. (*He kisses his palm.*) So how the fuck are you?

BARNEY: Tired, broke, depressed, and Tim is moving out this afternoon. Well, you asked. I hear you have a new PWA.*

PAT: Sorry about Tim. Yes, I have a new baby, a writer. Why do I get all the tough customers?

BARNEY: Because you're so tough.

PAT: So butch.

BARNEY: So mean.

PAT: Weathered by life like the saddle under a cowboy's ass.

BARNEY: Ooooh. I could never be a CMP.** Where do you get your energy?

PAT: Drugs. I don't do that anymore either. What *do* I do? I wait tables, answer phones, and work with ingrates like Rich. Boy, is he pissed. He calls me Miss Nightingale or Florence and throws dishes and curses his roommate and won't cooperate with the doctor and won't see his shrink and isn't interested in support groups *and he shit in the fucking bathtub!* He shit—

BARNEY: Is he incontinent?

PAT: Fuck, no. He ain't that sick yet. He said it was "convenient." I don't know why he shit in the tub.

BARNEY: A real sweetheart.

PAT: I'm going out of my mind. Thank God they put him in the hospital.

BARNEY: First time?

PAT: Yep.

BARNEY: I'd probably be a real bastard.

PAT: I wouldn't take it lying down.

BARNEY: You'd take it any way you can get it.

PAT: Go on, girlfriend.

BARNEY: Me, if I learned I had it, I'd shove a time bomb up my tush and drop in on Timmy for tea and meet his new lover: Jimmy.

*Person With Aids.
**Crisis Management Partner.

PAT: Jimmy?

BARNEY: I swear: Jimmy. (*Visiting* TIMMY *and* JIMMY *for high tea.*) "Timmy has told me so much about you. I've been *dying* to meet you." And kaboom! There goes Timmy and Jimmy.

PAT: Timmy and Jimmy? (*The telephone rings.*)

BARNEY: Ain't it a gas?

PAT: Gag me, for sure.

BARNEY: For sure.

PAT (*answering the phone*): Hotline. Pat speaking.

BARNEY (*raging*): When are we going to get some more help around here??!! I'm going out of my mind! (*Suddenly, sweet and sultry as he answers the phone.*) Hotline, Barney speaking.

PAT: Are you a gay man?

BARNEY: Are you a gay man?

(*The lights quickly fade on the two men. The curtain opens, revealing a hospital room, with bed, chair, and bed table. The loft space and bar have disappeared.* RICH *is in bed.* LILY, SAUL, *and a nurse are standing nearby.*)

NURSE: Temperature and blood pressure, Mr. Farrell.

LILY: Can you come back later?

SAUL: He's had some bad news.

NURSE: He's last on my rounds.

RICH (*to* SAUL): You lied to me.

SAUL: I didn't know.

LILY: He didn't know. I swear.

NURSE: It'll just take a minute.

RICH: What other little details are you keeping from me? They let him lie there like a dog. What else? (*A* Hispanic hospital worker comes in to empty the waste basket.*) You! *Váyase!* Get the wetback out of here! *Váyase!*

HOSPITAL WORKER: I not do nothing! He crazy.

RICH: You, get out of here before I breathe on you! *Ahora! Ahora! Váyase!*

NURSE: Mr. Farrell, please.

SAUL: Come back later. *Más tarde, por favor.*

RICH: Go back to your picket line. (*To* SAUL:) They want a wage hike, no less. He tried to get me to bribe him to clean my room—

HOSPITAL WORKER: *Qué coño estás diciendo?* [What the fuck are you saying?]

NURSE: Please cooperate.

LILY: He didn't say anything.

RICH: He won't go near my bed, but he's not afraid to touch my money.

SAUL: You misunderstood him.

RICH: *El dinero está limpio, ah? Tu madre.* [Money is clean, huh, motherfucker?]

HOSPITAL WORKER: *Maricón.* [Faggot.]

RICH (*to* SAUL): They're unionizing primates now.

LILY (*to* RICH): Sh!

HOSPITAL WORKER: *No entiendo.* [I don't understand.] I going. (*He exits.*)

LILY (*aside to* SAUL): I shouldn't have told him about Chet.

SAUL (*aside to* LILY): Better you than someone else.

RICH (*imitating* LILY *and* SAUL): Bzzz bzzz bzzz.

NURSE (*trying to put a blood pressure cuff on* RICH's *arm*): Will you be still a moment so I can check your blood pressure?

RICH: Are you a union member, too?

NURSE (*to* SAUL): What shall I do?

LILY: A good friend of his just passed away.

NURSE: AIDS? (*She resumes struggling with the cuff.*)

RICH: The undertakers' union. Go away, I'm on strike, too; I refuse to participate in the documentation of my own demise.

SAUL: She's only trying to help you.

RICH (*to the nurse, ripping off the cuff*): Go find another statistic for the Center for Disease Control.

NURSE (*to* SAUL): I'm a patient woman, but he wants me to lose it. I swear that's what he's after.

RICH: Lady, fuck off!

SAUL (*to the nurse*): Please. Can't you see he's upset?

NURSE (*to* RICH): Okay, you win. I'm losing it. Are you happy? I'm *angry*, angry, Mr. Farrell.

LILY: Will you please go!

NURSE: A person can take only so much. I give up. I don't have to put up with this shit. I'm gonna speak to my supervisor. (*The* NURSE *exits.*)

RICH (*applauding*): Three gold stars for self-assertion!

LILY (*to* SAUL): I should have kept my mouth shut.

RICH: Having brought Romeo the news that Juliet is dead, Balthasar makes a tearful exit.

LILY: I don't know what to say. (LILY *looks at* RICH, *then* SAUL.)

RICH: I said: Balthasar makes a tearful exit.

LILY: I know how you're feeling.

RICH: No matter. Get thee gone and hire those horses.

LILY: I loved Chet, too.

RICH: Tush, thou art deceived.

LILY: He told me he was sorry for the way he treated you.

RICH: Do the thing I bid thee.

LILY: He didn't belong in New York. He thought he was so sophisticated, but he was just a kid from Mendocino. I'm sorry I let him go home.

RICH: The messenger must go. The hero wishes to be alone with his confidant. (RICH *turns his back on* SAUL *and* LILY.)

LILY: I'll be back tomorrow. (*Aside to* SAUL:) I've got half a crown roast from Margo. She went vegetarian. I'll be up. I have to have a talk with Mick. He's irrational on the subject of AIDS. He can go to hell. If he's so afraid, let him move out. (*To* RICH:) I won't let him come between us. You're my buddy. (SAUL *indicates that* LILY *should leave. She gathers up her belongings, mimes dialing a telephone, and blows* SAUL *a kiss.*) Rich? (SAUL *shakes his head no. She leaves.* SAUL *tries to think of something to say to* RICH. *He abandons the effort and picks up the Sunday* New York Times *crossword puzzle.*)

SAUL: "African quadruped." (*Writing.*) G-n-u . . . "Hitler's father." (*Counting on his fingers.*) One, two . . . five letters. Let's see: Herman? Herman Hitler? (*Counting.*) That's six . . . Otto? . . . Werner? . . . Rudi? . . . Putzi? (*He shrugs.*) Fuck. (*He reads on.*) Thank God: "Jewish rolls." Starts with a *b*, six letters: bagels. (*He starts to write it in.*) Shit, that won't work. I need a *y*.

RICH (*without turning*): Bialys.

SAUL: *B-i-a-l-y-s.*

RICH: Short for Bialystok, a large industrial city in eastern Poland . . . (*turning to*

SAUL) hometown of Ludwig Zamenhof, inventor of Esperanto, an artificial international language. Alois Hitler! A-*l-o*—

SAUL (*putting down the puzzle*): Outclassed again. Why do I bother? He knows everything.

RICH: When I was a kid I used to spend all my time in libraries. My childhood was—

SAUL: If I had a father like yours I would have done the same thing.

RICH: But thanks to that son of a bitch I could tell you how many metric tons of coal the Benelux countries produced per annum, and the capital city of the Grand Duchy of Liechtenstein.

SAUL: I give up.

RICH: Vaduz.

SAUL: Miss Trivial Pursuit.

RICH: I knew to which great linguistic family the Telegu language of South India belongs.

SAUL: Telegu? Isn't that the national dish of Botswana?

RICH (*ignoring him*): The Dravidian. (SAUL *straightens up the bed table.*) I've always loved words . . . I wrote poetry when I was a kid. My brother used to make fun of me . . .

Winter, winter,
How you glinter,
With holidays' array.
And the snow
We all know
Is here all day.

(SAUL *smiles.*)

I was eight, nine when I wrote that. I had just come in from sledding down Indian Hill—a steep road that connects Jefferson Heights to the valley.

SAUL: You showed it to me on our grand tour of West Jersey.

RICH: It was a late afternoon just before sundown and the sky was intensely blue and intensely cold and you could see the stars already. For some reason nobody was home when I came back, so I stood there at the stamped enamel-top kitchen table dripping in my frozen corduroys and wrote that poem.

SAUL: Are you comfortable? (RICH *shrugs.* SAUL *fixes his pillows.*)

RICH: I was a good kid, but I was lonely and scared all the time. I was so desperate to find people like myself that I looked for them in the indexes of books—under *H*. I eventually found them—

SAUL: But not in books.

RICH: The next thing you know I moved to the city and was your typical office-worker-slash-writer. I hated my job, so I grew a beard and wore sandals, hoping they would fire me and give me permanent unemployment. I wanted to stay at home in my rent-controlled apartment and drink bourbon and write poems. I did that for a period. I loved it. The apartment got filthy and I did, too, and I'd go out only at night—to pick up guys. And then I found you—in a porno theater—(*he takes* SAUL's *hand*) and we semi-settled down and you took my picture and I started to jog. We bought a loft—

SAUL: And raised a cat—

RICH: —and loved each other. But that wasn't enough for me. I don't think you ever understood this: you weren't my muse, you were . . . (*he searches for the word*) Saul. (SAUL *rises and looks out the window.*) I loved you but I wanted someone to write poems to. During our marriage I had almost stopped writing and felt stifled even though our loft had appeared in *New York* magazine. And then I met Chet and left you in the lurch and lived with him at the Chelsea Hotel. He was shallow, callow, and selfish, and I loved him, too.

   We did a lot of coke and I wrote a lot of poetry and the catering was booming and the *New Yorker* published a story of mine and I ran in the marathon. I was on a roll. (*With mounting excitement as he relives the experience.*) I remember training on the East River Drive for the first time. I didn't realize how narrow and dark the city streets were until I got to the river and all of a sudden there was the fucking river. The sky was the same color as that twilight when I was a kid. I came from the darkness into the light. I'm running downtown and I make this bend and out of nowhere straight up ahead is the Manhattan Bridge and then the Brooklyn Bridge, one after another, and my earphones are playing Handel's *Royal Fireworks Music*. It can't get better than this, I know it. I'm running and crying from gratitude. I came from the darkness into the light. I'm running and telling God I didn't know He was *that* good or *that* big, thank you, Jesus, thanks, thanks . . . (*He slumps back, exhausted from the effort.*)

   The next morning I woke up with the flu and stayed in bed for a couple of days and felt much better. But my throat stayed a little sore and my glands were a little swollen . . . (*Long silence. Casually.*) Saul, I want you to do something for me. Will you do something for me, baby?

SAUL: Sure, babe.

RICH: Now listen. I want you to go out of here and go to the doctor and tell him you aren't sleeping so hot—

SAUL: I'm sleeping okay.

RICH: Sh! Now listen: you tell him you want something to make you sleep and Valium doesn't work on you, but a friend once gave you some Seconal—

SAUL: *No!* I won't do it!

RICH (*pressuring* SAUL *relentlessly*): I tried hoarding the pills here, but every night the nurse stays to watch me swallow them down.

SAUL: I can't do that.

RICH: I don't want to end up like Chet.

SAUL: I won't listen.

RICH: If you love me, you'll help me. I have something that's eating me up. I don't want to go on. I'm scared to go on.

SAUL: Don't do this to me! I can't handle it. I'll go out the window, I swear, don't do this—

RICH: Don't you see, it's the only way. Just get the pills.

SAUL: No!

RICH: Just have them around. You'll get used to the idea. And when the lesions spread above my neck so that I don't look the same, you'll want me to have them.

SAUL: Help me, help me!

RICH: It's all right. Not now.

SAUL: No.

RICH: Tomorrow.

SAUL: No.

RICH: The day after.

SAUL: No.

RICH: We'll see.

(RICH's *brother, wearing a surgical mask, gown, and gloves and carrying a small shopping bag, tiptoes in, stopping when he notices* RICH *and* SAUL.)

SAUL: Oh, my God. I think it's your brother.

BROTHER: I'll come back later.

SAUL (*pulling himself together*): No, I was just going.

BROTHER: It's all right, really.

SAUL: I've been here for a while.

BROTHER: I'm interrupting.

SAUL: Really.

RICH (*to his* BROTHER): Unless you're planning to come into intimate contact with me or my body fluids, none of that shit you have on is necessary.

BROTHER: The sign says—

RICH: But please restrain your brotherly affection for my sake; who knows what diseases you might have brought in with you? (*The* BROTHER *removes the mask, gown, and gloves.*)

SAUL: You two haven't seen each other for a while, so why don't I just—

RICH: By all means. You need a break, kid. Think about what I said.

SAUL: It stopped raining. I'll take a walk.

RICH: Have a nice walk.

BROTHER: Good seeing ya . . . ? (*He has forgotten* SAUL'S *name.*)

SAUL: Saul. Yeah.

(SAUL *exits. Beat.*)

BROTHER: I owe you an apology . . . (RICH *won't help him.*) I was very frightened . . . I'm afraid I panicked . . . Please forgive me.

RICH: Nothing to forgive.

BROTHER (*brightly*): Betty sends her love. She sent along a tin of butter crunch. (*He offers* RICH *a tin, which* RICH *ignores.*) You're not on any special diet? I told Betty I thought maybe you'd be on one of those macrobiotic diets. I read in the papers that it's helped some people with . . .

RICH: AIDS.

BROTHER: Yes. I keep a file of clippings on all the latest medical developments. (*He takes a clipping out of his wallet.*) Looks like they're going to have a vaccine soon. The French—

RICH: That's to *prevent* AIDS. I already *have* AIDS.

BROTHER: They have this new drug, AZT.

RICH: That's for the pneumonia. I don't have pneumonia.

BROTHER: Right . . . So how are you doing?

RICH (*smiling cheerfully*): I have Kaposi's sarcoma, a hitherto rare form of skin cancer. It's spreading. I have just begun chemotherapy. It nauseates me. I expect my hair will fall out. I also have a fungal infection of the throat called candidiasis, or thrush. My life expectancy is . . . I have a greater chance of winning the lottery. Otherwise I'm fine. How are you?

BROTHER: I'm sorry . . . (*Brightly again, after a long pause.*) Mary Pat sends her love. She won her school swimming competition and I registered her for the South Jersey championship. Oh, I forgot, she made this for you . . . (*He takes a large handmade fold-out card from the shopping bag. It opens downward a full two feet.*)

RICH: Say, have you heard about the miracle of AIDS?

BROTHER: What?

RICH: It can turn a fruit into a vegetable. What's the worst thing about getting AIDS? (*The* BROTHER *lets the card fall to the floor.*)

BROTHER: Stop it!

RICH: Trying to convince your parents that you're Haitian. Get it?

BROTHER: I came here to see if I could help you.

RICH: Skip it. So what do you want?

BROTHER: I don't want anything.

RICH: Everything I own is going to Saul—

BROTHER: I don't want anything.

RICH: Except for the stuff Mom left us. I told Saul that it's to go to you. Except for the Barcelona chair—

BROTHER: I don't care about—

RICH: I'm leaving Saul the copyright to my book—

BROTHER: Why are you doing this to me?

RICH: So you don't want my worldly possessions, such as they are; you want me to relieve your guilt.

BROTHER: Stop it.

RICH (*making the sign of the cross over his* BROTHER, *chanting*): I hereby exonerate you of the sin of being ashamed of your queer brother and being a coward in the face of—

BROTHER: Stop! Don't! (*The* BROTHER *grabs* RICH's *hand.*)

RICH: No!

BROTHER: Richard, don't! . . . (*He attempts to hug* RICH, *who resists with all his strength.*) I don't care . . . I don't care! . . . Rich! . . . Richie . . . Richie . . . (RICH *relents. They hug.*)

RICH: I'm so . . . [frightened]

BROTHER: Forgive me. Forgive me.

RICH: I don't want to . . . [die]

BROTHER: It's all right. I'm here . . . I'm here . . .

(*They hold each other close for a beat. The* HOSPITAL WORKER *rushes into the room.*)

HOSPITAL WORKER: Psst. Oye. Psst.

(RICH *and his* BROTHER *notice the* WORKER.)

RICH: What do you want now?

HOSPITAL WORKER (*shakes his head no*): Viene. Viene. He come. He come. (*He pulls the* BROTHER *from* RICH.)

RICH: Who come?

HOSPITAL WORKER: *Su amigo.* Your freng. He no like.

BROTHER: What's he saying?

(RICH *starts to laugh. Enter* SAUL. *The* WORKER *starts sweeping and whistling with an air of exuberant nonchalance. The following is overlapping.*)

RICH (*laughing*): He . . . he . . .

SAUL: What's going on?

BROTHER: Richie, what's so damned funny?

RICH: He thought we . . . (*he breaks up*) that he and I were cheating on you.

BROTHER: He thought that you and I were . . . (*He laughs.*)

RICH: He came in to warn me that you were coming! (*He laughs. To the worker:*) Gracias! Muchas gracias!

SAUL: He thought you two were . . . (*He laughs.*)

HOSPITAL WORKER (*to* RICH): *De nada.* [You're welcome.] Why you laugh? (*The* WORKER *laughs.*) *Como hay maricones.* [What a bunch of faggots.]

RICH: *Es mi hermano.* [He's my brother.]

HOSPITAL WORKER: *Coño.* [Fuck.]

RICH: *Perdona por lo que dije antes. Yo* (*pointing to himself*) *era mucho estupido.* [Forgive me for what I said to you before. I was being very stupid.]

HOSPITAL WORKER: *De nada. Somos todos estúpidos, chico.* [We're all stupid, my friend.] (*He exits. The giggles subside.*)

BROTHER (*checking watch, stiffening his spine*): I've got to be going now.

RICH: I'm glad you came by.

BROTHER: I'll be back tomorrow with Mary Pat. She's been dying—wanting to come by. She's been writing poetry and—

RICH: I'd love to see her. And tell Betty thanks for the . . . ?

BROTHER: Butter crunch. (*Exiting, shaking hands with* SAUL.) Good seeing ya . . . ? (*He has forgotten* SAUL's *name again.*)

SAUL: Saul.

BROTHER: Sorry. Bye. (*He exits.*)

SAUL: I won't get upset. I won't get upset.

RICH: What's the matter?

SAUL: It's *my* problem.

RICH: What?

SAUL: Rich, I've thought about things.

RICH: What?

SAUL (*suddenly exploding*): Goddamn it! That prick doesn't know my name after— how many years are we together?

RICH: *Were* together.

SAUL: Pardon me, I forgot we got an annulment from the pope. Fuck it, I won't get upset.

RICH (*overlapping*): My brother finds it hard to deal with the fact that—

SAUL: I said fuck it.

RICH: Don't you see, it was a big step for him—

SAUL: Your brother hates my fucking guts. Haven't you ever told him I didn't turn you queer?

RICH: My brother—

SAUL: I didn't give you AIDS either.

RICH: My brother—

SAUL: Why're you always defending him? What about me?

RICH: My brother's got a few feelings, too, even if he isn't a card-carrying member of the lavender elite.

SAUL: Let's hear it for our working-class hero.

RICH: You've never tried talking to him. You're so self-centered that it never occurred to you—

SAUL: I'm self—Now wait one minute! I'm so self-centered that I was willing to buy the pills for you.

RICH: You have the pills?

(*The other actors create the sleazy atmosphere of Christopher Street near the Hudson River.*)

DEALER 1: Yo, my man.

SAUL: I was willing to go down to Christopher Street, where all the drug dealers hang out.

DEALER 2: What's 'attenin', what's 'attenin'?

(SAUL *turns his back to* RICH *and immediately he is on Christopher Street.*)

SAUL (*to* DEALER 2): Nice night.

RICH: I told you to go to the doctor's.

DEALER 1: Smoke 'n' acid, MDA 'n' DEALER 2: Smoke 'n' coke, smoke 'n' speed, Smoke 'n' acid, MDA 'n'   coke, smoke 'n' coke . . . speed. . . .

SAUL (*to* DEALER 1): I said, "Nice night."

DEALER 1: Real nice. What's shakin', babe?

RICH: All you would've had to say to the doctor was "My roommate has AIDS and I'm not sleeping well."

SAUL (*to* DEALER 1): I'm not sleeping well.

DEALER 1: I have just the thing. Step right into my office.

DEALER 3: Speed, acid, mesc, ups, downs, crack . . .

SAUL: I'll take one hundred.

DEALER 1: Two dollars a cap.

RICH: Forty's enough.

SAUL: I wanted enough for both of us.

DEALER 1: You got the cash, I got the stash.

RICH: Tristan and Isolde.

DEALER 1: Hey, man, you want them or not?

SAUL: You don't understand anything!

DEALER 1: Look, man, I can't handle all that emotiating.

SAUL (*near the breaking point*): You've never understood anything!

DEALER 1: Gimme the greens, I'll give you the reds.

RICH: The widow throws herself on her husband's funeral pyre.

SAUL (*hitting the bed with his fists. If* RICH *were the bed he'd be dead*): SHIT! SHIT! SHIT! You selfish bastard!

RICH: What stopped you?

SAUL: From hitting you?

RICH: From buying the pills.

SAUL: The pills? Nothing stopped me. I bought them.

RICH: Thank you. Where are they?

SAUL: I threw them away.

RICH: Why?

SAUL: Let me help you live!

RICH: What's so hot about living when you're covered with lesions and you're coming down with a new infection every day? . . . If it gets too bad, I want to be able to quietly disappear.

SAUL: I won't argue the logic of it. I can't do what you want me to do.

RICH: I just want them around. You keep them for me—just in case.

SAUL: I won't.

RICH: Then I'll get them myself. I'll go out of here and get them. (*He climbs out of bed. He's shaky.*)

SAUL: You're crazy.

RICH: I don't need you to do my dirty work. (*He takes a few steps.*) Where're my clothes? Where'd they put them?

SAUL: Get back in bed!

RICH: I want to get out of here! (*He puts on his robe.*) This place is a death machine! (*He starts to leave but collapses on the floor.*)

SAUL (*rushing to his aid*): You idiot.

RICH (*catching his breath*): Well, here we are again. (SAUL *tries to help him back to bed.*) No. Let me sit . . . Fuck . . . (*He sits in chair.*) "Dependent": from the Late Latin "to hang from."

SAUL: I tried to do what you asked me to do. Just like always.

RICH: You don't have to apologize.

SAUL: I want you to understand something.

RICH: I understand.

SAUL: It's important. Listen. I had made up my mind to give you half of the pills and keep the other half for myself. I was walking past Sheridan Square. It was starting to drizzle again. You've never seen Sheridan Square look grungier: a drunk was pissing on the pathetic little flowers. And that crazy lady—you know the one that sings off-key at the top of her lungs—she was there, too. And my favorite, the guy with his stomach out to here—

RICH: I get the picture.

SAUL: There I was walking with the pills in my pocket, contemplating our suicides. And I was getting wet and cold. As I passed the square, Seconal seemed too slow to me. You don't have a monopoly on pain.

RICH: I never thought—

SAUL: Shut up. Anyway, I had stopped in front of the Pleasure Chest. I looked up and there in the window were sex toys and multicolored jockstraps, lit by a red neon sign. I said, "Help me, God." Which is funny coming from an atheist, let me tell you . . . I said it out loud.

RICH: And you could walk again.

SAUL: Well, it wasn't exactly a miracle.

RICH: Thank God.

SAUL: Anyway, there I was in front of a sex shop, and I looked down and there was a puddle. Now this'll sound stupid.

RICH: Couldn't sound stupider than the rest.

SAUL: In this dirty little puddle was a reflection of the red neon sign. It was beautiful. And the whole street was shining with the incredible colors. They kept changing as the different signs blinked on and off . . . I don't know how long I stood there. A phrase came to my head: "The Lord taketh and the Lord giveth."

RICH: You blew your punch line.

SAUL: It's the other way around. Anyway, there went two hundred bucks down the sewer.

RICH: Take it off your taxes.

SAUL: Don't you see, I just don't have the right to take your life or mine.

RICH: The Miracle of the Pleasure Chest.

SAUL: Hang in there, Rich.

RICH: Our Lady of Christopher Street.

SAUL: Maybe I'm being selfish, but I want you here. I need you.

RICH: My future isn't exactly promising.

SAUL: I'll take you as is.

RICH: But what happens when it gets worse? It's gonna get worse.

SAUL: I'll be here for you no matter what happens.

RICH: Will you?

SAUL: I promise.

RICH: Shit.

SAUL: What do you want me to say?

RICH: You're so goddamned noble.

SAUL: How do you want me to be?

RICH: I can't afford to be noble. The only thing holding me together is rage. It's not fair! Why me?

SAUL: Why *not* you? Maybe I'm next. No one knows.

RICH: I reserve the right to put an end to all this shit.

SAUL: All right, but if you kill yourself they won't bury you in hallowed ground and you'll go to hell with all us Jews.

RICH: I bet they have a separate AIDS section in the cemetery so I don't infect the other corpses. (*Beat, then suddenly he speaks fiercely.*) Do you promise to stick with me no matter what happens?

SAUL: I do.

RICH: *Do you?* (*He searches* SAUL's *face for the answer.*) I need you. (*Long silence. He releases* SAUL.) Paradise in a puddle.

SAUL: You couldn't resist that, could you?

RICH: Prodigies and signs, why not? It's the end of an era.

SAUL: What do you think'll come next?

RICH: Next? After I'm gone?

SAUL: Don't be maudlin. You know I didn't mean that.

RICH: I know you didn't . . . I've been wondering what happens after I die . . . Do you think things go on and on? I don't know. Is this all the time I have? I hope not . . . Do you think anywhere out there is a place as sweet as this one? I like it here—even though right now I am going through a lot of . . . (*searching for the word*) difficulty. (*He goes back to bed.*) And if we get to come back, where do we get to come back to? I don't feature leaving here and going to a goddamned naphtha swamp in the Z sector of some provincial galaxy to live as some kind of weird insect . . . But if life is a kind of educational process in which each piece of the universe eventually gets to discover its own true divine nature, if it is, then a methane bog on Jupiter might serve just as well as a meadow in the Berkshires . . . I want to be cremated and I want my ashes to fertilize the apple tree in the middle of Jake's pasture. When you take a bite of an apple from that tree, think of me.

SAUL: You'd be the worm in it.

RICH: Saul?

SAUL: What, Rich?

RICH: There's a café way over by Tompkins Square Park, off of B. It holds maybe ten tables and has the scuzziest art on the walls.

SAUL: What about it?

RICH: I want to read my work there.

SAUL: You turned down the Y.

RICH: People go there, gay, straight, with their weird hair and their ears pierced ninety-nine different ways, they go there late in the evening, and there's a guitarist, and they sit there politely and listen. They look newborn, but slightly depraved. I want to read there when I get out of here. And you'll take pictures. Okay?

SAUL: Sounds okay. Sounds good to me.

RICH: Forgive me for being such a fuck.

SAUL: You really are a fuck.

RICH: I'm a real prick.

SAUL: You're an asshole.

RICH: You're a faggot.

SAUL: You're a fruit.

RICH: You know, if we took precautions . . .

SAUL: If what? What? You always do that.

RICH: I don't know.

SAUL: Would you like to?

RICH: If we're careful. Do you want to?

SAUL: I'd love to. What do you think?

RICH: I think it'd be okay.

SAUL: What'll we do?

RICH: I don't know. Something safe.

SAUL: We'll think of something.

RICH: Close the curtain.

SAUL: Do you think we should?

RICH: Well, we can't do it like this.

SAUL: Right.

RICH: Right.

SAUL: What if someone comes in?

RICH: So what?

SAUL: Right. (SAUL *doesn't move.*)

RICH: So what are you waiting for?

SAUL: I'm scared.

RICH: So am I. Do you think we should?

SAUL: God, I want to.

RICH: Well, close the fucking curtain! (*The* HOSPICE WORKER *ends the impasse by closing the curtain.*) Thanks.

SAUL: Thanks.

(*When the curtain is completely shut, the* HOSPICE WORKER *walks down center.*)

HOSPICE WORKER: I have a new AIDS patient. Richard. He still has a lot of denial about his condition. Which is normal. I think most of us would go crazy if we had to face our own deaths squarely. He's a wonderful man. He writes extraordinarily funny poems about the ward. His lover's there all the time, and he's got a lot of friends visiting, and both families. I only hope it keeps up. It's only his second time in the hospital. They get a lot of support at first, but as the illness goes on, the visitors stop coming—and they're left with only me.

But something tells me it's not going to happen in his case. You should see how his lover takes care of him. God forbid they treat Rich badly, Saul swoops down and lets them have it. He's making a real pain in the ass of himself, which is sometimes how you have to be in this situation.

Rich should be out of the hospital again in a week or so. For a while. He's a fighter . . . The angry phase is just about over and the bargaining phase is beginning. If he behaves like a good little boy, God will do what Rich tells Him to do . . . I certainly hope that God does.

I don't know anymore. Sometimes I think I'm an atheist. No. Not really. It's more that I'm angry at God: how can He do this? (*Pause.*) I have a lot of denial, I am angry, and I bargain with God. I have a long way to go towards acceptance. Maybe it's time for me to resign. Maybe I'm suffering from burnout.

But what would I do if I didn't go to St. Vincent's? And it's a privilege to be with people when they are dying. Sometimes they tell you the most amazing things. The other night Jean-Jacques—he's this real queen, there's no other word for it—he told me what he misses most in the hospital is his corset and high heels. I mean he weighs all of ninety pounds and he's half-dead. But I admire his spirit. The way they treat him. Sometimes they won't even bring the food to his bed. And I'm afraid to complain for fear they take it out on him! Damn them! . . . I've lost some of my idealism, as I said. Last night I painted his nails for him. (*She shows the audience her vividly painted fingernails.*) Flaming red. He loved it.

BIBLIOGRAPHY

RESOURCES:

Brecht, Stefan. *Queer Theatre*. Frankfurt: Suhrkamp, 1978.

Chinoy, Helen Krich, and Linda Walsh Jenkins (eds.). *Women in American Theatre*. New York: Crown, 1981.

Curtin, Kaier. *We Can Always Call Them Bulgarians: The Emergence of Lesbians and Gay Men on the American Stage*. New York: Alyson Publications, 1987.

Helbing, Terry (ed.). *Gay Theatre Alliance Directory of Gay Plays*. New York: JH Press, 1982.

Hoffman, William M. (ed.). *Gay Plays: The First Collection*. New York: Avon, 1979.

McDermott, Kate (ed.). *Places, Please!* Iowa City: Aunt Lute Book Company, 1985.

Wilcox, Michael (ed.).*Gay Plays*. London: Methuen, 1984.

—*Gay Plays Volume Two*. London: Methuen, 1985.

PLAYS:

NOTE: *Several of the abovementioned volumes contain bibliographies listing plays that feature gay characters or themes. The Helbing directory and the Hoffman anthology are especially thorough in this regard. Any plays noted in those volumes are omitted from the bibliography that follows. I would like to be able to say that the list of plays below is a complete account of contemporary gay plays. At the same time, I am pleased to acknowledge that gay plays have proliferated so rapidly in the last ten years that it would be foolish for me to claim to know about all of them. I have tried to include all the major plays originally written in English that have been published by major houses or received major productions in the American theater, as well as titles that I have discovered from articles about theater in Canada, Australia, England, and all over the United States. However, I am certain that they represent only part of the theater's contribution to the free exploration of gay identity—past, present, and future.*

The productions noted are the original ones, as far as I know. Plays in this volume are omitted for obvious reasons. Publications are marked with an asterisk.

Abatemarco, Tony, and others. *Plato's Symposium*. Powerhouse Theater, Santa Monica, 1986.

Adams, John, and William Kromm. *The Marlowe Show*. Boston Arts Group, Boston, 1978.

Andersen, D. R. *Dancing in the Dark*. Shandol Theater, New York, 1986.

*Archer, Robyn. *Pack of Women*. Melbourne: Penguin, 1986.

*Arnold, C. D. *The Dinosaur Plays*. New York: JH Press, 1983.

—*Delivery*. Theatre Rhinoceros, San Francisco, 1982.

—*A Night at the Blue Moon*. Earnest Players, San Francisco, 1980.

*Artists Involved in Death and Survival. *The AIDS Show*. Los Angeles: West Coast Plays 17/18, 1985.

—*Unfinished Business: The New AIDS Show*. Theatre Rhinoceros, San Francisco, 1986.

Ayanoglu, Byron. *Friendship*. Buddies in Bad Times Theater, Toronto, 1985.

Barnett, Robert. *The Fifth Square*. Tyson Studio, New York, 1984.

Bartlett, Neil. *A Vision of Love Revealed in Sleep*. Battersea Arts Centre, London, 1987.

Bartlett, Neil, Duncan Roy, and Robin Whitmore. *Pornography*. Institute of Contemporary Arts, London, 1984.

*Baum, Terry. *Immediate Family* in *Places, Please!* Iowa City: Aunt Lute Book Company, 1985.

*Baum, Terry, and Carolyn Myers. *Dos Lesbos* in *Places, Please!* Iowa City: Aunt Lute Book Company, 1985.

*Bell, Neal. *Raw Youth*. New York: Dramatists Play Service, 1986.

Bentley, Eric. *Round Two*. Celebration Theater, Los Angeles, 1987.

Bernard, Kenneth. *The 60-Minute Queer Show*. La Mama ETC, New York, 1977.

Bishop, John. *The Musical Comedy Murders of 1940*. Circle Repertory Theatre, New York, 1987.

Bommer, Lawrence, and Rick Paul. *Gunsel, or Love on the Lam*. Celebration Theatre, Los Angeles, 1985.

*Bowne, Alan. *Forty Deuce*. New York: Sea Horse Press, 1983.

—*Beirut*. Bay Area Playwrights Festival, San Francisco, 1986.

Bray, Errol. *The Choir*. Nimrod Theatre, Sydney, 1980.

Briggs, Donald. *Phil and Mac*. Los Angeles Actors Theatre, 1983.

*Brown, Arch. *News Boy*. New York: JH Press, 1982.

Buford, Lorenzo. *Tea Time*. Celebration Theatre, Los Angeles, 1985.

—*Grease Your Legs and Let 'Em Shine*. A Different Light, Los Angeles, 1985.

*Bumbalo, Victor. *Niagara Falls and Other Plays* (also includes *Kitchen Duty* and *After Eleven*). New York: Calamus Books, 1984.

*Busch, Charles. *Vampire Lesbians of Sodom*. New York: Samuel French, 1985.

—*Times Square Angel*. Limbo Theater, New York, 1985.

—*Pardon My Inquisition*. Limbo Theater, New York, 1986.

—*Psycho Beach Party*. Limbo Theater, New York, 1986.

Case, Sue-Ellen. *Jo*. Julian Theatre, San Francisco, 1979.

*Chambers, Jane. *Last Summer at Bluefish Cove*. New York: JH Press, 1982.

*—*My Blue Heaven*. New York: JH Press, 1982.

—*The Quintessential Image*. Town Hall, New York, 1984.

*Chesley, Robert. *Stray Dog Story*. New York: JH Press, 1984.

—*Hell, I Love You*. Theatre Rhinoceros, San Francisco, 1980.

—*Night Sweat*. Meridian Gay Theater, New York, 1984.

Davison, Anthony. *Screamers*. Croydon Warehouse, London, 1985.

Dickler, Gloria. *Dry Wells*. Eccentric Circles Theater, New York, 1985.

*Dreher, Sarah. *8 x 10 Glossy*. See McDermott, *Places, Please!*

*—*Ruby Christmas*. See McDermott, *Places, Please!*

Dubois, René-Daniel. *Being at Home with Claude*. Théâtre de Quat 'Sous, Montreal, 1985.

*Durang, Christopher. *Beyond Therapy*. In *Christopher Durang Explains It All for You*. New York: Avon, 1983.

*—*Sister Mary Ignatius Explains It All for You*. New York: Avon, 1982.

Dwyer, Sandy. *Cheese and Crackers*. Cast Theater, Los Angeles, 1982.

Elverman, Bill. *Particular Friendships*. Astor Place, New York, 1982.

Evans, Jon Morgan. *Pool Play*. Cast Theater, Los Angeles, 1982.

*Fierstein, Harvey. *Torch Song Trilogy*. New York: Gay Presses of New York, 1980.

*—*Safe Sex*. New York: Atheneum, 1987.

—*Spookhouse*. Playhouse 91, New York, 1982.

—*La Cage aux Folles*. Palace Theater, New York, 1983.

*Finn, William. *In Trousers*. New York: Samuel French, 1986.

*—*March of the Falsettos*. New York: Samuel French, 1981.

Fleming, Justin. *The Cobra*. Sydney Theatre Company, Sydney, 1983.

Forrester, Alice. *Heart of the Scorpion*. WOW Café, New York, 1985.

Foster, Emmett. *Emmett: A One Morman Show*. Public Theater, New York, 1983.

Fulford, Robin. *Steel Kiss.* Buddies in Bad Times, Toronto, 1986.

Garvey, Ellen Gruber. *Soup* in *Places, Please!*

Gay Actors' Ensemble. *This Is Not a Stage I'm Going Through.* Guild Theatre, Melbourne, 1985.

Giantvalley, Scott. *The Wedding.* Déjà Vu Coffeehouse, Los Angeles, 1985.

—*Fracture.* Fifth Estate Theatre, Los Angeles, 1985.

Gilbert, Sky. *The Dressing Gown.* Buddies in Bad Times Theater, Toronto.

—*Drag Queens on Trial.* Buddies in Bad Times Theater, Toronto.

—*Drag Queen in Outer Space.* Buddies in Bad Times Theater, Toronto.

—*Gloria in Excelsis Deo.* Theatre Centre, Toronto, 1983.

—*Radiguet.* Buddies in Bad Times Theater, Toronto.

Gormley, Fred. *Elmo's Driving Lesson.* Gay and Lesbian Playwrights, New York, 1986.

*Gow, Michael. *The Kid.* Sydney: Currency Press, 1983.

Grattan, Simon. *Magpie's Nest.* Belvoir Theatre, Sydney, 1987.

Green, Wayne. *Ticking!* Celebration Theatre, Los Angeles, 1985.

Greenspan, David. *Recent Hemispheres.* Home, New York, 1987.

*Greig, Noel. *Poppies.* London: Gay Men's Press, 1983.

Hagedorn, Jeff. *One.* Lionheart Theatre, Chicago, 1983.

Harders, Robert. *Bill and Eddie.* Los Angeles Actors Theater, 1984.

Hartog, Patricia. *Cadylee.* Sanford Meisner Theater, New York, 1986.

*Harwood, Ronald. *The Dresser.* New York: Grove Press, 1981.

Hoffman, Frank. *Smiling Travelers, Gorgeous Lies.* Meridian Gay Theatre, New York, 1983.

Holsclaw, Doug. *The Life of the Party.* Theatre Rhinoceros, San Francisco, 1986.

Holt, Stephen. *The Blonde Leading the Blonde.* Theater for the New City, New York, 1982.

—*A Fever of Unknown Origin.* Theater for the New City, New York, 1984.

Hoskins, Tam. *Friends Like You.* Finborough Arms Theatre, London, 1985.

Hughes, Holly. *The Lady Dick.* WOW Café, New York, 1986.

—*Dress Suits for Hire.* WOW Café, New York, 1987.

*Innaurato, Albert. *Coming of Age in Soho.* New York: Dramatists Play Service, 1984.

Jacker, Corinne. *Dancing in the Dark.* Long Wharf Theater, New Haven, 1987.

Kantrowitz, Stephen. *Arrivals.* 18th Street Playhouse, New York, 1983.

Katz, Michael, Steven Twiss, and Jerry Campbell. *Something More.* Meridian Gay Theater, New York, 1982.

Kearns, Michael. *The Truth Is Bad Enough.* Cast Theater, Los Angeles, 1983.

*Kenna, Peter. *Mates* in *Drag Show,* edited and published by Currency Press, Sydney, 1977.

—A Hard God. Sydney: Currency Press, 1974.

—Furtive Love. Sydney: Currency Press, 1980.

*Kesselman, Wendy. *My Sister in This House.* New York: Samuel French, 1982.

*Kondoleon, Harry. *Christmas on Mars.* New York: Dramatists Play Service, 1983.

—Anteroom. New York: Dramatists Play Service, 1986.

Kreiger, Donald. *A Boy's Life.* Cast Theater, Los Angeles, 1983.

Kreitman, Margery. *Please Wait for the Beep.* Stonewall Repertory Theater, New York, 1986.

Laurents, Arthur. *A Loss of Memory.* The Glines, Town Hall, 1982.

*Levin, Ira. *Deathtrap.* New York: Dramatists Play Service, 1979.

*Linney, Romulus. *Childe Byron.* New York: Dramatists Play Service, 1981.

—*April Snow.* Ensemble Studio Theater, New York, 1987.

Lotman, Loretta. *Thanksgiving.* Stonewall Repertory Theater, New York, 1982.

*Lowe, Barry. *Writer's Cramp.* Sydney: Appollyon Press, 1983.

*Lucas, Craig. *Blue Window.* New York: Samuel French, 1985.

*Lucie, Doug. *Progress*. London: Methuen, 1986.

Ludlam, Charles. *Secret Lives of the Sexists*. Ridiculous Theatrical Company, New York, 1984.

—*The Mystery of Irma Vep*. New York, 1985.

—*Salammbo*. New York, 1986.

—*The Artificial Jungle*. New York. 1986.

*Lyssa, Alison. *Pinball* in *Plays by Women* (ed. Michelene Wandor). London: Methuen, 1985.

—*The Boiling Frog*. Nimrod Theatre, Sydney, 1983.

MacIvor, Daniel. *Material Benefits*. Buddies in Bad Times, Toronto, 1986.

*Malpede, Karen. *Sappho and Aphrodite* in *A Monster Has Stolen the Sun and Other Plays*. Marlboro, VT: Marlboro Press, 1987.

*Mamet, David. *Edmond*. New York: Grove Press, 1985.

*—*A Life in the Theatre*. New York: Grove Press, 1977.

*—*The Shawl*. New York: Grove Press, 1985.

*Mason, Timothy. *Levitation*. New York: Dramatists Play Service, 1986.

—*Bearclaw*. See Wilcox, *Gay Plays, Volume Two*.

Mauriello, David. *But Mostly Because It's Raining*. Boston Arts Group, Boston, 1977.

McDonald, Bryden. *Remission*. Buddies in Bad Times, Toronto, 1986.

McLane, Robert. *Do Rattlesnakes Bite in the Dark?* Celebration Theater, Los Angeles, 1985.

Mehrten, Greg. *Pretty Boy*. Performing Garage, New York, 1984.

—*It's a Man's World*. L.A. Theater Center, Los Angeles, 1985.

Miller, Susan. *Flux*. Phoenix Repertory Company, New York, 1977.

*Miller, Terry. *Pines '79*. New York: JH Press, 1984.

*Mitchell, Julian. *Another Country*. New York: Samuel French, 1982.

Moch, Cheryl. *Cinderella: The Real True Story*. WOW Café, New York, 1986.

—*Snow White Unadorned*. WOW Café, New York, 1986.

Moore, Stephen. *Dream Boy*. Celebration Theater, Los Angeles, 1985.

Morris, Bob. *Waving Goodbye*. Jewish Repertory Theatre, New York, 1987.

*Morris, Sidney. *If This Isn't Love!* New York: JH Press, 1982.

—*The Demolition of Harry Fay*. Meridian Gay Theater, New York, 1983.

—*Last Chance at the Brass Ring*. Shakespeare Studio Theatre, New York, 1983.

Mushroom, Merrill. *Bar Dykes*. Déjà Vu Coffeehouse, Los Angeles, 1984.

*Nelson, Mariah Burton. *Out of Bounds* in *Places, Please!*

Oxendine, Bill. *Stuck*. Déjà Vu Coffeehouse, Los Angeles, 1980.

—*BBQ Pork*. Déjà Vu Coffeehouse, Los Angeles, 1981.

—*Beach Head*. Fifth Estate Theatre, Los Angeles, 1981.

—*Pumps*. Fifth Estate Theatre, Los Angeles, 1984.

*Parnell, Peter. *Romance Language*. New York: Samuel French, 1985.

Patrick, Robert. *Blue Is For Boys*. Theater for the New City, New York, 1983.

—*50s, 60s, 70s, 80s*. Fifth Estate, Los Angeles, 1984.

—*Bread Alone*. Wings Theater Company, New York, 1986.

—*The Hostages*. Wings Theater Company, New York, 1986.

—*Michelangelo's Models*. Fifth Estate, Los Angeles, 1982.

—*Orpheus & Amerika*. Theater for the New City, New York, 1981.

Perring, Robert. *Caged Men*. 18th Street Playhouse, New York, 1987.

—*Trade*. 18th Street Playhouse, New York, 1983.

Picano, Felice, and Jerry Campbell. *Immortal!* Meridian Gay Theater, New York, 1986.

Pickett, James Carroll. *Dream Man*. Celebration Theatre, Los Angeles, 1985.
—*Bathhouse Benediction*. Celebration Theatre, Los Angeles, 1984.
Pike, Frank. *Smaller Heartaches*. Triangle Theater, Boston, 1985.
Pintauro, Joseph. *Snow Orchid*. Circle Repertory Theatre, New York, 1982.
Pliura, Vytautas. *Conspiracy of Feeling*. Fifth Street Studio Theatre, Los Angeles, 1982.
Pressman, Kenneth. *Sand Dancing*. Hudson Guild, New York, 1983.
Preston, John. *Franny, the Queen of Provincetown*. Meridian Gay Theatre, New York, 1984.
Pugh, Nigel. *Skin Deep*. Fallen Angel Theatre, London, 1986.
Ranson, Rebecca. *Warren*. Southeastern Arts Media and Education (SANE), Atlanta, 1984.
Rifkin, Don. *Delusion of Angels*. Actors Outlet, New York, 1987.
Rooney, Alison. *Rabbit Plantation*. WOW Café, New York, 1987.
Rudet, Jacqueline. *Basin*. Royal Court, London, 1986.
Rutherford, Stanley. *Tongue Dance*. Off Ramp, San Francisco, 1985.
Saleem, Adele. *John*. Oval House Theatre, London, 1984.
*Schein, David. *Out Comes Butch*. Los Angeles: *West Coast Plays* 17/18, 1985.
Schiowitz, Josh. *The Truth Is Bad Enough*. Cast Theater, Los Angeles, 1983.
Schpak, Helene, Beryl Rotchatka, and Cathie Bauer. *Peacocks*. Déjà Vu Coffeehouse, Los Angeles, 1984.
Schulman, Sarah, and Robin Epstein. *Art Failures*. More Fire! Productions, New York, 1984.
Schwartz, Joel. *Powerlines*. Odyssey Theater, Los Angeles, 1982.
Selig, Paul. *Terminal Bar*. En Garde Arts, New York, 1986.
Sewell, Stephen. *Dreams in an Empty City*. State Theater of South Australia, Adelaide, 1986.
Shank, Adele Edling. *Winterplay*. Magic Theatre, San Francisco, 1982.
*Shawn, Wallace. *Aunt Dan and Lemon*. New York: Grove Press, 1986.
Sherman, Martin. *Cracks*. See Wilcox, *Gay Plays, Volume Two*.
*Spears, Steve. *The Elocution of Benjamin Franklin* in *Drag Show*. Sydney: Currency Press, 1983.
Spencer, Stuart. *Cash*. Ensemble Studio Theater, New York, 1985.
—*The Last Outpost at the End of the World*. Ensemble Studio Theater, New York, 1987.
Steppling, John. *Close*. Factory Place Theatre, Los Angeles, 1984.
*—*Neck* in *Plays from Padua Hills 1982*. Claremont, CA: Pomona College, 1982.
—*The Dream Coast*. Mark Taper Forum, Los Angeles, 1986.
St. Lubin, Yves Assoto. *Risin' to the Love We Need*. Stonewall Repertory Theater, New York, 1981.
Suncircle, Pat. *Cory*. Lavender Cellar Theatre, Minneapolis, 1975.
Swados, Robin. *A Quiet End*. Offstage Theatre, London, 1986.
Tierney, Rod. *Love In Bloom*. Earnest Players, San Francisco, 1980.
Type, David. *Just Us Indians*. Théâtre Passe Muraille, Toronto, 1984.
Upton, Phyllis. *A Portrait of Michael*. Celebration Theatre, Los Angeles, 1985.
Van Maanen, James. *Better Living*. StageArts Theater, New York, 1987.
*Wagner, Jane. *The Search for Signs of Intelligent Life in the Universe*. New York: Harper & Row, 1986.
Weaver, Neal. *Initiation Rites*. Meat and Potatoes Company, New York, 1986.
Weinberg, Tom Wilson. *Ten Percent Revue*. Provincetown, 1986.
Wells, Win. *Gertrude Stein and a Companion*. Bush Theatre, London, 1984.
*White, Patrick. *Netherwood*. Sydney: Currency Press, 1983.
*Whitemore, Hugh. *Breaking the Code*. London: Unwin, 1986.

Williams, Tennessee. *Something Cloudy, Something Clear.* Jean Cocteau Rep, New York, 1981.

*—*Vieux Carre.* New York: New Directions, 1979.

*Willis, Julia. *Going Up.* See McDermott, *Places, Please!*

Wojnarowicz, David. *Sounds in the Distance.* BACA Downtown, Brooklyn, 1984.

Yeomans, Cal. *Sunsets.* Stonewall Repertory Theater, New York, 1981.

ABOUT THE AUTHORS

ROBERT CHESLEY was born in 1943 in Jersey City, New Jersey. He has been writing plays for gay theater since 1980, when his one-act *Hell, I Love You* was produced by San Francisco's Theatre Rhinoceros. His plays have been seen in New York since 1981, when the Chelsea Gay Association Theatre Project presented three of his one-acts under the title *City Pieces*. His *Stray Dog Story* had a four-month run as the premiere production of Meridian Gay Theatre and has also been produced in San Francisco, Indianapolis, and Portland, Oregon. His *Night Sweat*, produced by Meridian in 1984, was the first play dealing with AIDS to be produced in New York and has subsequently had successful, extended runs in Los Angeles and San Francisco. *Jerker* ran for four months at Los Angeles's Celebration Theatre, in a production which was also presented in Atlanta. His other work includes *Pigman* and a collaboration with choreographer Christopher Beck titled *Nocturnes*. Chesley lives in San Francisco and is a member of the Dramatists Guild.

HARVEY FIERSTEIN was born June 6, 1954, in Bensonhurst in Brooklyn, New York City. A graduate of Pratt Institute with a fine arts degree, he made his professional acting debut in 1971 with Andy Warhol at La Mama E.T.C. He has since worked on stage and screen with Woody Allen, Ron Tavel, Garrett Morris, Robert Patrick, Megan Terry, Danny DeVito, and Tom O'Horgan, to name a few. Fierstein began his playwriting career in 1973 with *In Search of the Cobra Jewels*, for which the *Village Voice* dubbed him "the devil come to earth." That triumph was followed by *Freaky Pussy* and *Flatbush Tosca*. In 1978 La Mama E.T.C. began producing the three plays which constitute *Torch Song Trilogy*. In 1983 he wrote the libretto for the musical *La Cage aux Folles*. In 1984 his play *Spookhouse* premiered Off Broadway, and in 1987 *Safe Sex* bowed on Broadway. He is the recipient of three Tony Awards, two Drama Desk Awards, an Obie, an Oppy (*Newsday* playwriting award), four Villager Awards, the 1981 Fund for Human Dignity Award, and the Dramatists Guild/Hull Warriner Award, as well as grants from the Ford Foundation, the Rockefeller Foundation, and CAPS. Mr. Fierstein's plays have been produced around the world from the West End to the West Bank. He is very gay about it all.

WILLIAM M. HOFFMAN was born April 12, 1939, in New York City. He started writing for the theater at the legendary Off Off Broadway showcase, the Caffe Cino. He is a member of the Circle Repertory Company but has also worked at La Mama, Playwrights Horizons, and the Manhattan Theater Club. He is co-author (with Anthony Holland) of three comedies, *Cornbury*, *Shoe Palace Murray*, and *The Cherry Orchard, Part Two*. He wrote the book and co-wrote the lyrics (with composer John Braden) to the musicals *Gulliver's Travels* and *Etiquette*. In recognition of his work, Hoffman has received Guggenheim and New York Foundation for the Arts fellowships and two National Endowment for the Arts grants. He has written for both film and television and is the editor of four play anthologies, including *Gay Plays: The First Collection*. He wrote the libretto for *A Figaro for Antonia* (music by John Corigliano), commissioned by the Metropolitan Opera.

As Is received the 1985 Drama Desk Award for Outstanding New Play, an Obie Award for Distinguished Playwriting, and three Tony nominations, including one for Best Play.

HOLLY HUGHES was born March 10, 1955, in the Navy Bean Capital of the World: Saginaw, Michigan. Her earliest exposure to the thespian arts came at the Christian leadership camps she attended each year. She worked on set crew for a production of *The Sound of Music.* She remembers to this day the beaverboard Alps she helped construct and, less fondly, their demise when a flatulent von Trapp family member farted into a microphone during "Edelweiss." Recognition came as early as high school, when Ms. Hughes received the coveted Lion's Club Citizenship Award. With a fifty dollar savings bond and a patty-melt-plate luncheon under her belt, she attended Kalamazoo College, graduating in 1977. In 1978, Ms. Hughes briefly attended Burger College, but the call of the muse was stronger than her love of all things fried. Off to New York she went, to a New Life and the thrill of big-city waitressing. She attended the New York Feminist Institute in a program directed by Miriam Schapiro. One day she took a wrong turn on the way to Balducci's and ended up in the quaint East Village, specifically the WOW Café. After a few weeks of volunteering, Ms. Hughes assumed artistic directorship when the rest of the "collective" skipped the country. In 1983, she presented her first piece, *Shrimp in a Basket (A Personal History of Seafood). The Well of Horniness* followed in the form of fifteen- to twenty-minute chunks presented ad nauseam throughout the East Village. Her second play, *The Lady Dick,* premiered at WOW in November 1985. *Dress Suits for Hire,* written for Lois Weaver and Peggy Shaw, was performed at P.S. 122 and the Women's Interart Theater in 1987.

HARRY KONDOLEON was born February 26, 1955, in New York City. While a graduate student at the Yale School of Drama (where he twice won the Molly Kazan Award for playwriting), he had two plays produced: *Rococo,* which premiered at the Yale Repertory Theater's first Winterfest of New American Plays in 1981, and *The Brides,* published in *Wordplays 2,* which was later produced by the Lenox Arts Center/Music-Theater Group. He spent a summer at the Eugene O'Neill Playwrights' Conference where his play *Clara Toil* was developed and presented. *Slacks and Tops* appeared soon after in New York at the Manhattan Theater Club. The Double Image Theater put on four of his one-acts in repertory, including *Self Torture and Strenuous Exercise,* which was selected for publication in *Best Short Plays 1984.* The same season his play *Christmas on Mars* premiered at Playwrights Horizons. His next play *The Vampires* opened first at the Empty Space in Seattle and was produced Off Broadway at the Astor Place Theater. The Second Stage produced *Linda Her* and *The Fairy Garden* in 1984, and in 1985 *Anteroom* opened at Playwrights Horizons. Thanks to support from the MacDowell Colony and Yaddo, he has completed three new plays, *The Poets' Corner, Play Yourself,* and *Zero Positive,* which were produced in 1988 at Theater for the New City, Virginia Stage Company, and the New York Shakespeare Festival's Public Theatre, respectively. He is the recipient of an Obie Award for "Most Promising Young Playwright," a *Newsday* Oppenheimer Award, and a Los Angeles DramaLogue Award, as well as grants from

the Rockefeller Foundation, the National Endowment for the Arts and the New York Foundation for the Arts.

Other publications include the novels, *The Whore of Tjampuan*, published by Performing Arts Journal Publications, and *Appear and Disappear*, part of which was published by Wedge Press; *The Death of Understanding*, a book of poems published by Caliban Press; and an edition of his play *Andrea Rescued* with illustrations by Alison Seiffer. In addition, he collaborated with artist Mark Beard on an elaborate edition of his play *The Cote d'Azur Triangle* (first performed at the Actors Studio), which has been exhibited internationally and is part of the permanent collection of the Museum of Modern Art.

EMILY MANN was born in Boston on April 12, 1952. She received a B.A. from Harvard and an M.F.A. from the University of Minnesota. Her first play, *Annulla, An Autobiography*, premiered at the Guthrie Theater's Guthrie 2 under her direction in 1977 and was later produced at Chicago's Goodman Theater and on National Public Radio's *Earplay* series. *Still Life*, her probing play about the Vietnam War, premiered at the Goodman Studio Theatre and opened at New York's American Place Theatre in 1981 under the author's direction, winning six Obie Awards, including those for playwriting and direction. The play was later published in *New Plays USA 1* and *Coming to Terms: American Plays & the Vietnam War* and has been performed around the world. Mann began work on *Execution of Justice* on a commission from San Francisco's Eureka Theater in 1982. First produced in March 1984 by the Actors Theatre of Louisville, the piece was co-winner of the Great American Play Contest and was subsequently presented by the Center Stage in Baltimore, Theater Cornell, Seattle's The Empty Space, the Arena Stage in Washington, D.C., the Alley Theatre in Houston, Berkeley Rep, and the San Jose Rep in association with the Eureka Theater. The play was also produced at the Guthrie Theater and on Broadway under Mann's direction. *Execution of Justice* won the Helen Hayes Award, the Bay Area Theatre Critics Circle Award, the HBO/USA Award, a Drama Desk nomination, and the Playwriting Award from the Women's Committee of the Dramatists Guild for "dramatizing issues of conscience."

Mann's other directorial credits include the BAM Theater Company's production of *He and She* and *Oedipus the King*, the Guthrie's *The Glass Menagerie*, *A Weekend Near Madison* at the Actors Theatre of Louisville and the Astor Place Theater in New York, *A Doll's House* at the Hartford Stage Company, and *Hedda Gabler* at the La Jolla Playhouse. Her screenplays include two movies for television, *Naked* and *The Deep End*, and an original screenplay, *Fanny Kelly*. She wrote the premiere episode of *The Clinic* for Lorimar Television. A member of New Dramatists, she has received numerous awards, including a Guggenheim fellowship, NEA Artistic Associates grant, NEA Playwrights Fellowship, CAPS awards, and a McKnight Fellowship. In 1983 Mann received the Rosamond Gilder Award from the New Drama Forum for "outstanding creative achievement in the theater."

TERRENCE MCNALLY was born November 3, 1939, in St. Petersburg, Florida, grew up in Corpus Christi, Texas, and attended Columbia College in New York City. His work has been seen on Broadway (*And Things That Go Bump in the Night, The Ritz,*

Bad Habits, and *Noon*), Off Broadway (*Where Has Tommy Flowers Gone?*, *Next*, *Sweet Eros/Witness*, and *Whiskey*), film (*The Ritz*), and television (*The 5:48* and *Apple Pie* for PBS and *Mama Malone* for CBS). He wrote the book for *The Rink*, which had a score by John Kander and Fred Ebb and was presented on Broadway with Chita Rivera and Liza Minnelli in the leading roles. His recent work includes *It's Only a Play*, *Frankie and Johnny in the Clair de Lune*, and *The Lisbon Traviata*. He has received two Guggenheim fellowships, an Obie Award, and a citation from the American Academy of Arts and Letters. McNally is Vice President of the Dramatists Guild, an organization he cherishes.

MARTIN SHERMAN was born December 22, 1938, in Philadelphia and educated at Boston University. He has received grants from the National Endowment for the Arts and the Rockefeller Foundation. His plays *Passing By*, *Soaps*, *Cracks*, and *Rio Grande* have all been produced by Playwrights Horizons in New York, and he was resident playwright there for the 1976–77 season. His play *Bent* was first seen as a staged reading at the Eugene O'Neill Playwrights Conference; in 1979 it was produced at the Royal Court Theatre in London with Ian McKellen and Tom Bell, and then transferred to the Criterion Theatre on the West End. It opened on Broadway the following season with Richard Gere, David Dukes, and David Marshall Grant, where it received a Tony nomination for Best Play and the Hull-Warriner Award. It has subsequently been presented in over thirty countries. *Bent* was followed by *Messiah*, produced first at the Hampstead Theatre in London in 1982 and later transferred to the Aldwych Theatre on the West End. It was subsequently presented in New York at the Manhattan Theatre Club. *When She Danced* premiered at the Yvonne Arnaud Theatre in Guildford, England, and has been produced in theaters throughout Europe. His newest play is *A Madhouse in Goa*. He resides in London.

EVAN SMITH was born May 21, 1967, in Washington, D.C., and grew up in Savannah, Georgia, where he attended St. James and Blessed Sacrament elementary schools and Benedictine Military School. *Remedial English* was written for the Young Playwrights Festival open to playwrights under the age of eighteen and was the first of Smith's plays to be produced professionally. He wrote the piece on time stolen from his job mapping the graves at the Catholic cemetery in Savannah. No longer a Young Playwright, Smith is now a student at Vassar College.

KATHLEEN TOLAN was born in Milwaukee in 1950. She studied acting at New York University and was a member of André Gregory's Manhattan Project from 1971–1973. She wrote *A Weekend Near Madison* in 1979 and rewrote it every six months for a few years until the play was produced in 1983 at the Actors Theatre of Louisville and the Astor Place Theater in New York. She wrote *Digging to China* in 1981 and directed it at the Omaha Magic Theatre; it was later produced at the Williamstown Theater Festival. Her other plays include *Remote Conflict* (1985) and *Pages from a Diary* (1987).

DORIC WILSON was born February 24, 1939, and raised on his grandparents' ranch on the Columbia River of Washington State. His first play *And He Made a Her*

opened at the Caffe Cino in 1961 and moved to the Cherry Lane Theatre the following year. A founding member of the Barr/Wilder/Albee Playwrights' Unit and the Circle Repertory Theater Company, he was artistic director of the New York Theatre Ensemble (1965–1968) and TOSOS Theatre Company (1972–1977). His plays *The West Street Gang* (1977) and *A Perfect Relationship* (1979) are published by Sea Horse Press. *Forever After,* which opened in New York in 1980 and won San Francisco's Cable Car Award in 1981, is published by JH Press. *Street Theater* opened in New York in 1982, where it won the Villager Best Play Award in 1983 and the Jane Chambers/Billy Blackwell Best Play Award, 1982/1983. He has written, directed, and produced over a hundred productions Off and Off Off Broadway. He has taught playwriting and directing in Portland and Seattle and currently lives in Los Angeles. His latest play is *An Object of Affection.*

ABOUT THE EDITOR

DON SHEWEY is a theater critic and journalist who lives in New York City. Born May 12, 1954, in Denver, Colorado, he studied classical languages at Rice University in Houston and received a B.F.A. in acting from Boston University. Formerly theater editor of the *Soho News* and contributing editor to *Rolling Stone*, he is currently arts editor of *Seven Days*. He also frequently writes about theater for the Arts and Leisure section of the *New York Times* and the *Village Voice*. His articles have also appeared in the *New York Times Magazine, Esquire, American Film, American Theater, Performing Arts Magazine, Next Wave Journal 1986, Newsday, Theater Crafts, Stagebill,* the *Boston Phoenix,* and other publications. He has taught dramaturgy to New York University students at the Playwrights Horizons Theater School. He is the author of *Sam Shepard,* a biography published by Dell Books, and *Caught in the Act: New York Actors Face to Face,* a collaboration with photographer Susan Shacter, published by NAL Books.